THE ROMAN HISTORIANS

OLD WESTERN CULTURE READER

VOLUME 6

The Roman Historians

Old Western Culture Reader

Volume 6

ROMAN ROADS PRESS

The Roman Historians: Old Western Culture Reader, Vol. 6

Published by Roman Roads Press
Moscow, Idaho, USA
romanroadspress.com
info@romanroadsmedia.com

General Editor: Daniel Foucachon
Interior Layout: Carissa Hale
Illustrations: Cooper Salmon
Cover Design, Valerie Anne Bost, Daniel Foucachon, and Rachel Rosales

The Roman Historians: Old Western Culture Reader, Volume 6
Roman Roads Press, an imprint of Roman Roads Media, LLC.
ISBN: 978-1-944482-05-3

Version 3.0.0 May 2021

This is a compantion reader for the *Old Western Culture* curriculum by Roman Roads Press. To find out more about this course, visit www.romanroadspress.com.

OLD WESTERN CULTURE

Great Books Reader Series

THE GREEKS

VOLUME 1	*The Epics*
VOLUME 2	*Drama & Lyric*
VOLUME 3	*The Histories*
VOLUME 4	*The Philosophies*

THE ROMANS

VOLUME	*The Aeneid*
VOLUME 6	*The Historians*
VOLUME 7	*Early Christianity*
VOLUME 8	*Nicene Christianity*

CHRISTENDOM

VOLUME 9	*Early Medievals*
VOLUME 10	*Defense of the Faith*
VOLUME 11	*The Medieval Mind*
VOLUME 12	*The Reformation*

EARLY MODERNS

VOLUME 13	*Rise of England*
VOLUME 14	*Politics and Poetry*
VOLUME 15	*The Enlightenment*
VOLUME 16	*The Novels*

Contents

LIVY

THE EARLY HISTORY OF ROME

LIVY

Translated by Rev. Canon Roberts

Book I: The Earliest Legends

Preface

WHETHER the task I have undertaken of writing a complete history of the Roman people from the very commencement of its existence will reward me for the labour spent on it, I neither know for certain, nor if I did know would I venture to say. For I see that this is an old-established and a common practice, each fresh writer being invariably persuaded that he will either attain greater certainty in the materials of his narrative, or surpass the rudeness of antiquity in the excellence of his style. However this may be, it will still be a great satisfaction to me to have taken my part, too, in investing, to the utmost of my abilities, the annals of the foremost nation in the world with a deeper interest; and if in such a crowd of writers my own reputation is thrown into the shade, I would console myself with the renown and greatness of those who eclipse my fame. The subject, moreover, is one that demands immense labour. It goes back beyond 700 years and, after starting from small and humble beginnings, has grown to such dimensions that it begins to be overburdened by its greatness. I have very little doubt, too, that for the majority of my readers the earliest times and those immediately succeeding, will possess little attraction; they will hurry on to these modern days in which the might of a long paramount nation is wasting by internal decay. I, on the other hand, shall look for a further reward of my labours in being able to close my eyes to the evils which our generation has witnessed for so many years; so long, at least, as I am devoting all my thoughts to retracing those pristine records, free from all the anxiety which can disturb the historian of his own times even if it cannot warp him from the truth.

The traditions of what happened prior to the foundation of the City or whilst it was being built, are more fitted to adorn the creations of the poet than the authentic records of the historian, and I have no intention of establishing either their truth or their falsehood. This much license is conceded to the ancients, that by intermingling human actions with divine they may confer a more august dignity on the origins of states. Now, if any nation ought to be allowed to claim a sacred origin and point back to a divine paternity that nation is Rome. For such is her renown in war that when she chooses to represent Mars as her own and her founder's father, the nations of the world accept the statement with the same equanimity with which they accept her dominion. But whatever opinions may be formed or criticisms passed upon these and similar traditions, I regard them as of small importance. The subjects to which I would ask each of my readers to devote his earnest attention are these—the life and morals of the community; the men and the qualities by which through domestic policy and foreign war dominion was won and extended. Then as the standard of morality gradually lowers, let him follow the decay of the national character, observing how at first it slowly sinks, then slips downward more and more rapidly, and finally begins to plunge into headlong ruin, until he reaches these days, in which we can bear neither our diseases nor their remedies.

There is this exceptionally beneficial and fruitful advantage to be derived from the study of the past, that you see, set in the clear light of historical truth, examples of every possible type. From these you may select for yourself and your country what to imitate, and also what, as being mischievous in its inception and disastrous in its issues, you are to avoid. Unless, however, I am misled by affection for my undertaking, there has never existed any commonwealth greater in power, with a purer morality, or more fertile in good examples; or any state in which avarice and luxury have been so late in making their inroads, or poverty and frugality so highly and continuously honoured, showing so clearly that the less wealth men possessed the less they coveted. In these latter years wealth has brought avarice in its train, and the unlimited command of pleasure has created in men a passion for ruining themselves and everything else through self-indulgence and licentiousness. But criticisms which will be unwelcome, even when perhaps necessary, must not appear in the commencement at all events of this extensive work. We should much prefer to start with favourable omens, and if we could have adopted the poets' custom, it would have been much pleasanter to commence with prayers and supplications to gods and goddesses that they would grant a favourable and successful issue to the great task before us.

1.1

TO begin with, it is generally admitted that after the capture of Troy, whilst the rest of the Trojans were massacred, against two of them—Aeneas and Antenor—the Achivi refused to exercise the rights of war, partly owing to old ties of hospitality, and partly because these men had always been in favour of making peace and surrendering Helen. Their subsequent fortunes were different. Antenor sailed into the furthest part of the Adriatic, accompanied by a number of Enetians who had been driven from Paphlagonia by a revolution, and after losing their king Pylaemenes before Troy were looking for a settlement and a leader. The combined force of Enetians and Trojans defeated the Euganei, who dwelt between the sea and the Alps and occupied their land. The place where they disembarked was called Troy, and the name was extended to the surrounding district; the whole nation were called Veneti. Similar misfortunes led to Aeneas becoming a wanderer, but the Fates were preparing a higher destiny for him. He first visited Macedonia, then was carried down to Sicily in quest of a settlement; from Sicily he directed his course to the Laurentian territory. Here, too, the name of Troy is found, and here the Trojans disembarked, and as their almost infinite wanderings had left them nothing but their arms and their ships, they began to plunder the neighbourhood. The Aborigines, who occupied the country, with their king Latinus at their head, came hastily together from the city and the country districts to repel the inroads of the strangers by force of arms.

From this point there is a twofold tradition. According to the one, Latinus was defeated in battle, and made peace with Aeneas, and subsequently a family alliance. According to the other, whilst the two armies were standing ready to engage and waiting for the signal, Latinus advanced in front of his lines and invited the leader of the strangers to a conference. He inquired of him what manner of men they were, whence they came, what had happened to make them leave their homes, what were they in quest of when they landed in Latinus' territory. When he heard that the men were Trojans, that their leader was Aeneas, the son of Anchises and Venus, that their city had been burnt, and that the homeless exiles were now looking for a place to settle in and build a city, he was so struck with the noble bearing of the men and their leader, and their readiness to accept alike either peace or war, that he gave his right hand as a solemn pledge of friendship for the future. A formal treaty was made between the leaders and mutual greetings exchanged between the armies. Latinus received Aeneas as a guest in his house, and there, in the presence of his tutelary deities, completed the political alliance by a domestic one, and gave his daughter in marriage to Aeneas. This incident confirmed the Trojans in the hope that they had reached the term of their wanderings and won a permanent home. They built a town, which Aeneas called Lavinium after his wife. In a short time a boy was born of the new marriage, to whom his parents gave the name of Ascanius.

1.2

IN a short time the Aborigines and Trojans became involved in war with Turnus, the king of the Rutulians. Lavinia had been betrothed to him before the arrival of Aeneas, and, furious at finding a stranger preferred to him, he declared war against both Latinus and Aeneas. Neither side could congratulate themselves on the result of the battle; the Rutulians were defeated, but the victorious Aborigines and Trojans lost their leader Latinus. Feeling their need of allies, Turnus and the Rutulians had recourse to the celebrated power of the Etruscans and Mezentius, their king, who was reigning at Caere, a wealthy city in those days. From the first he had felt anything but pleasure at the rise of the new city, and now he regarded the growth of the Trojan state as much too rapid to be safe to its neighbours, so he welcomed the proposal to join forces with the Rutulians. To keep the Aborigines from abandoning him in the face of this strong coalition and to secure their being not only under the same laws, but also the same designation, Aeneas called both nations by the common name of Latins. From that time the Aborigines were not behind the Trojans in their loyal devotion to Aeneas. So great was the power of Etruria that the renown of her people had filled not only the inland parts of Italy but also the coastal districts along the whole length of the land from the Alps to the Straits of Messina. Aeneas, however, trusting to the loyalty of the two nations who were day by day growing into one, led his forces into the field, instead of awaiting the enemy behind his walls. The battle resulted in favour of the Latins, but it was the last mortal act of Aeneas. His tomb—whatever it is lawful and right to call him—is situated on the bank of the Numicius. He is addressed as "Jupiter Indiges."

1.3

HIS son, Ascanius, was not old enough to assume the government; but his throne remained secure throughout his minority. During that interval—such was Lavinia's force of character—though a woman was regent, the Latin State, and the kingdom of his father and grandfather, were preserved unimpaired for her son. I will not discuss the question—for who could speak decisively about a matter of such extreme antiquity?—whether the man whom the Julian house claim, under the name of Iulus, as the founder of their name, was this Ascanius or an older one than he, born of Creusa, whilst

Ilium was still intact, and after its fall a sharer in his father's fortunes. This Ascanius, where ever born, or of whatever mother—it is generally agreed in any case that he was the son of Aeneas—left to his mother (or his stepmother) the city of Lavinium, which was for those days a prosperous and wealthy city, with a superabundant population, and built a new city at the foot of the Alban hills, which from its position, stretching along the side of the hill, was called "Alba Longa." A interval of thirty years elapsed between the foundation of Lavinium and the colonization of Alba Longa. Such had been the growth of the Latin power, mainly through the defeat of the Etruscans, that neither at the death of Aeneas, nor during the regency of Lavinia, nor during the immature years of the reign of Ascanius, did either Mezentius and the Etruscans or any other of their neighbours venture to attack them. When terms of peace were being arranged, the river Albula, now called the Tiber, had been fixed as the boundary between the Etruscans and the Latins.

Ascanius was succeeded by his son Silvius, who by some chance had been born in the forest. He became the father of Aeneas Silvius, who in his turn had a son, Latinus Silvius. He planted a number of colonies: the colonists were called Prisci Latini. The cognomen of Silvius was common to all the remaining kings of Alba, each of whom succeeded his father. Their names are Alba, Atys, Capys, Capetus, Tiberinus, who was drowned in crossing the Albula, and his name transferred to the river, which became henceforth the famous Tiber. Then came his son Agrippa, after him his son Romulus Silvius. He was struck by lightning and left the crown to his son Aventinus, whose shrine was on the hill which bears his name and is now a part of the city of Rome. He was succeeded by Proca, who had two sons, Numitor and Amulius. To Numitor, the elder, he bequeathed the ancient throne of the Silvian house. Violence, however, proved stronger than either the father's will or the respect due to the brother's seniority; for Amulius expelled his brother and seized the crown. Adding crime to crime, he murdered his brother's sons and made the daughter, Rea Silvia, a Vestal virgin; thus, under the presence of honouring her, depriving her of all hopes of issue.

1.4

BUT the Fates had, I believe, already decreed the origin of this great city and the foundation of the mightiest empire under heaven. The Vestal was forcibly violated and gave birth to twins. She named Mars as their father, either because she really believed it, or because the fault might appear less heinous if a deity were the cause of it. But neither gods nor men sheltered her or her babes from the king's cruelty; the priestess was thrown into prison, the boys were ordered to be thrown into the river. By a heaven-sent chance it happened that the Tiber was then overflowing its banks, and stretches of standing water prevented any approach to the main channel. Those who were carrying the children expected that this stagnant water would be sufficient to drown them, so under the impression that they were carrying out the king's orders they exposed the boys at the nearest point of the overflow, where the Ficus Ruminalis (said to have been formerly called Romularis) now stands. The locality was then a wild solitude. The tradition goes on to say that after the floating cradle in which the boys had been exposed had been left by the retreating water on dry land, a thirsty she-wolf from the surrounding hills, attracted by the crying of the children, came to them, gave them her teats to suck and was so gentle towards them that the king's flock-master found her licking the boys with her tongue. According to the story, his name was Faustulus. He took the children to his hut and gave them to his wife Larentia to bring up. Some writers think that Larentia, from her unchaste life, had got the nickname of "She-wolf" amongst the shepherds, and that this was the origin of the marvelous story. As soon as the boys, thus born and thus brought up, grew to be young men they did not neglect their pastoral duties, but their special delight was roaming through the woods on hunting expeditions. As their strength and courage were thus developed, they used not only to lie in wait for fierce beasts of prey, but they even attacked brigands when loaded with plunder. They distributed what they took amongst the shepherds, with whom, surrounded by a continually increasing body of young men, they associated themselves in their serious undertakings and in their sports and pastimes.

1.5

IT is said that the festival of the Lupercalia, which is still observed, was even in those days celebrated on the Palatine hill. This hill was originally called Pallantium from a city of the same name in Arcadia; the name was afterwards changed to Palatium. Evander, an Arcadian, had held that territory many ages before, and had introduced an annual festival from Arcadia in which young men ran about naked for sport and wantonness, in honour of the Lycaean Pan, whom the Romans afterwards called Inuus. The existence of this festival was widely recognised, and it was while the two brothers were engaged in it that the brigands, enraged at losing their plunder, ambushed them. Romulus successfully defended himself, but Remus was taken prisoner and brought before Amulius, his captors impudently accusing him of their own crimes. The principal charge brought against them was that of invading Numitor's lands with a body of young men whom they had got together, and carrying off plunder as though in regular warfare. Remus accordingly was handed over to Numitor for punishment. Faustulus had from the beginning suspected that it was royal offspring that he was bringing up, for he was aware that the boys had been exposed at the king's command and the time at which he had taken them away exactly corresponded with that of their exposure. He had, however, refused to divulge the matter prematurely, until either a fitting opportunity occurred or necessity demanded its disclosure. The necessity came first. Alarmed for the safety of Remus he revealed the state of the case to Romulus. It so happened that Numitor also, who had Remus in his custody, on hearing that he and his brother were twins and comparing their ages and the character and bearing so unlike that of one in a servile condition, began to recall the memory of his grandchildren, and further inquiries brought him to the same conclusion as Faustulus; nothing was wanting to the recognition of Remus. So the king Amulius was being enmeshed on all sides by hostile purposes. Romulus shrunk from a direct attack with his body of shepherds, for he was no match for the king in open fight. They were instructed to approach the palace by different routes and meet there at a given time, whilst from Numitor's house Remus lent his assistance with a second band he had collected. The attack succeeded and the king was killed.

1.6

AT the beginning of the fray, Numitor gave out that an enemy had entered the City and was attacking the palace, in order to draw off the Alban soldiery to the citadel, to defend it. When he saw the young men coming to congratulate him after the assassination, he at once called a council of his people and explained his brother's infamous conduct towards him, the story of his grandsons, their parentage and bringing up, and how he recognised them. Then he proceeded to inform them of the tyrant's death and his responsibility for it. The young men marched in order through the midst of the assembly and saluted their grandfather as king; their action was approved by the whole population, who with one voice ratified the title and sovereignty of the king. After the government of Alba was thus transferred to Numitor, Romulus and Remus were seized with the desire of building a city in the locality where they had been exposed. There was the superfluous population of the Alban and Latin towns, to these were added the shepherds: it was natural to hope that with all these Alba would be small and Lavinium small in comparison with the city which was to be founded. These pleasant anticipations were disturbed by the ancestral curse—ambition—which led to a deplorable quarrel over what was at first a trivial matter. As they were twins and no claim to precedence could be based on seniority, they decided to consult the tutelary deities of the place by means of augury as to who was to give his name to the new city, and who was to rule it after it had been founded. Romulus accordingly selected the Palatine as his station for observation, Remus the Aventine.

1.7

REMUS is said to have been the first to receive an omen: six vultures appeared to him. The augury had just been announced to Romulus when double the number appeared to him. Each was saluted as king by his own party. The one side based their claim on the priority of the appearance, the other on the number of the birds. Then followed an angry altercation; heated passions led to bloodshed; in the tumult Remus was killed. The more common report is that Remus contemptuously jumped over the newly raised walls and was forthwith killed by the enraged Romulus, who exclaimed, "So shall it be henceforth with every one who leaps over my walls." Romulus thus became sole ruler, and the city was called after him, its founder. His first work was to fortify the Palatine hill where he had been brought up. The worship of the other deities he conducted according to the use of Alba, but that of Hercules in accordance with the Greek rites as they had been instituted by Evander. It was into this neighbourhood, according to the tradition, that Hercules, after he had killed Geryon, drove his oxen, which were of marvelous beauty. He swam across the Tiber, driving the oxen before him, and wearied with his journey, lay down in a grassy place near the river to rest himself and the oxen, who enjoyed the rich pasture. When sleep had overtaken him, as he was heavy with food and wine, a shepherd living near, called Cacus, presuming on his strength, and captivated by the beauty of the oxen, determined to secure them. If he drove them before him into the cave, their hoof-marks would have led their owner on his search for them in the same direction, so he dragged the finest of them backwards by their tails into his cave. At the first streak of dawn Hercules awoke, and on surveying his herd saw that some were missing. He proceeded towards the nearest cave, to see if any tracks pointed in that direction, but he found that every hoofmark led from the cave and none towards it. Perplexed and bewildered he began to drive the herd away from so dangerous a neighbourhood. Some of the cattle, missing those which were left behind, lowed as they often do, and an answering low sounded from the cave. Hercules turned in that direction, and as Cacus tried to prevent him by force from entering the cave, he was killed by a blow from Hercules' club, after vainly appealing for help to his comrades.

The king of the country at that time was Evander, a refugee from Peloponnesus, who ruled more by personal ascendancy than by the exercise of power. He was looked up to with reverence for his knowledge of letters—a new and marvelous thing for uncivilized men—but he was still more revered because of his mother Carmenta, who was believed to be a divine being and regarded with wonder by all as an interpreter of Fate, in the days before the arrival of the Sibyl in Italy. This Evander, alarmed by the crowd of excited shepherds standing round a stranger whom they accused of open murder, ascertained from them the nature of his act and what led to it. As he observed the bearing and stature of the man to be more than human in greatness and august dignity, he asked who he was. When he heard his name, and learnt his father and his country he said, "Hercules, son of Jupiter, hail! My mother, who speaks truth in the name of the gods, has prophesied that thou shalt join the company of the gods, and that here a shrine shall be dedicated to thee, which in ages to come the most powerful nation in all the world shall call their Ara Maxima and honour with shine own special worship." Hercules grasped Evander's right hand and said that he took the omen to himself and would fulfill the prophecy by building and consecrating the altar. Then a heifer of conspicuous beauty was taken from the herd, and the first sacrifice was offered; the Potitii and Pinarii, the two principal families in those parts, were invited by Hercules to assist in the sacrifice and at the feast which followed. It so happened that the Potitii were present at the appointed time, and the entrails were placed before them; the Pinarii arrived after these were consumed and came in for the rest of the banquet. It became a permanent institution from that time, that as long as the family of the Pinarii survived they should not eat of the entrails of the victims. The Potitii, after being instructed by Evander, presided over that rite for many ages, until they handed over this ministerial office to public servants after which the whole race of the Potitii perished. This out of all foreign rites, was the only one which Romulus adopted, as though he felt that an immortality won through courage, of which this was the memorial, would one day be his own reward.

1.8

AFTER the claims of religion had been duly acknowledged, Romulus called his people to a council. As nothing could unite them into one political body but the observance of common laws and customs, he gave them a body of laws, which he thought would only be respected by a rude and uncivilized race of men if he inspired them with awe by assuming the outward symbols of power. He surrounded himself with greater state, and in particular he called into his service twelve lictors. Some think that he fixed upon this number from the number of the birds who foretold his sovereignty; but I am inclined to agree with those who think that as this class of public officers was borrowed from the same people from whom the *sella curulis* and the *toga praetexta* were adopted—their neighbours, the Etruscans—so the number itself also was taken from them. Its use amongst the Etruscans is traced to the custom of the twelve sovereign cities of Etruria, when jointly electing a king, furnishing him each with one lictor. Meantime the City was growing by the extension of its walls in various directions; an increase due rather to the anticipation of its future population than to any present overcrowding. His next care was to secure an addition to the population that the size of the City might not be a source of weakness. It had been the ancient policy of the founders of cities to get together a multitude of people of obscure and low origin and then to spread the fiction that they were the children of the soil. In accordance with this policy, Romulus opened a place of refuge on the spot where, as you go down from the Capitol, you find an enclosed space between two groves. A promiscuous crowd of freemen and slaves, eager for change, fled thither from the neighbouring states. This was the first accession of strength to the nascent greatness of the city. When he was satisfied as to its strength, his next step was to provide for that strength being wisely directed. He created a hundred senators; either because that number was adequate, or because there were only a hundred heads of houses who could be created. In any case they were called the "Patres" in virtue of their rank, and their descendants were called "Patricians."

1.9

THE Roman State had now become so strong that it was a match for any of its neighbours in war, but its greatness threatened to last for only one generation, since through the absence of women there was no hope of offspring, and there was no right of intermarriage with their neighbours. Acting on the advice of the senate, Romulus sent envoys amongst the surrounding nations to ask for alliance and the right of intermarriage on behalf of his new community. It was represented that cities, like everything else, sprung from the humblest beginnings, and those who were helped on by their own courage and the favour of heaven won for themselves great power and great renown. As to the origin of Rome, it was well known that whilst it had received divine assistance, courage and self-reliance were not wanting. There should, therefore, be no reluctance for men to mingle their blood with their fellow-men. Nowhere did the envoys meet with a favourable reception. Whilst their proposals were treated with contumely, there was at the same time a general feeling of alarm at the power so rapidly growing in their midst. Usually they were dismissed with the question, "whether they had opened an asylum for women, for nothing short of that would secure for them intermarriage on equal terms." The Roman youth could ill brook such insults, and matters began to look like an appeal to force. To secure a favourable place and time for such an attempt, Romulus, disguising his resentment, made elaborate preparations for the celebration of games in honour of "Equestrian Neptune," which he called "the Consualia." He ordered public notice of the spectacle to be given amongst the adjoining cities, and his people supported him in making the celebration as magnificent as their knowledge and resources allowed, so that expectations were raised to the highest pitch. There was a great gathering; people were eager to see the new City, all their nearest neighbours—the people of Caenina, Antemnae, and Crustumerium—were there, and the whole Sabine population came, with their wives and families. They were invited to accept hospitality at the different houses, and after examining the situation of the City, its walls and the large number of dwelling-houses it included, they were astonished at the rapidity with which the Roman State had grown.

When the hour for the games had come, and their eyes and minds were alike riveted on the spectacle before them, the pre-concerted signal was given and the Roman youth dashed in all directions to carry off the maidens who were present. The larger part were carried off indiscriminately, but some particularly beautiful girls who had been marked out for the leading patricians were carried to their houses by plebeians told off for the task. One, conspicuous amongst them all for grace and beauty, is reported to have been carried off by a group led by a certain Talassius, and to the many inquiries as to whom she was intended for, the invariable answer was given, "For Talassius." Hence the use of this word in the marriage rites. Alarm and consternation broke up the games, and the parents of the maidens fled, distracted with grief, uttering bitter reproaches on the violators of the laws of hospitality and appealing to the god to whose solemn games they had come, only to be the victims of impious perfidy. The abducted maidens were quite as despondent and indignant. Romulus, however, went round in person, and pointed out to them that it was all owing to the pride of their parents in denying right of intermarriage to their neighbours. They would live in honourable wedlock, and share all their property and civil rights, and—dearest of all to human nature—would be the mothers of freemen. He begged them to lay aside their feelings of resentment and give their affections to those whom fortune had made masters of their persons. An injury had often led to reconciliation and love; they would find their husbands all the more affectionate, because each would do his utmost, so far as in him lay, to make up for the loss of parents and country. These arguments were reinforced by the endearments of their husbands, who excused their conduct by pleading the irresistible force of their passion—a plea effective beyond all others in appealing to a woman's nature.

1.10

THE feelings of the abducted maidens were now pretty completely appeased, but not so those of their parents. They went about in mourning garb, and tried by their tearful complaints to rouse their countrymen to action. Nor did they confine their remonstrances to their own cities; they flocked from all sides to Titus Tatius, the king of the Sabines, and sent formal deputations to him, for his was the most influential name in those parts. The people of Caenina, Crustumerium, and Antemnae were the greatest sufferers;

they thought Tatius and his Sabines were too slow in moving, so these three cities prepared to make war conjointly. Such, however, were the impatience and anger of the Caeninensians that even the Crustuminians and Antemnates did not display enough energy for them, so the men of Caenina made an attack upon Roman territory on their own account. Whilst they were scattered far and wide, pillaging and destroying, Romulus came upon them with an army, and after a brief encounter taught them that anger is futile without strength. He put them to a hasty flight, and following them up, killed their king and despoiled his body; then after slaying their leader took their city at the first assault. He was no less anxious to display his achievements than he had been great in performing them, so, after leading his victorious army home, he mounted to the Capitol with the spoils of his dead foe borne before him on a frame constructed for the purpose. He hung them there on an oak, which the shepherds looked upon as a sacred tree, and at the same time marked out the site for the temple of Jupiter, and addressing the god by a new title, uttered the following invocation: "Jupiter Feretrius! these arms taken from a king, I, Romulus a king and conqueror, bring to thee, and on this domain, whose bounds I have in will and purpose traced, I dedicate a temple to receive the *spolia opima* which posterity following my example shall bear hither, taken from the kings and generals of our foes slain in battle." Such was the origin of the first temple dedicated in Rome. And the gods decreed that though its founder did not utter idle words in declaring that posterity would thither bear their spoils, still the splendour of that offering should not be dimmed by the number of those who have rivaled his achievement. For after so many years have elapsed and so many wars been waged, only twice have the *spolia opima* been offered. So seldom has Fortune granted that glory to men.

1.11

WHILST the Romans were thus occupied, the army of the Antemnates seized the opportunity of their territory being unoccupied and made a raid into it. Romulus hastily led his legion against this fresh foe and surprised them as they were scattered over the fields.

At the very first battle-shout and charge the enemy were routed and their city captured. Whilst Romulus was exulting over this double victory, his wife, Hersilia, moved by the entreaties of the abducted maidens, implored him to pardon their parents and receive them into citizenship, for so the State would increase in unity and strength. He readily granted her request. He then advanced against the Crustuminians, who had commenced war, but their eagerness had been damped by the successive defeats of their neighbours, and they offered but slight resistance. Colonies were planted in both places; owing to the fertility of the soil of the Crustumine district, the majority gave their names for that colony. On the other hand there were numerous migrations to Rome mostly of the parents and relatives of the abducted maidens. The last of these wars was commenced by the Sabines and proved the most serious of all, for nothing was done in passion or impatience; they masked their designs till war had actually commenced. Strategy was aided by craft and deceit, as the following incident shows. Spurius Tarpeius was in command of the Roman citadel. Whilst his daughter had gone outside the fortifications to fetch water for some religious ceremonies, Tatius bribed her to admit his troops within the citadel. Once admitted, they crushed her to death beneath their shields, either that the citadel might appear to have been taken by assault, or that her example might be left as a warning that no faith should be kept with traitors. A further story runs that the Sabines were in the habit of wearing heavy gold armlets on their left arms and richly jeweled rings, and that the girl made them promise to give her "what they had on their left arms," accordingly they piled their shields upon her instead of golden gifts. Some say that in bargaining for what they had in their left hands, she expressly asked for their shields, and being suspected of wishing to betray them, fell a victim to her own bargain.

1.12

HOWEVER this may be, the Sabines were in possession of the citadel. And they would not come down from it the next day, though the Roman army was drawn up in battle array over the whole of the ground between the Palatine and the Capitoline hill, until, exasperated at the loss of their citadel and determined to recover it, the Romans mounted to the attack. Advancing before the rest, Mettius Curtius, on the side of the Sabines, and Hostius Hostilius, on the side of the Romans, engaged in single combat. Hostius, fighting on disadvantageous ground, upheld the fortunes of Rome by his intrepid bravery, but at last he fell; the Roman line broke and fled to what was then the gate of the Palatine. Even Romulus was being swept away by the crowd of fugitives, and lifting up his hands to heaven he exclaimed: "Jupiter, it was thy omen that I obeyed when I laid here on the Palatine the earliest foundations of the City. Now the Sabines hold its citadel, having bought it by a bribe, and coming thence have seized the valley and are pressing hitherwards in battle. Do thou, Father of gods and men, drive hence our foes, banish terror from Roman hearts, and stay our shameful flight! Here do I vow a temple to thee, 'Jove the Stayer,' as a memorial for the generations to come that it is through thy present help that the City has been saved." Then, as though he had become aware that his prayer had been heard, he cried, "Back, Romans! Jupiter Optimus Maximus bids you stand and renew the battle." They stopped as though commanded by a voice from heaven—Romulus dashed up to the foremost line, just as Mettius Curtius had run down from the citadel in front of the Sabines and driven the Romans in headlong flight over the whole of the ground now occupied by the Forum. He was now not far from the gate of the Palatine, and was shouting: "We have conquered our faithless hosts, our cowardly foes; now they know that to carry off maidens is a very different thing from fighting with men." In the midst of these vaunts Romulus, with a compact body of valiant troops, charged down on him. Mettius happened to be on horseback, so he was the more easily driven back, the Romans followed in pursuit, and, inspired by the courage of their king, the rest of the Roman army routed the Sabines. Mettius, unable to control his horse, maddened by the noise of his pursuers, plunged into a morass. The danger of their general drew off the attention of the Sabines for a moment from the battle; they called out and made signals to encourage him, so, animated to fresh efforts, he succeeded in extricating himself. Thereupon the Romans and Sabines renewed the fighting in the middle of the valley, but the fortune of Rome was in the ascendant.

1.13

THEN it was that the Sabine women, whose wrongs had led to the war, throwing off all womanish fears in their distress, went boldly into the midst of the flying missiles with disheveled hair and rent garments. Running across the space between the two armies they tried to stop any further fighting and calm the excited passions by appealing to their fathers in the one army and their husbands in the other not to bring upon themselves a curse by staining their hands with the blood of a father-in-law or a son-in-law, nor upon their posterity the taint of parricide. "If," they cried, "you are weary of these ties of kindred, these marriage-bonds, then turn your anger upon us; it is we who are the cause of the war, it is we who have wounded and slain our husbands and fathers. Better for us to perish rather than live without one or the other of you, as widows or as orphans." The armies and their leaders were alike moved by this appeal. There was a sudden hush and silence. Then the generals advanced to arrange the terms of a treaty. It was not only peace that was made, the two nations were united into one State, the royal power was shared between them, and the seat of government for both nations was Rome. After thus doubling the City, a concession was made to the Sabines in the new appellation of Quirites, from their old capital of Cures. As a memorial of the battle, the place where Curtius got his horse out of the deep marsh on to safer ground was called the Curtian lake. The joyful peace, which put an abrupt close to such a deplorable war, made the Sabine women still dearer to their husbands and fathers, and most of all to Romulus himself. Consequently when he effected the distribution of the people into the thirty curiae, he affixed their names to the curiae. No doubt there were many more than thirty women, and tradition is silent as to whether those whose names were given to the curiae were selected on the ground of age, or on that of personal distinction—either their own or their husbands'—or merely by lot. The enrollment of the three centuries of knights took place at the same time; the Ramnenses were called after Romulus, the Titienses from T. Tatius. The origin of the Luceres and why they were so called is uncertain. Thenceforward the two kings exercised their joint sovereignty with perfect harmony.

1.18

THERE was living, in those days, at Cures, a Sabine city, a man of renowned justice and piety—Numa Pompilius. He was as conversant as any one in that age could be with all divine and human law. His master is given as Pythagoras of Samos, as tradition speaks of no other. But this is erroneous, for it is generally agreed that it was more than a century later, in the reign of Servius Tullius, that Pythagoras gathered round him crowds of eager students, in the most distant part of Italy, in the neighbourhood of Metapontum, Heraclea, and Crotona. Now, even if he had been contemporary with Numa, how could his reputation have reached the Sabines? From what places, and in what common language could he have induced any one to become his disciple? Who could have guaranteed the safety of a solitary individual traveling through so many nations differing in speech and character? I believe rather that Numa's virtues were the result of his native temperament and self-training, moulded not so much by foreign influences as by the rigorous and austere discipline of the ancient Sabines, which was the purest type of any that existed in the old days. When Numa's name was mentioned, though the Roman senators saw that the balance of power would be on the side of the Sabines if the king were chosen from amongst them, still no one ventured to propose a partisan of his own, or any senator, or citizen in preference to him. Accordingly they all to a man decreed that the crown should be offered to Numa Pompilius. He was invited to Rome, and following the precedent set by Romulus, when he obtained his crown through the augury which sanctioned the founding of the City, Numa ordered that in his case also the gods should be consulted. He was solemnly conducted by an augur, who was afterwards honoured by being made a State functionary for life, to the Citadel, and took his seat on a stone facing south. The augur seated himself on his left hand, with his head covered, and holding in his right hand a curved staff without any knots, which they called a *lituus*. After surveying the prospect over the City and surrounding country, he offered prayers and marked out the heavenly regions by an imaginary line from east to west; the southern he defined as "the right hand," the northern as "the left hand." He then fixed upon an object, as far as he could see, as a corresponding mark, and then transferring the *lituus* to his left hand, he laid his right upon Numa's head and offered this prayer: "Father Jupiter, if it be heaven's will that this Numa Pompilius, whose head I hold, should be king of Rome, do thou signify it to us by sure signs within those boundaries which I have traced." Then he described in the usual formula the augury which he desired should be sent. They were sent, and Numa being by them manifested to be king, came down from the "templum."

1.19

HAVING in this way obtained the crown, Numa prepared to found, as it were, anew, by laws and customs, that City which had so recently been founded by force of arms. He saw that this was impossible whilst a state of war lasted, for war brutalized men. Thinking that the ferocity of his subjects might be mitigated by the disuse of arms, he built the temple of Janus at the foot of the Aventine as an index of peace and war, to signify when it was open that the State was under arms, and when it was shut that all the surrounding nations were at peace. Twice since Numa's reign has it been shut, once after the first Punic war in the consulship of T. Manlius, the second time, which heaven has allowed our generation to witness, after the battle of Actium, when peace on land and sea was secured by the emperor Caesar Augustus. After forming treaties of alliance with all his neighbours and closing the temple of Janus, Numa turned his attention to domestic matters. The removal of all danger from without would induce his subjects to luxuriate in idleness, as they would be no longer restrained by the fear of an enemy or by military discipline. To prevent this, he strove to inculcate in their minds the fear of the gods, regarding this as the most powerful influence which could act upon an uncivilized and, in those ages, a barbarous people. But, as this would fail to make a deep impression without some claim to supernatural wisdom, he pretended that he had nocturnal interviews with the nymph Egeria: that it was on her advice that he was instituting the ritual most acceptable to the gods and appointing for each deity his own special priests. First of all he divided the year into twelve months, corresponding to the moon's revolutions. But as the moon does not complete thirty days in each month, and so there are fewer days in the lunar year than in that measured by the course of the sun, he interpolated intercalary months and so arranged them that every twentieth year the days should coincide with the same position of the sun as when they started, the whole twenty years being thus complete. He also established a distinction between the days on which legal business could be transacted and those on which it could not, because it would sometimes be advisable that there should be no business transacted with the people.

1.20

NEXT he turned his attention to the appointment of priests. He himself, however, conducted a great many religious services, especially those which belong to the Flamen of Jupiter. But he thought that in a warlike state there would be more kings of the type of Romulus than of Numa who would take the field in person. To guard, therefore, against the sacrificial rites which the king performed being interrupted, he appointed a Flamen as perpetual priest to Jupiter, and ordered that he should wear a distinctive dress and sit in the royal curule chair. He appointed two additional Flamens, one for Mars, the other for Quirinus, and also chose virgins as priestesses to Vesta. This order of priestesses came into existence originally in Alba and was connected with the race of the founder. He assigned them a public stipend that they might give their whole time to the temple, and made their persons sacred and inviolable by a vow of chastity and other religious sanctions. Similarly he chose twelve "Salii" for Mars Gradivus, and assigned to them the distinctive dress of an embroidered tunic and over it a brazen cuirass. They were instructed to march in solemn procession through the City, carrying the twelve shields called the "Ancilia," and singing hymns accompanied by a solemn dance in triple time. The next office to be filled was that of the Pontifex Maximus. Numa appointed the son of Marcus, one of the senators—Numa Marcius—and all the regulations bearing on religion, written out and sealed, were placed in his charge. Here was laid down with what victims, on what days, and at what temples the various sacrifices were to be offered, and from what sources the expenses connected with them were to be defrayed. He placed all other sacred functions, both public and private, under the supervision of the Pontifex, in order that there might be an authority for the people to consult, and so all trouble and confusion arising through foreign rites being adopted and their ancestral ones neglected might be avoided. Nor were his functions confined to directing the worship of the celestial gods; he was to instruct the people how to conduct funerals and appease the spirits of the departed, and what prodigies sent by lightning or in any other way were to be attended to and expiated. To elicit these signs of the divine will, he dedicated an altar to Jupiter Elicius on the Aventine, and consulted the god through auguries, as to which prodigies were to receive attention.

1.21

THE deliberations and arrangements which these matters involved diverted the people from all thoughts of war and provided them with ample occupation. The watchful care of the gods, manifesting itself in the providential guidance of human affairs, had kindled in all hearts such a feeling of piety that the sacredness of promises and the sanctity of oaths were a controlling force for the community scarcely less effective than the fear inspired by laws and penalties. And whilst his subjects were moulding their characters upon the unique example of their king, the neighbouring nations, who had hitherto believed that it was a fortified camp and not a city that was placed amongst them to vex the peace of all, were now induced to respect them so highly that they thought it sinful to injure a State so entirely devoted to the service of the gods. There was a grove through the midst of which a perennial stream flowed, issuing from a dark cave. Here Numa frequently retired unattended as if to meet the goddess, and he consecrated the grove to the Camaenae, because it was there that their meetings with his wife Egeria took place. He also instituted a yearly sacrifice to the goddess Fides and ordered that the Flamens should ride to her temple in a hooded chariot, and should perform the service with their hands covered as far as the fingers, to signify that Faith must be sheltered and that her seat is holy even when it is in men's right hands. There were many other sacrifices appointed by him and places dedicated for their performance which the pontiffs call the Argei. The greatest of all his works was the preservation of peace and the security of his realm throughout the whole of his reign. Thus by two successive kings the greatness of the State was advanced; by each in a different way, by the one through war, by the other through peace. Romulus reigned thirty-seven years, Numa forty-three. The State was strong and disciplined by the lessons of war and the arts of peace.

1.43

THOSE whose property amounted to, or exceeded 100,000 lbs. weight of copper were formed into eighty centuries, forty of juniors and forty of seniors. These were called the First Class. The seniors were to defend the City, the juniors to serve in the field. The armour which they were to provide themselves with comprised helmet, round shield, greaves, and coat of mail, all of brass; these were to protect the person. Their offensive weapons were spear and sword. To this class were joined two centuries of carpenters whose duty it was to work the engines of war; they were without arms. The Second Class consisted of those whose property amounted to between 75,000 and 100,000 lbs. weight of copper; they were formed, seniors and juniors together, into twenty centuries. Their regulation arms were the same as those of the First Class, except that they had an oblong wooden shield instead of the round brazen one and no coat of mail. The Third Class he formed of those whose property fell as low as 50,000 lbs.; these also consisted of twenty centuries, similarly divided into seniors and juniors. The only difference in the armour was that they did not wear greaves. In the Fourth Class were those whose property did not fall below 25,000 lbs. They also formed twenty centuries; their only arms were a spear and a javelin. The Fifth Class was larger it formed thirty centuries. They carried slings and stones, and they included the supernumeraries, the horn-blowers, and the trumpeters, who formed three centuries. This Fifth Class was assessed at 11,000 lbs. The rest of the population whose property fell below this were formed into one century and were exempt from military service.

After thus regulating the equipment and distribution of the infantry, he re-arranged the cavalry. He enrolled from amongst the principal men of the State twelve centuries. In the same way he made six other centuries (though only three had been formed by Romulus) under the same names under which the first had been inaugurated. For the purchase of the horse, 10,000 lbs. were assigned them from the public treasury; whilst for its keep certain widows were assessed to pay 2000 lbs. each, annually. The burden of all these expenses was shifted from the poor on to the rich. Then additional privileges were conferred. The former kings had maintained the constitution as handed down by Romulus, viz., manhood suffrage in which all alike possessed the same weight and enjoyed the same rights. Servius introduced a graduation; so that whilst no one was ostensibly deprived of his vote, all the voting power was in the hands of the principal men of the State. The knights were first summoned to record their vote, then the eighty centuries of the infantry of the First Class; if their votes were divided, which seldom happened, it was arranged for the Second Class to be summoned; very seldom did the voting extend to the lowest Class. Nor need it occasion any surprise, that the arrangement which now exists since the completion of the thirty-five tribes, their number being doubled by the centuries of juniors and seniors, does not agree with the total as instituted by Servius Tullius. For, after dividing the City with its districts and the hills which were inhabited into four parts, he called these divisions "tribes," I think from the tribute they paid, for he also introduced the practice of collecting it at an equal rate according to the assessment. These tribes had nothing to do with the distribution and number of the centuries.

1.44

THE work of the census was accelerated by an enactment in which Servius denounced imprisonment and even capital punishment against those who evaded assessment. On its completion he issued an order that all the citizens of Rome, knights and infantry alike, should appear in the Campus Martius, each in their centuries. After the whole army had been drawn up there, he purified it by the triple sacrifice of a swine, a sheep, and an ox. This was called "a closed lustrum," because with it the census was completed. Eighty thousand citizens are said to have been included in that census. Fabius Pictor, the oldest of our historians, states that this was the number of those who could bear arms. To contain that population it was obvious that the City would have to be enlarged. He added to it the two hills—the Quirinal and the Viminal—and then made a further addition by including the Esquiline, and to give it more importance he lived there himself. He surrounded the City with a mound and moats and wall; in this way he extended the "pomoerium." Looking only to the etymology of the word, they explain "pomoerium" as "postmoerium"; but it is rather a "circamoerium." For the space which the Etruscans of old, when founding their cities, consecrated in accordance with auguries and marked off by boundary stones at intervals on each side, as the part where the wall was to be carried, was to be kept vacant so that no buildings might connect with the wall on the inside (whilst now they generally touch), and on the outside some ground might remain virgin soil untouched by cultivation. This space, which it was forbidden either to build upon or to plough, and which could not be said to be behind the wall any more than the wall could be said to be behind it, the Romans called the "pomoerium." As the City grew, these sacred boundary stones were always moved forward as far as the walls were advanced.

1.45

AFTER the State was augmented by the expansion of the City and all domestic arrangements adapted to the requirements of both peace and war, Servius endeavoured to extend his dominion by state-craft, instead of aggrandizing it by arms, and at the same time made an addition to the adornment of the City. The temple of the Ephesian Diana was famous at that time, and it was reported to have been built by the co-operation of the states of Asia. Servius had been careful to form ties of hospitality and friendship with the chiefs of the Latin nation, and he used to speak in the highest praise of that co-operation and the common recognition of the same deity. By constantly dwelling on this theme he at length induced the Latin tribes to join with the people of Rome in building a temple to

Diana in Rome. Their doing so was an admission of the predominance of Rome; a question which had so often been disputed by arms. Though the Latins, after their many unfortunate experiences in war, had as a nation laid aside all thoughts of success, there was amongst the Sabines one man who believed that an opportunity presented itself of recovering the supremacy through his own individual cunning. The story runs that a man of substance belonging to that nation had a heifer of marvelous size and beauty. The marvel was attested in after ages by the horns which were fastened up in the vestibule of the temple of Diana. The creature was looked upon as—what it really was—a prodigy, and the soothsayers predicted that, whoever sacrificed it to Diana, the state of which he was a citizen should be the seat of empire. This prophecy had reached the ears of the official in charge of the temple of Diana. When the first day on which the sacrifice could properly be offered arrived, the Sabine drove the heifer to Rome, took it to the temple, and placed it in front of the altar. The official in charge was a Roman, and, struck by the size of the victim, which was well known by report, he recalled the prophecy and addressing the Sabine, said, "Why, pray, are you, stranger, preparing to offer a polluted sacrifice to Diana? Go and bathe yourself first in running water. The Tiber is flowing down there at the bottom of the valley." Filled with misgivings, and anxious for everything to be done properly that the prediction might be fulfilled, the stranger promptly went down to the Tiber. Meanwhile the Roman sacrificed the heifer to Diana. This was a cause of intense gratification to the king and to his people.

1.48

SERVIUS had been summoned by a breathless messenger, and arrived on the scene while Tarquin was speaking. As soon as he reached the vestibule, he exclaimed in loud tones, "What is the meaning of this, Tarquin? How dared you, with such insolence, convene the senate or sit in that chair whilst I am alive?" Tarquin replied fiercely that he was occupying his father's seat, that a king's son was a much more legitimate heir to the throne than a slave, and that he, Servius, in playing his reckless game, had insulted his masters long enough. Shouts arose from their respective partisans, the people made a rush to the senate-house, and it was evident that he who won the fight would reign. Then Tarquin, forced by sheer necessity into proceeding to the last extremity, seized Servius round the waist, and being a much younger and stronger man, carried him out of the senate-house and flung him down the steps into the Forum below. He then returned to call the senate to order. The officers and attendants of the king fled. The king himself, half dead from the violence, was put to death by those whom Tarquin had sent in pursuit of him. It is the current belief that this was done at Tullia's suggestion, for it is quite in keeping with the rest of her wickedness. At all events, it is generally agreed that she drove down to the Forum in a two-wheeled car, and, unabashed by the presence of the crowd, called her husband out of the senate-house and was the first to salute him as king. He told her to make her way out of the tumult, and when on her return she had got as far as the top of the Cyprius Vicus, where the temple of Diana lately stood, and was turning to the right on the Urbius Clivus, to get to the Esquiline, the driver stopped horror-struck and pulled up, and pointed out to his mistress the corpse of the murdered Servius. Then, the tradition runs, a foul and unnatural crime was committed, the memory of which the place still bears, for they call it the Vicus Sceleratus. It is said that Tullia, goaded to madness by the avenging spirits of her sister and her husband, drove right over her father's body, and carried back some of her father's blood with which the car and she herself were defiled to her own and her husband's household gods, through whose anger a reign which began in wickedness was soon brought to a close by a like cause. Servius Tullius reigned forty-four years, and even a wise and good successor would have found it difficult to fill the throne as he had done. The glory of his reign was all the greater because with him perished all just and lawful kingship in Rome. Gentle and moderate as his sway had been, he had nevertheless, according to some authorities, formed the intention of laying it down, because it was vested in a single person, but this purpose of giving freedom to the State was cut short by that domestic crime.

1.49

LUCIUS Tarquinius now began his reign. His conduct procured for him the nickname of "Superbus," for he deprived his father-in-law of burial, on the plea that Romulus was not buried, and he slew the leading nobles whom he suspected of being partisans of Servius. Conscious that the precedent which he had set, of winning a throne by violence, might be used against himself, he surrounded himself with a guard. For he had nothing whatever by which to make good his claim to the crown except actual violence; he was reigning without either being elected by the people, or confirmed by the senate. As, moreover, he had no hope of winning the affections of the citizens, he had to maintain his dominion by fear. To make himself more dreaded, he conducted the trials in capital cases without any assessors, and under this presence he was able to put to death, banish, or fine not only those whom he suspected or disliked, but also those from whom his only object was to extort money. His main object was so to reduce the number of senators, by refusing to fill up any vacancies, that the dignity of the order itself might be lowered through the smallness of its numbers, and less indignation felt at all public business being taken out of its hands. He was the first of the kings to break through the traditional custom of consulting the senate on all questions, the first to conduct the government on the advice of his palace favourites. War, peace, treaties, alliances were made or broken off by him, just as he thought good, without any authority from either people or senate. He made a special point of securing the Latin nation, that through his power and influence abroad he might be safer amongst his subjects at home; he not only formed ties of hospitality with their chief men, but established family connections. He gave his daughter in marriage to Octavius Mamilius of Tusculum, who was quite the foremost man of the Latin race, descended, if we are to believe traditions, from Ulysses and the goddess Circe; through that connection he gained many of his son-in-law's relations and friends.

1.50

TARQUIN had now gained considerable influence amongst

the Latin nobility, and he sent word for them to meet on a fixed date at the Grove of Ferentina, as there were matters of mutual interest about which he wished to consult them. They assembled in considerable numbers at daybreak; Tarquin kept his appointment, it is true, but did not arrive till shortly before sunset. The council spent the whole day in discussing many topics. Turnus Herdonius, from Aricia, had made a fierce attack on the absent Tarquin. It was no wonder, he said, that the epithet "Tyrant" had been bestowed upon him at Rome—for this was what people commonly called him, though only in whispers—could anything show the tyrant more than his thus trifling with the whole Latin nation? After summoning the chiefs from distant homes, the man who had called the council was not present. He was in fact trying how far he could go, so that if they submitted to the yoke he might crush them. Who could not see that he was making his way to sovereignty over the Latins? Even supposing that his own countrymen did well to entrust him with supreme power, or rather that it was entrusted and not seized by an act of parricide, the Latins ought not, even in that case, to place it in the hands of an alien. But if his own people bitterly rue his sway, seeing how they are being butchered, sent into exile, stripped of all their property, what better fate can the Latins hope for? If they followed the speaker's advice they would go home and take as little notice of the day fixed for the council as he who had fixed it was taking. Just while these and similar sentiments were being uttered by the man who had gained his influence in Aricia by treasonable and criminal practice, Tarquin appeared on the scene. That put a stop to his speech, for all turned from the speaker to salute the king. When silence was restored, Tarquin was advised by those near to explain why he had come so late. He said that having been chosen as arbitrator between a father and a son, he had been detained by his endeavours to reconcile them, and as that matter had taken up the whole day, he would bring forward the measures he had decided upon the next day. It is said that even this explanation was not received by Turnus without his commenting on it; no case, he argued, could take up less time than one between a father and a son, it could be settled in a few words; if the son did not comply with the father's wishes he would get into trouble.

1.51

WITH these censures on the Roman king he left the council. Tarquin took the matter more seriously than he appeared to do and at once began to plan Turnus' death, in order that he might inspire the Latins with the same terror through which he had crushed the spirits of his subjects at home. As he had not the power to get him openly put to death, he compassed his destruction by bringing a false charge against him. Through the agency of some of the Aricians who were opposed to Turnus, he bribed a slave of his to allow a large quantity of swords to be carried secretly into his quarters. This plan was executed in one night. Shortly before daybreak Tarquin summoned the Latin chiefs into his presence, as though something had happened to give him great alarm. He told them that his delay on the previous day had been brought about by some divine providence, for it had proved the salvation both of them and himself. He was informed that Turnus was planning his murder and that of the leading men in the different cities, in order that he might hold sole rule over the Latins. He would have attempted it the previous day in the council; but the attempt was deferred owing to the absence of the convener of the council, the chief object of attack. Hence the abuse leveled against him in his absence, because his delay had frustrated the hopes of success. If the reports which reached him were true, he had no doubt that, on the assembling of the council at daybreak, Turnus would come armed and with a strong body of conspirators. It was asserted that a vast number of swords had been conveyed to him. Whether this was an idle rumour or not could very soon be ascertained, he asked them to go with him to Turnus. The restless, ambitious character of Turnus, his speech of the previous day, and Tarquin's delay, which easily accounted for the postponement of the murder, all lent colour to their suspicions. They went, inclined to accept Tarquin's statement, but quite prepared to regard the whole story as baseless, if the swords were not discovered. When they arrived, Turnus was roused from sleep and placed under guard, and the slaves who from affection to their master were preparing to defend him were seized. Then, when the concealed swords were produced from every corner of his lodgings, the matter appeared only too certain and Turnus was thrown into chains. Amidst great excitement a council of the Latins was at once summoned. The sight of the swords, placed in the midst, aroused such furious resentment that he was condemned, without being heard in his defense, to an unprecedented mode of death. He was thrown into the fountain of Ferentina and drowned by a hurdle weighted with stones being placed over him.

1.52

AFTER the Latins had reassembled in council and had been commended by Tarquin for having inflicted on Turnus a punishment befitting his revolutionary and murderous designs, Tarquin addressed them as follows: It was in his power to exercise a long-established right, since, as all the Latins traced their origin to Alba, they were included in the treaty made by Tullus under which the whole of the Alban State with its colonies passed under the suzerainty of Rome. He thought, however, that it would be more advantageous for all parties if that treaty were renewed, so that the Latins could enjoy a share in the prosperity of the Roman people, instead of always looking out for, or actually suffering, the demolition of their towns and the devastation of their fields, as happened in the reign of Ancus and afterwards whilst his own father was on the throne. The Latins were persuaded without much difficulty, although by that treaty Rome was the predominant State, for they saw that the heads of the Latin League were giving their adhesion to the king, and Turnus afforded a present example of the danger incurred by any one who opposed the king's wishes. So the treaty was renewed, and orders were issued for the "juniors" amongst the Latins to muster under arms, in accordance with the treaty, on a given day, at the Grove of Ferentina. In compliance with the order contingents assembled from all the thirty towns, and with a view to depriving them of their own general or a separate command, or distinctive standards, he formed one Latin and one Roman century into a maniple, thereby making one unit out of the two, whilst he doubled the strength of the maniples, and placed a centurion over each half.

1.53

HOWEVER tyrannical the king was in his domestic administration he was by no means a despicable general; in military skill he would have rivaled any of his predecessors had not the degeneration of his character in other directions prevented him from attaining distinction here also. He was the first to stir up war with the Volscians—a war which was to last for more than two hundred years after his time—and took from them the city of Pomptine Suessa. The booty was sold and he realized out of the proceeds forty talents of silver. He then sketched out the design of a temple to Jupiter, which in its extent should be worthy of the king of gods and men, worthy of the Roman empire, worthy of the majesty of the City itself. He set apart the above-mentioned sum for its construction. The next war occupied him longer than he expected. Failing to capture the neighbouring city of Gabii by assault and finding it useless to attempt an investment, after being defeated under its walls, he employed methods against it which were anything but Roman, namely, fraud and deceit. He pretended to have given up all thoughts of war and to be devoting himself to laying the foundations of his temple and other undertakings in the City. Meantime, it was arranged that Sextus, the youngest of his three sons, should go as a refugee to Gabii, complaining loudly of his father's insupportable cruelty, and declaring that he had shifted his tyranny from others on to his own family, and even regarded the presence of his children as a burden and was preparing to devastate his own family as he had devastated the senate, so that not a single descendant, not a single heir to the crown might be left. He had, he said, himself escaped from the murderous violence of his father, and felt that no place was safe for him except amongst Lucius Tarquin's enemies. Let them not deceive themselves, the war which apparently was abandoned was hanging over them, and at the first chance he would attack them when they least expected it. If amongst them there was no place for suppliants, he would wander through Latium, he would petition the Volsci, the Aequi, the Hernici, until he came to men who know how to protect children against the cruel and unnatural persecutions of parents. Perhaps he would find people with sufficient spirit to take up arms against a remorseless tyrant backed by a warlike people. As it seemed probable that if they paid no attention to him he would, in his angry mood, take his departure, the people of Gabii gave him a kind reception. They told him not to be surprised if his father treated his children as he had treated his own subjects and his allies; failing others he would end by murdering himself. They showed pleasure at his arrival and expressed their belief that with his assistance the war would be transferred from the gates of Gabii to the walls of Rome.

1.54

HE was admitted to the meetings of the national council. Whilst expressing his agreement with the elders of Gabii on other subjects, on which they were better informed, he was continually urging them to war, and claimed to speak with special authority, because he was acquainted with the strength of each nation, and knew that the king's tyranny, which even his own children had found insupportable, was certainly detested by his subjects. So after gradually working up the leaders of the Gabinians to revolt, he went in person with some of the most eager of the young men on foraging and plundering expeditions. By playing the hypocrite both in speech and action, he gained their mistaken confidence more and more; at last he was chosen as commander in the war. Whilst the mass of the population were unaware of what was intended, skirmishes took place between Rome and Gabii in which the advantage generally rested with the latter, until the Gabinians from the highest to the lowest firmly believed that Sextus Tarquin had been sent by heaven to be their leader. As for the soldiers, he became so endeared to them by sharing all their toils and dangers, and by a lavish distribution of the plunder, that the elder Tarquin was not more powerful in Rome than his son was in Gabii.

When he thought himself strong enough to succeed in anything that he might attempt, he sent one of his friends to his father at Rome to ask what he wished him to do now that the gods had given him sole and absolute power in Gabii. To this messenger no verbal reply was given, because, I believe, he mistrusted him. The king went into the palace-garden, deep in thought, his son's messenger following him. As he walked along in silence it is said that he struck off the tallest poppy-heads with his stick. Tired of asking and waiting for an answer, and feeling his mission to be a failure, the messenger returned to Gabii, and reported what he had said and seen, adding that the king, whether through temper or personal aversion or the arrogance which was natural to him, had not uttered a single word. When it had become clear to Sextus what his father meant him to understand by his mysterious silent action, he proceeded to get rid of the foremost men of the State by traducing some of them to the people, whilst others fell victims to their own unpopularity. Many were publicly executed, some against whom no plausible charges could be brought were secretly assassinated. Some were allowed to seek safety in flight or were driven into exile; the property of these as well as of those who had been put to death was distributed in grants and bribes. The gratification felt by each who received a share blunted the sense of the public mischief that was being wrought, until, deprived of all counsel and help, the State of Gabii was surrendered to the Roman king without a single battle.

1.55

AFTER the acquisition of Gabii, Tarquin made peace with the Aequi and renewed the treaty with the Etruscans. Then he turned his attention to the business of the City. The first thing was the temple of Jupiter on the Tarpeian Mount, which he was anxious to leave behind as a memorial of his reign and name; both the Tarquins were concerned in it, the father had vowed it, the son completed it. That the whole of the area which the temple of Jupiter was to occupy might be wholly devoted to that deity, he decided to deconsecrate the fanes and chapels, some of which had been originally vowed by King Tatius at the crisis of his battle with Romulus, and subsequently consecrated and inaugurated. Tradition records that at the commencement of this work the gods sent a divine intimation of the future vastness of the empire, for whilst the omens were favourable for the deconsecration of all the other shrines, they were unfavourable for that of the fane of Terminus. This was interpreted to mean that as the abode of Terminus was not moved and he alone of all the deities was not called forth from his consecrated borders, so all would be firm and immovable in the future empire. This augury of lasting dominion was followed by a prodigy which portended the greatness of the empire. It is said that whilst they were digging the foundations of the temple, a human head came to light with the face perfect; this appearance unmistakably portended that the spot would be the stronghold of empire and the head of all the world. This was the interpretation given by the soothsayers in the City, as well as by those who had been called into council from Etruria. The king's designs were now much more extensive; so much so that his share of the spoils of Pometia, which had been set apart to complete the work, now hardly met the cost of the foundations. This makes me inclined to trust Fabius—who, moreover is the older authority—when he says that the amount was only forty talents, rather than Piso, who states that forty thousand pounds of silver were set apart for that object. For not only is such a sum more than could be expected from the spoils of any single city at that time, but it would more than suffice for the foundations of the most magnificent building of the present day.

1.56

DETERMINED to finish his temple, he sent for workmen from all parts of Etruria, and not only used the public treasury to defray the cost, but also compelled the plebeians to take their share of the work. This was in addition to their military service, and was anything but a light burden. Still they felt it less of a hardship to build the temples of the gods with their own hands, than they did afterwards when they were transferred to other tasks less imposing, but involving greater toil—the construction of the "ford" in the Circus and that of the Cloaca Maxima, a subterranean tunnel to receive all the sewage of the City. The magnificence of these two works could hardly be equaled by anything in the present day. When the plebeians were no longer required for these works, he considered that such a multitude of unemployed would prove a burden to the State, and as he wished the frontiers of the empire to be more widely colonised, he sent colonists to Signia and Circeii to serve as a protection to the

City by land and sea. While he was carrying out these undertakings a frightful portent appeared; a snake gliding out of a wooden column created confusion and panic in the palace. The king himself was not so much terrified as filled with anxious forebodings. The Etruscan soothsayers were only employed to interpret prodigies which affected the State; but this one concerned him and his house personally, so he decided to send to the world-famed oracle of Delphi. Fearing to entrust the oracular response to any one else, he sent two of his sons to Greece, through lands at that time unknown and over seas still less known. Titus and Arruns started on their journey. They had as a traveling companion L. Junius Brutus, the son of the king's sister, Tarquinia, a young man of a very different character from that which he had assumed. When he heard of the massacre of the chiefs of the State, amongst them his own brother, by his uncle's orders, he determined that his intelligence should give the king no cause for alarm nor his fortune any provocation to his avarice, and that as the laws afforded no protection, he would seek safety in obscurity and neglect. Accordingly he carefully kept up the appearance and conduct of an idiot, leaving the king to do what he liked with his person and property, and did not even protest against his nickname of "Brutus"; for under the protection of that nickname the soul which was one day to liberate Rome was awaiting its destined hour. The story runs that when brought to Delphi by the Tarquins, more as a butt for their sport than as a companion, he had with him a golden staff enclosed in a hollow one of corner wood, which he offered to Apollo as a mystical emblem of his own character. After executing their father's commission the young men were desirous of ascertaining to which of them the kingdom of Rome would come. A voice came from the lowest depths of the cavern: "Whichever of you, young men, shall be the first to kiss his mother, he shall hold supreme sway in Rome." Sextus had remained behind in Rome, and to keep him in ignorance of this oracle and so deprive him of any chance of coming to the throne, the two Tarquins insisted upon absolute silence being kept on the subject. They drew lots to decide which of them should be the first to kiss his mother on their return to Rome. Brutus, thinking that the oracular utterance had another meaning, pretended to stumble, and as he fell kissed the ground, for the earth is of course the common mother of us all. Then they returned to Rome, where preparations were being energetically pushed forward for a war with the Rutulians.

1.57

THIS people, who were at that time in possession of Ardea, were, considering the nature of their country and the age in which they lived, exceptionally wealthy. This circumstance really originated the war, for the Roman king was anxious to repair his own fortune, which had been exhausted by the magnificent scale of his public works, and also to conciliate his subjects by a distribution of the spoils of war. His tyranny had already produced disaffection, but what moved their special resentment was the way they had been so long kept by the king at manual and even servile labour. An attempt was made to take Ardea by assault; when that failed recourse was had to a regular investment to starve the enemy out. When troops are stationary, as is the case in a protracted more than in an active campaign, furloughs are easily granted, more so to the men of rank, however, than to the common soldiers. The royal princes sometimes spent their leisure hours in feasting and entertainments, and at a wine party given by Sextus Tarquinius at which Collatinus, the son of Egerius, was present, the conversation happened to turn upon their wives, and each began to speak of his own in terms of extraordinarily high praise. As the dispute became warm, Collatinus said that there was no need of words, it could in a few hours be ascertained how far his Lucretia was superior to all the rest. "Why do we not," he exclaimed, "if we have any youthful vigour about us, mount our horses and pay our wives a visit and find out their characters on the spot? What we see of the behaviour of each on the unexpected arrival of her husband, let that be the surest test." They were heated with wine, and all shouted: "Good! Come on!" Setting spur to their horses they galloped off to Rome, where they arrived as darkness was beginning to close in. Thence they proceeded to Collatia, where they found Lucretia very differently employed from the king's daughters-in-law, whom they had seen passing their time in feasting and luxury with their acquaintances. She was sitting at her wool work in the hall, late at night, with her maids busy round her. The palm in this competition of wifely virtue was awarded to Lucretia. She welcomed the arrival of her husband and the Tarquins, whilst her victorious spouse courteously invited the royal princes to remain as his guests. Sextus Tarquin, inflamed by the beauty and exemplary purity of Lucretia, formed the vile project of effecting her dishonour. After their youthful frolic they returned for the time to camp.

1.58

A FEW days afterwards Sextus Tarquin went, unknown to Collatinus, with one companion to Collatia. He was hospitably received by the household, who suspected nothing, and after supper was conducted to the bedroom set apart for guests. When all around seemed safe and everybody fast asleep, he went in the frenzy of his passion with a naked sword to the sleeping Lucretia, and placing his left hand on her breast, said, "Silence, Lucretia! I am Sextus Tarquin, and I have a sword in my hand; if you utter a word, you shall die." When the woman, terrified out of her sleep, saw that no help was near, and instant death threatening her, Tarquin began to confess his passion, pleaded, used threats as well as entreaties, and employed every argument likely to influence a female heart. When he saw that she was inflexible and not moved even by the fear of death, he threatened to disgrace her, declaring that he would lay the naked corpse of the slave by her dead body, so that it might be said that she had been slain in foul adultery. By this awful threat, his lust triumphed over her inflexible chastity, and Tarquin went off exulting in having successfully attacked her honour. Lucretia, overwhelmed with grief at such a frightful outrage, sent a messenger to her father at Rome and to her husband at Ardea, asking them to come to her, each accompanied by one faithful friend; it was necessary to act, and to act promptly; a horrible thing had happened. Spurius Lucretius came with Publius Valerius, the son of Volesus; Collatinus with Lucius Junius Brutus, with whom he happened to be returning to Rome when he was met by his wife's messenger. They found Lucretia sitting in her room prostrate with grief. As they entered, she burst into tears, and to her husband's inquiry whether all was well, replied, "No! what can be well with a woman when her honour is lost? The marks of a stranger, Collatinus, are in your bed. But it is only the body that has been violated, the soul is pure; death shall bear witness to that. But pledge me your solemn word that the adulterer shall not go unpunished. It is Sextus Tarquin, who, coming as an enemy instead of a guest, forced from me last night by brutal violence a pleasure fatal to me, and, if you are men, fatal to him." They all successively pledged their word, and tried to console the distracted woman by turning the guilt from the victim of the outrage to the perpetrator, and urging that it is the mind that sins, not the body, and where there has been no consent there is no guilt. "It is for you," she said, "to see that he gets his deserts; although I acquit myself of the sin, I do not free myself from the penalty; no unchaste woman shall henceforth live and plead Lucretia's example." She had a knife concealed in her dress which she plunged into her heart, and fell dying on the floor. Her father and husband raised the death-cry.

1.59

WHILST they were absorbed in grief, Brutus drew the knife from Lucretia's wound, and holding it, dripping with blood, in front of him, said, "By this blood—most pure before the outrage wrought by the king's son—I swear, and you, O gods, I call to witness that I will drive hence Lucius Tarquinius Superbus, together with his cursed wife and his whole brood, with fire and sword and every means in my power, and I will not suffer them or any one else to reign in Rome." Then he handed the knife to Collatinus and then to Lucretius and Valerius, who were all astounded at the marvel of the thing, wondering whence Brutus had acquired this new character. They swore as they were directed; all their grief changed to wrath, and they followed the lead of Brutus, who summoned them to abolish the monarchy forthwith. They carried the body of Lucretia from her home down to the Forum, where, owing to the unheard-of atrocity of the crime, they at once collected a crowd. Each had his own complaint to make of the wickedness and violence of the royal house. Whilst all were moved by the father's deep distress, Brutus bade them stop their tears and idle laments, and urged them to act as men and Romans and take up arms against their insolent foes. All the high-spirited amongst the younger men came forward as armed volunteers, the rest followed their example. A portion of this body was left to hold Collatia, and guards were stationed at the gates to prevent any news of the movement from reaching the king; the rest marched in arms to Rome with Brutus in command. On their arrival, the sight of so many men in arms spread panic and confusion wherever they marched, but when again the people saw that the foremost men of the State were leading the way, they realized that whatever the movement was it was a serious one. The terrible occurrence created no less excitement in Rome than it had done in Collatia; there was a rush from all quarters of the City to the Forum. When they had gathered there, the herald summoned them to attend the "Tribune of the Celeres"; this was the office which Brutus happened at the time to be holding. He made a speech quite out of keeping with the character and temper he had up to that day assumed. He dwelt upon the brutality and licentiousness of Sextus Tarquin, the infamous outrage on Lucretia and her pitiful death, the bereavement sustained by her father, Tricipitinus, to whom the cause of his daughter's death was more shameful and distressing than the actual death itself. Then he dwelt on the tyranny of the king, the toils and sufferings of the plebeians kept underground clearing out ditches and sewers—Roman men, conquerors of all the surrounding nations, turned from warriors into artisans and stonemasons! He reminded them of the shameful murder of Servius Tullius and his daughter driving in her accursed chariot over her father's body, and solemnly invoked the gods as the avengers of murdered parents. By enumerating these and, I believe, other still more atrocious incidents which his keen sense of the present injustice suggested, but which it is not easy to give in detail, he goaded on the incensed multitude to strip the king of his sovereignty and pronounce a sentence of banishment against Tarquin with his wife and children. With a picked body of the "Juniors," who volunteered to follow him, he went off to the camp at Ardea to incite the army against the king, leaving the command in the City to Lucretius, who had previously been made Prefect of the City by the king. During the commotion Tullia fled from the palace amidst the execrations of all whom she met, men and women alike invoking her father's avenging spirit against her.

1.60

WHEN the news of these proceedings reached the camp, the king, alarmed at the turn affairs were taking, hurried to Rome to quell the outbreak. Brutus, who was on the same road had become aware of his approach, and to avoid meeting him took another route, so that he reached Ardea and Tarquin Rome almost at the same time, though by different ways. Tarquin found the gates shut, and a decree of banishment passed against him; the Liberator of the City received a joyous welcome in the camp, and the king's sons were expelled from it. Two of them followed their father into exile amongst the Etruscans in Caere. Sextus Tarquin proceeded to Gabii, which he looked upon as his kingdom, but was killed in revenge for the old feuds he had kindled by his rapine and murders. Lucius Tarquinius Superbus reigned twenty-five years. The whole duration of the regal government from the foundation of the City to its liberation was two hundred and forty-four years. Two consuls were then elected in the assembly of centuries by the prefect of the City, in accordance with the regulations of Servius Tullius. They were Lucius Junius Brutus and Lucius Tarquinius Collatinus.

Book II: The Early Years of the Republic

2.1

IT is of a Rome henceforth free that I am to write the history—her civil administration and the conduct of her wars, her annually elected magistrates, the authority of her laws supreme over all her citizens. The tyranny of the last king made this liberty all the more welcome, for such had been the rule of the former kings that they might not undeservedly be counted as founders of parts, at all events, of the city; for the additions they made were required as abodes for the increased population which they themselves had augmented. There is no question that the Brutus who won such glory through the expulsion of Superbus would have inflicted the gravest injury on the State had he wrested the sovereignty from any of the former kings, through desire of a liberty for which the people were not ripe. What would have been the result if that horde of shepherds and immigrants, fugitives from their own cities, who had secured liberty, or at all events impunity, in the shelter of an inviolable sanctuary,—if, I say, they had been freed from the restraining power of kings and, agitated by tribunician storms, had begun to foment quarrels with the patricians in a City where they were aliens before sufficient time had elapsed for either family ties or a growing love for the very soil to effect a union of hearts? The infant State would have been torn to pieces by internal dissension. As it was, however, the moderate and tranquilizing authority of the kings had so fostered it that it was at last able to bring forth the fair fruits of liberty in the maturity of its strength. But the origin of liberty may be referred to this time rather because the consular authority was limited to one year than because there was any weakening of the authority which the kings had possessed. The first consuls retained all the old jurisdiction and insignia of office, one only, however, had the "fasces," to prevent the fear which might have been inspired by the sight of both with those dread symbols. Through the concession of his colleague, Brutus had them first, and he was not less zealous in guarding the public liberty than he had been in achieving it. His first act was to secure the people, who were now jealous of their newly-recovered liberty, from being influenced by any entreaties or bribes from the king. He therefore made them take an oath that they would not suffer any man to reign in Rome. The senate had been thinned by the murderous cruelty of Tarquin, and Brutus' next care was to strengthen its influence by selecting some of the leading men of equestrian rank to fill the vacancies; by this means he brought it up to the old number of three hundred. The new members were known as "conscripti," the old ones retained their designation of "patres." This measure had a wonderful effect in promoting harmony in the State and bringing the patricians and plebeians together.

2.2

HE next gave his attention to the affairs of religion. Certain public functions had hitherto been executed by the kings in person; with the view of supplying their place a "king for sacrifices" was created, and lest he should become king in anything more than name, and so threaten that liberty which was their first care, his office was made subordinate to the Pontifex Maximus. I think that they went to unreasonable lengths in devising safeguards for their liberty, in all, even the smallest points. The second consul, L. Tarquinius Collatinus, bore an unpopular name—this was his sole offence—and men said that the Tarquins had been too long in power. They began with Priscus; then Servius Tullius reigned, and Superbus Tarquinius, who even after this interruption had not lost sight of the throne which another filled, regained it by crime and violence as the hereditary possession of his house. And now that he was expelled, their power was being wielded by Collatinus; the Tarquins did not know how to live in a private station, the very name was a danger to liberty. What were at first whispered hints became the common talk of the City, and as the people were becoming suspicious and alarmed, Brutus summoned an assembly. He first of all rehearsed the people's oath, that they would suffer no man to reign or to live in Rome by whom the public liberty might be imperiled. This was to be guarded with the utmost care, no means of doing so were to be neglected. Personal regard made him reluctant to speak, nor would he have spoken had not his affection for the commonwealth compelled him. The Roman people did consider that their freedom was not yet fully won; the royal race, the royal name, was still there, not only amongst the citizens but in the government; in that fact lay an injury, an obstacle to full liberty. Turning to his brother consul: "These apprehensions it is for you, L. Tarquinius, to banish of your own free will. We have not forgotten, I assure you, that you expelled the king's family, complete your good work, remove their very name. Your fellow-citizens will, on my authority, not only hand over your property, but if you need anything, they will add to it with lavish generosity. Go, as our friend, relieve the commonwealth from a, perhaps groundless, fear: men are persuaded that only with the family will the tyranny of the

Tarquins depart." At first the consul was struck dumb with astonishment at this extraordinary request; then, when he was beginning to speak, the foremost men in the commonwealth gathered round him and repeatedly urged the same plea, but with little success. It was not till Spurius Lucretius, his superior in age and rank, and also his father-in-law, began to use every method of entreaty and persuasion that he yielded to the universal wish. The consul, fearing lest after his year of office had expired and he returned to private life, the same demand should be made upon him, accompanied with loss of property and the ignominy of banishment, formally laid down the consulship, and after transferring all his effects to Lanuvium, withdrew from the State. A decree of the senate empowered Brutus to propose to the people a measure exiling all the members of the house of Tarquin. He conducted the election of a new consul, and the centuries elected as his colleague Publius Valerius, who had acted with him in the expulsion of the royal family.

2.3

THOUGH no one doubted that war with the Tarquins was imminent, it did not come as soon as was universally expected. What was not expected, however, was that through intrigue and treachery the newly won liberty was almost lost. There were some young men of high birth in Rome who during the late reign had done pretty much what they pleased, and being boon companions of the young Tarquins were accustomed to live in royal fashion. Now that all were equal before the law, they missed their former license and complained that the liberty which others enjoyed had become slavery for them; as long as there was a king, there was a person from whom they could get what they wanted, whether lawful or not, there was room for personal influence and kindness, he could show severity or indulgence, could discriminate between his friends and his enemies. But the law was a thing, deaf and inexorable, more favourable to the weak than to the powerful, showing no indulgence or forgiveness to those who transgressed; human nature being what it was, it was a dangerous plan to trust solely to one's innocence. When they had worked themselves into a state of disaffection, envoys from the royal family arrived, bringing a demand for the restoration of their property without any allusion to their possible return. An audience was granted them by the senate, and the matter was discussed for some days; fears were expressed that the non-surrender would be taken as a pretext for war, while if surrendered it might provide the means of war. The envoys, meantime, were engaged on another task: whilst ostensibly seeking only the surrender of the property they were secretly hatching schemes for regaining the crown. Whilst canvassing the young nobility in favour of their apparent object, they sounded them as to their other proposals, and meeting with a favourable reception, they brought letters addressed to them by the Tarquins and discussed plans for admitting them secretly at night into the City.

2.4

THE project was at first entrusted to the brothers Vitellii and Aquilii. The sister of the Vitellii was married to the consul Brutus, and there were grown-up children from this marriage—Titus and Tiberius. Their uncles took them into the conspiracy, there were others besides, whose names have been lost. In the meantime the opinion that the property ought to be restored was adopted by the majority of the senate, and this enabled the envoys to prolong their stay, as the consuls required time to provide vehicles for conveying the goods. They employed their time in consultations with the conspirators and they insisted on getting a letter which they were to give to the Tarquins, for without such a guarantee, they argued, how could they be sure that their envoys had not brought back empty promises in a matter of such vast importance? A letter was accordingly given as a pledge of good faith, and this it was that led to the discovery of the plot. The day previous to the departure of the envoys they happened to be dining at the house of the Vitellii. After all who were not in the secret had left, the conspirators discussed many details respecting their projected treason, which were overheard by one of the slaves who had previously suspected that something was afoot, but was waiting for the moment when the letter should be given, as its seizure would be a complete proof of the plot When he found that it had been given, he disclosed the affair to the consuls. They at once proceeded to arrest the envoys and the conspirators, and crushed the whole plot without exciting any alarm. Their first care was to secure the letter before it was destroyed. The traitors were forthwith thrown into prison; there was some hesitation in dealing with the envoys, and although they had evidently been guilty of a hostile act, the rights of international law were accorded them.

2.5

THE question of the restoration of the property was referred anew to the senate, who yielding to their feelings of resentment prohibited its restoration, and forbade its being brought into the treasury; it was given as plunder to the plebs, that their share in this spoliation might destroy for ever any prospect of peaceable relations with the Tarquins. The land of the Tarquins, which lay between the City and the Tiber, was henceforth sacred to Mars and known as the Campus Martius. There happened, it is said, to be a crop of corn there which was ripe for the harvest, and as it would have been sacrilege to consume what was growing on the Campus, a large body of men were sent to cut it. They carried it, straw and all, in baskets to the Tiber and threw it into the river. It was the height of the summer and the stream was low, consequently the corn stuck in the shallows, and heaps of it were covered with mud; gradually as the debris which the river brought down collected there, an island was formed. I believe that it was subsequently raised and strengthened so that the surface might be high enough above the water and firm enough to carry temples and colonnades. After the royal property had been disposed of, the traitors were sentenced and executed. Their punishment created a great sensation owing to the fact that the consular office imposed upon a father the duty of inflicting punishment on his own children; he who ought not to have witnessed it was destined to be the one to see it duly carried out. Youths belonging to the noblest families were standing tied to the post, but all eyes were turned to the consul's children, the others were unnoticed. Men did not grieve more for their punishment than for the crime which had incurred it—that they should have conceived the idea, in that year above all, of betraying to one, who had been a ruthless tyrant and was now an exile and an enemy, a newly liberated country, their father who had liberated it, the consulship which had originated in the Junian house, the senate, the plebs, all that Rome possessed of human or divine. The consuls took their seats, the lictors were told off to inflict the penalty; they scourged their bared backs with rods and then beheaded them. During the whole time, the father's countenance betrayed his feelings, but the father's stern resolution was still more apparent as he superintended the public execution. After the guilty had paid the penalty, a notable example of a different nature was provided to act as a deterrent of crime, the informer was assigned a sum of money from the treasury and he was given his liberty and the rights of citizenship. He is said to have been the first to be made free by the "vindicta." Some suppose this designation to have been derived from him, his name being Vindicius. After him it was the rule that those who were made free in this way were considered to be admitted to the citizenship.

2.6

A DETAILED report of these matters reached Tarquin. He was not only furious at the failure of plans from which he had hoped so much, but he was filled with rage at finding the way blocked against secret intrigues; and consequently determined upon open war. He visited the cities of Etruria and appealed for help; in particular, he implored the people of Veii and Tarquinii not to allow one to perish before their eyes who was of the same blood with them, and from being a powerful monarch was now, with his children, homeless and destitute. Others, he said, had been invited from abroad to reign in Rome; he, the king, whilst extending the rule of Rome by a successful war, had been driven out by the infamous conspiracy of his nearest kinsmen. They had no single person amongst them deemed worthy to reign, so they had distributed the kingly authority amongst themselves, and had given his property as plunder to the people, that all might be involved in the crime. He wanted to recover his country and his throne and punish his ungrateful subjects. The Veientines must help him and furnish him with resources, they must set about avenging their own wrongs also, their legions so often cut to pieces, their territory torn from them. This appeal decided the Veientines, they one and all loudly demanded that their former humiliations should be wiped out and their losses made good, now that they had a Roman to lead them. The people of Tarquinii were won over by the name and nationality of the exile; they were proud of having a countryman as king in Rome. So two armies from these cities followed Tarquin to recover his crown and chastise the Romans. When they had entered the Roman territory the consuls advanced against them; Valerius with the infantry in phalanx formation, Brutus reconnoitering in advance with the cavalry. Similarly the enemy's cavalry was in front of his main body, Arruns Tarquin, the king's sons, in command; the king himself followed with the legionaries. Whilst still at a distance Arruns distinguished the consul by his escort of lictors; as they drew nearer he clearly recognised Brutus by his features, and in a transport of rage exclaimed, "That is the man who drove us from our country; see him proudly advancing, adorned with our insignia! Ye gods, avengers of kings, aid me!" With these words, he dug spurs into his horse and rode straight at the consul. Brutus saw that he was making for him. It was a point of honour in those days for the leaders to engage in single combat, so he eagerly accepted the challenge, and they charged with such fury, neither of them thinking of protecting himself, if only he could wound his foe, that each drove his spear at the same moment through the other's shield, and they fell dying from their horses, with the spears sticking in them. The rest of the cavalry at once engaged, and not long after the infantry came up. The battle raged with varying fortune, the two armies being fairly matched; the right wing of each was victorious, the left defeated. The Veientes, accustomed to defeat at the hands of the Romans, were scattered in flight, but the Tarquinians, a new foe, not only held their ground, but forced the Romans to give way.

2.7

AFTER the battle had gone in this way, so great a panic seized Tarquin and the Etruscans that the two armies of Veii and Tarquinii, on the approach of night, despairing of success, left the field and departed for their homes. The story of the battle was enriched by marvels. In the silence of the next night a great voice is said to have come from the forest of Arsia, believed to be the voice of Silvanus, which spoke thus: "The fallen of the Tusci are one more than those of their foe; the Roman is conqueror." At all events the Romans left the field as victors; the Etruscans regarded themselves as vanquished, for when daylight appeared not a single enemy was in sight. P. Valerius, the consul, collected the spoils and returned in triumph to Rome. He celebrated his colleague's obsequies with all the pomp possible in those days, but far greater honour was done to the dead by the universal mourning, which was rendered specially noteworthy by the fact that the matrons were a whole year in mourning for him, because he had been such a determined avenger of violated chastity. After this the surviving consul, who had been in such favour with the multitude, found himself—such is its fickleness—not only unpopular but an object of suspicion, and that of a very grave character. It was rumoured that he was aiming at monarchy, for he had held no election to fill Brutus' place, and he was building a house on the top of the Velia, an impregnable fortress was being constructed on that high and strong position. The consul felt hurt at finding these rumours so widely believed, and summoned the people to an assembly. As he entered the "fasces" were lowered, to the great delight of the multitude, who understood that it was to them that they were lowered as an open avowal that the dignity and might of the people were greater than those of the consul. Then, after securing silence, he began to eulogise the good fortune of his colleague who had met his death, as a liberator of his country, possessing the highest honour it could bestow, fighting for the commonwealth, whilst his glory was as yet undimmed by jealousy and distrust. Whereas he himself had outlived his glory and fallen on days of suspicion and opprobrium; from being a liberator of his country he had sunk to the level of the Aquilii and Vitellii. "Will you," he cried, "never deem any man's merit so assured that it cannot be tainted by suspicion? Am I, the most determined foe to kings to dread the suspicion of desiring to be one myself? Even if I were dwelling in the Citadel on the Capitol, am I to believe it possible that I should be feared by my fellow-citizens? Does my reputation amongst you hang on so slight a thread? Does your confidence rest upon such a weak foundation that it is of greater moment where I am than who I am? The house of Publius Valerius shall be no check upon your freedom, your Velia shall be safe. I will not only move my house to level ground, but I will move it to the bottom of the hill that you may dwell above the citizen whom you suspect. Let those dwell on the Velia who are regarded as truer friends of liberty than Publius Valerius." All the materials were forthwith carried below the Velia and his house was built at the very bottom of the hill where now stands the temple of Vica Pota.

2.8

LAWS were passed which not only cleared the consul from suspicion but produced such a reaction that he won the people's affections, hence his soubriquet of Publicola. The most popular of these laws were those which granted a right of appeal from the magistrate to the people and devoted to the gods the person and property of any one who entertained projects of becoming king. Valerius secured the passing of these laws while still sole consul, that the people might feel grateful solely to him; afterwards he held the elections for the appointment of a colleague. The consul elected was Sp. Lucretius. But he had not, owing to his great age, strength enough to discharge the duties of his office, and within a few days he died. M. Horatius Pulvillus was elected in his place. In some ancient authors I find no mention of Lucretius, Horatius being named immediately after Brutus; as he did nothing of any note during his office, I suppose, his memory has perished. The temple of Jupiter on the Capitol had not yet been dedicated, and the consuls drew lots to decide which should dedicate it. The lot fell to Horatius. Publicola set out for the Veientine war. His friends showed unseemly annoyance at the dedication of so illustrious a fane being assigned to Horatius, and tried every means of preventing it. When all else failed, they tried to alarm the consul, whilst he was actually holding the door-post during the dedicatory prayer, by a wicked message that his son was dead, and he could not dedicate a temple while death was in his house. As to whether he disbelieved the message, or whether his conduct simply showed extraordinary self-control, there is no definite tradition, and it is not easy to decide from the records. He only allowed the message to interrupt him so far that he gave orders for the body to be burnt; then, with his hand still on the door-post, he finished the prayer and dedicated the temple. These were the principal incidents at home and in the field during the first year after the expulsion of the royal family. The consuls elected for the next year were P. Valerius, for the second time, and T. Lucretius.

2.9

THE Tarquins had now taken refuge with Porsena, the king of Clusium, whom they sought to influence by entreaty mixed with warnings. At one time they entreated him not to allow men of Etruscan race, of the same blood as himself, to wander as penniless exiles; at another they would warn him not to let the new fashion of expelling kings go unpunished. Liberty, they urged, possessed fascination enough in itself; unless kings defend their authority with as much energy as their subjects show in quest of liberty, all things come to a dead level, there will be no one thing preeminent or superior to all else in the State; there will soon be an end of kingly power, which is the most beautiful thing, whether amongst gods or amongst mortal men. Porsena considered that the presence of an Etruscan upon the Roman throne would be an honour to his nation; accordingly he advanced with an army against Rome. Never before had the senate been in such a state of alarm, so great at that time was the power of Clusium and the reputation of Porsena. They feared not only the enemy but even their own fellow-citizens, lest the plebs, overcome by their fears, should admit the Tarquins into the City, and accept peace even though it meant slavery. Many concessions were made at that time to the plebs by the senate. Their first care was to lay in a stock of corn, and commissioners were despatched to Vulsi and Cumae to collect supplies. The sale of salt, hitherto in the hands of private individuals who had raised the price to a high figure, was now wholly transferred to the State. The plebs were exempted from the payment of harbour-dues and the war-tax, so that they might fall on the rich, who could bear the burden; the poor were held to pay sufficient to the State if they brought up their children. This generous action of the senate maintained the harmony of the commonwealth through the subsequent stress of siege and famine so completely that the name of king was not more abhorrent to the highest than it was to the lowest, nor did any demagogue ever succeed in becoming so popular in after times as the senate was then by its beneficent legislation.

2.10

ON the appearance of the enemy the country people fled into the City as best they could. The weak places in the defenses were occupied by military posts; elsewhere the walls and the Tiber were deemed sufficient protection. The enemy would have forced their way over the Sublician bridge had it not been for one man, Horatius Cocles. The good fortune of Rome provided him as her bulwark on that memorable day. He happened to be on guard at the bridge when he saw the Janiculum taken by a sudden assault and the enemy rushing down from it to the river, whilst his own men, a panic-struck mob, were deserting their posts and throwing away their arms. He reproached them one after another for their cowardice, tried to stop them, appealed to them in heaven's name to stand, declared that it was in vain for them to seek safety in flight whilst leaving the bridge open behind them, there would very soon be more of the enemy on the Palatine and the Capitol than there were on the Janiculum. So he shouted to them to break down the bridge by sword or fire, or by whatever means they could, he would meet the enemies' attack so far as one man could keep them at bay. He advanced to the head of the bridge. Amongst the fugitives, whose backs alone were visible to the enemy, he was conspicuous as he fronted them armed for fight at close quarters. The enemy were astounded at his preternatural courage. Two men were kept by a sense of shame from deserting him—Sp. Lartius and T. Herminius—both of them men of high birth and renowned courage. With them he sustained the first tempestuous shock and wild confused onset, for a brief interval. Then, whilst only a small portion of the bridge remained and those who were cutting it down called upon them to retire, he insisted upon these, too, retreating. Looking round with eyes dark with menace upon the Etruscan chiefs, he challenged them to single combat, and reproached them all with being the slaves of tyrant kings, and whilst unmindful of their own liberty coming to attack that of others. For some time they hesitated, each looking round upon the others to begin. At length shame roused them to action, and raising a shout they hurled their javelins from all sides on their solitary foe. He caught them on his outstretched shield, and with unshaken resolution kept his place on the bridge with firmly planted foot. They were just attempting to dislodge him by a charge when the crash of the broken bridge and the shout which the Romans raised at seeing the work completed stayed the attack by filling them with sudden panic. Then Cocles said, "Tiberinus, holy father, I pray thee to receive into thy propitious stream these arms and this thy warrior." So, fully armed, he leaped into the Tiber, and though many missiles fell over him he swam across in safety to his friends: an act of daring more famous than credible with posterity. The State showed its gratitude for such courage; his statue was set up in the Comitium, and as much land given to him as he could drive the plough round in one day. Besides this public honour, the citizens individually showed their feeling; for, in spite of the great scarcity, each, in proportion to his means, sacrificed what he could from his own store as a gift to Cocles.

2.11

REPULSED in his first attempt, Porsena changed his plans from assault to blockade. After placing a detachment to hold the Janiculum he fixed his camp on the plain between that hill and the Tiber, and sent everywhere for boats, partly to intercept any attempt to get corn into Rome and partly to carry his troops across to different spots for plunder, as opportunity might serve. In a short time he made the whole of the district round Rome so insecure that not only were all the crops removed from the fields but even the cattle were all driven into the City, nor did any one venture to take them outside the gates. The impunity with which the Etruscans committed their depredations was due to strategy on the part of the Romans more than to fear. For the consul Valerius, determined to get an opportunity of attacking them when they were scattered in large numbers over the fields, allowed small forages to pass unnoticed, whilst he was reserving himself for vengeance on a larger scale. So to draw on the pillagers, he gave orders to a considerable body of his men to drive cattle out of the Esquiline gate, which was the furthest from the enemy, in the expectation that they would gain intelligence of it through the slaves who were deserting, owing to the scarcity produced by the blockade. The information was duly conveyed, and in consequence they crossed the river in larger numbers than usual in the hope of securing the whole lot. P. Valerius ordered T. Herminius with a small body of troops to take up a concealed position at a distance of two miles on the Gabian road, whilst Sp. Lartius with some light-armed infantry was to post himself at the Colline gate until the enemy had passed him and then to intercept their retreat to the river. The other consul, T. Lucretius, with a few maniples made a sortie from the Naevian gate; Valerius himself led some picked cohorts from the Caelian hill, and these were the first to attract the enemy's notice. When Herminius became aware that fighting was begun, he rose from ambush and took the enemy who were engaged with Valerius in rear. Answering cheers arose right and left, from the Colline and the Naevian gates and the pillagers, hemmed in, unequal to the fight, and with every way of escape blocked, were cut to pieces. That put an end to these irregular and scattered excursions on the part of the Etruscans.

2.12

THE blockade, however, continued, and with it a growing scarcity of corn at famine prices. Porsena still cherished hopes of capturing the City by keeping up the investment. There was a young noble, C. Mucius, who regarded it as a disgrace that whilst Rome in the days of servitude under her kings had never been blockaded in any war or by any foe, she should now, in the day of her freedom, be besieged by those very Etruscans whose armies she had often routed. Thinking that this disgrace ought to be avenged by some great deed of daring, he determined in the first instance to penetrate into the enemy's camp on his own responsibility. On second thoughts, however, he became apprehensive that if he went without orders from the consuls, or unknown to any one, and happened to be arrested by the Roman outposts, he might be brought back as a deserter, a charge which the condition of the City at the time would make only too probable. So he went to the senate. "I wish," he said, "Fathers, to swim the Tiber, and, if I can, enter the enemy's camp, not as a pillager nor to inflict retaliation for their pillagings. I am purposing, with heaven's help, a greater deed." The senate gave their approval. Concealing a sword in his robe, he started. When he reached the camp he took his stand in the densest part of the crowd near the royal tribunal. It happened to be the soldiers' pay-day, and a secretary, sitting by the king and dressed almost exactly like him, was busily engaged, as the soldiers kept coming to him incessantly. Afraid to ask which of the two was the king, lest his ignorance should betray him, Mucius struck as fortune directed the blow and killed the secretary instead of the king. He tried to force his way back with his blood-stained dagger through the dismayed crowd, but the shouting caused a rush to be made to the spot; he was seized and dragged back by the king's bodyguard to the royal tribunal. Here, alone and helpless, and in the utmost peril, he was still able to inspire more fear than he felt. "I am a citizen of Rome," he said, "men call me C. Mucius. As an enemy I wished to kill an enemy, and I have as much courage to meet death as I had to inflict it. It is the Roman nature to act bravely and to suffer bravely. I am not alone in having made this resolve against you, behind me there is a long list of those who aspire to the same distinction. If then it is your pleasure, make up your mind for a struggle in which you will every hour have to fight for your life and find an armed foe on the threshold of your royal tent. This is the war which we the youth of Rome, declare against you. You have no serried ranks, no pitched battle to fear, the matter will be settled between you alone and each one of us singly." The king, furious with anger, and at the same time terrified at the unknown danger, threatened that if he did not promptly explain the nature of the plot which he was darkly hinting at he should be roasted alive. "Look," Mucius cried, "and learn how lightly those regard their bodies who have some great glory in view." Then he plunged his right hand into a fire burning on the altar. Whilst he kept it roasting there as if he were devoid of all sensation, the king, astounded at his preternatural conduct, sprang from his seat and ordered the youth to be removed from the altar. "Go," he said, "you have been a worse enemy to yourself than to me. I would invoke blessings on your courage if it were displayed on behalf of my country; as it is, I send you away exempt from all rights of war, unhurt, and safe." Then Mucius, reciprocating, as it were, this generous treatment, said, "Since you honour courage, know that what you could not gain by threats you have obtained by kindness. Three hundred of us, the foremost amongst the Roman youth, have sworn to attack you in this way. The lot fell to me first, the rest, in the order of their lot, will come each in his turn, till fortune shall give us a favourable chance against you."

2.13

MUCIUS was accordingly dismissed; afterwards he received the soubriquet of Scaevola, from the loss of his right hand. Envoys from Porsena followed him to Rome. The king's narrow escape from the first of many attempts; which was owing solely to the mistake of his assailant, and the prospect of having to meet as many attacks as there were conspirators, so unnerved him that he made proposals of peace to Rome. One for the restoration of the Tarquins was put forward, more because he could not well refuse their request than because he had any hope of its being granted. The demand for the restitution of their territory to the Veientines, and that for the surrender of hostages as a condition of the withdrawal of the detachment from the Janiculum, were felt by the Romans to be inevitable, and on their being accepted and peace concluded, Porsena moved his troops from the Janiculum and evacuated the Roman territory. As a recognition of his courage the senate gave C. Mucius a piece of land across the river, which was afterwards known as the Mucian Meadows. The honour thus paid to courage incited even women to do glorious things for the State. The Etruscan camp was situated not far from the river, and the maiden Cloelia, one of the hostages, escaped, unobserved, through the guards and at the head of her sister hostages swam across the river amidst a shower of javelins and restored them all safe to their relatives. When the news of this incident reached him, the king was at first exceedingly angry and sent to demand the surrender of Cloelia; the others he did not care about. Afterwards his feelings changed to admiration; he said that the exploit surpassed those of Cocles and

Mucius, and announced that whilst on the one hand he should consider the treaty broken if she were not surrendered, he would on the other hand, if she were surrendered, send her back to her people unhurt. Both sides behaved honourably; the Romans surrendered her as a pledge of loyalty to the terms of the treaty; the Etruscan king showed that with him courage was not only safe but honoured, and after eulogizing the girl's conduct, told her that he would make her a present of half the remaining hostages, she was to choose whom she would. It is said that after all had been brought before her, she chose the boys of tender age; a choice in keeping with maidenly modesty, and one approved by the hostages themselves, since they felt that the age which was most liable to ill-treatment should have the preference in being rescued from hostile hands. After peace was thus re-established, the Romans rewarded the unprecedented courage shown by a woman by an unprecedented honour, namely an equestrian statue. On the highest part of the Sacred Way a statue was erected representing the maiden sitting on horseback.

Book III:
The Decemvirate

3.11

THUS far the tribunes. The consuls at the other end of the Forum, however, placed their chairs in full view of the tribunes and proceeded with the levy. The tribunes ran to the spot, carrying the Assembly with them. A few were cited, apparently as an experiment, and a tumult arose at once. As soon as any one was seized by the consuls' orders, a tribune ordered him to be released. None of them confined himself to his legal rights; trusting to their strength they were bent upon getting what they set their minds upon by main force. The methods of the tribunes in preventing the enrollment were followed by the patricians in obstructing the Law, which was brought forward every day that the Assembly met. The trouble began when the tribunes had ordered the people to proceed to vote—

the patricians refused to withdraw. The older members of the order were generally absent from proceedings which were certain not to be controlled by reason, but given over to recklessness and license; the consuls, too, for the most part kept away, lest in the general disorder the dignity of their office might be exposed to insult. Caeso was a member of the Quinctian house, and his noble descent and great bodily strength and stature made him a daring and intrepid young man. To these gifts of the gods he added brilliant military qualities and eloquence as a public speaker, so that no one in the State was held to surpass him either in speech or action. When he took his stand in the middle of a group of patricians, conspicuous amongst them all, carrying as it were in his voice and personal strength all dictatorships and consulships combined, he was the one to withstand the attacks of the tribunes and the storms of popular indignation. Under his leadership the tribunes were often driven from the Forum, the plebeians routed and chased away, anybody who stood in his way went off stripped and beaten. It became quite clear that if this sort of thing were allowed to go on, the Law would be defeated. When the other tribunes were now almost in despair, Aulus Verginius, one of the college, impeached Caeso on a capital charge. This procedure inflamed more than it intimidated his violent temper; he opposed the Law and harassed the plebeians more fiercely than ever, and declared regular war against the tribunes. His accuser allowed him to rush to his ruin and fan the flame of popular hatred, and so supply fresh material for the charges to be brought against him. Meantime he continued to press the Law, not so much in the hope of carrying it as in order to provoke Caeso to greater recklessness. Many wild speeches and exploits of the younger patricians were fastened on Caeso to strengthen the suspicions against him. Still the opposition to the Law was kept up. A. Verginius frequently said to the plebeians, "Are you now aware, Quirites, that you cannot have the Law which you desire, and Caeso as a citizen, together? Yet, why do I talk of the Law? He is a foe to liberty, he surpasses all the Tarquins in tyranny. Wait till you see the man who now, in private station, acts the king in audacity and violence—wait till you see him made consul, or dictator." His words were endorsed by many who complained of having been beaten, and the tribune was urged to bring the matter to a decision.

3.12

THE day of trial was now at hand, and it was evident that men generally believed that their liberty depended upon the condemnation of Caeso. At last, to his great indignation, he was constrained to approach individual members of the plebs; he was followed by his friends, who were amongst the foremost men of the State. Titus Quinctius Capitolinus, who had three times been consul, after recounting his own numerous distinctions and those of his family, asserted that neither in the Quinctian house nor in the Roman State did there exist another such example of personal merit and youthful courage. He had been the foremost soldier in his army; he had often fought under his own eyes. Sp. Furius said that Caeso had been sent by Quinctius Capitolinus to his assistance when in difficulties, and that no single person had done more to retrieve the fortunes of the day. L. Lucretius, the consul of the previous year, in the splendour of his newly-won glory, associated Caeso with his own claim to distinction, enumerated the actions in which he had taken part, recounted his brilliant exploits on the march and in the field, and did his utmost to persuade them to retain as their own fellow-citizen a young man furnished with every advantage that nature and fortune could give, who would be an immense power in any state of which he became a member, rather than drive him to an alien people. As to what had given such offence—his hot temper and audacity—these faults were being continually lessened; what was wanting in him—prudence—was increasing day by day. As his faults were decaying and his virtues maturing, they ought to allow such a man to live out his years in the commonwealth. Among those who spoke for him was his father, L. Quinctius Cincinnatus. He did not go over all his merits again, for fear of aggravating the feeling against him, but he pleaded for indulgence to the errors of youth; he himself had never injured any one either by word or deed, and for his own sake he implored them to pardon his son. Some refused to listen to his prayers, lest they should incur the displeasure of their friends; others complained of the maltreatment they had received, and by their angry replies showed beforehand what their verdict would be.

3.13

OVER and above the general exasperation, one charge in particular weighed heavily against him. M. Volscius Fictor, who had some years previously been tribune of the plebs, had come forward to give evidence that not long after the epidemic had visited the City, he had met some young men strolling in the Suburra. A quarrel broke out and his elder brother, still weak from illness, was knocked down by a blow from Caeso's fist, and carried home in a critical condition, and afterwards died, he believed, in consequence of the blow. He had not been allowed by the consuls, during the years that had elapsed, to obtain legal redress for the outrage. Whilst Volscius was telling this story in a loud tone of voice, so much excitement was created that Caeso was very near losing his life at the hands of the people. Verginius ordered him to be arrested and taken to prison. The patricians met violence by violence. T. Quinctius called out that when the day of trial has been fixed for any one indicted on a capital charge and is near at hand, his personal liberty ought not to be interfered with before the case is heard and sentence given. The tribune replied that he was not going to inflict punishment upon a man not yet found guilty; but he should keep him in prison till the day of the trial, that the Roman people might be in a position to punish one who has taken a man's life. The other tribunes were appealed to, and they saved their prerogative by a compromise; they forbade him to be cast into prison, and announced as their decision that the accused should appear in court, and if he failed to do so, he should forfeit a sum of money to the people. The question was, what sum would it be fair to fix? The matter was referred to the senate, the accused was detained in the Assembly whilst the senators were deliberating. They decided that he should give sureties, and each surety was bound in 3000 "ases" It was left to the tribunes to decide how many should be given; they fixed the number at ten. The prosecutor released the accused on that bail. Caeso was the first who gave securities on a state trial. After leaving the Forum, he went the following night into exile amongst the Tuscans. When the day for the trial came, it was pleaded in defense of his non-appearance that he had changed his domicile by going into exile. Verginius, nevertheless, went on with the proceedings, but his colleagues, to whom an appeal was made, dismissed the Assembly. The money was unmercifully extorted from the father, who had to sell all his property and live for some time like a banished man in an out-of-the-way hut on the other side of the Tiber.

3.14

THIS trial and the discussions on the Law kept the State employed; there was a respite from foreign troubles. The patricians were cowed by the banishment of Caeso, and the tribunes, having, as they thought, gained the victory, regarded the Law as practically carried. As far as the senior senators were concerned, they abandoned the control of public affairs, but the younger members of the order, mostly those who had been Caeso's intimates, were more bitter than ever against the plebeians, and quite as aggressive. They made much more progress by conducting the attack in a methodical manner. The first time that the Law was brought forward after Caeso's flight they were organized in readiness, and on the tribunes furnishing them with a pretext, by ordering them to withdraw, they attacked them with a huge army of clients in such a way that no single individual could carry home any special share of either glory or odium. The plebeians complained that for one Caeso thousands had sprung up. During the intervals when the tribunes were not agitating the Law, nothing could be more quiet or peaceable than these same men; they accosted the plebeians affably, entered into conversation with them, invited them to their houses, and when present in the Forum even allowed the tribunes to bring all other questions forward without interrupting them. They were never disagreeable to any one either in public or private, except when a discussion commenced on the Law; on all other occasions they were friendly with the people. Not only did the tribunes get through all their other business quietly, but they were even re-elected for the following year, without any offensive remark being made, still less any violence being offered. By gentle handling they gradually made the plebs tractable, and through these methods the Law was cleverly evaded throughout the year.

3.25

THE new consuls, L. Minucius and C. Nautius, took over the two subjects which remained from the previous year. As before, they obstructed the Law, the tribunes obstructed the trial of Volscius; but the new quaestors possessed greater energy and greater weight. T. Quinctius Capitolinus, who had been thrice consul, was quaestor with M. Valerius, the son of Valerius and grandson of Volesus. As Caeso could not be restored to the house of the Quinctii, nor could the greatest of her soldiers be restored to the State, Quinctius was bound in justice and by loyalty to his family to prosecute the false witness who had deprived an innocent man of the power to plead in his own defense. As Verginius, most of all the tribunes, was agitating for the Law, an interval of two months was granted the consuls for an examination of it, in order that when they had made the people understand what insidious dishonesty it contained, they might allow them to vote upon it. During this interval matters were quiet in the City. The Aequi, however, did not allow much respite. In violation of the treaty made with Rome the year before, they made predatory incursions into the territory of Labici and then into that of Tusculum. They had placed Gracchus Cloelius in command, their foremost man at that time. After loading themselves with plunder they fixed their camp on Mount Algidus. Q. Fabius, P. Volumnius, and A. Postumius were sent from Rome to demand satisfaction, under the terms of the treaty. The general's quarters were located under an enormous oak, and he told the Roman envoys to deliver the instructions they had received from the senate to the oak under whose shadow he was sitting, as he was otherwise engaged. As they withdrew, one of the envoys exclaimed, "May this consecrated oak, may each offended deity hear that you have broken the treaty! May they look upon our complaint now, and may they presently aid our arms when we seek to redress the outraged rights of gods as well as men!" On the return of the envoys, the senate ordered one of the consuls to march against Gracchus on Algidus; the other was instructed to ravage the territory of the Aequi. As usual, the tribunes attempted to obstruct the levy and probably would in the end have succeeded, had there not been fresh cause for alarm.

3.26

AN immense body of Sabines came in their ravages almost up to the walls of the City. The fields were ruined, the City thoroughly alarmed. Now the plebeians cheerfully took up arms, the tribunes remonstrated in vain, and two large armies were levied. Nautius led one of them against the Sabines, formed an entrenched camp, sent out, generally at night, small bodies who created such destruction in the Sabine territory that the Roman borders appeared in comparison almost untouched by war. Minucius was not so fortunate, nor did he conduct the campaign with the same energy; after taking up an entrenched position not far from the enemy, he remained timidly within his camp, though he had not suffered any important defeat. As usual, the enemy were emboldened by the lack of courage on the other side. They made a night attack on his camp, but as they gained little by a direct assault they proceeded the following day to invest it. Before all the exits were closed by the circumvallation, five mounted men got through the enemies' outposts and brought to Rome the news that the consul and his army were blockaded. Nothing could have happened so unlooked for, so undreamed of; the panic and confusion were as great as if it had been the City and not the camp that was invested. The consul Nautius was summoned home, but as he did nothing equal to the emergency, they decided to appoint a Dictator to retrieve the threatening position of affairs. By universal consent L. Quinctius Cincinnatus was called to the office.

It is worth while for those who despise all human interests in comparison with riches, and think that there is no scope for high honours or for virtue except where lavish wealth abounds, to listen to this story. The one hope of Rome, L. Quinctius, used to cultivate a four-acre field on the other side of the Tiber, just opposite the place where the dockyard and arsenal are now situated; it bears the name of the " Quinctian Meadows." There he was found by the deputation from the senate either digging out a ditch or ploughing, at all events, as is generally agreed, intent on his husbandry. After mutual salutations he was requested to put on his toga that he might hear the mandate of the senate, and they expressed the hope that it might turn out well for him and for the State. He asked them, in surprise, if all was well, and bade his wife, Racilia, bring him his toga quickly from the cottage. Wiping off the dust and perspiration, he put it on and came forward, on which the deputation saluted him as Dictator and congratulated him, invited him to the City and explained the state of apprehension in which the army were. A vessel had been provided for him by the government, and after he had crossed over, he was welcomed by his three sons, who had come out to meet him. They were followed by other relatives and friends, and by the majority of the senate. Escorted by this numerous gathering and preceded by the lictors, he was conducted to his house. There was also an enormous gathering of the plebs, but they were by no means so pleased to see Quinctius; they regarded the power with which he was invested as excessive, and the man himself more dangerous than his power. Nothing was done that night beyond adequately guarding the City.

3.27

THE following morning the Dictator went, before daylight, into the Forum and named as his Master of the Horse, L. Tarquitius, a member of a patrician house, but owing to his poverty he had served in the infantry, where he was considered by far the finest of the Roman soldiers. In company with the Master of the Horse the Dictator proceeded to the Assembly, proclaimed a suspension of all public business, ordered the shops to be closed throughout the City, and forbade the transaction of any private business whatever. Then he ordered all who were of military age to appear fully armed in the Campus Martius before sunset, each with five days' provisions and twelve palisades. Those who were beyond that age were required to cook the rations for their neighbours, whilst they were getting their arms ready and looking for palisades. So the soldiers dispersed to hunt for palisades; they took them from the nearest places, no one was interfered with, all were eager to carry out the Dictator's edict. The formation of the army was equally adapted for marching or, if circumstances required, for fighting; the Dictator led the legions in person, the Master of the Horse was at the head of his cavalry. To both bodies words of encouragement were addressed suitable to the emergency, exhorting them to march at extra speed, for there was need of haste if they were to reach the enemy at night; a Roman army with its consul had been now invested for three days, it was uncertain what a day or a night might bring forth, tremendous issues often turned on a moment of time. The men shouted to one another, "Hurry on, standard-bearer!" "Follow up, soldiers!" to the great gratification of their leaders. They reached Algidus at midnight, and on finding that they were near the enemy, halted.

3.28

THE Dictator, after riding round and reconnoitering as well as he could in the night the position and shape of the camp, commanded the military tribunes to give orders for the baggage to be collected together and the soldiers with their arms and palisades to resume their places in the ranks. His orders were carried out. Then, keeping the formation in which they had marched, the whole army, in one long column, surrounded the enemies' lines. At a given signal all were ordered to raise a shout; after raising the shout each man was to dig a trench in front of him and fix his palisade. As soon as the order reached the men, the signal followed. The men obeyed the order, and the shout rolled round the enemies' line and over them into the consul's camp. In the one it created panic, in the other rejoicing. The Romans recognised their fellow citizens' shout, and congratulated one another on help being at hand. They even made sorties from their outposts against the enemy and so increased their alarm. The consul said there must be no delay, that shout meant that their friends had not only arrived but were engaged, he should be surprised if the outside of the enemies' lines was not already attacked. He ordered his men to seize their arms and follow him. A nocturnal battle began. They notified the Dictator's legions by their shouts that on their side too the action had commenced. The Aequi were already making preparations to prevent themselves from being surrounded when the enclosed enemy began the battle; to prevent their lines from being broken through, they turned from those who were investing them to fight the enemy within, and so left the night free for the Dictator to complete his work. The fighting with the consul went on till dawn. By this time they were completely invested by the Dictator, and were hardly able to keep up the fight against one army. Then their lines were attacked by Quinctius' army, who had completed the circumvallation and resumed their arms. They had now to maintain a fresh conflict, the previous one was in no way slackened. Under the stress of the double attack they turned from fighting to supplication, and implored the Dictator on the one side and the consul on the other not to make their extermination the price of victory, but to allow them to surrender their arms and depart. The consul referred them to the Dictator, and he, in his anger, determined to humiliate his defeated enemy. He ordered Gracchus Cloelius and others of their principal men to be brought to him in chains, and the town of Corbio to be evacuated. He told the Aequi he did not require their blood, they were at liberty to depart; but, as an open admission of the defeat and subjugation of their nation, they would have to pass under the yoke. This was made of three spears, two fixed upright in the ground, and the third tied to them across the top. Under this yoke the Dictator sent the Aequi.

3.29

THEIR camp was found to be full of everything—for they had been sent away with only their shirts on—and the Dictator gave the whole of the spoil to his own soldiers alone. Addressing the consul and his army in a tone of severe rebuke, "You, soldiers," he said, "will go without your share of the spoil, for you all but fell a spoil yourselves to the enemy from whom it was taken; and you, L. Minucius, will command these legions as a staff officer, until you begin to show the spirit of a consul." Minucius laid down his consulship and remained with the army under the Dictator's orders. But such unquestioning obedience did men in those days pay to authority when ably and wisely exercised, that the soldiers, mindful of the service he had done them rather than of the disgrace inflicted on them, voted to the Dictator a gold crown a pound in weight, and when he left they saluted him as their "patron." Quintus Fabius, the prefect of the City, convened a meeting of the senate, and they decreed that Quinctius, with the army he was bringing home, should enter the City in triumphal procession. The commanding officers of the enemy were led in front, then the military standards were borne before the general's chariot, the army followed loaded with spoil. It is said that tables spread with provisions stood before all the houses, and the feasters followed the chariot with songs of triumph and the customary jests and lampoons. On that day the freedom of the City was bestowed on L. Mamilius the Tusculan, amidst universal approval. The Dictator would at once have laid down his office had not the meeting of the Assembly for the trial of M. Volscius detained him: fear of the Dictator prevented the tribunes from obstructing it. Volscius was condemned and went into exile at Lanuvium. Quinctius resigned on the sixteenth day the dictatorship which had been conferred upon him for six months. During that period the consul Nautius fought a brilliant action with the Sabines at Eretum, who suffered a severe defeat, in addition to the ravaging of their fields. Fabius Quintus was sent to succeed Minucius in command at Algidus. Towards the end of the year, the tribunes began to agitate the Law, but as two armies were absent, the senate succeeded in preventing any measure from being brought before the plebs. The latter gained their point, however, in securing the re-election of the tribunes for the fifth time. It is said that wolves pursued by dogs were seen in the Capitol; this prodigy necessitated its purification. These were the events of the year.

3.30

THE next consuls were Quintus Minucius and C. Horatius Pulvillus. As there was peace abroad at the beginning of the year, the domestic troubles began again; the same tribunes agitating for the same Law. Matters would have gone further—so inflamed were the passions on both sides—had not news arrived, as though it had been purposely arranged, of the loss of the garrison at Corbio in a night attack of the Aequi. The consuls summoned a meeting of the senate; they were ordered to form a force of all who could bear arms and march to Algidus. The contest about the Law was suspended, and a fresh struggle began about the enlistment. The consular authority was on the point of being overborne by the interference of the tribunes when a fresh alarm was created. A Sabine army had descended on the Roman fields for plunder, and were approaching the City. Thoroughly alarmed, the tribunes allowed the enrollment to proceed; not, however, without insisting on an agreement that since they had been foiled for five years and but slight protection to the plebeians had so far been afforded, there should henceforth be ten tribunes of the plebs elected. Necessity extorted this from the senate, with only one condition, that for the future they should not see the same tribunes in two successive years. That this agreement might not, like all the others, prove illusory, when once the war was over, the elections for tribunes were held at once. The office of tribune had existed for thirty-six years when for the first time ten were created, two from each class. It was definitely laid down that this should be the rule in all future elections. When the enrollment was completed Minucius advanced against the Sabines, but did not find the enemy. After massacring the garrison at Corbio, the Aequi had captured Ortona; Horatius fought them on Algidus, inflicting great slaughter, and drove them not only from Algidus but also out of Corbio and Ortona; Corbio he totally destroyed on account of their having betrayed the garrison.

3.31

M. VALERIUS and Sp. Vergilius were the new consuls. There was quiet at home and abroad. Owing to excessive rain there was a scarcity of provisions. A law was carried making the Aventine a part of the State domain. The tribunes of the plebs were re-elected. These men in the following year, when T. Romilius and C. Veturius were the consuls, were continually making the Law the staple of all their harangues, and said that they should be ashamed of their number being increased to no purpose, if that matter made as little progress during their two years of office as it had made during the five preceding years. Whilst the agitation was at its height, a hurried message came from Tusculum to the effect that the Aequi were in the Tusculan territory. The good services which that nation had so lately rendered made the people ashamed to delay sending assistance. Both consuls were sent against the enemy, and found him in his usual position on Algidus. An action was fought there;

above 7000 of the enemy were killed, the rest were put to flight; immense booty was taken. This, owing to the low state of the public treasury, the consuls sold. Their action, however, created ill-feeling in the army, and afforded the tribunes material on which to base an accusation against them. When, therefore, they went out of office, in which they were succeeded by Spurius Tarpeius and A. Aeternius, they were both impeached—Romilius by C. Calvius Cicero, plebeian tribune, and Veturius by L. Alienus, plebeian aedile. To the intense indignation of the senatorial party, both were condemned and fined; Romilius had to pay 10,000 "ases," and Veturius 15,000. The fate of their predecessors did not shake the resolution of the new consuls; they said that while it was quite possible that they might also be condemned, it was not possible for the plebs and its tribunes to carry the Law. Through long discussion it had become stale, the tribunes now threw it over and approached the patricians in a less aggressive spirit. They urged that an end should be put to their disputes, and if they objected to the measures adopted by the plebeians, they should consent to the appointment of a body of legislators, chosen in equal numbers from plebeians and patricians, to enact what would be useful to both orders and secure equal liberty for each. The patricians thought the proposal worth consideration; they said, however, that no one should legislate unless he were a patrician, since they were agreed as to the laws and only differed as to who should enact them. Commissioners were sent to Athens with instructions to make a copy of the famous laws of Solon, and to investigate the institutions, customs, and laws of other Greek States. Their names were Spurius Postumius Albus, A. Manlius, P. Sulpicius Camerinus.

3.32

AS regards foreign war, the year was a quiet one. The following one, in which P. Curiatius and Sextus Quinctilius were consuls, was still quieter owing to the continued silence of the tribunes. This was due to two causes: first, they were waiting for the return of the commissioners who had gone to Athens, and the foreign laws which they were to bring; and secondly, two fearful disasters came together, famine and a pestilence which was fatal to men and fatal to cattle.

The fields lay waste, the City was depleted by an unbroken series of deaths, many illustrious houses were in mourning. The Flamen Quirinalis, Servius Cornelius, died, also the augur C. Horatius Pulvillus, in whose place the augurs chose C. Veturius, all the more eagerly because he had been condemned by the plebs. The consul Quinctilius and four tribunes of the plebs died. The year was a gloomy one owing to the numerous losses. There was a respite from external enemies. The succeeding consuls were C. Menenius and P. Sestius Capitolinus. This year also was free from war abroad, but commotions began at home. The commissioners had now returned with the laws of Athens; the tribunes, in consequence, were more insistent that a commencement should at last be made in the compilation of the laws. It was decided that a body of Ten (hence called the "Decemvirs") should be created, from whom there should be no appeal, and that all other magistrates should be suspended for the year. There was a long controversy as to whether plebeians should be admitted; at last they gave way to the patricians on condition that the Icilian Law concerning the Aventine and the other sacred laws should not be repealed.

3.33

FOR the second time—in the 301st year from the foundation of Rome—was the form of government changed; the supreme authority was transferred from consuls to decemvirs, just as it had previously passed from kings to consuls. The change was the less noteworthy owing to its short duration, for the happy beginnings of that government developed into too luxuriant a growth; hence its early failure and the return to the old practice of entrusting to two men the name and authority of consul. The decemvirs were Appius Claudius, T. Genucius, P. Sestius, L. Veturius, C. Julius, A. Manlius, P. Sulpicius, P. Curiatius, T. Romilius, and Sp. Postumius. As Claudius and Genucius were the consuls designate, they received the honour in place of the honour of which they were deprived. Sestius, one of the consuls the year before, was honoured because he had, against his colleague, brought that subject before the senate. Next to them were placed the three commissioners who had gone to Athens, as a reward for their undertaking so distant an embassage, and also because it was thought that those who were familiar with the laws of foreign States would be useful in the compilation of new ones. It is said that in the final voting for the four required to complete the number, the electors chose aged men, to prevent any violent opposition to the decisions of the others. The presidency of the whole body was, in accordance with the wishes of the plebs, entrusted to Appius. He had assumed such a new character that from being a stern and bitter enemy of the people he suddenly appeared as their advocate, and trimmed his sails to catch every breath of popular favour. They administered justice each in turn, the one who was presiding judge for the day was attended by the twelve lictors, the others had only a single usher each. Notwithstanding the singular harmony which prevailed amongst them—a harmony which under other circumstances might be dangerous to individuals—the most perfect equity was shown to others. It will be sufficient to adduce a single instance as proof of the moderation with which they acted. A dead body had been discovered and dug up in the house of Sestius, a member of a patrician family. It was brought into the Assembly. As it was clear that an atrocious crime had been committed, Caius Julius, a decemvir, indicted Sestius, and appeared before the people to prosecute in person, though he had the right to act as sole judge in the case. He waived his right in order that the liberties of the people might gain what he surrendered of his power.

3.34

WHILST highest and lowest alike were enjoying their prompt and impartial administration of justice, as though delivered by an oracle, they were at the same time devoting their attention to the framing of the laws. These eagerly looked for laws were at length inscribed on ten tables which were exhibited in an Assembly specially convened for the purpose. After a prayer that their work might bring welfare and happiness to the State, to them and to their children, the decemvirs bade them go and read the laws which were exhibited. "As far as the wisdom and foresight of ten men admitted, they had established equal laws for all, for highest and lowest alike; there was, however, more weight in the intelligence and advice of many men. They should turn over each separate item in their minds, discuss them in conversations with each other, and bring forward for public debate what appeared to them superfluous or defective in each enactment. The future laws for Rome should be such as would appear to have been no less unanimously proposed by the people themselves than ratified by them on the proposal of others." When it appeared that they had been sufficiently amended in accordance with the expression of public opinion on each head, the Laws of the Ten Tables were passed by the Assembly of Centuries. Even in the mass of legislation today, where laws are piled one upon another in a confused heap, they still form the source of all public and private jurisprudence. After their ratification, the remark was generally made that two tables were still wanting; if they were added, the body, as it might be called, of Roman law would be complete. As the day for the elections approached, this impression created a desire to appoint decemvirs for a second year. The plebeians had learnt to detest the name of "consul" as much as that of "king," and now as the decemvirs allowed an appeal from one of their body to another, they no longer required the aid of their tribunes.

3.35

BUT after notice had been given that the election of decemvirs would be held on the third market day, such eagerness to be amongst those elected displayed itself, that even the foremost men of the State began an individual canvass as humble suitors for an office which they had previously with all their might opposed, seeking it at the hands of that very plebs with which they had hitherto been in conflict. I think they feared that if they did not fill posts of such great authority, they would be open to men who were not worthy of them. Appius Claudius was keenly alive to the chance that he might not be re-elected, in spite of his age and the honours he had enjoyed. You could hardly tell whether to consider him as a decemvir or a candidate. Sometimes he was more like one who sought office than one who actually held it; he abused the nobility, and extolled all the candidates who had neither birth nor personal weight to recommend them; he used to bustle about the Forum surrounded by ex-tribunes of the Duellius and Scilius stamp and through them made overtures to the plebeians, until even his colleagues, who till then had been wholly devoted to him, began to watch him, wondering what he meant. They were convinced that there was no sincerity about it, it was certain that so haughty a man would not exhibit such affability for nothing. They regarded this demeaning of himself and hobnobbing with private individuals as the action of a man who was not so keen to resign office as to discover some way of prolonging it. Not venturing to thwart his aims openly, they tried to moderate his violence by humouring him. As he was the youngest member of their body, they unanimously conferred on him the office of presiding over the elections. By this artifice they hoped to prevent him from getting himself elected; a thing which no one except the tribunes of the plebs had ever done, setting thereby the worst of precedents. However, he gave out that, if all went well, he should hold the elections, and he seized upon what should have been an impediment as a good opportunity for effecting his purpose. By forming a coalition he secured the rejection of the two Quinctii—Capitolinus and Cincinnatus—his own uncle, C. Claudius, one of the firmest supporters of the nobility, and other citizens of the same rank. He procured the election of men who were very far from being their equals either socially or politically, himself amongst the first, a step which respectable men disapproved of, all the more because no one had supposed that he would have the audacity to take it. With him were elected M. Cornelius Maluginensis, M. Sergius, L. Minucius, Q. Fabius Vibulanus, Q. Poetilius, T. Antonius Merenda, K. Duillius, Sp. Oppius Cornicen, and Manlius Rabuleius.

3.36

THIS was the end of Appius' assumption of a part foreign to his nature. From that time his conduct was in accordance with his natural disposition, and he began to mould his new colleagues, even before they entered on office, into the lines of his own character. They held private meetings daily; then, armed with plans hatched in absolute secrecy for exercising unbridled power, they no longer troubled to dissemble their tyranny, but made themselves difficult of access, harsh and stern to those to whom they granted interviews. So matters went on till the middle of May. At that period, May 15, was the proper time for magistrates to take up their office. At the outset, the first day of their government was marked by a demonstration which aroused great fears. For, whereas the previous decemvirs had observed the rule of only one having the "fasces" at a time and making this emblem of royalty go to each in turn, now all the Ten suddenly appeared, each with his twelve lictors. The Forum was filled with one hundred and twenty lictors, and they bore the axes tied up in the "fasces." The decemvirs explained it by saying that as they were invested with absolute power of life and death, there was no reason for the axes being removed. They presented the appearance of ten kings, and manifold fears were entertained not only by the lowest classes but even by the foremost of the senators. They felt that a pretext for commencing bloodshed was being sought for, so that if any one uttered, either in the senate or amongst the people, a single word which reminded them of liberty, the rods and axes would instantly be made ready for him, to intimidate the rest. For not only was there no protection in the people now that the right of appeal to them was withdrawn, but the decemvirs had mutually agreed not to interfere with each other's sentences, whereas the previous decemvirs had allowed their judicial decisions to be revised on appeal to a colleague, and certain matters which they considered to be within the jurisdiction of the people they had referred to them. For some time they inspired equal terror in all, gradually it rested wholly on the plebs. The patricians were unmolested; it was the men in humble life for whom they reserved their wanton and cruel treatment. They were solely swayed by personal motives, not by the justice of a cause, since influence had with them the force of equity. They drew up their judgments at home and pronounced them in the Forum; if any one appealed to a colleague, he left the presence of the one to whom he had appealed bitterly regretting that he had not abided by the first sentence. A belief, not traceable to any authoritative source, had got abroad that their conspiracy against law and justice was not for the present only, a secret and sworn agreement existed amongst them not to hold any elections, but to keep their power, now they had once obtained it, by making the decemvirate perpetual.

3.37

THE plebeians now began to study the faces of the patricians, to catch haply some gleam of liberty from the men from whom they had dreaded slavery and through that dread had brought the commonwealth into its present condition. The leaders of the senate hated the decemvirs, and hated the plebs; they did not approve of what was going on, but they thought that the plebeians deserved all that they got, and refused to help men who by rushing too eagerly after liberty had fallen into slavery. They even increased the wrongs they suffered, that through their disgust and impatience at the present conditions they might begin to long for the former state of things and the two consuls as of old. The greater part of the year had now elapsed; two tables had been added to the ten of the previous year; if these additional laws were passed by the "Comitia Centuriata" there was no reason why the decemvirate should be any longer considered necessary. Men were wondering how soon notice would be given of the election of consuls; the sole anxiety of the plebeians was as to the method by which they could re-establish that bulwark of their liberties, the power of the tribunes, which was now suspended. Meantime nothing was said about any elections. At first the decemvirs had bid for popularity by appearing before the plebs, surrounded by ex-tribunes, but now they were accompanied by an escort of young patricians, who crowded round the tribunals, maltreated the plebeians and plundered their property, and being the stronger, succeeded in getting whatever they had taken a fancy to. They did not stop short of personal violence, some were scourged, others beheaded, and that this brutality might not be gratuitous, the punishment of the owner was followed by a grant of his effects. Corrupted by such bribes, the young nobility not only declined to oppose the lawlessness of the decemvirs, but they openly showed that they preferred their own freedom from all restraints to the general liberty.

3.38

THE fifteenth of May arrived, the decemvirs' term of office expired, but no new magistrates were appointed. Though now only private citizens, the decemvirs came forward as determined as ever to enforce their authority and retain all the emblems of power. It was now in truth undisguised monarchy. Liberty was looked upon as for ever lost, none stood forth to vindicate it, nor did it seem likely that any one would do so. Not only had the people sunk into despondency themselves but they were beginning to be despised by their neighbours, who scorned the idea of sovereign power existing where there was no liberty. The Sabines made an incursion into Roman territory in great force, and carrying their ravages far and wide, drove away an immense quantity of men and cattle to Eretum, where they collected their scattered forces and encamped in the hope that the distracted state of Rome would prevent an army from being raised. Not only the messengers who brought the information but the country people who were flying into the City created a panic. The decemvirs, hated alike by the senate and the plebs, were left without any support, and whilst they were consulting as to the necessary measures, Fortune added a fresh cause of alarm. The Aequi, advancing in a different direction, had entrenched themselves on Algidus, and from there were making predatory incursions into the territory of Tusculum. The news was brought by envoys from Tusculum who implored assistance. The panic created unnerved the decemvirs, and seeing the City encompassed by two separate wars they were driven to consult the senate. They gave orders for the senators to be summoned, quite realizing what a storm of indignant resentment was awaiting them, and that they would be held solely responsible for the wasted territory and the threatening dangers. This, they expected, would lead to an attempt to deprive them of office, unless they offered a unanimous resistance, and by a sharp exercise of authority on a few of the most daring spirits repress the attempts of the others.

When the voice of the crier was heard in the Forum calling the patricians to the Senate-house to meet the decemvirs, the novelty of it, after so long a suspension of the meetings of the senate, filled the plebeians with astonishment. "What," they asked, "has happened to revive a practice so long disused? We ought to be grateful to the enemy who are menacing us with war, for causing anything to happen which belongs to the usage of a free State." They looked in every part of the Forum for a senator, but seldom was one recognised; then they contemplated the Senate-house and the solitude round the decemvirs. The latter put it down to the universal hatred felt for their authority, the plebeians explained it by saying that the senators did not meet because private citizens had not the right to summon them. If the plebs made common cause with the senate, those who were bent on recovering their liberty would have men to lead them, and as the senators when summoned would not assemble, so the plebs must refuse to be enrolled for service. Thus the plebeians expressed their opinions. As to the senators, there was hardly a single member of the order in the Forum, and very few in the City. Disgusted with the state of matters they had retired to their country homes and were attending to their own affairs, having lost all interest in those of the State. They felt that the more they kept away from any meeting and intercourse with their tyrannical masters the safer would it be for them. As, on being summoned, they did not come, the ushers were despatched to their houses to exact the penalties for non-attendance and to ascertain whether they absented themselves of set purpose. They took back word that the senate was in the country. This was less unpleasant for the decemvirs than if they had been in the City and had refused to recognize their authority. Orders were issued for all to be summoned for the following day. They assembled in greater numbers than they themselves expected. This led the plebeians to think that their liberty had been betrayed by the senate, since they had obeyed men whose term of office had expired and who, apart from the force at their disposal, were only private citizens; thus recognizing their right to convene the senate.

3.39

THIS obedience, however, was shown more by their coming to the Senate-house than by any servility in the sentiments which we understand that they expressed. It is recorded that after the question of the war had been introduced by Appius Claudius, and before the formal discussion began, L. Valerius Potitus created a scene by demanding that he should be allowed to speak on the political question, and on the decemvirs forbidding him in threatening tones to do so, he declared that he would present himself before the people.

Marcus Horatius Barbatus showed himself an equally determined opponent, called the decemvirs "ten Tarquins," and reminded them that it was under the leadership of the Valerii and the Horatii that monarchy had been expelled from Rome. It was not the name of "king" that men had now grown weary of, for it was the proper title of Jupiter, Romulus the founder of the City and his successors were called "kings," and the name was still retained for religious purposes. It was the tyranny and violence of kings that men detested. If these were insupportable in a king or a king's son, who would endure them in ten private citizens? They should see to it that they did not, by forbidding freedom of speech in the House, compel them to speak outside its walls. He could not see how it was less permissible for him as a private citizen to convene an Assembly of the people than for them to summon the senate. They might find out whenever they chose how much more powerful a sense of wrong is to vindicate liberty than greedy ambition is to support tyranny. They were bringing up the question of the Sabine war as if the Roman people had any more serious war to wage than one against men who, appointed to draw up laws, left no vestige of law or justice in the State; who had abolished the elections, the annual magistrates, the regular succession of rulers, which formed the sole guarantee of equal liberty for all; who, though simple citizens, still retained the fasces and the power of despotic monarchs. After the expulsion of the kings, the magistrates were patricians; after the secession of the plebs, plebeian magistrates were appointed. "What party did these men belong to?" he asked. "The popular party? Why, what have they ever done in conjunction with the people? The nobility? What! these men, who have not held a meeting of the senate for nearly a year, and now that they are holding one, forbid any speaking on the political situation? Do not place too much reliance on the fears of others. The ills that men are actually suffering from seem to them much more grievous than any they may fear in the future."

3.40

WHILST Horatius was delivering this impassioned speech, and the decemvirs were in doubt how far they ought to go, whether in the direction of angry resistance or in that of concession, and unable to see what the issue would be, C. Claudius, the uncle of the decemvir Appius, made a speech more in the nature of entreaty than of censure. He implored him by the shade of his father to think rather of the social order under which he had been born than of the nefarious compact made with his colleagues. It was much more, he said, for the sake of Appius than of the State that he made this appeal, for the State would assert its rights in spite of them, if it could not do so with their consent. But great controversies generally kindle great and bitter passions, and it was what these might lead to that he dreaded. Though the decemvirs forbade the discussion of any subject save the one they had introduced, their respect for Claudius prevented them from interrupting him, so he concluded with a resolution that no decree should be passed by the senate. This was universally taken to mean that Claudius adjudged them to be private citizens, and many of the consulars expressed their concurrence. Another proposal, apparently more drastic, but in reality less effective, was that the senate should order the patricians to hold a special meeting to appoint an "interrex." For by voting for this, they decided that those who were presiding over the senate were lawful magistrates, whoever they were, whereas the proposal that no decree should be passed made them private citizens.

The cause of the decemvirs was on the point of collapsing, when L. Cornelius Maluginensis, the brother of M. Cornelius the decemvir, who had been purposely selected from among the consulars to wind up the debate, undertook to defend his brother and his brother's colleagues by professing great anxiety about the war. He was wondering, he said, by what fatality it had come about that the decemvirs should be attacked by those who had sought the office or by their allies or in particular by these men, or why, during all the months that the commonwealth was undisturbed, no one questioned whether those at the head of affairs were lawful magistrates or not, whereas now, when the enemy were almost at their gates, they were fomenting civic discord—unless indeed they supposed that the nature of their proceeding would be less apparent in the general confusion. No one was justified in importing prejudice into a matter of such moment whilst they were preoccupied with much more serious anxieties. He gave it as his opinion that the point raised by Valerius and Horatius, namely, that the decemvirs had ceased to hold office by May 15, should be submitted to the senate for decision after the impending wars had been brought to a close and the tranquility of the State restored. And further, that Ap. Claudius must at once understand that he must be prepared to make a proper return of the election which he held for the appointment of decemvirs, stating whether they were elected only for a year, or until such time as the laws which were still required should be passed. In his opinion every matter but the war should for the present be laid aside. If they thought that the reports of it which had got abroad were false, and that not only the messengers which had come in but even the Tuscan envoys had invented the story, then they ought to send out reconnoitering parties to bring back accurate information. If, however, they believed the messengers and the envoys, a levy ought to be made at the earliest possible moment, the decemvirs should lead the armies in whatever direction each thought best, and nothing else should take precedence.

3.41

WHILST a division was being taken and the younger senators were carrying this proposition, Valerius and Horatius rose again in great excitement and loudly demanded leave to discuss the political situation. If, they said, the faction in the senate prevented them, they would bring it before the people, for private citizens had no power to silence them either in the Senate-house or in the Assembly, and they were not going to give way before the fasces of a mock authority. Appius felt that unless he met their violence with equal audacity, his authority was practically at an end. "It will be better," he said, "not to speak on any subject but the one we are now considering," and as Valerius insisted that he should not keep silent for a private citizen, Appius ordered a lictor to go to him. Valerius ran to the doors of the Senate-house and invoked "the protection of the Quirites." L. Cornelius put an end to the scene by throwing his arms round Appius as though to protect Valerius, but really to protect Appius from further mischief. He obtained permission for Valerius to say what he wanted, and as this liberty did not go beyond words, the decemvirs achieved their purpose. The consulars and senior senators felt that the tribunitian authority, which they still regarded with detestation, was much more eagerly desired by the plebs than the restoration of the consular authority, and they would almost rather have had the decemvirs voluntarily resigning office at a subsequent period than that the plebs should recover power through their unpopularity. If matters could be quietly arranged and the consuls restored without any popular disturbance, they thought that either the preoccupation of war or the moderate exercise of power on the part of the consuls would make the plebs forget all about their tribunes. The levy was proclaimed without any protest from the senate. The men of age for active service answered to their names, as there was no appeal from the authority of the decemvirs. When the legions were enrolled, the decemvirs arranged among themselves their respective commands. The prominent men amongst them were Q. Fabius and Appius Claudius. The war at home threatened to be more serious than the one abroad, and the violent disposition of Appius was deemed more fitted to repress commotions in the City, whilst Fabius was looked upon as more inclined to evil practices than to be any permanent good to them. This man, at one time so distinguished both at home and in the field, had been so changed by office and the influence of his colleagues that he preferred to take Appius as his model rather than be true to himself. He was entrusted with the Sabine war, and Manlius Rabuleius and Q. Poetilius were associated with him in its conduct. M. Cornelius was sent to Algidus, together with L. Minucius, T. Antonius, Kaeso Duillius, and M. Sergius. It was decreed that Sp. Oppius should assist Ap. Claudius in the defense of the City, with an authority co-ordinate with that of the other decemvirs.

3.42

THE military operations were not any more satisfactory than the domestic administration. The commanders were certainly at fault in having made themselves objects of detestation to the citizens, but otherwise the whole of the blame rested on the soldiers, who, to prevent anything from succeeding under the auspices and leadership of the decemvirs, disgraced both themselves and their generals by allowing themselves to be defeated. Both armies had been routed, the one by the Sabines at Eretum, the other by the Aequi on Algidus. Fleeing from Eretum in the silence of the night, they had entrenched themselves on some high ground near the City between Fidenae and Crustumeria. They refused to meet the pursuing enemy anywhere on equal terms, and trusted for safety to their entrenchments and the nature of the ground, not to arms or courage. On Algidus they behaved more disgracefully, suffered a heavier defeat, and even lost their camp. Deprived of all their stores, the soldiers made their way to Tusculum, looking for subsistence to the good faith and compassion of their hosts, and their confidence was not misplaced. Such alarming reports were brought to Rome that the senate, laying aside their feeling against the decemvirs, resolved that guards should be mounted in the City, ordered that all who were of age to bear arms should man the walls and undertake outpost duty before the gates, and decreed a supply of arms to be sent to Tusculum to replace those which had been lost, whilst the decemvirs were to evacuate Tusculum and keep their soldiers encamped. The other camp was to be transferred from Fidenae on to the Sabine territory, and by assuming the offensive deter the enemy from any project of attacking the City.

3.43

TO these defeats at the hands of the enemy have to be added two infamous crimes on the part of the decemvirs. L. Siccius was serving in the campaign against the Sabines. Seeing the bitter feeling against the decemvirs, he used to hold secret conversations with the soldiery and threw out hints about the creation of tribunes and resorting to a secession. He was sent to select and survey a site for a camp, and the soldiers who had been told off to accompany him were instructed to choose a favourable opportunity for attacking and despatching him. They did not effect their purpose with impunity, several of the assassins fell around him whilst he was defending himself with courage equal to his strength, and that was exceptional.

The rest brought a report back to camp that Siccius had fallen into an ambush and had died fighting bravely, whilst some soldiers had been lost with him. At first the informants were believed; but subsequently a cohort which had gone out by permission of the decemvirs to bury those who had fallen, found, when they reached the spot, no corpse despoiled, but the body of Siccius lying in the centre fully armed with those around all turned towards him, whilst there was not a single body belonging to the enemy nor any trace of their having retired. They brought the body back and declared that, as a matter of fact, he had been killed by his own men. The camp was filled with deep resentment, and it was decided that Siccius should be forthwith carried to Rome. The decemvirs anticipated this resolve by hastily burying him with military honours at the cost of the State. The soldiers manifested profound grief at his funeral, and the worst possible suspicions were everywhere entertained against the decemvirs.

3.44

THIS was followed by a second atrocity, the result of brutal lust, which occurred in the City and led to consequences no less tragic than the outrage and death of Lucretia, which had brought about the expulsion of the royal family. Not only was the end of the decemvirs the same as that of the kings, but the cause of their losing their power was the same in each case. Ap. Claudius had conceived a guilty passion for a girl of plebeian birth. The girl's father, L. Verginius, held a high rank in the army on Algidus; he was a man of exemplary character both at home and in the field. His wife had been brought up on equally high principles, and their children were being brought up in the same way. He had betrothed his daughter to L. Icilius, who had been tribune, an active and energetic man whose courage had been proved in his battles for the plebs. This girl, now in the bloom of her youth and beauty, excited Appius' passions, and he tried to prevail on her by presents and promises. When he found that her virtue was proof against all temptation, he had recourse to unscrupulous and brutal violence. He commissioned a client, M. Claudius, to claim the girl as his slave, and to bar any claim on the part of her friends to retain possession of her till the case was tried, as he thought that the father's absence afforded a good opportunity for this illegal action. As the girl was going to her school in the Forum—the grammar schools were held in booths there—the decemvir's pander laid his hand upon her, declaring that she was the daughter of a slave of his, and a slave herself. He then ordered her to follow him, and threatened, if she hesitated, to carry her off by force. While the girl was stupefied with terror, her maid's shrieks, invoking "the protection of the Quirites," drew a crowd together. The names of her father Verginius and her betrothed lover, Icilius, were held in universal respect. Regard for them brought their friends, feelings of indignation brought the crowd to the maiden's support. She was now safe from violence; the man who claimed her said that he was proceeding according to law, not by violence, there was no need for any excited gathering. He cited the girl into court. Her supporters advised her to follow him; they came before the tribunal of Appius. The claimant rehearsed a story already perfectly familiar to the judge as he was the author of the plot, how the girl had been born in his house, stolen from there, transferred to the house of Verginius and fathered on him; these allegations would be supported by definite evidence, and he would prove them to the satisfaction of Verginius himself, who was really most concerned, as an injury had been done to him. Meanwhile, he urged, it was only right that a slave girl should follow her master. The girl's advocates contended that Verginius was absent on the service of the State, he would be present in two days' time if information were sent to him, and it was contrary to equity that in his absence he should incur risk with regard to his children. They demanded that he should adjourn the whole of the proceedings till the father's arrival, and in accordance with the law which he himself had enacted, grant the custody of the girl to those who asserted her freedom, and not suffer a maiden of ripe age to incur danger to her reputation before her liberty was imperiled.

3.45

BEFORE giving judgment, Appius showed how liberty was upheld by that very law to which the friends of Verginia had appealed in support of their demand. But, he went on to say, it guaranteed liberty only so far as its provisions were strictly adhered to as regarded both persons and cases. For where personal freedom is the matter of claim, that provision holds good, because any one can lawfully plead, but in the case of one who is still in her father's power, there is none but her father to whom her master need renounce possession. His decision, therefore, was that the father should be summoned, and in the meanwhile the man who claimed her should not forego his right to take the girl and give security to produce her on the arrival of her reputed father. The injustice of this sentence called forth many murmurs, but no one ventured on open protest, until P. Numitorius, the girl's grandfather, and Icilius, her betrothed, appeared on the scene. The intervention of Icilius seemed to offer the best chance of thwarting Appius, and the crowd made way for him. The lictor said that judgment had been given, and as Icilius continued loudly protesting he attempted to remove him. Such rank injustice would have fired even a gentle temper. He exclaimed, "I am, at your orders, Appius, to be removed at the point of the sword, that you may stifle all comment on what you want to keep concealed. I am going to marry this maiden, and I am determined to have a chaste wife. Summon all the lictors of all your colleagues, give orders for the axes and rods to be in readiness—the betrothed of Icilius shall not remain outside her father's house. Even if you have deprived us of the two bulwarks of our liberty—the aid of our tribunes and the right of appeal to the Roman plebs—that has given you no right to our wives and children, the victims of your lust. Vent your cruelty upon our backs and necks; let female honour at least be safe. If violence is offered to this girl, I shall invoke the aid of the Quirites here for my betrothed, Verginius that of the soldiers for his only daughter; we shall all invoke the aid of gods and men, and you shall not carry out that judgment except at the cost of our lives. Reflect, Appius, I demand of you, whither you are going! When Verginius has come, he must decide what action to take about his daughter; if he submits to this man's claim, he must look out another husband for her. Meantime I will vindicate her liberty at the price of my life, sooner than sacrifice my honour."

3.46

THE people were excited and a conflict appeared imminent. The lictors had closed round Icilius, but matters had not got beyond threats on both sides when Appius declared that it was not the defense of Verginia that was Icilius' main object; a restless intriguer, even yet breathing the spirit of the tribuneship, was looking out for a chance of creating sedition. He would not, however, afford him material for it that day, but that he might know that it was not to his insolence that he was making a concession, but to the absent Verginius, to the name of father, and to liberty, he would not adjudicate on that day, or issue any decree. He would ask M. Claudius to forego his right, and allow the girl to be in the custody of her friends till the morrow. If the father did not then appear, he warned Icilius and men of his stamp that neither as legislator would he be disloyal to his own law, nor as decemvir would he lack firmness to execute it. He certainly would not call upon the lictors of his colleagues to repress the ringleaders of sedition, he should be content with his own. The time for perpetrating this illegality was thus postponed, and after the girl's supporters had withdrawn, it was decided as the very first thing to be done that the brother of Icilius and one of Numitor's sons, both active youths, should make their way straight to the gate and summon Verginius from the camp with all possible speed. They knew that the girl's safety turned upon her protector against lawlessness being present in time. They started on their mission, and riding at full speed brought the news to the father. While the claimant of the girl was pressing Icilius to enter his plea and name his sureties, and Icilius kept asserting that this very thing was being arranged, purposely spinning out the time to allow of his messengers getting first to the camp, the crowd everywhere held up their hands to show that every one of them was ready to be security for him. With tears in his eyes, he said, "It is most kind of you. Tomorrow I may need your help, now I have sufficient securities." So Verginia was bailed on the security of her relatives. Appius remained for some time on the bench, to avoid the appearance of having taken his seat for that one case only. When he found that owing to the universal interest in this one case no other suitors appeared, he withdrew to his home and wrote to his colleagues in camp not to grant leave of absence to Verginius, and actually to keep him under arrest. This wicked advice came too late, as it deserved to do; Verginius had already obtained leave, and started in the first watch. The letter ordering his detention was delivered the next morning, and was therefore useless.

3.47

IN the City, the citizens were standing in the Forum in the early dawn, on the tiptoe of expectation. Verginius, in mourning garb, brought his daughter, similarly attired, and accompanied by a number of matrons, into the Forum. An immense body of sympathizers stood round him. He went amongst the people, took them by the hand and appealed to them to help him, not out of compassion only but because they owed it to him; he was at the front day by day, in defense of their children and their wives; of no man could they recount more numerous deeds of endurance and of daring than of him. What good was it all, he asked, if while the City was safe, their children were exposed to what would be their worst fate if it were actually captured? Men gathered round him, whilst he spoke as though he were addressing the Assembly. Icilius followed in the same strain. The women who accompanied him made a profounder impression by their silent weeping than any words could have made. Unmoved by all this—it was really madness rather than love that had clouded his judgment—Appius mounted the tribunal. The claimant began by a brief protest against the proceedings of the previous day; judgment, he said, had not been given owing to the partiality of the judge. But before he could proceed with his claim or any opportunity was given to Verginius of replying, Appius intervened. It is possible that the ancient writers may have correctly stated some ground which he alleged for his decision, but I do not find one anywhere that would justify such an iniquitous decision. The one thing which can be propounded as being generally admitted is the judgment itself. His decision was that the girl was a slave. At first all were stupefied with amazement at this atrocity, and for a few moments there was a dead silence. Then, as M. Claudius approached the matrons standing round the girl, to seize her amidst their outcries and tears,

Verginius, pointing with outstretched arm to Appius, cried, "It is to Icilius and not to you, Appius, that I have betrothed my daughter; I have brought her up for wedlock, not for outrage. Are you determined to satisfy your brutal lusts like cattle and wild beasts? Whether these people will put up with this, I know not, but I hope that those who possess arms will refuse to do so." Whilst the man who claimed the maiden was being pushed back by the group of women and her supporters who stood round, the crier called for silence.

3.48

THE decemvir, utterly abandoned to his passion, addressed the crowd and told them that he had ascertained not only through the insolent abuse of Icilius on the previous day and the violent behaviour of Verginius, which the Roman people could testify to, but mainly from certain definite information received, that all through the night meetings had been held in the City to organize a seditious movement. Forewarned of the likelihood of disturbance, he had come down into the Forum with an armed escort, not to injure peaceable citizens, but to uphold the authority of the government by putting down the disturbers of public tranquility. "It will therefore," he proceeded, "be better for you to keep quiet. Go, lictor, remove the crowd and clear a way for the master to take possession of his slave." When, in a transport of rage, he had thundered out these words, the people fell back and left the deserted girl a prey to injustice. Verginius, seeing no prospect of help anywhere, turned to the tribunal. "Pardon me, Appius, I pray you, if I have spoken disrespectfully to you, pardon a father's grief. Allow me to question the nurse here, in the maiden's presence, as to what are the real facts of the case, that if I have been falsely called her father, I may leave her with the greater resignation." Permission being granted, he took the girl and her nurse aside to the booths near the temple of Venus Cloacina, now known as the "New Booths," and there, snatching up a butcher's knife, he plunged it into her breast, saying, "In this the only way in which I can, I vindicate, my child, thy freedom." Then, looking towards the tribunal, "By this blood, Appius, I devote thy head to the infernal gods." Alarmed at the outcry which arose at this terrible deed, the decemvir ordered

Verginius to be arrested. Brandishing the knife, he cleared the way before him, until, protected by a crowd of sympathizers, he reached the city gate. Icilius and Numitorius took up the lifeless body and showed it to the people; they deplored the villainy of Appius, the ill-starred beauty of the girl, the terrible compulsion under which the father had acted. The matrons, who followed with angry cries, asked, "Was this the condition on which they were to rear children, was this the reward of modesty and purity?" with other manifestations of that womanly grief, which, owing to their keener sensibility, is more demonstrative, and so expresses itself in more moving and pitiful fashion. The men, and especially Icilius, talked of nothing but the abolition of the tribunitian power and the right of appeal and loudly expressed their indignation at the condition of public affairs.

3.49

THE people were excited partly by the atrocity of the deed, partly by the opportunity now offered of recovering their liberties. Appius first ordered Icilius to be summoned before him, then, on his refusal to come, to be arrested. As the lictors were not able to get near him, Appius himself with a body of young patricians forced his way through the crowd and ordered him to be taken to prison. By this time Icilius was not only surrounded by the people, but the people's leaders were there—L. Valerius and M. Horatius. They drove back the lictors and said, if they were going to proceed by law, they would undertake the defense of Icilius against one who was only a private citizen, but if they were going to attempt force, they would be no unequal match for him. A furious scuffle began, the decemvir's lictors attacked Valerius and Horatius; their "fasces" were broken up by the people; Appius mounted the platform, Horatius and Valerius followed him; the Assembly listened to them, Appius was shouted down. Valerius, assuming the tone of authority, ordered the lictors to cease attendance on one who held no official position, on which Appius, thoroughly cowed, and fearing for his life, muffled his head with his toga and retreated into a house near the Forum, without his adversaries perceiving his flight. Sp. Oppius burst into the Forum from the other side to support his colleague, and saw that their authority was overcome by main force. Uncertain what to do and distracted by the conflicting advice given him on all sides, he gave orders for the senate to be summoned. As a great number of the senators were thought to disapprove of the conduct of the decemvirs, the people hoped that their power would be put an end to through the action of the senate, and consequently became quiet. The senate decided that nothing should be done to irritate the plebs, and, what was of much more importance, that every precaution should be taken to prevent the arrival of Verginius from creating a commotion in the army.

3.50

ACCORDINGLY, some of the younger senators were sent to the camp, which was then on Mount Vecilius. They informed the three decemvirs who were in command that by every possible means they were to prevent the soldiers from mutinying. Verginius caused a greater commotion in the camp than the one he had left behind in the City. The sight of his arrival with a body of nearly 400 men from the City, who, fired with indignation, had enlisted themselves as his comrades, still more the weapon still clenched in his hand and his blood-besprinkled clothes, attracted the attention of the whole camp. The civilian garb seen in all directions in the camp made the number of the citizens who had accompanied him seem greater than it was. Questioned as to what had happened, Verginius for a long time could not speak for weeping; at length when those who had run up stood quietly round him and there was silence, he explained everything in order just as it happened. Then lifting up his hands to heaven he appealed to them as his fellow-soldiers and implored them not to attribute to him what was really the crime of Appius, nor to look upon him with abhorrence as the murderer of his children. His daughter's life was dearer to him than his own, had she been allowed to live in liberty and purity; when he saw her dragged off as a slave girl to be outraged, he thought it better to lose his child by death than by dishonour. It was through compassion for her that he had fallen into what looked like cruelty, nor would he have survived her had he not entertained the hope of avenging her death by the aid of his fellow-soldiers. For they, too, had daughters and sisters and wives; the lust of Appius was not quenched with his daughter's life, nay rather, the more impunity it met with the more unbridled would it be. Through the sufferings of another they had received a warning how to guard themselves against a like wrong. As for him, his wife had been snatched from him by Fate, his daughter, because she could no longer live in chastity, had met a piteous but an honourable death. There was no longer in his house any opportunity for Appius to gratify his lust, from any other violence on that man's part he would defend himself with the same resolution with which he had defended his child; others must look out for themselves and for their children.

To this impassioned appeal of Verginius the crowd replied with a shout that they would not fail him in his grief or in the defense of his liberty. The civilians mingling in the throng of soldiers told the same tragic story, and how much more shocking the incident was to behold than to hear about; at the same time they announced that affairs were in fatal confusion at Rome, and that some had followed them into camp with the tidings that Appius after being almost killed had gone into exile. The result was a general call to arms, they plucked up the standards and started for Rome. The decemvirs, thoroughly alarmed at what they saw and at what they heard of the state of things in Rome, went to different parts of the camp to try and allay the excitement. Where they tried persuasion no answer was returned, but where they attempted to exercise authority, the reply was, "We are men and have arms." They marched in military order to the City and occupied the Aventine. Every one whom they met was urged to recover the liberties of the plebs and appoint tribunes; apart from this, no appeals to violence were heard. The meeting of the senate was presided over by Sp. Oppius. They decided not to adopt any harsh measures, as it was through their own lack of energy that the sedition had arisen. Three envoys of consular rank were sent to the army to demand in the name of the senate by whose orders they had abandoned their camp, and what they meant by occupying the Aventine in arms, and diverting the war from foreign foes to their own country, which they had taken forcible possession of. They were at no loss for an answer, but they were at a loss for some one to give it, since they had as yet no regular leader, and individual officers did not venture to expose themselves to the dangers of such a position. The only reply was a loud and general demand that L. Valerius and M. Horatius should be sent to them, to these men they would give a formal reply.

3.51

AFTER the envoys were dismissed, Verginius pointed out to the soldiers that they had a few moments ago felt themselves embarrassed in a matter of no great importance, because they were a multitude without a head, and the answer they had given, though it served their turn, was the outcome rather of the general feeling at the time than of any settled purpose. He was of opinion that ten men should be chosen to hold supreme command, and by virtue of their military rank should be called tribunes of the soldiers. He himself was the first to whom this distinction was offered, but he replied, "Reserve the opinion you have formed of me till both you and I are in more favourable circumstances; so long as my daughter is unavenged no honour can give me pleasure, nor in the present disturbed state of the commonwealth is it any advantage for those men to be at your head who are most obnoxious to party malice. If I am to be of any use, I shall be none the less so in a private capacity." Ten military tribunes, accordingly, were appointed. The army acting against the Sabines did not remain passive. There, too, at the instigation of Icilius and Numitorius, a revolt against the decemvirs took place. The feelings of the soldiery were roused by the recollection of the murdered Siccius no less than by the fresh story of the maiden whom it had been sought to make a victim of foul lust. When Icilius heard that tribunes of the soldiers had been elected on the Aventine, he anticipated from what he knew of the plebs that when they came. to elect their tribunes they would follow the lead of the army and choose those who were already elected as military tribunes. As he was looking to a tribuneship himself, he took care to get the same number appointed and invested with similar powers by his own men, before they entered the City. They made their entry through the Colline gate in military order, with standards displayed, and proceeded through the heart of the City to the Aventine. There the two armies united, and the twenty military tribunes were requested to appoint two of their number to take the supreme direction of affairs. They appointed M. Oppius and Sex. Manlius. Alarmed at the direction affairs were talking, the senate held daily meetings, but the time was spent in mutual reproaches rather than in deliberation. The decemvirs were openly charged with the murder of Siccius, the profligacy of Appius, and the disgrace incurred in the field. It was proposed that Valerius and Horatius should go to the Aventine, but they refused to go unless the decemvirs gave up the insignia of an office which had expired the previous year. The decemvirs protested against this attempt to coerce them, and said that they would not lay down their authority until the laws which they were appointed to draw up were duly enacted.

3.52

M. DUILLIUS, a former tribune, informed the plebs that, owing to incessant wranglings, no business was being transacted in the senate. He did not believe that the senators would trouble about them till they saw the City deserted; the Sacred Hill would remind them of the firm determination once shown by the plebs, and they would learn that unless the tribunitian power was restored there could be no concord in the State. The armies left the Aventine and, going out by the Nomentan—or, as it was then called, the Ficulan—road, they encamped on the Sacred Hill, imitating the moderation of their fathers by abstaining from all injury. The plebeian civilians followed the army, no one whose age allowed him to go hung back. Their wives and children followed them, asking in piteous tones, to whom would they leave them in a City where neither modesty nor liberty were respected? The unwonted solitude gave a dreary and deserted look to every part of Rome; in the Forum there were only a few of the older patricians, and when the senate was in session it was wholly deserted. Many besides Horatius and Valerius were now angrily asking, "What are you waiting for, senators? If the decemvirs do not lay aside their obstinacy, will you allow everything to go to wrack and ruin? And what, pray; is that authority, decemvirs, to which you cling so closely? Are you going to administer justice to walls and roofs? Are you not ashamed to see a greater number of lictors in the Forum than of all other citizens put together? What will you do if the enemy approach the City? What if the plebs, seeing that their secession has no effect, come shortly against us in arms? Do you want to end your power by the fall of the City? Either you will have to do without the plebeians or you will have to accept their tribunes; sooner than they will go without their magistrates, we shall have to go without ours. That power which they wrested from our fathers, when it was an untried novelty, they will not submit to be deprived of, now that they have tasted the sweets of it, especially as we are not making that moderate use of our power which would prevent their needing its protection." Remonstrances like these came from all parts of the House; at last the decemvirs, overborne by the unanimous opposition, asserted that since it was the general wish, they would submit to the authority of the senate. All they asked for was that they might be protected against the popular rage; they warned the senate against the plebs becoming by their death habituated to inflicting punishment on the patricians.

3.53

VALERIUS and Horatius were then sent to the plebs with terms which it was thought would lead to their return and the adjustment of all differences; they were also instructed to procure guarantees for the protection of the decemvirs against popular violence. They were welcomed in the camp with every expression of delight, for they were unquestionably regarded as liberators from the commencement of the disturbance to its close. Thanks therefore were offered to them on their arrival. Icilius was the spokesman. A policy had been agreed upon before the arrival of the envoys, so when the discussion of the terms commenced, and the envoys asked what the demands of the plebs were, Icilius put forward proposals of such a nature as to show clearly that their hopes lay in the justice of their cause rather than in an appeal to arms. They demanded the re-establishment of the tribunitian power and the right of appeal, which before the institution of decemvirs had been their main security. They also demanded an amnesty for those who had incited the soldiers or the plebs to recover their liberties by a secession. The only vindictive demand made was with reference to the punishment of the decemvirs. They insisted, as an act of justice, that they should be surrendered, and they threatened to burn them alive. The envoys replied to these demands as follows: "The demands you have put forward as the result of your deliberations are so equitable that they would have been voluntarily conceded, for you ask for them as the safeguards of your liberties, not as giving you license to attack others. Your feelings of resentment are to be excused rather than indulged; for it is through hatred of cruelty that you are actually hurrying into cruelty, and almost before you are free yourselves you want to act the tyrant over your adversaries. Is our State never to enjoy any respite from punishments inflicted either by the patricians on the Roman plebs, or by the plebs on the patricians? You need the shield rather than the sword. He is humble enough who lives in the State under equal laws, neither inflicting nor suffering injury. Even if the time should come when you will make yourselves formidable, when, after recovering your magistrates and your laws, you will have judicial power over our lives and property—even then you will decide each case on its merits, it is enough now that your liberties are won back."

3.54

PERMISSION having been unanimously granted them to do as they thought best, the envoys announced that they would return shortly after matters were arranged. When they laid the demands of the plebs before the senate, the other decemvirs, on finding that no mention was made of inflicting punishment on them, raised no objection whatever. The stern Appius, who was detested most of all, measuring the hatred of others towards him by his hatred towards them, said, "I am quite aware of the fate that is hanging over me. I see that the struggle against us is only postponed till our weapons are handed over to our opponents. Their rage must be appeased with blood. Still, even I do not hesitate to lay down my decemvirate." A decree was passed for the decemvirs to resign office as soon as possible, Q. Furius, the Pontifex Maximus, to appoint tribunes of the plebs, and an amnesty to be granted for the secession of the soldiers and the plebs. After these decrees were passed, the senate broke up, and the decemvirs proceeded to the Assembly and formally laid down their office, to the immense delight of all. This was reported to the plebs on the Sacred Hill. The envoys who carried the intelligence were followed by everybody who was left in the City; this mass of people was met by another rejoicing multitude who issued from the camp. They exchanged mutual congratulations on the restoration of liberty and concord. The envoys, addressing the multitude as an Assembly, said, "Prosperity, fortune, and happiness to you and to the State! Return to your fatherland, your homes, your wives, and your children! But carry into the City the same self-control which you have exhibited here, where no man's land has been damaged, notwithstanding the need of so many things necessary for so large a multitude. Go to the Aventine, whence you came; there, on the auspicious spot where you laid the beginnings of your liberty, you will appoint your tribunes; the Pontifex Maximus will be present to hold the election." Great was the delight and eagerness with which they applauded everything. They plucked up the standards and started for Rome, outdoing those they met in their expressions of joy. Marching under arms through the City in silence, they reached the Aventine. There the Pontifex Maximus at once proceeded to hold the election for tribunes. The first to be elected was L. Verginius; next, the organizers of the secession, L. Icilius and P. Numitorius, the uncle of Verginius; then, C. Sicinius, the son of the man who is recorded as the first to be elected of the tribunes on the Sacred Hill, and M. Duillius, who had filled that office with distinction before the appointment of the decemvirs, and through all the struggles with them had never failed to support the plebs. After these came M. Titinius, M. Pomponius, C. Apronius, Appius Villius, and Caius Oppius, all of whom were elected rather in hope of their future usefulness than for any services actually rendered. When he had entered on his tribuneship L. Icilius at once proposed a resolution which the plebs accepted, that no one should suffer for the secession. Marcus Duillius immediately carried a measure for the election of consuls and the right of appeal from them to the people. All these measures were passed in a council of the plebs which was held in the Flaminian Meadows, now called the Circus Flaminius.

3.55

THE election of consuls took place under the presidency of an "interrex." Those elected were L. Valerius and M. Horatius, and they at once assumed office. Their consulship was a popular one, and inflicted no injustice upon the patricians, though they regarded it with suspicion, for whatever was done to safeguard the liberties of the plebs they looked upon as an infringement of their own powers. First of all, as it was a doubtful legal point whether the patricians were bound by the ordinances of the plebs, they carried a law in the Assembly of Centuries that what the plebs had passed in their Tribes should be binding on the whole people. By this law a very effective weapon was placed in the hands of the tribunes. Then another consular law, confirming the right of appeal, as the one defense of liberty, which had been annulled by the decemvirs, was not only restored but strengthened for the future by a fresh enactment. This forbade the appointment of any magistrate from whom there was no right of appeal, and provided that any one who did so appoint might be rightly and lawfully put to death, nor should the man who put him to death be held guilty of murder. When they had sufficiently strengthened the plebs by the right of appeal on the one hand and the protection afforded by the tribunes on the other, they proceeded to secure the personal inviolability of the tribunes themselves. The memory of this had almost perished, so they renewed it with certain sacred rites revived from a distant past, and in addition to securing their inviolability by the sanctions of religion, they enacted a law that whoever offered violence to the magistrates of the plebs, whether tribunes, aediles, or decemviral judges, his person should be devoted to Jupiter, his possessions sold and the proceeds assigned to the temples of Ceres, Liber, and Liberal Jurists say that by this law no one was actually "sacrosanct," but that when injury was offered to any of those mentioned above the offender was "sacer." If an aedile, therefore, were arrested and sent to prison by superior magistrates, though this could not be done by law—for by this law it would not be lawful for him to be injured—yet it is a proof that an aedile is not held to be "sacrosanct," whereas the tribunes of the plebs were "sacrosanct" by the ancient oath taken by the plebeians when that office was first created. There were some who interpreted the law as including even the consuls in its provisions, and the praetors, because they were elected under the same auspices as the consuls, for a consul was called a "judge." This interpretation is refuted by the fact that in those times it was the custom for a judge to be called not "consul" but "praetor." These were the laws enacted by the consuls. They also ordered that the decrees of the senate, which used formerly to be suppressed and tampered with at the pleasure of the consuls, should henceforth be taken to the aediles at the temple of Ceres. Marcus Duillius, the tribune, then proposed a resolution which the plebs adopted, that any one who should leave the plebs without tribunes, or who should create a magistrate from whom there was no appeal, should be scourged and beheaded. All these transactions were distasteful to the patricians, but they did not actively oppose them, as none of them had yet been marked out for vindictive proceedings.

3.56

THE power of the tribunes and the liberties of the plebs were now on a secure basis. The next step was taken by the tribunes, who thought the time had come when they might safely proceed against individuals. They selected Verginius to take up the first prosecution, which was that of Appius. When the day had been fixed, and Appius had come down to the Forum with a bodyguard of young patricians, the sight of him and his satellites reminded all present of the power he had used so vilely. Verginius began: "Oratory was invented for doubtful cases. I will not, therefore, waste time by a long indictment before you of the man from whose cruelty you have vindicated yourselves by force of arms, nor will I allow him to add to his other crimes an impudent defense. So I will pass over, Appius Claudius, all the wicked and impious things that you had the audacity to do, one after another, for the last two years. One charge only will I bring against you, that contrary to law you have adjudged a free person to be a slave, and unless you name an umpire before whom you can prove your innocence, I shall order you to be taken to prison." Appius had nothing to hope for in the protection of the tribunes or the verdict of the people. Nevertheless he called upon the tribunes, and when none intervened to stay proceedings and he was seized by the apparitor, he said, "I appeal." This single word, the protection of liberty, uttered by those lips which had so lately judicially deprived a person of her freedom, produced a general silence. Then the people remarked to one another that there were gods after all who did not neglect the affairs of men; arrogance and cruelty were visited by punishments which, though lingering, were not light; that man was appealing who had taken away the power of appeal; that man was imploring the protection of the people who had trampled underfoot all their rights; he was losing his own liberty and being carried off to prison who had sentenced a free person to slavery. Amidst the murmur of the Assembly the voice of Appius himself was heard imploring "the protection of the Roman people."

He began by enumerating the services of his ancestors to the State, both at home and in the field; his own unfortunate devotion to the plebs, which had led him to resign his consulship in order to enact equal laws for all, giving thereby the greatest offence to the patricians; his laws which were still in force, though their author was being carried to prison. As to his own personal conduct and his good and evil deeds, however, he would bring them to the test when he had the opportunity of pleading his cause. For the present he claimed the common right of a Roman citizen to be allowed to plead on the appointed day and submit himself to the judgment of the Roman people. He was not so apprehensive of the general feeling against him as to abandon all hope in the impartiality and sympathy of his fellow citizens. If he was to be taken to prison before his case was heard, he would once more appeal to the tribunes, and warn them not to copy the example of those whom they hated. If they admitted that they were bound by the same agreement to abolish the right of appeal which they accused the decemvirs of having formed, then he would appeal to the people and invoke the laws which both consuls and tribunes had enacted that very year to protect that right. For if before the case is heard and judgment given there is no power of appeal, who would appeal ? What plebeian, even the humblest, would find protection in the laws, if Appius Claudius could not? His case would show whether it was tyranny or freedom that was conferred by the new laws, and whether the right of challenge and appeal against the injustice of magistrates was only displayed in empty words or was actually granted.

3.57

VERGINIUS replied. Appius Claudius, he said, alone was outside the laws, outside all the bonds that held States or even human society together. Let men cast their eyes on that tribunal, the fortress of all villainies, where that perpetual decemvir, surrounded by hangmen not lictors, in contempt of gods and men alike, wreaked his vengeance on the goods, the backs, and the lives of the citizens, threatening all indiscriminately with the rods and axes, and then when his mind was diverted from rapine and murder to lust, tore a freeborn maiden from her father's arms, before the eyes of Rome, and gave her to a client, the minister of his intrigues—that tribunal where by a cruel decree and infamous judgment he armed the father's hand against the daughter, where he ordered those who took up the maiden's lifeless body—her betrothed lover and her grandfather—to be thrown into prison, moved less by her death than by the check to his criminal gratification. For him as much as for others was that prison built which he used to call "the domicile of the Roman plebs." Let him appeal again and again, he (the speaker) would always refer him to an umpire on the charge of having sentenced a free person to slavery. If he would not go before an umpire he should order him to be imprisoned as though found guilty. He was accordingly thrown into prison, and though no one actually opposed this step, there was a general feeling of anxiety, since even the plebeians themselves thought it an excessive use of their liberty to inflict punishment on so great a man. The tribune adjourned the day of trial. During these proceedings ambassadors came from the Latins and Hernicans to offer their congratulations on the restoration of harmony between the patriciate and the plebs. As a memorial of it, they brought an offering to Jupiter Optimus Maximus, in the shape of a golden crown. It was not a large one, as they were not wealthy States; their religious observances were characterised by devotion rather than magnificence. They also brought information that the Aequi and Volscians were devoting all their energies to preparing for war. The consuls were thereupon ordered to arrange their respective commands. The Sabines fell to Horatius, the Aequi to Valerius. They proclaimed a levy for these wars, and so favourable was the attitude of the plebs that not only did the men liable for service promptly give in their names, but a large part of the levy consisted of men who had served their time and came forward as volunteers. In this way the army was strengthened not only in numbers but in the quality of the soldiers, as veterans took their places in the ranks. Before they left the City, the laws of the decemvirs, known as the "Twelve Tables," were engraved in brass and publicly exhibited; some writers assert that the aediles discharged this task under orders from the tribunes.

Book IV: The Growing Power of the Plebs

4.1

THE consuls who succeeded were M. Genucius and C. Curtius. The year was a troubled one both at home and abroad. In the beginning of the year C. Canuleius, a tribune of the plebs, introduced a law with regard to the intermarriage of patricians and plebeians. The patricians considered that their blood would be contaminated by it and the special rights of the houses thrown into confusion. Then the tribunes began to throw out hints about one consul being elected from the plebs, and matters advanced so far that nine tribunes brought in a measure empowering the people to elect consuls from the plebeians or the patricians as they chose. The patricians believed that, if this were carried, the supreme power would not only be degraded by being shared with the lowest of the people, but would entirely pass away from the chief men in the State into the hands of the plebs. The senate were not sorry, therefore, to hear that Ardea had revolted as a consequence of the unjust decision about the territory, that the Veientines had ravaged the districts on the Roman frontier, and that the Volscians and Aequi were protesting against the fortifying of Verrugo; so much did they prefer war, even when unsuccessful, to an ignominious peace. On receiving these reports—which were somewhat exaggerated—the senate tried to drown the voice of the tribunes in the uproar of so many wars by ordering a levy to be made and all preparations for war pushed on with the utmost vigour, more so, if possible, than during the consulship of T. Quinctius. Thereupon C. Canuleius addressed the senate in a short and angry speech. It was, he said, useless for the consuls to hold out threats in the hope of distracting the attention of the plebs from the proposed law; as long as he was alive they should never hold a levy until the plebs had adopted the measures brought forward by himself and his colleagues. He at once convened an Assembly.

4.2

THE consuls began to rouse the senate to take action against the tribunes, and at the same time the tribunes were getting up an agitation against the consuls. The consuls declared that the revolutionary proceedings of the tribunes could no longer be tolerated, matters had come to a crisis, there was a more bitter war going on at home than abroad. This was not the fault of the plebs so much as of the senate, nor of the tribunes more than of the consuls. Those things in a State which attain the highest development are those which are encouraged by rewards; it is thus that men become good citizens in times of peace, good soldiers in times of war. In Rome the greatest rewards are won by seditious agitations, these have always brought honour to men both individually and in the mass. Those present should reflect upon the greatness and dignity of the senate as they had received it from their fathers, and consider what they were going to hand on to their children, in order that they might be able to feel pride in the extension and growth of its influence, as the plebs felt pride in theirs. There was no final settlement in sight, nor would there be as long as agitators were honoured in proportion to the success of their agitation. What enormous questions had C. Canuleius raised! He was advocating the breaking up of the houses, tampering with the auspices, both those of the State and those of individuals, so that nothing would be pure, nothing free from contamination, and in the effacing of all distinctions of rank, no one would know either himself or his kindred. What other result would mixed marriages have except to make unions between patricians and plebeians almost like the promiscuous association of animals? The offspring of such marriages would not know whose blood flowed in his veins, what sacred rites he might perform; half of him patrician, half plebeian, he would not even be in harmony with himself. And as though it were a small matter for all things human and divine to be thrown into confusion, the disturbers of the people were now making an onslaught on the consulship. At first the question of one consul being elected from the plebs was only mooted in private conversations, now a measure was brought forward giving the people power to elect consuls from either patricians or plebeians as they chose. And there was no shadow of doubt that they would elect all the most dangerous revolutionaries in the plebs; the Canuleii and the Icilii would be consuls. Might Jupiter Optimus Maximus never allow a power truly royal in its majesty to sink so low! They would rather die a thousand deaths than suffer such an ignominy to be perpetrated. Could their ancestors have divined that all their concessions only served to make the plebs more exacting, not more friendly, since their first success only emboldened them to make more and more urgent demands, it was quite certain that they would have gone any lengths in resistance sooner than allow these laws to be forced upon them. Because a concession was once made in the matter of tribunes, it had been made again; there was no end to it. Tribunes of the plebs and the senate could not exist in the same State, either that office or this order (i.e. the nobility) must go. Their insolence and recklessness must be opposed, and better late than never. Were they to be allowed with impunity to stir up our neighbours to war by sowing the seeds of discord and then prevent the State from arming in its defense against those whom they had stirred up, and after all but summoning the enemy not allow armies to be enrolled against the enemy? Was Canuleius, forsooth, to have the audacity to give out before the senate that unless it was prepared to accept his conditions, like those of a conqueror, he would stop a levy being held? What else was that but threatening to betray his country and allowing it to be attacked and captured ? What courage would his words inspire, not in the Roman plebs but in the Volscians and Aequi and Veientines! Would they not hope, with Canuleius as their leader, to be able to scale the Capitol and the Citadel, if the tribunes, after stripping the senate of its rights and its authority, deprived it also of its courage? The consuls were ready to be their leaders against criminal citizens before they led them against the enemy in arms.

4.3

AT the very time when this was going on in the senate, Canuleius delivered the following speech in defense of his laws and in opposition to the consuls: "I fancy, Quirites, that I have often noticed in the past how greatly the patricians despise you, how unworthy they deem you to live in the same City, within the same walls, as they. Now, however, it is perfectly obvious, seeing how bitter an opposition they have raised to our proposed laws. For what is our purpose in framing them except to remind them that we are their fellow-citizens, and though we do not possess the same power, we still inhabit the same country? In one of these laws we demand the right of intermarriage, a right usually granted to neighbours and foreigners—indeed we have granted citizenship, which is more than intermarriage, even to a conquered enemy—in the other we are bringing forward nothing new, but simply demanding back what belongs to the people and claiming that the Roman people should confer its honours on whom it will. What possible reason is there why they should embroil heaven and earth, why recently in the Senate-house I was on the point of being subjected to personal violence, why they declare they will not keep their hands off, and threaten to attack our inviolable authority? Will this City be no longer able to stand, is our dominion at an end, if a free vote is allowed to the Roman people so that they may entrust the consulship to whomsoever they will, and no plebeian may be shut out from the hope of attaining the highest honour if only he be worthy of the highest honour? Does the phrase 'Let no plebeian be made consul' mean just the same as 'No slave or freedman shall be consul'? Do you ever realize in what contempt you are living? They would rob you of your share in this daylight, if they could. They are indignant because you breathe and utter speech and wear the form of men. Why! Heaven forgive me, they actually say that it would be an act of impiety for a plebeian to be made consul! Though we are not allowed access to the "Fasti" or the records of the pontiffs, do we not, pray, know what every stranger knows, that the consuls have simply taken the place of the kings, and possess no right or privilege which was not previously vested in the kings? I suppose you have never heard tell that Numa Pompilius, who was not only no patrician but not even a Roman citizen, was summoned from the land of the Sabines, and after being accepted by the people and confirmed by the senate, reigned as king of Rome? Or that, after him, L. Tarquinius, who belonged to no Roman house, not even to an Italian one, being the son of Demaratus of Corinth, who had settled in Tarquinii, was made king while the sons of Ancus were still alive? Or that, after him again, Servius Tullius, the illegitimate son of a female slave captured at Corniculum, gained the crown by sheer merit and ability? Why need I mention the Sabine Titus Tatius, with whom Romulus himself, the Father of the City, shared his throne? As long as no class of person in which conspicuous merit appeared was rejected, the Roman dominion grew. Are you then to regard a plebeian consul with disgust, when our ancestors showed no aversion to strangers as their kings? Not even after the expulsion of the kings was the City closed to foreign merit. The Claudian house, at all events, who migrated from the Sabines, was received by us not only into citizenship, but even into the ranks of the patricians. Shall a man who was an alien become a patrician and afterwards consul, and a Roman citizen, if he belongs to the plebs, be cut off from all hope of the consulship? Do we believe that it is impossible for a plebeian to be brave and energetic and capable both in peace and war, or if there be such a man, are we not to allow him to touch the helm of the State; are we to have, by preference, consuls like the decemvirs, those vilest of mortals—who, nevertheless, were all patricians—rather than men who resemble the best of the kings, new men though they were?

4.4

"BUT, I may be told, no consul, since the expulsion of the kings, has ever been elected from the plebs. What then? Ought no innovation ever to be introduced; and because a thing has not yet been done—and in a new community there are many things which have not yet been done—ought they not to be done, even when they are advantageous? In the reign of Romulus there were no pontiffs, no college of augurs; they were created by Numa Pompilius. There was no census in the State, no register of the centuries and classes; it was made by Servius Tullius. There were never any consuls; when the kings had been expelled they were created. Neither the power nor the name of Dictator was in existence; it originated with the senate. There were no tribunes of the plebs, no aediles, no quaestors; it was decided that these offices should be created. Within the last ten years we appointed decemvirs to commit the laws to writing and then we abolished their office. Who doubts that in a City built for all time and without any limits to its growth new authorities have to be established, new priesthoods, modifications in the rights and privileges of the houses as well as of individual citizens? Was not this very prohibition of intermarriage between patricians and plebeians, which inflicts such serious injury on the commonwealth and such a gross injustice on the plebs, made by the decemvirs within these last few years? Can there be a greater or more signal disgrace than for a part of the community to be held unworthy of intermarriage, as though contaminated? What is this but to suffer exile and banishment within the same walls? They are guarding against our becoming connected with them by affinity or relationship, against our blood being allied with theirs. Why, most of you are descended from Albans and Sabines, and that nobility of yours you hold not by birth or blood, but by co-optation into the patrician ranks, having been selected for that honour either by the kings, or after their expulsion by the mandate of the people. If your nobility is tainted by union with us, could you not have kept it pure by private regulations, by not seeking brides from the plebs, and not suffering your sisters or daughters to marry outside your order? No plebeian will offer violence to a patrician maiden, it is the patricians who indulge in those criminal practices. None of us would have compelled any one to enter into a marriage contract against his will. But, really, that this should be prohibited by law and the intermarriage of patricians and plebeians made impossible is indeed insulting to the plebs. Why do you not combine to forbid intermarriage between rich and poor? Everywhere and in all ages there has been an understanding that a woman might marry into any house in which she has been betrothed, and a man might marry from any house the woman to whom he has become engaged, and this understanding you are fettering by the manacles of a most insolent law, through which you may break up civil society and rend one State into two. Why do you not enact a law that no plebeian shall live in the neighbourhood of a patrician, or go along the same road, or take his place at the same banquet, or stand in the same Forum? For, as a matter of fact, what difference is there, if a patrician marries a plebeian woman or a plebeian marries a patrician? What rights are infringed, pray? Of course, the children follow the father. There is nothing that we are seeking in intermarriage with you, except that we may be reckoned amongst men and citizens; there is nothing for you to fight about, unless you delight in trying how far you can insult and degrade us.

4.5

"IN a word, does the supreme power belong to you or to the Roman people? Did the expulsion of the kings mean absolute ascendancy for you or equal liberty for all? Is it right and proper for the Roman people to enact a law, if it wishes to do so, or are you going, whenever a measure is proposed, to order a levy by way of punishment? Am I to call the tribes up to vote, and as soon as I have begun, are you, the consuls, going to compel those who are liable for service to take the military oath, and then march them off to camp, threatening alike the plebs and the tribunes? Why, have you not on two occasions found out what your threats are worth against a united plebs? Was it, I wonder, in our interest that you abstained from an open conflict, or was it because the stronger party was also the more moderate one that there was no fighting? Nor will there be any conflict now, Quirites; they will always try your courage, they will not test your strength. And so, consuls, the plebeians are ready to follow you to these wars, whether real or imaginary, on condition that by restoring the right of intermarriage you at last make this commonwealth a united one, that it be in their power to be allied with you by family ties, that the hope of attaining high office be granted to men of ability and energy, that it be open to them to be associated with you in taking their share of the government, and—which is the essence of equal liberty—to rule and obey in turn, in the annual succession of magistrates. If any one is going to obstruct these measures, you may talk about wars and exaggerate them by rumour, no one is going to give in his name, no one is going to take up arms, no one is going to fight for domineering masters with whom they have in public life no partnership in honours, and in private life no right of intermarriage."

4.6

AFTER the two consuls had come forward into the Assembly, set speeches gave place to a personal altercation. The tribune asked why it was not right for a plebeian to be elected consul. The consuls gave a reply which, though perhaps true, was an unfortunate one in view of the present controversy. They said, "Because no plebeian could have the auspices, and the reason why the decemvirs had put an end to intermarriage was to prevent the auspices from being vitiated through the uncertainty of descent." This bitterly exasperated the plebeians, for they believed that they were held incompetent to take the auspices because they were hateful to the immortal gods. As they had got a most energetic leader in their tribune and were supporting him with the utmost determination, the controversy ended in the defeat of the patricians. They consented to the intermarriage law being passed, mainly in the belief that the tribunes would either abandon the struggle for plebeian consuls altogether, or would at least postpone it till after the war, and that the plebeians, contented with what they had gained, would be ready to enlist. Owing to his victory over the patricians Canuleius was now immensely popular. Fired by his example, the other tribunes fought with the utmost energy to secure the passing of their measure, and though the rumours of war became more serious every day they obstructed the enlistment. As no business could be transacted in the senate owing to the intervention of the tribunes, the consuls held councils of the leaders at their own houses.

It was evident that they would have to yield the victory either to their foreign foes or to their own countrymen. Valerius and Horatius were the only men of consular rank who did not attend these councils. C. Claudius was in favour of empowering the consuls to use armed force against the tribunes; the Quinctii, Cincinnatus and Capitolinus, were averse from bloodshed or injury to those whom in their treaty with the plebs they had agreed to hold inviolable. The result of their deliberations was that they allowed tribunes of the soldiers with consular powers to be elected from the patricians and plebeians indiscriminately; no change was made in the election of consuls. This arrangement satisfied the tribunes and it satisfied the plebs. Notice was published that an Assembly would be held for the election of three tribunes with consular powers. No sooner was this announcement made than everybody who had ever acted or spoken as a fomenter of sedition, especially those who had been tribunes, came forward as candidates, and began to bustle about the Forum, canvassing for votes. The patricians were at first deterred from seeking election, as in the exasperated mood of the plebeians they regarded their chances as hopeless, and they were disgusted at the prospect of having to hold office with these men. At last, under compulsion from their leaders, lest they should appear to have withdrawn from any share in the government, they consented to stand. The result of the election showed that when men are contending for liberty and the right to hold office their feelings are different from what they are when the contest is over and they can form an unbiased judgment. The people were satisfied now that votes were allowed for plebeians, and they elected none but patricians. Where in these days will you find in a single individual the moderation, fairness, and loftiness of mind which then characterized the people as a whole?

4.7

IN the 310th year after the foundation of Rome (444 B.C.), military tribunes with consular powers for the first time took office. Their names were Aulus Sempronius Atratinus, L. Atilius, and T. Caecilius, and during their tenure of office concord at home procured peace abroad. Some writers omit all mention of the proposal to elect consuls from the plebs, and assert that the creation of three military tribunes invested with the insignia and authority of consuls was rendered necessary by the inability of two consuls to cope at the same time with the Veientine war in addition to the war with the Aequi and Volscians and the defection of Ardea. The jurisdiction of that office was not yet, however, firmly established, for in consequence of the decision of the augurs they resigned office after three months, owing to some irregularity in their election. C. Curtius, who had presided over their election, had not rightly selected his position for taking the auspices. Ambassadors came from Ardea to complain of the injustice done them; they promised that if it were removed by the restoration of their territory they would abide by the treaty and remain good friends with Rome. The senate replied that they had no power to rescind a judgment of the people, there was no precedent or law to allow it, the necessity of preserving harmony between the two orders made it impossible. If the Ardeates were willing to wait their time and leave the redress of their wrongs in the hands of the senate, they would afterwards congratulate themselves on their moderation, and would discover that the senators were just as anxious that no injustice should be done them as that whatever had been done should speedily be repaired. The ambassadors said that they would bring the whole matter again before their senate, and were then courteously dismissed.

As the State was now without any curule magistrate, the patricians met together and appointed an interrex. Owing to a dispute whether consuls or military tribunes should be elected, the interregnum lasted several days. The interrex and the senate tried to secure the election of consuls; the plebs and their tribunes that of military tribunes. The senate conquered, for the plebeians were sure to confer either honour on the patricians and so refrained from an idle contest, whilst their leaders preferred an election in which no votes could be received for them to one in which they would be passed over as unworthy to hold office. The tribunes, too, gave up the fruitless contest out of complaisance to the leaders of the senate. T. Quinctius Barbatus, the interrex, elected as consuls Lucius Papirius Mugilanus and L. Sempronius Atratinus. During their consulship the treaty with Ardea was renewed. This is the sole proof that they were the consuls for that year, for they are not found in the ancient annals nor in the official list of magistrates. The reason, I believe, was that since at the beginning of the year there were military tribunes, the names of the consuls who replaced them were omitted as though the tribunes had continued in office through the year. According to Licinius Macer, their names were found in the copy of the treaty with Ardea, as well as in the "Linen Rolls." In spite of so many alarming symptoms of unrest amongst the neighbouring nations, things were quiet both abroad and at home.

4.8

WHETHER there were tribunes this year, or whether they were replaced by consuls, there is no doubt that the following year the consuls were M. Geganius Macerinus and T. Quinctius Capitolinus; the former consul for the second time, the latter for the fifth time. This year saw the beginning of the censorship, an office which, starting from small beginnings, grew to be of such importance that it had the regulation of the conduct and morals of Rome, the control of the senate and the equestrian order; the power of honouring and degrading was also in the hands of these magistrates; the legal rights connected with public places and private property, and the revenues of the Roman people, were under their absolute control. Its origin was due to the fact that no census had been taken of the people for many years, and it could no longer be postponed, whilst the consuls, with so many wars impending, did not feel at liberty to undertake the task. It was suggested in the senate that as the business would be a complicated and laborious one, not at all suitable for the consuls, a special magistrate was needed who should superintend the registrars and have the custody of the lists and assessment schedules and fix the valuation of property and the status of citizens at his discretion. Though the suggestion was not of great importance, the senate gladly adopted it, as it would add to the number of patrician magistrates in the State, and I think that they anticipated what actually happened, that the influence of those who held the office would soon enhance its authority and dignity.

The tribunes, too, looking more at the need which certainly existed for such an office than at the lustre which would attend its administration, offered no opposition, lest they should appear to be raising troublesome difficulties even in small matters. The foremost men of the State declined the honour, so Papirius and Sempronius—about whose consulship doubts were entertained—were elected by the suffrages of the people to conduct the census. Their election to this magistracy made up for the incompleteness of their consulship. From the duties they had to discharge they were called Censors.

4.9

WHILST this was going on in Rome, ambassadors came from Ardea, appealing, in the name of the ancient alliance and recently renewed treaty, for help for their city which was almost destroyed. They were not allowed, they said, to enjoy the peace which in pursuance of the soundest policy they had maintained with Rome, owing to internal disputes. The origin and occasion of these is said to have been party struggles, which have been and will be more ruinous to the majority of States than external wars or famine and pestilence or whatever else is ascribed to the wrath of the gods as the last evil which a State can suffer. Two young men were courting a maiden of plebeian descent celebrated for her beauty. One of them, the girl's equal in point of birth, was encouraged by her guardians, who belonged to the same class; the other, a young noble captivated solely by her beauty, was supported by the sympathy and good-will of the nobility. Party feeling had even penetrated into the girl's home, for the mother, who wanted her daughter to make as splendid a match as possible, preferred the young noble, whilst the guardians, carrying their partisanship even into such a matter as this, were working for the man of their own class. As the matter could not be settled within the four walls of the house, they brought it into court. After hearing the appeals of the mother and of the guardians, the magistrates granted the disposal of the girl's hand in accordance with the mother's wishes. But violence won the day, for the guardians, after haranguing a number of their partisans in the Forum on the iniquity of the verdict, collected a body of men and carried off the maiden from her mother's house. They were met by a still more determined troop of nobles, assembled to follow their young comrade, who was furious at the outrage. A desperate fight ensued and the plebeians got the worst of it. In a very different spirit from the Roman plebs they marched, fully armed, out of the city and took possession of a hill from which they raided the lands of the nobles and laid them waste with fire and sword. A multitude of artisans who had previously taken no part in the conflict, excited by the hope of plunder, joined them, and preparations were made to besiege the city. All the horrors of war were present in the city, as though it had been infected with the madness of the two young men who were seeking fatal nuptials out of their country's ruin. Both sides felt the need of an addition to their strength; the nobles prevailed on the Romans to come to the relief of their beleaguered city; the plebs induced the Volscians to join them in attacking Ardea. The Volscians, under the leadership of Cluilius, the Aequian, were the first to come, and drew lines of circumvallation round the enemy's walls. When news of this reached Rome the consul M. Geganius at once left with an army and fixed his camp three miles distant from the enemy, and as the day was declining he ordered his men to rest. At the fourth watch he ordered an advance, and so expeditiously was the task undertaken and completed, that at sunrise the Volscians saw themselves enclosed by a stronger circumvallation than the one which they had themselves carried round the city. In another direction the consul constructed a covered way up to the wall of Ardea by which his friends in the city could go to and fro.

4.10

UP to that time the Volscian commander had not laid in any stock of provisions, as he had been able to maintain his army upon the corn carried off each day from the surrounding country. Now, however, that he was suddenly shut in by the Roman lines, he found himself destitute of everything. He invited the consul to a conference, and said that if the object for which the Romans had come was to raise the siege, he would withdraw the Volscians. The consul replied that it was for the defeated side to submit to terms, not to impose them, and as the Volscians had come at their own pleasure to attack the allies of Rome, they should not depart on the same terms. He required them to lay down their arms, surrender their general, and make acknowledgment of their defeat by placing themselves under his orders; otherwise, whether they remained or departed, he would prove a relentless foe, and would rather carry back to Rome a victory over them than a faithless peace. The only hope of the Volscians lay in their arms, and slight as it was they risked it. The ground was unfavourable to them for fighting, still more so for flight. As they were being cut down in all directions, they begged for quarter, but they were only allowed to get away after their general had been surrendered, their arms given up, and they themselves sent under the yoke. Covered with disgrace and disaster, they departed with only one garment apiece. They halted not far from the city of Tusculum, and owing to an old grudge which that city had against them, they were suddenly attacked, and defenseless as they were, suffered severe punishment, few being left to carry the news of the disaster. The consul settled the troubles in Ardea by beheading the ringleaders of the disturbance and confiscating their property to the treasury of the city. The citizens considered that the injustice of the recent decision was removed by the great service that Rome had rendered, but the senate thought that something ought still to be done to wipe out the record of national avarice. The consul Quinctius achieved the difficult task of rivaling in his civil administration the military renown of his colleague. He showed such care to maintain peace and concord by tempering justice equally for the highest and the lowest, that whilst the senate looked upon him as a stern consul, the plebeians regarded him as a lenient one. He held his ground against the tribunes more by personal authority than by active opposition. Five consulships marked by the same even tenor of conduct, a whole lifetime passed in a manner worthy of a consul, invested the man himself with almost more reverence than the office he filled. Whilst these two men were consuls there was no talk of military tribunes.

4.11

THE new consuls were Marcus Fabius Vibulanus and Postumius Aebutius Cornicinen. The previous year was regarded by the neighbouring peoples, whether friendly or hostile, as chiefly memorable because of the trouble taken to help Ardea in its peril. The new consuls, aware that they were succeeding men distinguished both at home and abroad, were all the more anxious to obliterate from men's minds the infamous judgment. Accordingly, they obtained a senatorial decree ordering that as the population of Ardea had been seriously reduced through the internal disturbances, a body of colonists should be sent there as a protection against the Volscians. This was the reason alleged in the text of the decree, to prevent their intention of rescinding the judgment from being suspected by the plebs and tribunes. They had, however, privately agreed that the majority of the colonists should consist of Rutulians, that no land should be allotted other than what had been appropriated under the infamous judgment, and that not a single sod should be assigned to a Roman till all the Rutulians had received their share. So the land went back to the Ardeates. Agrippa Menenius, T. Cluilius Siculus, and M. Aebutius Helva were the triumvirs appointed to superintend the settlement of the colony. Their office was not only extremely unpopular, but they gave great offence to the plebs by assigning to allies land which the Roman people had formally adjudged to be their own. Even with the leaders of the patricians they were out of favour, because they had refused to allow themselves to be influenced by any of them. The tribunes impeached them, but they avoided all further vexatious proceedings by enrolling themselves amongst the settlers and remaining in the colony which they now possessed as a testimony to their justice and integrity.

4.12

THERE was peace abroad and at home during this and the following year when C. Furius Pacilus and M. Papirius Crassus were consuls. The Sacred Games, which in accordance with a decree of the senate had been vowed by the decemvirs on the occasion of the secession of the plebs, were celebrated this year. Poetilius, who had again raised the question of the division of territory, was made tribune. He made fruitless efforts to create sedition, and was unable to prevail upon the consuls to bring the question before the senate.

After a great struggle he succeeded so far that the senate should be consulted as to whether the next elections should be held for consuls or for consular tribunes. They ordered consuls to be elected. The tribune's menaces were laughed at when he threatened to obstruct the levy at a time when all the neighbouring States were quiet and there was no necessity for war or for any preparations for war. Proculus Geganius Macerinus and Lucius Menenius Lanatus were the consuls for the year which followed this state of tranquility; a year remarkable for a multiplicity of disasters and dangers, seditions, famine, and the imminent risk of the people being bribed to bow their necks to despotic power. A foreign war alone was wanting. Had this come to aggravate the universal distress, resistance would hardly have been possible even with the help of all the gods.

The misfortunes began with a famine, owing either to the year being unfavourable to the crops, or to the cultivation of the land being abandoned for the attractions of political meetings and city life; both causes are assigned. The senate blamed the idleness of the plebeians, the tribunes charged the consuls at one time with dishonesty, at another with negligence. At last they induced the plebs, with the acquiescence of the senate, to appoint as Prefect of the Corn-market L. Minucius. In that capacity he was more successful in guarding liberty than in the discharge of his office, though in the end he deservedly won gratitude and reputation for having relieved the scarcity. He despatched numerous agents by sea and land to visit the surrounding nations, but as, with the sole exception of Etruria, who furnished a small supply, their mission was fruitless, he made no impression on the market. He then devoted himself to the careful adjustment of the scarcity, and obliged all who possessed any corn to declare the amount, and after retaining a month's supply for themselves, sell the rest to the Government. By cutting down the daily rations of the slaves to one half, by holding up the corn merchants to public execration, by rigorous and inquisitorial methods, he revealed the prevailing distress more than he relieved it. Many of the plebs lost all hope, and rather than drag on a life of misery muffled their heads and threw themselves into the Tiber.

4.13

IT was at that time that Spurius Maelius, a member of the equestrian order and a very wealthy man for those days, entered upon an undertaking, serviceable in itself, but forming a very bad precedent and dictated by still worse motives. Through the instrumentality of his clients and foreign friends he purchased corn in Etruria, and this very circumstance, I believe, hampered the Government in their efforts to cheapen the market. He distributed this corn gratis, and so won the hearts of the plebeians by this generosity that wherever he moved, conspicuous and consequential beyond an ordinary mortal, they followed him, and this popularity seemed to his hopes a sure earnest of a consulship. But the minds of men are never satisfied with Fortune's promises, and he began to entertain loftier and unattainable aims; he knew the consulship would have to be won in the teeth of the patricians, so he began to dream of royalty. After all his grand schemes and efforts he looked upon that as the only fitting reward which owing to its greatness must be won by the greatest exertions. The consular elections were now close at hand, and as his plans were not yet matured, this circumstance proved his ruin. T. Quinctius Capitolinus, a very awkward man for any one meditating a revolution, was chosen consul for the sixth time, and Agrippa Menenius, surnamed Lanatus, was assigned to him as his colleague. Lucius Minucius was either reappointed prefect of the corn-market, or his original appointment was for an indefinite period as long as circumstances required; there is nothing definitely stated beyond the fact that the name of the prefect was entered on the "Linen Rolls" among the magistrates for both years. Minucius was discharging the same function as a State official which Maelius had undertaken as a private citizen, and the same class of people frequented both their houses. He made a discovery which he brought to the notice of the senate, viz., that arms were being collected in Maelius' house, and that he was holding secret meetings at which plans were being undoubtedly formed to establish a monarchy. The moment for action was not yet fixed, but everything else had been settled; the tribunes had been bought over to betray the liberties of the people, and these leaders of the populace had had their various parts assigned to them. He had, he said, delayed making his report till it was almost too late for the public safety, lest he should appear to be the author of vague and groundless suspicions.

On hearing this the leaders of the senate censured the consuls of the previous year for having allowed those free distributions of corn and secret meetings to go on, and they were equally severe on the new consuls for having waited till the prefect of the corn-market had made his report, for the matter was of such importance that the consuls ought not only to have reported it, but also dealt with it. In reply, Quinctius said that the censure on the consuls was undeserved, for, hampered as they were by the laws giving the right of appeal, which were passed to weaken their authority, they were far from possessing as much power as will to punish the atrocious attempt with the severity it deserved. What was wanted was not only a strong man, but one who was free to act, unshackled by the laws. He should therefore nominate Lucius Quinctius as Dictator, for he had the courage and resolution which such great powers demanded. This met with universal approval. Quinctius at first refused and asked them what they meant by exposing him at the close of his life to such a bitter struggle. At last, after well-merited commendations were showered upon him from all parts of the House and he was assured that "in that aged mind there was not only more wisdom but more courage than in all the rest," whilst the consul adhered to his decision, he yielded. After a prayer to heaven that in such a time of danger his old age might not prove a source of harm or discredit to the republic, Cincinnatus was made Dictator. He appointed Caius Servilius Ahala as his Master of the Horse.

4.14

THE next day, after posting guards at different points, he came down to the Forum. The novelty and mystery of the thing drew the attention of the plebs towards him. Maelius and his confederates recognised that this tremendous power was directed against them, whilst those who knew nothing of the plot asked what disturbance or sudden outbreak of war called for the supreme authority of a

Dictator or required Quinctius, after reaching his eightieth year, to assume the government of the republic. Servilius, the Master of the Horse, was despatched by the Dictator to Maelius with the message: "The Dictator summons you." Alarmed at the summons, he inquired what it meant. Servilius explained that he had to stand his trial and clear himself of the charge brought against him by Minucius in the senate. On this Maelius retreated amongst his troop of adherents, and looking round at them began to slink away, when an officer by order of the Master of the Horse seized him and began to drag him away. The bystanders rescued him, and as he fled he implored "the protection of the Roman plebs," and said that he was the victim of a conspiracy amongst the patricians, because he had acted generously towards the plebs. He entreated them to come to his help in this terrible crisis, and not suffer him to be butchered before their eyes. Whilst he was making these appeals, Servilius overtook him and slew him. Besprinkled with the dead man's blood, and surrounded by a troop of young patricians, he returned to the Dictator and: reported that Maelius after being summoned to appear before him had driven away his officer and incited the populace to riot, and had now met with the punishment he deserved. "Well done!" said the Dictator, "C. Servilius, you have delivered the republic."

4.15

THE populace did not know what to make of the deed and were becoming excited. The Dictator ordered them to be summoned to an Assembly. He declared that Maelius had been lawfully slain, even if he were guiltless of treason, because he had refused to come to the Dictator when summoned by the Master of the Horse. He, Cincinnatus, had sat to investigate the case, after it had been investigated Maelius would have been treated in accordance with the result. He was not to be dealt with like an ordinary citizen. For, though born amongst a free people under laws and settled rights, in a City from which he knew that royalty had been expelled, and in the very same year, the sons of the king's sister, children of the consul who liberated his country, had, on the discovery of a conspiracy for restoring royalty, been beheaded by their own father—a City from which Collatinus Tarquin the consul had been ordered to lay down his office and go into exile, because the very name of Tarquin was detested—a City in which some years later Spurius Cassius had been punished for entertaining designs of sovereignty—a City in which recently the decemvirs had been punished by confiscation, exile, and death because of a tyranny as despotic as that of kings—in that City Maelius had conceived hopes of sovereignty! And who was this man? Although no nobility of birth, no honours, no services to the State paved the way for any man to sovereign power, still it was their consulships, their decemvirates, the honours achieved by them and their ancestors and the splendour of their families that raised the ambitions of the Claudii and the Cassii to an impious height. But Spurius Maelius, to whom the tribuneship of the plebs was a thing to be wished for rather than hoped for, a wealthy corn-factor, hoped to buy the liberty of his fellow-citizens for a couple of pounds of spelt, and imagined that by throwing a little corn to them he could reduce to slavery the men who had conquered all the neighbouring States, and that he whom the State could hardly stomach as a senator would be tolerated as a king, possessing the power and insignia of Romulus, who had sprung from the gods and been carried back to the gods! His act must be regarded as a portent quite as much as a crime; for that portent his blood was not sufficient expiation, those walls within which such madness had been conceived must be leveled to the ground, and his property, contaminated by the price of treason, confiscated to the State.

4.16

SO far the Dictator. He then gave orders for the house to be forthwith razed to the ground, that the place where it stood might be a perpetual reminder of impious hopes crushed. It was afterwards called the Aequimaelium. L. Minucius was presented with the Image of a golden ox set up outside the Trigeminan gate. As he distributed the corn which had belonged to Maelius at the price of one "as" per bushel, the plebs raised no objection to his being thus honoured. I find it stated in some authorities that this Minucius went over from the patricians to the plebeians and after being co-opted as an eleventh tribune quelled a disturbance which arose in consequence of the death of Maelius. It is, however, hardly credible that the senate would have allowed this increase in the number of the tribunes, or that such a precedent, above all others, should have been introduced by a patrician, or that if that concession had been once made, the plebs should not have adhered to it, or at all events tried to do so. But the most conclusive refutation of the lying inscription on his image is to be found in a provision of the law passed a few years previously that it should not be lawful for tribunes to co-opt a colleague. Q. Caecilius, Q. Junius, and Sex. Titinius were the only members of the college of tribunes who did not support the proposal to honour Minucius, and they never ceased to attack Minucius and Servilius in turn before the Assembly and charge them with the undeserved death of Maelius. They succeeded in securing the creation of military tribunes instead of consuls at the next election, for they felt no doubt that for the six vacancies—that number could now be elected—some of the plebeians, by giving out that they would avenge the death of Maelius, would be elected. But in spite of the excitement amongst the plebeians owing to the numerous commotions through the year, they did not create more than three tribunes with consular powers; amongst them L. Quinctius the son of the Cincinnatus who as Dictator incurred such odium that it was made the pretext for disturbances. Mam. Aemilius polled the highest number of votes, L. Julius came in third.

4.59

MEANTIME the consular tribunes decided to lead the army into the territory of the Volscians; Cnaeus Cornelius was left in charge of the City. The three tribunes ascertained that there was no camp of the Volscians anywhere, and that they would not risk a battle, so they divided into three separate forces to ravage the country. Valerius made Antium his objective; Cornelius, Ecetrae. Wherever they marched they destroyed the homesteads and crops far and wide to divide the forces of the Volscians. Fabius marched to Anxur, which was the chief objective, without losing time in devastating the country. This city is now called Terracina; it was built on the side of a hill and sloped down to the marshes. Fabius made a show of attacking the city on that side. Four cohorts were despatched with C. Servilius Ahala by a circuitous route to seize the hill which overhung the town on the other side. After doing so they made an attack amidst loud shouts and uproar from their higher position upon that part of the town where there was no defense. Those who were holding the lower part of the city against Fabius were stupefied with astonishment at the noise, and this gave him time to plant his scaling ladders. The Romans were soon in all parts of the city, and for some time a ruthless slaughter went on of fugitives and fighters, armed and unarmed alike. As there was no hope of quarter, the defeated enemy were compelled to keep up the fight, till suddenly an order was issued that none but those taken with arms should be injured. On this the whole of the population threw down their arms; prisoners to the number of 2500 were taken. Fabius would not allow his men to touch the other spoils of war until the arrival of his colleagues, for those armies too had taken their part in the capture of Anxur, since they had prevented the Volscians from coming to its relief. On their arrival the three armies sacked the town, which, owing to its long-continued prosperity, contained much wealth. This generosity on the part of the generals was the first step towards the reconciliation of the plebs and the senate. This was followed by a boon which the senate, at a most opportune moment, conferred on the plebeians. Before the question was mooted either by the plebs or their tribunes, the senate decreed that the soldiery should receive pay from the public treasury. Previously, each man had served at his own expense.

4.60

NOTHING, it is recorded, was ever welcomed by the plebs with such delight; they crowded round the Senate-house, grasped the hands of the senators as they came out, acknowledged that they were rightly called "Fathers," and declared that after what they had done no one would ever spare his person or his blood, as long as any strength remained, for so generous a country. They saw with pleasure that their private property at all events would rest undisturbed at such times as they were impressed and actively employed in the public service, and the fact of the boon being spontaneously offered, without any demand on the part of their tribunes, increased their happiness and gratitude immensely. The only people who did not share the general feeling of joy and goodwill were the tribunes of the plebs. They asserted that the arrangement would not turn out such a pleasant thing for the senate or such a benefit to the whole community as they supposed. The policy was more attractive at first sight than it would prove in actual practice. From what source, they asked, could the money be raised; except by imposing a tax on the people? They were generous at other people's expense. Besides, those who had served their time would not, even if the rest approved, permit others to serve on more favourable terms than they themselves had done and after having had to provide for their own expenses, now provide for those of others. These arguments influenced some of the plebeians. At last, after the tax had been imposed, the tribunes actually gave notice that they would protect any one who refused to contribute to the war tax. The senators were determined to uphold a measure so happily inaugurated, they were themselves the first to contribute, and as coined money was not yet introduced, they carried the copper by weight in wagons to the treasury, thereby drawing public attention to the fact of their contributing. After the senators had contributed most conscientiously the full amount at which they were assessed, the leading plebeians, personal friends of the nobles, began, as had been agreed, to pay in their share. When the crowd saw these men applauded by the senate and looked up to by the men of military age as patriotic citizens, they hastily rejected the proffered protection of the tribunes and vied with one another in their eagerness to contribute. The proposal authorizing the declaration of war against Veii was carried, and the new consular tribunes marched thither an army composed to a large extent of men who volunteered for service.

Book V: The Veii and the Destruction of Rome by the Gauls

5.15

DURING this period many portents were announced, but as they rested on the testimony of single individuals, and there were no soothsayers to consult as to how to expiate them, owing to the hostile attitude of the Etruscans, these reports were generally disbelieved and disregarded. One incident, however, caused universal anxiety. The Alban Lake rose to an unusual height, without any rainfall or other cause which could prevent the phenomenon from appearing supernatural. Envoys were sent to the oracle of Delphi to ascertain why the gods sent the portent. But an explanation was afforded nearer at hand. An aged Veientine was impelled by destiny to announce, amidst the jeers of the Roman and Etruscan outposts, in prophetic strain, that the Romans would never get possession of Veii until the water had been drawn off from the Alban Lake. This was at first treated as a wild utterance, but afterwards it began to be talked about. Owing to the length of the war, there were frequent conversations between the troops on both sides, and a Roman on outpost duty asked one of the townsmen who was nearest to him who the man was who was throwing out such dark hints about the Alban Lake. When he heard that he was a soothsayer, being himself a man not devoid of religious fears, he invited the prophet to an interview on the pretext of wishing to consult him, if he had time, about a portent which demanded his own personal expiation. When the two had gone some distance from their respective lines, unarmed, apprehending no danger, the Roman, a young man of immense strength, seized the feeble old man in the sight of all, and in spite of the outcry of the Etruscans, carried him off to his own side. He was brought before the commander-in-chief and then sent to the senate in Rome. In reply to inquiries as to what he wanted people to understand by his remark about the Alban Lake, he said that the gods must certainly have been wroth with the people of Veii on the day when they inspired him with the resolve to disclose the ruin which the Fates had prepared for his native city. What he had then predicted under divine inspiration he could not now recall or unsay, and perhaps he would incur as much guilt by keeping silence about things which it was the will of heaven should be revealed as by uttering what ought to be concealed. It stood recorded in the Books of Fate, and had been handed down by the occult science of the Etruscans, that whenever the water of the Alban Lake overflowed and the Romans drew it off in the appointed way, the victory over the Veientines would be granted them; until that happened the gods would not desert the walls of Veii. Then he explained the prescribed mode of drawing off the water. The senate, however, did not regard their informant as sufficiently trustworthy in a matter of such importance, and determined to wait for the return of their embassy with the oracular reply of the Pythian god.

5.16

PREVIOUS to their return, and before any way of dealing with the Alban portent was discovered, the new consular tribunes entered upon office. They were L. Julius Julus, L. Furius Medullinus—for the fourth time—L. Sergius Fidenas, A. Postumius Regillensis, P. Cornelius Maluginensis, and A. Manlius. This year a new enemy arose. The people of Tarquinii saw that the Romans were engaged in numerous campaigns—against the Volscians at Anxur, where the garrison was blockaded; against the Aequi at Labici, who were attacking the Roman colonists, and, in addition to these, at Veii, Falerii, and Capenae, whilst, owing to the contentions between the plebs and the senate, things were no quieter within the walls of the City. Regarding this as a favourable opportunity for mischief, they despatched some light-armed cohorts to harry the Roman territory, in the belief that the Romans would either let the outrage pass unpunished to avoid having another war on their shoulders, or would resent it with a small and weak force. The Romans felt more indignation than anxiety at the raid, and without making any great effort, took prompt steps to avenge it. A. Postumius and L. Julius raised a force, not by a regular levy—for they were obstructed by the tribunes of the plebs—but consisting mostly of volunteers whom they had induced by strong appeals to come forward. With this they advanced by cross marches through the territory of Caere and surprised the Tarquinians as they were returning heavily laden with booty. They slew great numbers, stripped the whole force of their baggage, and returned with the recovered possessions from their farms to Rome. Two days were allowed for the owners to identify their property; what was unclaimed on the third day, most of it belonging to the enemy, was sold "under the spear," and the proceeds distributed amongst the soldiers. The issues of the other wars, especially of that against Veii, were still undecided, and the Romans were already despairing of success through their own efforts, and were looking to the Fates and the gods, when the embassy returned from Delphi with the sentence of the oracle. It was in accord with the answer given by the Veientine soothsayer, and ran as follows:

"See to it, Roman, that the rising flood
At Alba flow not o'er its banks and shape
Its channel seawards. Harmless through thy fields
Shalt thou disperse it, scattered into rills.
Then fiercely press upon thy foeman's walls,
For now the Fates have given thee victory.
That city which long years thou hast besieged
Shall now be thine. And when the war hath end,
Do thou, the victor, bear an ample gift
Into my temple, and the ancestral rites
Now in disuse, see that thou celebrate
Anew with all their wonted pomp."

5.17

FROM that time the captive prophet began to be held in very high esteem, and the consular tribunes, Cornelius and Postumius, began to make use of him for the expiation of the Alban portent and the proper method of appeasing the gods. At length it was discovered why the gods were visiting men for neglected ceremonies and religious duties unperformed. It was in fact due to nothing else but the fact that there was a flaw in the election of the magistrates, and consequently they had not proclaimed the Festival of the Latin League and the sacrifice on the Alban Mount with the due formalities. There was only one possible mode of expiation, and that was that the consular tribunes should resign office, the auspices to be taken entirely afresh, and an interrex appointed. All these measures were earned out by a decree of the senate. There were three interreges in succession—L. Valerius, Q. Servilius Fidenas, and M. Furius Camillus. During all this time there were incessant disturbances owing to the tribunes of the plebs hindering the elections until an understanding was come to that the majority of the consular tribunes should be elected from the plebeians. Whilst this was going on the national council of Etruria met at the Fane of Voltumna. The Capenates and the Faliscans demanded that all the cantons of Etruria should unite in common action to raise the siege of Veii; they were told in reply that assistance had been previously refused to the Veientines because they had no right to seek help from those whose advice they had not sought in a matter of such importance. Now, however, it was their unfortunate circumstances and not their will that compelled them to refuse. The Gauls, a strange and unknown race, had recently overrun the greatest part of Etruria, and they were not on terms of either assured peace or open war with them. They would, however, do this much for those of their blood and name, considering the imminent danger of their kinsmen—if any of their younger men volunteered for the war they would not prevent their going. The report spread in Rome that a large number had reached Veii, and in the general alarm the internal dissensions, as usual, began to calm down.

5.18

THE prerogative centuries elected P. Licinius Calvus consular tribune, though he was not a candidate. His appointment was not at all distasteful to the senate, for when in office before he had shown himself a man of moderate views. He was, however, advanced in years. As the voting proceeded it became clear that all who had been formerly his colleagues in office were being reappointed one after another. They were L. Titinius, P. Maenius, Q. Manlius, Cnaeus Genucius, and L. Atilius. After the tribes had been duly summoned to hear the declaration of the poll, but before it was actually published, P. Licinius Calvus, by permission of the interrex, spoke as follows: "I see, Quirites, that from what you remember of our former tenure of office, you are seeking in these elections an omen of concord for the coming year, a thing most of all helpful in the present state of affairs. But, whilst you are re-electing my old comrades, who have become wiser and stronger by experience, you see in me not the man I was, but only a mere shadow and name of P. Licinius. My bodily powers are worn out, my sight and hearing are impaired, my memory is failing, my mental vigour is dulled. Here," he said, holding his son by the hand, "is a young man, the image and counterpart of him whom in days gone by you elected as the first consular tribune taken from the ranks of the plebs. This young man whom I have trained and moulded I now hand over and dedicate to the republic to take my place, and I beg you, Quirites, to confer this honour which you have bestowed unsought on me, on him who is seeking it, and whose candidature I would fain support and further by my prayers." His request was granted, and his son P. Licinius was formally announced as consular tribune with those above mentioned. Titinius and Genucius marched against the Faliscans and Capenates, but they proceeded with more courage than caution and fell into an ambuscade. Genucius atoned for his rashness by an honourable death, and fell fighting amongst the foremost. Titinius rallied his men from the disorder into which they had fallen and gained some rising ground where he reformed his line, but would not come down to continue the fight on level terms.

More disgrace was incurred than loss, but it almost resulted in a terrible disaster, so great was the alarm it created not only in Rome, where very exaggerated accounts were received, but also in the camp before Veii. Here a rumour had gained ground that after the destruction of the generals and their army, the victorious Capenates and Faliscans and the whole military strength of Etruria had proceeded to Veii and were at no great distance; in consequence of this the soldiers were with difficulty restrained from taking to flight. Still more disquieting rumours were current in Rome; at one moment they imagined that the camp before Veii had been stormed, at another that a part of the enemies' forces was in full march to the City. They hurried to the walls; the matrons, whom the general alarm had drawn from their homes, made prayers and supplications in the temples; solemn petitions were offered up to the gods that they would ward off destruction from the houses and temples of the City and from the walls of Rome, and divert the fears and alarms to Veii if the sacred rites had been duly restored and the portents expiated.

5.19

BY this time the Games and the Latin Festival had been celebrated afresh, and the water drawn off from the Alban Lake on the fields, and now the fated doom was closing over Veii. Accordingly the commander destined by the Fates for the destruction of that city and the salvation of his country—M. Furius Camillus—was nominated Dictator. He appointed as his Master of the Horse P. Cornelius Scipio. With the change in the command everything else suddenly changed; men's hopes were different, their spirits were different, even the fortunes of the City wore a different aspect. His first measure was to execute military justice upon those who had fled during the panic from the camp, and he made the soldiers realize that it was not the enemy who was most to be feared. He then appointed a day for the enrollment of troops, and in the interim went to Veii to encourage the soldiers, after which he returned to Rome to raise a fresh army. Not a man tried to escape enlistment. Even foreign troops—Latins and Hernicans—came to offer assistance for the war. The Dictator formally thanked them in the senate, and as all the preparations for war were now sufficiently advanced, he vowed, in pursuance of a senatorial decree, that on the capture of Veii he would celebrate the Great Games and restore and dedicate the temple of Matuta the Mother, which had been originally dedicated by Servius Tullius. He left the City with his army amid a general feeling of anxious expectation rather than of hopeful confidence on the part of the citizens, and his first engagement was with the Faliscans and Capenates in the territory of Nepete. As usual where everything was managed with consummate skill and prudence, success followed. He not only defeated the enemy in the field, but he stripped them of their camp and secured immense booty. The greater part was sold and the proceeds paid over to the quaestor, the smaller share was given to the soldiers. From there the army was led to Veii. The forts were constructed more closely together. Frequent skirmishes had occurred at random in the space between the city wall and the Roman lines, and an edict was issued that none should fight without orders, thereby keeping the soldiers to the construction of the siege works. By far the greatest and most difficult of these was a mine which was commenced, and designed to lead into the enemies' citadel. That the work might not be interrupted, or the troops exhausted by the same men being continuously employed in underground labour, he formed the army into six divisions. Each division was told off in rotation to work for six hours at a time; the work went on without any intermission until they had made a way into the citadel.

5.20

WHEN the Dictator saw that victory was now within his grasp, that a very wealthy city was on the point of capture, and that there would be more booty than had been amassed in all the previous wars taken together, he was anxious to avoid incurring the anger of the soldiers through too niggardly a distribution of it on the one hand, and the jealousy of the senate through too lavish a grant of it on the other. He sent a despatch to the senate in which he stated that through the gracious favour of heaven, his own generalship, and the persevering efforts of his soldiers, Veii would in a very few hours be in the power of Rome, and he asked for their decision as to the disposal of the booty. The senate were divided. It is reported that the aged P. Licinius, who was the first to be asked his opinion by his son, urged that the people should receive public notice that whoever wanted to share in the spoils should go to the camp at Veii. Appius Claudius took the opposite line. He stigmatised the proposed largesse as unprecedented, wasteful, unfair, reckless. If, he said, they once thought it sinful for money taken from the enemy to lie in the treasury, drained as it had been by the wars, he would advise that the pay of the soldiers be supplied from that source, so that the plebs might have so much less tax to pay. "The homes of all would feel alike the benefit of a common boon, the rewards won by brave warriors would not be filched by the hands of city loafers, ever greedy for plunder, for it so constantly happens that those who usually seek the foremost place in toil and danger are the least active in appropriating the spoils." Licinius on the other hand said that "this money would always be regarded with suspicion and aversion, and would supply material for indictments before the plebs, and consequently bring about disturbances and revolutionary measures. It was better, therefore, that the plebs should be conciliated by this gift, that those who had been crushed and exhausted by so many years of taxation should be relieved and get some enjoyment from the spoils of a war in which they had almost become old men. When any one brings home something he has taken from the enemy with his own hand, it affords him more pleasure and gratification than if he were to receive many times its value at the bidding of another. The Dictator had referred the question to the senate because he wanted to avoid the odium and misrepresentations which it might occasion; the senate, in its turn, ought to entrust it to the plebs and allow each to keep what the fortune of war has given him." This was felt to be the safer course, as it would make the senate popular. Notice accordingly was given that those who thought fit should go to the Dictator in camp to share in the plunder of Veii.

5.21

AN enormous crowd went and filled the camp. After the Dictator had taken the auspices and issued orders for the soldiers to arm for battle, he uttered this prayer: "Pythian Apollo, guided and inspired by thy will I go forth to destroy the city of Veii, and a tenth part of its spoils I devote to thee. Thee too, Queen Juno, who now dwellest in Veii, I beseech, that thou wouldst follow us, after our victory, to the City which is ours and which will soon be shine, where a temple worthy of thy majesty will receive thee." After this prayer, finding himself superior in numbers, he attacked the city on all sides, to distract the enemies' attention from the impending danger of the mine. The Veientines, all unconscious that their doom had already been sealed by their own prophets and by oracles in foreign lands, that some of the gods had already been invited to their share in the spoils, whilst others, called upon in prayer to leave their city, were looking to new abodes in the temples of their foes; all unconscious that they were spending their last day, without the slightest suspicion that their walls had been undermined and their citadel already filled with the enemy, hurried with their weapons to the walls, each as best he could, wondering what had happened to make the Romans, after never stirring from their lines for so many days, now run recklessly up to the walls as though struck with sudden frenzy.

At this point a tale is introduced to the effect that whilst the king of the Veientines was offering sacrifice, the soothsayer announced that victory would be granted to him who had cut out the sacrificial parts of the victim, His words were heard by the soldiers in the mine, they burst through, seized the parts and carried them to the Dictator. But in questions of such remote antiquity I should count it sufficient if what bears the stamp of probability be taken as true. Statements like this, which are more fitted to adorn a stage which delights in the marvelous than to inspire belief, it is not worth while either to affirm or deny. The mine, which was now full of picked soldiers, suddenly discharged its armed force in the temple of Juno, which was inside the citadel of Veii. Some attacked the enemy on the walls from behind, others forced back the bars of the gates, others again set fire to the houses from which stones and tiles were being hurled by women and slaves. Everything resounded with the confused noise of terrifying threats and shrieks of despairing anguish blended with the wailing of women and children. In a very short time the defenders were driven from the walls and the city gates flung open. Some rushed in in close order, others scaled the deserted walls; the city was filled with Romans; fighting went on everywhere. At length, after great carnage, the fighting slackened, and the Dictator ordered the heralds to proclaim that the unarmed were to be spared. That put a stop to the bloodshed, those who were unarmed began to surrender, and the soldiers dispersed with the Dictator's permission in quest of booty. This far surpassed all expectation both in its amount and its value, and when the Dictator saw it before him he is reported to have raised his hands to heaven and prayed that if any of the gods deemed the good fortune which had befallen him and the Romans to be too great, the jealousy which it caused might be allayed by such a calamity as would be least injurious to him and to Rome. The tradition runs that whilst he was turning round during this devotion he stumbled and fell. To those who judged after the event it appeared as if that omen pointed to Camillus' own condemnation and the subsequent capture of Rome which occurred a few years later. That day was spent in the massacre of the enemy and the sack of the city with its enormous wealth.

5.22

THE following day the Dictator sold all freemen who had been spared, as slaves. The money so realized was the only amount paid into the public treasury, but even that proceeding roused the ire of the plebs. As for the spoil they brought home with them, they did not acknowledge themselves under any obligation for it either to their general, who, they thought, had referred a matter within his own competence to the senate in the hope of getting their authority for his niggardliness, nor did they feel any gratitude to the senate. It was the Licinian family to whom they gave the credit, for it was the father who had advocated the popular measure and the son who had taken the opinion of the senate upon it. When all that belonged to man had been carried away from Veii, they began to remove from the temples the votive gifts that had been made to the gods, and then the gods themselves; but this they did as worshipers rather than as plunderers. The deportation of Queen Juno to Rome was entrusted to a body of men selected from the whole army, who after performing their ablutions and arraying themselves in white vestments, reverently entered the temple and in a spirit of holy dread placed their hands on the statue, for it was as a rule only the priest of one particular house who, by Etruscan usage, touched it. Then one of them, either under a sudden inspiration, or in a spirit of youthful mirth, said, "Art thou willing, Juno, to go to Rome?" The rest exclaimed that the goddess nodded assent. An addition to the story was made to the effect that she was heard to say, "I am willing." At all events we have it that she was moved from her place by appliances of little power, and proved light and easy of transport, as though she were following of her own accord. She was brought without mishap to the Aventine, her everlasting seat, whither the prayers of the Roman Dictator had called her, and where this same Camillus afterwards dedicated the temple which he had vowed. Such was the fall of Veii, the most wealthy city of the Etruscan league, showing its greatness even in its final overthrow, since after being besieged for ten summers and winters and inflicting more loss than it sustained, it succumbed at last to destiny, being after all carried by a mine and not by direct assault.

5.23

ALTHOUGH the portents had been averted by due expiation and the answers given by the soothsayer and the oracle were matters of common knowledge, and all that man could do had been done by the selection of M. Furius, the greatest of all commanders—notwithstanding all this, when the capture of Veii was announced in Rome, after so many years of undecided warfare and numerous defeats, the rejoicing was as great as if there had been no hope of success. Anticipating the order of the senate, all the temples were filled with Roman mothers offering thanksgivings to the gods. The senate ordered that the public thanksgivings should be continued for four days, a longer period than for any previous war. The arrival of the Dictator, too, whom all classes poured out to meet, was welcomed by a greater concourse than that of any general before. His triumph went far beyond the usual mode of celebrating the day; himself the most conspicuous object of all, he was drawn into the City by a team of white horses, which men thought unbecoming even for a mortal man, let alone a Roman citizen. They saw with superstitious alarm the Dictator putting himself on a level in his equipage with Jupiter and Sol, and this one circumstance made his triumph more brilliant than popular. After this he signed a contract for building the temple of Queen Juno on the Aventine and dedicated one to Matuta the Mother. After having thus discharged his duties to gods and men he resigned his Dictatorship. Subsequently a difficulty arose about the offering to Apollo. Camillus stated that he had vowed a tenth of the spoils to the deity, and the college of pontiffs decided that the people must fulfill their religious obligation. But it was not easy to find a way of ordering the people to restore their share of booty so that the due proportion might be set apart for sacred purposes. At length recourse was had to what seemed the smoothest plan, namely, that any one who wished to discharge the obligation for himself and his household should make a valuation of his share and contribute the value of a tenth of it to the public treasury, in order that out of the proceeds a golden crown might be made, worthy of the grandeur of the temple and the august divinity of the god, and such as the honour of the Roman people demanded. This contribution still further estranged the feelings of the plebeians from Camillus. During these occurrences envoys from the Volscians and Aequi came to sue for peace. They succeeded in obtaining it, not so much because they deserved it as that the commonwealth, wearied with such a long war, might enjoy repose.

5.34

ABOUT the passage of the Gauls into Italy we have received the following account. Whilst Tarquinius Priscus was king of Rome, the supreme power amongst the Celts, who formed a third part of the whole of Gaul, was in the hands of the Bituriges; they used to furnish the king for the whole Celtic race. Ambigatus was king at that time, a man eminent for his own personal courage and prosperity as much as for those of his dominions. During his sway the harvests were so abundant and the population increased so rapidly in Gaul that the government of such vast numbers seemed almost impossible. He was now an old man, and anxious to relieve his realm from the burden of over-population. With this view he signified his intention of sending his sister's sons Bellovesus and Segovesus, both enterprising young men, to settle in whatever locality the gods should by augury assign to them. They were to invite as many as wished to accompany them, sufficient to prevent any nation from repelling their approach. When the auspices were taken, the Hercynian forest was assigned to Segovesus; to Bellovesus the gods gave the far pleasanter way into Italy. He invited the surplus population of six tribes—the Bituriges, the Averni, the Senones, the Aedui, the Ambarri, the Carnutes, and the Aulerci. Starting with an enormous force of horse and foot, he came to the Tricastini. Beyond stretched the barrier of the Alps, and I am not at all surprised that they appeared insurmountable, for they had never yet been surmounted by any route, as far at least as unbroken memory reaches, unless you choose to believe the fables about Hercules. Whilst the mountain heights kept the Gauls fenced in as it were there, and they were looking everywhere to see by what path they could cross the peaks which reached to heaven and so enter a new world, they were also prevented from advancing by a sense of religious obligation, for news came that some strangers in quest of territory were being attacked by the Salyi. These were Massilians who had sailed from Phocaea. The Gauls, looking upon this as an omen of their own fortunes, went to their assistance and enabled them to fortify the spot where they had first landed, without any interference from the Salyi. After crossing the Alps by the passes of the Taurini and the valley of the Douro, they defeated the Tuscans in battle not far from the Ticinus, and when they learnt that the country in which they had settled belonged to the Insubres, a name also borne by a canton of the Haedui, they accepted the omen of the place and built a city which they called Mediolanum.

5.35

SUBSEQUENTLY another body, consisting of the Cenomani, under the leadership of Elitovius, followed the track of the former and crossed the Alps by the same pass, with the goodwill of Bellovesus. They had their settlements where the cities of Brixia and Verona now stand. The Libui came next and the Saluvii; they settled near the ancient tribe of the Ligurian Laevi, who lived about the Ticinus. Then the Boii and Lingones crossed the Pennine Alps, and as all the country between the Po and the Alps was occupied, they crossed the Po on rafts and expelled not only the Etruscans but the Umbrians as well. They remained, however, north of the Apennines. Then the Senones, the last to come, occupied the country from the Utis to the Aesis. It was this last tribe, I find, that came to Clusium, and from there to Rome; but it is uncertain whether they came alone or helped by contingents from all the Cisalpine peoples. The people of Clusium were appalled by this strange war, when they saw the numbers, the extraordinary appearance of the men, and the kind of weapons they used, and heard that the legions of Etruria had been often routed by them on both sides of the Po. Although they had no claim on Rome, either on the ground of alliance or friendly relations, unless it was that they had not defended their kinsmen at Veii against the Romans, they nevertheless sent ambassadors to ask the senate for assistance. Active assistance they did not obtain. The three sons of M. Fabius Ambustus were sent as ambassadors to negotiate with the Gauls and warn them not to attack those from whom they had suffered no injury, who were allies and friends of Rome, and who, if circumstances compelled them, must be defended by the armed force of Rome. They preferred that actual war should be avoided, and that they should make acquaintance with the Gauls, who were strangers to them, in peace rather than in arms.

5.36

A PEACEABLE enough mission, had it not contained envoys of a violent temper, more like Gauls than Romans. After they had delivered their instructions in the council of the Gauls, the following reply was given: "Although we are hearing the name of Romans for the first time, we believe nevertheless that you are brave men, since the Clusines are imploring your assistance in their time of danger. Since you prefer to protect your allies against us by negotiation rather than by armed force, we on our side do not reject the peace you offer, on condition that the Clusines cede to us Gauls, who are in need of land, a portion of that territory which they possess to a greater extent than they can cultivate. On any other conditions peace cannot be granted. We wish to receive their reply in your presence, and if territory is refused us we shall fight, whilst you are still here, that you may report to those at home how far the Gauls surpass all other men in courage." The Romans asked them what right they had to demand, under threat of war, territory from those who were its owners, and what business the Gauls had in Etruria. The haughty answer was returned that they carried their right in their weapons, and that everything belonged to the brave. Passions were kindled on both sides; they flew to arms and joined battle. Thereupon, contrary to the law of nations, the envoys seized their weapons, for the Fates were already urging Rome to its ruin. The fact of three of the noblest and bravest Romans fighting in the front line of the Etruscan army could not be concealed, so conspicuous was the valour of the strangers. And what was more, Q. Fabius rode forward at a Gaulish chieftain, who was impetuously charging right at the Etruscan standards, ran his spear through his side and slew him. Whilst he was in the act of despoiling the body the Gauls recognised him, and the word was passed through the whole army that it was a Roman ambassador. Forgetting their rage against the Clusines, and breathing threats against the Romans, they sounded the retreat.

Some were for an instant advance on Rome. The older men thought that ambassadors should first be sent to Rome to make a formal complaint and demand the surrender of the Fabii as satisfaction for the violation of the law of nations. After the ambassadors had stated their case, the senate, whilst disapproving of the conduct of the Fabii, and recognizing the justice of the demand which the barbarians made, were prevented by political interests from placing their convictions on record in the form of a decree in the case of men of such high rank. In order, therefore, that the blame for any defeat which might be incurred in a war with the Gauls might not rest on them alone, they referred the consideration of the Gauls' demands to the people. Here personal popularity and influence had so much more weight that the very men whose punishment was under discussion were elected consular tribunes for the next year. The Gauls regarded this procedure as it deserved to be regarded, namely, as an act of hostility, and after openly threatening war, returned to their people. The other consular tribunes elected with the Fabii were Q. Sulpicius Longus, Q. Servilius—for the fourth time—and P. Cornelius Maluginensis.

5.37

TO such an extent does Fortune blind men's eyes when she will not have her threatened blows parried, that though such a weight of disaster was hanging over the State, no special steps were taken to avert it. In the wars against Fidenae and Veii and other neighbouring States, a Dictator had on many occasions been nominated as a last resource. But now when an enemy, never seen or even heard of before, was rousing up war from ocean and the furthest corners of the world, no recourse was had to a Dictator, no extraordinary efforts were made. Those men through whose recklessness the war had been brought about were in supreme commands as tribunes, and the levy they raised was not larger than had been usual in ordinary campaigns, they even made light of the resorts as to the seriousness of the war. Meantime the Gauls learnt that their embassy had been treated with contempt, and that honours had actually been conferred upon men who had violated the law of nations. Burning with rage—as a nation they cannot control their passions—they seized their standards and hurriedly set out on their march. At the sound of their tumult as they swept by, the affrighted cities flew to arms and the country folk took to flight. Horses and men, spread far and wide, covered an immense tract of country; wherever they went they made it understood by loud shouts that they were going to Rome. But though they were preceded by rumours and by messages from Clusium, and then from one town after another, it was the swiftness of their approach that created most alarm in Rome. An army hastily raised by a levy en masse marched out to meet them. The two forces met hardly eleven miles from Rome, at a spot where the Alia, flowing in a very deep channel from the Crustuminian mountains, joins the river Tiber a little below the road to Crustumerium. The whole country in front and around was now swarming with the enemy, who, being as a nation given to wild outbreaks, had by their hideous howls and discordant clamour filled everything with dreadful noise.

5.38

THE consular tribunes had secured no position for their camp, had constructed no entrenchments behind which to retire, and had shown as much disregard of the gods as of the enemy, for they formed their order of battle without having obtained favourable auspices. They extended their line on either wing to prevent their being outflanked, but even so they could not make their front equal to the enemy's, whilst by thus thinning their line they weakened the centre so that it could hardly keep in touch. On their right was a small eminence which they decided to hold with reserves, and this disposition, though it was the beginning of the panic and flight, proved to be the only means of safety to the fugitives. For Bennus, the Gaulish chieftain, fearing some ruse in the scanty numbers of the enemy, and thinking that the rising ground was occupied in order that the reserves might attack the flank and rear of the Gauls while their front was engaged with the legions, directed his attack upon the reserves, feeling quite certain that if he drove them from their position, his overwhelming numbers would give him an easy victory on the level ground. So not only Fortune but tactics also were on the side of the barbarians. In the other army there was nothing to remind one of Romans either amongst the generals or the private soldiers. They were terrified, and all they thought about was flight, and so utterly had they lost their heads that a far greater number fled to Veii, a hostile city, though the Tiber lay in their way, than by the direct road to Rome, to their wives and children. For a short time the reserves were protected by their position. In the rest of the army, no sooner was the battle-shout heard on their flank by those nearest to the reserves, and then by those at the other end of the line heard in their rear, than they fled, whole and unhurt, almost before they had seen their untried foe, without any attempt to fight or even to give back the battle-shout. None were slain while actually fighting; they were cut down from behind whilst hindering one another's flight in a confused, struggling mass. Along the bank of the Tiber, whither the whole of the left wing had fled, after throwing away their arms, there was great slaughter. Many who were unable to swim or were hampered by the weight of their cuirasses and other armour were sucked down by the current. The greater number, however, reached Veii in safety, yet not only were no troops sent from there to defend the City, but not even was a messenger despatched to report the defeat to Rome. All the men on the right wing, which had been stationed some distance from the river, and nearer to the foot of the hill, made for Rome and took refuge in the Citadel without even closing the City gates.

5.39

THE Gauls for their part were almost dumb with astonishment at so sudden and extraordinary a victory. At first they did not dare to move from the spot, as though puzzled by what had happened, then they began to fear a surprise, at last they began to despoil the dead, and, as their custom is, to pile up the arms in heaps. Finally, as no hostile movement was anywhere visible, they commenced their march and reached Rome shortly before sunset. The cavalry, who had ridden on in front, reported that the gates were not shut, there were no pickets on guard in front of them, no troops on the walls. This second surprise, as extraordinary as the previous one, held them back, and fearing a nocturnal conflict in the streets of an unknown City, they halted and bivouacked between Rome and the Anio. Reconnoitering parties were sent out to examine the circuit of the walls and the other gates, and to ascertain what plans their enemies were forming in their desperate plight. As for the Romans, since the greater number had fled from the field in the direction of Veii instead of Rome, it was universally believed that the only survivors were those who had found refuge in Rome, and the mourning for all who were lost, whether living or dead, filled the whole City with the cries of lamentation. But the sounds of private grief were stifled by the general terror when it was announced that the enemy were at hand. Presently the yells and wild war-whoops of the squadrons were heard as they rode round the walls. All the time until the next day's dawn the citizens were in such a state of suspense that they expected from moment to moment an attack on the City. They expected it first when the enemy approached the walls, for they would have remained at the Alia had not this been their object; then just before sunset they thought the enemy would attack because there was not much daylight left; and then when night was fallen they imagined that the attack was delayed till then to create all the greater terror. Finally, the approach of the next day deprived them of their senses; the entrance of the enemy's standards within the gates was the dreadful climax to fears that had known no respite.

But all through that night and the following day the citizens afforded an utter contrast to those who had fled in such terror at the Alia. Realizing the hopelessness of attempting any defense of the City with the small numbers that were left, they decided that the men of military age and the able-bodied amongst the senators should, with their wives and children, withdraw into the Citadel and the Capitol, and after getting in stores of arms and provisions, should from that fortified position defend their gods, themselves, and the great name of Rome. The Flamen and priestesses of Vesta were to carry the sacred things of the State far away from the bloodshed and the fire, and their sacred cult should not be abandoned as long as a single person survived to observe it. If only the Citadel and the Capitol, the abode of gods; if only the senate, the guiding mind of the national policy; if only the men of military age survived the impending ruin of the City, then the loss of the crowd of old men left behind in the City could be easily borne; in any case, they were certain to perish. To reconcile the aged plebeians to their fate, the men who had been consuls and enjoyed triumphs gave out that they would meet their fate side by side with them, and not burden the scanty force of fighting men with bodies too weak to carry arms or defend their country.

5.40

THUS they sought to comfort one another—these aged men doomed to death. Then they turned with words of encouragement to the younger men on their way to the Citadel and Capitol, and solemnly commended to their strength and courage all that was left of the fortunes of a City which for 360 years had been victorious in all its wars. As those who were carrying with them all hope and succour finally separated from those who had resolved not to survive the fall of the City the misery of the scene was heightened by the distress of the women. Their tears, their distracted running about as they followed first their husbands then their sons, their imploring appeals to them not to leave them to their fate, made up a picture in which no element of human misery was wanting. A great many of them actually followed their sons into the Capitol, none forbidding or inviting them, for though to diminish the number of non-combatants would have helped the besieged, it was too inhuman a step to take. Another crowd, mainly of plebeians, for whom there was not room on so small a hill or food enough in the scanty store of corn, poured out of the City in one continuous line and made for the Janiculum. From there they dispersed, some over the country, others towards the neighbouring cities, without any leader or concerted action, each following his own aims, his own ideas. and all despairing of the public safety. While all this was going on, the Flamen of Quirinus and the Vestal virgins, without giving a thought to their own property, were deliberating as to which of the sacred things they ought to take with them, and which to leave behind, since they had not strength enough to carry all, and also what place would be the safest for their custody. They thought best to conceal what they could not take in earthen jars and bury them under the chapel next to the Flamen's house, where spitting is now forbidden. The rest they divided amongst them and carried off, taking the road which leads by the Pons Sublicius to the Janiculum. Whilst ascending that hill they were seen by L. Albinius, a Roman plebeian who with the rest of the crowd who were unfit for war was leaving the City. Even in that critical hour the distinction between sacred and profane was not forgotten. He had his wife and children with him in a wagon, and it seemed to him an act of impiety for him and his family to be seen in a vehicle whilst the national priests should be trudging along on foot, bearing the sacred vessels of Rome. He ordered his wife and children to get down, put the virgins and their sacred burden in the wagon, and drove them to Caere, their destination.

5.41

AFTER all the arrangements that circumstances permitted had been made for the defense of the Capitol, the old men returned to their respective homes and, fully prepared to die, awaited the coming of the enemy. Those who had filled curule offices resolved to meet their fate wearing the insignia of their former rank and honour and distinctions. They put on the splendid dress which they wore when conducting the chariots of the gods or riding in triumph through the City, and thus arrayed, they seated themselves in their ivory chairs in front of their houses. Some writers record that, led by M. Fabius, the

Pontifex Maximus, they recited the solemn formula in which they devoted themselves to death for their country and the Quirites. As the Gauls were refreshed by a night's rest after a battle which had at no point been seriously contested, and as they were not now taking the City by assault or storm, their entrance the next day was not marked by any signs of excitement or anger. Passing the Colline gate which was standing open, they came to the Forum and gazed round at the temples and at the Citadel, which alone wore any appearance of war. They left there a small body to guard against any attack from the Citadel or Capitol whilst they were scattered, and then they dispersed in quest of plunder through streets in which they did not meet a soul. Some poured in a body into all the houses near, others made for the most distant ones, expecting to find them untouched and full of spoils. Appalled by the very desolation of the place and dreading lest some stratagem should surprise the stragglers, they returned to the neighbourhood of the Forum in close order. The houses of the plebeians were barricaded, the halls of the patricians stood open, but they felt greater hesitation about entering the open houses than those which were closed. They gazed with feelings of real veneration upon the men who were seated in the porticoes of their mansions, not only because of the superhuman magnificence of their apparel and their whole bearing and demeanor, but also because of the majestic expression of their countenances, wearing the very aspect of gods. So they stood, gazing at them as if they were statues, till, as it is asserted, one of the patricians, M. Papirius, roused the passion of a Gaul, who began to stroke his beard—which in those days was universally worn long—by smiting him on the head with his ivory staff. He was the first to be killed, the others were butchered in their chairs. After this slaughter of the magnates, no living being was thenceforth spared; the houses were rifled, and then set on fire.

5.42

NOW—whether it was that the Gauls were not all animated by a passion for the destruction of the City, or whether their chiefs had decided on the one hand to present the spectacle of a few fires as a means of intimidating the besieged into surrender from a desire to save their homes, and on the other, by abstaining from a universal conflagration, hold what remained of the City as a pledge by which to weaken their enemies' determination—certain it is that the fires were far from being so indiscriminate or so extensive as might be expected on the first day of a captured city. As the Romans beheld from the Citadel the City filled with the enemy who were running about in all the streets, while some new disaster was constantly occurring, first in one quarter then in another, they could no longer control their eyes and ears, let alone their thoughts and feelings. In whatever direction their attention was drawn by the shouts of the enemy, the shrieks of the women and boys, the roar of the flames, and the crash of houses falling in, thither they turned their eyes and minds as though set by Fortune to be spectators of their country's fall, powerless to protect anything left of all they possessed beyond their lives. Above all others who have ever stood a siege were they to be pitied, cut off as they were from the land of their birth and seeing all that had been theirs in the possession of the enemy. The day which had been spent in such misery was succeeded by a night not one whit more restful, this again by a day of anguish, there was not a single hour free from the sight of some ever fresh calamity. And yet, though, weighed down and overwhelmed with so many misfortunes, they had watched everything laid low in flame and ruin, they did not for a moment relax their determination to defend by their courage the one spot still left to freedom, the hill which they held, however small and poor it might be. At length, as this state of things went on day by day, they became as it were hardened to misery, and turned their thoughts from the circumstances round them to their arms and the sword in their right hand, which they gazed upon as the only things left to give them hope.

5.43

FOR some days the Gauls had been making useless war merely upon the houses of the City. Now that they saw nothing surviving amidst the ashes and ruin of the captured City except an armed foe whom all these disasters had failed to appall, and who would entertain no thought of surrender unless force were employed, they determined as a last resort to make an assault on the Citadel. At daybreak the signal was given and the whole of their number formed up in the Forum. Raising their battle-shout and locking their shields together over their heads, they advanced. The Romans awaited the attack without excitement or fear, the detachments were strengthened to guard all the approaches, and in whatever direction they saw the enemy advancing, there they posted a picked body of men and allowed the enemy to climb up, for the steeper the ground they got on to, the easier they thought it would be to fling them down the slope. About midway up the hill the Gauls halted; then from the higher ground, which of itself almost hurled them against the enemy, the Romans charged, and routed the Gauls with such loss and overthrow that they never again attempted that mode of fighting either with detachments or in full strength. All hope, therefore, of forcing a passage by direct assault being laid aside, they made preparations for a blockade. Up to that time they had never thought of one; all the corn in the City had been destroyed in the conflagrations, whilst that in the fields around had been hastily carried off to Veii since the occupation of the City. So the Gauls decided to divide their forces; one division was to invest the Citadel, the other to forage amongst the neighbouring States so that they could supply corn to those who were keeping up the investment. It was Fortune herself who led the Gauls after they left the City to Ardea, that they might have some experience of Roman courage. Camillus was living there as an exile, grieving more over his country's fortunes than his own, eating his heart out in reproaches to gods and men, asking in indignant wonder where the men were with whom he had taken Veii and Falerii; men whose valour in all their wars was greater even than their success. Suddenly he heard that the Gaulish army was approaching, and that the Ardeates were engaged in anxious deliberation about it. He had generally avoided the council meetings, but now, seized with an inspiration nothing short of divine, he hastened to the assembled councilors and addressed them as follows:

5.44

"MEN of Ardea! friends of old, and now my fellow citizens—

for this your kindness has granted, this my fortunes have compelled—let none of you imagine that I have come here in forgetfulness of my position. The force of circumstances and the common danger constrain every man to contribute what help he can to meet the crisis. When shall I ever be able to show my gratitude for all the obligations you have conferred if I fail in my duty now? When shall I ever be of any use to you if not in war? It was by that that I held my position in my native City as having never known defeat; in times of peace my ungrateful countrymen banished me. Now the chance is offered to you, men of Ardea, of proving your gratitude for all the kindness that Rome has shown you—you have not forgotten how great it is, nor need I bring it up against those who so well remember it—the chance of winning for your city a vast reputation for war at the expense of our common foe. Those who are coming here in loose and disorderly fashion are a race to whom nature has given bodies and minds distinguished by bulk rather than by resolution and endurance. It is for this reason that they bring into every battle a terrifying appearance rather than real force. Take the disaster of Rome as a proof. They captured the City because it lay open to them; a small force repelled them from the Citadel and Capitol. Already the irksomeness of an investment has proved too much for them, they are giving it up and wandering through the fields in straggling parties. When they are gorged with food and the wine they drink so greedily, they throw themselves down like wild beasts, on the approach of night, in all directions by the streams, without entrenching themselves, or setting any outposts or pickets on guard. And now after their success they are more careless than ever. If it is your intention to defend your walls and not to allow all this country to become a second Gaul, seize your arms and muster in force by the first watch and follow me to what will be a massacre, not a battle. If I do not deliver them, whilst enchained by sleep, into your hands to be slaughtered like cattle, I am ready to accept the same fate in Ardea which I met with in Rome."

5.45

FRIENDS and foes were alike persuaded that nowhere else was there at that time so great a master of war. After the council broke up they refreshed themselves and waited eagerly for the signal to be given. When it was given in the silence of the night they were at the gates ready for Camillus. After marching no great distance from the city they came upon the camp of the Gauls, unprotected, as he had said, and carelessly open on every side. They raised a tremendous shout and rushed in; there was no battle, it was everywhere sheer massacre; the Gauls, defenseless and dissolved in sleep, were butchered as they lay. Those in the furthest part of the camp, however, startled from their lairs, and not knowing whence or what the attack was, fled in terror, and some actually rushed, unawares, amongst their assailants. A considerable number were carried into the neighbourhood of Antium, where they were surrounded by the townsmen. A similar slaughter of Etruscans took place in the district of Veii. So far were these people from feeling sympathy with a City which for almost four centuries had been their neighbour, and was now crushed by an enemy never seen or heard of before, that they chose that time for making forays into Roman territory, and after loading themselves with plunder, intended to attack Veii, the bulwark and only surviving hope of the Roman name. The Roman soldiers at Veii had seen them dispersed through the fields, and afterwards, with their forces collected, driving their booty in front of them. Their first feelings were those of despair, then indignation and rage took possession of them. "Are even the Etruscans," they exclaimed, "from whom we have diverted the arms of Gaul on to ourselves, to find amusement in our disasters?" With difficulty they restrained themselves from attacking them. Caedicius, a centurion whom they had placed in command, induced them to defer operations till nightfall. The only thing lacking was a commander like Camillus, in all other respects the ordering of the attack and the success achieved were the same as if he had been present. Not content with this, they made some prisoners who had survived the night's massacre act as guides, and, led by them, surprised another body of Tuscans at the salt works and inflicted a still greater loss upon them. Exultant at this double victory they returned to Veii.

5.46

DURING these days there was little going on in Rome; the investment was maintained for the most part with great slackness; both sides were keeping quiet, the Gauls being mainly intent on preventing any of the enemy from slipping through their lines. Suddenly a Roman warrior drew upon himself the admiration of foes and friends alike. The Fabian house had an annual sacrifice on the Quirinal, and C. Fabius Dorsuo, wearing his toga in the "Gabine cincture," and bearing in his hands the sacred vessels, came down from the Capitol, passed through the middle of the hostile pickets, unmoved by either challenge or threat, and reached the Quirinal. There he duly performed all the solemn rites and returned with the same composed expression and gait, feeling sure of the divine blessing, since not even the fear of death had made him neglect the worship of the gods; finally he re-entered the Capitol and rejoined his comrades. Either the Gauls were stupefied at his extraordinary boldness, or else they were restrained by religious feelings, for as a nation they are by no means inattentive to the claims of religion. At Veii there was a steady accession of strength as well as courage. Not only were the Romans who had been dispersed by the defeat and the capture of the City gathering there, but volunteers from Latium also flocked to the place that they might be in for a share of the booty. The time now seemed ripe for the recovery of their native City out of the hands of the enemy. But though the body was strong it lacked a head. The very place reminded men of Camillus, the majority of the soldiers had fought successfully under his auspices and leadership, and Caedicius declared that he would give neither gods nor men any pretext for terminating his command; he would rather himself, remembering his subordinate rank, ask for a commander-in-chief. It was decided by general consent that Camillus should be invited from Ardea, but the senate was to be consulted first; to such an extent was everything regulated by reverence for law; the proper distinctions of things were observed, even though the things themselves were almost lost.

Frightful risk would have to be incurred in passing through the enemies' outposts. Pontius Cominius, a fine soldier, offered himself for the task. Supporting himself on a cork float, he was carried down the Tiber to the City. Selecting the nearest way from the bank of the river, he scaled a precipitous rock which, owing to its steepness, the enemy had left unguarded, and found his way into the Capitol. On being brought before the supreme magistrates he delivered his instructions from the army. After receiving the decree of the senate, which was to the effect that after being recalled from exile by the *comitia curiata*, Camillus should be forthwith nominated Dictator by order of the people, and the soldiers should have the commander they wanted, the messenger returned by the same route and made the best of his way to Veii. A deputation was sent to Ardea to conduct Camillus to Veii. The law was passed in the *comitia curiata* annulling his banishment and nominating him Dictator, and it is, I think, more likely that he did not start from Ardea until he learnt that this law had been passed, because he could not change his domicile without the sanction of the people, nor could he take the auspices in the name of the army until he had been duly nominated Dictator.

5.47

WHILE these proceedings were taking place at Veii, the Citadel and Capitol of Rome were in imminent danger. The Gauls had either noticed the footprints left by the messenger from Veii, or had themselves discovered a comparatively easy ascent up the cliff to the temple of Carmentis. Choosing a night when there was a faint glimmer of light, they sent an unarmed man in advance to try the road; then handing one another their arms where the path was difficult, and supporting each other or dragging each other up as the ground required, they finally reached the summit. So silent had their movements been that not only were they unnoticed by the sentinels, but they did not even wake the dogs, an animal peculiarly sensitive to nocturnal sounds. But they did not escape the notice of the geese, which were sacred to Juno and had been left untouched in spite of the extremely scanty supply of food. This proved the safety of the garrison, for their clamour and the noise of their wings aroused M. Manlius, the distinguished soldier, who had been consul three years before. He snatched up his weapons and ran to call the rest to arms, and while the rest hung back he struck with the boss of his shield a Gaul who had got a foothold on the summit and knocked him down. He fell on those behind and upset them, and Manlius slew others who had laid aside their weapons and were clinging to the rocks with their hands. By this time others had joined him, and they began to dislodge the enemy with volleys of stones and javelins till the whole body fell helplessly down to the bottom. When the uproar had died away, the remainder of the night was given to sleep, as far as was possible under such disturbing circumstances, whilst their peril, though past, still made them anxious.

At daybreak the soldiers were summoned by sound of trumpet to a council in the presence of the tribunes, when the due rewards for good conduct and for bad would be awarded. First, Manlius was commended for his bravery, and rewarded not by the tribunes alone but by the soldiers as a body, for every man brought to him at his quarters, which were in the Citadel, half a pound of meal and a quarter of a pint of wine. This does not sound much, but the scarcity made it an overwhelming proof of the affection felt for him, since each stinted himself of food and contributed in honour of that one man what had to be taken from his necessaries of life. Next, the sentinels who had been on duty at the spot where the enemy had climbed up without their noticing it were called forward. Q. Sulpicius, the consular tribune, declared that he should punish them all by martial law. He was, however, deterred from this course by the shouts of the soldiers, who all agreed in throwing the blame upon one man. As there was no doubt of his guilt, he was amidst general approval flung from the top of the cliff. A stricter watch was now kept on both sides; by the Gauls because it had become known that messengers were passing between Rome and Veii; by the Romans, who had not forgotten the danger they were in that night.

5.48

BUT the greatest of all the evils arising from the siege and the war was the famine which began to afflict both armies, whilst the Gauls were also visited with pestilence. They had their camp on low-lying ground between the hills, which had been scorched by the fires and was full of malaria, and the least breath of wind raised not dust only but ashes. Accustomed as a nation to wet and cold, they could not stand this at all, and tortured as they were by heat and suffocation, disease became rife among them, and they died off like sheep. They soon grew weary of burying their dead singly, so they piled the bodies into heaps and burned them indiscriminately, and made the locality notorious; it was afterwards known as the Busta Gallica. Subsequently a truce was made with the Romans, and with the sanction of the commanders, the soldiers held conversations with each other. The Gauls were continually bringing up the famine and calling upon them to yield to necessity and surrender. To remove this impression it is said that bread was thrown in many places from the Capitol into the enemies' pickets. But soon the famine could neither be concealed nor endured any longer. So, at the very time that the Dictator was raising his own levy at Ardea, and ordering his Master of the Horse, L. Valerius, to withdraw his army from Veii, and making preparations for a sufficient force with which to attack the enemy on equal terms, the army of the Capitol, worn out with incessant duty, but still superior to all human ills, had nature not made famine alone insuperable by them, were day by day eagerly watching for signs of any help from the Dictator. At last not only food but hope failed them. Whenever the sentinels went on duty, their feeble frames almost crushed by the weight of their armour, the army insisted that they should either surrender or purchase their ransom on the best terms they could, for the Gauls were throwing out unmistakable hints that they could be induced to abandon the siege for a moderate consideration. A meeting of the senate was now held, and the consular tribunes were empowered to make terms. A conference took place between Q. Sulpicius, the consular tribune, and Brennus, the Gaulish chieftain, and an agreement was arrived at by which 1000 lbs. of gold was fixed as the ransom of a people destined ere long to rule the world. This humiliation was great enough as it was, but it was aggravated by the despicable meanness of the Gauls, who produced unjust weights, and when the tribune protested, the insolent Gaul threw his sword into the scale, with an exclamation intolerable to Roman ears, "Woe to the vanquished!"

5.49

BUT gods and men alike prevented the Romans from living as a ransomed people. By a dispensation of Fortune it came about that before the infamous ransom was completed and all the gold weighed out, whilst the dispute was still going on, the Dictator appeared on the scene and ordered the gold to be carried away and the Gauls to move off. As they declined to do so, and protested that a definite compact had been made, he informed them that when he was once appointed Dictator no compact was valid which was made by an inferior magistrate without his sanction. He then warned the Gauls to prepare for battle, and ordered his men to pile their baggage into a heap, get their weapons ready, and win their country back by steel, not by gold. They must keep before their eyes the temples of the gods, their wives and children, and their country's soil, disfigured by the ravages of war—everything, in a word, which it was their duty to defend, to recover or to avenge. He then drew up his men in the best formation that the nature of the ground, naturally uneven and now half burnt, admitted, and made every provision that his military skill suggested for securing the advantage of position and movement for his men. The Gauls, alarmed at the turn things had taken, seized their weapons and rushed upon the Romans with more rage than method. Fortune had now turned, divine aid and human skill were on the side of Rome. At the very first encounter the Gauls were routed as easily as they had conquered at the Alia. In a second and more sustained battle at the eighth milestone on the road to Gabii, where they had rallied from their flight, they were again defeated under the generalship and auspices of Camillus. Here the carnage was complete; the camp was taken, and not a single man was left to carry tidings of the disaster. After thus recovering his country from the enemy, the Dictator returned in triumph to the City, and amongst the homely jests which soldiers are wont to bandy, he was called in no idle words of praise, "A Romulus," "The Father of his country," "The Second Founder of the City." He had saved his country in war, and now that peace was restored, he proved, beyond all doubt, to be its saviour again, when he prevented the migration to Veii. The tribunes of the plebs were urging this course more strongly than ever now that the City was burnt, and the plebs were themselves more in favour of it. This movement and the pressing appeal which the senate made to him not to abandon the republic while the position of affairs was so doubtful, determined him not to lay down his dictatorship after his triumph.

5.50

AS he was most scrupulous in discharging religious obligations, the very first measures he introduced into the senate were those relating to the immortal gods. He got the senate to pass a resolution containing the following provisions: All the temples, so far as they had been in possession of the enemy, were to be restored and purified, and their boundaries marked out afresh; the ceremonies of purification were to be ascertained from the sacred books by the decemvirs. Friendly relations as between State and State were to be established with the people of Caere, because they had sheltered the sacred treasures of Rome and her priests, and by this kindly act had prevented any interruption to the divine worship. Capitoline Games were to be instituted, because Jupiter Optimus Maximus had protected his dwelling-place and the Citadel of Rome in the time of danger, and the Dictator was to form a college of priests for that object from amongst those who were living on the Capitol and in the Citadel. Mention was also made of offering propitiation for the neglect of the nocturnal Voice which was heard announcing disaster before the war began, and orders were given for a temple to be built in the Nova Via to AIUS LOCUTIUS. The gold which had been rescued from the Gauls and that which during the confusion had been brought from the other temples, had been collected in the temple of Jupiter. As no one remembered what proportion ought to be returned to the other temples, the whole was declared sacred, and ordered to be deposited under the throne of Jupiter. The religious feeling of the citizens had already been shown in the fact that when there was not sufficient gold in the treasury to make up the sum agreed upon with the Gauls, they accepted the contribution of the matrons, to avoid touching that which was sacred. The matrons received public thanks, and the distinction was conferred upon them of having funeral orations pronounced over them as in the case of men. It was not till after those matters were disposed of which concerned the gods, and which therefore were within the province of the senate, that Camillus' attention was drawn to the tribunes, who were making incessant harangues to persuade the plebs to leave the ruins and migrate to Veii, which was ready for them. At last he went up to the Assembly, followed by the whole of the senate, and delivered the following speech:-

5.51

"SO painful to me, Quirites, are controversies with the tribunes of the plebs, that all the time I lived at Ardea my one consolation in my bitter exile was that I was far removed from these conflicts. As far as they are concerned I would never have returned even if you recalled me by a thousand senatorial decrees and popular votes. And now that I am returned, it was not change of mind on my part but change of fortune on yours that compelled me. The question at stake was whether my country was to remain unshaken in her seat, not whether I was to be in my country at any cost. Even now I would gladly remain quiet and hold my peace, if I were not fighting another battle for my country. To be wanting to her, as long as life shall last, would be for other men a disgrace, for Camillus a downright sin. Why did we win her back, why did we, when she was beset by foes, deliver her from their hands, if, now that she is recovered, we desert her? Whilst the Gauls were victorious and the whole of the City in their power, the gods and men of Rome still held, still dwelt in, the Capitol and the Citadel. And now that the Romans are victorious and the City recovered, are the Citadel and Capitol to be abandoned? Shall our good fortune inflict greater desolation on this City than our evil fortune wrought? Even had there been no religious institutions established when the City was founded and passed down from hand to hand, still, so clearly has Providence been working in the affairs of Rome at this time, that I for one would suppose that all neglect of divine worship has been banished from human life. Look at the alternations of prosperity and adversity during these late years; you will find that all went well with us when we followed the divine guidance, and all was disastrous when we neglected it. Take first of all the war with Veii. For what a number of years and with what immense exertions it was carried on! It did not come to an end before the water was drawn off from the Alban Lake at the bidding of the gods. What, again, of this unparalleled disaster to our City? Did it burst upon us before the Voice sent from heaven announcing the approach of the Gauls was treated with contempt, before the law of nations had been outraged by our ambassadors, before we had, in the same irreligious spirit, condoned that outrage when we ought to have punished it? And so it was that, defeated, captured, ransomed, we received such punishment at the hands of gods and men that we were a lesson to the whole world. Then, in our adversity, we bethought us of our religious duties. We fled to the gods in the Capitol, to the seat of Jupiter Optimus Maximus; amidst the ruin of all that we possessed we concealed some of the sacred treasures in the earth, the rest we carried out of the enemies' sight to neighbouring cities; abandoned as we were by gods and men, we still did not intermit the divine worship. It is because we acted thus that they have restored to us our native City, and victory and the renown in war which we had lost; but against the enemy, who, blinded by avarice, broke treaty and troth in the weighing of the gold, they have launched terror and rout and death.

5.52

"WHEN you see such momentous consequences for human affairs flowing from the worship or the neglect of the gods, do you not realize, Quirites, how great a sin we are meditating whilst hardly yet emerging from the shipwreck caused by our former guilt and fall? We possess a City which was founded with the divine approval as revealed in auguries and auspices; in it there is not a spot which is not full of religious associations and the presence of a god; the regular sacrifices have their appointed places no less than they have their appointed days. Are you, Quirites, going to desert all these gods—those whom the State honours, those whom you worship, each at your own altars? How far does your action come up to that of the glorious youth C. Fabius, during the siege, which was watched by the enemy with no less admiration than by you, when he went down from the Citadel through the missiles of the Gauls and celebrated the appointed sacrifice of his house on the Quirinal? Whilst the sacred rites of the patrician houses are not interrupted even in time of war, are you content to see the State offices of religion and the gods of Rome abandoned in a time of peace? Are the Pontiffs and Flamens to be more neglectful of their public functions than a private individual is of the religious obligations of his house?

"Some one may possibly reply that we can either discharge these duties at Veii or send priests to discharge them here. But neither of these things can be done if the rites are to be duly performed. Not to mention all the ceremonies or all the deities individually, where else, I would ask, but in the Capitol can the couch of Jupiter be prepared on the day of his festal banquet? What need is there for me to speak about the perpetual fire of Vesta, and the Image—the pledge of our dominion—which is in the safe keeping of her temple? And you, Mars Gradivus, and you, Father Quirinus, what need to speak of your sacred shields? Is it your wish that all these holy things, coeval with the City, some of even greater antiquity, should be abandoned and left on unhallowed soil? See, too, how great the difference between us and our ancestors. They left to us certain rites and ceremonies which we can only duly perform on the Alban Mount or at Lavinium. If it was a matter of religion that these rites should not be transferred from cities which belonged to an enemy to us at Rome, shall we transfer them from here to the enemies' city, Veii, without offending heaven? Call to mind, I pray you, how often ceremonies are repeated, because through negligence or accident some detail of the ancestral ritual has been omitted. What remedy was there for the republic, when crippled by the war with Veii after the portent of the Alban Lake, except the revival of sacred rites and the taking of fresh auspices? And more than that, as though after all we reverenced the ancient faiths, we have transferred foreign deities to Rome, and have established new ones. Queen Juno was lately carried from Veii and dedicated on the Aventine, and how splendidly that day was celebrated through the grand enthusiasm of our matrons! We ordered a temple to be built to Aius Locutius because of the divine Voice which was heard in the Via Nova. We have added to our annual festivals the Capitoline Games, and on the authority of the senate we have founded a college of priests to superintend them. What necessity was there for all these undertakings if we intended to leave the City of Rome at the same time as the Gauls, if it was not of our own free will that we remained in the Capitol through all those months, but the fear of the enemy which shut us up there?

"We are speaking about the temples and the sacred rites and ceremonies. But what, pray, about the priests? Do you not realize what a heinous sin will be committed? For the Vestals surely there is only that one abode, from which nothing has ever removed them but the capture of the City. The Flamen of Jupiter is forbidden by divine law to stay a single night outside the City. Are you going to make these functionaries priests of Veii instead of priests of Rome? Will thy Vestals desert thee, Vesta ? Is the Flamen to bring fresh guilt upon himself and the State for every night he sojourns abroad? Think of the other proceedings which, after the auspices have been duly taken, we conduct almost entirely within the City boundaries—to what oblivion, to what neglect are we consigning them! The Assembly of the Curies, which confers the supreme command, the Assembly of the Centuries, in which you elect the consuls and consular tribunes—where can they be held and the auspices taken except where they are wont to be held? Shall we transfer these to Veii, or are the people, when an Assembly is to be held, to meet at vast inconvenience in this City after it has been deserted by gods and men?

5.53

"BUT, you may say, it is obvious that the whole City is polluted, and no expiatory sacrifices can purify it; circumstances themselves compel us to quit a City devastated by fire, and all in ruins, and migrate to Veii where everything is untouched. We must not distress the poverty-stricken plebs by building here. I fancy, however, Quirites, that it is evident to you, without my telling you, that this suggestion is a plausible excuse rather than a true reason. You remember how this same question of migrating to Veii was mooted before the Gauls came, whilst public and private buildings were still safe and the City stood secure. And mark you, tribunes, how widely my view differs from yours. Even supposing it ought not to have been done then, you think that at any rate it ought to be done now, whereas—do not express surprise at what I say before you have grasped its purport—I am of opinion that even had it been right to migrate then when the City was wholly unhurt, we ought not to abandon these ruins now. For at that time the reason for our migrating to a captured city would have been a victory glorious for us and for our posterity, but now this migration would be glorious for the Gauls, but for us shame and bitterness. For we shall be thought not to have left our native City as victors, but to have lost it because we were vanquished; it will look as though it was the flight at the Alia, the capture of the City, the beleaguering of the Capitol, which had laid upon us the necessity of deserting our household gods and dooming ourselves to banishment from a place which we were powerless to defend. Was it possible for Gauls to overthrow Rome and shall it be deemed impossible for Romans to restore it?

"What more remains except for them to come again with fresh forces—we all know that their numbers surpass belief—and elect to live in this City which they captured, and you abandoned, and for you to allow them to do so? Why, if it were not Gauls who were doing this, but your old enemies, the Aequi and Volscians, who migrated to Rome, would you wish them to be Romans and you Veientines? Or would you rather that this were a desert of your own than the city of your foes? I do not see what could be more infamous. Are you prepared to allow this crime and endure this disgrace because of the trouble of building? If no better or more spacious dwelling could be put up in the whole City of Rome than that hut of our Founder, would it not be better to live in huts after the manner of herdsmen and peasants, surrounded by our temples and our gods, than to go forth as a nation of exiles? Our ancestors, shepherds and refugees, built a new City in a few years, when there was nothing in these parts but forests and swamps; are we shirking the labour of rebuilding what has been burnt, though the Citadel and Capitol are intact, and the temples of the gods still stand? What we would each have done in our own case, had our houses caught fire, are we as a community refusing to do now that the City has been burnt?

5.54

"WELL now, suppose that either through crime or accident a fire broke out in Veii, and the flames, as is quite possible, fanned by the wind, consumed a great part of the city, are we going to look out for Fidenae or Gabii, or any other city you please, as a place to which to migrate? Has our native soil, this land we call our motherland, so slight a hold upon us? Does our love for our country cling only to its buildings? Unpleasant as it is to recall my sufferings, still more your injustice, I will nevertheless confess to you that whenever I thought of my native City all these things came into my mind—the hills, the plains, the Tiber, this landscape so familiar to me, this sky beneath which I was born and bred—and I pray that they may now move you by the affection they inspire to remain in your City, rather than that, after you have abandoned it, they should make you pine with homesickness. Not without good reason did gods and men choose this spot as the site of a City, with its bracing hills, its commodious river, by means of which the produce of inland countries may be brought down and over-sea supplies obtained; a sea near enough for all useful purposes, but not so near as to be exposed to danger from foreign fleets; a district in the very centre of Italy—in a word, a position singularly adapted by nature for the expansion of a city. The mere size of so young a City is a proof of this. This is the 365th year of the City, Quirites, yet in all the wars you have for so long been carrying on amongst all those ancient nations—not to mention the separate cities—the Volscians in conjunction with the Aequi and all their strongly fortified towns, the whole of Etruria, so powerful by land and sea, and stretching across Italy from sea to sea—none have proved a match for you in war. This has hitherto been your Fortune; what sense can there be—perish the thought!—in making trial of another Fortune? Even granting that your valour can pass over to another spot, certainly the good Fortune of this place cannot be transferred. Here is the Capitol where in the old days a human head was found, and this was declared to be an omen, for in that place would be fixed the head and supreme sovereign power of the world. Here it was that whilst the Capitol was being cleared with augural rites, Juventas and Terminus, to the great delight of your fathers, would not allow themselves to be moved. Here is the Fire of Vesta; here are the Shields sent down from heaven; here are all the gods, who, if you remain, will be gracious to you."

5.55

IT is stated that this speech of Camillus made a profound impression, particularly that part of it which appealed to the religious feelings. But whilst the issue was still uncertain, a sentence, opportunely uttered, decided the matter. The senate, shortly afterwards, were discussing the question in the Curia Hostilia, and some cohorts returning from guard happened to be marching through the Forum. They had just entered the Comitium, when the centurion shouted, "Halt, standardbearer! Plant the standard; it will be best for us to stop here." On hearing these words, the senators rushed out of the Senate-house, exclaiming that they welcomed the omen, and the people crowding round them gave an emphatic approval. The proposed measure for migration was dropped, and they began to rebuild the City in a haphazard way. Tiling was provided at the public expense; every one was given the right to cut stone and timber where he pleased, after giving security that the building should be completed within the year. In their haste, they took no trouble to plan out straight streets; as all distinctions of ownership in the soil were lost, they built on any ground that happened to be vacant. That is the reason why the old sewers, which originally were carried under public ground, now run everywhere under private houses, and why the conformation of the City resembles one casually built upon by settlers rather than one regularly planned out.

SALLUST

THE WAR WITH JUGURTHA

SALLUST

1

WITHOUT reason do mankind complain of their nature, on the ground that it is weak and of short duration and ruled rather by chance than by virtue. For reflection would show on the contrary that nothing is greater or more excellent, and that nature has more often found diligence lacking in men than strength or endurance in itself. But the leader and ruler of man's life is the mind, and when this advances to glory by the path of virtue, it has power and potency in abundance, as well as fame; and it needs not fortune, since fortune can neither give to any man honesty, diligence, and other good qualities, nor can she take them away. But if through the lure of base desires the mind has sunk into sloth and the pleasures of the body, when it has enjoyed ruinous indulgence for a season, when strength, time, and talents have been wasted through indolence, the weakness of human nature is accused, and the guilty shift their own blame to circumstances.

But if men had as great regard for honourable enterprises as they have ardour in pursuing what is foreign to their interests, and bound to be unprofitable and often even dangerous, they would control fate rather than be controlled by it, and would attain to that height of greatness where from mortals their glory would make them immortal.

2

FOR just as mankind is made up of body and soul, so all our acts and pursuits partake of the nature either of the body or of the mind. Therefore notable beauty and great riches, as well as bodily strength and all other gifts of that kind, soon pass away, but the splendid achievements of the intellect, like the soul, are everlasting. In short, the goods of the body and of fortune have an end as well as a beginning, and they all rise and fall, wax and wane; but the mind, incorruptible, eternal, ruler of mankind, animates and controls all things, yet is itself not controlled. Therefore we can marvel the more at the perversity of those who pass their life in riotous living and idleness, given over to the pleasures of the body, but allow the mind, which is better and greater than anything else in man's nature, to grow dull from neglect and inaction; especially when there are so many and so varied intellectual pursuits by which the highest distinction may be won.

3

BUT among these pursuits, in my opinion, magistracies and military commands, in short all public offices, are least desirable in these times, since honour is not bestowed upon merit, while those who have gained it wrongfully are neither safe nor the more honourable because of it. For to rule one's country or subjects by force, although you both have the power to correct abuses, and do correct them, is nevertheless tyrannical; especially since all attempts at change foreshadow bloodshed, exile, and other horrors of war. Moreover, to struggle in vain and after wearisome exertion to gain nothing but hatred, is the height of folly, unless haply one is possessed by a dishonourable and pernicious passion for sacrificing one's personal honour and liberty to the power of a few men.

4

BUT among intellectual pursuits, the recording of the events of the past is especially serviceable; but of that it becomes me to say nothing, both because many men have already spoken of its value, and in order that no one may suppose that I am led by vanity to eulogize my own favourite occupation. I suppose, too, that since I have resolved to pass my life aloof from public affairs, some will apply to this arduous and useful employment of mine the name of idleness, certainly those who regard courting the people and currying favour by banquets as the height of industriousness. But if such men will only bear in mind in what times I was elected to office, what men of merit were unable to attain the same honour and what sort of men have since come into the senate, they will surely be convinced that it is rather from justifiable motives than from indolence that I have changed my opinion, and that greater profit will accrue to our country from my inactivity than from others' activity.

I have often heard that Quintus Maximus, Publius Scipio, and other eminent men of our country, were in the habit of declaring that their hearts were set mightily aflame for the pursuit of virtue whenever they gazed upon the masks of their ancestors. Of course they did not mean to imply that the wax or the effigy had any such power over them, but rather that it is the memory of great deeds that kindles in the breasts of noble men this flame that cannot be quelled until they by their own prowess have equaled the fame and glory of their forefathers.

But in these degenerate days, on the contrary, who is there that does not vie with his ancestors in riches and extravagance rather than in uprightness and diligence? Even the "new men," who in former times already relied upon worth to outdo the nobles, now make their way to power and distinction by intrigue and open fraud rather than by noble practices; just as if a praetorship, a consulship, or anything else of the kind were distinguished and illustrious in and of itself and were not valued according to the merit of those who live up to it. But in giving expression to my sorrow and indignation at the morals of our country I have spoken too freely and wandered too far from my subject. To this I now return.

5

I PROPOSE to write of the war which the people of Rome waged with Jugurtha, king of the Numidians: first, because it was long, sanguinary and of varying fortune; and secondly, because then for the first time resistance was offered to the insolence of the nobles—the beginning of a struggle which threw everything, human and divine, into confusion, and rose to such a pitch of frenzy that civil discord ended in war and the devastation of Italy. But before actually beginning such a narrative, let me recall a few earlier events, in order that everything may be placed in a better light for our understanding and may be the more clearly revealed.

During the second Punic war, when Hannibal, leader of the Carthaginians, had dealt Italy's power the heaviest blow since the Roman nation attained its full stature, Masinissa, king of Numidia, had become the friend of Publius Scipio, afterwards surnamed Africanus because of his prowess, and performed many illustrious deeds of arms. In return for this, after the defeat of the Carthaginians and the capture of Syphax, whose dominion in Africa was great and extensive, the Roman people gave Masinissa as a free gift all the cities and territories that he had taken in war. Consequently Masinissa was ever our true and loyal friend. But his reign and his life ended together. His son Micipsa then became sole ruler, since his brothers Mastanabal and Gulussa had fallen ill and died. Micipsa begot Adherbal and Hiempsal, and brought up in the palace, in the same manner as his own children, a son of his brother Mastanabal called Jugurtha, whom Masinissa in his will had allowed to remain a commoner because he was the offspring of a concubine.

6

AS soon as Jugurtha grew up, endowed as he was with physical strength, a handsome person, but above all with a vigorous intellect, he did not allow himself to be spoiled by luxury or idleness, but following the custom of that nation, he rode, he hurled the javelin, he contended with his fellows in foot-races; and although he surpassed them all in renown, he nevertheless won the love of all. Besides this, he devoted much time to the chase, he was the first or among the first to strike down the lion and other wild beasts, he distinguished himself greatly, but spoke little of his own exploits.

At first Micipsa was delighted with this conduct, believing that the prowess of Jugurtha would contribute to the glory of his kingdom; but when he realized that the man was young and constantly growing in power, while he himself was advanced in years and his children were small, he was seriously troubled by the situation and gave it constant thought. He dreaded the natural disposition of mankind, which is greedy for power and eager to gratify its heart's desire, while his own years and the youthfulness of his sons offered that opportunity which through the hope of gain leads astray even men of moderate ambition. He observed too the devotion which Jugurtha had inspired in the Numidians, and was apprehensive of some rebellion or war from that source, if by treachery he should cause the death of such a man.

7

EMBARRASSED by these problems, and seeing that one so dear to the people could not be put out of way by violence or by stratagem, he resolved, inasmuch as Jugurtha was full of energy and eager for military glory, to expose him to dangers and thus put fortune to the proof. Accordingly, when Micipsa sent cavalry and infantry to aid the Romans in the war with Numantia, he gave Jugurtha command of the Numidians whom he sent to Spain, hoping that he would easily fall a victim either to a desire to display his valour or to the ruthless foe.

But the result was not at all what he had expected; for Jugurtha, who had an active and keen intellect, soon became acquainted with the character of Publius Scipio, who then commanded the Romans, and with the tactics of the enemy. Then by hard labour and attention to duty, at the same time by showing strict obedience and often courting dangers, he shortly acquired such a reputation that he became very popular with our soldiers and a great terror to the Numantians. In fact, he was both valiant in war and wise in counsel, a thing most difficult to achieve, for most often wisdom through caution leads to timorousness and valour through boldness to rashness. Therefore Scipio relied upon Jugurtha for almost all difficult undertakings, treated him as a friend, and grew more and more attached to him every day, since the young Numidian failed neither in judgment nor in any enterprise. He had, besides, a generous nature and a ready wit, qualities by which he had bound many Romans to him in intimate friendship.

8

AT that time there were a great many in our army, both new men and nobles, who cared more for riches than for virtue and self-respect; they were intriguers at home, influential with our allies, rather notorious than respected. These men fired Jugurtha's ambitious spirit by holding out hopes that if king Micipsa should die, he might gain the sole power in Numidia, since he himself stood first in merit, while at Rome anything could be bought.

Now when Numantia had been destroyed and Publius Scipio determined to disband his auxiliary troops and return to Rome himself, after giving Jugurtha gifts and commending him in the highest terms before the assembled soldiers, he took him into his tent. There he privately advised the young man to cultivate the friendship of the Roman people at large rather than that of individual Roman citizens, and not to form the habit of bribery. It was dangerous, he said, to buy from a few what belonged to the many. If Jugurtha would continue as he had begun, fame and a throne would come to him unsought; but if he acted too hastily, he would bring about his ruin by means of his own money.

9

AFTER speaking in this way, Scipio dismissed the young man with a letter to be delivered to Micipsa, the purport of which was this: "The valour of your Jugurtha in the Numantine war was most conspicuous, as I am sure you will be glad to learn. To us he is dear because of his services, and we shall use our best efforts to make him beloved also by the senate and people of Rome. As your friend I congratulate you; in him you have a hero worthy of yourself and of his grandfather Masinissa."

Then the king, upon learning from the general's letter that the reports which had come to his ears were true, was led both by Jugurtha's merits and by his influential position to change his plans and attempt to win the young man by kindness. He adopted him at once and in his will named joint heir with his sons. But a few years later and upon his own motion the king, then enfeebled by years and illness and realizing that the end of his life was near, is said to have talked with Jugurtha in the presence of his friends and kinsfolk, including his sons Adherbal and Hiempsal, in some such terms as the following:-

10

"WHEN you were a small boy, Jugurtha, an orphan without prospects or means, I took you into the royal household, believing that because of my kindness you would love me as if you were my own child. And I was not mistaken; for, to say training of your other great and noble actions, of late on your return from Numantia you have conferred honour upon me and my realm by your glory, and by your prowess have made the Romans still more friendly to Numidia than before; while in Spain the name of our family has been given new life. Finally, by the glory you have won you have overcome envy, a most difficult feat for mortal man. Now, since nature is bringing my life to its close, I conjure and implore you by this right hand, by the loyalty due to the kingdom, hold dear these youths who are your kinsmen by birth and through my favour are your brothers; and do not desire to make new friends among strangers in preference to keeping the love of those who are bound to you by ties of blood. Neither armies nor treasure form the bulwarks of a throne, but friends; these you can neither acquire by force of arms nor buy with gold; it is by devotion and loyalty that they are won. But who is more bound by ties of friendship than brother to brother, or what stranger will you find loyal, if you become the enemy of your kindred? I deliver to you three a realm that is strong if you prove virtuous, but weak if you do ill; for harmony makes small states great, while discord undermines the mightiest empires. As for the rest, it devolves upon you, Jugurtha, rather than upon these children, since you are older and wiser than they, to see to it that my hopes are not disappointed. For in all strife the stronger, even though he suffer wrong, is looked upon as the aggressor because of his superior power. As for you, Adherbal and Hiempsal, love and respect this great man, emulate his virtues, and strive to show that I did not adopt better children than I begat."

11

ALTHOUGH Jugurtha knew that the king spoke insincerely, and though he had very different designs in his own mind, yet he returned a gracious answer, suited to the occasion. A few days later Micipsa died. After the princes had performed his obsequies with regal splendour, they met together for a general discussion of their affairs. Then Hiempsal, the youngest of the three, who was naturally haughty and even before this had shown his contempt for Jugurtha's inferior birth because he was not his equal on the maternal side, sat down on the right of Adherbal, in order to prevent Jugurtha from taking his place between the two, a position which is regarded as an honour among the Numidians. Afterwards, however, when his brother begged him to show respect to greater years, he was reluctantly induced to move to the other side.

At this meeting, in the course of a long discussion about the government of the kingdom, Jugurtha suggested, among other measures, that they ought to annul all laws and decrees passed within the past five years, on the ground that during that time Micipsa was far gone in years and hardly of sound mind. Thereupon Hiempsal again spoke up and declared that he approved the suggestion; for it was within the last three years, he said, that Jugurtha himself had been adopted and thus given a share in the kingdom. This remark sank more deeply into Jugurtha's mind than anyone would have supposed. So, from that moment he was a prey to resentment and fear, planned and schemed, and thought of nothing except some means by which he might outwit and ensnare Hiempsal. But since his plans moved too slowly and his proud spirit retained its anger, he resolved to effect his design in any possible way.

12

AT the first meeting of the princes, which I have already mentioned, they failed to agree and therefore determined to divide the treasures and partition the kingdom among the three. Accordingly, they set a time for both events, that for the division of the money being the earlier, and meanwhile came by different routes to a place near the treasury. Now it chanced that Hiempsal was occupying a house in the town of Thirmida which belonged to Jugurtha's most confidential attendant, who had always been his master's dear and beloved friend. This man, whom chance threw in his way as an agent, Jugurtha loaded with promises, and induced him to go to his house on the pretext of inspecting it and to have false keys made for the doors; for the true ones used to be delivered to Hiempsal. As to the rest, Jugurtha himself promised to be at hand at the proper time with a strong force. The Numidian promptly carried out his instructions, and, as he had been directed, let in Jugurtha's soldiers by night. They rushed into the house, scattered in search of the king, slew some of the household in their sleep and others as they offered resistance, ransacked all hiding-places, broke down doors, and filled the whole place with noise and confusion. Meanwhile, Hiempsal was found hiding in the cell of a maid-servant, where in his first terror, unacquainted as he was with the premises, he had taken refuge. The Numidians did as they were ordered, and brought his head to Jugurtha.

13

NOW, in a short time the news of this awful crime spread over all Africa. Fear seized Adherbal and all the former subjects of

Micipsa. The Numidians were divided into two parties, the greater number siding with Adherbal, but the better soldiers with his rival. Jugurtha then armed the largest possible number of troops, brought some cities under his sway by force and others with their consent, and prepared to make himself ruler of all Numidia. Although Adherbal had at once dispatched envoys to Rome, to inform the senate of his brother's murder and his own position, yet he prepared to take the field, relying upon the superior number of his troops. But he was defeated in the very first engagement, fled to our province, and thence made his way to Rome.

Then Jugurtha, when he had carried out his plans and was in possession of all Numidia, having leisure to think over what he had done, began to be afraid of the Roman people and to despair of escaping their anger except through the avarice of the Roman nobles and his own wealth. Accordingly, a few days later, he sent envoys to Rome with a great amount of gold and silver, directing them first to load his old friends with presents, and then to win new one—in short, to make haste to accomplish by largess whatever they could.

But when the envoys arrived at Rome, and, as the king had commanded, sent magnificent presents to his friends and to other of the senate whose influence at the time was powerful, such a change of sentiment ensued that in place of the pronounced hostility of the nobles Jugurtha gained their favour and support. Induced in some cases by hope, in others by bribery, they went about to individual members of the senate and urged them not to take too severe measures against Jugurtha. When, because of this, the envoys came to feel sufficient confidence, a time was appointed for the appearance of both parties before the senate. Thereupon Adherbal is said to have spoken in the following terms:-

14

"FATHERS of the Senate, my sire Micipsa admonished me on his deathbed to consider that I was only a steward of the kingdom of Numidia, but that the right and authority were in your hands; at the same time he bade me strive to be as helpful as possible to the Roman people in peace and in war and to regard you as my kindred and relatives. He declared that if I did this, I should find in your friendship an army, and wealth, and bulwarks for my kingdom. As I was following these injunctions of my father, Jugurtha, wickedest of all men on the face of the earth, in despite of your power robbed me, the grandson of Masinissa and hereditary friend and ally of the Roman people, of my throne and all my fortunes.

"And for myself, Fathers of the Senate, since I was doomed to such a depth of wretchedness, I could wish that I might ask your help rather because of my own services than those of my ancestors; I could wish above all that favours were due to me from the Roman people which I did not need; and failing this, that if they were needed I might accept them as my due. But since virtue alone is not its own protection, and since it was not in my power to mould the character of Jugurtha, I have had recourse to you, Fathers of the Senate, to whom (and this is greatest part of my wretchedness) I am compelled to be a burden before I have been an aid. All other kings have been admitted to your friendship when they were vanquished in war, or have sought your alliance in their time of peril; our family established friendly relations with Rome during the war with Carthage, at a time when the plighted word of Rome was a greater inducement to us than her fortune. Therefore do not allow me, their descendant and the grandson of Masinissa, to implore your aid in vain.

"If I had no other reason for asking the favour than my pitiable lot—of late a king, mighty in family, fame and fortune; now broken by woes, destitute and appealing to others for help—it would nevertheless be becoming to the majesty of the Roman people to defend me against wrong and not to allow any man's power to grow great through crime. But in fact I am driven from the lands which the people of Rome gave to my forefathers and from which my father and grandfather helped you to drive Syphax and the Carthaginians. It is your gift, Fathers of the Senate, which has been wrested from me, and in the wrong done to me you have been scorned. Woe's me! O my father Micipsa, has this been the effect of your kindness, that the man whom you put on an equality with your own children, whom you made a partner in your kingdom, should of all men be the destroyer of your house?

"Shall my family then never find rest? Shall we always dwell amid bloodshed, arms and exile? While the Carthaginians were unconquered, we naturally suffered all kinds of hardship; the enemy were upon our flank, you, our friends, were far away; all our hope was in our arms. After Africa had been freed from that pestilence, we enjoyed the delights of peace, since we had no enemy, unless haply at your command. But lo! on a sudden, Jugurtha, carried away by intolerable audacity, wickedness and arrogance, after killing my brother, who was also his kinsman, first made Hiempsal's realm the spoil of his crime; then, when he had failed to outwit me by the same wiles, and when under your sovereignty I was looking for anything rather than violence or war, he has made me, as you see, an exile from home and country, a prey to want and wretchedness, and safer anywhere than in my own kingdom.

"I always used to think, Fathers of the Senate, as I had heard my father maintain, that those who diligently cultivated your friendship undertook an arduous duty, indeed, but were safe beyond all others. Our family has done its best to aid you in all your wars; that we may enjoy peace and safety, Fathers of the Senate, is in your power. Our father left two of us brothers; a third, Jugurtha, he hoped to add to our number by his favours. One of the three has been slain; I myself have barely escaped the sacrilegious hands of the other. What shall I do, or to what special protection shall I appeal in my troubles? All the defenses of my house are destroyed. My father, as was inevitable, has paid the debt of nature. My brother has lost his life through the crime of a kinsman, the last man who ought to have raised a hand against him. Relatives, friends, and others who were near to me have fallen by one blow or another. Of those taken by Jugurtha some have been crucified, others thrown to wild beasts; a few, whose lives were spared, in gloomy dungeons amid sorrow and lamentation drag out an existence worse than death. But if all that I have lost, or all that has turned from affection to hostility, remained untouched, even then, if any unexpected misfortune had befallen me, I should appeal to you, Fathers of the Senate, whom it befits, because of the extent of your dominion, to take under your care all matters of right and wrong everywhere. As it is, however, an exile from home and country, alone, and stripped of all that becomes my station, where shall I take refuge or to whom shall I appeal? To nations or kings, all of whom are hostile to our family because of our friendship for you? To what land can I turn and not find there many a record of my ancestors' acts of hostility? Can anyone feel compassion for us who was ever your enemy? Finally, Fathers of the Senate, Masinissa instructed us to attach ourselves to none save the Roman people and to contract no new leagues and alliances; he declared that in your friendship there would be for us all an ample protection, and that, if the fortune of your empire should change, we must fall with it.

"Through valour and the favour of the gods you are mighty and powerful, all things are favourable and yield obedience to you; hence you may the more readily have regard to the wrongs of your allies. My only fear is lest private friendship for Jugurtha, the true character of which is not evident, may lead some of your number astray; for I hear that his partisans are using every effort, and are soliciting and entreating each of you separately not to pass any judgment upon him in his absence without a hearing. They declare that I am speaking falsely and feigning the necessity for flight, when I might have remained in my own kingdom. As to that, I hope that I may yet see the man through whose impious crime I have been subjected to these woes making the same pretense, and that at last either you or the immortal gods may begin to take thought for human affairs! Then of a truth that wretch, who now exults and glories in his crimes, will be tortured by ills of every kind and pay a heavy penalty for his treachery to our father, for the murder of my brother, and for my unhappiness.

"At last, brother dearest to my heart, although life has been taken from you untimely by the last hand that should have been raised against you, yet your fate seems to me a cause for joy rather than for sorrow. For when you lost your life it was not your throne you lost, but it was flight, exile, want and all these woes which weigh me down. While I, poor wretch, hurled from my father's throne into this sea of troubles, present a tragedy of human vicissitude, being at a loss what course to take, whether to try to avenge your wrongs when I myself am in need of aid, or to take thought for my throne when the very question of my life or death hangs upon the help of others. Would that death were an honourable means of escape for one of my estate! Would that, worn out by affliction, I could succumb to oppression without appearing justly contemptible! As it is, life has no charms for me, but death is impossible without shame.

"Fathers of the Senate, I beseech you in your own name, by your children and parents, and by the majesty of the Roman people, aid me in my distress, set your faces against injustice, do not permit the kingdom of Numidia, which belongs to you, to be ruined by villainy and the blood-guiltiness of our family."

15

AFTER the king had finished speaking, the envoys of Jugurtha, who relied rather upon bribery than upon the justice of their cause, replied briefly. They declared that Hiempsal had been slain by the Numidians because of his savage cruelty; the Adherbal after making war without provocation and suffering defeat, was complaining because he had been prevented from inflicting injury. Jugurtha, they said, begged the senate not to think him other than he had shown himself at Numantia, or let the words of an enemy outweigh his own actions.

Then both parties left the House and the matter was at once laid before the senate. The partisans of the envoys, and a large number of other senators who had been corrupted by their influence, derided the words of Adherbal and lauded the virtues of Jugurtha; exerting their influence, their eloquence, in short every possible means, they laboured as diligently in defense of the shameful crime of a foreigner as though they were striving to win honour. A few, on the other hand, to whom right and justice were more precious than riches, recommended that aid be given to Adherbal and that the death of Hiempsal be severely punished. Conspicuous among these was Aemilius Scaurus, a noble full of energy, a partisan, greedy for power, fame, and riches, but clever in concealing his faults. As soon as this man saw the king's bribery, so notorious and so brazen, fearing the usual result in such cases, namely, that such gross corruption would arouse popular resentment, he curbed his habitual cupidity.

16

IN spite of all, that faction of the senate prevailed which rated money and favour higher than justice. It was voted that ten commissioners should divide Micipsa's former kingdom between Jugurtha and Adherbal. The head of this commission was Lucius Opimius, a distinguished man, who was influential in the senate at that time because in his consulship, after bringing about the death of Gaius Gracchus and Marcus Fulvius Flaccus, he had made cruel use of the victory of the nobles over the people. Although at Rome Opimius had been one of Jugurtha's opponents, the king received him with the greatest respect, and soon induced him, by many gifts and promises, to consider Jugurtha's advantage of more consequence than his own fair fame, his honour, and in short, than all personal considerations. Then adopting the same tactics with the other envoys, Jugurtha won over the greater number of them; only a few held their honour dearer than gold. When the division was made, the part of Numidia adjoining Mauretania, which was the more fertile and thickly populated, was assigned to Jugurtha; the other part, preferable in appearance rather than in reality, having more harbours and being provided with more buildings, fell to Adherbal.

26

WHEN this was reported at Cirta, the Italiotes, on whose valour the defense of the town depended, were confident that in the event of surrender they would escape injury because of the prestige of Rome. They therefore advised Adherbal to deliver himself and the town to Jugurtha, stipulating merely that his life should be spared and leaving the rest to the senate. But Adherbal, though he thought that anything was better than trusting to Jugurtha, yet because the Italiotes were in a position to use compulsion if he opposed them, surrendered on the terms which they had advised. Thereupon Jugurtha first tortured Adherbal to death and then made an indiscriminate massacre of all the adult Numidians and of traders whom he found with arms in their hands.

27

WHEN this outrage became known at Rome and the matter was brought up for discussion in the senate, those same tools of the king, by interrupting the discussions and wasting time, often through their personal influence, often by wrangling, tried to disguise the atrocity of the deed. And had not Gaius Memmius, tribune of the commons elect, a man of spirit who was hostile to the domination of the nobles, made it clear to the populace of Rome that the motive of these tactics was to condone Jugurtha's crime through the influence of a few of his partisans, the deliberations would undoubtedly have been protracted until all indignation had evaporated: so great was the power of the king's influence and money. But when the senate from consciousness of guilt began to fear the people, Numidia and Italy, as the Sempronian law required, were assigned to the consuls who should next be elected. The consuls in question were Publius Scipio Nasica and Lucius Calpurnius Bestia; Numidia fell to Bestia, Italy to Scipio. An army was then enrolled to be transported to Africa, the soldiers' pay and other necessaries of war were voted.

28

WHEN Jugurtha heard this unexpected news (for he had a firm conviction that at Rome anything could be bought) he sent his son, and with him two friends, as envoys to the senate, giving them the same directions that he had given those whom he sent after murdering Hiempsal, namely, to try the power of money on everybody. As this deputation drew near the city, Bestia referred to the senate the question whether they would consent to receive Jugurtha's envoys within the walls. The members thereupon decreed that unless the envoys had come to surrender the king and his kingdom, they must leave Italy within the next ten days. The consul gave orders that the Numidians should be notified of the senate's action; they therefore went home without fulfilling their mission.

Meanwhile Calpurnius, having levied his army, chose as his lieutenants men of noble rank and strong party spirit, by whose influence he hoped that any misdeeds of his would be upheld. Among these was Scaurus, whose character and conduct I described a short time ago. For though our consul possessed many excellent qualities of mind and body, they were all nullified by avarice. He had great endurance, a keen intellect, no little foresight, considerable military experience, and a stout heart in the face of dangers and plots. Now the legions were transported across Italy to Rhegium, from there to Sicily, from Sicily to Africa. Then Calpurnius, having provided himself with supplies, began by making a vigorous attack on the Numidians, taking many prisoners and storming several of their towns.

29

BUT when Jugurtha through his emissaries began to try the power of money upon Calpurnius and to point out the difficulty of the war which he was conducting, the consul's mind, demoralized as it was by avarice, was easily turned from its purpose. Moreover, he took Scaurus as an accomplice and tool in all his designs; for although at first, even after many of his own party had been seduced, Scaurus had vigorously opposed the king, a huge bribe had turned him from honour and virtue to criminality. At first, however, Jugurtha merely purchased a delay in hostilities, thinking that he could meanwhile effect something at Rome by bribery or by his personal interest. But as soon as he learned that Scaurus was implicated, he conceived a strong hope of gaining peace, and decided to discuss all the conditions in person with the envoys.

But meanwhile, as a token of good faith, the consul sent his quaestor Sextius to Vaga, a town of Jugurtha's, ostensibly to receive the grain which Calpurnius had publicly demanded of the envoys in return for observing an armistice until a surrender should be arranged. Thereupon the king, as he had agreed, came to the camp and after he had spoken a few words in the presence of the council in justification of his conduct and had asked to be received in surrender, he arranged the rest privately with Bestia and Scaurus. Then on the next day an irregular vote was taken and the surrender accepted. As had been ordered before the council, thirty elephants, many cattle and horses, with a small amount of silver were handed over to the quaestor. Calpurnius went to Rome to preside at the elections. In Numidia and in our army peace reigned.

The Conspiracy of Catiline

Sallust

Trnaslated by J. C. Rolfe

1

IT behooves all men who wish to excel other animals to strive with might and main not to pass through life unheralded, like the beasts, which Nature has fashioned groveling and slaves to the belly. All our power, on the contrary, lies in both mind and body; we employ the mind to rule, the body rather to serve; the one we have in common with the Gods, the other with the brutes. Therefore I find it becoming, in seeking renown, that we should employ the resources of the intellect rather than those of brute strength, to the end that, since the span of life which we enjoy is short, we may make the memory of our lives as long as possible. For the renown which riches or beauty confer is fleeting and frail; mental excellence is a splendid and lasting possession.

Yet for a long time mortal men have discussed the question whether success in arms depends more on strength of body or excellence of mind; for before you begin, deliberation is necessary, when you have deliberated, prompt action. Thus each of these, being incomplete in itself, requires the other's aid.

2

ACCORDINGLY in the beginning kings (for that was the first title of sovereignty among men), took different courses, some training their minds and others their bodies. Even at that time men's lives were still free from covetousness; each was quite content with his own possessions. But when Cyrus in Asia and in Greece the Athenians and Lacedaemonians began to subdue cities and nations, to make the lust for dominion a pretext for war, to consider the greatest empire the greatest glory, then at last men learned from perilous enterprises that qualities of mind availed most in war.

Now if the mental excellence with which kings and rulers are endowed were as potent in peace as in war, human affairs would run an evener and steadier course, and you would not see power passing from hand to hand and everything in turmoil and confusion; for empire is easily retained by the qualities by which it was first won. But when sloth has usurped the place of industry, and lawlessness and insolence have superseded self-restraint and justice, the fortune of princes changes with their character. Thus the sway is always passing to the best man from the hands of his inferior.

Success in agriculture, navigation, and architecture depends invariably upon mental excellence. Yet many men, being slaves to appetite and sleep, have passed through life untaught and untrained, like mere wayfarers in these men we see, contrary to Nature's intent, the body a source of pleasure, the soul a burden. For my own part, I consider the lives and deaths of such men as about alike, since no record is made of either. In very truth that man alone lives and makes the most of life, as it seems to me, who devotes himself to some occupation, courting the fame of a glorious deed or a noble career. But amid the wealth of opportunities Nature points out one path to one and another to another.

3

IT is glorious to serve one's country by deeds; even to serve her by words is a thing not to be despised; one may become famous in peace as well as in war. Not only those who have acted, but those also who have recorded the acts of others oftentimes receive our approbation. And for myself, although I am well aware that by no means equal repute attends the narrator and the doer of deeds, yet I regard the writing of history as one of the most difficult of tasks: first, because the style and diction must be equal to the deeds recorded; and in the second place, because such criticism as you make of others' shortcomings are thought by most men to be due to malice and envy. Furthermore, when you commemorate the distinguished merit and fame of good men, while every one is quite ready to believe you when you tell of things which he thinks he could easily do himself, everything beyond that he regards as fictitious, if not false.

When I myself was a young man, my inclinations at first led me, like many another, into public life, and there I encountered man obstacles; for instead of modesty, incorruptibility and honesty, shamelessness, bribery and rapacity held sway. And although my soul, a stranger to evil ways, recoiled from such faults, yet amid so many vices my youthful weakness was led astray and held captive my ambition; for while I of took no part in the evil practices of the others, yet the desire for preferment made me the victim of the same ill-repute and jealousy as they.

4

ACCORDINGLY, when my mind found peace after many troubles and perils and I had determined that I must pass what was left of my life aloof from public affairs, it was not my intention to waste my precious leisure in indolence and sloth, nor yet by turning to farming or the chase, to lead a life devoted to slavish employments. On the contrary, I resolved to return to a cherished purpose from which ill-starred ambition had diverted me, and write a history of the Roman people, selecting such portions as seemed to me worthy of record; and I was confirmed in this resolution by the fact that my mind was free from hope, and fear, and partisanship. I shall therefore write briefly and as truthfully as possible of the conspiracy of

Catiline; for I regard that event as worthy of special notice because of the extraordinary nature of the crime and of the danger arising from it. But before beginning my narrative I must say a few words about the man's character.

5

LUCIUS Catiline, scion of a noble family, had great vigour both of mind and body, but an evil and depraved nature. From youth up he reveled in civil wars, murder, pillage, and political dissension, and amid these he spent his early manhood. His body could endure hunger, cold and want of sleep to an incredible degree; his mind was reckless, cunning, treacherous, capable of any form of pretense or concealment. Covetous of others' possessions, he was prodigal of his own; he was violent in his passions. He possessed a certain amount of eloquence, but little discretion. His disordered mind ever craved the monstrous, incredible, gigantic.

After the domination of Lucius Sulla the man had been seized with a mighty desire of getting control of the government, recking little by what manner he should achieve it, provided he made himself supreme. His haughty spirit was goaded more and more every day by poverty and a sense of guilt, both of which he had augmented by the practices of which I have already spoken. He was spurred on, also, by the corruption of the public morals, which were being ruined by two great evils of an opposite character, extravagance and avarice.

Since the occasion has arisen to speak of the morals of our country, the nature of my theme seems to suggest that I go farther back and give a brief account of the institutions of our forefathers in peace and in war, how they governed the commonwealth, how great it was when they bequeathed it to us, and how by gradual changes it has ceased to be the noblest and best, and has become the worst and most vicious.

6

THE city of Rome, according to my understanding, was at the outset founded and inhabited by Trojans, who were wandering about in exile under the leadership of Aeneas and had no fixed abode; the were joined by the Aborigines, a rustic folk, without laws or government, free and unrestrained. After these two peoples, different in race, unlike in speech and mode of life, were united within the same walls, they were merged into one with incredible facility, so quickly did harmony change a heterogeneous and roving band into a commonwealth. But when this new community had grown in numbers, civilization, and territory, and was beginning to seem amply rich and amply strong, then, as is usual with mortal affairs, prosperity gave birth to envy. As a result, neighbouring kings and peoples made war upon them, and but few of their friends lent them aid; for the rest were smitten with fear and stood aloof from the danger. But the Romans, putting forth their whole energy at home and in the field, made all haste, got ready, encouraged one another, went to meet he foe, and defended their liberty, their country, and their parents by arms. Afterwards, when their prowess had averted the danger, they lent aid to their allies and friends, and established friendly relations rather by conferring than by accepting favours.

They had a constitution founded upon law, which was in name a monarchy; a chosen few, whose bodies were enfeebled by age but whose minds were fortified with wisdom, took counsel for the welfare of the state. These were called Fathers, by reason either of their age or of the similarity of their duties. Later, when the rule of the kings, which at first had tended to preserve freedom and advance the state, had degenerated into a lawless tyranny, they altered their form of government and appointed two rulers with annual power, thinking that this device would prevent men's minds from growing arrogant through unlimited authority.

7

NOW at that time every man began to lift his head higher and to have his talents more in readiness. For kings hold the good in greater suspicion than the wicked, and to them the merit of others is always fraught with danger; still the free state, once liberty was won, waxed incredibly strong and great in a remarkably short time, such was the thirst for glory that had filled men's minds. To begin with, as soon as the young men could endure the hardships of war, they were taught a soldier's duties in camp under a vigorous discipline, and they took more pleasure in handsome arms and war horses than in harlots and revelry. To such men consequently no labour was unfamiliar, no region too rough or too steep, no armed foeman was terrible; valour was all in all. Nay, their hardest struggle for glory was with one another; each man strove to be the first to strike down the foe, to scale a wall, to be seen of all while doing such a deed. This they considered riches, this fair fame and high nobility. It was praise they coveted, but they were lavish of money; their aim was unbounded renown, but only such riches as could be gained honourably. I might name the battlefields on which the Romans with a mere handful of men routed great armies of their adversaries, and the cities fortified by nature which they took by assault, were it not that such a theme could carry me too far from my subject.

8

BUT beyond question Fortune holds sway everywhere. It is she that makes all events famous or obscure according to her caprice rather than in accordance with the truth. The acts of the Athenians, in my judgment, were indeed great and glorious enough, but nevertheless somewhat less important than fame represents them. But because Athens produced writers of exceptional talent, the exploits of the men of Athens are heralded throughout the world as unsurpassed. Thus the merit of those who did the deeds is rated as high as brilliant minds have been able to exalt the deeds themselves by words of praise. But the Roman people never had that advantage, since their ablest men were always most engaged with affairs;

their minds were never employed apart from their bodies; the best citizen preferred action to words, and thought that his own brave deeds should be lauded by others rather than that theirs should be recounted by him.

9

ACCORDINGLY, good morals were cultivated at home and in the field; there was the greatest harmony and little or no avarice; justice and probity prevailed among them, thanks not so much to laws as to nature. Quarrels, discord, and strife were reserved for their enemies; citizen vied with citizen only for the prize of merit. They were lavish in their offerings to the gods, frugal in the home, loyal to their friends. By practicing these two qualities, boldness in warfare and justice when peace came, they watched over themselves and their country. In proof of these statements I present this convincing evidence: firstly, in time of war punishment was more often inflicted for attacking the enemy contrary to orders, or for withdrawing too tardily when recalled from the field, than for venturing to abandon the standards or to give ground under stress; and secondly, in time of peace they ruled by kindness rather than fear, and when wronged preferred forgiveness to vengeance.

10

BUT when our country had grown great through toil and the practice of justice, when great kings had been vanquished in war, savage tribes and mighty peoples subdued by force of arms, when Carthage, the rival of Rome's sway, had perished root and branch, and all seas and lands were open, then Fortune began to grow cruel and to bring confusion into all our affairs. Those who had found it easy to bear hardship and dangers, anxiety and adversity, found leisure and wealth, desirable under other circumstances, a burden and a curse. Hence the lust for money first, then for power, grew upon them; these were, I may say, the root of all evils. For avarice destroyed honour, integrity, and all other noble qualities; taught in their place insolence, cruelty, to neglect the gods, to set a price on everything. Ambition drove many men to become false; to have one thought locked in the breast, another ready on the tongue; to value friendships and enmities not on their merits but by the standard of self-interest, and to show a good front rather than a good heart. At first these vices grew slowly, from time to time they were punished; finally, when the disease had spread like a deadly plague, the state was changed and a government second to none in equity and excellence became cruel and intolerable.

11

BUT at first men's souls were actuated less by avarice than by ambition—a fault, it is true, but not so far removed from virtue; for the noble and the base alike long for glory, honour, and power, but the former mount by the true path, whereas the latter, being destitute of noble qualities, rely upon craft and deception. Avarice implies a desire for money, which no wise man covets; steeped as it were with noxious poisons, it renders the most manly body and soul effeminate; it is ever unbounded and insatiable, nor can either plenty or want make it less. But after Lucius Sulla, having gained control of the state by arms, brought everything to a bad end from a good beginning, all men began to rob and pillage. One coveted a house, another lands; the victors showed neither moderation nor restraint, but shamefully and cruelly wronged their fellow citizens. Besides all this, Lucius Sulla, in order to secure the loyalty of the army which he led into Asia, had allowed it a luxury and license foreign to the manners of our forefathers; and in the intervals of leisure those charming and voluptuous lands had easily demoralized the warlike spirit of his soldiers. There it was that an army of the Roman people first learned to indulge in women and drink; to admire statues, paintings, and chased vases, to steal them from private houses and public places, to pillage shrines, and to desecrate everything, both sacred and profane. These soldiers, therefore, after they had won the victory, left nothing to the vanquished. In truth, prosperity tries the souls of even the wise; how then should men of depraved character like these make a moderate use of victory?

12

AS soon as riches came to be held in honour, when glory, dominion, and power followed in their train, virtue began to lose its lustre, poverty to be considered a disgrace, blamelessness to be termed malevolence. Therefore as the result of riches, luxury and greed, united with insolence, took possession of our young manhood. They pillaged, squandered; set little value on their own, coveted the goods of others; they disregarded modesty, chastity, everything human and divine; in short, they were utterly thoughtless and reckless.

It is worth your while, when you look upon houses and villas reared to the size of cities, to pay a visit to the temples of the gods built by our forefathers, most reverent of men. But they adorned the shrines of the gods with piety, their own homes with glory, while from the vanquished they took naught save the power of doing harm. The men of to-day, on the contrary, basest of creatures, with supreme wickedness are robbing our allies of all that those heroes in the hour of victory had left them; they act as though the one and only way to rule were to wrong.

13

WHY, pray, should I speak of things which are incredible except to those who have seen them, that a host of private men have leveled mountains and built upon the seas? To such men their riches seem to me to have been but a plaything; for while they might have enjoyed them honourably, they made haste to squander them shamefully. Nay more, the passion which arose for lewdness, gluttony, and the other attendants of luxury was equally strong; men played the woman, women offered their chastity for sale; to gratify their palates they scoured land and sea; they slept before they needed sleep; they did not await the coming of hunger or thirst, of cold or of weariness, but all these things their self-indulgence anticipated. Such were the vices that incited the young men to crime, as soon as they had run through their property. Their minds, habituated to evil practices, could not easily refrain from self-indulgence, and so they abandoned themselves the more recklessly to every means of gain as well as of extravagance.

14

IN a city so great and so corrupt Catiline found it a very easy matter to surround himself, as by a bodyguard, with troops of criminals and reprobates of every kind. For whatever wanton, glutton, or gamester had wasted his patrimony in play, feasting, or debauchery; anyone who had contracted an immense debt that he might buy immunity from disgrace or crime; all, furthermore, from every side who had been convicted of murder or sacrilege, or feared prosecution for their crimes; those, too, whom hand and tongue supported by perjury or the blood of their fellow citizens; finally, all who were hounded by disgrace, poverty, or an evil conscience—all these were nearest and dearest to Catiline. And if any guiltless man did chance to become his friend, daily intercourse and the allurements of vice soon made him as bad or almost as bad as the rest. But most of all Catiline sought the intimacy of the young; their minds, still pliable as they were and easily moulded, were without difficulty ensnared by his wiles. For carefully noting the passion which burned in each, according to his time of life, he found harlots for some or bought dogs and horses for others; in fine, he spared neither expense nor his own decency, provided he could make them submissive and loyal to himself. I am aware that some have believed that the young men who frequented Catiline's house set but little store by their chastity; but that report became current rather for other reasons than because anyone had evidence of its truth.

15

EVEN in youth Catiline had many shameful intrigues—with a maiden of noble rank, with a priestess of Vesta—and other affairs equally unlawful and impious. At last he was seized with a passion for Aurelia Orestilla, in whom no good man ever commended anything save her beauty; and when she hesitated to marry him because she was afraid of his stepson, then a grown man, it is generally believed that he murdered the young man in order to make an empty house for this criminal marriage. In fact, I think that this was his special motive for hastening his plot; for his guilt-stained soul, at odds with gods and men, could find rest neither waking nor sleeping, so cruelly did conscience ravage his overwrought mind. Hence his pallid complexion, his bloodshot eyes, his gait now fast, now slow; in short, his face and his every glance showed the madman.

16

TO the young men whom he had ensnared, as I have described, he taught many forms of wickedness. From their number he supplied false witnesses and forgers; he bade them make light of honour, fortune, and dangers; then, when he had sapped their good repute and modesty, he called for still greater crimes. If there was no immediate motive for wrong doing, he nevertheless waylaid and murdered innocent as well as guilty; indeed, he preferred to be needlessly vicious and cruel rather than to allow their hands and spirits to grow weak through lack of practice.

Relying upon such friends and accomplices as these, Catiline formed the plan of overthrowing the government, both because his own debt was enormous in all parts of the world and because the greater number of Sulla's veterans, who had squandered their property and now thought with longing of their former pillage and victories, were eager for civil war. There was no army in Italy; Gnaeus Pompeius was waging war in distant parts of the world; Catiline himself had high hopes as a candidate for the consulship; the senate was anything but alert; all was peaceful and quiet; this was his golden opportunity.

17

ACCORDINGLY, towards the first of June in the consulate of Lucius Caesar and Gaius Figulus, he addressed his followers at first one by one, encouraging some and sounding others. He pointed out his own resources, the unprepared condition of the state, the great prizes of conspiracy. When he had such information as he desired, he assembled all those who were most desperate and most reckless. There were present from the senatorial order Publius Lentulus Sura, Publius Autronius, Lucius Cassius Longinus, Gaius Cethegus, Publius and Servius Sulla, sons of Servius, Lucius Vargunteius, Quintus Annius, Marcus Porcius Laeca, Lucius Bestia, Quintus Curius; also of the equestrian order, Marcus Fulvius Nobilior, Lucius Statilius, Publius Gabinius Capito, Gaius Cornelius; besides these there were many men from the colonies and free towns who were of noble rank at home. There were, moreover, several nobles who had a somewhat more secret connection with the plot, men who were prompted rather by the hope of power than by want or any other exigency. The greater part of the young men also, in particular those of high position, were favourable to Catiline's project; for although in quiet times they had the means of living elegantly or luxuriously, they preferred uncertainty to certainty, war to peace. There were also at that time some who believed that Marcus Licinius Crassus was not wholly ignorant of the plot; that because his enemy Gaius Pompeius was in command of a large army, he was willing to see anyone's influence grow in opposition to the power of his rival, fully believing meanwhile that if the conspirators should be successful, he would easily be the leading man among them.

23

NOW one of the members of the conspiracy was Quintus Curius, a man of no mean birth but guilty of many shameful crimes, whom the censors had expelled from the senate because of his immorality. This man was as untrustworthy as he was reckless; he could neither keep secret what he had heard nor conceal even his own misdeeds; he was utterly regardless of what he did or said. He had an intrigue of long standing with Fulvia, a woman of quality, and when he began to lose her favour because poverty compelled him to be less lavish, he suddenly fell to boasting, began to promise her seas and mountains, and sometimes to threaten his mistress with the steel if she did not bow to his will; in brief, to show much greater assurance than before. But Fulvia, when she learned the cause of her lover's overbearing conduct, had no thought of concealing such a peril to her country, but without mentioning the name of her informant she told a number of people what she had heard of Catiline's conspiracy from various sources.

It was this discovery in particular which aroused a general desire to confer the consulate upon Marcus Tullius Cicero; for before that most of the nobles were consumed with jealousy and thought the office in a way prostituted if a "new man," however excellent, should obtain it. But when danger came, jealousy and pride fell into the background.

24

ACCORDINGLY, when the elections had been held Marcus Tullius and Gaius Antonius were proclaimed consuls, and this at first filled the conspirators with consternation. And yet Catiline's frenzy did not abate. On the contrary, he increased his activity every day, made collections of arms at strategic points in Italy, and borrowed money on his own credit or that of his friends, sending it to Faesulae to a certain Manlius, who afterwards was the first to take the field. At that time Catiline is said to have gained the support of many men of all conditions and even of some women; the latter at first had met their enormous expenses by prostitution, but later, when their time of life had set a limit to their traffic but not to their extravagance, had contracted a huge debt. Through their help Catiline believed that he could tempt the city slaves to his side and set fire to Rome; and then either attach the women's husbands to his cause or make away with them.

25

NOW among these women was Sempronia, who had often committed many crimes of masculine daring. In birth and beauty, in her husband also and children, she was abundantly favoured by fortune; well read in the literature of Greece and Rome, able to play the lyre and dance more skilfully than an honest woman need, and having many other accomplishments which minister to voluptuousness. But there was nothing which she held so cheap as modesty and chastity; you could not easily say whether she was less sparing of her money or her honour; her desires were so ardent that she sought men more often than she was sought by them. Even before the time of the conspiracy she had often broken her word, repudiated her debts, been privy to murder; poverty and extravagance combined had driven her headlong. Nevertheless, she was a woman of no mean endowments; she could write verses, bandy jests, and use language which was modest, or tender, or wanton; in fine, she possessed a high degree of wit and of charm.

26

AFTER making these preparations Catiline nevertheless became a candidate for the consulship of the following year, hoping that if he should be elected he could easily do whatever he wished with Antonius. In the meantime he was not idle, but kept laying plots of all kinds against Cicero, who, however, did not lack the craft and address to escape them. For immediately after the beginning of his consulate, by dint of many promises made through Fulvia, Cicero had induced Quintus Curius, the man whom I mentioned a little while ago, to reveal Catiline's designs to him. Furthermore, he had persuaded his colleague Antonius, by agreeing to make over his province to him, not to entertain schemes hostile to the public weal, and he also had surrounded himself secretly with a bodyguard of friends and dependents.

When the day of the elections came and neither Catiline's suit nor the plots which he had made against the consuls in the Campus Martius were successful, he resolved to take the field and dare the uttermost, since his covert attempts had resulted in disappointment and disgrace.

27

HE therefore dispatched Gaius Manlius to Faesulae and the adjacent part of Etruria, a certain Septimius of Camerinum to the Picene district, and Gaius Julius to Apulia; others too to other places, wherever he thought that each would be serviceable to his project. Meanwhile he himself was busy at Rome with many attempts at once, laying traps for the consul, planning fires, posting armed men in commanding places. He went armed himself, bade others to do the same, conjured them to be always alert and ready, kept on the move night and day, took no rest yet succumbed neither to wakefulness nor fatigue. Finally, when his manifold attempts met with no success, again in the dead of night he summoned the ringleaders of the conspiracy to the house of Marcus Porcius Laeca. There, after reproaching them bitterly for their inaction, he stated that had sent Manlius on ahead to the force which he had prepared for war, and also other men to other important points to commence hostilities, explaining that he himself was eager to go to the front if he could first make away with Cicero, who was a serious obstacle to his plans.

28

UPON this the rest were terrified and hesitated; but Gaius Cornelius, a Roman knight, offered his services and was joined by Lucius Vargunteius, a senator. These two men determined that very night, a little later, to get access to Cicero, accompanied by a band of armed men, as if for a ceremonial call and taking him by surprise to murder the defenseless consul in his own house. When Curius learned of the great danger which threatened the consul, he hastened to report to Cicero through Fulvia the trap which was being set for him. Hence the would-be assassins were refused admission and proved to have undertaken this awful crime to no purpose.

Meanwhile Manlius in Etruria was working upon the populace, who were already ripe for revolution because of penury and resentment at their wrongs; for during Sulla's supremacy they had lost their lands and all their property. He also approached brigands of various nationalities, who were numerous in that part of the country, and some members of Sulla's colonies who had been stripped by prodigal and luxurious living of the last of their great booty.

29

WHEN these events were reported to Cicero, he was greatly disturbed by the twofold peril, since he could no longer by his unaided efforts protect the city against these plots, nor gain any exact information as to the size and purpose of Manlius's army; he therefore formally called the attention of the senate to the matter, which had already been the subject of popular gossip. Thereupon, as is often done in a dangerous emergency, the senate voted "that the consuls would take heed that the commonwealth suffer no harm." The power which according to Roman usage is thus conferred upon a magistrate by the senate is supreme, allowing him to raise an army, wage war, exert any kind of compulsion upon allies and citizens, and exercise unlimited command and jurisdiction at home and in the field; otherwise the consul has none of these privileges except by the order of the people.

30

A FEW days later, in a meeting of the senate, Lucius Saenius, one of its members, read a letter which he said had been brought to him from Faesulae, stating that Gaius Manlius had taken the field with a large force on the twenty-seventh day of October. At the same time, as is usual in such a crisis, omens and portents were reported by some, while others told of the holding of meetings, of the transportation of arms, and of insurrections of the slaves at Capua and in Apulia.

Thereupon by decree of the senate Quintus Marcius Rex was sent to Faesulae and Quintus Metellus Creticus to Apulia and its neighbourhood. Both these generals were at the gates in command of their armies, being prevented from celebrating a triumph by the intrigues of a few men, whose habit it was to make everything, honourable and dishonourable, a matter of barter. Of the praetors, Quintus Pompeius Rufus was sent to Capua and Quintus Metellus Celer to the district of Pisa, with permission to raise an army suited to the emergency and the danger. The senate also voted that if anyone should give information as to the plot which had been made against the state, he should, if a slave, be rewarded with his freedom and a hundred thousand sesterces, and if a free man, with immunity for complicity therein, and two hundred thousand sesterces; further, that the troops of gladiators should be quartered on Capua and the other free towns according to the resources of each place; that at Rome watch should be kept by night in all parts of the city under the direction of the minor magistrates.

31

THESE precautions struck the community with terror, and the aspect of the city was changed. In place of extreme gaiety and frivolity, the fruit of long-continued peace, there was sudden and general gloom. Men were uneasy and apprehensive, put little confidence in any place of security or in any human being, were neither at war nor at peace, and measured the peril each by his own fears. The women, too, whom the greatness of our country had hitherto shielded from the terrors of war, were in a pitiful state of anxiety, raised suppliant hands to heaven, bewailed the fate of their little children, asked continual questions, trembled at everything, and throwing aside haughtiness and self-indulgence, despaired of themselves and of their country.

But Catiline's pitiless spirit persisted in the same attempts, although defenses were preparing, and he himself had been arraigned by Lucius Paulus under the Plautian law. Finally, in order to conceal his designs or to clear himself, as though he had merely been the object of some private slander, he came into the senate. Then the consul Marcus Tullius, either fearing his presence or carried away by indignation, delivered a brilliant speech of great service to the state, which he later wrote out and published. When he took his seat,

Catiline, prepared as he was to deny everything, with downcast eyes and pleading accents began to beg the Fathers of the Senate not to believe any unfounded charge against him; he was sprung from such a family, he said, and had so ordered his life from youth up, that he had none save the best of prospects. They must not suppose that he, a patrician, who like his forefathers had rendered great service to the Roman people, would be benefited by the overthrow of the government, while its saviour was Marcus Tullius, a resident alien in the city of Rome. When he would have added other insults, he was shouted down by the whole body, who called him traitor and assassin. Then in a transport of fury he cried: "Since I am brought to bay by my enemies and driven desperate, I will put out my fire by general devastation."

36

CATILINE himself, after spending a few days with Gaius Flaminius in the vicinity of Arretium, where he supplied arms to the populace, which had already been roused to revolt, hastened to join Manlius in his camp, taking with him the fasces and the other emblems of authority. As soon as this became known at Rome, the senate pronounced Catiline and Manlius traitors and named a day before which the rest of the conspirators might lay down their arms and escape punishment, excepting those under sentence for capital offenses. It was further voted that the consuls should hold a levy and that Antonius with an army should at once pursue Catiline, while Cicero defended the capital.

At no other time has the condition of imperial Rome, as it seems to me, been more pitiable. The whole world, from the rising of the sun to its setting, subdued by her arms, rendered obedience to her; at home there was peace and an abundance of wealth, which mortal men deem the chiefest of blessings. Yet there were citizens who from sheer perversity were bent upon their own ruin and that of their country. For in spite of the two decrees of the senate not one man of all that great number was led by the promised reward to betray the conspiracy, and not a single one deserted Catiline's camp;

such was the potency of the malady which like a plague had infected the minds of many of our countrymen.

37

THIS insanity was not confined to those who were implicated in the plot, but the whole body of the commons through desire for change favoured the designs of Catiline. In this very particular they seemed to act as the populace usually does; for in every community those who have no means envy the good, exalt the base, hate what is old and established, long for something new, and from disgust with their own lot desire a general upheaval. Amid turmoil and rebellion they maintain themselves without difficulty, since poverty is easily provided for and can suffer no loss. But the city populace in particular acted with desperation for many reasons. To begin with, all who were especially conspicuous for their shamelessness and impudence, those too who had squandered their patrimony in riotous living, finally all whom disgrace or crime had forced to leave home, had all flowed into Rome as into a cesspool. Many, too, who recalled Sulla's victory, when they saw common soldiers risen to the rank of senator, and others become so rich that they feasted and lived like kings, hoped each for himself for like fruits of victory, if he took the field. Besides this, the young men who had maintained a wretched existence by manual labour in the country, tempted by public and private doles had come to prefer idleness in the city to their hateful toil; these, like all the others, battened on the public ills. Therefore it is not surprising that men who were beggars and without character, with illimitable hopes, should respect their country as little as they did themselves. Moreover, those to whom Sulla's victory had meant the proscription of their parents, loss of property, and curtailment of their rights, looked forward in a similar spirit to the issue of a war. Finally, all who belonged to another party than that of the senate preferred to see the government overthrown rather than be out of power themselves. Such, then, was the evil which after many years had returned upon the state.

56

WHILE this was taking place in Rome, Catiline combined the forces which he had brought with him with those which Manlius already had, and formed two legions, filling up the cohorts so far as the number of his soldiers permitted. Then distributing among them equally such volunteers or conspirators as came to the camp, he soon completed the full quota of the legions, although in the beginning he had no more than two thousand men. But only about a fourth part of the entire force was provided with regular arms. The others carried whatever weapons chance had given them; namely, javelins or lances, or in some cases pointed stakes.

When Antonius was drawing near with his army, Catiline marched through the mountains, moved his camp now towards the city and now in the direction of Gaul, and gave the enemy no opportunity for battle, hoping shortly to have a large force if the conspirators at Rome succeeded in carrying out their plans. Meanwhile he refused to enroll slaves, a great number of whom flocked to him at first, because he had confidence in the strength of the conspiracy and at the same time thought it inconsistent with his designs to appear to have given runaway slaves a share in a citizens' cause.

57

BUT when news reached the camp that the plot had been discovered at Rome, and that Lentulus, Cethegus, and the others whom I mentioned had been done to death, very many of those whom the hope of pillage or desire for revolution had led to take up arms began to desert. The remainder Catiline led by forced marches over rugged mountains to the neighbourhood of Pistoria, intending to escape secretly by cross-roads into Transalpine Gaul. But Quintus Metellus Celer, with three legions, was on the watch in the district of Pisa, inferring from the difficulty of the enemy's position that he would take the very course which I have mentioned. Accordingly, when he learned through deserters in what direction Catiline was going, he quickly moved his camp and took up a position at the foot of the very mountains from which the conspirator would have to descend in his flight into Gaul. Antonius also was not far distant, since he was following the fleeing rebels over more level ground with an army which, though large, was lightly equipped. Now, when Catiline perceived that he was shut in between the mountains and the forces of his enemies, that his plans in the city had failed, and that he had hope neither of escape nor reinforcements, thinking it best in such a crisis to try the fortune of battle, he decided to engage Antonius as soon as possible. Accordingly he assembled his troops and addressed them in a speech of the following purport:-

58

"I AM well aware, soldiers, that words do not supply valour, and that a spiritless army is not made vigorous, or a timid one stout-hearted, by a speech from its commander. Only that degree of courage which is in each man's heart either by disposition or by habit, is wont to be revealed in battle. It is vain to exhort one who is roused neither by glory nor by dangers; the fear he feels in his heart closes ears. I have, however, called you together to offer a few words of advice, and at the same time to explain the reason for my resolution.

"You know perfectly well, soldiers, how great is the disaster that the incapacity and cowardice of Lentulus have brought upon himself and us, and how, waiting for reinforcements from the city, I could not march into Gaul. At this present time, moreover, you understand as well as I do in what condition our affairs stand. Two hostile armies, one towards Rome, the other towards Gaul, block our way. We cannot remain longer where we are, however much we may desire it, because of lack of grain and other necessities. Wherever we decide to go, we must hew a path with the sword. Therefore I counsel you to be brave and ready of spirit, and when you enter the battle to remember that you carry in your own right hands riches, honour, glory; yea, even freedom and your nature land. If we win, complete security will be ours, supplies will abound, free towns and colonies will open their gates; but if we yield to fear, the very reverse will be true: no place and no friend will guard the man whom arms could not protect. Moreover, soldiers, we and our opponents are not facing the same exigency. We are battling for country, for freedom, for life; theirs is a futile contest, to uphold the power of a few men. March on, therefore, with the greater courage, mindful of your former valour.

"You might have passed your life in exile and in utter infamy, at Rome some of you might look to others for aid after losing your estates; but since such conditions seemed base and intolerable to true men, you decided upon this course. If you wish to forsake it, you have need of boldness; none save the victor exchanges war for peace. To hope for safety in flight when you have turned away from the enemy the arms which should protect your body, is surely the height of madness. In battle the greatest danger always threatens those who show the greatest fear; boldness is a breastwork.

"When I think on you, my soldiers, and weigh your deeds, I have high hopes of victory. Your spirit, youth, and valour give me heart, not to mention necessity, which makes even the timid brave. In this narrow defile the superior numbers of the enemy cannot surround us. But if Fortune frowns upon your bravery, take care not to die unavenged. Do not be captured and slaughtered like cattle, but, fighting like heroes, leave the enemy a bloody and tearful victory."

[59]

WHEN he had thus spoken, after a brief pause he ordered the trumpets to sound and led his army in order of battle down into the plain. Then, after sending away all the horses, in order to make the danger equal for all and thus to increase the soldiers' courage, himself on foot like the rest he drew up the army as the situation and his numbers demanded. Since, namely, the plain was shut in on the left by mountains and on the right by rough, rocky ground, he posted eight cohorts in front and held the rest in reserve in closer order. From these he took the centurions, all picked men and reservists, as well as the best armed of the ordinary soldiers, and placed them in the front rank. He gave the charge of the right wing to Gaius Manlius, and that of the left to a man of Faesulae. He himself with his freedmen and the camp-servants took his place beside the eagle, which, it was said, had been in the army of Gaius Marius during the war with the Cimbri.

On the other side Gaius Antonius, who was ill with the gout and unable to enter the battle, he trusted his army to Marcus Petreius, his lieutenant. Petreius placed in the van the veteran cohorts which he had enrolled because of the outbreak, and behind them the rest of his army in reserve. Riding up and down upon his horse, he addressed each his men by name, exhorted him, and begged him to remember that he was fighting against unarmed highwaymen in defense of his country, his children, his altars, and his hearth. Being a man of military experience, who had served in the army with high distinction for more than thirty years as tribune, prefect, lieutenant, or commander, he personally knew the greater number of his soldiers and their valorous deeds of arms, and by mentioning these he fired the spirits of his men.

[60]

WHEN Petreius, after making all his preparations, gave the signal with the trumpet, he ordered his cohorts to advance slowly; the army of the enemy followed their example. After they had reached a point where battle could be joined by the skirmishers, the hostile armies rushed upon each other with loud shouts, then threw down their pikes and took to the sword. The veterans, recalling their old-time prowess, advanced bravely to close quarters; the enemy, not lacking in courage, stood their ground, and there was a terrific struggle. Meanwhile Catiline, with his light-armed troops, was busy in the van, aided those who were hard pressed, summoned fresh troops to replace the wounded, had an eye to everything, and at the same time fought hard himself, often striking down the foe—thus performing at once the duties of a valiant soldier and of a skillful leader.

When Petreius saw that Catiline was making so much stronger a fight than he had expected, he led his praetorian cohort against the enemy's centre, threw them into confusion, and slew those who resisted in various parts of the field; then he attacked the rest on both flanks at once. Manlius and the man from Faesulae were among the first to fall, sword in hand. When Catiline saw that his army was routed and that he was left with a mere handful of men, mindful of his birth and former rank he plunged into the thickest of the enemy and there fell fighting, his body pierced through and through.

[61]

WHEN the battle was ended it became evident what boldness and resolution had pervaded Catiline's army. For almost every man covered with his body, when life was gone, the position which he had taken when alive at the beginning of the conflict. A few, indeed, in the centre, whom the praetorian cohort had scattered, lay a little apart from the rest, but the wounds even of these were in front. But Catiline was found far in advance of his men amid a heap of slain foemen, still breathing slightly, and showing in his face the indomitable spirit which had animated him when alive. Finally, out of the whole army not a single citizen of free birth was taken during the battle or in flight, showing that all had valued their own lives no more highly than those of their enemies.

But the army of the Roman people gained no joyful nor bloodless victory, for all the most valiant had either fallen in the fight or come off with severe wounds. Many, too, who had gone from the camp to visit the field or to pillage, on turning over the body of the rebels found now a friend, now a guest or kinsman; some also recognised their personal enemies. Thus the whole army was variously affected with sorrow and grief, rejoicing and lamentation.

JULIUS CAESAR

The Gallic Wars

Julius Caesar

Translated by W. A. McDevitte and W. S. Bohn

Book I

1

ALL Gaul is divided into three parts, one of which the Belgae inhabit, the Aquitani another, those who in their own language are called Celts, in our Gauls, the third. All these differ from each other in language, customs and laws. The river Garonne separates the Gauls from the Aquitani; the Marne and the Seine separate them from the Belgae. Of all these, the Belgae are the bravest, because they are furthest from the civilization and refinement of [our] Province, and merchants least frequently resort to them, and import those things which tend to effeminate the mind; and they are the nearest to the Germans, who dwell beyond the Rhine, with whom they are continually waging war; for which reason the Helvetii also surpass the rest of the Gauls in valor, as they contend with the Germans in almost daily battles, when they either repel them from their own territories, or themselves wage war on their frontiers. One part of these, which it has been said that the Gauls occupy, takes its beginning at the river Rhone; it is bounded by the river Garonne, the ocean, and the territories of the Belgae; it borders, too, on the side of the Sequani and the Helvetii, upon the river Rhine, and stretches toward the north. The Belgae rises from the extreme frontier of Gaul, extend to the lower part of the river Rhine; and look toward the north and the rising sun. Aquitania extends from the river Garonne to the Pyrenaean mountains and to that part of the ocean which is near Spain: it looks between the setting of the sun, and the north star.

2

AMONG the Helvetii, Orgetorix was by far the most distinguished and wealthy. He, when Marcus Messala and Marcus Piso were consuls, incited by lust of sovereignty, formed a conspiracy among the nobility, and persuaded the people to go forth from their territories with all their possessions, [saying] that it would be very easy, since they excelled all in valor, to acquire the supremacy of the whole of Gaul. To this he the more easily persuaded them, because the Helvetii, are confined on every side by the nature of their situation; on one side by the Rhine, a very broad and deep river, which separates the Helvetian territory from the Germans; on a second side by the Jura, a very high mountain, which is [situated] between the Sequani and the Helvetii; on a third by the Lake of Geneva, and by the river Rhone, which separates our Province from the Helvetii. From these circumstances it resulted, that they could range less widely, and could less easily make war upon their neighbors; for which reason men fond of war [as they were] were affected with great regret. They thought, that considering the extent of their population, and their renown for warfare and bravery, they had but narrow limits, although they extended in length 240, and in breadth 180 [Roman] miles.

3

INDUCED by these considerations, and influenced by the authority of Orgetorix, they determined to provide such things as were necessary for their expedition—to buy up as great a number as possible of beasts of burden and wagons—to make their sowings as large as possible, so that on their march plenty of corn might be in store—and to establish peace and friendship with the neighboring states. They reckoned that a term of two years would be sufficient for them to execute their designs; they fix by decree their departure for the third year. Orgetorix is chosen to complete these arrangements. He took upon himself the office of ambassador to the states: on this journey he persuades Casticus, the son of Catamantaledes (one of the Sequani, whose father had possessed the sovereignty among the people for many years, and had been styled "friend" by the senate of the Roman people), to seize upon the sovereignty in his own state, which his father had held before him, and he likewise persuades Dumnorix, an Aeduan, the brother of Divitiacus, who at that time possessed the chief authority in the state, and was exceedingly beloved by the people, to attempt the same, and gives him his daughter in marriage. He proves to them that to accomplish their attempts was a thing very easy to be done, because he himself would obtain the government of his own state; that there was no doubt that the Helvetii were the most powerful of the whole of Gaul; he assures them that he will, with his own forces and his own army, acquire the sovereignty for them. Incited by this speech, they give a pledge and oath to one another, and hope that, when they have seized the sovereignty, they will, by means of the three most powerful and valiant nations, be enabled to obtain possession of the whole of Gaul.

4

WHEN this scheme was disclosed to the Helvetii by informers, they, according to their custom, compelled Orgetorix to plead his cause in chains; it was the law that the penalty of being burned by fire should await him if condemned. On the day appointed for the pleading of his cause, Orgetorix drew together from all quarters to the court, all his vassals to the number of ten thousand persons; and led together to the same place all his dependents and debtor-bondsmen, of whom he had a great number; by means of those he rescued himself from [the necessity of] pleading his cause. While the state, incensed at this act, was endeavoring to assert its right by arms, and the magistrates were mustering a large body of men from the country, Orgetorix died; and there is not wanting a suspicion, as the Helvetii think, of his having committed suicide.

5

AFTER his death, the Helvetii nevertheless attempt to do that which they had resolved on, namely, to go forth from their territories. When they thought that they were at length prepared for this undertaking, they set fire to all their towns, in number about twelve—to their villages about four hundred—and to the private dwellings that remained; they burn up all the corn, except what they intend to carry with them; that after destroying the hope of a return home, they might be the more ready for undergoing all dangers. They order every one to carry forth from home for himself provisions for three months, ready ground. They persuade the Rauraci, and the Tulingi, and the Latobrigi, their neighbors, to adopt the same plan, and after burning down their towns and villages, to set out with them: and they admit to their party and unite to themselves as confederates the Boii, who had dwelt on the other side of the Rhine, and had crossed over into the Norican territory, and assaulted Noreia.

6

THERE were in all two routes, by which they could go forth from their country one through the Sequani narrow and difficult, between Mount Jura and the river Rhone (by which scarcely one wagon at a time could be led; there was, moreover, a very high mountain overhanging, so that a very few might easily intercept them; the other, through our Province, much easier and freer from obstacles, because the Rhone flows between the boundaries of the Helvetii and those of the Allobroges, who had lately been subdued, and is in some places crossed by a ford. The furthest town of the Allobroges, and the nearest to the territories of the Helvetii, is Geneva. From this town a bridge extends to the Helvetii. They thought that they should either persuade the Allobroges, because they did not seem as yet well-affected toward the Roman people, or compel them by force to allow them to pass through their territories. Having provided every thing for the expedition, they appoint a day, on which they should all meet on the bank of the Rhone. This day was the fifth before the kalends of April [i.e. the 28th of March], in the consulship of Lucius Piso and Aulus Gabinius [B.C. 58].

7

WHEN it was reported to Caesar that they were attempting to make their route through our Province he hastens to set out from the city, and, by as great marches as he can, proceeds to Further Gaul, and arrives at Geneva. He orders the whole Province [to furnish] as great a number of soldiers as possible, as there was in all only one legion in Further Gaul: he orders the bridge at Geneva to be broken down. When the Helvetii are apprised of his arrival they send to him, as ambassadors, the most illustrious men of their state (in which embassy Numeius and Verudoctius held the chief place), to say "that it was their intention to march through the Province without doing any harm, because they had" [according to their own representations,] "no other route: that they requested, they might be allowed to do so with his consent." Caesar, inasmuch as he kept in remembrance that Lucius Cassius, the consul, had been slain, and his army routed and made to pass under the yoke by the Helvetii, did not think that [their request] ought to be granted: nor was he of opinion that men of hostile disposition, if an opportunity of marching through the Province were given them, would abstain from outrage and mischief. Yet, in order that a period might intervene, until the soldiers whom he had ordered [to be furnished] should assemble, he replied to the ambassadors, that he would take time to deliberate; if they wanted any thing, they might return on the day before the ides of April [on April 12th].

8

MEANWHILE, with the legion which he had with him and the soldiers which had assembled from the Province, he carries along for nineteen [Roman, not quite eighteen English] miles a wall, to the height of sixteen feet, and a trench, from the Lake of Geneva, which flows into the river Rhone, to Mount Jura, which separates the territories of the Sequani from those of the Helvetii. When that work was finished, he distributes garrisons, and closely fortifies redoubts, in order that he may the more easily intercept them, if they should attempt to cross over against his will. When the day which he had appointed with the ambassadors came, and they returned to him; he says, that he can not, consistently with the custom and precedent of the Roman people, grant any one a passage through the Province; and he gives them to understand, that, if they should attempt to use violence he would oppose them. The Helvetii, disappointed in this hope, tried if they could force a passage (some by means of a bridge of boats and numerous rafts constructed for the purpose; others, by the fords of the Rhone, where the depth of the river was least, sometimes by day, but more frequently by night), but being kept at bay by the strength of our works, and by the concourse of the soldiers, and by the missiles, they desisted from this attempt.

9

THERE was left one way, [namely] through the Sequani, by which, on account of its narrowness, they could not pass without the consent of the Sequani. As they could not of themselves prevail on them, they send ambassadors to Dumnorix the Aeduan, that through his intercession, they might obtain their request from the Sequani. Dumnorix, by his popularity and liberality, had great influence among the Sequani, and was friendly to the Helvetii, because out of that state he had married the daughter of Orgetorix; and, incited by lust of sovereignty, was anxious for a revolution, and wished to have as many states as possible attached to him by his kindness toward them. He, therefore, undertakes the affair, and prevails upon the Sequani to allow the Helvetii to march through their territories, and arranges that they should give hostages to each other—the Sequani not to obstruct the Helvetii in their march—the Helvetii, to pass without mischief and outrage.

10

IT is again told Caesar, that the Helvetii intended to march through the country of the Sequani and the Aedui into the territories of the Santones, which are not far distant from those boundaries of the Tolosates, which [viz. Tolosa, Toulouse] is a state in the Province. If this took place, he saw that it would be attended with great danger to the Province to have warlike men, enemies of the Roman people, bordering upon an open and very fertile tract of country. For these reasons he appointed Titus Labienus, his lieutenant, to the command of the fortification which he had made. He himself proceeds to Italy by forced marches, and there levies two legions, and leads out from winter-quarters three which were wintering around Aquileia, and with these five legions marches rapidly by the nearest route across the Alps into Further Gaul. Here the Centrones and the Graioceli and the Caturiges, having taken possession of the higher parts, attempt to obstruct the army in their march. After having routed these in several battles, he arrives in the territories of the Vocontii in the Further Province on the seventh day from Ocelum, which is the most remote town of the Hither Province; thence he leads his army into the country of the Allobroges, and from the Allobroges to the Segusiani. These people are the first beyond the Province on the opposite side of the Rhone.

11

THE Helvetii had by this time led their forces over through the narrow defile and the territories of the Sequani, and had arrived at the territories of the Aedui, and were ravaging their lands. The Aedui, as they could not defend themselves and their possessions against them, send ambassadors to Caesar to ask assistance, [pleading] that they had at all times so well deserved of the Roman people, that their fields ought not to have been laid waste—their children carried off into slavery—their towns stormed, almost within sight of our army. At the same time the Ambarri, the friends and kinsmen of the Aedui, apprize Caesar, that it was not easy for them, now that their fields had been devastated, to ward off the violence of the enemy from their towns: the Allobroges likewise, who had villages and possessions on the other side of the Rhone, betake themselves in flight to Caesar, and assure him that they had nothing remaining, except the soil of their land. Caesar, induced by these circumstances, decides, that he ought not to wait until the Helvetii, after destroying all the property of his allies, should arrive among the Santones.

12

THERE is a river [called] the Saone, which flows through the territories of the Aedui and Sequani into the Rhone with such incredible slowness, that it can not be determined by the eye in which direction it flows. This the Helvetii were crossing by rafts and boats joined together. When Caesar was informed by spies that the Helvetii had already conveyed three parts of their forces across that river, but that the fourth part was left behind on this side of the Saone, he set out from the camp with three legions during the third watch, and came up with that division which had not yet crossed the river. Attacking them encumbered with baggage, and not expecting him, he cut to pieces a great part of them; the rest betook themselves to flight, and concealed themselves in the nearest woods. That canton [which was cut down] was called the Tigurine; for the whole Helvetian state is divided into four cantons. This single canton having left their country, within the recollection of our fathers, had slain Lucius Cassius the consul, and had made his army pass under the yoke. Thus, whether by chance, or by the design of the immortal gods, that part of the Helvetian state which had brought a signal calamity upon the Roman people, was the first to pay the penalty. In this Caesar avenged not only the public but also his own personal wrongs, because the Tigurini had slain Lucius Piso the lieutenant [of Cassius], the grandfather of Lucius Calpurnius Piso, his [Caesar's] father-in-law, in the same battle as Cassius himself.

13

THIS battle ended, that he might be able to come up with the remaining forces of the Helvetii, he procures a bridge to be made across the Saone, and thus leads his army over. The Helvetii, confused by his sudden arrival, when they found that he had effected in one day, what they, themselves had with the utmost difficulty accomplished in twenty namely, the crossing of the river, send ambassadors to him; at the head of which embassy was Divico, who had been commander of the Helvetii, in the war against Cassius. He thus treats with Caesar: that, "if the Roman people would make peace with the Helvetii they would go to that part and there remain, where Caesar might appoint and desire them to be; but if he should persist in persecuting them with war that he ought to remember both the ancient disgrace of the Roman people and the characteristic valor of the Helvetii. As to his having attacked one canton by surprise, [at a time] when those who had crossed the river could not bring assistance to their friends, that he ought not on that account to ascribe very much to his own valor, or despise them; that they had so learned from their sires and ancestors, as to rely more on valor than on artifice and stratagem. Wherefore let him not bring it to pass that the place, where they were standing, should acquire a name, from the disaster of the Roman people and the destruction of their army or transmit the remembrance [of such an event to posterity]."

14

TO these words Caesar thus replied that "on that very account he felt less hesitation, because he kept in remembrance those circumstances which the Helvetian ambassadors had mentioned, and that he felt the more indignant at them, in proportion as they had happened undeservedly to the Roman people: for if they had been conscious of having done any wrong, it would not have been difficult to be on their guard, but for that very reason had they been deceived, because neither were they aware that any offense had been given by them, on account of which they should be afraid, nor did they think that they ought to be afraid without cause. But even if he were willing to forget their former outrage, could he also lay aside the remembrance of the late wrongs, in that they had against his will attempted a route through the Province by force, in that they had molested the Aedui, the Ambarri, and the Allobroges? That as to their so insolently boasting of their victory, and as to their being astonished that they had so long committed their outrages with impunity, [both these things] tended to the same point; for the immortal gods are wont to allow those persons whom they wish to punish for their guilt sometimes a greater prosperity and longer impunity, in order that they may suffer the more severely from a reverse of circumstances. Although these things are so, yet, if hostages were to be given him by them in order that he may be assured these will do what they promise, and provided they will give satisfaction to the Aedui for the outrages which they had committed against them and their allies, and likewise to the Allobroges, he [Caesar] will make peace with them." Divico replied, that "the Helvetii had been so trained by their ancestors, that they were accustomed to receive, not to give hostages; of that fact the Roman people were witness." Having given this reply, he withdrew.

15

ON the following day they move their camp from that place; Caesar does the same, and sends forward all his cavalry, to the number of four thousand (which he had drawn together from all parts of the Province and from the Aedui and their allies), to observe toward what parts the enemy are directing their march. These, having too eagerly pursued the enemy's rear, come to a battle with the cavalry of the Helvetii in a disadvantageous place, and a few of our men fall. The Helvetii, elated with this battle, because they had with five hundred horse repulsed so large a body of horse, began to face us more boldly, sometimes too from their rear to provoke our men by an attack. Caesar [however] restrained his men from battle, deeming it sufficient for the present to prevent the enemy from rapine, forage, and depredation. They marched for about fifteen days in such a manner that there was not more than five or six miles between the enemy's rear and our van.

16

MEANWHILE, Caesar kept daily importuning the Aedui for the corn which they had promised in the name of their state; for, in consequence of the coldness (Gaul, being as before said, situated toward the north), not only was the corn in the fields not ripe, but there was not in store a sufficiently large quantity even of fodder: besides he was unable to use the corn which he had conveyed in ships up the river Saone, because the Helvetii, from whom he was unwilling to retire had diverted their march from the Saone. The Aedui kept deferring from day to day, and saying that it was being collected—brought in—on the road." When he saw that he was put off too long, and that the day was close at hand on which he ought to serve out the corn to his soldiers;—having called together their chiefs, of whom he had a great number in his camp, among them Divitiacus and Liscus who was invested with the chief magistracy (whom the Aedui style the Vergobretus, and who is elected annually and has power of life or death over his countrymen), he severely reprimands them, because he is not assisted by them on so urgent an occasion, when the enemy were so close at hand, and when [corn] could neither be bought nor taken from the fields, particularly as, in a great measure urged by their prayers, he had undertaken the war; much more bitterly, therefore does he complain of his being forsaken.

17

THEN at length Liscus, moved by Caesar's speech, discloses what he had hitherto kept secret: that there are some whose influences with the people is very great, who, though private men, have more power than the magistrates themselves: that these by seditions and violent language are deterring the populace from contributing the corn which they ought to supply; [by telling them] that, if they can not any longer retain the supremacy of Gaul, it were better to submit to the government of Gauls than of Romans, nor ought they to doubt that, if the Romans should overpower the Helvetii, they would wrest their freedom from the Aedui together with the remainder of Gaul. By these very men, [said he], are our plans and whatever is done in the camp, disclosed to the enemy; that they could not be restrained by him: nay more, he was well aware, that though compelled by necessity, he had disclosed the matter to Caesar, at how great a risk he had done it; and for that reason, he had been silent as long as he could."

18

CAESAR perceived that by this speech of Liscus, Dumnorix, the brother of Divitiacus, was indicated; but, as he was unwilling that these matters should be discussed while so many were present, he speedily dismisses: the council, but detains Liscus: he inquires from him when alone, about those things which he had said in the meeting. He [Liscus] speaks more unreservedly and boldly. He [Caesar] makes inquiries on the same points privately of others, and discovered that it is all true; that "Dumnorix is the person, a man of the highest daring, in great favor with the people on account of his liberality, a man eager for a revolution: that for a great many years he has been in the habit of contracting for the customs and all the other taxes of the Aedui at a small cost, because when he bids, no one dares to bid against him. By these means he has both increased his own private property, and amassed great means for giving largesses; that he maintains constantly at his own expense and keeps about his own person a great number of cavalry, and that not only at home, but even among the neighboring states, he has great influence, and for the sake of strengthening this influence has given his mother in marriage among the Bituriges to a man the most noble and most influential there; that he has himself taken a wife from among the Helvetii, and has given his sister by the mother's side and his female relations in marriage into other states; that he favors and wishes well to the Helvetii on account of this connection; and that he hates Caesar and the Romans, on his own account, because by their arrival his power was weakened, and his brother, Divitiacus, restored to his former position of influence and dignity: that, if any thing should happen to the Romans, he entertains the highest hope of gaining the sovereignty by means of the Helvetii, but that under the government of the Roman people he despairs not only of royalty, but even of that influence which he already has." Caesar discovered too, on inquiring into the unsuccessful cavalry engagement which had taken place a few days before, that the commencement of that flight had been made by Dumnorix and his cavalry (for Dumnorix was in command of the cavalry which the Aedui had sent for aid to Caesar); that by their flight the rest of the cavalry were dismayed.

19

AFTER learning these circumstances, since to these suspicions the most unequivocal facts were added, viz., that he had led the Helvetii through the territories of the Sequani; that he had provided that hostages should be mutually given; that he had done all these things, not only without any orders of his [Caesar's] and of his own state's, but even without their [the Aedui] knowing any thing of it themselves; that he [Dumnorix] was reprimanded: by the [chief] magistrate of the Aedui; he [Caesar] considered that there was sufficient reason, why he should either punish him himself, or order the state to do so. One thing [however] stood in the way of all this—that he had learned by experience his brother Divitiacus's very high regard for the Roman people, his great affection toward him, his distinguished faithfulness, justice, and moderation; for he was afraid lest by the punishment of this man, he should hurt the feelings of Divitiacus. Therefore, before he attempted any thing, he orders Divitiacus to be summoned to him, and, when the ordinary interpreters had been withdrawn, converses with him through Caius Valerius Procillus, chief of the province of Gaul, an intimate friend of his, in whom he reposed the highest confidence in every thing; at the same time he reminds him of what was said about Dumnorix in the council of the Gauls, when he himself was present, and shows what each had said of him privately in his [Caesar's] own presence; he begs and exhorts him, that, without offense to his feelings, he may either himself pass judgment on him [Dumnorix] after trying the case, or else order the [Aeduan] state to do so.

20

DIVITIACUS, embracing Caesar, begins to implore him, with many tears, that "he would not pass any very severe sentence upon his brother; saying, that he knows that those charges are true, and that nobody suffered more pain on that account than he himself did; for when he himself could effect a very great deal by his influence at home and in the rest of Gaul, and he [Dumnorix] very little on account of his youth, the latter had become powerful through his means, which power and strength he used not only to the lessening of his [Divitiacus] popularity, but almost to his ruin; that he, however, was influenced both by fraternal affection and by public opinion. But if any thing very severe from Caesar should befall him [Dumnorix], no one would think that it had been done without his consent, since he himself held such a place in Caesar's friendship: from which circumstance it would arise, that the affections of the whole of Gaul would be estranged from him." As he was with tears begging these things of Caesar in many words, Caesar takes his right hand, and, comforting him, begs him to make an end of entreating, and assures him that his regard for him is so great, that he forgives both the injuries of the republic and his private wrongs, at his desire and prayers. He summons Dumnorix to him; he brings in his brother; he points out what he censures in him; he lays before him what he of himself perceives, and what the state complains of; he warns him for the future to avoid all grounds of suspicion; he says that he pardons the past, for the sake of his brother, Divitiacus. He sets spies over Dumnorix that he may be able to know what he does, and with whom he communicates.

21

BEING on the same day informed by his scouts, that the enemy had encamped at the foot of a mountain eight miles from his own camp; he sent persons to ascertain what the nature of the mountain was, and of what kind the ascent on every side. Word was brought back, that it was easy. During the third watch he orders Titus Labienus, his lieutenant with praetorian powers, to ascend to the highest ridge of the mountain with two legions, and with those as guides who had examined the road; he explains what his plan is. He himself during the fourth watch, hastens to them by the same route by which the enemy had gone, and sends on all the cavalry before him. Publius Considius, who was reputed to be very experienced in military affairs, and had been in the army of Lucius Sulla, and afterward in that of Marcus Crassus, is sent forward with the scouts.

Book IV

20

DURING the short part of summer which remained, Caesar, although in these countries, as all Gaul lies toward the north, the winters are early, nevertheless resolved to proceed into Britain, because he discovered that in almost all the wars with the Gauls succors had been furnished to our enemy from that country; and even if the time of year should be insufficient for carrying on the war, yet he thought it would be of great service to him if he only entered the island, and saw into the character of the people, and got knowledge of their localities, harbors, and landing-places, all which were for the most part unknown to the Gauls. For neither does any one except merchants generally go thither, nor even to them was any portion of it known, except the sea-coast and those parts which are opposite to Gaul. Therefore, after having called up to him the merchants from all parts, he could learn neither what was the size of the island, nor what or how numerous were the nations which inhabited it, nor what system of war they followed, nor what customs they used, nor what harbors were convenient for a great number of large ships.

21

HE sends before him Caius Volusenus with a ship of war, to acquire a knowledge of these particulars before he in person should make a descent into the island, as he was convinced that this was a judicious measure. He commissioned him to thoroughly examine into all matters, and then return to him as soon as possible. He himself proceeds to the Morini with all his forces. He orders ships from all parts of the neighboring countries, and the fleet which the preceding summer he had built for the war with the Veneti, to assemble in this place. In the mean time, his purpose having been discovered, and reported to the Britons by merchants, ambassadors come to him from several states of the island, to promise that they will give hostages, and submit to the government of the Roman people. Having given them an audience, he after promising liberally, and exhorting them to continue in that purpose, sends them back to their own country, and [dispatches] with them Commius, whom, upon subduing the Atrebates, he had created king there, a man whose courage and conduct he esteemed, and who he thought would be faithful to him, and whose influence ranked highly in those countries. He orders him to visit as many states as he could, and persuade them to embrace the protection of the Roman people, and apprise them that he would shortly come thither. Volusenus, having viewed the localities as far as means could be afforded one who dared not leave his ship and trust himself to barbarians, returns to Caesar on the fifth day, and reports what he had there observed.

22

WHILE Caesar remains in these parts for the purpose of procuring ships, ambassadors come to him from a great portion of the Morini, to plead their excuse respecting their conduct on the late occasion; alleging that it was as men uncivilized, and as those who were unacquainted with our custom, that they had made war upon the Roman people, and promising to perform what he should command. Caesar, thinking that this had happened fortunately enough for him, because he neither wished to leave an enemy behind him, nor had an opportunity for carrying on a war, by reason of the time of year, nor considered that employment in such trifling matters was to be preferred to his enterprise on Britain, imposes a large number of hostages; and when these were brought, he received them to his protection. Having collected together, and provided about eighty transport ships, as many as he thought necessary for conveying over two legions, he assigned such [ships] of war as he had besides to the quaestor, his lieutenants, and officers of cavalry. There were in addition to these eighteen ships of burden which were prevented, eight miles from that place, by winds, from being able to reach the same port. These he distributed among the horse; the rest of the army, he delivered to Q. Titurius Sabinus and L. Aurunculeius Cotta, his lieutenants, to lead into the territories of the Menapii and those cantons of the Morini from which ambassadors had not come to him. He ordered P. Sulpicius Rufus, his lieutenant, to hold possession of the harbor, with such a garrison as he thought sufficient.

23

THESE matters being arranged, finding the weather favorable for his voyage, he set sail about the third watch, and ordered the horse to march forward to the further port, and there embark and follow him. As this was performed rather tardily by them, he himself reached Britain with the first squadron of ships, about the fourth hour of the day, and there saw the forces of the enemy drawn up in arms on all the hills. The nature of the place was this: the sea was confined by mountains so close to it that a dart could be thrown from their summit upon the shore. Considering this by no means a fit place for disembarking, he remained at anchor till the ninth hour, for the other ships to arrive there. Having in the mean time assembled the lieutenants and military tribunes, he told them both what he had learned from Volusenus, and what he wished to be done; and enjoined them (as the principle of military matters, and especially as maritime affairs, which have a precipitate and uncertain action, required) that all things should be performed by them at a nod and at the instant. Having dismissed them, meeting both with wind and tide favorable at the same time, the signal being given and the anchor weighed, he advanced about seven miles from that place, and stationed his fleet over against an open and level shore.

24

BUT the barbarians, upon perceiving the design of the Romans, sent forward their cavalry and charioteers, a class of warriors of whom it is their practice to make great use in their battles, and following with the rest of their forces, endeavored to prevent our men landing. In this was the greatest difficulty, for the following reasons, namely, because our ships, on account of their great size, could be stationed only in deep water; and our soldiers, in places unknown to them, with their hands embarrassed, oppressed with a large and heavy weight of armor, had at the same time to leap from the ships, stand amid the waves, and encounter the enemy; whereas they, either on dry ground, or advancing a little way into the water, free in all their limbs in places thoroughly known to them, could confidently throw their weapons and spur on their horses, which were accustomed to this kind of service. Dismayed by these circumstances and altogether untrained in this mode of battle, our men did not all exert the same vigor and eagerness which they had been wont to exert in engagements on dry ground.

25

WHEN Caesar observed this, he ordered the ships of war, the appearance of which was somewhat strange to the barbarians and the motion more ready for service, to be withdrawn a little from the transport vessels, and to be propelled by their oars, and be stationed toward the open flank of the enemy, and the enemy to be beaten off and driven away, with slings, arrows, and engines: which plan was of great service to our men; for the barbarians being startled by the form of our ships and the motions of our oars and the nature of our engines, which was strange to them, stopped, and shortly after retreated a little. And while our men were hesitating [whether they should advance to the shore], chiefly on account of the depth of the sea, he who carried the eagle of the tenth legion, after supplicating the gods that the matter might turn out favorably to the legion, exclaimed, "Leap, fellow soldiers, unless you wish to betray your eagle to the enemy. I, for my part, will perform my duty to the commonwealth and my general." When he had said this with a loud voice, he leaped from the ship and proceeded to bear the eagle toward the enemy. Then our men, exhorting one another that so great a disgrace should not be incurred, all leaped from the ship. When those in the nearest vessels saw them, they speedily followed and approached the enemy.

26

THE battle was maintained vigorously on both sides. Our men, however, as they could neither keep their ranks, nor get firm footing, nor follow their standards, and as one from one ship and another from another assembled around whatever standards they met, were thrown into great confusion. But the enemy, who were acquainted with all the shallows, when from the shore they saw any coming from a ship one by one, spurred on their horses, and attacked them while embarrassed; many surrounded a few, others threw their weapons upon our collected forces on their exposed flank. When Caesar observed this, he ordered the boats of the ships of war and the spy sloops to be filled with soldiers, and sent them up to the succor of those whom he had observed in distress. Our men, as soon as they made good their footing on dry ground, and all their comrades had joined them, made an attack upon the enemy, and put them to flight, but could not pursue them very far, because the horse had not been able to maintain their course at sea and reach the island. This alone was wanting to Caesar's accustomed success.

27

THE enemy being thus vanquished in battle, as soon as they recovered after their flight, instantly sent ambassadors to Caesar to negotiate about peace. They promised to give hostages and perform what he should command. Together with these ambassadors came Commius the Altrebatian, who, as I have above said, had been sent by Caesar into Britain. Him they had seized upon when leaving his ship, although in the character of ambassador he bore the general's commission to them, and thrown into chains: then after the battle was fought, they sent him back, and in suing for peace cast the blame of that act upon the common people, and entreated that it might be pardoned on account of their indiscretion. Caesar, complaining, that after they had sued for peace, and had voluntarily sent ambassadors into the continent for that purpose, they had made war without a reason, said that he would pardon their indiscretion, and imposed hostages, a part of whom they gave immediately; the rest they said they would give in a few days, since they were sent for from remote places. In the mean time they ordered their people to return to the country parts, and the chiefs assembled from all quarter, and proceeded to surrender themselves and their states to Caesar.

28

A PEACE being established by these proceedings four days after we had come into Britain, the eighteen ships, to which reference has been made above, and which conveyed the cavalry, set sail from the upper port with a gentle gale, when, however, they were approaching Britain and were seen from the camp, so great a storm suddenly arose that none of them could maintain their course at sea; and some were taken back to the same port from which they had started; others, to their great danger, were driven to the lower part of the island, nearer to the west; which, however, after having cast anchor, as they were getting filled with water, put out to sea through necessity in a stormy night, and made for the continent.

29

IT happened that night to be full moon, which usually occasions very high tides in that ocean; and that circumstance was unknown to our men. Thus, at the same time, the tide began to fill the ships of war which Caesar had provided to convey over his army, and which he had drawn up on the strand; and the storm began to dash the ships of burden which were riding at anchor against each other; nor was any means afforded our men of either managing them or of rendering any service. A great many ships having been wrecked, inasmuch as the rest, having lost their cables, anchors, and other tackling, were unfit for sailing, a great confusion, as would necessarily happen, arose throughout the army; for there were no other ships in which they could be conveyed back, and all things which are of service in repairing vessels were wanting, and, corn for the winter had not been provided in those places, because it was understood by all that they would certainly winter in Gaul.

30

ON discovering these things the chiefs of Britain, who had come up after the battle was fought to perform those conditions which Caesar had imposed, held a conference, when they perceived that cavalry, and ships, and corn were wanting to the Romans, and discovered the small number of our soldiers from the small extent of the camp (which, too, was on this account more limited than ordinary, because Caesar had conveyed over his legions without baggage), and thought that the best plan was to renew the war, and cut off our men from corn and provisions and protract the affair till winter; because they felt confident, that, if they were vanquished or cut off from a return, no one would afterward pass over into Britain for the purpose of making war. Therefore, again entering into a conspiracy, they began to depart from the camp by degrees and secretly bring up their people from the country parts.

31

BUT Caesar, although he had not as yet discovered their measures, yet, both from what had occurred to his ships, and from the circumstance that they had neglected to give the promised hostages, suspected that the thing would come to pass which really did happen. He therefore provided remedies against all contingencies; for he daily conveyed corn from the country parts into the camp, used the timber and brass of such ships as were most seriously damaged for repairing the rest, and ordered whatever things besides were necessary for this object to be brought to him from the continent. And thus, since that business was executed by the soldiers with the greatest energy, he effected that, after the loss of twelve ships, a voyage could be made well enough in the rest.

32

WHILE these things are being transacted, one legion had been sent to forage, according to custom, and no suspicion of war had arisen as yet, and some of the people remained in the country parts, others went backward and forward to the camp, they who were on duty at the gates of the camp reported to Caesar that a greater dust than was usual was seen in that direction in which the legion had marched. Caesar, suspecting that which was [really the case]—that some new enterprise was undertaken by the barbarians—ordered the two cohorts which were on duty, to march into that quarter with him, and two other cohorts to relieve them on duty; the rest to be armed and follow him immediately. When he had advanced some little way from the camp, he saw that his men were overpowered by the enemy and scarcely able to stand their ground, and that, the legion being crowded together, weapons were being cast on them from all sides. For as all the corn was reaped in every part with the exception of one, the enemy, suspecting that our men would repair to that, had concealed themselves in the woods during the night. Then attacking them suddenly, scattered as they were, and when they had laid aside their arms, and were engaged in reaping, they killed a small number, threw the rest into confusion, and surrounded them with their cavalry and chariots.

33

THEIR mode of fighting with their chariots is this: firstly, they drive about in all directions and throw their weapons and generally break the ranks of the enemy with the very dread of their horses and the noise of their wheels; and when they have worked themselves in between the troops of horse, leap from their chariots and engage on foot. The charioteers in the mean time withdraw some little distance from the battle, and so place themselves with the chariots that, if their masters are overpowered by the number of the enemy, they may have a ready retreat to their own troops. Thus they display in battle the speed of horse, [together with] the firmness of infantry; and by daily practice and exercise attain to such expertness that they are accustomed, even on a declining and steep place, to check their horses at full speed, and manage and turn them in an instant and run along the pole, and stand on the yoke, and thence betake themselves with the greatest celerity to their chariots again.

34

UNDER these circumstances, our men being dismayed by the

novelty of this mode of battle, Caesar most seasonably brought assistance; for upon his arrival the enemy paused, and our men recovered from their fear; upon which thinking the time unfavorable for provoking the enemy and coming to an action, he kept himself in his own quarter, and, a short time having intervened, drew back the legions into the camp. While these things are going on, and all our men engaged, the rest of the Britons, who were in the fields, departed. Storms then set in for several successive days, which both confined our men to the camp and hindered the enemy from attacking us. In the mean time the barbarians dispatched messengers to all parts, and reported to their people the small number of our soldiers, and how good an opportunity was given for obtaining spoil and for liberating themselves forever, if they should only drive the Romans from their camp. Having by these means speedily got together a large force of infantry and of cavalry they came up to the camp.

35

ALTHOUGH Caesar anticipated that the same thing which had happened on former occasions would then occur—that, if the enemy were routed, they would escape from danger by their speed; still, having got about thirty horse, which Commius the Atrebatian, of whom mention has been made, had brought over with him [from Gaul], he drew up the legions in order of battle before the camp. When the action commenced, the enemy were unable to sustain the attack of our men long, and turned their backs; our men pursued them as far as their speed and strength permitted, and slew a great number of them; then, having destroyed and burned every thing far and wide, they retreated to their camp.

36

THE same day, ambassadors sent by the enemy came to Caesar to negotiate a peace. Caesar doubled the number of hostages which he had before demanded; and ordered that they should be brought over to the continent, because, since the time of the equinox was near, he did not consider that, with his ships out of repair, the voyage ought to be deferred till winter. Having met with favorable weather, he set sail a little after midnight, and all his fleet arrived safe at the continent, except two of the ships of burden which could not make the same port which the other ships did, and were carried a little lower down.

37

WHEN our soldiers, about 300 in number, had been drawn out of these two ships, and were marching to the camp, the Morini, whom Caesar, when setting forth for Britain, had left in a state of peace, excited by the hope of spoil, at first surrounded them with a small number of men, and ordered them to lay down their arms, if they did not wish to be slain; afterward however, when they, forming a circle, stood on their defense, a shout was raised and about 6000 of the enemy soon assembled; which being reported, Caesar sent all the cavalry in the camp as a relief to his men. In the mean time our soldiers sustained the attack of the enemy, and fought most valiantly for more than four hours, and, receiving but few wounds themselves, slew several of them. But after our cavalry came in sight, the enemy, throwing away their arms, turned their backs, and a great number of them were killed.

38

THE day following Caesar sent Labienus, his lieutenant, with those legions which he had brought back from Britain, against the Morini, who had revolted; who, as they had no place to which they might retreat, on account of the drying up of their marshes (which they had availed themselves of as a place of refuge the preceding year), almost all fell into the power of Labienus. In the mean time Caesar's lieutenants, Q. Titurius and L. Cotta, who had led the legions into the territories of the Menapii, having laid waste all their lands, cut down their corn and burned their houses, returned to Caesar because the Menapii had all concealed themselves in their thickest woods. Caesar fixed the winter quarters of all the legions among the Belgae. Thither only two British states sent hostages; the rest omitted to do so. For these successes, a thanksgiving of twenty days was decreed by the senate upon receiving Caesar's letter.

Book V

1

LUCIUS Domitius and Appius Claudius being consuls, Caesar, when departing from his winter quarters into Italy, as he had been accustomed to do yearly, commands the lieutenants whom he appointed over the legions to take care that during the winter as many ships as possible should be built, and the old repaired. He plans the size and shape of them. For dispatch of lading, and for drawing them on shore, he makes them a little lower than those which we have been accustomed to use in our sea; and that so much the more, because he knew that, on account of the frequent changes of the tide, less swells occurred there; for the purpose of transporting burdens and a great number of horses, [he makes them] a little broader than those which we use in other seas. All these he orders to be constructed for lightness and expedition, to which object their lowness contributes greatly. He orders those things which are necessary for equipping ships to be brought thither from Spain. He himself, on the assizes of Hither Gaul being concluded, proceeds into Illyricum, because he heard that the part of the province nearest them was being laid waste by the incursions of the Pirustae. When he had arrived there, he levies soldiers upon the states, and orders them to assemble at an appointed place. Which circumstance having been reported [to them], the Pirustae send ambassadors to him to inform him that no part of those proceedings was done by public deliberation, and assert that they were ready to make compensation by all means for the injuries [inflicted]. Caesar, accepting their defense, demands hostages, and orders them to be brought to him on a specified day, and assures them that unless they did so he would visit their state with war. These being brought to him on the day which he had ordered, he appoints arbitrators between the states, who should estimate the damages and determine the reparation.

2

THESE things being finished, and the assizes being concluded, he returns into Hither Gaul, and proceeds thence to the army. When he had arrived there, having made a survey of the winter quarter, he finds that, by the extraordinary ardor of the soldiers, amid the utmost scarcity of all materials, about six hundred ships of that kind which we have described above and twenty-eight ships of war, had been built, and were not far from that state, that they might be launched in a few days. Having commended the soldiers and those who had presided over the work, he informs them what he wishes to be done, and orders all the ships to assemble at port Itius, from which port he had learned that the passage into Britain was shortest, [being only] about thirty miles from the continent. He left what seemed a sufficient number of soldiers for that design; he himself proceeds into the territories of the Treviri with four legions without baggage, and 800 horse, because they neither came to the general diets [of Gaul], nor obeyed his commands, and were moreover, said to be tampering with the Germans beyond the Rhine.

3

THIS state is by far the most powerful of all Gaul in cavalry, and has great forces of infantry, and as we have remarked above, borders on the Rhine. In that state, two persons, Indutiomarus and Cingetorix, were then contending with each other for the supreme power; one of whom, as soon as the arrival of Caesar and his legions was known, came to him; assures him that he and all his party would continue in their allegiance, and not revolt from the alliance of the Roman people, and informs him of the things which were going on among the Treviri. But Indutiomarus began to collect cavalry and infantry, and make preparations for war, having concealed those who by reason of their age could not be under arms, in the forest Arduenna, which is of immense size, [and] extends from the Rhine across the country of the Treviri to the frontiers of the Remi. But after that, some of the chief persons of the state, both influenced by their friendship for Cingetorix, and alarmed at the arrival of our army, came to Caesar and began to solicit him privately about their own interests, since they could not provide for the safety of the state; Indutiomarus, dreading lest he should be abandoned by all, sends ambassadors to Caesar, to declare that he absented himself from his countrymen, and refrained from coming to him on this account, that he might the more easily keep the state in its allegiance, lest on the departure of all the nobility the commonalty should, in their indiscretion, revolt. And thus the whole state was at his control; and that he, if Caesar would permit, would come to the camp to him, and would commit his own fortunes and those of the state to his good faith.

4

CAESAR, though he discerned from what motive these things were said, and what circumstances deterred him from his meditated plan, still, in order that he might not be compelled to waste the summer among the Treviri, while all things were prepared for the war with Britain, ordered Indutiomarus to come to him with 200 hostages. When they were brought, [and] among them his son and near relations, whom he had demanded by name, he consoled Indutiomarus, and enjoined him to continue in his allegiance; yet, nevertheless, summoning to him the chief men of the Treviri, he reconciled them individually to Cingetorix: this he both thought should be done by him in justice to the merits of the latter, and also judged that it was of great importance that the influence of one whose singular attachment toward him he had fully seen, should prevail as much as possible among his people. Indutiomarus was very much offended at this act, [seeing that] his influence was diminished among his countrymen; and he, who already before had borne a hostile mind toward us, was much more violently inflamed against us through resentment at this.

5

THESE matters being settled, Caesar went to port Itius with the legions. There he discovers that forty ships, which had been built in the country of the Meldi, having been driven back by a storm, had been unable to maintain their course, and had returned to the same port from which they had set out; he finds the rest ready for sailing, and furnished with every thing. In the same place, the cavalry of the whole of Gaul, in number 4,000, assembles, and [also] the chief persons of all the states; he had determined to leave in Gaul a very few of them, whose fidelity toward him he had clearly discerned, and take the rest with him as hostages; because he feared a commotion in Gaul when he should be absent.

6

THERE was together with the others, Dumnorix, the Aeduan, of whom we have made previous mention. Him, in particular, he had resolved to have with him, because he had discovered him to be fond of change, fond of power, possessing great resolution, and great influence among the Gauls. To this was added, that Dumnorix had before said in an assembly of Aeduans, that the sovereignty of the state had been made over to him by Caesar; which speech the Aedui bore with impatience and yet dared not send ambassadors to Caesar for the purpose of either rejecting or deprecating [that appointment]. That fact Caesar had learned from his own personal friends. He at first strove to obtain by every entreaty that he should be left in Gaul; partly, because, being unaccustomed to sailing, he feared the sea; partly because he said he was prevented by divine admonitions. After he saw that this request was firmly refused him, all hope of success being lost, he began to tamper with the chief persons of the Gauls, to call them apart singly and exhort them to remain on the continent; to agitate them with the fear that it was not without reason that Gaul should be stripped of all her nobility; that it was Caesar's design, to bring over to Britain and put to death all those whom he feared to slay in the sight of Gaul, to pledge his honor to the rest, to ask for their oath that they would by common deliberation execute what they should perceive to be necessary for Gaul. These things were reported to Caesar by several persons.

7

HAVING learned this fact, Caesar, because he had conferred so much honor upon the Aeduan state, determined that Dumnorix should be restrained and deterred by whatever means he could; and that, because he perceived his insane designs to be proceeding further and further, care should be taken lest he might be able to injure him and the commonwealth. Therefore, having stayed about twenty-five days in that place, because the north wind, which usually blows a great part of every season, prevented the voyage, he exerted himself to keep Dumnorix in his allegiance [and] nevertheless learn all his measures: having at length met with favorable weather, he orders the foot soldiers and the horse to embark in the ships. But, while the minds of all were occupied, Dumnorix began to take his departure from the camp homeward with the cavalry of the Aedui, Caesar being ignorant of it. Caesar, on this matter being reported to him, ceasing from his expedition and deferring all other affairs, sends a great part of the cavalry to pursue him, and commands that he be brought back; he orders that if he use violence and do not submit, that he be slain; considering that Dumnorix would do nothing as a rational man while he himself was absent, since he had disregarded his command even when present. He, however, when recalled, began to resist and defend himself with his hand, and implore the support of his people, often exclaiming that "he was free and the subject of a free state." They surround and kill the man as they had been commanded; but the Aeduan horsemen all return to Caesar.

8

WHEN these things were done [and] Labienus, left on the continent with three legions and 2,000 horse, to defend the harbors and provide corn, and discover what was going on in Gaul, and take measures according to the occasion and according to the circumstance; he himself, with five legions and a number of horse, equal to that which he was leaving on the continent, set sail at sun-set, and [though for a time] borne forward by a gentle south-west wind, he did not maintain his course, in consequence of the wind dying away about midnight, and being carried on too far by the tide, when the sun rose, espied Britain passed on his left. Then, again, following the change of tide, he urged on with the oars that he might make that part of the island in which he had discovered the preceding summer, that there was the best landing-place, and in this affair the spirit of our soldiers was very much to be extolled; for they with the transports and heavy ships, the labor of rowing not being [for a moment] discontinued, equaled the speed of the ships of war. All the ships reached Britain nearly at midday; nor was there seen a [single] enemy in that place, but, as Caesar afterward found from some prisoners, though large bodies of troops had assembled there, yet being alarmed by the great number of our ships, more than eight hundred of which, including the ships of the preceding year, and those private vessels which each had built for his own convenience, had appeared at one time, they had quitted the coast and concealed themselves among the higher points.

9

CAESAR, having disembarked his army and chosen a convenient place for the camp, when he discovered from the prisoners in what part the forces of the enemy had lodged themselves, having left ten cohorts and 300 horse at the sea, to be a guard to the ships, hastens to the enemy, at the third watch, fearing the less for the ships, for this reason because he was leaving them fastened at anchor upon an even and open shore; and he placed Q. Atrius over the guard of the ships. He himself, having advanced by night about twelve miles, espied the forces of the enemy. They, advancing to the river with their cavalry and chariots from the higher ground, began to annoy our men and give battle. Being repulsed by our cavalry, they concealed themselves in woods, as they had secured a place admirably fortified by nature and by art, which, as it seemed, they had before prepared on account of a civil war; for all entrances to it were shut up by a great number of felled trees. They themselves rushed out of the woods to fight here and there, and prevented our men from entering their fortifications. But the soldiers of the seventh legion, having formed a testudo and thrown up a rampart against the fortification, took the place and drove them out of the woods, receiving only a few wounds. But Caesar forbade his men to pursue them in their flight any great distance; both because he was ignorant of the nature of the ground, and because, as a great part of the day was spent, he wished time to be left for the fortification of the camp.

10

THE next day, early in the morning, he sent both foot-soldiers and horse in three divisions on an expedition to pursue those who had fled. These having advanced a little way, when already the rear [of the enemy] was in sight, some horse came to Caesar from Quintus Atrius, to report that the preceding night, a very great storm having arisen, almost all the ships were dashed to pieces and cast upon the shore, because neither the anchors and cables could resist, nor could the sailors and pilots sustain the violence of the storm; and thus great damage was received by that collision of the ships.

11

THESE things being known [to him], Caesar orders the legions and cavalry to be recalled and to cease from their march; he himself returns to the ships: he sees clearly before him almost the same things which he had heard of from the messengers and by letter, so that, about forty ships being lost, the remainder seemed capable of being repaired with much labor. Therefore he selects workmen from the legions, and orders others to be sent for from the continent; he writes to Labienus to build as many ships as he could with those legions which were with him. He himself, though the matter was one of great difficulty and labor, yet thought it to be most expedient for all the ships to be brought up on shore and joined with the camp by one fortification. In these matters he employed about ten days, the labor of the soldiers being unremitting even during the hours of night. The ships having been brought up on shore and the camp strongly fortified, he left the same forces as he did before as a guard for the ships; he sets out in person for the same place that he had returned from. When he had come thither, greater forces of the Britons had already assembled at that place, the chief command and management of the war having been entrusted to Cassivellaunus, whose territories a river, which is called the Thames, separates, from the maritime states at about eighty miles from the sea. At an earlier period perpetual wars had taken place between him and the other states; but, greatly alarmed by our arrival, the Britons had placed him over the whole war and the conduct of it.

12

THE interior portion of Britain is inhabited by those of whom they say that it is handed down by tradition that they were born in the island itself: the maritime portion by those who had passed over from the country of the Belgae for the purpose of plunder and making war; almost all of whom are called by the names of those states from which being sprung they went thither, and having waged war, continued there and began to cultivate the lands. The number of the people is countless, and their buildings exceedingly numerous, for the most part very like those of the Gauls: the number of cattle is great. They use either brass or iron rings, determined at a certain weight, as their money. Tin is produced in the midland regions; in the maritime, iron; but the quantity of it is small: they employ brass, which is imported. There, as in Gaul, is timber of every description, except beech and fir. They do not regard it lawful to eat the hare, and the cock, and the goose; they, however, breed them for amusement and pleasure. The climate is more temperate than in Gaul, the colds being less severe.

13

THE island is triangular in its form, and one of its sides is opposite to Gaul. One angle of this side, which is in Kent, whither almost all ships from Gaul are directed, [looks] to the east; the lower looks to the south. This side extends about 500 miles. Another side lies toward Spain and the west, on which part is Ireland, less, as is reckoned, than Britain, by one half: but the passage [from it] into Britain is of equal distance with that from Gaul. In the middle of this voyage, is an island, which is called Mona: many smaller islands besides are supposed to lie [there], of which islands some have written that at the time of the winter solstice it is night there for thirty consecutive days. We, in our inquiries about that matter, ascertained nothing, except that, by accurate measurements with water, we perceived the nights to be shorter there than on the continent. The length of this side, as their account states, is 700 miles. The third side is toward the north, to which portion of the island no land is opposite; but an angle of that side looks principally toward Germany. This side is considered to be 800 miles in length. Thus the whole island is [about] 2,000 miles in circumference.

14

THE most civilized of all these nations are they who inhabit Kent, which is entirely a maritime district, nor do they differ much from the Gallic customs. Most of the inland inhabitants do not sow corn, but live on milk and flesh, and are clad with skins. All the Britains, indeed, dye themselves with wood, which occasions a bluish color, and thereby have a more terrible appearance in fight. They wear their hair long, and have every part of their body shaved except their head and upper lip. Ten and even twelve have wives common to them, and particularly brothers among brothers, and parents among their children; but if there be any issue by these wives, they are reputed to be the children of those by whom respectively each was first espoused when a virgin.

15

THE horse and charioteers of the enemy contended vigorously in a skirmish with our cavalry on the march; yet so that our men were conquerors in all parts, and drove them to their woods and hills; but, having slain a great many, they pursued too eagerly, and lost some of their men. But the enemy, after some time had elapsed, when our men were off their guard, and occupied in the fortification of the camp, rushed out of the woods, and making an attack upon those who were placed on duty before the camp, fought in a determined manner; and two cohorts being sent by Caesar to their relief, and these severally the first of two legions, when these had taken up their position at a very small distance from each other, as our men were disconcerted by the unusual mode of battle, the enemy broke through the middle of them most courageously, and retreated thence in safety. That day, Q. Laberius Durus, a tribune of the soldiers, was slain. The enemy, since more cohorts were sent against them, were repulsed.

16

IN the whole of this method of fighting since the engagement took place under the eyes of all and before the camp, it was perceived that our men, on account of the weight of their arms, inasmuch as they could neither pursue [the enemy when] retreating, nor dare quit their standards, were little suited to this kind of enemy; that the horse also fought with great danger, because they [the Britons] generally retreated even designedly, and, when they had drawn off our men a short distance from the legions, leaped from their chariots and fought on foot in unequal [and to them advantageous] battle. But the system of cavalry engagement is wont to produce equal danger, and indeed the same, both to those who retreat and to those who pursue. To this was added, that they never fought in close order, but in small parties and at great distances, and had detachments placed [in different parts], and then the one relieved the other, and the vigorous and fresh succeeded the wearied.

17

THE following day the enemy halted on the hills, a distance from our camp, and presented themselves in small parties, and began to challenge our horse to battle with less spirit than the day before. But at noon, when Caesar had sent three legions, and all the cavalry, with C. Trebonius, the lieutenant, for the purpose of foraging, they flew upon the foragers suddenly from all quarters, so that they did not keep off [even] from the standards and the legions. Our men making an attack on them vigorously, repulsed them; nor did they cease to pursue them until the horse, relying on relief, as they saw the legions behind them, drove the enemy precipitately before them, and slaying a great number of them, did not give them the opportunity either of rallying, or halting, or leaping from their chariots. Immediately after this retreat, the auxiliaries who had assembled from all sides, departed; nor after that time did the enemy ever engage with us in very large numbers.

18

CAESAR, discovering their design, leads his army into the territories of Cassivellaunus to the river Thames; which river can be forded in one place only and that with difficulty. When he had arrived there, he perceives that numerous forces of the enemy were marshaled on the other bank of the river; the bank also was defended by sharp stakes fixed in front, and stakes of the same kind fixed under the water were covered by the river. These things being discovered from [some] prisoners and deserters, Caesar, sending forward the cavalry, ordered the legions to follow them immediately. But the soldiers advanced with such speed and such ardor, though they stood above the water by their heads only, that the enemy could not sustain the attack of the legions and of the horse, and quitted the banks, and committed themselves to flight.

19

CASSIVELLAUNUS, as we have stated above, all hope [rising out] of battle being laid aside, the greater part of his forces being dismissed, and about 4,000 charioteers only being left, used to observe our marches and retire a little from the road, and conceal himself in intricate and woody places, and in those neighborhoods in which he had discovered we were about to march, he used to drive the cattle and the inhabitants from the fields into the woods; and, when our cavalry, for the sake of plundering and ravaging the more freely, scattered themselves among the fields, he used to send out charioteers from the woods by all the well-known roads and paths, and to the great danger of our horse, engage with them; and this source of fear hindered them from straggling very extensively. The result was, that Caesar did not allow excursions to be made to a great distance from the main body of the legions, and ordered that damage should be done to the enemy in ravaging their lands, and kindling fires only so far as the legionary soldiers could, by their own exertion and marching, accomplish it.

20

IN the meantime, the Trinobantes, almost the most powerful state of those parts, from which the young man, Mandubratius embracing the protection of Caesar had come to the continent of Gaul to [meet] him (whose father, Imanuentius, had possessed the sovereignty in that state, and had been killed by Cassivellaunus; he himself had escaped death by flight), send ambassadors to Caesar, and promise that they will surrender themselves to him and perform his commands; they entreat him to protect Mandubratius from the violence of Cassivellaunus, and send to their state some one to preside over it, and possess the government. Caesar demands forty hostages from them, and corn for his army, and sends Mandubratius to them. They speedily performed the things demanded, and sent hostages to the number appointed, and the corn.

21

THE Trinobantes being protected and secured from any violence of the soldiers, the Cenimagni, the Segontiaci, the Ancalites, the Bibroci, and the Cassi, sending embassies, surrendered themselves to Caesar. From them he learns that the capital town of Cassivellaunus was not far from that place, and was defended by woods and morasses, and a very large number of men and of cattle had been collected in it. (Now the Britons, when they have fortified the intricate woods, in which they are wont to assemble for the purpose of avoiding the incursion of an enemy, with an entrenchment and a rampart, call them a town.) Thither he proceeds with his legions: he finds the place admirably fortified by nature and art; he, however, undertakes to attack it in two directions. The enemy, having remained only a short time, did not sustain the attack of our soldiers, and hurried away on the other side of the town. A great amount of cattle was found there, and many of the enemy were taken and slain in their flight.

22

WHILE these things are going forward in those places, Cassivellaunus sends messengers into Kent, which, we have observed above, is on the sea, over which districts four several kings reigned, Cingetorix, Carvilius, Taximagulus and Segonax, and commands them to collect all their forces, and unexpectedly assail and storm the naval camp. When they had come to the camp, our men, after making a sally, slaying many of their men, and also capturing a distinguished leader named Lugotorix, brought back their own men in safety. Cassivellaunus, when this battle was reported to him as so many losses had been sustained, and his territories laid waste, being alarmed most of all by the desertion of the states, sends ambassadors to Caesar [to treat] about a surrender through the mediation of Commius the Atrebatian. Caesar, since he had determined to pass the winter on the continent, on account of the sudden revolts of Gaul, and as much of the summer did not remain, and he perceived that even that could be easily protracted, demands hostages, and prescribes what tribute Britain should pay each year to the Roman people; he forbids and commands Cassivellaunus that he wage not war against Mandubratius or the Trinobantes.

23

WHEN he had received the hostages, he leads back the army to the sea, and finds the ships repaired. After launching these, because he had a large number of prisoners, and some of the ships had been lost in the storm, he determines to convey back his army at two embarkations. And it so happened, that out of so large a number of ships, in so many voyages, neither in this nor in the previous year was any ship missing which conveyed soldiers; but very few out of those which were sent back to him from the continent empty, as the soldiers of the former convoy had been disembarked, and out of those (sixty in number) which Labienus had taken care to have built, reached their destination; almost all the rest were driven back, and when Caesar had waited for them for some time in vain, lest he should be debarred from a voyage by the season of the year, inasmuch as the equinox was at hand, he of necessity stowed his soldiers the more closely, and, a very great calm coming on, after he had weighed anchor at the beginning of the second watch, he reached land at break of day and brought in all the ships in safety.

Book VI

11

SINCE we have come to the place, it does not appear to be foreign to our subject to lay before the reader an account of the manners of Gaul and Germany, and wherein these nations differ from each other. In Gaul there are factions not only in all the states, and in all the cantons and their divisions, but almost in each family, and of these factions those are the leaders who are considered according to their judgment to possess the greatest influence, upon whose will and determination the management of all affairs and measures depends. And that seems to have been instituted in ancient times with this view, that no one of the common people should be in want of support against one more powerful; for, none [of those leaders] suffers his party to be oppressed and defrauded, and if he do otherwise, he has no influence among his party. This same policy exists throughout the whole of Gaul; for all the states are divided into two factions.

12

WHEN Caesar arrived in Gaul, the Aedui were the leaders of one faction, the Sequani of the other. Since the latter were less powerful by themselves, inasmuch as the chief influence was from of old among the Aedui, and their dependencies were great, they had united to themselves the Germans and Ariovistus, and had brought them over to their party by great sacrifices and promises. And having fought several successful battles and slain all the nobility of the Aedui, they had so far surpassed them in power, that they brought over, from the Aedui to themselves, a large portion of their dependents and received from them the sons of their leading men as hostages, and compelled them to swear in their public character that they would enter into no design against them; and held a portion of the neighboring land, seized on by force, and possessed the sovereignty of the whole of Gaul. Divitiacus urged by this necessity, had proceeded to Rome to the senate, for the purpose of entreating assistance, and had returned without accomplishing his object. A change of affairs ensued on the arrival of Caesar, the hostages were returned to the Aedui, their old dependencies restored, and new acquired through Caesar (because those who had attached themselves to their alliance saw that they enjoyed a better state and a milder government), their other interests, their influence, their reputation were likewise increased, and in consequence, the Sequani lost the sovereignty. The Remi succeeded to their place, and, as it was perceived that they equaled the Aedui in favor with Caesar, those, who on account of their old animosities could by no means coalesce with the Aedui, consigned themselves in clientship to the Remi. The latter carefully protected them. Thus they possessed both a new and suddenly acquired influence. Affairs were then in that position that the Aedui were considered by far the leading people, and the Remi held the second post of honor.

13

THROUGHOUT all Gaul there are two orders of those men who are of any rank and dignity: for the commonality is held almost in the condition of slaves, and dares to undertake nothing of itself, and is admitted to no deliberation. The greater part, when they are pressed either by debt, or the large amount of their tributes, or the oppression of the more powerful, give themselves up in vassalage to the nobles, who possess over them the same rights without exception as masters over their slaves. But of these two orders, one is that of the Druids, the other that of the knights. The former are engaged in things sacred, conduct the public and the private sacrifices, and interpret all matters of religion. To these a large number of the young men resort for the purpose of instruction, and they [the Druids] are in great honor among them. For they determine respecting almost all controversies, public and private; and if any crime has been perpetrated, if murder has been committed, if there be any dispute about an inheritance, if any about boundaries, these same persons decide it; they decree rewards and punishments; if any one, either in a private or public capacity, has not submitted to their decision, they interdict him from the sacrifices. This among them is the most heavy punishment. Those who have been thus interdicted are esteemed in the number of the impious and the criminal: all shun them, and avoid their society and conversation, lest they receive some evil from their contact; nor is justice administered to them when seeking it, nor is any dignity bestowed on them. Over all these Druids one presides, who possesses supreme authority among them. Upon his death, if any individual among the rest is preeminent in dignity, he succeeds; but, if there are many equal, the election is made by the suffrages of the Druids; sometimes they even contend for the presidency with arms. These assemble at a fixed period of the year in a consecrated place in the territories of the Carnutes, which is reckoned the central region of the whole of Gaul. Hither all, who have disputes, assemble from every part, and submit to their decrees and determinations. This institution is supposed to have been devised in Britain, and to have been brought over from it into Gaul; and now those who desire to gain a more accurate knowledge of that system generally proceed thither for the purpose of studying it.

14

THE Druids do not go to war, nor pay tribute together with the rest; they have an exemption from military service and a dispensation in all matters. Induced by such great advantages, many embrace this profession of their own accord, and [many] are sent to it by their parents and relations. They are said there to learn by heart a great number of verses; accordingly some remain in the course of training twenty years. Nor do they regard it lawful to commit these to writing, though in almost all other matters, in their public and private transactions, they use Greek characters. That practice they seem to me to have adopted for two reasons; because they neither desire their doctrines to be divulged among the mass of the people, nor those who learn, to devote themselves the less to the efforts of memory, relying on writing; since it generally occurs to most men, that, in their dependence on writing, they relax their diligence in learning thoroughly, and their employment of the memory. They wish to inculcate this as one of their leading tenets, that souls do not become extinct, but pass after death from one body to another, and they think that men by this tenet are in a great degree excited to valor, the fear of death being disregarded. They likewise discuss and impart to the youth many things respecting the stars and their motion, respecting the extent of the world and of our earth, respecting the nature of things, respecting the power and the majesty of the immortal gods.

15

THE other order is that of the knights. These, when there is occasion and any war occurs (which before Caesar's arrival was for the most part wont to happen every year, as either they on their part were inflecting injuries or repelling those which others inflected on them), are all engaged in war. And those of them most distinguished by birth and resources, have the greatest number of vassals and dependents about them. They acknowledge this sort of influence and power only.

16

THE nation of all the Gauls is extremely devoted to superstitious rites; and on that account they who are troubled with unusually severe diseases, and they who are engaged in battles and dangers, either sacrifice men as victims, or vow that they will sacrifice them, and employ the Druids as the performers of those sacrifices; because they think that unless the life of a man be offered for the life of a man, the mind of the immortal gods can not be rendered propitious, and they have sacrifices of that kind ordained for national purposes. Others have figures of vast size, the limbs of which formed of osiers they fill with living men, which being set on fire, the men perish enveloped in the flames. They consider that the oblation of such as have been taken in theft, or in robbery, or any other offense, is more acceptable to the immortal gods; but when a supply of that class is wanting, they have recourse to the oblation of even the innocent.

17

THEY worship as their divinity, Mercury in particular, and have many images of him, and regard him as the inventor of all arts, they consider him the guide of their journeys and marches, and believe him to have great influence over the acquisition of gain and mercantile transactions. Next to him they worship Apollo, and Mars, and Jupiter, and Minerva; respecting these deities they have for the most part the same belief as other nations: that Apollo averts diseases, that Minerva imparts the invention of manufactures, that Jupiter possesses the sovereignty of the heavenly powers; that Mars presides over wars. To him, when they have determined to engage in battle, they commonly vow those things which they shall take in war. When they have conquered, they sacrifice whatever captured animals may have survived the conflict, and collect the other things into one place. In many states you may see piles of these things heaped up in their consecrated spots; nor does it often happen that any one, disregarding the sanctity of the case, dares either to secrete in his house things captured, or take away those deposited; and the most severe punishment, with torture, has been established for such a deed.

18

ALL the Gauls assert that they are descended from the god Dis, and say that this tradition has been handed down by the Druids. For that reason they compute the divisions of every season, not by the number of days, but of nights; they keep birthdays and the beginnings of months and years in such an order that the day follows the night. Among the other usages of their life, they differ in this from almost all other nations, that they do not permit their children to approach them openly until they are grown up so as to be able to bear the service of war; and they regard it as indecorous for a son of boyish age to stand in public in the presence of his father.

19

WHATEVER sums of money the husbands have received in the name of dowry from their wives, making an estimate of it, they add the same amount out of their own estates. An account is kept of all this money conjointly, and the profits are laid by: whichever of them shall have survived [the other], to that one the portion of both reverts together with the profits of the previous time. Husbands have power of life and death over their wives as well as over their children: and when the father of a family, born in a more than commonly distinguished rank, has died, his relations assemble, and, if the circumstances of his death are suspicious, hold an investigation upon the wives in the manner adopted toward slaves; and, if proof be obtained, put them to severe torture, and kill them. Their funerals, considering the state of civilization among the Gauls, are magnificent and costly; and they cast into the fire all things, including living creatures, which they suppose to have been dear to them when alive; and, a little before this period, slaves and dependents, who were ascertained to have been beloved by them, were, after the regular funeral rites were completed, burnt together with them.

20

THOSE states which are considered to conduct their commonwealth more judiciously, have it ordained by their laws, that, if any person shall have heard by rumor and report from his neighbors any thing concerning the commonwealth, he shall convey it to the magistrate, and not impart it to any other; because it has been discovered that inconsiderate and inexperienced men were often alarmed by false reports, and driven to some rash act, or else took hasty measures in affairs of the highest importance. The magistrates conceal those things which require to be kept unknown; and they disclose to the people whatever they determine to be expedient. It is not lawful to speak of the commonwealth, except in council.

21

THE Germans differ much from these usages, for they have neither Druids to preside over sacred offices, nor do they pay great regard to sacrifices. They rank in the number of the gods those alone whom they behold, and by whose instrumentality they are obviously benefited, namely, the sun, fire, and the moon; they have not heard of the other deities even by report. Their whole life is occupied in hunting and in the pursuits of the military art; from childhood they devote themselves to fatigue and hardships. Those who have remained chaste for the longest time, receive the greatest commendation among their people; they think that by this the growth is promoted, by this the physical powers are increased and the sinews are strengthened. And to have had knowledge of a woman before the twentieth year they reckon among the most disgraceful acts; of which matter there is no concealment, because they bathe promiscuously in the rivers and [only] use skins or small cloaks of deer's hides, a large portion of the body being in consequence naked.

22

THEY do not pay much attention to agriculture, and a large portion of their food consists in milk, cheese, and flesh; nor has any one a fixed quantity of land or his own individual limits; but the magistrates and the leading men each year apportion to the tribes and families, who have united together, as much land as, and in the place in which, they think proper, and the year after compel them to remove elsewhere. For this enactment they advance many reasons—lest seduced by long-continued custom, they may exchange their ardor in the waging of war for agriculture; lest they may be anxious to acquire extensive estates, and the more powerful drive the weaker from their possessions; lest they construct their houses with too great a desire to avoid cold and heat; lest the desire of wealth spring up, from which cause divisions and discords arise; and that they may keep the common people in a contented state of mind, when each sees his own means placed on an equality with [those of] the most powerful.

23

IT is the greatest glory to the several states to have as wide deserts as possible around them, their frontiers having been laid waste. They consider this the real evidence of their prowess, that their neighbors shall be driven out of their lands and abandon them, and that no one dare settle near them; at the same time they think that they shall be on that account the more secure, because they have removed the apprehension of a sudden incursion. When a state either repels war waged against it, or wages it against another, magistrates are chosen to preside over that war with such authority, that they have power of life and death. In peace there is no common magistrate, but the chiefs of provinces and cantons administer justice and determine controversies among their own people. Robberies which are committed beyond the boundaries of each state bear no infamy, and they avow that these are committed for the purpose of disciplining their youth and of preventing sloth. And when any of their chiefs has said in an assembly "that he will be their leader, let those who are willing to follow, give in their names;" they who approve of both the enterprise and the man arise and promise their assistance and are applauded by the people; such of them as have not followed him are accounted in the number of deserters and traitors, and confidence in all matters is afterward refused them. To injure guests they regard as impious; they defend from wrong those who have come to them for any purpose whatever, and esteem them inviolable; to them the houses of all are open and maintenance is freely supplied.

24

AND there was formerly a time when the Gauls excelled the Germans in prowess, and waged war on them offensively, and, on account of the great number of their people and the insufficiency of their land, sent colonies over the Rhine. Accordingly, the Volcae Tectosages, seized on those parts of Germany which are the most fruitful [and lie] around the Hercynian forest, (which, I perceive, was known by report to Eratosthenes and some other Greeks, and which they call Orcynia), and settled there. Which nation to this time retains its position in those settlements, and has a very high character for justice and military merit; now also they continue in the same scarcity, indigence, hardihood, as the Germans, and use the same food and dress; but their proximity to the Province and knowledge of commodities from countries beyond the sea supplies to the Gauls many things tending to luxury as well as civilization. Accustomed by degrees to be overmatched and worsted in many engagements, they do not even compare themselves to the Germans in prowess.

25

THE breadth of this Hercynian forest, which has been referred to above, is to a quick traveler, a journey of nine days. For it can not be otherwise computed, nor are they acquainted with the measures of roads. It begins at the frontiers of the Helvetii, Nemetes, and Rauraci, and extends in a right line along the river Danube to the territories of the Daci and the Anartes; it bends thence to the left in a different direction from the river, and owing to its extent touches the confines of many nations; nor is there any person belonging to this part of Germany who says that he either has gone to the extremity of that forest, though he had advanced a journey of sixty days, or has heard in what place it begins. It is certain that many kinds of wild beast are produced in it which have not been seen in other parts; of which the following are such as differ principally from other animals, and appear worthy of being committed to record.

26

THERE is an ox of the shape of a stag, between whose ears a horn rises from the middle of the forehead, higher and straighter than those horns which are known to us. From the top of this, branches, like palms, stretch out a considerable distance. The shape of the female and of the male is the, same; the appearance and the size of the horns is the same.

27

THERE are also [animals] which are called elks. The shape of these, and the varied color of their skins, is much like roes, but in size they surpass them a little and are destitute of horns, and have legs without joints and ligatures; nor do they lie down for the purpose of rest, nor, if they have been thrown down by any accident, can they raise or lift themselves up. Trees serve as beds to them; they lean themselves against them, and thus reclining only slightly, they take their rest; when the huntsmen have discovered from the footsteps of these animals whither they are accustomed to betake themselves, they either undermine all the trees at the roots, or cut into them so far that the upper part of the trees may appear to be left standing. When they have leant upon them, according to their habit, they knock down by their weight the unsupported trees, and fall down themselves along with them.

28

THERE is a third kind, consisting of those animals which are called uri. These are a little below the elephant in size, and of the appearance, color, and shape of a bull. Their strength and speed are extraordinary; they spare neither man nor wild beast which they have espied. These the Germans take with much pains in pits and kill them. The young men harden themselves with this exercise, and practice themselves in this kind of hunting, and those who have slain the greatest number of them, having produced the horns in public, to serve as evidence, receive great praise. But not even when taken very young can they be rendered familiar to men and tamed. The size, shape, and appearance of their horns differ much from the horns of our oxen. These they anxiously seek after, and bind at the tips with silver, and use as cups at their most sumptuous entertainments.

Book VII

1

GAUL being tranquil, Caesar, as he had determined, sets out for Italy to hold the provincial assizes. There he receives intelligence of the death of Clodius; and, being informed of the decree of the senate, [to the effect] that all the youth of Italy should take the military oath, he determined to hold a levy throughout the entire province. Report of these events is rapidly borne into Transalpine Gaul. The Gauls themselves add to the report, and invent what the case seemed to require, [namely] that Caesar was detained by commotions in the city, and could not, amid so violent dissensions, come to his army. Animated by this opportunity, they who already, previously to this occurrence, were indignant that they were reduced beneath the dominion of Rome, begin to organize their plans for war more openly and daringly. The leading men of Gaul, having convened councils among themselves in the woods, and retired places, complain of the death of Acco: they point out that this fate may fall in turn on themselves: they bewail the unhappy fate of Gaul; and by every sort of promises and rewards, they earnestly solicit some to begin the war, and assert the freedom of Gaul at the hazard of their lives. They say that special care should be paid to this, that Caesar should be cut off from his army before their secret plans should be divulged. That this was easy, because neither would the legions, in the absence of their general, dare to leave their winter quarters, nor could the general reach his army without a guard: finally, that it was better to be slain in battle, than not to recover their ancient glory in war, and that freedom which they had received from their forefathers.

2

WHILE these things are in agitation, the Carnutes declare "that they would decline no danger for the sake of the general safety, and promise" that they would be the first of all to begin the war; and since they can not at present take precautions, by giving and receiving hostages, that the affair shall not be divulged, they require that a solemn assurance be given them by oath and plighted honor, their military standards being brought together (in which manner their most sacred obligations are made binding), that they should not be deserted by the rest of the Gauls on commencing the war.

3

WHEN the appointed day came, the Carnutes, under the command of Cotuatus and Conetodunus, desperate men, meet together at Genabum, and slay the Roman citizens who had settled there for the purpose of trading (among the rest, Caius Fusius Cita, a distinguished Roman knight, who by Caesar's orders had presided over the provision department), and plunder their property. The report is quickly spread among all the states of Gaul; for, whenever a more important and remarkable event takes place, they transmit the intelligence through their lands and districts by a shout; the others take it up in succession, and pass it to their neighbors, as happened on this occasion; for the things which were done at Genabum at sunrise, were heard in the territories of the Arverni before the end of the first watch, which is an extent of more than a hundred and sixty miles.

4

THERE in like manner, Vercingetorix the son of Celtillus the Arvernian, a young man of the highest power (whose father had held the supremacy of entire Gaul, and had been put to death by his fellow-citizens, for this reason, because he aimed at sovereign power), summoned together his dependents, and easily excited them. On his design being made known, they rush to arms: he is expelled from the town of Gergovia, by his uncle Gobanitio and the rest of the nobles, who were of opinion, that such an enterprise ought not to be hazarded: he did not however desist, but held in the country a levy of the needy and desperate. Having collected such a body of troops, he brings over to his sentiments such of his fellow-citizens as he has access to: he exhorts them to take up arms in behalf of the general freedom, and having assembled great forces he drives from the state his opponents, by whom he had been expelled a short time previously. He is saluted king by his partisans; he sends ambassadors in every direction, he conjures them to adhere firmly to their promise. He quickly attaches to his interests the Senones, Parisii, Pictones, Cadurci, Turones, Aulerci, Lemovice, and all the others who border on the ocean; the supreme command is conferred on him by unanimous consent. On obtaining this authority, he demands hostages from all these states, he orders a fixed number of soldiers to be sent to him immediately; he determines what quantity of arms each state shall prepare at home, and before what time; he pays particular attention to the cavalry. To the utmost vigilance he adds the utmost rigor of authority; and by the severity of his punishments brings over the wavering: for on the commission of a greater crime he puts the perpetrators to death by fire and every sort of tortures; for a slighter cause, he sends home the offenders with their ears cut off, or one of their eyes put out, that they may be an example to the rest, and frighten others by the severity of their punishment.

5

HAVING quickly collected an army by their punishments, he sends Lucterius, one of the Cadurci, a man the utmost daring, with part of his forces, into the territory of the Ruteni; and marches in person into the country of the Bituriges. On his arrival, the Bituriges send ambassadors to the Aedui, under whose protection they were, to solicit aid in order that they might more easily resist the forces of the enemy. The Aedui, by the advice of the lieutenants whom Caesar had left with the army, send supplies of horse and foot to succor the Bituriges. When they came to the river Loire, which separates the Bituriges from the Aedui, they delayed a few days there, and, not daring to pass the river, return home, and send back word to the lieutenants that they had returned through fear of the treachery of the Bituriges, who, they ascertained, had formed this design, that if the Aedui should cross the river, the Bituriges on the one side, and the Arverni on the other, should surround them. Whether they did this for the reason which they alleged to the lieutenants, or influenced by treachery, we think that we ought not to state as certain, because we have no proof. On their departure, the Bituriges immediately unite themselves to the Arverni.

6

THESE affairs being announced to Caesar in Italy, at the time when he understood that matters in the city had been reduced to a more tranquil state by the energy of Cneius Pompey, he set out for Transalpine Gaul. After he had arrived there, he was greatly at a loss to know by what means he could reach his army. For if he should summon the legions into the province, he was aware that on their march they would have to fight in his absence; he foresaw too that if he himself should endeavor to reach the army, he would act injudiciously, in trusting his safety even to those who seemed to be tranquilized.

32

CAESAR, after delaying several days at Avaricum, and, finding there the greatest plenty of corn and other provisions, refreshed his army after their fatigue and privation. The winter being almost ended, when he was invited by the favorable season of the year to prosecute the war and march against the enemy, [and try] whether he could draw them from the marshes and woods, or else press them by a blockade; some noblemen of the Aedui came to him as ambassadors to entreat "that in an extreme emergency he should succor their state; that their affairs were in the utmost danger, because, whereas single magistrates had been usually appointed in ancient times and held the power of king for a single year, two persons now exercised this office, and each asserted that he was appointed according to their laws. That one of them was Convictolitanis, a powerful and illustrious youth; the other Cotus, sprung from a most ancient family, and personally a man of very great influence and extensive connections. His brother Valetiacus had borne the same office during the last year: that the whole state was up in arms; the senate divided, the people divided; that each of them had his own adherents; and that, if the animosity would be fomented any longer, the result would be that one part of the state would come to a collision with the other; that it rested with his activity and influence to prevent it."

33

ALTHOUGH Caesar considered it ruinous to leave the war and the enemy, yet, being well aware what great evils generally arise from internal dissensions, lest a state so powerful and so closely connected with the Roman people, which he himself had always fostered and honored in every respect, should have recourse to violence and arms, and that the party which had less confidence in its own power should summon aid from Vercingetorix, he determined to anticipate this movement; and because, by the laws of the Aedui, it was not permitted those who held the supreme authority to leave the country, she determined to go in person to the Aedui, lest he should appear to infringe upon their government and laws, and summoned all the senate, and those between whom the dispute was, to meet him at Decetia. When almost all the state had assembled there, and he was informed that one brother had been declared magistrate by the other, when only a few persons were privately summoned for the purpose, at a different time and place from what he ought, whereas the laws not only forbade two belonging to one family to be elected magistrates while each was alive, but even deterred them from being in the senate, he compelled Cotus to resign his office; he ordered Convictolitanis, who had been elected by the priests, according to the usage of the state, in the presence of the magistrates, to hold the supreme authority.

34

HAVING pronounced this decree between [the contending parties], he exhorted the Aedui to bury in oblivion their disputes and dissensions, and, laying aside all these things, devote themselves to the war, and expect from him, on the conquest of Gaul, those rewards which they should have earned, and send speedily to him all their cavalry and ten thousand infantry, which he might place in different garrisons to protect his convoys of provisions, and then divided his army into two parts: he gave Labienus four legions to lead into the country of the Senones and Parisii; and led in person six into the country of the Arverni, in the direction of the town of Gergovia, along the banks of the Allier. He gave part of the cavalry to Labienus and kept part to himself. Vercingetorix, on learning this circumstance, broke down all the bridges over the river and began to march on the other bank of the Allier.

35

WHEN each army was in sight of the other, and was pitching their camp almost opposite that of the enemy, scouts being distributed in every quarter, lest the Romans should build a bridge and bring over their troops; it was to Caesar a matter attended with great difficulties, lest he should be hindered from passing the river during the greater part of the summer, as the Allier can not generally be forded before the autumn. Therefore, that this might not happen, having pitched his camp in a woody place opposite to one of those bridges which Vercingetorix had taken care should be broken down, the next day he stopped behind with two legions in a secret place; he sent on the rest of the forces as usual, with all the baggage, after having selected some cohorts, that the number of the legions might appear to be complete. Having ordered these to advance as far as they could, when now, from the time of day, he conjectured they had come to an encampment, he began to rebuild the bridge on the same piles, the lower part of which remained entire. Having quickly finished the work and led his legions across, he selected a fit place for a camp, and recalled the rest of his troops. Vercingetorix, on ascertaining this fact, went before him by forced marches, in order that he might not be compelled to come to an action against his will.

36

CAESAR, in five days' march, went from that place to Gergovia, and after engaging in a slight cavalry skirmish that day, on viewing the situation of the city, which, being built on a very high mountain, was very difficult of access, he despaired of taking it by storm, and determined to take no measures with regard to besieging it before he should secure a supply of provisions. But Vercingetorix, having pitched his camp on the mountain near the town, placed the forces of each state separately and at small intervals around himself, and having occupied all the hills of that range as far as they commanded a view [of the Roman encampment], he presented a formidable appearance; he ordered the rulers of the states, whom he had selected as his council of war, to come to him daily at the dawn, whether any measure seemed to require deliberation or execution. Nor did he allow almost any day to pass without testing in a cavalry action, the archers being intermixed, what spirit and valor there was in each of his own men. There was a hill opposite the town, at the very foot of that mountain, strongly fortified and precipitous on every side (which if our men could gain, they seemed likely to exclude the enemy from a great share of their supply of water, and from free foraging; but this place was occupied by them with a weak garrison): however, Caesar set out from the camp in the silence of night, and dislodging the garrison before succor could come from the town, he got possession of the place and posted two legions there, and drew from the greater camp to the less a double trench twelve feet broad, so that the soldiers could even singly pass secure from any sudden attack of the enemy.

37

WHILE these affairs were going on at Gergovia, Convictolanis, the Aeduan, to whom we have observed the magistracy was adjudged by Caesar, being bribed by the Arverni, holds a conference with certain young men, the chief of whom were Litavicus and his brothers, who were born of a most noble family. He shares the bribe with them, and exhorts them to "remember that they were free and born for empire; that the state of the Aedui was the only one which retarded the most certain victory of the Gauls; that the rest were held in check by its authority; and, if it was brought over, the Romans would not have room to stand on in Gaul; that he had received some kindness from Caesar, only so far, however, as gaining a most just cause by his decision; but that he assigned more weight to the general freedom; for, why should the Aedui go to Caesar to decide concerning their rights and laws, rather than the Romans come to the Aedui?" The young men being easily won over by the speech of the magistrate and the bribe, when they declared that they would even be leaders in the plot, a plan for accomplishing it was considered, because they were confident their state could not be induced to undertake the war on slight grounds. It was resolved that Litavicus should have the command of the ten thousand, which were being sent to Caesar for the war, and should have charge of them on their march, and that his brothers should go before him to Caesar. They arrange the other measures, and the manner in which they should have them done.

38

LITAVICUS, having received the command of the army, suddenly convened the soldiers, when he was about thirty miles distant from Gergovia, and, weeping, said, "Soldiers, whither are we going? All our knights and all our nobles have perished. Eporedirix and Viridomarus, the principal men of the state, being accused of treason, have been slain by the Romans without any permission to plead their cause. Learn this intelligence from those who have escaped from the massacre; for I, since my brothers and all my relations have been slain, am prevented by grief from declaring what has taken place. Persons are brought forward whom he had instructed in what he would have them say, and make the same statements to the soldiery as Litavicus had made: that all the knights of the Aedui were slain because they were said to have held conferences with the Arverni; that they had concealed themselves among the multitude of soldiers, and had escaped from the midst of the slaughter. The Aedui shout aloud and conjure Litavicus to provide for their safety. As if, said he, it were a matter of deliberation, and not of necessity, for us to go to Gergovia and unite ourselves to the Arverni. Or have we any reasons to doubt that the Romans, after perpetrating the atrocious crime, are now hastening to slay us? Therefore, if there be any spirit in us, let us avenge the death of those who have perished in a most unworthy manner, and let us slay these robbers." He points to the Roman citizens, who had accompanied them, in reliance on his protection. He immediately seizes a great quantity of corn and provisions, cruelly tortures them, and then puts them to death, sends messengers throughout the entire state of the Aedui, and rouses them completely by the same falsehood concerning the slaughter of their knights and nobles; he earnestly advises them to avenge, in the same manner as he did, the wrongs, which they had received.

39

EPOREDIRIX, the Aeduan, a young man born in the highest rank and possessing very great influence at home, and, along with Viridomarus, of equal age and influence, but of inferior birth, whom Caesar had raised from a humble position to the highest rank, on being recommended to him by Divitiacus, had come in the number of horse, being summoned by Caesar by name. These had a dispute with each other for precedence, and in the struggle between the magistrates they had contended with their utmost efforts, the one for Convictolitanis, the other for Cotus. Of these Eporedirix, on learning the design of Litavicus, lays the matter before Caesar almost at midnight; he entreats that Caesar should not suffer their state to swerve from the alliance with the Roman people, owing to the depraved counsels of a few young men which he foresaw would be the consequence if so many thousand men should unite themselves to the enemy, as their relations could not neglect their safety, nor the state regard it as a matter of slight importance.

40

CAESAR felt great anxiety on this intelligence, because he had always especially indulged the state of the Aedui, and, without any hesitation, draws out from the camp four light-armed legions and all the cavalry: nor had he time, at such a crisis, to contract the camp, because the affair seemed to depend upon dispatch. He leaves Caius Fabius, his lieutenant, with two legions to guard the camp. When he ordered the brothers of Litavicus to be arrested, he discovers that they had fled a short time before to the camp of the enemy. He encouraged his soldiers "not to be disheartened by the labor of the journey on such a necessary occasion," and, after advancing twenty-five miles, all being most eager, he came in sight of the army of the Aedui, and, by sending on his cavalry, retards and impedes their march; he then issues strict orders to all his soldiers to kill no one. He commands Eporedirix and Viridomarus, who they thought were killed, to move among the cavalry and address their friends. When they were recognised and the treachery of Litavicus discovered, the Aedui began to extend their hands to intimate submission, and, laying down their arms, to deprecate death. Litavicus, with his clansmen, who after the custom of the Gauls consider it a crime to desert their patrons, even in extreme misfortune, flees forth to Gergovia.

41

CAESAR, after sending messengers to the state of the Aedui, to inform them that they whom he could have put to death by the right of war were spared through his kindness, and after giving three hours of the night to his army for his repose, directed his march to Gergovia. Almost in the middle of the journey, a party of horse that were sent by Fabius stated in how great danger matters were, they inform him that the camp was attacked by a very powerful army, while fresh men were frequently relieving the wearied, and exhausting our soldiers by the incessant toil, since on account of the size of the camp, they had constantly to remain on the rampart; that many had been wounded by the immense number of arrows and all kinds of missiles; that the engines were of great service in withstanding them; that Fabius, at their departure, leaving only two gates open, was blocking up the rest, and was adding breast-works to the ramparts, and was preparing himself for a similar casualty on the following day. Caesar, after receiving this information, reached the camp before sunrise owing to the very great zeal of his soldiers.

42

WHILE these things are going on at Gergovia, the Aedui, on receiving the first announcements from Litavicus, leave themselves no time to ascertain the truth of those statements. Some are stimulated by avarice, others by revenge and credulity, which is an innate propensity in that race of men to such a degree that they consider a slight rumor as an ascertained fact. They plunder the property of the Roman citizens, and either massacre them or drag them away to slavery. Convictolitanis increases the evil state of affairs, and goads on the people to fury, that by the commission of some outrage they may be ashamed to return to propriety. They entice from the town of Cabillonus, by a promise of safety, Marcus Aristius, a military tribune, who was on his march to his legion; they compel those who had settled there for the purpose of trading to do the same. By constantly attacking them on their march they strip them of all their baggage; they besiege day and night those that resisted; when many were slain on both sides, they excite a great number to arms.

43

IN the meantime, when intelligence was brought that all their soldiers were in Caesar's power, they run in a body to Aristius; they assure him that nothing had been done by public authority; they order an inquiry to be made about the plundered property; they confiscate the property of Litavicus and his brothers; they send ambassadors to Caesar for the purpose of clearing themselves. They do all this with a view to recover their soldiers; but being contaminated by guilt, and charmed by the gains arising from the plundered property, as that act was shared in by many, and being tempted by the fear of punishment, they began to form plans of war and stir up the other states by embassies. Although Caesar was aware of this proceeding, yet he addresses the ambassadors with as much mildness as he can: "That he did not think worse of the state on account of the ignorance and fickleness of the mob, nor would diminish his regard for the Aedui." He himself, fearing a greater commotion in Gaul, in order to prevent his being surrounded by all the states, began to form plans as to the manner in which he should return from Gergovia and again concentrate his forces, lest a departure arising from the fear of a revolt should seem like a flight.

44

WHILE he was considering these things an opportunity of acting successfully seemed to offer. For, when he had come into the smaller camp for the purpose of securing the works, he noticed that the hill in the possession of the enemy was stripped of men, although, on the former days, it could scarcely be seen on account of the numbers on it. Being astonished, he inquires the reason of it from the deserters, a great number of whom flocked to him daily. They all concurred in asserting, what Caesar himself had already ascertained by his scouts, that the back of that hill was almost level; but likewise woody an narrow, by which there was a pass to the other side of the town; that they had serious apprehensions for this place, and had no other idea, on the occupation of one hill by the Romans, than that, if they should lose the other, they would be almost surrounded, and cut off from all egress and foraging; that they were all summoned by Vercingetorix to fortify this place.

45

CAESAR, on being informed of this circumstance, sends several troops of horse to the place immediately after midnight; he orders them to range in every quarter with more tumult than usual. At dawn he orders a large quantity of baggage to be drawn out of the camp, and the muleteers with helmets, in the appearance and guise of horsemen, to ride round the hills. To these he adds a few cavalry, with instructions to range more widely to make a show. He orders them all to seek the same quarter by a long circuit; these proceedings were seen at a distance from the town, as Gergovia commanded a view of the camp, nor could the Gauls ascertain at so great a distance, what certainty there was in the maneuver. He sends one legion to the same hill, and after it had marched a little, stations it in the lower ground, and congeals it in the woods. The suspicion of the Gauls are increased, and all their forces are marched to that place to defend it. Caesar, having perceived the camp of the enemy deserted, covers the military insignia of his men, conceals the standards, and transfers his soldiers in small bodies from the greater to the less camp, and points out to the lieutenants whom he had placed in command over the respective legions, what he should wish to be done; he particularly advises them to restrain their men from advancing too far, through their desire of fighting, or their hope of plunder, he sets before them what disadvantages the unfavorable nature of the ground carries with it; that they could be assisted by dispatch alone: that success depended on a surprise, and not on a battle. After stating these particulars, he gives the signal for action, and detaches the Aedui at the same time by another ascent on the right.

46

THE town wall was 1200 paces distant from the plain and foot of the ascent, in a straight line, if no gap intervened; whatever circuit was added to this ascent, to make the hill easy, increased the length of the route. But almost in the middle of the hill, the Gauls had previously built a wall six feet high, made of large stones, and extending in length as far as the nature of the ground permitted, as a barrier to retard the advance of our men; and leaving all the lower space empty, they had filled the upper part of the hill, as far as the wall of the town, with their camps very close to one another. The soldiers, on the signal being given, quickly advance to this fortification, and passing over it, make themselves masters of the separate camps. And so great was their activity in taking the camps, that Teutomarus, the king of the Nitiobriges, being suddenly surprised in his tent, as he had gone to rest at noon, with difficulty escaped from the hands of the plunderers, with the upper part of his person naked, and his horse wounded.

47

CAESAR, having accomplished the object which he had in view, ordered the signal to be sounded for a retreat; and the soldiers of the tenth legion, by which he was then accompanied, halted. But the soldiers of the other legions, not hearing the sound of the trumpet, because there was a very large valley between them, were however kept back by the tribunes of the soldiers and the lieutenants, according to Caesar's orders; but being animated by the prospect of speedy victory, and the flight of the enemy, and the favorable battles of former periods, they thought nothing so difficult that their bravery could not accomplish it; nor did they put an end to the pursuit, until they drew nigh to the wall of the town and the gates. But then, when a shout arose in every quarter of the city, those who were at a distance being alarmed by the sudden tumult, fled hastily from the town, since they thought that the enemy were within the gates. The matrons begin to cast their clothes and silver over the wall, and bending over as far as the lower part of the bosom, with outstretched hands beseech the Romans to spare them, and not to sacrifice to their resentment even women and children, as they had done at Avaricum. Some of them let themselves down from the walls by their hands, and surrendered to our soldiers. Lucius Fabius a centurion of the eighth legion, who, it was ascertained, had said that day among his fellow soldiers that he was excited by the plunder of Avaricum, and would not allow any one to mount the wall before him, finding three men of his own company, and being raised up by them, scaled the wall. He himself, in turn, taking hold of them one by one drew them up to the wall.

48

IN the meantime those who had gone to the other part of the town to defend it, as we have mentioned above, at first, aroused by hearing the shouts, and, afterward, by frequent accounts, that the town was in possession of the Romans, sent forward their cavalry, and hastened in larger numbers to that quarter. As each first came he stood beneath the wall, and increased the number of his countrymen engaged in action. When a great multitude of them had assembled, the matrons, who a little before were stretching their hands from the walls to the Romans, began to beseech their countrymen, and after the Gallic fashion to show their disheveled hair, and bring their children into public view. Neither in position nor in numbers was the contest an equal one to the Romans; at the same time, being exhausted by running and the long continuation of the fight, they could not easily withstand fresh and vigorous troops.

49

CAESAR, when he perceived that his soldiers were fighting on unfavorable ground, and that the enemy's forces were increasing, being alarmed for the safety of his troops, sent orders to Titus Sextius, one of his lieutenants, whom he had left to guard the smaller camp, to lead out his cohorts quickly from the camp, and post them at the foot of the hill, on the right wing of the enemy; that if he should see our men driven from the ground, he should deter the enemy from following too closely. He himself, advancing with the legion a little from that place where he had taken his post, awaited the issue of the battle.

50

WHILE the fight was going on most vigorously, hand to hand, and the enemy depended on their position and numbers, our men on their bravery, the Aedui suddenly appeared on our exposed flank, as Caesar had sent them by another ascent on the right, for the sake of creating a diversion. These, from the similarity of their arms, greatly terrified our men; and although they were discovered to have their right shoulders bare, which was usually the sign of those reduced to peace, yet the soldiers suspected that this very thing was done by the enemy to deceive them. At the same time Lucius Fabius the centurion, and those who had scaled the wall with him, being surrounded and slain, were cast from the wall. Marcus Petreius, a centurion of the same legion, after attempting to hew down the gates, was overpowered by numbers, and, despairing of his safety, having already received many wounds, said to the soldiers of his own company who followed him: "Since I can not save you as well as myself, I shall at least provide for your safety, since I, allured by the love of glory, led you into this danger, do you save yourselves when an opportunity is given." At the same time he rushed into the midst of the enemy, and slaying two of them, drove back the rest a little from the gate. When his men attempted to aid him, "In vain," he says, "you endeavor to procure me safety, since blood and strength are now failing me, therefore leave this, while you have the opportunity, and retreat to the legion." Thus he fell fighting a few moments after, and saved his men by his own death.

51

OUR soldiers, being hard pressed on every side, were dislodged from their position, with the loss of forty-six centurions; but the tenth legion, which had been posted in reserve on ground a little more level, checked the Gauls in their eager pursuit. It was supported by the cohorts of the thirteenth legion, which, being led from the smaller camp, had, under the command of Titus Sextius, occupied the higher ground. The legions, as soon as they reached the plain, halted and faced the enemy. Vercingetorix led back his men from the part of the hill within the fortifications. On that day little less than seven hundred of the soldiers were missing.

52

ON the next day, Caesar, having called a meeting, censured the rashness and avarice of his soldiers, "In that they had judged for themselves how far they ought to proceed, or what they ought to do, and could not be kept back by the tribunes of the soldiers and the lieutenants;" and stated, "what the disadvantage of the ground could effect, what opinion he himself had entertained at Avaricum, when having surprised the enemy without either general or cavalry, he had given up a certain victory, lest even a trifling loss should occur in the contest owing to the disadvantage of position. That as much as he admired the greatness of their courage, since neither the fortifications of the camp, nor the height of the mountain, nor the wall of the town could retard them; in the same degree he censured their licentiousness and arrogance, because they thought that they knew more than their general concerning victory, and the issue of actions: and that he required in his soldiers forbearance and self-command, not less than valor and magnanimity."

67

THIS proposal receiving general approbation, and all being forced to take the oath, on the next day the cavalry were divided into three parts, and two of these divisions made a demonstration on our two flanks; while one in front began to obstruct our march. On this circumstance being announced, Caesar orders his cavalry also to form three divisions and charge the enemy. Then the action commences simultaneously in every part: the main body halts; the baggage is received within the ranks of the legions. If our men seemed to be distressed, or hard pressed in any quarter, Caesar usually ordered the troops to advance, and the army to wheel round in that quarter; which conduct retarded the enemy in the pursuit, and encouraged our men by the hope of support. At length the Germans, on the right wing, having gained the top of the hill, dislodge the enemy from their position and pursue them even as far as the river at which Vercingetorix with the infantry was stationed, and slay several of them. The rest, on observing this action, fearing lest they should be surrounded, betake themselves to flight. A slaughter ensues in every direction, and three of the noblest of the Aedui are taken and brought to Caesar: Cotus, the commander of the cavalry, who had been engaged in the contest with Convictolitanis the last election, Cavarillus, who had held the command of the infantry after the revolt of Litavicus, and Eporedirix, under whose command the Aedui had engaged in war against the Sequani, before the arrival of Caesar.

68

ALL his cavalry being routed, Vercingetorix led back his troops in the same order as he had arranged them before the camp, and immediately began to march to Alesia, which is a town of the Mandubii, and ordered the baggage to be speedily brought forth from the camp, and follow him closely. Caesar, having conveyed his baggage to the nearest hill, and having left two legions to guard it, pursued as far as the time of day would permit, and after slaying about three thousand of the rear of the enemy, encamped at Alesia on the next day. On reconnoitering the situation of the city, finding that the enemy were panic-stricken, because the cavalry in which they placed their chief reliance, were beaten, he encouraged his men to endure the toil, and began to draw a line of circumvallation round Alesia.

69

THE town itself was situated on the top of a hill, in a very lofty position, so that it did not appear likely to be taken, except by a regular siege. Two rivers, on two different sides, washed the foot of the hill. Before the town lay a plain of about three miles in length; on every other side hills at a moderate distance, and of an equal degree of height, surrounded the town. The army of the Gauls had filled all the space under the wall, comprising a part of the hill which looked to the rising sun, and had drawn in front a trench and a stone wall six feet high. The circuit of that fortification, which was commenced by the Romans, comprised eleven miles. The camp was pitched in a strong position, and twenty-three redoubts were raised in it, in which sentinels were placed by day, lest any sally should be made suddenly; and by night the same were occupied by watches and strong guards.

70

THE work having been begun, a cavalry action ensues in that plain, which we have already described as broken by hills, and extending three miles in length. The contest is maintained on both sides with the utmost vigor; Caesar sends the Germans to aid our troops when distressed, and draws up the legions in front of the camp, lest any sally should be suddenly made by the enemy's infantry. The courage of our men is increased by the additional support of the legions; the enemy being put to flight, hinder one another by their numbers, and as only the narrower gates were left open, are crowded together in them; then the Germans pursue them with vigor even to the fortifications. A great slaughter ensues; some leave their horses, and endeavor to cross the ditch and climb the wall. Caesar orders the legions which he had drawn up in front of the rampart to advance a little. The Gauls, who were within the fortifications, were no less panic-stricken, thinking that the enemy were coming that moment against them, and unanimously shout "to arms;" some in their alarm rush into the town; Vercingetorix orders the gates to be shut, lest the camp should be left undefended. The Germans retreat, after slaying many and taking several horses.

71

VERCINGETORIX adopts the design of sending away all his cavalry by night, before the fortifications should be completed by the Romans. He charges them when departing "that each of them should go to his respective state, and press for the war all who were old enough to bear arms; he states his own merits, and conjures them to consider his safety, and not surrender him who had deserved so well of the general freedom, to the enemy for torture; he points out to them that, if they should be remiss, eighty thousand chosen men would perish with him; that upon making a calculation, he had barely corn for thirty days, but could hold out a little longer by economy." After giving these instructions he silently dismisses the cavalry in the second watch, [on that side] where our works were not completed; he orders all the corn to be brought to himself; he ordains capital punishment to such as should not obey; he distributes among them, man by man, the cattle, great quantities of which had been driven there by the Mandubii; he began to measure out the corn sparingly, and by little and little; he receives into the town all the forces which he had posted in front of it. In this manner he prepares to await the succors from Gaul, and carry on the war.

72

CAESAR, on learning these proceedings from the deserters and captives, adopted the following system of fortification; he dug a trench twenty feet deep, with perpendicular sides, in such a manner that the base of this trench should extend so far as the edges were apart at the top. He raised all his other works at a distance of four hundred feet from that ditch; [he did] that with this intention, lest (since he necessarily embraced so extensive an area, and the whole works could not be easily surrounded by a line of soldiers) a large number of the enemy should suddenly, or by night, sally against the fortifications; or lest they should by day cast weapons against our men while occupied with the works. Having left this interval, he drew two trenches fifteen feet broad, and of the same depth; the innermost of them, being in low and level ground, he filled with water conveyed from the river. Behind these he raised a rampart and wall twelve feet high; to this he added a parapet and battlements, with large stakes cut like stags' horns, projecting from the junction of the parapet and battlements, to prevent the enemy from scaling it, and surrounded the entire work with turrets, which were eighty feet distant from one another.

73

IT was necessary, at one and the same time, to procure timber [for the rampart], lay in supplies of corn, and raise also extensive fortifications, and the available troops were in consequence of this reduced in number, since they used to advance to some distance from the camp, and sometimes the Gauls endeavored to attack our works, and to make a sally from the town by several gates and in great force. Caesar thought that further additions should be made to these works, in order that the fortifications might be defensible by a small number of soldiers. Having, therefore, cut down the trunks of trees or very thick branches, and having stripped their tops of the bark, and sharpened them into a point, he drew a continued trench every where five feet deep. These stakes being sunk into this trench, and fastened firmly at the bottom, to prevent the possibility of their being torn up, had their branches only projecting from the ground. There were five rows in connection with, and intersecting each other; and whoever entered within them were likely to impale themselves on very sharp stakes. The soldiers called these "cippi." Before these, which were arranged in oblique rows in the form of a quincunx, pits three feet deep were dug, which gradually diminished in depth to the bottom. In these pits tapering stakes, of the thickness of a man's thigh; sharpened at the top and hardened in the fire, were sunk in such a manner as to project from the ground not more than four inches; at the same time for the purpose of giving them strength and stability, they were each filled with trampled clay to the height of one foot from the bottom: the rest of the pit was covered over with osiers and twigs, to conceal the deceit. Eight rows of this kind were dug, and were three feet distant from each other. They called this a lily from its resemblance to that flower. Stakes a foot long, with iron hooks attached to them, were entirely sunk in the ground before these, and were planted in every place at small intervals; these they called spurs.

74

AFTER completing these works, saving selected as level ground as he could, considering the nature of the country, and having enclosed an area of fourteen miles, he constructed, against an external enemy, fortifications of the same kind in every respect, and separate from these, so that the guards of the fortifications could not be surrounded even by immense numbers, if such a circumstance should take place owing to the departure of the enemy's cavalry; and in order that the Roman soldiers might not be compelled to go out of the camp with great risk, he orders all to provide forage and corn for thirty days.

75

WHILE those things are carried on at Alesia, the Gauls, having convened a council of their chief nobility, determine that all who could bear arms should not be called out, which was the opinion of Vercingetorix, but that a fixed number should be levied from each state; lest, when so great a multitude assembled together, they could neither govern nor distinguish their men, nor have the means of supplying them with corn. They demand thirty-five thousand men from the Aedui and their dependents, the Segusiani, Ambivareti, and Aulerci Brannovices; an equal number from the Arverni in conjunction with the Eleuteti Cadurci, Gabali, and Velauni, who were accustomed to be under the command of the Arverni; twelve thousand each from the Senones, Sequani, Bituriges, Sentones, Ruteni, and Carnutes; ten thousand from the Bellovaci; the same number from the Lemovici; eight thousand each from the Pictones, and Turoni, and Parisii, and Helvii; five thousand each from the Suessiones, Ambiani, Mediomatrici, Petrocorii, Nervii, Morini, and Nitiobriges; the same number from the Aulerci Cenomani; four thousand from the Atrebates; three thousand each from the Bellocassi, Lexovii, and Aulerci Eburovices; thirty thousand from the Rauraci, and Boii; six thousand from all the states together, which border on the Atlantic, and which in their dialect are called Armoricae (in which number are comprehended the Curisolites, Rhedones, Ambibari, Caltes, Osismii, Lemovices, Veneti, and Unelli). Of these the Bellovaci did not contribute their number, as they said that they would wage war against the Romans on their own account, and at their own discretion, and would not obey the order of any one: however, at the request of Commius, they sent two thousand, in consideration of a tie of hospitality which subsisted between him and them.

76

CAESAR had, as we have previously narrated, availed himself of the faithful and valuable services of this Commius, in Britain, in former years: in consideration of which merits he had exempted from taxes his [Commius's] state, and had conferred on Commius himself the country of the Morini. Yet such was the unanimity of the Gauls in asserting their freedom, and recovering their ancient renown in war, that they were influenced neither by favors, nor by the recollection of private friendship; and all earnestly directed their energies and resources to that war, and collected eight thousand cavalry, and about two hundred and forty thousand infantry. These were reviewed in the country of the Aedui, and a calculation was made of their numbers: commanders were appointed: the supreme command is entrusted to Commius the Atrebatian, Viridomarus and Eporedirix the Aeduans, and Vergasillaunus the Arvernan, the cousin-german of Vercingetorix. To them are assigned men selected from each state, by whose advice the war should be conducted. All march to Alesia, sanguine and full of confidence: nor was there a single individual who imagined that the Romans could withstand the sight of such an immense host: especially in an action carried on both in front and rear, when [on the inside] the besieged would sally from the town and attack the enemy, and on the outside so great forces of cavalry and infantry would be seen.

77

BUT those who were blockaded at Alesia, the day being past, on which they had expected auxiliaries from their countrymen, and all their corn being consumed ignorant of what was going on among the Aedui, convened an assembly and deliberated on the exigency of their situation. After various opinions had been expressed among them, some of which proposed a surrender, others a sally, while their strength would support it, the speech of Critognatus ought not to be omitted for its singular and detestable cruelty. He sprung from the noblest family among the Arverni, and possessing great influence, says, "I shall pay no attention to the opinion of those who call a most disgraceful surrender by the name of a capitulation; nor do I think that they ought to be considered as citizens, or summoned to the council. My business is with those who approve of a sally: in whose advice the memory of our ancient prowess seems to dwell in the opinion of you all. To be unable to bear privation for a short time is disgraceful cowardice, not true valor. Those who voluntarily offer themselves to death are more easily found than those who would calmly endure distress. And I would approve of this opinion (for honor is a powerful motive with me), could I foresee no other loss, save that of life; but let us, in adopting our design, look back on all Gaul, which we have stirred up to our aid. What courage do you think would our relatives and friends have, if eighty thousand men were butchered in one spot, supposing that they should be forced to come to an action almost over our corpses? Do not utterly deprive them of your aid, for they have spurned all thoughts of personal danger on account of your safety; nor by your folly, rashness, and cowardice, crush all Gaul and doom it to an eternal slavery. Do you doubt their fidelity and firmness because they have not come at the appointed day? What then? Do you suppose that the Romans are employed every day in the outer fortifications for mere amusement? If you can not be assured by their dispatches, since every avenue is blocked up, take the Romans as evidence that there approach is drawing near; since they, intimidated by alarm at this, labor night and day at their works. What, therefore, is my design? To do as our ancestors did in the war against the Cimbri and Teutones, which was by no means equally momentous who, when driven into their towns, and oppressed by similar privations, supported life by the corpses of those who appeared useless for war on account of their age, and did not surrender to the enemy: and even if we had not a precedent for such cruel conduct, still I should consider it most glorious that one should be established, and delivered to posterity. For in what was that war like this? The Cimbri, after laying Gaul waste, and inflicting great calamities, at length departed from our country, and sought other lands; they left us our rights, laws, lands, and liberty. But what other motive or wish have the Romans, than, induced by envy, to settle in the lands and states of those whom they have learned by fame to be noble and powerful in war, and impose on them perpetual slavery? For they never have carried on wars on any other terms. But if you know not these things which are going on in distant countries, look to the neighboring Gaul, which being reduced to the form of a province, stripped of its rights and laws, and subjected to Roman despotism, is oppressed by perpetual slavery."

78

WHEN different opinions were expressed, they determined that those who, owing to age or ill health, were unserviceable for war, should depart from the town, and that themselves should try every expedient before they had recourse to the advice of Critognatus: however, that they would rather adopt that design, if circumstances should compel them and their allies should delay, than accept any terms of a surrender or peace. The Mandubii, who had admitted them into the town, are compelled to go forth with their wives and children. When these came to the Roman fortifications, weeping, they begged of the soldiers by every entreaty to receive them as slaves and relieve them with food. But Caesar, placing guards on the rampart, forbade them to be admitted.

79

IN the meantime, Commius and the rest of the leaders, to whom the supreme command had been entrusted, came with all their forces to Alesia, and having occupied the entire hill, encamped not more than a mile from our fortifications. The following day, having led forth their cavalry from the camp, they fill all that plain, which, we have related, extended three miles in length, and drew out their infantry a little from that place, and post them on the higher ground. The town Alesia commanded a view of the whole plain. The besieged run together when these auxiliaries were seen; mutual congratulations ensue, and the minds of all are elated with joy. Accordingly, drawing out their troops, they encamp before the town, and cover the nearest trench with hurdles and fill it up with earth, and make ready for a sally and every casualty.

80

CAESAR, having stationed his army on both sides of the fortifications, in order that, if occasion should arise, each should hold and know his own post, orders the cavalry to issue forth from the camp and commence action. There was a commanding view from the entire camp, which occupied a ridge of hills; and the minds of all the soldiers anxiously awaited the issue of the battle. The Gauls had scattered archers and light-armed infantry here and there, among their cavalry, to give relief to their retreating troops, and sustain the impetuosity of our cavalry. Several of our soldiers were unexpectedly wounded by these, and left the battle. When the Gauls were confident that their countrymen were the conquerors in the action, and beheld our men hard pressed by numbers, both those who were hemmed in by the line of circumvallation and those who had come to aid them, supported the spirits of their men by shouts and yells from every quarter. As the action was carried on in sight of all, neither a brave nor cowardly act could be concealed; both the desire of praise and the fear of ignominy, urged on each party to valor. After fighting from noon almost to sunset, without victory inclining in favor of either, the Germans, on one side, made a charge against the enemy in a compact body, and drove them back; and, when they were put to flight, the archers were surrounded and cut to pieces. In other parts, likewise, our men pursued to the camp the retreating enemy, and did not give them an opportunity of rallying. But those who had come forth from Alesia returned into the town dejected and almost despairing of success.

81

THE Gauls, after the interval of a day and after making, during that time, an immense number of hurdles, scaling-ladders, and iron hooks, silently went forth from the camp at midnight and approached the fortifications in the plain. Raising a shout suddenly, that by this intimation those who were besieged in the town might learn their arrival, they began to cast down hurdles and dislodge our men from the rampart by slings, arrows, and stones, and executed the other movements which are requisite in storming. At the same time, Vercingetorix, having heard the shout, gives the signal to his troops by a trumpet, and leads them forth from the town. Our troops, as each man's post had been assigned him some days before, man the fortifications; they intimidate the Gauls by slings, large stones, stakes which they had placed along the works, and bullets. All view being prevented by the darkness, many wounds are received on both sides; several missiles, are thrown from the engines. But Marcus Antonius, and Caius Trebonius, the lieutenants, to whom the defense of these parts had been allotted, draughted troops from the redoubts which were more remote, and sent them to aid our troops, in whatever direction they understood that they were hard pressed.

82

WHILE the Gauls were at a distance from the fortification, they did more execution, owing to the immense number of their weapons: after they came nearer, they either unawares impaled themselves on the spurs, or were pierced by the mural darts from the ramparts and towers, and thus perished. After receiving many wounds on all sides, and having forced no part of the works, when day drew nigh, fearing lest they should be surrounded by a sally made from the higher camp on the exposed flank, they retreated to their countrymen. But those within, while they bring forward those things which had been prepared by Vercingetorix for a sally, fill up the nearest trenches; having delayed a long time in executing these movements, they learned the retreat of their countrymen before they drew nigh to the fortifications. Thus they returned to the town without accomplishing their object.

83

THE Gauls, having been twice repulsed with great loss, consult what they should do; they avail themselves of the information of those who were well acquainted with the country; from them they ascertain the position and fortification of the upper camp. There was, on the north side, a hill, which our men could not include in their works, on account of the extent of the circuit, and had necessarily made their camp in ground almost disadvantageous, and pretty steep. Caius Antistius Reginus, and Caius Caninius Rebilus, two of the lieutenants, with two legions, were in possession of this camp. The leaders of the enemy, having reconnoitered the country by their scouts, select from the entire army sixty thousand men, belonging to those states, which bear the highest character for courage; they privately arrange among themselves what they wished to be done, and in what manner; they decide that the attack should take place when it should seem to be noon. They appoint over their forces Vergasillaunus, the Arvernian, one of the four generals, and a near relative of Vercingetorix. He, having issued from the camp at the first watch, and having almost completed his march a little before the dawn, hid himself behind the mountain, and ordered his soldiers to refresh themselves after their labor during the night. When noon now seemed to draw nigh, he marched hastily against that camp which we have mentioned before; and, at the same time, the cavalry began to approach the fortifications in the plain, and the rest of the forces to make a demonstration in front of the camp.

84

VERCINGETORIX, having beheld his countrymen from the citadel of Alesia, issues forth from the town; he brings forth from the camp long hooks, movable pent-houses, mural hooks, and other things, which he had prepared for the purpose of making a sally. They engage on all sides at once and every expedient is adopted. They flocked to whatever part of the works seemed weakest. The army of the Romans is distributed along their extensive lines, and with difficulty meets the enemy in every quarter. The shouts which were raised by the combatants in their rear, had a great tendency to intimidate our men, because they perceived that their danger rested on the valor of others: for generally all evils which are distant most powerfully alarm men's minds.

85

CAESAR, having selected a commanding situation, sees distinctly whatever is going on in every quarter, and sends assistance to his troops when hard pressed. The idea uppermost in the minds of both parties is, that the present is the time in which they would have the fairest opportunity of making a struggle; the Gauls despairing of all safety, unless they should succeed in forcing the lines: the Romans expecting an end to all their labors if they should gain the day. The principal struggle is at the upper lines, to which as we have said Vergasillaunus was sent. The least elevation of ground, added to a declivity, exercises a momentous influence. Some are casting missiles, others, forming a testudo, advance to the attack; fresh men by turns relieve the wearied. The earth, heaped up by all against the fortifications, gives the means of ascent to the Gauls, and covers those works which the Romans had concealed in the ground. Our men have no longer arms or strength.

86

CAESAR, on observing these movements, sends Labienus

with six cohorts to relieve his distressed soldiers: he orders him, if he should be unable to withstand them, to draw off the cohorts and make a sally; but not to do this except through necessity. He himself goes to the rest, and exhorts them not to succumb to the toil; he shows them that the fruits of all former engagements depend on that day and hour. The Gauls within, despairing of forcing the fortifications in the plains on account of the greatness of the works, attempt the places precipitous in ascent: hither they bring the engines which they had prepared; by the immense number of their missiles they dislodge the defenders from the turrets: they fill the ditches with clay and hurdles, then clear the way; they tear down the rampart and breast-work with hooks.

87

CAESAR sends at first young Brutus, with six cohorts, and afterward Caius Fabius, his lieutenant, with seven others: finally, as they fought more obstinately, he leads up fresh men to the assistance of his soldiers. After renewing the action, and repulsing the enemy, he marches in the direction in which he had sent Labienus, drafts four cohorts from the nearest redoubt, and orders part of the cavalry to follow him, and part to make the circuit of the external fortifications and attack the enemy in the rear. Labienus, when neither the ramparts or ditches could check the onset of the enemy, informs Caesar by messengers of what he intended to do. Caesar hastens to share in the action.

88

HIS arrival being known from the color of his robe, and the troops of cavalry, and the cohorts which he had ordered to follow him being seen, as these low and sloping grounds were plainly visible from the eminences, the enemy join battle. A shout being raised by both sides, it was succeeded by a general shout along the ramparts and whole line of fortifications. Our troops, laying aside their javelins, carry on the engagement with their swords. The cavalry is suddenly seen in the rear of the Gauls; the other cohorts advance rapidly; the enemy turn their backs; the cavalry intercept them in their flight, and a great slaughter ensues. Sedulius the general and chief of the Lemovices is slain; Vergasillaunus the Arvernian, is taken alive in the flight, seventy-four military standards are brought to Caesar, and few out of so great a number return safe to their camp. The besieged, beholding from the town the slaughter and flight of their countrymen, despairing of safety, lead back their troops from the fortifications. A flight of the Gauls from their camp immediately ensues on hearing of this disaster, and had not the soldiers been wearied by sending frequent reinforcements, and the labor of the entire day, all the enemy's forces could have been destroyed. Immediately after midnight, the cavalry are sent out and overtake the rear, a great number are taken or cut to pieces, the rest by flight escape in different directions to their respective states. Vercingetorix, having convened a council the following day, declares, "That he had undertaken that war, not on account of his own exigences, but on account of the general freedom; and since he must yield to fortune, he offered himself to them for either purpose, whether they should wish to atone to the Romans by his death, or surrender him alive. Ambassadors are sent to Caesar on this subject. He orders their arms to be surrendered, and their chieftains delivered up. He seated himself at the head of the lines in front of the camp, the Gallic chieftains are brought before him. They surrender Vercingetorix, and lay down their arms. Reserving the Aedui and Arverni, [to try] if he could gain over, through their influence, their respective states, he distributes one of the remaining captives to each soldier, throughout the entire army, as plunder.

90

AFTER making these arrangements, he marches into the [country of the] Aedui, and recovers that state. To this place ambassadors are sent by the Arveni, who promise that they will execute his commands. He demands a great number of hostages. He sends the legions to winter-quarters; he restores about twenty thousand captives to the Aedui and Arverni; he orders Titus Labienus to march into the [country of the] Sequani with two legions and the cavalry, and to him he attaches Marcus Sempronius Rutilus; he places Caius Fabius, and Lucius Minucius Basilus, with two legions in the country of the Remi, lest they should sustain any loss from the Bellovaci in their neighborhood. He sends Caius Antistius Reginus into the [country of the] Ambivareti, Titus Sextius into the territories of the Bituriges, and Caius Caninius Rebilus into those of the Ruteni, with one legion each. He stations Quintus Tullius Cicero, and Publius Sulpicius among the Aedui at Cabillo and Matisco on the Saone, to procure supplies of corn. He himself determines to winter at Bibracte. A supplication of twenty days is decreed by the senate at Rome, on learning these successes from Caesar's dispatches.

TACITUS

THE ANNALS

TACITUS

Book I

1

ROME at the beginning was ruled by kings. Freedom and the consulship were established by Lucius Brutus. Dictatorships were held for a temporary crisis. The power of the decemvirs did not last beyond two years, nor was the consular jurisdiction of the military tribunes of long duration. The despotisms of Cinna and Sulla were brief; the rule of Pompeius and of Crassus soon yielded before Caesar; the arms of Lepidus and Antonius before Augustus; who, when the world was wearied by civil strife, subjected it to empire under the title of "Prince." But the successes and reverses of the old Roman people have been recorded by famous historians; and fine intellects were not wanting to describe the times of Augustus, till growing sycophancy scared them away. The histories of Tiberius, Caius, Claudius, and Nero, while they were in power, were falsified through terror, and after their death were written under the irritation of a recent hatred. Hence my purpose is to relate a few facts about Augustus—more particularly his last acts, then the reign of Tiberius, and all which follows, without either bitterness or partiality, from any motives to which I am far removed.

2

WHEN after the destruction of Brutus and Cassius there was no longer any army of the Commonwealth, when Pompeius was crushed in Sicily, and when, with Lepidus pushed aside and Antonius slain, even the Julian faction had only Caesar left to lead it, then, dropping the title of triumvir, and giving out that he was a Consul, and was satisfied with a tribune's authority for the protection of the people, Augustus won over the soldiers with gifts, the populace with cheap corn, and all men with the sweets of repose, and so grew greater by degrees, while he concentrated in himself the functions of the Senate, the magistrates, and the laws. He was wholly unopposed, for the boldest spirits had fallen in battle, or in the proscription, while the remaining nobles, the readier they were to be slaves, were raised the higher by wealth and promotion, so that, aggrandized by revolution, they preferred the safety of the present to the dangerous past. Nor did the provinces dislike that condition of affairs, for they distrusted the government of the Senate and the people, because of the rivalries between the leading men and the rapacity of the officials, while the protection of the laws was unavailing, as they were continually deranged by violence, intrigue, and finally by corruption.

3

AUGUSTUS meanwhile, as supports to his despotism, raised to the pontificate and curule aedileship Claudius Marcellus, his sister's son, while a mere stripling, and Marcus Agrippa, of humble birth, a good soldier, and one who had shared his victory, to two consecutive consulships, and as Marcellus soon afterwards died, he also accepted him as his son-in-law. Tiberius Nero and Claudius Drusus, his stepsons, he honoured with imperial tides, although his own family was as yet undiminished. For he had admitted the children of Agrippa, Caius and Lucius, into the house of the Caesars; and before they had yet laid aside the dress of boyhood he had most fervently desired, with an outward show of reluctance, that they should be entitled "princes of the youth," and be consuls-elect. When Agrippa died, and Lucius Caesar as he was on his way to our armies in

Spain, and Caius while returning from Armenia, still suffering from a wound, were prematurely cut off by destiny, or by their step-mother Livia's treachery, Drusus too having long been dead, Nero remained alone of the stepsons, and in him everything tended to centre. He was adopted as a son, as a colleague in empire and a partner in the tribunitian power, and paraded through all the armies, no longer through his mother's secret intrigues, but at her open suggestion. For she had gained such a hold on the aged Augustus that he drove out as an exile into the island of Planasia, his only grandson, Agrippa Postumus, who, though devoid of worthy qualities, and having only he brute courage of physical strength, had not been convicted of any gross offence. And yet Augustus had appointed Germanicus, Drusus's offspring, to the command of eight legions on the Rhine, and required Tiberius to adopt him, although Tiberius had a son, now a young man, in his house; but he did it that he might have several safeguards to rest on. He had no war at the time on his hands except against the Germans, which was rather to wipe out the disgrace of the loss of Quintilius Varus and his army than out of an ambition to extend the empire, or for any adequate recompense. At home all was tranquil, and there were magistrates with the same titles; there was a younger generation, sprung up since the victory of Actium, and even many of the older men had been born during the civil wars. How few were left who had seen the republic!

4

THUS the State had been revolutionized, and there was not a vestige left of the old sound morality. Stripped of equality, all looked up to the commands of a sovereign without the least apprehension for the present, while Augustus in the vigour of life, could maintain his own position, that of his house, and the general tranquility. When in advanced old age, he was worn out by a sickly frame, and the end was near and new prospects opened, a few spoke in vain of the blessings of freedom, but most people dreaded and some longed for war. The popular gossip of the large majority fastened itself variously on their future masters. "Agrippa was savage, and had been exasperated by insult, and neither from age nor experience in affairs was equal to so great a burden. Tiberius Nero was of mature years, and had established his fame in war, but he had the old arrogance inbred in the Claudian family, and many symptoms of a cruel temper, though they were repressed, now and then broke out. He had also from earliest infancy been reared in an imperial house; consulships and triumphs had been heaped on him in his younger days; even in the years which, on the pretext of seclusion he spent in exile at Rhodes, he had had no thoughts but of wrath, hypocrisy, and secret sensuality. There was his mother too with a woman caprice. They must, it seemed, be subject to a female and to two striplings besides, who for a while would burden, and some day rend asunder the State."

5

WHILE these and like topics were discussed, the infirmities of Augustus increased, and some suspected guilt on his wife's part. For a rumour had gone abroad that a few months before he had sailed to Planasia on a visit to Agrippa, with the knowledge of some chosen friends, and with one companion, Fabius Maximus; that many tears were shed on both sides, with expressions of affection, and that thus there was a hope of the young man being restored to the home of his grandfather. This, it was said, Maximus had divulged to his wife Marcia, she again to Livia. All was known to Caesar, and when Maximus soon afterwards died, by a death some thought to be self-inflicted, there were heard at his funeral wailings from Marcia, in which she reproached herself for having been the cause of her husband's destruction. Whatever the fact was, Tiberius as he was just entering Illyria was summoned home by an urgent letter from his mother, and it has not been thoroughly ascertained whether at the city of Nola he found Augustus still breathing or quite lifeless. For Livia had surrounded the house and its approaches with a strict watch, and favourable bulletins were published from time to time, till, provision having been made for the demands of the crisis, one and the same report told men that Augustus was dead and that Tiberius Nero was master of the State.

6

THE first crime of the new reign was the murder of Postumus Agrippa. Though he was surprised and unarmed, a centurion of the firmest resolution despatched him with difficulty. Tiberius gave no explanation of the matter to the Senate; he pretended that there were directions from his father ordering the tribune in charge of the prisoner not to delay the slaughter of Agrippa, whenever he should himself have breathed his last. Beyond a doubt, Augustus had often complained of the young man's character, and had thus succeeded in obtaining the sanction of a decree of the Senate for his banishment. But he never was hard-hearted enough to destroy any of his kinsfolk, nor was it credible that death was to be the sentence of the grandson in order that the stepson might feel secure. It was more probable that Tiberius and Livia, the one from fear, the other from a stepmother's enmity, hurried on the destruction of a youth whom they suspected and hated. When the centurion reported, according to military custom, that he had executed the command, Tiberius replied that he had not given the command, and that the act must be justified to the Senate. As soon as Sallustius Crispus who shared the secret (he had, in fact, sent the written order to the tribune) knew this, fearing that the charge would be shifted on himself, and that his peril would be the same whether he uttered fiction or truth, he advised Livia not to divulge the secrets of her house or the counsels of friends, or any services performed by the soldiers, nor to let Tiberius weaken the strength of imperial power by referring everything to the Senate, for "the condition," he said, "of holding empire is that an account cannot be balanced unless it be rendered to one person."

7

MEANWHILE at Rome people plunged into slavery—consuls, senators, knights. The higher a man's rank, the more eager his hypocrisy, and his looks the more carefully studied, so as neither to betray joy at the decease of one emperor nor sorrow at the rise of another, while he mingled delight and lamentations with his flattery. Sextus Pompeius and Sextus Apuleius, the consuls, were the first to swear allegiance to Tiberius Caesar, and in their presence the oath was taken by Seius Strabo and Caius Turranius, respectively the commander of the praetorian cohorts and the superintendent of the corn supplies. Then the Senate, the soldiers and the people did the same. For Tiberius would inaugurate everything with the consuls, as though the ancient constitution remained, and he hesitated about being emperor. Even the proclamation by which he summoned the senators to their chamber, he issued merely with the title of Tribune, which he had received under Augustus. The wording of the proclamation was brief, and in a very modest tone. "He would," it said, "provide for the honours due to his father, and not leave the lifeless body, and this was the only public duty he now claimed." As soon, however, as Augustus was dead, he had given the watchword to the praetorian cohorts, as commander-in-chief. He had the guard under arms, with all the other adjuncts of a court; soldiers attended him to the forum; soldiers went with him to the Senate House. He sent letters to the different armies, as though supreme power was now his, and showed hesitation only when he spoke in the Senate. His chief motive was fear that Germanicus, who had at his disposal so many legions, such vast auxiliary forces of the allies, and such wonderful popularity, might prefer the possession to the expectation of empire. He looked also at public opinion, wishing to have the credit of having been called and elected by the State rather than of having crept into power through the intrigues of a wife and a dotard's adoption. It was subsequently understood that he assumed a wavering attitude, to test likewise the temper of the nobles. For he would twist a word or a look into a crime and treasure it up in his memory.

8

ON the first day of the Senate he allowed nothing to be discussed but the funeral of Augustus, whose will, which was brought in by the Vestal Virgins, named as his heirs Tiberius and Livia. The latter was to be admitted into the Julian family with the name of Augusta; next in expectation were the grand and great-grandchildren. In the third place, he had named the chief men of the State, most of whom he hated, simply out of ostentation and to win credit with posterity. His legacies were not beyond the scale of a private citizen, except a bequest of forty-three million five hundred thousand sesterces "to the people and populace of Rome," of one thousand to every praetorian soldier, and of three hundred to every man in the legionary cohorts composed of Roman citizens. Next followed a deliberation about funeral honours. Of these the most imposing were thought fitting. The procession was to be conducted through "the gate of triumph," on the motion of Gallus Asinius; the titles of the laws passed, the names of the nations conquered by Augustus were to be borne in front, on that of Lucius Arruntius. Messala Valerius further proposed that the oath of allegiance to Tiberius should be yearly renewed, and when Tiberius asked him whether it was at his bidding that he had brought forward this motion, he replied that he had proposed it spontaneously, and that in whatever concerned the State he would use only his own discretion, even at the risk of offending. This was the only style of adulation which yet remained. The Senators unanimously exclaimed that the body ought to be borne on their shoulders to the funeral pile. The emperor left the point to them with disdainful moderation, he then admonished the people by a proclamation not to indulge in that tumultuous enthusiasm which had distracted the funeral of the Divine Julius, or express a wish that Augustus should be burnt in the Forum instead of in his appointed resting-place in the Campus Martius. On the day of the funeral soldiers stood round as a guard, amid much ridicule from those who had either themselves witnessed or who had heard from their parents of the famous day when slavery was still something fresh, and freedom had been re-sought in vain, when the slaying of Caesar, the Dictator, seemed to some the vilest, to others, the most glorious of deeds. "Now," they said, "an aged sovereign, whose power had lasted long, who had provided his heirs with abundant means to coerce the State, requires forsooth the defense of soldiers that his burial may be undisturbed."

9

THEN followed much talk about Augustus himself, and many expressed an idle wonder that the same day marked the beginning of his assumption of empire and the close of his life, and, again, that he had ended his days at Nola in the same house and room as his father Octavius. People extolled too the number of his consulships, in which he had equaled Valerius Corvus and Caius Marius combined, the continuance for thirty-seven years of the tribunitian power, the title of Imperator twenty-one times earned, and his other honours which had either frequently repeated or were wholly new. Sensible men, however, spoke variously of his life with praise and censure. Some said "that dutiful feeling towards a father, and the necessities of the State in which laws had then no place, drove him into civil war, which can neither be planned nor conducted on any right principles. He had often yielded to Antonius, while he was taking vengeance on his father's murderers, often also to Lepidus. When the latter sank into feeble dotage and the former had been ruined by his profligacy, the only remedy for his distracted country was the rule of a single man. Yet the State had been organized under the name neither of a kingdom nor a dictatorship, but under that of a prince. The ocean and remote rivers were the boundaries of the empire; the legions, provinces, fleets, all things were linked together; there was law for the citizens; there was respect shown to the allies. The capital had been embellished on a grand scale; only in a few instances had he resorted to force, simply to secure general tranquility."

10

IT was said, on the other hand, "that filial duty and State necessity were merely assumed as a mask. It was really from a lust of sovereignty that he had excited the veterans by bribery, had, when a young man and a subject, raised an army, tampered with the Consul's legions, and feigned an attachment to the faction of Pompeius. Then, when by a decree of the Senate he had usurped the high functions and authority of Praetor when Hirtius and Pansa were slain—whether they were destroyed by the enemy, or Pansa by poison infused into a wound, Hirtius by his own soldiers and Caesar's treacherous machinations—he at once possessed himself of both their armies, wrested the consulate from a reluctant Senate, and turned against the State the arms with which he had been entrusted against Antonius. Citizens were proscribed, lands divided, without so much as the approval of those who executed these deeds. Even granting that the deaths of Cassius and of the Bruti were sacrifices to a hereditary enmity (though duty requires us to waive private feuds for the sake of the public welfare), still Pompeius had been deluded by the phantom of peace, and Lepidus by the mask of friendship. Subsequently, Antonius had been lured on by the treaties of Tarentum and Brundisium, and by his marriage with the sister, and paid by his death the penalty of a treacherous alliance. No doubt, there was peace after all this, but it was a peace stained with blood; there were the disasters of Lollius and Varus, the murders at Rome of the Varros, Egnatii, and Juli." The domestic life too of Augustus was not spared. "Nero's wife had been taken from him, and there had been the farce of consulting the pontiffs, whether, with a child conceived and not yet born, she could properly marry. There were the excesses of Quintus Tedius and Vedius Pollio; last of all, there was Livia, terrible to the State as a mother, terrible to the house of the Caesars as a stepmother. No honour was left for the gods, when Augustus chose to be himself worshiped with temples and statues, like those of the deities, and with flamens and priests. He had not even adopted Tiberius as his successor out of affection or any regard to the State, but, having thoroughly seen his arrogant and savage temper, he had sought glory for himself by a contrast of extreme wickedness." For, in fact, Augustus, a few years before, when he was a second time asking from the Senate the tribunitian power for Tiberius, though his speech was complimentary, had thrown out certain hints as to his manners, style, and habits of life, which he meant as reproaches, while he seemed to excuse. However, when his obsequies had been duly performed, a temple with a religious ritual was decreed him.

11

AFTER this all prayers were addressed to Tiberius. He, on his part, urged various considerations, the greatness of the empire, his distrust of himself. "Only," he said, "the intellect of the Divine Augustus was equal to such a burden. Called as he had been by him to share his anxieties, he had learnt by experience how exposed to fortune's caprices was the task of universal rule. Consequently, in a state which had the support of so many great men, they should not put everything on one man, as many, by uniting their efforts would more easily discharge public functions." There was more grand sentiment than good faith in such words. Tiberius's language even in matters which he did not care to conceal, either from nature or habit, was always hesitating and obscure, and now that he was struggling to hide his feelings completely, it was all the more involved in uncertainty and doubt. The Senators, however, whose only fear was lest they might seem to understand him, burst into complaints, tears, and prayers. They raised their hands to the gods, to the statue of Augustus, and to the knees of Tiberius, when he ordered a document to be produced and read. This contained a description of the resources of the State, of the number of citizens and allies under arms, of the fleets, subject kingdoms, provinces, taxes, direct and indirect, necessary expenses and customary bounties. All these details Augustus had written with his own hand, and had added a counsel, that the empire should be confined to its present limits, either from fear or out of jealousy.

12

MEANTIME, while the Senate stooped to the most abject supplication, Tiberius happened to say that although he was not equal to the whole burden of the State, yet he would undertake the charge of whatever part of it might be entrusted to him. Thereupon Asinius Gallus said, "I ask you, Caesar, what part of the State you wish to have entrusted to you?" Confounded by the sudden inquiry he was silent for a few moments; then, recovering his presence of mind, he replied that it would by no means become his modesty to choose or to avoid in a case where he would prefer to be wholly excused. Then Gallus again, who had inferred anger from his looks, said that the question had not been asked with the intention of dividing what could not be separated, but to convince him by his own admission that the body of the State was one, and must be directed by a single mind. He further spoke in praise of Augustus, and reminded Tiberius himself of his victories, and of his admirable deeds for many years as a civilian. Still, he did not thereby soften the emperor's resentment, for he had long been detested from an impression that, as he had married Vipsania, daughter of Marcus Agrippa, who had once been the wife of Tiberius, he aspired to be more than a citizen, and kept up the arrogant tone of his father, Asinius Pollio.

13

NEXT, Lucius Arruntius, who differed but little from the speech of Gallus, gave like offence, though Tiberius had no old grudge against him, but simply mistrusted him, because he was rich and daring, had brilliant accomplishments, and corresponding popularity. For Augustus, when in his last conversations he was discussing who would refuse the highest place, though sufficiently capable, who would aspire to it without being equal to it, and who would unite both the ability and ambition, had described Marcus Lepidus as able but contemptuously indifferent, Gallus Asinius as ambitious and incapable, Lucius Arruntius as not unworthy of it, and, should the chance be given him, sure to make the venture. About the two first there is a general agreement, but instead of Arruntius some have mentioned Cneius Piso, and all these men, except Lepidus, were soon afterwards destroyed by various charges through the contrivance of Tiberius. Quintus Haterius too and Mamercus Scaurus ruffled his suspicious temper, Haterius by having said—"How long, Caesar, will you suffer the State to be without a head?" Scaurus by the remark that there was a hope that the Senate's prayers would not be fruitless, seeing that he had not used his right as Tribune to negative the motion of the Consuls. Tiberius instantly broke out into invective against Haterius; Scaurus, with whom he was far more deeply displeased, he passed over in silence. Wearied at last by the assembly's clamorous importunity and the urgent demands of individual Senators, he gave way by degrees, not admitting that he undertook empire, but yet ceasing to refuse it and to be entreated. It is known that Haterius having entered the palace to ask pardon, and thrown himself at the knees of Tiberius as he was walking, was almost killed by the soldiers, because Tiberius fell forward, accidentally or from being entangled by the suppliant's hands. Yet the peril of so great a man did not make him relent, till Haterius went with entreaties to Augusta, and was saved by her very earnest intercessions.

14

GREAT too was the Senate's sycophancy to Augusta. Some would have her styled "parent"; others "mother of the country," and a majority proposed that to the name of Caesar should be added "son of Julia." The emperor repeatedly asserted that there must be a limit to the honours paid to women, and that he would observe similar moderation in those bestowed on himself, but annoyed at the invidious proposal, and indeed regarding a woman's elevation as a slight to himself, he would not allow so much as a lictor to be assigned her, and forbade the erection of an altar in memory of her adoption, and any like distinction. But for Germanicus Caesar he asked pro-consular powers, and envoys were despatched to confer them on him, and also to express sympathy with his grief at the death of Augustus. The same request was not made for Drusus, because he was consul elect and present at Rome. Twelve candidates were named for the praetorship, the number which Augustus had handed down, and when the Senate urged Tiberius to increase it, he bound himself by an oath not to exceed it.

15

IT was then for the first time that the elections were transferred from the Campus Martius to the Senate. For up to that day, though the most important rested with the emperor's choice, some were settled by the partialities of the tribes. Nor did the people complain of having the right taken from them, except in mere idle talk, and the Senate, being now released from the necessity of bribery and of degrading solicitations, gladly upheld the change, Tiberius confining himself to the recommendation of only four candidates who were to be nominated without rejection or canvass. Meanwhile the tribunes of the people asked leave to exhibit at their own expense games to be named after Augustus and added to the Calendar as the Augustales. Money was, however, voted from the exchequer, and though the use of the triumphal robe in the circus was prescribed, it was not allowed them to ride in a chariot. Soon the annual celebration was transferred to the praetor, to whose lot fell the administration of justice between citizens and foreigners.

Book II

27

ABOUT the same time Libo Drusus, of the family of Scribonii, was accused of revolutionary schemes. I will explain, somewhat minutely, the beginning, progress, and end of this affair, since then first were originated those practices which for so many years have eaten into the heart of the State. Firmius Catus, a senator, an intimate friend of Libo's, prompted the young man, who was thoughtless and an easy prey to delusions, to resort to astrologers' promises, magical rites, and interpreters of dreams, dwelling ostentatiously on his great-grandfather Pompeius, his aunt Scribonia, who had formerly been wife of Augustus, his imperial cousins, his house crowded with ancestral busts, and urging him to extravagance and debt, himself the companion of his profligacy and desperate embarrassments, thereby to entangle him in all the more proofs of guilt.

28

AS soon as he found enough witnesses, with some slaves who knew the facts, he begged an audience of the emperor, after first indicating the crime and the criminal through Flaccus Vescularius, a Roman knight, who was more intimate with Tiberius than himself. Caesar, without disregarding the information, declined an interview, for the communication, he said, might be conveyed to him through the same messenger, Flaccus. Meanwhile he conferred the praetorship on Libo and often invited him to his table, showing no unfriendliness in his looks or anger in his words (so thoroughly had he concealed his resentment); and he wished to know all his saying and doings, though it was in his power to stop them, till one Junius, who had been tampered with by Libo for the purpose of evoking by incantations spirits of the dead, gave information to Fulcinius Trio. Trio's ability was conspicuous among informers, as well as his eagerness for an evil notoriety. He at once pounced on the accused, went to the consuls, and demanded an inquiry before the Senate. The Senators were summoned, with a special notice that they must consult on a momentous and terrible matter.

29

LIBO meanwhile, in mourning apparel and accompanied by ladies of the highest rank, went to house after house, entreating his relatives, and imploring some eloquent voice to ward off his perils; which all refused, on different pretexts, but from the same apprehension. On the day the Senate met, jaded with fear and mental anguish, or, as some have related, feigning illness, he was carried in a litter to the doors of the Senate House, and leaning on his brother he raised his hands and voice in supplication to Tiberius, who received him with unmoved countenance. The emperor then read out the charges and the accusers' names, with such calmness as not to seem to soften or aggravate the accusations.

30

BESIDES Trio and Catus, Fonteius Agrippa and Caius Vibius were among his accusers, and claimed with eager rivalry the privilege of conducting the case for the prosecution, till Vibius, as they would not yield one to the other, and Libo had entered without counsel, offered to state the charges against him singly, and produced an extravagantly absurd accusation, according to which Libo had consulted persons whether he would have such wealth as to be able to cover the Appian road as far as Brundisium with money. There were other questions of the same sort, quite senseless and idle; if leniently regarded, pitiable. But there was one paper in Libo's handwriting, so the prosecutor alleged, with the names of Caesars and of Senators, to which marks were affixed of dreadful or mysterious significance. When the accused denied this, it was decided that his slaves who recognised the writing should be examined by torture. As an ancient statute of the Senate forbade such inquiry in a case affecting a master's life, Tiberius, with his cleverness in devising new law, ordered Libo's slaves to be sold singly to the State-agent, so that, forsooth, without an infringement of the Senate's decree, Libo might be tried on their evidence. As a consequence, the defendant asked an adjournment till next day, and having gone home he charged his kinsman, Publius Quirinus, with his last prayer to the emperor.

31

THE answer was that he should address himself to the Senate. Meanwhile his house was surrounded with soldiers; they crowded noisily even about the entrance, so that they could be heard and seen; when Libo, whose anguish drove him from the very banquet he had prepared as his last gratification, called for a minister of death, grasped the hands of his slaves, and thrust a sword into them. In their confusion, as they shrank back, they overturned the lamp on the table at his side, and in the darkness, now to him the gloom of death, he aimed two blows at a vital part. At the groans of the falling man his freedmen hurried up, and the soldiers, seeing the bloody deed, stood aloof. Yet the prosecution was continued in the Senate with the same persistence, and Tiberius declared on oath that he would have interceded for his life, guilty though he was, but for his hasty suicide.

32

HIS property was divided among his accusers, and praetorships out of the usual order were conferred on those who were of senators' rank. Cotta Messalinus then proposed that Libo's bust should not be carried in the funeral procession of any of his descendants; and Cneius Lentulus, that no Scribonius should assume the surname of Drusus. Days of public thanksgiving were appointed on the suggestion of Pomponius Flaccus. Offerings were given to Jupiter, Mars, and Concord, and the 13th day of September, on which Libo had killed himself, was to be observed as a festival, on the motion of Gallus Asinius, Papius Mutilus, and Lucius Apronius. I have mentioned the proposals and sycophancy of these men, in order to bring to light this old-standing evil in the State. Decrees of the Senate were also passed to expel from Italy astrologers and magicians. One of their number, Lucius Pituanius, was hurled from the Rock. Another, Publius Marcius, was executed, according to ancient custom, by the consuls outside the Esquiline Gate, after the trumpets had been bidden to sound.

33

ON the next day of the Senate's meeting much was said against the luxury of the country by Quintus Haterius, an ex-consul, and by Octavius Fronto, an ex-praetor. It was decided that vessels of solid gold should not be made for the serving of food, and that men should not disgrace themselves with silken clothing from the East. Fronto went further, and insisted on restrictions being put on plate, furniture, and household establishments. It was indeed still usual with the Senators, when it was their turn to vote, to suggest anything they thought for the State's advantage. Gallus Asinius argued on the other side. "With the growth of the empire private wealth too," he said, "had increased, and there was nothing new in this, but it accorded with the fashions of the earliest antiquity. Riches were one thing with the Fabricii, quite another with the Scipios. The State was the standard of everything; when it was poor, the homes of the citizens were humble; when it reached such magnificence, private grandeur increased. In household establishments, and plate, and in whatever was provided for use, there was neither excess nor parsimony except in relation to the fortune of the possessor. A distinction had been made in the assessments of Senators and knights, not because they differed naturally, but that the superiority of the one class in places in the theatre, in rank and in honour, might be also maintained in everything else which insured mental repose and bodily recreation, unless indeed men in the highest position were to undergo more anxieties and more dangers, and to be at the same time deprived of all solace under those anxieties and dangers." Gallus gained a ready assent, under these specious phrases, by a confession of failings with which his audience sympathized. And Tiberius too had added that this was not a time for censorship, and that if there were any declension in manners, a promoter of reform would not be wanting.

34

DURING this debate Lucius Piso, after exclaiming against the corruption of the courts, the bribery of judges, the cruel threats of accusations from hired orators, declared that he would depart and quit the capital, and that he meant to live in some obscure and distant rural retreat. At the same moment he rose to leave the Senate House. Tiberius was much excited, and though he pacified Piso with gentle words, he also strongly urged his relatives to stop his departure by their influence or their entreaties. Soon afterwards this same Piso gave an equal proof of a fearless sense of wrong by suing Urgulania, whom Augusta's friendship had raised above the law. Neither did Urgulania obey the summons, for in defiance of Piso she went in her litter to the emperor's house; nor did Piso give way, though Augusta complained that she was insulted and her majesty slighted. Tiberius, to win popularity by so humouring his mother as to say that he would go to the praetor's court and support Urgulania, went forth from the palace, having ordered soldiers to follow him at a distance. He was seen, as the people thronged about him, to wear a calm face, while he prolonged his time on the way with various conversations, till at last when Piso's relatives tried in vain to restrain him, Augusta directed the money which was claimed to be handed to him. This ended the affair, and Piso, in consequence, was not dishonoured, and the emperor rose in reputation. Urgulania's influence, however, was so formidable to the State, that in a certain cause which was tried by the Senate she would not condescend to appear as a witness. The praetor was sent to question her at her own house, although the Vestal virgins, according to ancient custom, were heard in the courts, before judges, whenever they gave evidence.

35

I SHOULD say nothing of the adjournment of public business in this year, if it were not worth while to notice the conflicting opinions of Cneius Piso and Asinius Gallus on the subject. Piso, although the emperor had said that he would be absent, held that all the more ought the business to be transacted, that the State might have honour of its Senate and knights being able to perform their duties in the sovereign's absence. Gallus, as Piso had forestalled him in the display of freedom, maintained that nothing was sufficiently impressive or suitable to the majesty of the Roman people, unless done before Caesar and under his very eyes, and that therefore the gathering from all Italy and the influx from the provinces ought to be reserved for his presence. Tiberius listened to this in silence, and the matter was debated on both sides in a sharp controversy. The business, however, was adjourned.

36

A DISPUTE then arose between Gallus and the emperor. Gallus proposed that the elections of magistrates should be held every five years, and that the commanders of the legions who before receiving a praetorship discharged this military service should at once become praetor-select, the emperor nominating twelve candidates every year. It was quite evident that this motion had a deeper meaning and was an attempt to explore the secrets of imperial policy. Tiberius, however, argued as if his power would be thus increased. "It would," he said, "be trying to his moderation to have to elect so many and to put off so many. He scarcely avoided giving offence from year to year, even though a candidate's rejection was solaced by the near prospect of office. What hatred would be incurred from those whose election was deferred for five years! How could he foresee through so long an interval what would be a man's temper, or domestic relations, or estate? Men became arrogant even with this annual appointment. What would happen if their thoughts were fixed on promotion for five years? It was in fact a multiplying of the magistrates five-fold, and a subversion of the laws which had prescribed proper periods for the exercise of the candidate's activity and the seeking or securing office. With this seemingly conciliatory speech he retained the substance of power.

37

HE also increased the incomes of some of the Senators. Hence it was the more surprising that he listened somewhat disdainfully to the request of Marcus Hortalus, a youth of noble rank in conspicuous poverty. He was the grandson of the orator Hortensius, and had been induced by Augustus, on the strength of a gift of a million sesterces, to marry and rear children, that one of our most illustrious families might not become extinct. Accordingly, with his four sons standing at the doors of the Senate House, the Senate then sitting in the palace, when it was his turn to speak he began to address them as follows, his eyes fixed now on the statue of Hortensius which stood among those of the orators, now on that of Augustus: "Senators, these whose numbers and boyish years you behold I have reared, not by my own choice, but because the emperor advised me. At the same time, my ancestors deserved to have descendants. For myself, not having been able in these altered times to receive or acquire wealth or popular favour, or that eloquence which has been the hereditary possession of our house, I was satisfied if my narrow means were neither a disgrace to myself nor burden to others. At the emperor's bidding I married. Behold the offspring and progeny of a succession of consuls and dictators. Not to excite odium do I recall such facts, but to win compassion. While you prosper, Caesar, they will attain such promotion as you shall bestow. Meanwhile save from penury the great-grandsons of Quintus Hortensius, the foster-children of Augustus."

38

THE Senate's favourable bias was an incitement to Tiberius to offer prompt opposition, which he did in nearly these words: "If all poor men begin to come here and to beg money for their children, individuals will never be satisfied, and the State will be bankrupt. Certainly our ancestors did not grant the privilege of occasionally proposing amendments or of suggesting, in our turn for speaking, something for the general advantage in order that we might in this house increase our private business and property, thereby bringing odium on the Senate and on emperors whether they concede or refuse their bounty. In fact, it is not a request, but an importunity, a utterly unreasonable as it is unforeseen, for a senator, when the house has met on other matters, to rise from his place and, pleading the number and age of his children, put a pressure on the delicacy of the Senate, then transfer the same constraint to myself, and, as it were, break open the exchequer, which, if we exhaust it by improper favouritism, will have to be replenished by crimes. Money was given you, Hortalus, by Augustus, but without solicitation, and not on the condition of its being always given. Otherwise industry will languish and idleness be encouraged, if a man has nothing to fear, nothing to hope from himself, and every one, in utter recklessness, will expect relief from others, thus becoming useless to himself and a burden to me." These and like remarks, though listened to with assent by those who make it a practice to eulogise everything coming from sovereigns, both good and bad, were received by the majority in silence or with suppressed murmurs. Tiberius perceived it, and having paused a while, said that he had given Hortalus his answer, but that if the senators thought it right, he would bestow two hundred thousand sesterces on each of his children of the male sex. The others thanked him; Hortalus said nothing, either from alarm or because even in his reduced fortunes he clung to his hereditary nobility. Nor did Tiberius afterwards show any pity, though the house of Hortensius sank into shameful poverty.

39

THAT same year the daring of a single slave, had it not been promptly checked, would have ruined the State by discord and civil war. A servant of Postumus Agrippa, Clemens by name, having ascertained that Augustus was dead, formed a design beyond a slave's conception, of going to the island of Planasia and seizing Agrippa by craft or force and bringing him to the armies of Germany. The slowness of a merchant vessel thwarted his bold venture. Meanwhile the murder of Agrippa had been perpetrated, and then turning his thoughts to a greater and more hazardous enterprise, he stole the ashes of the deceased, sailed to Cosa, a promontory of Etruria, and there hid himself in obscure places till his hair and beard were long. In age and figure he was not unlike his master. Then through suitable emissaries who shared his secret, it was rumoured that Agrippa was alive, first in whispered gossip, soon, as is usual with forbidden topics, in vague talk which found its way to the credulous ears of the most ignorant people or of restless and revolutionary schemers. He himself went to the towns, as the day grew dark, without letting himself be seen publicly or remaining long in the same places, but, as he knew that truth gains strength by notoriety and time, falsehood by precipitancy and vagueness, he would either withdraw himself from publicity or else forestall it.

40

IT was rumoured meanwhile throughout Italy, and was believed at Rome, that Agrippa had been saved by the blessing of Heaven. Already at Ostia, where he had arrived, he was the centre of interest to a vast concourse as well as to secret gatherings in the capital, while Tiberius was distracted by the doubt whether he should crush this slave of his by military force or allow time to dissipate a silly credulity. Sometimes he thought that he must overlook nothing, sometimes that he need not be afraid of everything, his mind fluctuating between shame and terror. At last he entrusted the affair to Sallustius Crispus, who chose two of his dependents (some say they were soldiers) and urged them to go to him as pretended accomplices, offering money and promising faithful companionship in danger. They did as they were bidden; then, waiting for an unguarded hour of night, they took with them a sufficient force, and having bound and gagged him, dragged him to the palace. When Tiberius asked him how he had become Agrippa, he is said to have replied, "As you became Caesar." He could not be forced to divulge his accomplices.

Tiberius did not venture on a public execution, but ordered him to be slain in a private part of the palace and his body to be secretly removed. And although many of the emperor's household and knights and senators were said to have supported him with their wealth and helped him with their counsels, no inquiry was made.

41

AT the close of the year was consecrated an arch near the temple of Saturn to commemorate the recovery of the standards lost with Varus, under the leadership of Germanicus and the auspices of Tiberius; a temple of Fors Fortuna, by the Tiber, in the gardens which Caesar, the dictator, bequeathed to the Roman people; a chapel to the Julian family, and statues at Bovillae to the Divine Augustus. In the consulship of Caius Caecilius and Lucius Pomponius, Germanicus Caesar, on the 26th day of May, celebrated his triumph over the Cherusci, Chatti, and Angrivarii, and the other tribes which extend as far as the Elbe. There were borne in procession spoils, prisoners, representations of the mountains, the rivers and battles; and the war, seeing that he had been forbidden to finish it, was taken as finished. The admiration of the beholders was heightened by the striking comeliness of the general and the chariot which bore his five children. Still, there was a latent dread when they remembered how unfortunate in the case of Drusus, his father, had been the favour of the crowd; how his uncle Marcellus, regarded by the city populace with passionate enthusiasm, had been snatched from them while yet a youth, and how short-lived and ill-starred were the attachments of the Roman people.

42

TIBERIUS meanwhile in the name of Germanicus gave every one of the city populace three hundred sesterces, and nominated himself his colleague in the consulship. Still, failing to obtain credit for sincere affection, he resolved to get the young prince out of the way, under pretense of conferring distinction, and for this he invented reasons, or eagerly fastened on such as chance presented. King

Archelaus had been in possession of Cappadocia for fifty years, and Tiberius hated him because he had not shown him any mark of respect while he was at Rhodes. This neglect of Archelaus was not due to pride, but was suggested by the intimate friends of Augustus, because, when Caius Caesar was in his prime and had charge of the affairs of the East, Tiberius's friendship was thought to be dangerous. When, after the extinction of the family of the Caesars, Tiberius acquired the empire, he enticed Archelaus by a letter from his mother, who without concealing her son's displeasure promised mercy if he would come to beg for it. Archelaus, either quite unsuspicious of treachery, or dreading compulsion, should it be thought that he saw through it, hastened to Rome. There he was received by a pitiless emperor, and soon afterwards was arraigned before the Senate. In his anguish and in the weariness of old age, and from being unused, as a king, to equality, much less to degradation, not, certainly, from fear of the charges fabricated against him, he ended his life, by his own act or by a natural death. His kingdom was reduced into a province, and Caesar declared that, with its revenues, the one per cent. tax could be lightened, which, for the future, he fixed at one-half per cent. During the same time, on the deaths of Antiochus and Philopator, kings respectively of the Commageni and Cilicians, these nations became excited, a majority desiring the Roman rule, some, that of their kings. The provinces too of Syria and Judaea, exhausted by their burdens, implored a reduction of tribute.

43

TIBERIUS accordingly discussed these matters and the affairs of Armenia, which I have already related, before the Senate. "The commotions in the East," he said, "could be quieted only by the wisdom, of Germanicus; own life was on the decline, and Drusus had not yet reached his maturity." Thereupon, by a decree of the Senate, the provinces beyond sea were entrusted to Germanicus, with greater powers wherever he went than were given to those who obtained their provinces by lot or by the emperor's appointment. Tiberius had however removed from Syria Creticus Silanus, who was connected by a close tie with Germanicus, his daughter being betrothed to Nero, the eldest of Germanicus's children. He appointed to it Cneius Piso, a man of violent temper, without an idea of obedience, with indeed a natural arrogance inherited from his father Piso, who in the civil war supported with the most energetic aid against Caesar the reviving faction in Africa, then embraced the cause of Brutus and Cassius, and, when suffered to return, refrained from seeking promotion till, he was actually solicited to accept a consulship offered by Augustus. But beside the father's haughty temper there was also the noble rank and wealth of his wife Plancina, to inflame his ambition. He would hardly be the inferior of Tiberius, and as for Tiberius's children, he looked down on them as far beneath him. He thought it a certainty that he had been chosen to govern Syria in order to thwart the aspirations of Germanicus. Some believed that he had even received secret instructions from Tiberius, and it was beyond a question that Augusta, with feminine jealousy, had suggested to Plancina calumnious insinuations against Agrippina. For there was division and discord in the court, with unexpressed partialities towards either Drusus or Germanicus. Tiberius favoured Drusus as his son and born of his own blood. As for Germanicus, his uncle's estrangement had increased the affection which all others felt for him, and there was the fact too that he had an advantage in the illustrious rank of his mother's family, among whom he could point to his grandfather Marcus Antonius and to his great-uncle Augustus. Drusus, on the other hand, had for his great-grandfather a Roman knight, Pomponius Atticus, who seemed to disgrace the ancestral images of the Claudii. Again, the consort of Germanicus, Agrippina, in number of children and in character, was superior to Livia, the wife of Drusus. Yet the brothers were singularly united, and were wholly unaffected by the rivalries of their kinsfolk.

44

SOON afterwards Drusus was sent into Illyricum to be familiarised with military service, and to win the goodwill of the army. Tiberius also thought that it was better for the young prince, who was being demoralised by the luxury of the capital, to serve in a camp, while he felt himself the safer with both his sons in command of legions. However, he made a pretext of the Suevi, who were imploring help against the Cherusci. For when the Romans had departed and they were free from the fear of an invader, these tribes, according to the custom of the race, and then specially as rivals in fame, had turned their arms against each other. The strength of the two nations, the valour of their chiefs were equal. But the title of king rendered Maroboduus hated among his countrymen, while Arminius was regarded with favour as the champion of freedom.

45

THUS it was not only the Cherusci and their allies, the old soldiers of Arminius, who took up arms, but even the Semnones and Langobardi from the kingdom of Maroboduus revolted to that chief. With this addition he must have had an overwhelming superiority, had not Inguiomerus deserted with a troop of his dependents to Maroboduus, simply for the reason that the aged uncle scorned to obey a brother's youthful son. The armies were drawn up, with equal confidence on both sides, and there were not those desultory attacks or irregular bands, formerly so common with the Germans. Prolonged warfare against us had accustomed them to keep close to their standards, to have the support of reserves, and to take the word of command from their generals. On this occasion Arminius, who reviewed the whole field on horseback, as he rode up to each band, boasted of regained freedom, of slaughtered legions, of spoils and weapons wrested from the Romans, and still in the hands of many of his men. As for Maroboduus, he called him a fugitive, who had no experience of battles, who had sheltered himself in the recesses of the Hercynian forest and then with presents and embassies sued for a treaty; a traitor to his country, a satellite of Caesar, who deserved to be driven out, with rage as furious as that with which they had slain Quintilius Varus. They should simply remember their many battles, the result of which, with the final expulsion of the Romans, sufficiently showed who could claim the crowning success in war.

46

NOR did Maroboduus abstain from vaunts about himself or from revilings of the foe. Clasping the hand of Inguiomerus, he protested "that in the person before them centred all the renown of the Cherusci, that to his counsels was due whatever had ended successfully. Arminius in his infatuation and ignorance was taking to himself the glory which belonged to another, for he had treacherously surprised three unofficered legions and a general who had not an idea of perfidy, to the great hurt of Germany and to his own disgrace, since his wife and his son were still enduring slavery. As for himself, he had been attacked by twelve legions led by Tiberius, and had preserved untarnished the glory of the Germans, and then on equal terms the armies had parted. He was by no means sorry that they had the matter in their own hands, whether they preferred to war with all their might against Rome, or to accept a bloodless peace." To these words, which roused the two armies, was added the stimulus of special motives of their own. The Cherusci and Langobardi were fighting for ancient renown or newly-won freedom; the other side for the increase of their dominion. Never at any time was the shock of battle more tremendous or the issue more doubtful, as the right wings of both armies were routed. Further fighting was expected, when Maroboduus withdrew his camp to the hills. This was a sign of discomfiture. He was gradually stripped of his strength by desertions, and, having fled to the Marcomanni, he sent envoys to Tiberius with entreaties for help. The answer was that he had no right to invoke the aid of Roman arms against the Cherusci, when he had rendered no assistance to the Romans in their conflict with the same enemy. Drusus, however, was sent as I have related, to establish peace.

47

THAT same year twelve famous cities of Asia fell by an earthquake in the night, so that the destruction was all the more unforeseen and fearful. Nor were there the means of escape usual in, such a disaster, by rushing out into the open country, for there people were swallowed up by the yawning earth. Vast mountains, it is said, collapsed; what had been level ground seemed to be raised aloft, and fires blazed out amid the ruin. The calamity fell most fatally on the inhabitants of Sardis, and it attracted to them the largest share of sympathy. The emperor promised ten million sesterces, and remitted for five years all they paid to the exchequer or to the emperor's purse. Magnesia, under Mount Sipylus, was considered to come next in loss and in need of help. The people of Temnus, Philadelpheia, Aegae, Apollonis, the Mostenians, and Hyrcanian Macedonians, as they were called, with the towns of Hierocaesarea, Myrina, Cyme, and Tmolus were, it was decided, to be exempted from tribute for the same time, and some one was to be sent from the Senate to examine their actual condition and to relieve them. Marcus Aletus, one of the expraetors, was chosen, from a fear that, as an exconsul was governor of Asia, there might be rivalry between men of equal rank, and consequent embarrassment.

48

TO his splendid public liberality the emperor added bounties no less popular. The property of Aemilia Musa, a rich woman who died intestate, on which the imperial treasury had a claim, he handed over to Aemilius Lepidus, to whose family she appeared to belong; and the estate of Patuleius, a wealthy Roman knight, though he was himself left in part his heir, he gave to Marcus Servilius, whose name he discovered in an earlier and unquestioned will. In both these cases he said that noble rank ought to have the support of wealth. Nor did he accept a legacy from any one unless he had earned it by friendship. Those who were strangers to him, and who, because they were at enmity with others, made the emperor their heir, he kept at a distance. While, however, he relieved the honourable poverty of the virtuous, he expelled from the Senate or suffered voluntarily to retire spendthrifts whose vices had brought them to penury, like Vibidius Varro, Marius Nepos, Appius Appianus, Cornelius Sulla, and Quintus Vitellius.

49

ABOUT the same time he dedicated some temples of the gods, which had perished from age or from fire, and which Augustus had begun to restore. These were temples to Liber, Libera, and Ceres, near the Great Circus, which last Aulus Postumius, when Dictator, had vowed; a temple to Flora in the same place, which had been built by Lucius and Marcus Publicius, aediles, and a temple to Janus, which had been erected in the vegetable market by Caius Duilius, who was the first to make the Roman power successful at sea and to win a naval triumph over the Carthaginians. A temple to Hope was consecrated by Germanicus; this had been vowed by Atilius in that same war.

50

MEANTIME the law of treason was gaining strength. Appuleia Varilia, grand-niece of Augustus, was accused of treason by an informer for having ridiculed the Divine Augustus, Tiberius, and Tiberius's mother, in some insulting remarks, and for having been convicted of adultery, allied though she was to Caesar's house. Adultery, it was thought, was sufficiently guarded against by the Julian law. As to the charge of treason, the emperor insisted that it should be taken separately, and that she should be condemned if she had spoken irreverently of Augustus. Her insinuations against himself he did not wish to be the subject of judicial inquiry. When asked by the consul what he thought of the unfavourable speeches she was accused of having uttered against his mother, he said nothing. Afterwards, on the next day of the Senate's meeting, he even begged in his mother's name that no words of any kind spoken against her might in any case be treated as criminal. He then acquitted Appuleia of treason. For her adultery, he deprecated the severer penalty, and advised that she should be removed by her kinsfolk, after the example of our forefathers, to more than two hundred miles from Rome. Her paramour, Manlius, was forbidden to live in Italy or Africa.

51

A CONTEST then arose about the election of a praetor in the room of Vipstanus Gallus, whom death had removed. Germanicus and Drusus (for they were still at Rome) supported Haterius Agrippa, a relative of Germanicus. Many, on the other hand, endeavoured to make the number of children weigh most in favour of the candidates. Tiberius rejoiced to see a strife in the Senate between his sons and the law. Beyond question the law was beaten, but not at once, and only by a few votes, in the same way as laws were defeated even when they were in force.

52

IN this same year a war broke out in Africa, where the enemy was led by Tacfarinas. A Numidian by birth, he had served as an auxiliary in the Roman camp, then becoming a deserter, he at first gathered round him a roving band familiar with robbery, for plunder and for rapine. After a while, he marshaled them like regular soldiers, under standards and in troops, till at last he was regarded as the leader, not of an undisciplined rabble, but of the Musulamian people. This powerful tribe, bordering on the deserts of Africa, and even then with none of the civilization of cities, took up arms and drew their Moorish neighbours into the war. These too had a leader, Mazippa. The army was so divided that Tacfarinas kept the picked men who were armed in Roman fashion within a camp, and familiarized them with a commander's authority, while Mazippa, with light troops, spread around him fire, slaughter, and consternation. They had forced the Ciniphii, a far from contemptible tribe, into their cause, when Furius Camillus, proconsul of Africa, united in one force a legion and all the regularly enlisted allies, and, with an army insignificant indeed compared with the multitude of the Numidians and Moors, marched against the enemy. There was nothing however which he strove so much to avoid as their eluding an engagement out of fear. It was by the hope of victory that they were lured on only to be defeated. The legion was in the army's centre; the light cohorts and two cavalry squadrons on its wings. Nor did Tacfarinas refuse battle. The Numidians were routed, and after a number of years the name of Furius won military renown. Since the days of the famous deliverer of our city and his son Camillus, fame as a general had fallen to the lot of other branches of the family, and the man of whom I am now speaking was regarded as an inexperienced soldier. All the more willingly did Tiberius commemorate his achievements in the Senate, and the Senators voted him the ornaments of triumph, an honour which Camillus, because of his unambitious life, enjoyed without harm.

53

IN the following year Tiberius held his third, Germanicus his second, consulship. Germanicus, however, entered on the office at Nicopolis, a city of Achaia, whither he had arrived by the coast of Illyricum, after having seen his brother Drusus, who was then in Dalmatia, and endured a stormy voyage through the Adriatic and afterwards the Ionian Sea. He accordingly devoted a few days to the repair of his fleet, and, at the same time, in remembrance of his ancestors, he visited the bay which the victory of Actium had made famous, the spoils consecrated by Augustus, and the camp of Antonius. For, as I have said, Augustus was his great-uncle, Antonius his grandfather, and vivid images of disaster and success rose before him on the spot. Thence he went to Athens, and there, as a concession to our treaty with an allied and ancient city, he was attended only by a single lictor. The Greeks welcomed him with the most elaborate honours, and brought forward all the old deeds and sayings of their countrymen, to give additional dignity to their flattery.

54

THENCE he directed his course to Euboea and crossed to Lesbos, where Agrippina for the last time was confined and gave birth to Julia. He then penetrated to the remoter parts of the province of Asia, visited the Thracian cities, Perinthus and Byzantium; next, the narrow strait of the Propontis and the entrance of the Pontus, from an anxious wish to become acquainted with those ancient and celebrated localities. He gave relief, as he went, to provinces which had been exhausted by internal feuds or by the oppressions of governors. In his return he attempted to see the sacred mysteries of the Samothracians, but north winds which he encountered drove him aside from his course. And so after visiting Ilium and surveying a scene venerable from the vicissitudes of fortune and as the birthplace of our people, he coasted back along Asia, and touched at Colophon, to consult the oracle of the Clarian Apollo. There, it is not a woman, as at Delphi, but a priest chosen from certain families, generally from Miletus, who ascertains simply the number and the names of the applicants. Then descending into a cave and drinking a draught from a secret spring, the man, who is commonly ignorant of letters and of poetry, utters a response in verse answering to the thoughts conceived in the mind of any inquirer. It was said that he prophesied to Germanicus, in dark hints, as oracles usually do, an early doom.

55

CNEIUS Piso meanwhile, that he might the sooner enter on his design, terrified the citizens of Athens by his tumultuous approach, and then reviled them in a bitter speech, with indirect reflections on Germanicus, who, he said, had derogated from the honour of the Roman name in having treated with excessive courtesy, not the people of Athens, who indeed had been exterminated by repeated disasters, but a miserable medley of tribes. As for the men before him, they had been Mithridates's allies against Sulla, allies of Antonius against the Divine Augustus. He taunted them too with the past, with their ill-success against the Macedonians, their violence to their own countrymen, for he had his own special grudge against this city, because they would not spare at his intercession one Theophilus whom the Areopagus had condemned for forgery. Then, by sailing rapidly and by the shortest route through the Cyclades, he overtook Germanicus at the island of Rhodes. The prince was not ignorant of the slanders with which he had been assailed, but his good nature was such that when a storm arose and drove Piso on rocks, and his enemy's destruction could have been referred to chance, he sent some triremes, by the help of which he might be rescued from danger. But this did not soften Piso's heart.

Scarcely allowing a day's interval, he left Germanicus and hastened on in advance. When he reached Syria and the legions, he began, by bribery and favouritism, to encourage the lowest of the common soldiers, removing the old centurions and the strict tribunes and assigning their places to creatures of his own or to the vilest of the men, while he allowed idleness in the camp, licentiousness in the towns, and the soldiers to roam through the country and take their pleasure. He went such lengths in demoralizing them, that he was spoken of in their vulgar talk as the father of the legions. Plancina too, instead of keeping herself within the proper limits of a woman, would be present at the evolutions of the cavalry and the maneuvers of the cohorts, and would fling insulting remarks at Agrippina and Germanicus. Some even of the good soldiers were inclined to a corrupt compliance, as a whispered rumour gained ground that the emperor was not averse to these proceedings. Of all this Germanicus was aware, but his most pressing anxiety was to be first in reaching Armenia.

56

THIS had been of old an unsettled country from the character of its people and from its geographical position, bordering, as it does, to a great extent on our provinces and stretching far away to Media. It lies between two most mighty empires, and is very often at strife with them, hating Rome and jealous of Parthia. It had at this time no king, Vonones having been expelled, but the nation's likings inclined towards Zeno, son of Polemon, king of Pontus, who from his earliest infancy had imitated Armenian manners and customs, loving the chase, the banquet, and all the popular pastimes of barbarians, and who had thus bound to himself chiefs and people alike. Germanicus accordingly, in the city of Artaxata, with the approval of the nobility, in the presence of a vast multitude, placed the royal diadem on his head. All paid him homage and saluted him as King Artaxias, which name they gave him from the city. Cappadocia meanwhile, which had been reduced to the form of a province, received as its governor Quintus Veranius. Some of the royal tributes were diminished, to inspire hope of a gentler rule under Rome. Quintus Servaeus was appointed to Commagene, then first put under a praetor's jurisdiction.

57

SUCCESSFUL as was this settlement of all the interests of our allies, it gave Germanicus little joy because of the arrogance of Piso. Though he had been ordered to march part of the legions into Armenia under his own or his son's command, he had neglected to do either. At length the two met at Cyrrhus, the winter quarters of the tenth legion, each controlling his looks, Piso concealing his fears, Germanicus shunning the semblance of menace. He was indeed, as I have said, a kind-hearted man. But friends who knew well how to inflame a quarrel, exaggerated what was true and added lies, alleging various charges against Piso, Plancina, and their sons. At last, in the presence of a few intimate associates, Germanicus addressed him in language such as suppressed resentment suggests, to which Piso replied with haughty apologies. They parted in open enmity. After this Piso was seldom seen at Caesar's tribunal, and if he ever sat by him, it was with a sullen frown and a marked display of opposition. He was even heard to say at a banquet given by the king of the Nabataeans, when some golden crowns of great weight were presented to Caesar and Agrippina and light ones to Piso and the rest, that the entertainment was given to the son of a Roman emperor, not of a Parthian king. At the same time he threw his crown on the ground, with a long speech against luxury, which, though it angered Germanicus, he still bore with patience.

58

MEANTIME envoys arrived from Artabanus, king of the Parthians. He had sent them to recall the memory of friendship and alliance, with an assurance that he wished for a renewal of the emblems of concord, and that he would in honour of Germanicus yield the point of advancing to the bank of the Euphrates. He begged meanwhile that Vonones might not be kept in Syria, where, by emissaries from an easy distance, he might draw the chiefs of the tribes into civil strife. Germanicus' answer as to the alliance between Rome and Parthia was dignified; as to the king's visit and the respect shown to himself, it was graceful and modest. Vonones was removed to

Pompeiopolis, a city on the coast of Cilicia. This was not merely a concession to the request of Artabanus, but was meant as an affront to Piso, who had a special liking for Vonones, because of the many attentions and presents by which he had won Plancina's favour.

59

IN the consulship of Marcus Silanus and Lucius Norbanus, Germanicus set out for Egypt to study its antiquities. His ostensible motive however was solicitude for the province. He reduced the price of corn by opening the granaries, and adopted many practices pleasing to the multitude. He would go about without soldiers, with sandaled feet, and appareled after the Greek fashion, in imitation of Publius Scipio, who, it is said, habitually did the same in Sicily, even when the war with Carthage was still raging. Tiberius having gently expressed disapproval of his dress and manners, pronounced a very sharp censure on his visit to Alexandria without the emperor's leave, contrary to the regulations of Augustus. That prince, among other secrets of imperial policy, had forbidden senators and Roman knights of the higher rank to enter Egypt except by permission, and he had specially reserved the country, from a fear that any one who held a province containing the key of the land and of the sea, with ever so small a force against the mightiest army, might distress Italy by famine.

60

GERMANICUS, however, who had not yet learnt how much he was blamed for his expedition, sailed up the Nile from the city of Canopus as his starting-point. Spartans founded the place because Canopus, pilot of one of their ships, had been buried there, when Menelaus on his return to Greece was driven into a distant sea and to the shores of Libya. Thence he went to the river's nearest mouth, dedicated to a Hercules who, the natives say, was born in the country and was the original hero, others, who afterwards showed like valour, having received his name. Next he visited the vast ruins of ancient Thebes. There yet remained on the towering piles Egyptian inscriptions, with a complete account of the city's past grandeur. One of the aged priests, who was desired to interpret the language of his country, related how once there had dwelt in Thebes seven hundred thousand men of military age, and how with such an army king Rhamses conquered Libya, Ethiopia, Media, Persia, Bactria, and Scythia, and held under his sway the countries inhabited by the Syrians, Armenians, and their neighbours, the Cappadocians, from the Bithynian to the Lycian sea. There was also to be read what tributes were imposed on these nations, the weight of silver and gold, the tale of arms and horses, the gifts of ivory and of perfumes to the temples, with the amount of grain and supplies furnished by each people, a revenue as magnificent as is now exacted by the might of Parthia or the power of Rome.

61

BUT Germanicus also bestowed attention on other wonders. Chief of these were the stone image of Memnon, which, when struck by the sun's rays, gives out the sound of a human voice; the pyramids, rising up like mountains amid almost impassable wastes of shifting sand, raised by the emulation and vast wealth of kings; the lake hollowed out of the earth to be a receptacle for the Nile's overflow; and elsewhere the river's narrow channel and profound depth which no line of the explorer can penetrate. He then came to Elephantine and Syene, formerly the limits of the Roman empire, which now extends to the Red Sea.

62

WHILE Germanicus was spending the summer in visits to several provinces, Drusus gained no little glory by sowing discord among the Germans and urging them to complete the destruction of the now broken power of Maroboduus. Among the Gotones was a youth of noble birth, Catualda by name, who had formerly been driven into exile by the might of Maroboduus, and who now, when the king's fortunes were declining, ventured on revenge. He entered the territory of the Marcomanni with a strong force, and, having corruptly won over the nobles to join him, burst into the palace and into an adjacent fortress. There he found the long-accumulated plunder of the Suevi and camp followers and traders from our provinces who had been attracted to an enemy's land, each from their various homes, first by the freedom of commerce, next by the desire of amassing wealth, finally by forgetfulness of their fatherland.

63

MAROBODUUS, now utterly deserted, had no resource but in the mercy of Caesar. Having crossed the Danube where it flows by the province of Noricum, he wrote to Tiberius, not like a fugitive or a suppliant, but as one who remembered his past greatness. When as a most famous king in former days he received invitations from many nations, he had still, he said, preferred the friendship of Rome. Caesar replied that he should have a safe and honourable home in Italy, if he would remain there, or, if his interests required something different, he might leave it under the same protection under which he had come. But in the Senate he maintained that Philip had not been so formidable to the Athenians, or Pyrrhus or Antiochus to the Roman people, as was Maroboduus. The speech is extant, and in it he magnifies the man's power, the ferocity of the tribes under his sway, his proximity to Italy as a foe, finally his own measures for his overthrow. The result was that Maroboduus was kept at Ravenna, where his possible return was a menace to the Suevi, should they ever disdain obedience. But he never left Italy for eighteen years, living to old age and losing much of his renown through an excessive clinging to life. Catualda had a like downfall and no better refuge. Driven out soon afterwards by the overwhelming strength of the Hermundusi led by Vibilius, he was received and sent to Forum Julii, a colony of Narbonensian Gaul. The barbarians who followed the two kings, lest they might disturb the peace of the provinces by mingling with the population, were settled beyond the Danube between the rivers Marus and Cusus, under a king, Vannius, of the nation of the Quadi.

64

TIDINGS having also arrived of Artaxias being made king of Armenia by Germanicus, the Senate decreed that both he and Drusus should enter the city with an ovation. Arches too were raised round the sides of the temple of Mars the Avenger, with statues of the two Caesars. Tiberius was the more delighted at having established peace by wise policy than if he had finished a war by battle. And so next he planned a crafty scheme against Rhescuporis, king of Thrace. That entire country had been in the possession of Rhoemetalces, after whose death Augustus assigned half to the king's brother Rhescuporis, half to his son Cotys. In this division the cultivated lands, the towns, and what bordered on Greek territories, fell to Cotys; the wild and barbarous portion, with enemies on its frontier, to Rhescuporis. The kings too themselves differed, Cotys having a gentle and kindly temper, the other a fierce and ambitious spirit, which could not brook a partner. Still at first they lived in a hollow friendship, but soon Rhescuporis overstepped his bounds and appropriated to himself what had been given to Cotys, using force when he was resisted, though somewhat timidly under Augustus, who having created both kingdoms would, he feared, avenge any contempt of his arrangement. When however he heard of the change of emperor, he let loose bands of freebooters and razed the fortresses, as a provocation to war.

65

NOTHING made Tiberius so uneasy as an apprehension of the disturbance of any settlement. He commissioned a centurion to tell the kings not to decide their dispute by arms. Cotys at once dismissed the forces which he had prepared. Rhescuporis, with assumed modesty, asked for a place of meeting where, he said, they might settle their differences by an interview. There was little hesitation in fixing on a time, a place, finally on terms, as every point was mutually conceded and accepted, by the one out of good nature, by the other with a treacherous intent. Rhescuporis, to ratify the treaty, as he said, further proposed a banquet; and when their mirth had been prolonged far into the night, and Cotys amid the feasting and the wine was unsuspicious of danger, he loaded him with chains, though he appealed, on perceiving the perfidy, to the sacred character of a king, to the gods of their common house, and to the hospitable board. Having possessed himself of all Thrace, he wrote word to Tiberius that a plot had been formed against him, and that he had forestalled the plotter. Meanwhile, under pretext of a war against the Bastarnian and Scythian tribes, he was strengthening himself with fresh forces of infantry and cavalry. He received a conciliatory answer. If there was no treachery in his conduct, he could rely on his innocence, but neither the emperor nor the Senate would decide on the right or wrong of his cause without hearing it. He was therefore to surrender Cotys, come in person transfer from himself the odium of the charge.

66

THIS letter Latinius Pandus, propraetor of Moesia, sent to Thrace, with soldiers to whose custody Cotys was to be delivered. Rhescuporis, hesitating between fear and rage, preferred to be charged with an accomplished rather than with an attempted crime. He ordered Cotys to be murdered and falsely represented his death as self-inflicted. Still the emperor did not change the policy which he had once for all adopted. On the death of Pandus, whom Rhescuporis accused of being his personal enemy, he appointed to the government of Moesia Pomponius Flaccus, a veteran soldier, specially because of his close intimacy with the king and his consequent ability to entrap him.

67

FLACCUS on arriving in Thrace induced the king by great promises, though he hesitated and thought of his guilty deeds, to enter the Roman lines. He then surrounded him with a strong force under pretense of showing him honour, and the tribunes and centurions, by counsel, by persuasion, and by a more undisguised captivity the further he went, brought him, aware at last of his desperate plight, to Rome. He was accused before the Senate by the wife of Cotys, and was condemned to be kept a prisoner far away from his kingdom. Thrace was divided between his son Rhoemetalces, who, it was proved, had opposed his father's designs, and the sons of Cotys. As these were still minors, Trebellienus Rufus, an ex-praetor, was appointed to govern the kingdom in the meanwhile, after the precedent of our ancestors who sent Marcus Lepidus into Egypt as guardian to Ptolemy's children. Rhescuporis was removed to Alexandria, and there attempting or falsely charged with attempting escape, was put to death.

68

ABOUT the same time, Vonones, who, as I have related, had been banished to Cilicia, endeavoured by bribing his guards to escape into Armenia, thence to Albania and Heniochia, and to his kinsman, the king of Scythia. Quitting the sea-coast on the pretense of a hunting expedition, he struck into trackless forests, and was soon borne by his swift steed to the river Pyramus, the bridges over which had been broken down by the natives as soon as they heard of the king's escape. Nor was there a ford by which it could be crossed. And so on the river's bank he was put in chains by Vibius Fronto, an officer of cavalry; and then Remmius, an enrolled pensioner, who had previously been entrusted with the king's custody, in pretended rage, pierced him with his sword. Hence there was more ground for believing that the man, conscious of guilty complicity and fearing accusation, had slain Vonones.

69

GERMANICUS meanwhile, as he was returning from Egypt, found that all his directions to the legions and to the various cities had been repealed or reversed. This led to grievous insults on Piso, while he as savagely assailed the prince. Piso then resolved to quit Syria. Soon he was detained there by the failing health of Germanicus, but when he heard of his recovery, while people were paying the vows they had offered for his safety, he went attended by his lictors, drove away the victims placed by the altars with all the preparations for sacrifice, and the festal gathering of the populace of Antioch. Then he left for Seleucia and awaited the result of the illness which had again attacked Germanicus. The terrible intensity of the malady was increased by the belief that he had been poisoned by Piso. And certainly there were found hidden in the floor and in the walls disinterred remains of human bodies, incantations and spells, and the name of Germanicus inscribed on leaden tablets, half-burnt cinders smeared with blood, and other horrors by which in popular belief souls are devoted so the infernal deities. Piso too was accused of sending emissaries to note curiously every unfavourable symptom of the illness.

70

GERMANICUS heard of all this with anger, no less than with fear. "If my doors," he said, "are to be besieged, if I must gasp out my last breath under my enemies' eyes, what will then be the lot of my most unhappy wife, of my infant children? Poisoning seems tedious; he is in eager haste to have the sole control of the province and the legions. But Germanicus is not yet fallen so low, nor will the murderer long retain the reward of the fatal deed." He then addressed a letter to Piso, renouncing his friendship, and, as many also state, ordered him to quit the province. Piso without further delay weighed anchor, slackening his course that he might not have a long way to return should Germanicus' death leave Syria open to him.

71

FOR a brief space the prince's hopes rose; then his frame became exhausted, and, as his end drew near, he spoke as follows to the friends by his side: "Were I succumbing to nature, I should have just ground of complaint even against the gods for thus tearing me away in my youth by an untimely death from parents, children, country. Now, cut off by the wickedness of Piso and Plancina, I leave to your hearts my last entreaties. Describe to my father and brother, torn by what persecutions, entangled by what plots, I have ended by the worst of deaths the most miserable of lives. If any were touched by my bright prospects, by ties of blood, or even by envy towards me while I lived, they will weep that the once prosperous survivor of so many wars has perished by a woman's treachery. You will have the opportunity of complaint before the Senate, of an appeal to the laws. It is not the chief duty of friends to follow the dead with unprofitable laments, but to remember his wishes, to fulfill his commands. Tears for Germanicus even strangers will shed; vengeance must come from you, if you loved the man more than his fortune. Show the people of Rome her who is the granddaughter of the Divine Augustus, as well as my consort; set before them my six children. Sympathy will be on the side of the accusers, and to those who screen themselves under infamous orders belief or pardon will be refused." His friends clasped the dying man's right hand, and swore that they would sooner lose life than revenge.

72

HE then turned to his wife and implored her by the memory of her husband and by their common offspring to lay aside her high spirit, to submit herself to the cruel blows of fortune, and not, when she returned to Rome, to enrage by political rivalry those who were stronger than herself. This was said openly; other words were whispered, pointing, it was supposed, to his fears from Tiberius. Soon afterwards he expired, to the intense sorrow of the province and of the neighbouring peoples. Foreign nations and kings grieved over him, so great was his courtesy to allies, his humanity to enemies. He inspired reverence alike by look and voice, and while he maintained the greatness and dignity of the highest rank, he had escaped the hatred that waits on arrogance.

73

HIS funeral, though it lacked the family statues and procession, was honoured by panegyrics and a commemoration of his virtues. Some there were who, as they thought of his beauty, his age, and the manner of his death, the vicinity too of the country where he died, likened his end to that of Alexander the Great. Both had a graceful person and were of noble birth; neither had much exceeded thirty years of age, and both fell by the treachery of their own people in strange lands. But Germanicus was gracious to his friends, temperate in his pleasures, the husband of one wife, with only legitimate children. He was too no less a warrior, though rashness he had none, and, though after having cowed Germany by his many victories, he was hindered from crushing it into subjection. Had he had the sole control of affairs, had he possessed the power and title of a king, he would have attained military glory as much more easily as he had excelled Alexander in clemency, in self-restraint, and in all other virtues. As to the body which, before it was burnt, lay bare in the forum at Antioch, its destined place of burial, it is doubtful whether it exhibited the marks of poisoning. For men according as they pitied Germanicus and were prepossessed with suspicion or were biased by partiality towards Piso, gave conflicting accounts.

74

THEN followed a deliberation among the generals and other senators present about the appointment of a governor to Syria. The contest was slight among all but Vibius Marsus and Cneius Sentius, between whom there was a long dispute. Finally Marsus yielded to Sentius as an older and keener competitor. Sentius at once sent to Rome a woman infamous for poisonings in the province and a special favourite of Plancina, Martina by name, on the demand of Vitellius and Veranius and others, who were preparing the charges and the indictment as if a prosecution had already been commenced.

75

AGRIPPINA meantime, worn out though she was with sorrow and bodily weakness, yet still impatient of everything which might delay her vengeance, embarked with the ashes of Germanicus and with her children, pitied by all. Here indeed was a woman of the highest nobility, and but lately because of her splendid union wont to be seen amid an admiring and sympathizing throng, now bearing in her bosom the mournful relics of death, with an uncertain hope of revenge, with apprehensions for herself, repeatedly at fortune's mercy by reason of the ill-starred fruitfulness of her marriage. Piso was at the island of Coos when tidings reached him that Germanicus was dead. He received the news with extravagant joy, slew victims, visited the temples, with no moderation in his transports; while Plancina's insolence increased, and she then for the first time exchanged for the gayest attire the mourning she had worn for her lost sister.

76

CENTURIONS streamed in, and hinted to Piso that he had the sympathy of the legions at his command. "Go back," they said, "to the province which has not been rightfully taken from you, and is still vacant." While he deliberated what he was to do, his son, Marcus Piso, advised speedy return to Rome. "As yet," he said, "you have not contracted any inexpiable guilt, and you need not dread feeble suspicions or vague rumours. Your strife with Germanicus deserved hatred perhaps, but not punishment, and by your having been deprived of the province, your enemies have been fully satisfied. But if you return, should Sentius resist you, civil war is begun, and you will not retain on your side the centurions and soldiers, who are powerfully swayed by the yet recent memory of their general and by a deep-rooted affection for the Caesars."

77

AGAINST this view Domitius Celer, one of Piso's intimate friends, argued that he ought to profit by the opportunity. "It was Piso, not Sentius, who had been appointed to Syria. It was to Piso that the symbols of power and a praetor's jurisdiction and the legions had been given. In case of a hostile menace, who would more rightfully confront it by arms than the man who had received the authority and special commission of a governor? And as for rumours, it is best to leave time in which they may die away. Often the innocent cannot stand against the first burst of unpopularity. But if Piso possesses himself of the army, and increases his resources, much which cannot be foreseen will haply turn out in his favour. Are we hastening to reach Italy along with the ashes of Germanicus, that, unheard and undefended, you may be hurried to ruin by the wailings of Agrippina and the first gossip of an ignorant mob? You have on your side the complicity of Augusta and the emperor's favour, though in secret, and none mourn more ostentatiously over the death of Germanicus than those who most rejoice at it."

78

WITHOUT much difficulty Piso, who was ever ready for violent action, was led into this view. He sent a letter to Tiberius accusing Germanicus of luxury and arrogance, and asserting that, having been driven away to make room for revolution, he had resumed the command of the army in the same loyal spirit in which he had before held it. At the same time he put Domitius on board a trireme, with an order to avoid the coast and to push on to Syria through the open sea away from the islands. He formed into regular companies the deserters who flocked to him, armed the camp-followers, crossed with his ships to the mainland, intercepted a detachment of new levies on their way to Syria, and wrote word to the petty kings of Cilicia that they were to help him with auxiliaries, the young Piso actively assisting in all the business of war, though he had advised against undertaking it.

79

AND so they coasted along Lycia and Pamphylia, and on meeting the fleet which conveyed Agrippina, both sides in hot anger at first armed for battle, and then in mutual fear confined themselves to revilings, Marsus Vibius telling Piso that he was to go to Rome to defend himself. Piso mockingly replied that he would be there as soon as the praetor who had to try poisoning cases had fixed a day for the accused and his prosecutors. Meanwhile Domitius having landed at Laodicea, a city of Syria, as he was on his way to the winter quarters of the sixth legion, which was, he believed, particularly open to revolutionary schemes, was anticipated by its commander Pacuvius. Of this Sentius informed Piso in a letter, and warned him not to disturb the armies by agents of corruption or the province by war. He gathered round him all whom he knew to cherish the memory of Germanicus, and to be opposed to his enemies, dwelling repeatedly on the greatness of the general, with hints that the State was being threatened with an armed attack, and he put himself at the head of a strong force, prepared for battle.

80

PISO, too, though his first attempts were unsuccessful, did not omit the safest precautions under present circumstances, but occupied a very strongly fortified position in Cilicia, named, Celenderis. He had raised to the strength of a legion the Cilician auxiliaries which the petty kings had sent, by mixing with them some deserters, and the lately intercepted recruits with his own and Plancina's slaves. And he protested that he, though Caesar's legate, was kept out of the province which Caesar had given him, not by the legions (for he had come at their invitation) but by Sentius, who was veiling private animosity under lying charges. "Only," he said, "stand in battle array, and the soldiers will not fight when they see that Piso whom they themselves once called 'father,' is the stronger, if right is to decide; if arms, is far from powerless." He then deployed his companies before the lines of the fortress on a high and precipitous hill, with the sea surrounding him on every other side. Against him were the veteran troops drawn up in ranks and with reserves, a formidable soldiery on one side, a formidable position on the other. But his men had neither heart nor hope, and only rustic weapons, extemporized for sudden use. When they came to fighting, the result was doubtful only while the Roman cohorts were struggling up to level ground; then, the Cilicians turned their backs and shut themselves up within the fortress.

81

MEANWHILE Piso vainly attempted an attack on the fleet which waited at a distance; he then went back, and as he stood before the walls, now smiting his breast, now calling on individual soldiers by name, and luring them on by rewards, sought to excite a mutiny.

He had so far roused them that a standard bearer of the sixth legion went over to him with his standard. Thereupon Sentius ordered the horns and trumpets to be sounded, the rampart to be assaulted, the scaling ladders to be raised, all the bravest men to mount on them, while others were to discharge from the engines spears, stones, and brands. At last Piso's obstinacy was overcome, and he begged that he might remain in the fortress on surrendering his arms, while the emperor was being consulted about the appointment of a governor to Syria. The proposed terms were refused, and all that was granted him were some ships and a safe return to Rome.

82

THERE meantime, when the illness of Germanicus was universally known, and all news, coming, as it did, from a distance, exaggerated the danger, there was grief and indignation. There was too an outburst of complaint. "Of course this was the meaning," they said, "of banishing him to the ends of the earth, of giving Piso the province; this was the drift of Augusta's secret interviews with Plancina. What elderly men had said of Drusus was perfectly true, that rulers disliked a citizen-like temper in their sons, and the young princes had been put out of the way because they had the idea of comprehending in a restored era of freedom the Roman people under equal laws." This popular talk was so stimulated by the news of Germanicus's death that even before the magistrate's proclamation or the Senate's resolution, there was a voluntary suspension of business, the public courts were deserted, and private houses closed. Everywhere there was a silence broken only by groans; nothing was arranged for mere effect. And though they refrained not from the emblems of the mourner, they sorrowed yet the more deeply in their hearts. It chanced that some merchants who left Syria while Germanicus was still alive, brought more cheering tidings about his health. These were instantly believed, instantly published. Every one passed on to others whom he met the intelligence, ill-authenticated as it was, and they again to many more, with joyous exaggeration. They ran to and fro through the city and broke open the doors of the temples. Night assisted their credulity, and amid the darkness confident assertion was comparatively easy. Nor did Tiberius check the false reports till by lapse of time they died away.

83

AND so the people grieved the more bitterly as though Germanicus was again lost to them. New honours were devised and decreed, as men were inspired by affection for him or by genius. His name was to be celebrated in the song of the Salii; chairs of state with oaken garlands over them were to be set up in the places assigned to the priesthood of the Augustales; his image in ivory was to head the procession in the games of the circus; no flamen or augur, except from the Julian family, was to be chosen in the room of Germanicus. Triumphal arches were erected at Rome, on the banks of the Rhine, and on mount Amanus in Syria, with an inscription recording his achievements, and how he had died in the public service. A cenotaph was raised at Antioch, where the body was burnt, a lofty mound at Epidaphna, where he had ended his life. The number of his statues, or of the places in which they were honoured, could not easily be computed. When a golden shield of remarkable size was voted him as a leader among orators, Tiberius declared that he would dedicate to him one of the usual kind, similar to the rest, for in eloquence, he said, there was no distinction of rank, and it was a sufficient glory for him to be classed among ancient writers. The knights called the seats in the theatre known as "the juniors," Germanicus's benches, and arranged that their squadrons were to ride in procession behind his effigy on the fifteenth of July. Many of these honours still remain; some were at once dropped, or became obsolete with time.

84

WHILE men's sorrow was yet fresh, Germanicus's sister Livia, who was married to Drusus, gave birth to twin sons. This, as a rare event, causing joy even in humble homes, so delighted the emperor that he did not refrain from boasting before the senators that to no Roman of the same rank had twin offspring ever before been born. In fact, he would turn to his own glory every incident, however casual. But at such a time, even this brought grief to the people, who thought that the increase of Drusus's family still further depressed the house of Germanicus.

85

THAT same year the profligacy of women was checked by stringent enactments, and it was provided that no woman whose grandfather, father, or husband had been a Roman knight should get money by prostitution. Vistilia, born of a praetorian family, had actually published her name with this object on the aedile's list, according to a recognised custom of our ancestors, who considered it a sufficient punishment on unchaste women to have to profess their shame. Titidius Labeo, Vistilia's husband, was judicially called on to say why with a wife whose guilt was manifest he had neglected to inflict the legal penalty. When he pleaded that the sixty days given for deliberation had not yet expired, it was thought sufficient to decide Vistilia's case, and she was banished out of sight to the island of Seriphos. There was a debate too about expelling the Egyptian and Jewish worship, and a resolution of the Senate was passed that four thousand of the freedmen class who were infected with those superstitions and were of military age should be transported to the island of Sardinia, to quell the brigandage of the place, a cheap sacrifice should they die from the pestilential climate. The rest were to quit Italy, unless before a certain day they repudiated their impious rites.

86

NEXT the emperor brought forward a motion for the election of a Vestal virgin in the room of Occia, who for fifty-seven years had presided with the most immaculate virtue over the Vestal worship. He formally thanked Fonteius Agrippa and Domitius Pollio for offering their daughters and so vying with one another in zeal for the commonwealth. Pollio's daughter was preferred, only because her mother had lived with one and the same husband, while Agrippa had impaired the honour of his house by a divorce. The emperor consoled his daughter, passed over though she was, with a dowry of a million sesterces.

87

AS the city populace complained of the cruel dearness of corn, he fixed a price for grain to be paid by the purchaser, promising himself to add two sesterces on every peck for the traders. But he would not therefore accept the title of "father of the country" which once before too had been offered him, and he sharply rebuked those who called his work "divine" and himself "lord." Consequently, speech was restricted and perilous under an emperor who feared freedom while he hated sycophancy.

88

I FIND it stated by some writers and senators of the period that a letter from Adgandestrius, chief of the Chatti, was read in the Senate, promising the death of Arminius, if poison were sent for the perpetration of the murder, and that the reply was that it was not by secret treachery but openly and by arms that the people of Rome avenged themselves on their enemies. A noble answer, by which Tiberius sought to liken himself to those generals of old who had forbidden and even denounced the poisoning of king Pyrrhus. Arminius, meanwhile, when the Romans retired and Maroboduus was expelled, found himself opposed in aiming at the throne by his countrymen's independent spirit. He was assailed by armed force, and while fighting with various success, fell by the treachery of his kinsmen. Assuredly he was the deliverer of Germany, one too who had defied Rome, not in her early rise, as other kings and generals, but in the height of her empire's glory, had fought, indeed, indecisive battles, yet in war remained unconquered. He completed thirty-seven years of life, twelve years of power, and he is still a theme of song among barbarous nations, though to Greek historians, who admire only their own achievements, he is unknown, and to Romans not as famous as he should be, while we extol the past and are indifferent to our own times.

Book III

64

ABOUT this time Julia Augusta had an alarming illness, which compelled the emperor to hasten his return to Rome, for hitherto there had been a genuine harmony between the mother and son, or a hatred well concealed. Not long before, for instance, Julia in dedicating a statue to the Divine Augustus near the theatre of Marcellus had inscribed the name of Tiberius below her own, and it was surmised that the emperor, regarding this as a slight on a sovereign's dignity, had brooded over it with deep and disguised resentment. However the Senate now decreed supplications to the gods and the celebration of the Great Games, which were to be exhibited by the pontiffs, augurs, the colleges of the Fifteen and of the Seven, with the Augustal Brotherhood. Lucius Apronius moved that the heralds too should preside over these Games. This the emperor opposed, distinguishing the peculiar privileges of the sacred guilds, and quoting precedents. Never, he argued, had the heralds this dignity. "The Augustal priests were included expressly because their sacred office was specially attached to the family for which vows were being performed."

65

MY purpose is not to relate at length every motion, but only such as were conspicuous for excellence or notorious for infamy. This I regard as history's highest function, to let no worthy action be uncommemorated, and to hold out the reprobation of posterity as a terror to evil words and deeds. So corrupted indeed and debased was that age by sycophancy that not only the foremost citizens who were forced to save their grandeur by servility, but every ex-consul, most of the ex-praetors and a host of inferior senators would rise in eager rivalry to propose shameful and preposterous motions. Tradition says that Tiberius as often as he left the Senate-House used to exclaim in Greek, "How ready these men are to be slaves." Clearly, even he, with his dislike of public freedom, was disgusted at the abject abasement of his creatures.

66

FROM unseemly flatteries they passed by degrees to savage acts. Caius Silanus, pro-consul of Asia, was accused by our allies of extortion; whereupon Mamercus Scaurus, an ex-consul, Junius Otho, a praetor, Brutidius Niger, an aedile, simultaneously fastened on him and charged him with sacrilege to the divinity of Augustus, and contempt of the majesty of Tiberius, while Mamercus Scaurus quoted old precedents, the prosecutions of Lucius Cotta by Scipio Africanus, of Servius Galba by Cato the Censor and of Publius Rutilius by Scaurus. As if indeed Scipio's and Cato's vengeance fell on such offences, or that of the famous Scaurus, whom his great grandson, a blot on his ancestry, this Mamercus was now disgracing by his infamous occupation. Junius Otho's old employment had been the keeping of a preparatory school. Subsequently, becoming a senator by the influence of Sejanus, he shamed his origin, low as it was, by his unblushing effronteries. Brutidius who was rich in excellent accomplishments, and was sure, had he pursued a path of virtue, to reach the most brilliant distinction, was goaded on by an eager impatience, while he strove to outstrip his equals, then his superiors, and at last even his own aspirations. Many have thus perished, even good men, despising slow and safe success and hurrying on even at the cost of ruin to premature greatness.

67

GELLIUS Publicola and Marcus Paconius, respectively quaestor and lieutenant of Silanus, swelled the number of the accusers. No doubt was felt as to the defendant's conviction for oppression and extortion, but there was a combination against him, that must have been perilous even to an innocent man. Besides a host of adverse Senators there were the most accomplished orators of all Asia, who, as such, had been retained for the prosecution, and to these he had to reply alone, without any experience in pleading, and under that personal apprehension which is enough to paralyze even the most practiced eloquence. For Tiberius did not refrain from pressing him with angry voice and look, himself putting incessant questions, without allowing him to rebut or evade them, and he had often even to make admissions, that the questions might not have been asked in vain. His slaves too were sold by auction to the state-agent, to be examined by torture. And that not a friend might help him in his danger, charges of treason were added, a binding guarantee for sealed lips. Accordingly he begged a few days' respite, and at last abandoned his defense, after venturing on a memorial to the emperor, in which he mingled reproach and entreaty.

Book IV

1

THE year when Caius Asinius and Caius Antistius were consuls was the ninth of Tiberius's reign, a period of tranquillity for the State and prosperity for his own house, for he counted Germanicus's death a happy incident. Suddenly fortune deranged everything; the emperor became a cruel tyrant, as well as an abettor of cruelty in others. Of this the cause and origin was Aelius Sejanus, commander of the praetorian cohorts, of whose influence I have already spoken. I will now fully describe his extraction, his character, and the daring wickedness by which he grasped at power. Born at Vulsinii, the son of Seius Strabo, a Roman knight, he attached himself in his early youth to Caius Caesar, grandson of the Divine Augustus, and the story went that he had sold his person to Apicius, a rich debauchee. Soon afterwards he won the heart of Tiberius so effectually by various artifices that the emperor, ever dark and mysterious towards others, was with Sejanus alone careless and freespoken. It was not through his craft, for it was by this very weapon that he was overthrown; it was rather from heaven's wrath against Rome, to whose welfare his elevation and his fall were alike disastrous. He had a body which could endure hardships, and a daring spirit. He was one who screened himself, while he was attacking others; he was as cringing as he was imperious; before the world he affected humility; in his heart he lusted after supremacy, for the sake of which he sometimes lavish and luxurious, but oftener energetic and watchful, qualities quite as mischievous when hypocritically assumed for the attainment of sovereignty.

2

HE strengthened the hitherto moderate powers of his office by concentrating the cohorts scattered throughout the capital into one camp, so that they might all receive orders at the same moment, and that the sight of their numbers and strength might give confidence to themselves, while it would strike terror into the citizens. His pretexts were the demoralisation incident to a dispersed soldiery, the greater effectiveness of simultaneous action in the event of a sudden peril, and the stricter discipline which would be insured by the establishment of an encampment at a distance from the temptations of the city. As soon as the camp was completed, he crept gradually into the affections of the soldiers by mixing with them and addressing them by name, himself selecting the centurions and tribunes. With the Senate too he sought to ingratiate himself, distinguishing his partisans with offices and provinces, Tiberius readily yielding, and being so biased that not only in private conversation but before the senators and the people he spoke highly of him as the partner of his toils, and allowed his statues to be honoured in theatres, in forums, and at the head-quarters of our legions.

3

THERE were however obstacles to his ambition in the imperial house with its many princes, a son in youthful manhood and grownup grandsons. As it would be unsafe to sweep off such a number at once by violence, while craft would necessitate successive intervals in crime, he chose, on the whole, the stealthier way and to begin with Drusus, against whom he had the stimulus of a recent resentment. Drusus, who could not brook a rival and was somewhat irascible, had, in a casual dispute, raised his fist at Sejanus, and, when he defended himself, had struck him in the face. On considering every plan Sejanus thought his easiest revenge was to turn his attention to Livia, Drusus's wife. She was a sister of Germanicus, and though she was not handsome as a girl, she became a woman of surpassing beauty. Pretending an ardent passion for her, he seduced her, and having won his first infamous triumph, and assured that a woman after having parted with her virtue will hesitate at nothing, he lured her on to thoughts of marriage, of a share in sovereignty, and of her husband's destruction. And she, the niece of Augustus, the daughter-in-law of Tiberius, the mother of children by Drusus, for a provincial paramour, foully disgraced herself, her ancestors, and her descendants, giving up honour and a sure position for prospects as base as they were uncertain. They took into their confidence Eudemus, Livia's friend and physician, whose profession was a pretext for frequent secret interviews. Sejanus, to avert his mistress's jealousy, divorced his wife Apicata, by whom he had had three children. Still the magnitude of the crime caused fear and delay, and sometimes a conflict of plans.

4

MEANWHILE, at the beginning of this year, Drusus, one of the children of Germanicus, assumed the dress of manhood, with a repetition of the honours decreed by the Senate to his brother Nero. The emperor added a speech with warm praise of his son for sharing a father's affection to his brother's children. Drusus indeed, difficult as it is for power and mutual harmony to exist side by side, had the character of being kindly disposed or at least not unfriendly towards the lads. And now the old plan, so often insincerely broached, of a progress through the provinces, was again discussed. The emperor's pretext was the number of veterans on the eve of discharge and the necessity of fresh levies for the army. Volunteers were not forthcoming, and even if they were sufficiently numerous, they had not the same bravery and discipline, as it is chiefly the needy and the homeless who adopt by their own choice a soldier's life. Tiberius also rapidly enumerated the legions and the provinces which they had to garrison. I too ought, I think, to go through these details, and thus show what forces Rome then had under arms, what kings were our allies, and how much narrower then were the limits of our empire.

5

ITALY on both seas was guarded by fleets, at Misenum and at Ravenna, and the contiguous coast of Gaul by ships of war captured in the victory of Actium, and sent by Augustus powerfully manned to the town of Forojulium. But chief strength was on the Rhine, as a defense alike against Germans and Gauls, and numbered eight legions. Spain, lately subjugated, was held by three. Mauretania was king Juba's, who had received it as a gift from the Roman people. The rest of Africa was garrisoned by two legions, and Egypt by the same number. Next, beginning with Syria, all within the entire tract of country stretching as far as the Euphrates, was kept in restraint by four legions, and on this frontier were Iberian, Albanian, and other kings, to whom our greatness was a protection against any foreign power. Thrace was held by Rhoemetalces and the children of Cotys; the bank of the Danube by two legions in Pannonia, two in Moesia, and two also were stationed in Dalmatia, which, from the situation of the country, were in the rear of the other four, and, should Italy suddenly require aid, not to distant to be summoned. But the capital was garrisoned by its own special soldiery, three city, nine praetorian cohorts, levied for the most part in Etruria and Umbria, or ancient Latium and the old Roman colonies. There were besides, in commanding positions in the provinces, allied fleets, cavalry and light infantry, of but little inferior strength. But any detailed account of them would be misleading, since they moved from place to place as circumstances required, and had their numbers increased and sometimes diminished.

6

IT is however, I think, a convenient opportunity for me to review the hitherto prevailing methods of administration in the other departments of the State, inasmuch as that year brought with it the beginning of a change for the worse in Tiberius's policy. In the first place, public business and the most important private matters were managed by the Senate: the leading men were allowed freedom of discussion, and when they stooped to flattery, the emperor himself checked them. He bestowed honours with regard to noble ancestry, military renown, or brilliant accomplishments as a civilian, letting it be clearly seen that there were no better men to choose. The consul and the praetor retained their prestige; inferior magistrates exercised their authority; the laws too, with the single exception of cases of treason, were properly enforced. As to the duties on corn, the indirect taxes and other branches of the public revenue, they were in the hands of companies of Roman knights. The emperor entrusted his own property to men of the most tried integrity or to persons known only by their general reputation, and once appointed they were retained without any limitation, so that most of them grew old in the same employments. The city populace indeed suffered much from high prices, but this was no fault of the emperor, who actually endeavoured to counteract barren soils and stormy seas with every resource of wealth and foresight. And he was also careful not to distress the provinces by new burdens, and to see that in bearing the old they were safe from any rapacity or oppression on the part of governors. Corporal punishments and confiscations of property were unknown.

7

THE emperor had only a few estates in Italy, slaves on a moderate scale, and his household was confined to a few freedmen. If ever he had a dispute with a private person, it was decided in the law courts. All this, not indeed with any graciousness, but in a blunt fashion which often alarmed, he still kept up, until the death of Drusus changed everything. While he lived, the system continued, because Sejanus, as yet only in the beginning of his power, wished to be known as an upright counselor, and there was one whose vengeance he dreaded, who did not conceal his hatred and incessantly complained "that a stranger was invited to assist in the government while the emperor's son was alive. How near was the step of declaring the stranger a colleague! Ambition at first had a steep path before it; when once the way had been entered, zealous adherents were forthcoming. Already, at the pleasure of the commander of the guards, a camp had been established; the soldiers given into his hands; his statues were to be seen among the monuments of Cneius Pompeius; his grandsons would be of the same blood as the family of the Drusi. Henceforth they must pray that he might have self-control, and so be contented." So would Drusus talk, not infrequently, or only in the hearing of a few persons. Even his confidences, now that his wife had been corrupted, were betrayed.

8

SEJANUS accordingly thought that he must be prompt, and chose a poison the gradual working of which might be mistaken for a natural disorder. It was given to Drusus by Lygdus, a eunuch, as was ascertained eight years later. As for Tiberius, he went to the Senate house during the whole time of the prince's illness, either because he was not afraid, or to show his strength of mind, and even in the interval between his death and funeral. Seeing the consuls, in token of their grief, sitting on the ordinary benches, he reminded them of their high office and of their proper place; and when the Senate burst into tears, suppressing a groan, he revived their spirits with a fluent speech. "He knew indeed that he might be reproached for thus encountering the gaze of the Senate after so recent an affliction. Most mourners could hardly bear even the soothing words of kinsfolk or to look on the light of day. And such were not to be condemned as weak. But he had sought a more manly consolation in the bosom of the commonwealth." Then deploring the extreme age of Augusta, the childhood of his grandsons, and his own declining years, he begged the Senate to summon Germanicus's children, the only comfort under their present misery. The consuls went out, and having encouraged the young princes with kind words, brought them in and presented them to the emperor. Taking them by the hand he said: "Senators, when these boys lost their father, I committed them to their uncle, and begged him, though he had children of his own, to cherish and rear them as his own offspring, and train them for himself and for posterity. Drusus is now lost to us, and I turn my prayers to you, and before heaven and your country I adjure you to receive into your care and guidance the great-grandsons of Augustus, descendants of a most noble ancestry. So fulfill your duty and mine.

To you, Nero and Drusus, these senators are as fathers. Such is your birth that your prosperity and adversity must alike affect the State."

9

THERE was great weeping at these words, and then many a benediction. Had the emperor set bounds to his speech, he must have filled the hearts of his hearers with sympathy and admiration. But he now fell back on those idle and often ridiculed professions about restoring the republic, and the wish that the consuls or some one else might undertake the government, and thus destroyed belief even in what was genuine and noble. The same honours were decreed to the memory of Drusus as to that of Germanicus, and many more were added. Such is the way with flattery, when repeated. The funeral with its procession of statues was singularly grand. Aeneas, the father of the Julian house, all the Alban kings, Romulus, Rome's founder, then the Sabine nobility, Attus Clausus, and the busts of all the other Claudii were displayed in a long train.

10

IN relating the death of Drusus I have followed the narrative of most of the best historians. But I would not pass over a rumour of the time, the strength of which is not even yet exhausted. Sejanus, it is said, having seduced Livia into crime, next secured, by the foulest means, the consent of Lygdus, the eunuch, as from his youth and beauty he was his master's favourite, and one of his principal attendants. When those who were in the secret had decided on the time and place of the poisoning, Sejanus, with the most consummate daring, reversed his plan, and, whispering an accusation against Drusus of intending to poison his father, warned Tiberius to avoid the first draught offered him as he was dining at his son's house. Thus deceived, the old emperor, on sitting down to the banquet, took the cup and handed it to Drusus. His suspicions were increased when Drusus, in perfect unconsciousness, drank it off with youthful eagerness, apparently, out of fear and shame, bringing on himself the death which he had plotted against his father.

11

THESE popular rumours, over and above the fact that they are not vouched for by any good writer, may be instantly refuted. For who, with moderate prudence, far less Tiberius with his great experience, would have thrust destruction on a son, without even hearing him, with his own hand too, and with an impossibility of returning to better thoughts. Surely he would rather have had the slave who handed the poison, tortured, have sought to discover the traitor, in short, would have been as hesitating and tardy in the case of an only son hitherto unconvicted of any crime, as he was naturally even with strangers. But as Sejanus had the credit of contriving every sort of wickedness, the fact that he was the emperor's special favourite, and that both were hated by the rest of the world, procured belief for any monstrous fiction, and rumour too always has a dreadful side in regard to the deaths of men in power. Besides, the whole process of the crime was betrayed by Apicata, Sejanus's wife, and fully divulged, under torture, by Eudemus and Lygdus. No writer has been found sufficiently malignant to fix the guilt on Tiberius, though every circumstance was scrutinized and exaggerated. My object in mentioning and refuting this story is, by a conspicuous example, to put down hearsay, and to request all into whose hands my work shall come, not to catch eagerly at wild and improbable rumours in preference to genuine history which has not been perverted into romance.

32

MUCH of what I have related and shall have to relate, may perhaps, I am aware, seem petty trifles to record. But no one must compare my annals with the writings of those who have described Rome in old days. They told of great wars, of the storming of cities, of the defeat and capture of kings, or whenever they turned by preference to home affairs, they related, with a free scope for digression, the strifes of consuls with tribunes, land and corn-laws, and the struggles between the commons and the aristocracy. My labours are circumscribed and inglorious; peace wholly unbroken or but slightly disturbed, dismal misery in the capital, an emperor careless about the enlargement of the empire, such is my theme. Still it will not be useless to study those at first sight trifling events out of which the movements of vast changes often take their rise.

33

ALL nations and cities are ruled by the people, the nobility, or by one man. A constitution, formed by selection out of these elements, it is easy to commend but not to produce; or, if it is produced, it cannot be lasting. Formerly, when the people had power or when the patricians were in the ascendant, the popular temper and the methods of controlling it, had to be studied, and those who knew most accurately the spirit of the Senate and aristocracy, had the credit of understanding the age and of being wise men. So now, after a revolution, when Rome is nothing but the realm of a single despot, there must be good in carefully noting and recording this period, for it is but few who have the foresight to distinguish right from wrong or what is sound from what is hurtful, while most men learn wisdom from the fortunes of others. Still, though this is instructive, it gives very little pleasure. Descriptions of countries, the various incidents of battles, glorious deaths of great generals, enchain and refresh a reader's mind. I have to present in succession the merciless biddings of a tyrant, incessant prosecutions, faithless friendships, the ruin of innocence, the same causes issuing in the same results, and I am everywhere confronted by a wearisome monotony in my subject matter. Then, again, an ancient historian has but few disparagers, and no one cares whether you praise more heartily the armies of Carthage or Rome. But of many who endured punishment or disgrace under Tiberius, the descendants yet survive; or even though the families themselves may be now extinct, you will find those who, from a resemblance of character, imagine that the evil deeds of others are a reproach to themselves. Again, even honour and virtue make enemies, condemning, as they do, their opposites by too close a contrast. But I return to my work.

34

IN the year of the consulship of Cornelius Cossus and Asinius Agrippa, Cremutius Cordus was arraigned on a new charge, now for the first time heard. He had published a history in which he had praised Marcus Brutus and called Caius Cassius the last of the Romans. His accusers were Satrius Secundus and Pinarius Natta, creatures of Sejanus. This was enough to ruin the accused; and then too the emperor listened with an angry frown to his defense, which Cremutius, resolved to give up his life, began thus: "It is my words, Senators, which are condemned, so innocent am I of any guilty act; yet these do not touch the emperor or the emperor's mother, who are alone comprehended under the law of treason. I am said to have praised Brutus and Cassius, whose careers many have described and no one mentioned without eulogy. Titus Livius, preeminently famous for eloquence and truthfulness, extolled Cneius Pompeius in such a panegyric that Augustus called him Pompeianus, and yet this was no obstacle to their friendship. Scipio, Afranius, this very Cassius, this same Brutus, he nowhere describes as brigands and traitors, terms now applied to them, but repeatedly as illustrious men. Asinius Pollio's writings too hand down a glorious memory of them, and Messala Corvinus used to speak with pride of Cassius as his general. Yet both these men prospered to the end with wealth and preferment. Again, that book of Marcus Cicero, in which he lauded Cato to the skies, how else was it answered by Caesar the dictator, than by a written oration in reply, as if he was pleading in court? The letters Antonius, the harangues of Brutus contain reproaches against Augustus, false indeed, but urged with powerful sarcasm; the poems which we read of Bibaculus and Catullus are crammed with invectives on the Caesars. Yet the Divine Julius, the Divine Augustus themselves bore all this and let it pass, whether in forbearance or in wisdom I cannot easily say. Assuredly what is despised is soon forgotten; when you resent a thing, you seem to recognize it."

35

"OF the Greeks I say nothing; with them not only liberty, but even license went unpunished, or if a person aimed at chastising, he retaliated on satire by satire. It has, however, always been perfectly open to us without any one to censure, to speak freely of those whom death has withdrawn alike from the partialities of hatred or esteem. Are Cassius and Brutus now in arms on the fields of Philippi, and am I with them rousing the people by harangues to stir up civil war? Did they not fall more than seventy years ago, and as they are known to us by statues which even the conqueror did not destroy, so too is not some portion of their memory preserved for us by historians? To every man posterity gives his due honour, and, if a fatal sentence hangs over me, there will be those who will remember me as well as Cassius and Brutus." He then left the Senate and ended his life by starvation. His books, so the Senators decreed, were to be burnt by the aediles; but some copies were left which were concealed and afterwards published. And so one is all the more inclined to laugh at the stupidity of men who suppose that the despotism of the present can actually efface the remembrances of the next generation. On the contrary, the persecution of genius fosters its influence; foreign tyrants, and all who have imitated their oppression, have merely procured infamy for themselves and glory for their victims.

36

THAT year was such a continuous succession of prosecutions that on the days of the Latin festival when Drusus, as city-prefect, had ascended his tribunal for the inauguration of his office, Calpurnius Salvianus appeared before him against Sextus Marius. This the emperor openly censured, and it caused the banishment of Salvianus. Next, the people of Cyzicus were accused of publicly neglecting the established worship of the Divine Augustus, and also of acts of violence to Roman citizens. They were deprived of the franchise which they had earned during the war with Mithridates, when their city was besieged, and when they repulsed the king as much by their own bravery as by the aid of Lucullus. Then followed the acquittal of Fonteius Capito, the late proconsul of Asia, on proof that charges brought against him by Vibius Serenus were fictitious. Still this did not injure Serenus, to whom public hatred was actually a protection.

Indeed any conspicuously restless informer was, so to say, inviolable; only the insignificant and undistinguished were punished.

37

ABOUT the same time Further Spain sent a deputation to the Senate, with a request to be allowed, after the example of Asia, to erect a temple to Tiberius and his mother. On this occasion, the emperor, who had generally a strong contempt for honours, and now thought it right to reply to the rumour which reproached him with having yielded to vanity, delivered the following speech: "I am aware, Senators, that many deplore my want of firmness in not having opposed a similar recent petition from the cities of Asia. I will therefore both explain the grounds of my previous silence and my intentions for the future. Inasmuch as the Divine Augustus did not forbid the founding of a temple at Pergamos to himself and to the city of Rome, I who respect as law all his actions and sayings, have the more readily followed a precedent once approved, seeing that with the worship of myself was linked an expression of reverence towards the Senate. But though it may be pardonable to have allowed this once, it would be a vain and arrogant thing to receive the sacred honour of images representing the divine throughout all the provinces, and the homage paid to Augustus will disappear if it is vulgarized by indiscriminate flattery.

38

"FOR myself, Senators, I am mortal and limited to the functions of humanity, content if I can adequately fill the highest place; of this I solemnly assure you, and would have posterity remember it. They will more than sufficiently honour my memory by believing me to have been worthy of my ancestry, watchful over your interests, courageous in danger, fearless of enmity, when the State required it. These sentiments of your hearts are my temples, these my most glorious and abiding monuments. Those built of stone are despised as mere tombs, if the judgment of posterity passes into hatred. And therefore this is my prayer to our allies, our citizens, and to heaven itself; to the last, that, to my life's close, it grant me a tranquil mind, which can discern alike human and divine claims; to the first, that, when I die, they honour my career and the reputation of my name with praise and kindly remembrance." Henceforth Tiberius even in private conversations persisted in showing contempt for such homage to himself. Some attributed this to modesty; many to self-distrust; a few to a mean spirit. "The noblest men," it was said, "have the loftiest aspirations, and so Hercules and Bacchus among the Greeks and Quirinus among us were enrolled in the number of the gods. Augustus, did better, seeing that he had aspired. All other things princes have as a matter of course; one thing they ought insatiably to pursue, that their memory may be glorious. For to despise fame is to despise merit."

39

SEJANUS meanwhile, dazed by his extravagant prosperity and urged on too by a woman's passion, Livia now insisting on his promise of marriage, addressed a memorial to the emperor. For it was then the custom to apply to him by writing, even though he was at Rome. This petition was to the following effect: The kindness of Augustus, the father, and then the many favourable testimonies of Tiberius, the son, had engendered the habit of confiding his hopes and wishes to the ears of emperors as readily as to those of the gods. The splendour of high distinctions he had never craved; he had rather chosen watchings and hardships, like one of the common soldiers, for the emperor's safety. But there was one most glorious honour he had won, the reputation of being worthy of an alliance with a Caesar. This was the first motive of his ambition. As he had heard that Augustus, in marrying his daughter, had even entertained some thoughts of Roman knights, so if a husband were sought for Livia, he hoped Tiberius would bear in mind a friend who would find his reward simply in the glory of the alliance. He did not wish to rid himself of the duties imposed on him; he thought it enough for his family to be secured against the unjust displeasure of Agrippina, and this for the sake of his children. For, as for himself, enough and more than enough for him would be a life completed while such a sovereign still reigned.

40

TIBERIUS, in reply, after praising the loyal sentiments of Sejanus and briefly enumerating the favours he had bestowed on him, asked time for impartial consideration, adding that while other men's plans depended on their ideas of their own interest, princes, who had to regulate their chief actions by public opinion, were in a different position. "Hence," he said, "I do not take refuge in an answer which it would be easy to return, that Livia can herself decide whether she considers that, after Drusus, she ought again to marry or rather to endure life in the same home, and that she has in her mother and grandmother counselors nearer and dearer to her. I will deal more frankly. First, as to the enmity of Agrippina, I maintain that it will blaze out more fiercely if Livia's marriage rends, so to say, the house of the Caesars into two factions. Even as it is, feminine jealousies break out, and my grandsons are torn asunder by the strife. What will happen if the rivalry is rendered more intense by such a marriage? For you are mistaken, Sejanus, if you think that you will then remain in the same position, and that Livia, who has been the wife of Caius Caesar and afterwards of Drusus, will have the inclination to pass her old age with a mere Roman knight. Though I might allow it, do you imagine it would be tolerated by those who have seen her brother, her father, and our ancestors in the highest offices of state? You indeed desire to keep within your station; but those magistrates and nobles who intrude on you against your wishes and consult you on all matters, openly give out that you have long overstepped the rank of a knight and gone far beyond my father's friendships, and from their dislike of you they also condemn me. But, you say, Augustus had thoughts of giving his daughter to a Roman knight. Is it surprising that, with so many distracting cares, foreseeing too the immense elevation to which a man would be raised above others by such an alliance, he talked of Caius Proculeius and certain persons of singularly quiet life, wholly free from political entanglements? Still, if the hesitation of Augustus is to influence us, how much stronger is the fact that he bestowed his daughter on Marcus Agrippa, then on myself. All this, as a friend, I have stated without reserve, but I will not oppose your plans or those of Livia. My own earnest thoughts and the ties with which I am still purposing to unite you to myself, I shall for the present forbear to explain. This only I will declare, that nothing is too grand to be deserved by your merits and your goodwill towards me. When an opportunity presents itself, either in the Senate, or in a popular assembly, I shall not be silent."

41

SEJANUS, no longer thinking of his marriage but filled with a deeper alarm, rejoined by deprecating the whispers of suspicion, popular rumour and the gathering storm of odium. That he might not impair his influence by closing his doors on the throngs of his many visitors or strengthen the hands of accusers by admitting them, he made it his aim to induce Tiberius to live in some charming spot at a distance from Rome. In this he foresaw several advantages. Access to the emperor would be under his own control, and letters, for the most part being conveyed by soldiers, would pass through his hands. Caesar too, who was already in the decline of life, would soon, when enervated by retirement, more readily transfer to him the functions of empire; envy towards himself would be lessened when there was an end to his crowded levies and the reality of power would be increased by the removal of its empty show. So he began to declaim against the laborious life of the capital, the bustling crowds and streaming multitudes, while he praised repose and solitude, with their freedom from vexations and misunderstandings, and their special opportunities for the study of the highest questions.

42

IT happened that the trial at this time of Votienus Montanus, a popular wit, convinced the hesitating Tiberius that he ought to shun all assemblies of the Senate, where speeches, often true and offensive, were flung in his very face. Votienus was charged with insulting expressions towards the emperor, and while the witness, Aemilius, a military man, in his eagerness to prove the case, repeated the whole story and amid angry clamour struggled on with loud assertion, Tiberius heard the reproaches by which he was assailed in secret, and was so deeply impressed that he exclaimed that he would clear himself either at once or on a legal inquiry, and the entreaties of friends, with the flattery of the whole assembly, hardly restored his composure. As for Votienus, he suffered the penalty of treason; but the emperor, clinging all the more obstinately to the harshness with which he had been reproached in regard to accused persons, punished Aquilia with exile for the crime of adultery with Varius Ligur, although Lentulus Gaetulicus, the consul-elect, had proposed that she should be sentenced under the Julian law. He next struck off Apidius Merula from the register of the Senate for not having sworn obedience to the legislation of the Divine Augustus.

Book V

6

FORTY-FOUR speeches were delivered on this subject, a few of which were prompted by fear, most by the habit of flattery... "There is now a change of fortune, and even he who chose Sejanus to be his colleague and his son-in-law excuses his error. As for the rest, the man whom they encouraged by shameful baseness, they now wickedly revile. Which is the most pitiable, to be accused for friendship's sake or to have to accuse a friend, I cannot decide. I will not put any man's cruelty or compassion to the test, but, while I am free and have a clear conscience, I will anticipate peril. I implore you to cherish my memory with joy rather than with sorrow, numbering me too with those who by noble death have fled from the miseries of our country."

7

THEN detaining those of his friends who were minded to stay with him and converse, or, if otherwise, dismissing them, he thus spent part of the day, and with a numerous circle yet round him, all gazing on his fearless face, and imagining that there was still time to elapse before the last scene, he fell on a sword which he had concealed in his robe. The emperor did not pursue him after his death with either accusation or reproach, although he had heaped a number of foul charges on Blaesus.

8

NEXT were discussed the cases of Publius Vitellius and Pomponius Secundus. The first was charged by his accusers with having offered the keys of the treasury, of which he was prefect, and the military chest in aid of a revolution. Against the latter, Considius, an ex-praetor, alleged intimacy with Aelius Gallus, who, after the punishment of Sejanus, had fled to the gardens of Pomponius, as his safest refuge. They had no resource in their peril but in the courageous firmness of their brothers who became their sureties. Soon, after several adjournments, Vitellius, weary alike of hope and fear, asked for a penknife, avowedly, for his literary pursuits, and inflicted a slight wound in his veins, and died at last of a broken heart. Pomponius, a man of refined manners and brilliant genius, bore his adverse fortune with resignation, and outlived Tiberius.

9

IT was next decided to punish the remaining children of Sejanus, though the fury of the populace was subsiding, and people generally had been appeased by the previous executions. Accordingly they were carried off to prison, the boy, aware of his impending doom, and the little girl, who was so unconscious that she continually asked what was her offence, and whither she was being dragged, saying that she would do so no more, and a childish chastisement was enough for her correction. Historians of the time tell us that, as there was no precedent for the capital punishment of a virgin, she was violated by the executioner, with the rope on her neck. Then they were strangled and their bodies, mere children as they were, were flung down the Gemoniae.

10

ABOUT the same time Asia and Achaia were alarmed by a prevalent but short-lived rumour that Drusus, the son of Germanicus, had been seen in the Cyclades and subsequently on the mainland. There was indeed a young man of much the same age, whom some of the emperor's freedmen pretended to recognise, and to whom they attached themselves with a treacherous intent. The renown of the name attracted the ignorant, and the Greek mind eagerly fastens on what is new and marvelous. The story indeed, which they no sooner invented than believed, was that Drusus had escaped from custody, and was on his way to the armies of his father, with the design of invading Egypt or Syria. And he was now drawing to himself a multitude of young men and much popular enthusiasm, enjoying the present and cherishing idle hopes of the future, when Poppaeus Sabinus heard of the affair. At the time he was chiefly occupied with Macedonia, but he also had the charge of Achaia. So, to forestall the danger, let the story be true or false, he hurried by the bays of Torone and Thermae, then passed on to Euboea, an island of the Aegaean, to Piraeus, on the coast of Attica, thence to the shores of Corinth and the narrow Isthmus, and having arrived by the other sea at Nicopolis, a Roman colony, he there at last ascertained that the man, when skilfully questioned, had said that he was the son of Marcus Silanus, and that, after the dispersion of a number of his followers' he had embarked on a vessel, intending, it seemed, to go to Italy. Sabinus sent this account to Tiberius, and of the origin and issue of the affair nothing more is known to me.

11

AT the close of the year a long growing feud between the consuls broke out. Trio, a reckless man in incurring enmities and a practiced lawyer, had indirectly censured Regulus as having been half-hearted in crushing the satellites of Sejanus. Regulus, who, unless he was provoked, loved quietness, not only repulsed his colleague's attack, but was for dragging him to trial as a guilty accomplice in the conspiracy. And though many of the senators implored them to compose a quarrel likely to end fatally, they continued their enmity and their mutual menaces till they retired from office.

Book VI

1

CNEIUS Domitius and Camillus Scribonianus had entered on the consulship when the emperor, after crossing the channel which divides Capreae from Surrentum, sailed along Campania, in doubt whether he should enter Rome, or, possibly, simulating the intention of going thither, because he had resolved otherwise. He often landed at points in the neighborhood, visited the gardens by the Tiber, but went back again to the cliffs and to the solitude of the sea shores, in shame at the vices and profligacies into which he had plunged so unrestrainedly that in the fashion of a despot he debauched the children of free-born citizens. It was not merely beauty and a handsome person which he felt as an incentive to his lust, but the modesty of childhood in some, and noble ancestry in others. Hitherto unknown terms were then for the first time invented, derived from the abominations of the place and the endless phases of sensuality. Slaves too were set over the work of seeking out and procuring, with rewards for the willing, and threats to the reluctant, and if there was resistance from a relative or a parent, they used violence and force, and actually indulged their own passions as if dealing with captives.

2

AT Rome meanwhile, in the beginning of the year, as if Livia's crimes had just been discovered and not also long ago punished, terrible decrees were proposed against her very statues and memory, and the property of Sejanus was to be taken from the exchequer and transferred to the imperial treasury; as if there was any difference. The motion was being urged with extreme persistency, in almost the same or with but slightly changed language, by such men as Scipio, Silanus, and Cassius, when suddenly Togonius Gallus intruding his own obscurity among illustrious names, was heard with ridicule. He begged the emperor to select a number of senators, twenty out of whom should be chosen by lot to wear swords and to defend his person, whenever he entered the Senate House. The man had actually believed a letter from him in which he asked the protection of one of the consuls, so that he might go in safety from Capreae to Rome. Tiberius however, who usually combined jesting and seriousness, thanked the senators for their goodwill, but asked who could be rejected, who could be chosen? "Were they always to be the same, or was there to be a succession? Were they to be men who had held office or youths, private citizens or officials? Then, again, what a scene would be presented by persons grasping their swords on the threshold of the Senate House? His life was not of so much worth if it had to be defended by arms." This was his answer to Togonius, guarded in its expression, and he urged nothing beyond the rejection of the motion.

3

JUNIUS Gallio however, who had proposed that the praetorian soldiers, after having served their campaigns, should acquire the privilege of sitting in the fourteen rows of the theatre, received a savage censure. Tiberius, just as if he were face to face with him, asked what he had to do with the soldiers, who ought to receive the emperor's orders or his rewards except from the emperor himself? He had really discovered something which the Divine Augustus had not foreseen. Or was not one of Sejanus's satellites rather seeking to sow discord and sedition, as a means of prompting ignorant minds, under the pretense of compliment, to ruin military discipline? This was Gallio's recompense for his carefully prepared flattery, with immediate expulsion from the Senate, and then from Italy. And as men complained that he would endure his exile with equanimity, since he had chosen the famous and lovely island of Lesbos, he was dragged back to Rome, and confined in the houses of different officials. The emperor in the same letter crushed Sextius Paconianus, an ex-praetor, to the great joy of the senators, as he was a daring, mischievous man, who pryed into every person's secrets, and had been the chosen instrument of Sejanus in his treacherous designs against Caius Caesar. When this fact was divulged, there came an outburst of long-concealed hatreds, and there must have been a sentence of capital punishment, had he not himself volunteered a disclosure.

4

AS soon as he named Latinius Latiaris, accuser and accused, both alike objects of execration, presented a most welcome spectacle. Latiaris, as I have related, had been foremost in contriving the ruin of Titius Sabinus, and was now the first to pay the penalty. By way of episode, Haterius Agrippa inveighed against the consuls of the previous year for now sitting silent after their threats of impeaching one another. "It must be fear," he said, "and a guilty conscience which are acting as a bond of union. But the senators must not keep back what they have heard." Regulus replied that he was awaiting the opportunity for vengeance, and meant to press it in the emperor's presence. Trio's answer was that it was best to efface the memory of rivalries between colleagues, and of any words uttered in quarrels. When Agrippa still persisted, Sanquinius Maximus, one of the ex-consuls, implored the Senate not to increase the emperor's anxieties by seeking further occasions of bitterness, as he was himself competent to provide remedies. This secured the safety of Regulus and the postponement of Trio's ruin. Haterius was hated all the more. Wan with untimely slumbers and nights of riot, and not fearing in his indolence even the cruelest of princes, he yet plotted amid his gluttony and lust the destruction of illustrious men.

5

SEVERAL charges were next brought, as soon as the opportunity offered, against Cotta Messalinus, the author of every unusually cruel proposal, and consequently, regarded with inveterate hatred. He had spoken, it was said, of Caius Caesar, as if it were a question whether he was a man, and of an entertainment at which he was present on Augusta's birthday with the priests, as a funeral banquet. In remonstrating too against the influence of Marcus Lepidus and Lucius Arruntius, with whom he had disputes on many matters, he had added the remark, "They will have the Senate's support; I shall have that of my darling Tiberius." But the leading men of the State failed to convict him on all the charges. When they pressed the case, he appealed to the emperor. Soon afterwards, a letter arrived, in which Tiberius traced the origin of the friendship between himself and Cotta, enumerated his frequent services, and then requested that words perversely misrepresented and the freedom of table talk might not be construed into a crime.

6

THE beginning of the emperor's letter seemed very striking. It opened thus: "May all the gods and goddesses destroy me more miserably than I feel myself to be daily perishing, if I know at know at this moment what to write to you, Senators, how to write it, or what, in short, not to write." So completely had his crimes and infamies recoiled, as a penalty, on himself. With profound meaning was it often affirmed by the greatest teacher of philosophy that, could the minds of tyrants be laid bare, there would be seen gashes and wounds; for, as the body is lacerated by scourging, so is the spirit by brutality, by lust and by evil thoughts. Assuredly Tiberius was not saved by his elevation or his solitude from having to confess the anguish of his heart and his self-inflicted punishment.

7

AUTHORITY was then given to the Senate to decide the case of Caecilianus, one of its members, the chief witness against Cotta, and it was agreed that the same penalty should be inflicted as on Aruseius and Sanquinius, the accusers of Lucius Arruntius. Nothing ever happened to Cotta more to his distinction. Of noble birth, but beggared by extravagance and infamous for his excesses, he was now by dignity of his revenge, raised to a level with the stainless virtues of Arruntius. Quintus Servaeus and Minucius Thermus were next arraigned. Servaeus was an ex-praetor, and had formerly been a companion of Germanicus; Minucius was of equestrian rank, and both had enjoyed, though discreetly, the friendship of Sejanus. Hence they were the more pitied. Tiberius, on the contrary, denounced them as foremost in crime, and bade Caius Cestius, the elder, tell the Senate what he had communicated to the emperor by letter. Cestius undertook the prosecution. And this was the most dreadful feature of the age, that leading members of the Senate, some openly, some secretly employed themselves in the very lowest work of the informer. One could not distinguish between aliens and kinsfolk, between friends and strangers, or say what was quite recent, or what half-forgotten from lapse of time. People were incriminated for some casual remark in the forum or at the dinner-table, for every one was impatient to be the first to mark his victim, some to screen themselves, most from being, as it were, infected with the contagion of the malady. Minucius and Servaeus, on being condemned, went over to the prosecution, and then Julius Africanus with Seius Quadratus were dragged into the same ruin. Africanus was from the Santones, one of the states of Gaul; the origin of Quadratus I have not ascertained. Many authors, I am well aware, have passed over the perils and punishments of a host of persons, sickened by the multiplicity of them, or fearing that what they had themselves found wearisome and saddening would be equally fatiguing to their readers. For myself, I have lighted on many facts worth knowing, though other writers have not recorded them.

8

A ROMAN knight, Marcus Terentius, at the crisis when all others had hypocritically repudiated the friendship of Sejanus, dared, when impeached on that ground, to cling to it by the following avowal to the Senate: "In my position it is perhaps less to my advantage to acknowledge than to deny the charge. Still, whatever is to be the issue of the matter, I shall admit that I was the friend of Sejanus, that I anxiously sought to be such, and was delighted when I was successful. I had seen him his father's colleague in the command of the praetorian cohorts, and subsequently combining the duties of civil and military life. His kinsfolk and connections were loaded with honours; intimacy with Sejanus was in every case a powerful recommendation to the emperor's friendship. Those, on the contrary, whom he hated, had to struggle with danger and humiliation. I take no individual as an instance. All of us who had no part in his last design, I mean to defend at the peril of myself alone. It was really not Sejanus of Vulsinii, it was a member of the Claudian and Julian houses, in which he had taken a position by his marriage alliance, it was your son-in-law, Caesar, your partner in the consulship, the man who administered your political functions, whom we courted. It is not for us to criticize one whom you may raise above all others, or your motives for so doing. Heaven has entrusted you with the supreme decision of affairs, and for us is left the glory of obedience. And, again, we see what takes place before our eyes, who it is on whom you bestow riches and honours, who are the most powerful to help or to injure. That Sejanus was such, no one will deny. To explore the prince's secret thoughts, or any of his hidden plans, is a forbidden, a dangerous thing, nor does it follow that one could reach them. "Do not, Senators, think only of Sejanus's last day, but of his sixteen years of power. We actually adored a Satrius and a Pomponius. To be known even to his freedmen and hall-porters was thought something very grand. What then is my meaning? Is this apology meant to be offered for all without difference and discrimination? No; it is to be restricted within proper limits. Let plots against the State, murderous designs against the emperor be punished. As for friendship and its obligations, the same principle must acquit both you, Caesar, and us."

9

THE courage of this speech and the fact that there had been found a man to speak out what was in all people's thoughts, had such an effect that the accusers of Terentius were sentenced to banishment or death, their previous offenses being taken into account. Then came a letter from Tiberius against Sextus Vestilius, an ex-praetor, whom, as a special favourite of his brother Drusus, the emperor had admitted into his own select circle. His reason for being displeased with Vestilius was that he had either written an attack on Caius Caesar as a profligate, or that Tiberius believed a false charge. For this Vestilius was excluded from the prince's table. He then tried the knife with his aged hand, but again bound up his veins, opening them once more however on having begged for pardon by letter and received a pitiless answer. After him a host of persons were charged with treason, Annius Pollio, Appius Silanus, Scaurus Mamercus, Sabinus Calvisius, Vinicianus too, coupled with Pollio, his father, men all of illustrious descent, some too of the highest political distinction. The senators were panic-stricken, for how few of their number were not connected by alliance or by friendship with this multitude of men of rank! Celsus however, tribune of a city cohort, and now one of the prosecutors, saved Appius and Calvisius from the peril. The emperor postponed the cases of Pollio, Vinicianus, and Scaurus, intending to try them himself with the Senate, not however without affixing some ominous marks to the name of Scaurus.

10

EVEN women were not exempt from danger. Where they could not be accused of grasping at political power, their tears were made a crime. Vitia, an aged woman, mother of Fufius Geminus, was executed for bewailing the death of her son. Such were the proceedings in the Senate. It was the same with the emperor. Vescularius Atticus and Julius Marinus were hurried off to execution, two of his oldest friends, men who had followed him to Rhodes and been his inseparable companions at Capreae. Vescularius was his agent in the plot against Libo, and it was with the co-operation of Marinus that Sejanus had ruined Curtius Atticus. Hence there was all the more joy at the recoil of these precedents on their authors. About the same time Lucius Piso, the pontiff, died a natural death, a rare incident in so high a rank. Never had he by choice proposed a servile motion, and, whenever necessity was too strong for him, he would suggest judicious compromises. His father, as I have related, had been a censor. He lived to the advanced age of eighty, and had won in Thrace the honour of a triumph. But his chief glory rested on the wonderful tact with which as city-prefect he handled an authority, recently made perpetual and all the more galling to men unaccustomed to obey it.

11

IN former days, when the kings and subsequently the chief magistrates went from Rome, an official was temporarily chosen to administer justice and provide for emergencies, so that the capital might not be left without government. It is said that Denter Romulius was appointed by Romulus, then Numa Marcius by Tullus Hostilius, and Spurius Lucretius by Tarquinius Superbus. Afterwards, the consuls made the appointment. The shadow of the old practice still survives, whenever in consequence of the Latin festival some one is deputed to exercise the consul's functions. And Augustus too during the civil wars gave Cilnius Maecenas, a Roman knight, charge of everything in Rome and Italy. When he rose to supreme power, in consideration of the magnitude of the State and the slowness of legal remedies, he selected one of the ex-consuls to overawe the slaves and that part of the population which, unless it fears a strong hand, is disorderly and reckless. Messala Corvinus was the first to obtain the office, which he lost within a few days, as not knowing how to discharge it. After him Taurus Statilius, though in advanced years, sustained it admirably; and then Piso, after twenty years of similar credit, was, by the Senate's decree, honoured with a public funeral.

12

A MOTION was next brought forward in the Senate by Quintilianus, a tribune of the people, respecting an alleged book of the Sibyl. Caninius Gallus, a book of the College of the Fifteen, had asked that it might be received among the other volumes of the same prophetess by a decree on the subject. This having been carried by a division, the emperor sent a letter in which he gently censured the tribune, as ignorant of ancient usage because of his youth. Gallus he scolded for having introduced the matter in a thin Senate, notwithstanding his long experience in the science of religious ceremonies, without taking the opinion of the College or having the verses read and criticized, as was usual, by its presidents, though their authenticity was very doubtful. He also reminded him that, as many spurious productions were current under a celebrated name, Augustus had prescribed a day within which they should be deposited with the city-praetor, and after which it should not be lawful for any private person to hold them. The same regulations too had been made by our ancestors after the burning of the Capitol in the social war, when there was a search throughout Samos, Ilium, Erythrae, and even in Africa, Sicily and the Italian colonies for the verses of the Sibyl (whether there were but one or more) and the priests were charged with the business of distinguishing, as far as they could by human means, what were genuine. Accordingly the book in question was now also submitted to the scrutiny of the College of the Fifteen.

13

DURING the same consulship a high price of corn almost brought on an insurrection. For several days there were many clamorous demands made in the theatre with an unusual freedom of language towards the emperor. This provoked him to censure the magistrates and the Senate for not having used the authority of the State to put down the people. He named too the corn-supplying provinces, and dwelt on the far larger amount of grain imported by himself than by Augustus. So the Senate drew up a decree in the severe spirit of antiquity, and the consuls issued a not less stringent proclamation. The emperor's silence was not, as he had hoped, taken as a proof of patriotism, but of pride.

14

AT the year's close Geminius, Celsus and Pompeius, Roman knights, fell beneath a charge of conspiracy. Of these Caius Geminius, by lavish expenditure and a luxurious life, had been a friend of Sejanus, but with no serious result. Julius Celsus, a tribune, while in confinement, loosened his chain, and having twisted it around him, broke his neck by throwing himself in an opposite direction. Rubrius Fabatus was put under surveillance, on a suspicion that, in despair of the fortunes of Rome, he meant to throw himself on the mercy of the Parthians. He was, at any rate, found near the Straits of the Sicily, and, when dragged back by a centurion, he assigned no adequate reason for his long journey. Still, he lived on in safety, thanks to forgetfulness rather than to mercy.

15

IN the consulship of Servius Galba and Lucius Sulla, the emperor, after having long considered whom he was to choose to be husbands for his granddaughters, now that the maidens were of marriageable age, selected Lucius Cassius and Marcus Vinicius. Vinicius was of provincial descent; he was born at Cales, his father and grandfather having been consuls, and his family, on the other side, being of the rank of knights. He was a man of amiable temper and of cultivated eloquence. Cassius was of an ancient and honourable, though plebeian house, at Rome. Though he was brought up by his father under a severe training, he won esteem more frequently by his good-nature than by his diligence. To him and to Vinicius the emperor married respectively Drusilla and Julia, Germanicus's daughters, and addressed a letter on the subject to the Senate, with a slightly complimentary mention of the young men. He next assigned some very vague reasons for his absence, then passed to more important matters, the ill-will against him originating in his state policy, and requested that Macro, who commanded the praetorians, with a few tribunes and centurions, might accompany him whenever he entered the Senate-house. But though a decree was voted by the Senate on a liberal scale and without any restrictions as to rank or numbers, he never so much as went near the walls of Rome, much less the State council, for he would often go round and avoid his native city by circuitous routes.

16

MEANWHILE a powerful host of accusers fell with sudden fury on the class which systematically increased its wealth by usury in defiance of a law passed by Caesar the Dictator defining the terms of lending money and of holding estates in Italy, a law long obsolete because the public good is sacrificed to private interest. The curse of usury was indeed of old standing in Rome and a most frequent cause of sedition and discord, and it was therefore repressed even in the early days of a less corrupt morality. First, the Twelve Tables prohibited any one from exacting more than per cent., when, previously, the rate had depended on the caprice of the wealthy. Subsequently, by a bill brought in by the tribunes, interest was reduced to half that amount, and finally compound interest was wholly forbidden. A check too was put by several enactments of the people on evasions which, though continually put down, still, through strange artifices, reappeared. On this occasion, however, Gracchus, the praetor, to whose jurisdiction the inquiry had fallen, felt himself compelled by the number of persons endangered to refer the matter to the Senate. In their dismay the senators, not one of whom was free from similar guilt, threw themselves on the emperor's indulgence. He yielded, and a year and six months were granted, within which every one was to settle his private accounts conformable to the requirements of the law.

17

HENCE followed a scarcity of money, a great shock being given to all credit, the current coin too, in consequence of the conviction of so many persons and the sale of their property, being locked up in the imperial treasury or the public exchequer. To meet this, the Senate had directed that every creditor should have two-thirds his capital secured on estates in Italy. Creditors however were suing for payment in full, and it was not respectable for persons when sued to break faith. So, at first, there were clamorous meetings and importunate entreaties; then noisy applications to the praetor's court. And the very device intended as a remedy, the sale and purchase of estates, proved the contrary, as the usurers had hoarded up all their money for buying land. The facilities for selling were followed by a fall of prices, and the deeper a man was in debt, the more reluctantly did he part with his property, and many were utterly ruined. The destruction of private wealth precipitated the fall of rank and reputation, till at last the emperor interposed his aid by distributing throughout the banks a hundred million sesterces, and allowing freedom to borrow without interest for three years, provided the borrower gave security to the State in land to double the amount. Credit was thus restored, and gradually private lenders were found. The purchase too of estates was not carried out according to the letter of the Senate's decree, rigour at the outset, as usual with such matters, becoming negligence in the end.

18

FORMER alarms then returned, as there was a charge of treason against Considius Proculus. While he was celebrating his birthday without a fear, he was hurried before the Senate, condemned and instantly put to death. His sister Sancia was outlawed, on the accusation of Quintus Pomponius, a restless spirit, who pretended that he employed himself in this and like practices to win favour with the sovereign, and thereby alleviate the perils hanging over his brother Pomponius Secundus. Pompeia Macrina too was sentenced to banishment. Her husband Argolicus and her father-in-law Laco, leading men of Achaia, had been ruined by the emperor. Her father likewise, an illustrious Roman knight, and her brother, an ex-praetor, seeing their doom was near, destroyed themselves. It was imputed to them as a crime that their great-grandfather Theophanes of Mitylene had been one of the intimate friends of Pompey the Great, and that after his death Greek flattery had paid him divine honours.

19

SEXTUS Marius, the richest man in Spain, was next accused of incest with his daughter, and thrown headlong from the Tarpeian rock. To remove any doubt that the vastness of his wealth had proved the man's ruin, Tiberius kept his gold-mines for himself, though they were forfeited to the State. Executions were now a stimulus to his fury, and he ordered the death of all who were lying in prison under accusation of complicity with Sejanus. There lay, singly or in heaps, the unnumbered dead, of every age and sex, the illustrious with the obscure. Kinsfolk and friends were not allowed to be near them, to weep over them, or even to gaze on them too long. Spies were set round them, who noted the sorrow of each mourner and followed the rotting corpses, till they were dragged to the Tiber, where, floating or driven on the bank, no one dared to burn or to touch them. The force of terror had utterly extinguished the sense of human fellowship, and, with the growth of cruelty, pity was thrust aside.

20

ABOUT this time Caius Caesar, who became his grandfather's companion on his retirement to Capreae, married Claudia, daughter of Marcus Silanus. He was a man who masked a savage temper under an artful guise of self-restraint, and neither his mother's doom nor the banishment of his brothers extorted from him a single utterance. Whatever the humour of the day with Tiberius, he would assume the like, and his language differed as little. Hence the fame of a clever remark from the orator Passienus, that "there never was a better slave or a worse master." I must not pass over a prognostication of Tiberius respecting Servius Galba, then consul. Having sent for him and sounded him on various topics, he at last addressed him in Greek to this effect: "You too, Galba, will some day have a taste of empire." He thus hinted at a brief span of power late in life, on the strength of his acquaintance with the art of astrologers, leisure for acquiring which he had had at Rhodes, with Thrasyllus for instructor. This man's skill he tested in the following manner.

21

WHENEVER he sought counsel on such matters, he would make use of the top of the house and of the confidence of one freedman, quite illiterate and of great physical strength. The man always walked in front of the person whose science Tiberius had determined to test, through an unfrequented and precipitous path (for the house stood on rocks), and then, if any suspicion had arisen of imposture or of trickery, he hurled the astrologer, as he returned, into the sea beneath, that no one might live to betray the secret. Thrasyllus accordingly was led up the same cliffs, and when he had deeply impressed his questioner by cleverly revealing his imperial destiny and future career, he was asked whether he had also thoroughly ascertained his own horoscope, and the character of that particular year and day. After surveying the positions and relative distances of the stars, he first paused, then trembled, and the longer he gazed, the more was he agitated by amazement and terror, till at last he exclaimed that a perilous and well-nigh fatal crisis impended over him. Tiberius then embraced him and congratulated him on foreseeing his dangers and on being quite safe. Taking what he had said as an oracle, he retained him in the number of his intimate friends.

22

WHEN I hear of these and like occurrences, I suspend my judgment on the question whether it is fate and unchangeable necessity or chance which governs the revolutions of human affairs. Indeed, among the wisest of the ancients and among their disciples you will find conflicting theories, many holding the conviction that heaven does not concern itself with the beginning or the end of our life, or, in short, with mankind at all; and that therefore sorrows are continually the lot of the good, happiness of the wicked; while others, on the contrary, believe that though there is a harmony between fate and events, yet it is not dependent on wandering stars, but on primary elements, and on a combination of natural causes. Still, they leave us the capacity of choosing our life, maintaining that, the choice once made, there is a fixed sequence of events. Good and evil, again, are not what vulgar opinion accounts them; many who seem to be struggling with adversity are happy; many, amid great affluence, are utterly miserable, if only the first bear their hard lot with patience, and the latter make a foolish use of their prosperity. Most men, however, cannot part with the belief that each person's future is fixed from his very birth, but that some things happen differently from what has been foretold through the impostures of those who describe what they do not know, and that this destroys the credit of a science, clear testimonies to which have been given both by past ages and by our own. In fact, how the son of this same Thrasyllus predicted Nero's reign I shall relate when the time comes, not to digress too far from my subject.

23

THAT same year the death of Asinius Gallus became known. That he died of starvation, there was not a doubt; whether of his own choice or by compulsion, was a question. The emperor was asked whether he would allow him to be buried, and he blushed not to grant the favour, and actually blamed the accident which had proved fatal to the accused before he could be convicted in his presence. Just as if in a three years' interval an opportunity was wanting for the trial of an old ex-consul and the father of a number of ex-consuls. Next Drusus perished, after having prolonged life for eight days on the most wretched of food, even chewing the stuffing, his bed. According to some writers, Macro had been instructed that, in case of Sejanus attempting an armed revolt, he was to hurry the young prince out of the confinement in which he was detained in the Palace and put him at the head of the people. Subsequently the emperor, as a rumour was gaining ground that he was on the point of a reconciliation with his daughter-in-law and his grandson, chose to be merciless rather than to relent.

24

HE even bitterly reviled him after his death, taunting him with nameless abominations and with a spirit bent on his family's ruin and hostile to the State. And, what seemed most horrible of all, he ordered a daily journal of all that he said and did to be read in public. That there had been spies by his side for so many years, to note his looks, his sighs, and even his whispered thoughts, and that his grandfather could have heard read, and published all, was scarce credible. But letters of Attius, a centurion, and Didymus, a freedman, openly exhibited the names of slave after slave who had respectively struck or scared Drusus as he was quitting his chamber. The centurion had actually added, as something highly meritorious, his own language in all its brutality, and some utterances of the dying man in which, at first feigning loss of reason, he imprecated in seeming madness fearful things on Tiberius, and then, when hope of life was gone, denounced him with a studied and elaborate curse. "As he had slain a daughter-in-law, a brother's son, and son's sons, and filled his whole house with bloodshed, so might he pay the full penalty due to the name and race of his ancestors as well as to future generations." The Senate clamorously interrupted, with an affectation of horror, but they were penetrated by alarm and amazement at seeing that a hitherto cunning prince, who had shrouded his wickedness in mystery, had waxed so bold as to remove, so to speak, the walls of his house and display his grandson under a centurion's lash, amid the buffetings of slaves, craving in vain the last sustenance of life.

25

MEN'S grief at all this had not died away when news was heard of Agrippina. She had lived on, sustained by hope, I suppose, after the destruction of Sejanus, and, when she found no abatement of horrors, had voluntarily perished, though possibly nourishment was refused her and a fiction concocted of a death that might seem self-chosen. Tiberius, it is certain, vented his wrath in the foulest charges. He reproached her with unchastity, with having had Asinius Gallus as a paramour and being driven by his death to loathe existence. But Agrippina, who could not endure equality and loved to domineer, was with her masculine aspirations far removed from the frailties of women. The emperor further observed that she died on the same day on which Sejanus had paid the penalty of his crime two years before, a fact, he said, to be recorded; and he made it a boast that she had not been strangled by the halter and flung down the Gemonian steps. He received a vote of thanks, and it was decreed that on the seventeenth of October, the day on which both perished, through all future years, an offering should be consecrated to Jupiter.

26

SOON afterwards Cocceius Nerva, a man always at the emperor's side, a master of law both divine and human, whose position was secure and health sound, resolved to die. Tiberius, as soon as he knew it, sat by him and asked his reasons, adding entreaties, and finally protesting that it would be a burden on his conscience and a blot on his reputation, if the most intimate of his friends were to fly from life without any cause for death. Nerva turned away from his expostulations and persisted in his abstinence from all food. Those who knew his thoughts said that as he saw more closely into the miseries of the State, he chose, in anger and alarm, an honourable death, while he was yet safe and unassailed on. Meanwhile Agrippina's ruin, strange to say, dragged Plancina with it. Formerly the wife of Cneius Piso, and one who had openly exulted at the death of Germanicus, she had been saved, when Piso fell, by the entreaties of Augusta, and not less by the enmity of Agrippina. When hatred and favour had alike passed away, justice asserted itself. Pursued by charges universally notorious, she suffered by her own hand a penalty tardy rather than undeserved.

27

AMID the many sorrows which saddened Rome, one cause of grief was the marriage of Julia, Drusus's daughter and Nero's late wife, into the humbler family of Rubellius Blandus, whose grandfather many remembered as a Roman knight from Tibur. At the end of the year the death of Aelius Lamia, who, after being at last released from the farce of governing Syria, had become city-prefect, was celebrated with the honours of a censor's funeral. He was a man of illustrious descent, and in a hale old age; and the fact of the province having been withheld gained him additional esteem. Subsequently, on the death of Flaccus Pomponius, propraetor of Syria, a letter from the emperor was read, in which he complained that all the best men who were fit to command armies declined the service, and that he was thus necessarily driven to entreaties, by which some of the ex-consuls might be prevailed on to take provinces. He forgot that Arruntius had been kept at home now for ten years, that he might not go to Spain. That same year Marcus Lepidus also died. I have dwelt at sufficient length on his moderation and wisdom in my earlier books, and I need not further enlarge on his noble descent. Assuredly the family of the Aemilii has been rich in good citizens, and even the members of that house whose morals were corrupt, still lived with a certain splendour.

28

DURING the consulship of Paulus Fabius and Lucius Vitellius, the bird called the phoenix, after a long succession of ages, appeared in Egypt and furnished the most learned men of that country and of Greece with abundant matter for the discussion of the marvelous phenomenon. It is my wish to make known all on which they agree with several things, questionable enough indeed, but not too absurd to be noticed. That it is a creature sacred to the sun, differing from all other birds in its beak and in the tints of its plumage, is held unanimously by those who have described its nature. As to the number of years it lives, there are various accounts. The general tradition says five hundred years. Some maintain that it is seen at intervals of fourteen hundred and sixty-one years, and that the former birds flew into the city called Heliopolis successively in the reigns of Sesostris, Amasis, and Ptolemy, the third king of the Macedonian dynasty, with a multitude of companion birds marveling at the novelty of the appearance. But all antiquity is of course obscure. From Ptolemy to Tiberius was a period of less than five hundred years. Consequently some have supposed that this was a spurious phoenix, not from the regions of Arabia, and with none of the instincts which ancient tradition has attributed to the bird. For when the number of years is completed and death is near, the phoenix, it is said, builds a nest in the land of its birth and infuses into it a germ of life from which an offspring arises, whose first care, when fledged, is to bury its father. This is not rashly done, but taking up a load of myrrh and having tried its strength by a long flight, as soon as it is equal to the burden and to the journey, it carries its father's body, bears it to the altar of the Sun, and leaves it to the flames. All this is full of doubt and legendary exaggeration. Still, there is no question that the bird is occasionally seen in Egypt.

Book XII

1

THE destruction of Messalina shook the imperial house; for a strife arose among the freedmen, who should choose a wife for Claudius, impatient as he was of a single life and submissive to the rule of wives. The ladies were fired with no less jealousy. Each insisted on her rank, beauty, and fortune, and pointed to her claims to such a marriage. But the keenest competition was between Lollia Paulina, the daughter of Marcus Lollius, an ex-consul, and Julia Agrippina, the daughter of Germanicus. Callistus favoured the first, Pallas the second. Aelia Paetina however, of the family of the Tuberones, had the support of Narcissus. The emperor, who inclined now one way, now another, as he listened to this or that adviser, summoned the disputants to a conference and bade them express their opinions and give their reasons.

2

NARCISSUS dwelt on the marriage of years gone by, on the tie of offspring, for Paetina was the mother of Antonia, and on the advantage of excluding a new element from his household, by the return of a wife to whom he was accustomed, and who would assuredly not look with a stepmother's animosity on Britannicus and Octavia, who were next in her affections to her own children. Callistus argued that she was compromised by her long separation, and that were she to be taken back, she would be supercilious on the strength of it. It would be far better to introduce Lollia, for, as she had no children of her own, she would be free from jealousy, and would take the place of a mother towards her stepchildren. Pallas again selected Agrippina for special commendation because she would bring with her Germanicus's grandson, who was thoroughly worthy of imperial rank, the scion of a noble house and a link to unite the descendants of the Claudian family. He hoped that a woman who was the mother of many children and still in the freshness of youth, would not carry off the grandeur of the Caesars to some other house.

3

THIS advice prevailed, backed up as it was by Agrippina's charms. On the pretext of her relationship, she paid frequent visits to her uncle, and so won his heart, that she was preferred to the others, and, though not yet his wife, already possessed a wife's power. For as soon as she was sure of her marriage, she began to aim at greater things, and planned an alliance between Domitius, her son by Cneius Aenobarbus, and Octavia, the emperor's daughter. This could not be accomplished without a crime, for the emperor had betrothed Octavia to Lucius Silanus, a young man otherwise famous, whom he had brought forward as a candidate for popular favour by the honour of triumphal distinctions and by a magnificent gladiatorial show. But no difficulty seemed to be presented by the temper of a sovereign who had neither partialities nor dislikes, but such as were suggested and dictated to him.

4

VITELLIUS accordingly, who used the name of censor to screen a slave's trickeries, and looked forward to new despotisms, already impending, associated himself in Agrippina's plans, with a view to her favour, and began to bring charges against Silanus, whose sister, Junia Calvina, a handsome and lively girl, had shortly before become his daughter-in-law. Here was a starting point for an accuser. Vitellius put an infamous construction on the somewhat incautious though not criminal love between the brother and sister. The emperor listened, for his affection for his daughter inclined him the more to admit suspicions against his son-in-law. Silanus meanwhile, who knew nothing of the plot, and happened that year to be praetor, was suddenly expelled from the Senate by an edict of Vitellius, though the roll of Senators had been recently reviewed and the lustrum closed. Claudius at the same time broke off the connection; Silanus was forced to resign his office, and the one remaining day of his praetorship was conferred on Eprius Marcellus.

5

IN the year of the consulship of Caius Pompeius and Quintus Veranius, the marriage arranged between Claudius and Agrippina was confirmed both by popular rumour and by their own illicit love. Still, they did not yet dare to celebrate the nuptials in due form, for there was no precedent for the introduction of a niece into an uncle's house. It was positively incest, and if disregarded, it would, people feared, issue in calamity to the State. These scruples ceased not till Vitellius undertook the management of the matter in his own way. He asked the emperor whether he would yield to the recommendations of the people and to the authority of the Senate. When Claudius replied that he was one among the citizens and could not resist their unanimous voice, Vitellius requested him to wait in the palace, while he himself went to the Senate. Protesting that the supreme interest of the commonwealth was at stake, he begged to be allowed to speak first, and then began to urge that the very burdensome labours of the emperor in a world-wide administration, required assistance, so that, free from domestic cares, he might consult the public welfare. How again could there be a more virtuous relief for the mind of an imperial censor than the taking of a wife to share his prosperity and his troubles, to whom he might entrust his inmost thoughts and the care of his young children, unused as he was to luxury and pleasure, and wont from his earliest youth to obey the laws.

6

VITELLIUS, having first put forward these arguments in a conciliatory speech, and met with decided acquiescence from the Senate, began afresh to point out, that, as they all recommended the emperor's marriage, they ought to select a lady conspicuous for noble rank and purity, herself too the mother of children. "It cannot," he said, "be long a question that Agrippina stands first in nobility of birth. She has given proof too that she is not barren, and she has suitable moral qualities. It is, again, a singular advantage to us, due to divine providence, for a widow to be united to an emperor who has limited himself to his own lawful wives. We have heard from our fathers, we have ourselves seen that married women were seized at the caprice of the Caesars. This is quite alien to the propriety of our day. Rather let a precedent be now set for the taking of a wife by an emperor. But, it will be said, marriage with a brother's daughter is with us a novelty. True; but it is common in other countries, and there is no law to forbid it. Marriages of cousins were long unknown, but after a time they became frequent. Custom adapts itself to expediency, and this novelty will hereafter take its place among recognised usages."

7

THERE were some who rushed out of the Senate passionately protesting that if the emperor hesitated, they would use violence. A promiscuous throng assembled, and kept exclaiming that the same too was the prayer of the Roman people. Claudius without further delay presented himself in the forum to their congratulations; then entering the Senate, he asked from them a decree which should decide that for the future marriages between uncles and brothers' daughters should be legal. There was, however, found only one person who desired such a marriage, Alledius Severus, a Roman knight, who, as many said, was swayed by the influence of Agrippina. Then came a revolution in the State, and everything was under the control of a woman, who did not, like Messalina, insult Rome by loose manners. It was a stringent, and, so to say, masculine despotism; there was sternness and generally arrogance in public, no sort of immodesty at home, unless it conduced to power. A boundless greed of wealth was veiled under the pretext that riches were being accumulated as a prop to the throne.

8

ON the day of the marriage Silanus committed suicide, having up to that time prolonged his hope of life, or else choosing that day to heighten the popular indignation. His sister, Calvina, was banished from Italy. Claudius further added that sacrifices after the ordinances of King Tullius, and atonements were to be offered by the pontiffs in the grove of Diana, amid general ridicule at the idea devising penalties and propitiations for incest at such a time. Agrippina, that she might not be conspicuous only by her evil deeds, procured for Annaeus Seneca a remission of his exile, and with it the praetorship. She thought this would be universally welcome, from the celebrity of his attainments, and it was her wish too for the boyhood of Domitius to be trained under so excellent an instructor, and for them to have the benefit of his counsels in their designs on the throne. For Seneca, it was believed, was devoted to Agrippina from a remembrance of her kindness, and an enemy to Claudius from a bitter sense of wrong.

9

IT was then resolved to delay no longer. Memmius Pollio, the consul-elect, was induced by great promises to deliver a speech, praying Claudius to betroth Octavia to Domitius. The match was not unsuitable to the age of either, and was likely to develop still more important results. Pollio introduced the motion in much the same language as Vitellius had lately used. So Octavia was betrothed, and Domitius, besides his previous relationship, became now the emperor's affianced son-in-law, and an equal of Britannicus, through the exertions of his mother and the cunning of those who had been the accusers of Messalina, and feared the vengeance of her son.

10

ABOUT the same time an embassy from the Parthians, which had been sent, as I have stated, to solicit the return of Meherdates, was introduced into the Senate, and delivered a message to the following effect: "They were not," they said, "unaware of the treaty of alliance, nor did their coming imply any revolt from the family of the Arsacids; indeed, even the son of Vonones, Phraates's grandson, was with them in their resistance to the despotism of Gotarzes, which was alike intolerable to the nobility and to the people. Already brothers, relatives, and distant kin had been swept off by murder after murder; wives actually pregnant, and tender children were added to Gotarzes' victims, while, slothful at home and unsuccessful in war, he made cruelty a screen for his feebleness. Between the Parthians and ourselves there was an ancient friendship, founded on a state alliance, and we ought to support allies who were our rivals in strength, and yet yielded to us out of respect. Kings' sons were given as hostages, in order that when Parthia was tired of home rule, it might fall back on the emperor and the Senate, and receive from them a better sovereign, familiar with Roman habits."

11

IN answer to these and like arguments Claudius began to speak of the grandeur of Rome and the submissive attitude of the Parthians. He compared himself to the Divine Augustus, from whom, he reminded them, they had sought a king, but omitted to mention Tiberius, though he too had sent them sovereigns. He added some advice for Meherdates, who was present, and told him not to be thinking of a despot and his slaves, but rather of a ruler among fellow citizens, and to practice clemency and justice which barbarians would like the more for being unused to them. Then he turned to the envoys and bestowed high praise on the young foster-son of Rome, as one whose self-control had hitherto been exemplary. "Still," he said, "they must bear with the caprices of kings, and frequent revolutions were bad. Rome, sated with her glory, had reached such a height that, she wished even foreign nations to enjoy repose." Upon this Caius Cassius, governor of Syria, was commissioned to escort the young prince to the bank of the Euphrates.

12

CASSIUS was at that time preeminent for legal learning. The profession of the soldier is forgotten in a quiet period, and peace reduces the enterprising and indolent to an equality. But Cassius, as far as it was possible without war, revived ancient discipline, kept exercising the legions, in short, used as much diligence and precaution as if an enemy were threatening him. This conduct he counted worthy of his ancestors and of the Cassian family which had won renown even in those countries. He then summoned those at whose suggestion a king had been sought from Rome, and having encamped at Zeugma where the river was most easily fordable and awaited the arrival of the chief men of Parthia and of Acbarus, king of the Arabs, he reminded Meherdates that the impulsive enthusiasm of barbarians soon flags from delay or even changes into treachery, and that therefore he should urge on his enterprise. The advice was disregarded through the perfidy Acbarus, by whom the foolish young prince, who thought that the highest position merely meant self-indulgence, was detained for several days in the town of Edessa. Although a certain Carenes pressed them to come and promised easy success if they hastened their arrival, they did not make for Mesopotamia, which was close to them, but, by a long detour, for Armenia, then ill-suited to their movements, as winter was beginning.

13

AS they approached the plains, wearied with the snows and mountains, they were joined by the forces of Carenes, and having crossed the river Tigris they traversed the country of the Adiabeni, whose king Izates had avowedly embraced the alliance of Meherdates, though secretly and in better faith he inclined to Gotarzes. In their march they captured the city of Ninos, the most ancient capital of Assyria, and a fortress, historically famous, as the spot where the last battle between Darius and Alexander the power of Persia fell. Gotarzes meantime was offering vows to the local divinities on a mountain called Sambulos, with special worship of Hercules, who at a stated time bids the priests in a dream equip horses for the chase and place them near his temple. When the horses have been laden with quivers full of arrows, they scour the forest and at length return at night with empty quivers, panting violently. Again the god in a vision of the night reveals to them the track along which he roamed through the woods, and everywhere slaughtered beasts are found.

14

GOTARZES, his army not being yet in sufficient force, made the river Corma a line of defense, and though he was challenged to an engagement by taunting messages, he contrived delays, shifted his positions and sent emissaries to corrupt the enemy and bribe them to throw off their allegiance. Izates of the Adiabeni and then Acbarus of the Arabs deserted with their troops, with their countrymen's characteristic fickleness, confirming previous experience, that barbarians prefer to seek a king from Rome than to keep him. Meherdates, stripped of his powerful auxiliaries and suspecting treachery in the rest, resolved, as his last resource, to risk everything and try the issue of a battle. Nor did Gotarzes, who was emboldened by the enemy's diminished strength, refuse the challenge. They fought with terrible courage and doubtful result, till Carenes, who having beaten down all resistance had advanced too far, was surprised by a fresh detachment in his rear. Then Meherdates in despair yielded to promises from Parrhaces, one of his father's adherents, and was by his treachery delivered in chains to the conqueror. Gotarzes taunted him with being no kinsman of his or of the Arsacids, but a foreigner and a Roman, and having cut off his ears, bade him live, a memorial of his own clemency, and a disgrace to us. After this Gotarzes fell ill and died, and Vonones, who then ruled the Medes, was summoned to the throne. He was memorable neither for his good nor bad fortune; he completed a short and inglorious reign, and then the empire of Parthia passed to his son Vologeses.

15

MITHRIDATES of Bosporus, meanwhile, who had lost his power and was a mere outcast, on learning that the Roman general, Didius, and the main strength of his army had retired, and that Cotys, a young prince without experience, was left in his new kingdom with a few cohorts under Julius Aquila, a Roman knight, disdaining both, roused the neighbouring tribes, and drew deserters to his standard. At last he collected an army, drove out the king of the Dandaridae, and possessed himself of his dominions. When this was known, and the invasion of Bosporus was every moment expected, Aquila and Cotys, seeing that hostilities had been also resumed by Zorsines, king of the Siraci, distrusted their own strength, and themselves too sought the friendship of the foreigner by sending envoys to Eunones, who was then chief of the Adorsi. There was no difficulty about alliance, when they pointed to the power of Rome in contrast with the rebel Mithridates. It was accordingly stipulated that Eunones should engage the enemy with his cavalry, and the Romans undertake the siege of towns.

16

THEN the army advanced in regular formation, the Adorsi in the van and the rear, while the centre was strengthened by the cohorts, and native troops of Bosporus with Roman arms. Thus the enemy was defeated, and they reached Soza, a town in Dandarica, which Mithridates had abandoned, where it was thought expedient to leave a garrison, as the temper of the people was uncertain. Next they marched on the Siraci, and after crossing the river Panda besieged the city of Uspe, which stood on high ground, and had the defense of wall and fosses; only the walls, not being of stone, but of hurdles and wicker-work with earth between, were too weak to resist an assault. Towers were raised to a greater height as a means of annoying the besieged with brands and darts. Had not night stopped the conflict, the siege would have been begun and finished within one day.

17

NEXT day they sent an embassy asking mercy for the freeborn, and offering ten thousand slaves. As it would have been inhuman to slay the prisoners, and very difficult to keep them under guard, the conquerors rejected the offer, preferring that they should perish by the just doom of war. The signal for massacre was therefore given to the soldiers, who had mounted the walls by scaling ladders. The destruction of Uspe struck terror into the rest of the people, who thought safety impossible when they saw how armies and ramparts, heights and difficult positions, rivers and cities, alike yielded to their foe. And so Zorsines, having long considered whether he should still have regard to the fallen fortunes of Mithridates or to the kingdom of his fathers, and having at last preferred his country's interests, gave hostages and prostrated himself before the emperor's image, to the great glory of the Roman army, which all men knew to have come after a bloodless victory within three days' march of the river Tanais. In their return however fortune was not equally favourable; some of their vessels, as they were sailing back, were driven on the shores of the Tauri and cut off by the barbarians, who slew the commander of a cohort and several centurions.

18

MEANWHILE Mithridates, finding arms an unavailing resource, considered on whose mercy he was to throw himself. He feared his brother Cotys, who had once been a traitor, then become his open enemy. No Roman was on the spot of authority sufficient to make his promises highly valued. So he turned to Eunones, who had no personal animosity against him, and had been lately strengthened by his alliance with us. Adapting his dress and expression of countenance as much as possible to his present condition, he entered the palace, and throwing himself at the feet of Eunones he exclaimed, "Mithridates, whom the Romans have sought so many years by land and sea, stands before you by his own choice. Deal as you please with the descendant of the great Achaemenes, the only glory of which enemies have not robbed me."

19

THE great name of Mithridates, his reverse, his prayer, full of dignity, deeply affected Eunones. He raised the suppliant, and commended him for having chosen the nation of the Adorsi and his own good faith in suing for mercy. He sent at the same time envoys to Caesar with a letter to this effect, that friendship between emperors of Rome and sovereigns of powerful peoples was primarily based on a similarity of fortune, and that between himself and Claudius there was the tie of a common victory. Wars had glorious endings, whenever matters were settled by an amnesty. The conquered Zorsines had on this principle been deprived of nothing. For Mithridates, as he deserved heavier punishment, he asked neither power nor dominions, only that he might not be led in triumph, and pay the penalty of death.

20

CLAUDIUS, though merciful to foreign princes, was yet in doubt whether it were better to receive the captive with a promise of safety or to claim his surrender by the sword. To this last he was urged by resentment at his wrongs, and by thirst for vengeance. On the other hand it was argued that it would be undertaking a war in a country without roads, on a harbourless sea, against warlike kings and wandering tribes, on a barren soil; that a weary disgust would come of tardy movements, and perils of precipitancy; that the glory of victory would be small, while much disgrace would ensue on defeat. Why should not the emperor seize the offer and spare the exile, whose punishment would be the greater, the longer he lived in poverty? Moved by these considerations, Claudius wrote to Eunones that Mithridates had certainly merited an extreme and exemplary penalty, which he was not wanting in power to inflict, but it had been the principle of his ancestors to show as much forbearance to a suppliant as they showed persistence against a foe. As for triumphs, they were won over nations and kings hitherto unconquered.

21

AFTER this, Mithridates was given up and brought to Rome by Junius Cilo, the procurator of Pontus. There in the emperor's presence he was said to have spoken too proudly for his position, and words uttered by him to the following effect became the popular talk: "I have not been sent, but have come back to you; if you do not believe me, let me go and pursue me." He stood too with fearless countenance when he was exposed to the people's gaze near the Rostra, under military guard. To Cilo and Aquila were voted, respectively, the consular and praetorian decorations.

22

IN the same consulship, Agrippina, who was terrible in her hatred and detested Lollia, for having competed with her for the emperor's hand, planned an accusation, through an informer who was to tax her with having consulted astrologers and magicians and the image of the Clarian Apollo, about the imperial marriage. Upon this, Claudius, without hearing the accused, first reminded the Senate of her illustrious rank, that the sister of Lucius Volusius was her mother, Cotta Messalinus her granduncle, Memmius Regulus formerly her husband (for of her marriage to Caius Caesar he purposely said nothing), and then added that she had mischievous designs on the State, and must have the means of crime taken from her. Consequently, her property should be confiscated, and she herself banished from Italy. Thus out of immense wealth only five million sesterces were left to the exile. Calpurnia too, a lady of high rank, was ruined, simply because the emperor had praised her beauty in a casual remark, without any passion for her. And so Agrippina's resentment stopped short of extreme vengeance. A tribune was despatched to Lollia, who was to force her to suicide. Next on the prosecution of the Bithynians, Cadius Rufus, was condemned under the law against extortion.

23

NARBON Gaul, for its special reverence of the Senate, received a privilege. Senators belonging to the province, without seeking the emperor's approval, were to be allowed to visit their estates, a right enjoyed by Sicily. Ituraea and Judaea, on the death of their kings, Sohaemus and Agrippa, were annexed to the province of Syria. It was also decided that the augury of the public safety, which for twenty-five years had been neglected, should be revived and henceforth observed. The emperor likewise widened the sacred precincts of the capital, in conformity with the ancient usage, according to which, those who had enlarged the empire were permitted also to extend the boundaries of Rome. But Roman generals, even after the conquest of great nations, had never exercised this right, except Lucius Sulla and the Divine Augustus.

24

THERE are various popular accounts of the ambitious and vainglorious efforts of our kings in this matter. Still, I think, it is interesting to know accurately the original plan of the precinct, as it was fixed by Romulus. From the ox market, where we see the brazen statue of a bull, because that animal is yoked to the plough, a furrow was drawn to mark out the town, so as to embrace the great altar of Hercules; then, at regular intervals, stones were placed along the foot of the Palatine hill to the altar of Consus, soon afterwards, to the old Courts, and then to the chapel of Larunda. The Roman forum and the Capitol were not, it was supposed, added to the city by Romulus, but by Titus Tatius. In time, the precinct was enlarged with the growth of Rome's fortunes. The boundaries now fixed by Claudius may be easily recognised, as they are specified in the public records.

25

IN the consulship of Caius Antistius and Marcus Suilius, the adoption of Domitius was hastened on by the influence of Pallas. Bound to Agrippina, first as the promoter of her marriage, then as her paramour, he still urged Claudius to think of the interests of the State, and to provide some support for the tender years of Britannicus. "So," he said, "it had been with the Divine Augustus, whose stepsons, though he had grandsons to be his stay, had been promoted; Tiberius too, though he had offspring of his own, had adopted Germanicus. Claudius also would do well to strengthen himself with a young prince who could share his cares with him." Overcome by these arguments, the emperor preferred Domitius to his own son, though he was but two years older, and made a speech in the senate, the same in substance as the representations of his freedman. It was noted by learned men, that no previous example of adoption into the patrician family of the Claudii was to be found; and that from Attus Clausus there had been one unbroken line.

26

HOWEVER, the emperor received formal thanks, and still more elaborate flattery was paid to Domitius. A law was passed, adopting him into the Claudian family with the name of Nero. Agrippina too was honoured with the title of Augusta. When this had been done, there was not a person so void of pity as not to feel keen sorrow at the position of Britannicus. Gradually forsaken by the very slaves who waited on him, he turned into ridicule the ill-timed attentions of his stepmother, perceiving their insincerity. For he is said to have had by no means a dull understanding; and this is either a fact, or perhaps his perils won him sympathy, and so he possessed the credit of it, without actual evidence.

27

AGRIPPINA, to show her power even to the allied nations, procured the despatch of a colony of veterans to the chief town of the Ubii, where she was born. The place was named after her. Agrippa, her grandfather, had, as it happened, received this tribe, when they crossed the Rhine, under our protection. During the same time, there was a panic in Upper Germany through an irruption of plundering bands of Chatti. Thereupon Lucius Pomponius, who was in command, directed the Vangiones and Nemetes, with the allied cavalry, to anticipate the raid, and suddenly to fall upon them from every quarter while they were dispersed. The general's plan was backed up by the energy of the troops. These were divided into two columns; and those who marched to the left cut off the plunderers, just on their return, after a riotous enjoyment of their spoil, when they were heavy with sleep. It added to the men's joy that they had rescued from slavery after forty years some survivors of the defeat of Varus.

28

THE column which took the right-hand and the shorter route, inflicted greater loss on the enemy who met them, and ventured on a battle. With much spoil and glory they returned to Mount Taunus, where Pomponius was waiting with the legions, to see whether the Chatti, in their eagerness for vengeance, would give him a chance of fighting. They however fearing to be hemmed in on one side by the Romans, on the other by the Cherusci, with whom they are perpetually at feud, sent envoys and hostages to Rome. To Pomponius was decreed the honour of a triumph; a mere fraction of his renown with the next generation, with whom his poems constitute his chief glory.

29

AT this same time, Vannius, whom Drusus Caesar had made king of the Suevi, was driven from his kingdom. In the commencement of his reign he was renowned and popular with his countrymen; but subsequently, with long possession, he became a tyrant, and the enmity of neighbours, joined to intestine strife, was his ruin. Vibillius, king of the Hermunduri, and Vangio and Sido, sons of a sister of Vannius, led the movement. Claudius, though often entreated, declined to interpose by arms in the conflict of the barbarians, and simply promised Vannius a safe refuge in the event of his expulsion. He wrote instructions to Publius Atellius Hister, governor of Pannonia, that he was to have his legions, with some picked auxiliaries from the province itself, encamped on the riverbank, as a support to the conquered and a terror to the conqueror, who might otherwise, in the elation of success, disturb also the peace of our empire. For an immense host of Ligii, with other tribes, was advancing, attracted by the fame of the opulent realm which Vannius had enriched during thirty years of plunder and of tribute. Vannius's own native force was infantry, and his cavalry was from the Iazyges of Sarmatia; an army which was no match for his numerous enemy. Consequently, he determined to maintain himself in fortified positions, and protract the war.

30

BUT the Iazyges, who could not endure a siege, dispersed themselves throughout the surrounding country and rendered an engagement inevitable, as the Ligii and Hermunduri had there rushed to the attack. So Vannius came down out of his fortresses, and though he was defeated in battle, notwithstanding his reverse, he won some credit by having fought with his own hand, and received wounds on his breast. He then fled to the fleet which was awaiting him on the Danube, and was soon followed by his adherents, who received grants of land and were settled in Pannonia. Vangio and Sido divided his kingdom between them; they were admirably loyal to us, and among their subjects, whether the cause was in themselves or in the nature of despotism, much loved, while seeking to acquire power, and yet more hated when they had acquired it.

31

MEANWHILE, in Britain, Publius Ostorius, the propraetor, found himself confronted by disturbance. The enemy had burst into the territories of our allies with all the more fury, as they imagined that a new general would not march against them with winter beginning and with an army of which he knew nothing. Ostorius, well aware that first events are those which produce alarm or confidence, by a rapid movement of his light cohorts, cut down all who opposed him, pursued those who fled, and lest they should rally, and so an unquiet and treacherous peace might allow no rest to the general and his troops, he prepared to disarm all whom he suspected, and to occupy with encampments the whole country to the Avon and Severn. The Iceni, a powerful tribe, which war had not weakened, as they had voluntarily joined our alliance, were the first to resist. At their instigation the surrounding nations chose as a battlefield a spot walled in by a rude barrier, with a narrow approach, impenetrable to cavalry. Through these defenses the Roman general, though he had with him only the allied troops, without the strength of the legions, attempted to break, and having assigned their positions to his cohorts, he equipped even his cavalry for the work of infantry. Then at a given signal they forced the barrier, routing the enemy who were entangled in their own defenses. The rebels, conscious of their guilt, and finding escape barred, performed many noble feats. In this battle, Marius Ostorius, the general's son, won the reward for saving a citizen's life.

32

THE defeat of the Iceni quieted those who were hesitating between war and peace. Then the army was marched against the Cangi; their territory was ravaged, spoil taken everywhere without the enemy venturing on an engagement, or if they attempted to harass our march by stealthy attacks, their cunning was always punished. And now Ostorius had advanced within a little distance of the sea, facing the island Hibernia, when feuds broke out among the Brigantes and compelled the general's return, for it was his fixed purpose not to undertake any fresh enterprise till he had consolidated his previous successes. The Brigantes indeed, when a few who were beginning hostilities had been slain and the rest pardoned, settled down quietly; but on the Silures neither terror nor mercy had the least effect; they persisted in war and could be quelled only by legions encamped in their country. That this might be the more promptly effected, a colony of a strong body of veterans was established at Camulodunum on the conquered lands, as a defense against the rebels, and as a means of imbuing the allies with respect for our laws.

33

THE army then marched against the Silures, a naturally fierce people and now full of confidence in the might of Caractacus, who by many an indecisive and many a successful battle had raised himself far above all the other generals of the Britons. Inferior in military strength, but deriving an advantage from the deceptiveness of the country, he at once shifted the war by a stratagem into the territory of the Ordovices, where, joined by all who dreaded peace with us, he resolved on a final struggle. He selected a position for the engagement in which advance and retreat alike would be difficult for our men and comparatively easy for his own, and then on some lofty hills, wherever their sides could be approached by a gentle slope, he piled up stones to serve as a rampart. A river too of varying depth was in his front, and his armed bands were drawn up before his defenses.

34

THEN too the chieftains of the several tribes went from rank to rank, encouraging and confirming the spirit of their men by making light of their fears, kindling their hopes, and by every other warlike incitement. As for Caractacus, he flew hither and thither, protesting that that day and that battle would be the beginning of the recovery of their freedom, or of everlasting bondage. He appealed, by name, to their forefathers who had driven back the dictator Caesar, by whose valour they were free from the Roman axe and tribute, and still preserved inviolate the persons of their wives and of their children. While he was thus speaking, the host shouted applause; every warrior bound himself by his national oath not to shrink from weapons or wounds.

35

SUCH enthusiasm confounded the Roman general. The river too in his face, the rampart they had added to it, the frowning hill-tops, the stern resistance and masses of fighting men everywhere apparent, daunted him. But his soldiers insisted on battle, exclaiming that valour could overcome all things; and the prefects and tribunes, with similar language, stimulated the ardour of the troops. Ostorius having ascertained by a survey the inaccessible and the assailable points of the position, led on his furious men, and crossed the river without difficulty. When he reached the barrier, as long as it was a fight with missiles, the wounds and the slaughter fell chiefly on our soldiers; but when he had formed the military testudo, and the rude, ill-compacted fence of stones was torn down, and it was an equal hand-to-hand engagement, the barbarians retired to the heights. Yet even there, both light and heavy-armed soldiers rushed to the attack; the first harassed the foe with missiles, while the latter closed with them, and the opposing ranks of the Britons were broken, destitute as they were of the defense of breast-plates or helmets. When they faced the auxiliaries, they were felled by the swords and javelins of our legionaries; if they wheeled round, they were again met by the sabres and spears of the auxiliaries. It was a glorious victory; the wife and daughter of Caractacus were captured, and his brothers too were admitted to surrender.

36

THERE is seldom safety for the unfortunate, and Caractacus, seeking the protection of Cartismandua, queen of the Brigantes, was put in chains and delivered up to the conquerors, nine years after the beginning of the war in Britain. His fame had spread thence, and traveled to the neighbouring islands and provinces, and was actually celebrated in Italy. All were eager to see the great man, who for so many years had defied our power. Even at Rome the name of Caractacus was no obscure one; and the emperor, while he exalted his own glory, enhanced the renown of the vanquished. The people were summoned as to a grand spectacle; the praetorian cohorts were drawn up under arms in the plain in front of their camp; then came a procession of the royal vassals, and the ornaments and neck-chains and the spoils which the king had won in wars with other tribes, were displayed. Next were to be seen his brothers, his wife and daughter; last of all, Caractacus himself. All the rest stooped in their fear to abject supplication; not so the king, who neither by humble look nor speech sought compassion.

37

WHEN he was set before the emperor's tribunal, he spoke as follows: "Had my moderation in prosperity been equal to my noble birth and fortune, I should have entered this city as your friend rather than as your captive; and you would not have disdained to receive, under a treaty of peace, a king descended from illustrious ancestors and ruling many nations. My present lot is as glorious to you as it is degrading to myself. I had men and horses, arms and wealth. What wonder if I parted with them reluctantly? If you Romans choose to lord it over the world, does it follow that the world is to accept slavery? Were I to have been at once delivered up as a prisoner, neither my fall nor your triumph would have become famous. My punishment would be followed by oblivion, whereas, if you save my life, I shall be an everlasting memorial of your clemency." Upon this the emperor granted pardon to Caractacus, to his wife, and to his brothers. Released from their bonds, they did homage also to Agrippina who sat near, conspicuous on another throne, in the same language of praise and gratitude. It was indeed a novelty, quite alien to ancient manners, for a woman to sit in front of Roman standards. In fact, Agrippina boasted that she was herself a partner in the empire which her ancestors had won.

38

THE Senate was then assembled, and speeches were delivered full of pompous eulogy on the capture of Caractacus. It was as glorious, they said, as the display of Syphax by Scipio, or of Perses by Lucius Paulus, or indeed of any captive prince by any of our generals to the people of Rome. Triumphal distinctions were voted to Ostorius, who thus far had been successful, but soon afterwards met with reverses; either because, when Caractacus was out of the way, our discipline was relaxed under an impression that the war was ended, or because the enemy, out of compassion for so great a king, was more ardent in his thirst for vengeance. Instantly they rushed from all parts on the camp-prefect, and legionary cohorts left to establish fortified positions among the Silures, and had not speedy succour arrived from towns and fortresses in the neighbourhood, our forces would then have been totally destroyed. Even as it was, the camp-prefect, with eight centurions, and the bravest of the soldiers, were slain; and shortly afterwards, a foraging party of our men, with some cavalry squadrons sent to their support, was utterly routed.

39

OSTORIUS then deployed his light cohorts, but even thus he did not stop the flight, till our legions sustained the brunt of the battle. Their strength equalized the conflict, which after a while was in our favour. The enemy fled with trifling loss, as the day was on the decline. Now began a series of skirmishes, for the most part like raids, in woods and morasses, with encounters due to chance or to courage, to mere heedlessness or to calculation, to fury or to lust of plunder, under directions from the officers, or sometimes even without their knowledge. Conspicuous above all in stubborn resistance were the Silures, whose rage was fired by words rumoured to have been spoken by the Roman general, to the effect, that as the Sugambri had been formerly destroyed or transplanted into Gaul, so the name of the Silures ought to be blotted out. Accordingly they cut off two of our auxiliary cohorts, the rapacity of whose officers let them make incautious forays; and by liberal gifts of spoil and prisoners to the other tribes, they were luring them too into revolt, when Ostorius, worn out by the burden of his anxieties, died, to the joy of the enemy, who thought that a campaign at least, though not a single battle, had proved fatal to general whom none could despise.

40

THE emperor on hearing of the death of his representative appointed Aulus Didius in his place, that the province might not be left without a governor. Didius, though he quickly arrived, found matters far from prosperous, for the legion under the command of Manlius Valens had meanwhile been defeated, and the disaster had been exaggerated by the enemy to alarm the new general, while he again magnified it, that he might win the more glory by quelling the movement or have a fairer excuse if it lasted. This loss too had been inflicted on us by the Silures, and they were scouring the country far and wide, till Didius hurried up and dispersed them. After the capture of Caractacus, Venutius of the Brigantes, as I have already mentioned, was pre-eminent in military skill; he had long been loyal to Rome and had been defended by our arms while he was united in marriage to the queen Cartismandua. Subsequently a quarrel broke out between them, followed instantly by war, and he then assumed a hostile attitude also towards us. At first, however, they simply fought against each other, and Cartismandua by cunning stratagems captured the brothers and kinsfolk of Venutius. This enraged the enemy, who were stung with shame at the prospect of falling under the dominion of a woman. The flower of their youth, picked out for war, invaded her kingdom. This we had foreseen; some cohorts were sent to her aid and a sharp contest followed, which was at first doubtful but had a satisfactory termination. The legion under the command of Caesius Nasica fought with a similar result. For Didius, burdened with years and covered with honours, was content with acting through his officers and merely holding back the enemy. These transactions, though occurring under two propraetors, and occupying several years, I have closely connected, lest, if related separately, they might be less easily remembered. I now return to the chronological order.

41

IN the fifth consulship of Tiberius Claudius with Sextius Cornelius Orfitus for his colleague, Nero was prematurely invested with the dress of manhood, that he might be thought qualified for political life. The emperor willingly complied with the flatteries of the Senate who wished Nero to enter on the consulship in his twentieth year, and meanwhile, as consul-elect, to have pro-consular authority beyond the limits of the capital with the title of "prince of the youth of Rome." A donative was also given to the soldiery in Nero's name, and presents to the city populace. At the games too of the circus which were then being celebrated to win for him popular favour, Britannicus wore the dress of boyhood, Nero the triumphal robe, as they rode in the procession. The people would thus behold the one with the decorations of a general, the other in a boy's habit, and would accordingly anticipate their respective destinies. At the same time those of the centurions and tribunes who pitied the lot of Britannicus were removed, some on false pretexts, others by way of a seeming compliment. Even of the freedmen, all who were of incorruptible fidelity were discarded on the following provocation. Once when they met, Nero greeted Britannicus by that name and was greeted in return as Domitius. Agrippina reported this to her husband, with bitter complaint, as the beginning of a quarrel, as implying, in fact, contempt of Nero's adoption and a canceling at home of the Senate's decree and the people's vote. She said, too, that, if the perversity of such malignant suggestions were not checked, it would issue in the ruin of the State. Claudius, enraged by what he took as a grave charge, punished with banishment or death all his son's best instructors, and set persons appointed by his stepmother to have the care of him.

42

STILL Agrippina did not yet dare to attempt her greatest

scheme, unless Lusius Geta and Rufius Crispinus were removed from the command of the praetorian cohorts; for she thought that they cherished Messalina's memory and were devoted to her children. Accordingly, as the emperor's wife persistently affirmed that faction was rife among these cohorts through the rivalry of the two officers, and that there would be stricter discipline under one commander, the appointment was transferred to Burrus Afranius, who had a brilliant reputation as a soldier, but knew well to whose wish he owed his promotion. Agrippina, too, continued to exalt her own dignity; she would enter the Capitol in a chariot, a practice, which being allowed of old only to the priests and sacred images, increased the popular reverence for a woman who up to this time was the only recorded instance of one who, an emperor's daughter, was sister, wife, and mother of a sovereign. Meanwhile her foremost champion, Vitellius, in the full tide of his power and in extreme age (so uncertain are the fortunes of the great) was attacked by an accusation of which Junius Lupus, a senator, was the author. He was charged with treason and designs on the throne. The emperor would have lent a ready ear, had not Agrippina, by threats rather than entreaties, induced him to sentence the accuser to outlawry. This was all that Vitellius desired.

43

SEVERAL prodigies occurred in that year. Birds of evil omen perched on the Capitol; houses were thrown down by frequent shocks of earthquake, and as the panic spread, all the weak were trodden down in the hurry and confusion of the crowd. Scanty crops too, and consequent famine were regarded as a token of calamity. Nor were there merely whispered complaints; while Claudius was administering justice, the populace crowded round him with a boisterous clamour and drove him to a corner of the forum, where they violently pressed on him till he broke through the furious mob with a body of soldiers. It was ascertained that Rome had provisions for no more than fifteen days, and it was through the signal bounty of heaven and the mildness of the winter that its desperate plight was relieved. And yet in past days Italy used to send supplies for the legions into distant provinces, and even now it is not a barren soil which causes distress.

But we prefer to cultivate Africa and Egypt, and trust the life of the Roman people to ships and all their risks.

44

IN the same year war broke out between the Armenians and Iberians, and was the cause of very serious disturbances between Parthia and Rome. Vologeses was king of the Parthians; on the mother's side, he was the offspring of a Greek concubine, and he obtained the throne by the retirement of his brothers. Pharasmanes had been long in possession of Iberia, and his brother, Mithridates, ruled Armenia with our powerful support. There was a son of Pharasmanes named Rhadamistus, tall and handsome, of singular bodily strength, trained in all the accomplishments of his countrymen and highly renowned among his neighbours. He boasted so arrogantly and persistently that his father's prolonged old age kept back from him the little kingdom of Iberia as to make no concealment of his ambition. Pharasmanes accordingly seeing the young prince had power in his grasp and was strong in the attachment of his people, fearing too his own declining years, tempted him with other prospects and pointed to Armenia, which, as he reminded him, he had given to Mithridates after driving out the Parthians. But open violence, he said, must be deferred; artful measures, which might crush him unawares, were better. So Rhadamistus pretended to be at feud with his father as though his stepmother's hatred was too strong for him, and went to his uncle. While he was treated by him like a son, with excessive kindness, he lured the nobles of Armenia into revolutionary schemes, without the knowledge of Mithridates, who was actually loading him with honours.

45

HE then assumed a show of reconciliation with his father, to whom he returned, telling him all that could be accomplished by treachery was now ready and that he must complete the affair by the sword. Meanwhile Pharasmanes invented pretexts for war; when he was fighting with the king of the Albanians and appealing to the

Romans for aid, his brother, he said, had opposed him, and he would now avenge that wrong by his destruction. At the same time he gave a large army to his son, who by a sudden invasion drove Mithridates in terror from the open country and forced him into the fortress of Gorneas, which was strongly situated and garrisoned by some soldiers under the command of Caelius Pollio, a camp-prefect, and Casperius, a centurion. There is nothing of which barbarians are so ignorant as military engines and the skilful management of sieges, while that is a branch of military science which we especially understand. And so Rhadamistus having attempted the fortified walls in vain or with loss, began a blockade, and, finding that his assaults were despised, tried to bribe the rapacity of the camp-prefect. Casperius protested earnestly against the overthrow of an allied king and of Armenia, the gift of the Roman people, through iniquity and greed of gain. At last, as Pollio pleaded the overpowering numbers of the enemy and Rhadamistus the orders of his father, the centurion stipulated for a truce and retired, intending, if he could not deter Pharasmanes from further hostilities, to inform Ummidius Quadratus, the governor of Syria, of the state of Armenia.

46

BY the centurion's departure the camp prefect was released, so to say, from surveillance; and he now urged Mithridates to conclude a treaty. He reminded him of the tie of brotherhood, of the seniority in age of Pharasmanes, and of their other bonds of kindred, how he was united by marriage to his brother's daughter, and was himself the father-in-law of Rhadamistus. "The Iberians," he said, "were not against peace, though for the moment they were the stronger; the perfidy of the Armenians was notorious, and he had nothing to fall back on but a fortress without stores; so he must not hesitate to prefer a bloodless negotiation to arms." As Mithridates wavered, and suspected the intentions of the camp-prefect, because he had seduced one of the king's concubines and was reputed a man who could be bribed into any wickedness, Casperius meantime went to Pharasmanes, and required of him that the Iberians should raise the blockade. Pharasmanes, to his face, replied vaguely and often in a conciliatory tone, while by secret messages he recommended Rhadamistus to hurry on the siege by all possible means. Then the price of infamy was raised, and Pollio by secret corruption induced the soldiers to demand peace and to threaten that they would abandon the garrison. Under this compulsion, Mithridates agreed to a day and a place for negotiation and quitted the fortress.

47

RHADAMISTUS at first threw himself into his embraces, feigning respect and calling him father-in-law and parent. He swore an oath too that he would do him no violence either by the sword or by poison. At the same time he drew him into a neighbouring grove, where he assured him that the appointed sacrifice was prepared for the confirmation of peace in the presence of the gods. It is a custom of these princes, whenever they join alliance, to unite their right hands and bind together the thumbs in a tight knot; then, when the blood has flowed into the extremities, they let it escape by a slight puncture and suck it in turn. Such a treaty is thought to have a mysterious sanctity, as being sealed with the blood of both parties. On this occasion he who was applying the knot pretended that it had fallen off, and suddenly seizing the knees of Mithridates flung him to the ground. At the same moment a rush was made by a number of persons, and chains were thrown round him. Then he was dragged along by a fetter, an extreme degradation to a barbarian; and soon the common people, whom he had held under a harsh sway, heaped insults on him with menacing gestures, though some, on the contrary, pitied such a reverse of fortune. His wife followed him with his little children, and filled every place with her wailings. They were hidden away in different covered carriages till the orders of Pharasmanes were distinctly ascertained. The lust of rule was more to him than his brother and his daughter, and his heart was steeled to any wickedness. Still he spared his eyes the seeing them slain before his face. Rhadamistus too, seemingly mindful of his oath, neither unsheathed the sword nor used poison against his sister and uncle, but had them thrown on the ground and then smothered them under a mass of heavy clothes. Even the sons of Mithridates were butchered for having shed tears over their parent's murder.

48

QUADRATUS, learning that Mithridates had been betrayed and that his kingdom was in the hands of his murderers, summoned a council, and, having informed them of what had occurred, consulted them whether he should take vengeance. Few cared for the honour of the State; most argued in favour of a safe course, saying "that any crime in a foreign country was to be welcomed with joy, and that the seeds of strife ought to be actually sown, on the very principle on which Roman emperors had often under a show of generosity given away this same kingdom of Armenia to excite the minds of the barbarians. Rhadamistus might retain his ill-gotten gains, as long as he was hated and infamous; for this was more to Rome's interest than for him to have succeeded with glory." To this view they assented, but that they might not be thought to have approved the crime and receive contrary orders from the emperor, envoys were sent to Pharasmanes, requiring him to withdraw from Armenian territory and remove his son.

49

JULIUS Pelignus was then procurator of Cappadocia, a man despised alike for his feebleness of mind and his grotesque personal appearance. He was however very intimate with Claudius, who, when in private life, used to beguile the dullness of his leisure with the society of jesters. This Pelignus collected some provincial auxiliaries, apparently with the design of recovering Armenia, but, while he plundered allies instead of enemies, finding himself, through the desertion of his men and the raids of the barbarians, utterly defenseless, he went to Rhadamistus, whose gifts so completely overcame him that he positively encouraged him to assume the ensigns of royalty, and himself assisted at the ceremony, authorizing and abetting. When the disgraceful news had spread far and wide, lest the world might judge of other governors by Pelignus, Helvidius Priscus was sent in command of a legion to regulate, according to circumstances, the disordered state of affairs. He quickly crossed Mount Taurus, and had restored order to a great extent more by moderation than by force, when he was ordered to return to Syria, that nothing might arise to provoke a war with Parthia.

50

FOR Vologeses, thinking that an opportunity presented itself of invading Armenia, which, though the possession of his ancestors, was now through a monstrous crime held by a foreign prince, raised an army and prepared to establish Tiridates on the throne, so that not a member of his house might be without kingly power. On the advance of the Parthians, the Iberians dispersed without a battle, and the Armenian cities, Artaxata and Tigranocerta, submitted to the yoke. Then a frightful winter or deficient supplies, with pestilence arising from both causes, forced Vologeses to abandon his present plans. Armenia was thus again without a king, and was invaded by Rhadamistus, who was now fiercer than ever, looking on the people as disloyal and sure to rebel on the first opportunity. They however, though accustomed to be slaves, suddenly threw off their tameness and gathered round the palace in arms.

51

RHADAMISTUS had no means of escape but in the swiftness of the horses which bore him and his wife away. Pregnant as she was, she endured, somehow or other, out of fear of the enemy and love of her husband, the first part of the flight, but after a while, when she felt herself shaken by its continuous speed, she implored to be rescued by an honourable death from the shame of captivity. He at first embraced, cheered, and encouraged her, now admiring her heroism, now filled with a sickening apprehension at the idea of her being left to any man's mercy. Finally, urged by the intensity of his love and familiarity with dreadful deeds, he unsheathed his scimitar, and having stabbed her, dragged her to the bank of the Araxes and committed her to the stream, so that her very body might be swept away. Then in headlong flight he hurried to Iberia, his ancestral kingdom. Zenobia meanwhile (this was her name), as she yet breathed and showed signs of life on the calm water at the river's edge, was perceived by some shepherds, who inferring from her noble appearance that she was no base-born woman, bound up her wound and applied to it their rustic remedies. As soon as they knew her name and her adventure, they conveyed her to the city of Artaxata, whence she was conducted at the public charge to Tiridates, who received her kindly and treated her as a royal person.

52

IN the consulship of Faustus Sulla and Salvius Otho, Furius Scribonianus was banished on the ground that he was consulting the astrologers about the emperor's death. His mother, Junia, was included in the accusation, as one who still resented the misfortune of exile which she had suffered in the past. His father, Camillus, had raised an armed insurrection in Dalmatia, and the emperor in again sparing a hostile family sought the credit of clemency. But the exile did not live long after this; whether he was cut off by a natural death, or by poison, was matter of conflicting rumours, according to people's belief. A decree of the Senate was then passed for the expulsion of the astrologers from Italy, stringent but ineffectual. Next the emperor, in a speech, commended all who, from their limited means, voluntarily retired from the Senatorian order, while those were degraded from it who, by retaining their seats, added effrontery to poverty.

53

DURING these proceedings he proposed to the Senate a penalty on women who united themselves in marriage to slaves, and it was decided that those who had thus demeaned themselves, without the knowledge of the slave's master, should be reduced to slavery; if with his consent, should be ranked as freedwomen. To Pallas, who, as the emperor declared, was the author of this proposal, were offered on the motion of Barea Soranus, consul-elect, the decorations of the praetorship and fifteen million sesterces. Cornelius Scipio added that he deserved public thanks for thinking less of his ancient nobility as a descendant from the kings of Arcadia, than of the welfare of the State, and allowing himself to be numbered among the emperor's ministers. Claudius assured them that Pallas was content with the honour, and that he limited himself to his former poverty. A decree of the Senate was publicly inscribed on a bronze tablet, heaping the praises of primitive frugality on a freedman, the possessor of three hundred million sesterces.

54

NOT equally moderate was his brother, surnamed Felix, who had for some time been governor of Judaea, and thought that he could do any evil act with impunity, backed up as he was by such power. It is true that the Jews had shown symptoms of commotion in a seditious outbreak, and when they had heard of the assassination of Caius, there was no hearty submission, as a fear still lingered that any of the emperors might impose the same orders. Felix meanwhile, by ill-timed remedies, stimulated disloyal acts; while he had, as a rival in the worst wickedness, Ventidius Cumanus, who held a part of the province, which was so divided that Galilea was governed by Cumanus, Samaria by Felix. The two peoples had long been at feud, and now less than ever restrained their enmity, from contempt of their rulers. And accordingly they plundered each other, letting loose bands of robbers, forming ambuscades, and occasionally fighting battles, and carrying the spoil and booty to the two procurators, who at first rejoiced at all this, but, as the mischief grew, they interposed with an armed force, which was cut to pieces. The flame of war would have spread through the province, but it was saved by Quadratus, governor of Syria. In dealing with the Jews, who had been daring enough to slay our soldiers, there was little hesitation about their being capitally punished. Some delay indeed was occasioned by Cumanus and Felix; for Claudius on hearing the causes of the rebellion had given authority for deciding also the case of these procurators. Quadratus, however, exhibited Felix as one of the judges, admitting him to the bench with the view of cowing the ardour of the prosecutors. And so Cumanus was condemned for the crimes which the two had committed, and tranquility was restored to the province.

55

NOT long afterwards some tribes of the wild population of Cilicia, known as the Clitae, which had often been in commotion, established a camp, under a leader Troxobor, on their rocky mountains, whence rushing down on the coast, and on the towns, they dared to do violence to the farmers and townsfolk, frequently even to the merchants and shipowners. They besieged the city Anemurium, and routed some troopers sent from Syria to its rescue under the command of Curtius Severus; for the rough country in the neighbourhood, suited as it is for the fighting of infantry, did not allow of cavalry operations. After a time, Antiochus, king of that coast, having broken the unity of the barbarian forces, by cajolery of the people and treachery to their leader, slew Troxobor and a few chiefs, and pacified the rest by gentle measures.

56

ABOUT the same time, the mountain between Lake Fucinus and the river Liris was bored through, and that this grand work might be seen by a multitude of visitors, preparations were made for a naval battle on the lake, just as formerly Augustus exhibited such a spectacle, in a basin he had made this side the Tiber, though with light vessels, and on a smaller scale. Claudius equipped galleys with three and four banks of oars, and nineteen thousand men; he lined the circumference of the lake with rafts, that there might be no means of escape at various points, but he still left full space for the strength of the crews, the skill of the pilots, the impact of the vessels, and the usual operations of a sea fight. On the raft stood companies of the praetorian cohorts and cavalry, with a breastwork in front of them, from which catapults and balistas might be worked. The rest of the lake was occupied by marines on decked vessels. An immense multitude from the neighbouring towns, others from Rome itself, eager to see the sight or to show respect to the emperor, crowded the banks, the hills, and mountain tops, which thus resembled a theatre. The emperor, with Agrippina seated near him, presided; he wore a splendid military cloak, she, a mantle of cloth of gold. A battle was fought with all the courage of brave men, though it was between condemned criminals. After much bloodshed they were released from the necessity of mutual slaughter.

57

WHEN the sight was over, the outlet of the water was opened. The careless execution of the work was apparent, the tunnel not having been bored down so low as the bottom, or middle of the lake. Consequently after an interval the excavations were deepened, and to attract a crowd once more, a show of gladiators was exhibited, with floating pontoons for an infantry engagement. A banquet too was prepared close to the outflow of the lake, and it was the means of greatly alarming the whole company, for the water, in the violence of its outburst, swept away the adjoining parts, shook the more remote, and spread terror with the tremendous crash. At the same time, Agrippina availed herself of the emperor's fright to charge Narcissus, who had been the agent of the work, with avarice and peculation. He too was not silent, but inveighed against the domineering temper of her sex, and her extravagant ambition.

58

IN the consulship of Didius Junius and Quintus Haterius, Nero, now sixteen years of age, married Octavia, the emperor's daughter. Anxious to distinguish himself by noble pursuits, and the reputation of an orator, he advocated the cause of the people of Ilium, and having eloquently recounted how Rome was the offspring of Troy, and Aeneas the founder of the Julian line, with other old traditions akin to myths, he gained for his clients exemption from all public burdens. His pleading too procured for the colony of Bononia, which had been ruined by a fire, a subvention of ten million sesterces. The Rhodians also had their freedom restored to them, which had often been taken away, or confirmed, according to their services to us in our foreign wars, or their seditious misdeeds at home. Apamea, too, which had been shaken by an earthquake, had its tribute remitted for five years.

59

CLAUDIUS, on the other hand, was being prompted to exhibit the worst cruelty by the artifices of the same Agrippina. On the accusation of Tarquitius Priscus, she ruined Statilius Taurus, who was famous for his wealth, and at whose gardens she cast a greedy eye. Priscus had served under Taurus in his proconsular government of Africa, and after their return charged him with a few acts of extortion, but particularly with magical and superstitious practices. Taurus, no longer able to endure a false accusation and an undeserved humiliation, put a violent end to his life before the Senate's decision was pronounced. Tarquitius was however expelled from the Senate, a point which the senators carried, out of hatred for the accuser, notwithstanding the intrigues of Agrippina.

60

THAT same year the emperor was often heard to say that the legal decisions of the commissioners of the imperial treasury ought to have the same force as if pronounced by himself. Lest it might be supposed that he had stumbled inadvertently into this opinion, its principle was also secured by a decree of the Senate on a more complete and ample scale than before. It had indeed already been arranged by the Divine Augustus that the Roman knights who governed Egypt should hear causes, and that their decisions were to be as binding as those of Roman magistrates, and after a time most of the cases formerly tried by the praetors were submitted to the knights. Claudius handed over to them the whole administration of justice for which there had been by sedition or war so many struggles; the Sempronian laws vesting judicial power in the equestrian order, and those of Servilius restoring it to the Senate, while it was for this above everything else that Marius and Sulla fought of old. But those were days of political conflict between classes, and the results of victory were binding on the State. Caius Oppius and Cornelius Balbus were the first who were able, with Caesar's support, to settle conditions of peace and terms of war. To mention after them the Matii, Vedii, and other too influential names of Roman knights would be superfluous, when Claudius, we know, raised freedmen whom he had set over his household to equality with himself and with the laws.

61

NEXT the emperor proposed to grant immunity from taxation to the people of Cos, and he dwelt much on their antiquity. "The Argives or Coeus, the father of Latona, were the earliest inhabitants of the island; soon afterwards, by the arrival of Aesculapius, the art of the physician was introduced and was practiced with much fame by his descendants." Claudius named them one by one, with the periods in which they had respectively flourished. He said too that Xenophon, of whose medical skill he availed himself, was one of the same family, and that they ought to grant his request and let the people of Cos dwell free from all tribute in their sacred island, as a place devoted to the sole service of their god. It was also certain that many obligations under which they had laid Rome and joint victories with her might have been recounted. Claudius however did not seek to veil under any external considerations a concession he had made, with his usual good nature, to an individual.

62

ENVOYS from Byzantium having received audience, in complaining to the Senate of their heavy burdens, recapitulated their whole history. Beginning with the treaty which they concluded with us when we fought against that king of Macedonia whose supposed spurious birth acquired for him the name of the Pseudo Philip, they reminded us of the forces which they had afterwards sent against Antiochus, Perses and Aristonicus, of the aid they had given Antonius in the pirate-war, of their offers to Sulla, Lucullus, and Pompeius, and then of their late services to the Caesars, when they were in occupation of a district peculiarly convenient for the land or sea passage of generals and armies, as well as for the conveyance of supplies.

63

IT was indeed on that very narrow strait which parts Europe from Asia, at Europe's furthest extremity, that the Greeks built Byzantium. When they consulted the Pythian Apollo as to where they should found a city, the oracle replied that they were to seek a home opposite to the blind men's country. This obscure hint pointed to the people of Chalcedon, who, though they arrived there first and saw before others the advantageous position, chose the worse. For Byzantium has a fruitful soil and productive seas, as immense shoals of fish pour out of the Pontus and are driven by the sloping surface of the rocks under water to quit the windings of the Asiatic shore and take refuge in these harbours. Consequently the inhabitants were at first moneymaking and wealthy traders, but afterwards, under the pressure of excessive burdens, they petitioned for immunity or at least relief, and were supported by the emperor, who argued to the Senate that, exhausted as they were by the late wars in Thrace and Bosporus, they deserved help. So their tribute was remitted for five years.

64

IN the year of the consulship of Marcus Asinius and Manius Acilius it was seen to be portended by a succession of prodigies that there were to be political changes for the worse. The soldiers' standards and tents were set in a blaze by lightning. A swarm of bees settled on the summit of the Capitol; births of monsters, half man, half beast, and of a pig with a hawk's talons, were reported. It was accounted a portent that every order of magistrates had had its number reduced, a quaestor, an aedile, a tribune, a praetor and consul having died within a few months. But Agrippina's terror was the most conspicuous. Alarmed by some words dropped by Claudius when half intoxicated, that it was his destiny to have to endure his wives' infamy and at last punish it, she determined to act without a moment's delay. First she destroyed Lepida from motives of feminine jealousy. Lepida indeed as the daughter of the younger Antonia, as the grandniece of Augustus, the cousin of Agrippina, and sister of her husband Cneius, thought herself of equally high rank. In beauty, youth, and wealth they differed but slightly. Both were shameless, infamous, and intractable, and were rivals in vice as much as in the advantages they had derived from fortune. It was indeed a desperate contest whether the aunt or the mother should have most power over Nero. Lepida tried to win the young prince's heart by flattery and lavish liberality, while Agrippina on the other hand, who could give her son empire but could not endure that he should be emperor, was fierce and full of menace.

65

IT was charged on Lepida that she had made attempts on the Emperor's consort by magical incantations, and was disturbing the peace of Italy by an imperfect control of her troops of slaves in Calabria. She was for this sentenced to death, notwithstanding the vehement opposition of Narcissus, who, as he more and more suspected Agrippina, was said to have plainly told his intimate friends that "his destruction was certain, whether Britannicus or Nero were to be emperor, but that he was under such obligations to Claudius that he would sacrifice life to his welfare. Messalina and Silius had been convicted, and now again there were similar grounds for accusation. If Nero were to rule, or Britannicus succeed to the throne, he would himself have no claim on the then reigning sovereign. Meanwhile, a stepmother's treacherous schemes were convulsing the whole imperial house, with far greater disgrace than would have resulted from his concealment of the profligacy of the emperor's former wife. Even as it was, there was shamelessness enough, seeing that Pallas was her paramour, so that no one could doubt that she held honour, modesty and her very person, everything, in short, cheaper than sovereignty." This, and the like, he was always saying, and he would embrace Britannicus, expressing earnest wishes for his speedy arrival at a mature age, and would raise his hand, now to heaven, now to the young prince, with entreaty that as he grew up, he would drive out his father's enemies and also take vengeance on the murderers of his mother.

66

UNDER this great burden of anxiety, he had an attack of illness, and went to Sinuessa to recruit his strength with its balmy climate and salubrious waters. Thereupon, Agrippina, who had long decided on the crime and eagerly grasped at the opportunity thus offered, and did not lack instruments, deliberated on the nature of the poison to be used. The deed would be betrayed by one that was sudden and instantaneous, while if she chose a slow and lingering poison, there was a fear that Claudius, when near his end, might, on detecting the treachery, return to his love for his son. She decided on some rare compound which might derange his mind and delay death. A person skilled in such matters was selected, Locusta by name, who had lately been condemned for poisoning, and had long been retained as one of the tools of despotism. By this woman's art the poison was prepared, and it was to be administered by an eunuch, Halotus, who was accustomed to bring in and taste the dishes.

67

ALL the circumstances were subsequently so well known, that writers of the time have declared that the poison was infused into some mushrooms, a favourite delicacy, and its effect not at the instant perceived, from the emperor's lethargic, or intoxicated condition. His bowels too were relieved, and this seemed to have saved him. Agrippina was thoroughly dismayed. Fearing the worst, and defying the immediate obloquy of the deed, she availed herself of the complicity of Xenophon, the physician, which she had already secured. Under pretense of helping the emperor's efforts to vomit, this man, it is supposed, introduced into his throat a feather smeared with some rapid poison; for he knew that the greatest crimes are perilous in their inception, but well rewarded after their consummation.

68

MEANWHILE the Senate was summoned, and prayers rehearsed by the consuls and priests for the emperor's recovery, though the lifeless body was being wrapped in blankets with warm applications, while all was being arranged to establish Nero on the throne. At first Agrippina, seemingly overwhelmed by grief and seeking comfort, clasped Britannicus in her embraces, called him the very image of his father, and hindered him by every possible device from leaving the chamber. She also detained his sisters, Antonia and Octavia, closed every approach to the palace with a military guard, and repeatedly gave out that the emperor's health was better, so that the soldiers might be encouraged to hope, and that the fortunate moment foretold by the astrologers might arrive.

69

AT last, at noon on the 13th of October, the gates of the palace were suddenly thrown open, and Nero, accompanied by Burrus, went forth to the cohort which was on guard after military custom. There, at the suggestion of the commanding officer, he was hailed with joyful shouts, and set on a litter. Some, it is said, hesitated, and looked round and asked where Britannicus was; then, when there was no one to lead a resistance, they yielded to what was offered them. Nero was conveyed into the camp, and having first spoken suitably to the occasion and promised a donative after the example of his father's bounty, he was unanimously greeted as emperor. The decrees of the Senate followed the voice of the soldiers, and there was no hesitation in the provinces. Divine honours were decreed to Claudius, and his funeral rites were solemnized on the same scale as those of Augustus; for Agrippina strove to emulate the magnificence of her great-grandmother, Livia. But his will was not publicly read, as the preference of the stepson to the son might provoke a sense of wrong and angry feeling in the popular mind.

Book XIII

1

THE first death under the new emperor, that of Junius Silanus, proconsul of Asia, was, without Nero's knowledge, planned by the treachery of Agrippina. Not that Silanus had provoked destruction by any violence of temper, apathetic as he was, and so utterly despised under former despotisms, that Caius Caesar used to call him the golden sheep. The truth was that Agrippina, having contrived the murder of his brother Lucius Silanus, dreaded his vengeance; for it was the incessant popular talk that preference ought to be given over Nero, who was scarcely out of his boyhood and had gained the empire by crime, to a man of mature age, of blameless life, of noble birth, and, as a point then much regarded, of the line of the Caesars. Silanus in fact was the son of a great-grandson of Augustus. This was the cause of his destruction. The agents of the deed were Publius Celer, a Roman knight, and Helius, a freedman, men who had the charge of the emperor's domains in Asia. They gave the proconsul poison at a banquet, too openly to escape discovery. With no less precipitation, Narcissus, Claudius's freedman, whose quarrels with Agrippina I have mentioned, was driven to suicide by his cruel imprisonment and hopeless plight, even against the wishes of Nero, with whose yet concealed vices he was wonderfully in sympathy from his rapacity and extravagance.

2

AND now they had proceeded to further murders but for the opposition of Afranius Burrus and Annaeus Seneca. These two men guided the emperor's youth with an unity of purpose seldom found where authority is shared, and though their accomplishments were wholly different, they had equal influence. Burrus, with his soldier's discipline and severe manners, Seneca, with lessons of eloquence and a dignified courtesy, strove alike to confine the frailty of the prince's youth, should he loathe virtue, within allowable indulgences.

They had both alike to struggle against the domineering spirit of Agrippina, who inflamed with all the passions of an evil ascendency had Pallas on her side, at whose suggestion Claudius had ruined himself by an incestuous marriage and a fatal adoption of a son. Nero's temper however was not one to submit to slaves, and Pallas, by a surly arrogance quite beyond a freedman, had provoked disgust. Still every honour was openly heaped on Agrippina, and to a tribune who according to military custom asked the watchword, Nero gave "the best of mothers." The Senate also decreed her two lictors, with the office of priestess to Claudius, and voted to the late emperor a censor's funeral, which was soon followed by deification.

3

ON the day of the funeral the prince pronounced Claudius's panegyric, and while he dwelt on the antiquity of his family and on the consulships and triumphs of his ancestors, there was enthusiasm both in himself and his audience. The praise of his graceful accomplishments, and the remark that during his reign no disaster had befallen Rome from the foreigner, were heard with favour. When the speaker passed on to his foresight and wisdom, no one could refrain from laughter, though the speech, which was composed by Seneca, exhibited much elegance, as indeed that famous man had an attractive genius which suited the popular ear of the time. Elderly men who amuse their leisure with comparing the past and the present, observed that Nero was the first emperor who needed another man's eloquence. The dictator Caesar rivaled the greatest orators, and Augustus had an easy and fluent way of speaking, such as became a sovereign. Tiberius too thoroughly understood the art of balancing words, and was sometimes forcible in the expression of his thoughts, or else intentionally obscure. Even Caius Caesar's disordered intellect did not wholly mar his faculty of speech. Nor did Claudius, when he spoke with preparation, lack elegance. Nero from early boyhood turned his lively genius in other directions; he carved, painted, sang, or practiced the management of horses, occasionally composing verses which showed that he had the rudiments of learning.

4

WHEN he had done with his mimicries of sorrow he entered the Senate, and having first referred to the authority of the senators and the concurrence of the soldiery, he then dwelt on the counsels and examples which he had to guide him in the right administration of empire. "His boyhood," he said, "had not had the taint of civil wars or domestic feuds, and he brought with him no hatreds, no sense of wrong, no desire of vengeance." He then sketched the plan of his future government, carefully avoiding anything which had kindled recent odium. "He would not," he said, "be judge in all cases, or, by confining the accuser and the accused within the same walls, let the power of a few favourites grow dangerously formidable. In his house there should be nothing venal, nothing open to intrigue; his private establishment and the State should be kept entirely distinct. The Senate should retain its ancient powers; Italy and the State-provinces should plead their causes before the tribunals of the consuls, who would give them a hearing from the senators. Of the armies he would himself take charge, as specially entrusted to him."

5

HE was true to his word and several arrangements were made on the Senate's authority. No one was to receive a fee or a present for pleading a cause; the quaestors-elect were not to be under the necessity of exhibiting gladiatorial shows. This was opposed by Agrippina, as a reversal of the legislation of Claudius, but it was carried by the senators who used to be summoned to the palace, in order that she might stand close to a hidden door behind them, screened by a curtain which was enough to shut her out of sight, but not out of hearing. When envoys from Armenia were pleading their nation's cause before Nero, she actually was on the point of mounting the emperor's tribunal and of presiding with him; but Seneca, when every one else was paralysed with alarm, motioned to the prince to go and meet his mother. Thus, by an apparently dutiful act, a scandalous scene was prevented.

6

WITH the close of the year came disquieting rumours that the Parthians had again broken their bounds and were ravaging Armenia, from which they had driven Rhadamistus, who, having often possessed himself of the kingdom and as often been thrust out of it, had now relinquished hostilities. Rome with its love of talking began to ask how a prince of scarce seventeen was to encounter and avert this tremendous peril, how they could fall back on one who was ruled by a woman; or whether battles and sieges and the other operations of war could be directed by tutors. "Some, on the contrary, argued that this was better than it would have been, had Claudius in his feeble and spiritless old age, when he would certainly have yielded to the bidding of slaves, been summoned to the hardships of a campaign. Burrus, at least, and Seneca were known to be men of very varied experience, and, as for the emperor himself, how far was he really short of mature age, when Cneius Pompeius and Caesar Octavianus, in their eighteenth and nineteenth years respectively, bore the brunt of civil wars? The highest rank chiefly worked through its prestige and its counsels more than by the sword and hand. The emperor would give a plain proof whether he was advised by good or bad friends by putting aside all jealousy and selecting some eminent general, rather than by promoting out of favouritism, a rich man backed up by interest."

7

AMIDST this and like popular talk, Nero ordered the young recruits levied in the adjacent provinces to be brought up for the supply of the legions of the East, and the legions themselves to take up a position on the Armenian frontier while two princes of old standing, Agrippa and Antiochus, were to prepare a force for the invasion of the Parthian territories. The Euphrates too was to be spanned by bridges; Lesser Armenia was entrusted to Aristobulus, Sophene to Sohaemus, each with the ensigns of royalty. There rose up at this crisis a rival to Vologeses in his son Vardanes, and the Parthians quitted Armenia, apparently intending to defer hostilities.

8

ALL this however was described with exaggeration to the Senate, in the speeches of those members who proposed a public thanksgiving, and that on the days of the thanksgiving the prince should wear the triumphal robe and enter Rome in ovation, lastly, that he should have statues on the same scale as those of Mars the Avenger, and in the same temple. To their habitual flattery was added a real joy at his having appointed Domitius Corbulo to secure Armenia, thus opening, as it seemed, a field to merit. The armies of the East were so divided that half the auxiliaries and two legions were to remain in the province of Syria under its governor, Quadratus Ummidius; while Corbulo was to have an equal number of citizen and allied troops, together with the auxiliary infantry and cavalry which were in winter quarters in Cappadocia. The confederate kings were instructed to obey orders, just as the war might require. But they had a specially strong liking for Corbulo. That general, with a view to the prestige which in a new enterprise is supremely powerful, speedily accomplished his march, and at Aegeae, a city of Cilicia, met Quadratus who had advanced to the place under an apprehension that, should Corbulo once enter Armenia to take command of the army, he would draw all eyes on himself, by his noble stature, his imposing eloquence, and the impression he would make, not only by his wisdom and experience, but also by the mere display of showy attributes.

9

MEANTIME both sent messages to king Vologeses, advising him to choose peace rather than war, and to give hostages and so continue the habitual reverence of his ancestors towards the people of Rome. Vologeses, wishing to prepare for war at an advantage, or to rid himself of suspected rivals under the name of hostages, delivered up some of the noblest of the Arsacids. A centurion, Insteius, sent perhaps by Ummidius on some previous occasion, received them after an interview with the king. Corbulo, on knowing this, ordered Arrius Varus, commander of a cohort, to go and take the hostages. Hence arose a quarrel between the commander and the centurion, and to stop such a scene before foreigners, the decision of the matter was left to the hostages and to the envoys who conducted them. They preferred Corbulo, for his recent renown, and from a liking which even enemies felt for him. Then there was a feud between the two generals; Ummidius complained that he was robbed of what his prudence had achieved, while Corbulo on the other hand appealed to the fact that Vologeses had not brought himself to offer hostages till his own appointment to the conduct of the war turned the king's hopes into fears. Nero, to compose their differences, directed the issue of a proclamation that for the successes of Quadratus and Corbulo the laurel was to be added to the imperial "fasces." I have closely connected these events, though they extend into another consulship.

10

THE emperor in the same year asked the Senate for a statue to his father Domitius, and also that the consular decorations might be conferred on Asconius Labeo, who had been his guardian. Statues to himself of solid gold and silver he forbade, in opposition to offers made, and although the Senate passed a vote that the year should begin with the month of December, in which he was born, he retained for its commencement, the old sacred associations of the first of January. Nor would he allow the prosecution of Carinas Celer, a senator, whom a slave accused, or of Julius Densus, a knight, whose partiality for Britannicus was construed into a crime.

11

IN the year of his consulship with Lucius Antistius, when the magistrates were swearing obedience to imperial legislation, he forbade his colleague to extend the oath to his own enactments, for which he was warmly praised by the senators, in the hope that his youthful spirit, elated with the glory won by trifles, would follow on to nobler aspirations. Then came an act of mercy to Plautius Lateranus, who had been degraded from his rank for adultery with Messalina, and whom he now restored, assuring them of his clemency in a number of speeches which Seneca, to show the purity of his teaching or to display his genius, published to the world by the emperor's mouth.

12

MEANWHILE the mother's influence was gradually weakened, as Nero fell in love with a freed woman, Acte by name, and took into his confidence Otho and Claudius Senecio, two young men of fashion, the first of whom was descended from a family of consular rank, while Senecio's father was one of the emperor's freedmen. Without the mother's knowledge, then in spite of her opposition, they had crept into his favour by debaucheries and equivocal secrets, and even the prince's older friends did not thwart him, for here was a girl who without harm to any one gratified his desires, when he loathed his wife Octavia, high born as she was, and of approved virtue, either from some fatality, or because vice is overpoweringly attractive. It was feared too that he might rush into outrages on noble ladies, were he debarred from this indulgence.

13

AGRIPPINA, however, raved with a woman's fury about having a freed woman for a rival, a slave girl for a daughter-in-law, with like expressions. Nor would she wait till her son repented or wearied of his passion. The fouler her reproaches, the more powerfully did they inflame him, till completely mastered by the strength of his desire, he threw off all respect for his mother, and put himself under the guidance of Seneca, one of whose friends, Annaeus Serenus, had veiled the young prince's intrigue in its beginning by pretending to be in love with the same woman, and had lent his name as the ostensible giver of the presents secretly sent by the emperor to the girl. Then Agrippina, changing her tactics, plied the lad with various blandishments, and even offered the seclusion of her chamber for the concealment of indulgences which youth and the highest rank might claim. She went further; she pleaded guilty to an ill-timed strictness, and handed over to him the abundance of her wealth, which nearly approached the imperial treasures, and from having been of late extreme in her restraint of her son, became now, on the other hand, lax to excess. The change did not escape Nero; his most intimate friends dreaded it, and begged him to beware of the arts of a woman, was always daring and was now false. It happened at this time that the emperor after inspecting the apparel in which wives and mothers of the imperial house had been seen to glitter, selected a jeweled robe and sent it as a gift to his mother, with the unsparing liberality of one who was bestowing by preference on her a choice and much coveted present. Agrippina, however, publicly declared that so far from her wardrobe being furnished by these gifts, she was really kept out of the remainder, and that her son was merely dividing with her what he derived wholly from herself.

14

SOME there were who put even a worse meaning on her words. And so Nero, furious with those who abetted such arrogance in a woman, removed Pallas from the charge of the business with which he had been entrusted by Claudius, and in which he acted, so to say, as the controller of the throne. The story went that as he was departing with a great retinue of attendants, the emperor rather wittily remarked that Pallas was going to swear himself out of office. Pallas had in truth stipulated that he should not be questioned for anything he had done in the past, and that his accounts with the State were to be considered as balanced. Thereupon, with instant fury, Agrippina rushed into frightful menaces, sparing not the prince's ears her solemn protest "that Britannicus was now of full age, he who was the true and worthy heir of his father's sovereignty, which a son, by mere admission and adoption, was abusing in outrages on his mother. She shrank not from an utter exposure of the wickedness of that ill-starred house, of her own marriage, to begin with, and of her poisoner's craft. All that the gods and she herself had taken care of was that her stepson was yet alive; with him she would go to the camp, where on one side should be heard the daughter of Germanicus; on the other, the crippled Burrus and the exile Seneca, claiming, forsooth, with disfigured hand, and a pedant's tongue, the government of the world." As she spoke, she raised her hand in menace and heaped insults on him, as she appealed to the deified Claudius, to the infernal shades of the Silani, and to those many fruitless crimes.

15

NERO was confounded at this, and as the day was near on which Britannicus would complete his fourteenth year, he reflected, now on the domineering temper of his mother, and now again on the character of the young prince, which a trifling circumstance had lately tested, sufficient however to gain for him wide popularity. During the feast of Saturn, amid other pastimes of his playmates, at a game of lot drawing for king, the lot fell to Nero, upon which he gave all his other companions different orders, and such as would not put them to the blush; but when he told Britannicus to step forward and begin a song, hoping for a laugh at the expense of a boy who knew nothing of sober, much less of riotous society, the lad with perfect coolness commenced some verses which hinted at his expulsion from his father's house and from supreme power. This procured him pity, which was the more conspicuous, as night with its merriment had stripped off all disguise. Nero saw the reproach and redoubled his hate. Pressed by Agrippina's menaces, having no charge against his brother and not daring openly to order his murder, he meditated a secret device and directed poison to be prepared through the agency of Julius Pollio, tribune of one of the praetorian cohorts, who had in his custody a woman under sentence for poisoning, Locusta by name, with a vast reputation for crime. That every one about the person of Britannicus should care nothing for right or honour, had long ago been provided for. He actually received his first dose of poison from his tutors and passed it off his bowels, as it was rather weak or so qualified as not at once to prove deadly. But Nero, impatient at such slow progress in crime, threatened the tribune and ordered the poisoner to execution for prolonging his anxiety while they were thinking of the popular talk and planning their own defense. Then they promised that death should be as sudden as if it were the hurried work of the dagger, and a rapid poison of previously tested ingredients was prepared close to the emperor's chamber.

16

IT was customary for the imperial princes to sit during their meals with other nobles of the same age, in the sight of their kinsfolk, at a table of their own, furnished somewhat frugally. There Britannicus was dining, and as what he ate and drank was always tested by the taste of a select attendant, the following device was contrived, that the usage might not be dropped or the crime betrayed by the death of both prince and attendant. A cup as yet harmless, but extremely hot and already tasted, was handed to Britannicus; then, on his refusing it because of its warmth, poison was poured in with some cold water, and this so penetrated his entire frame that he lost alike voice and breath. There was a stir among the company; some, taken by surprise, ran hither and thither, while those whose discernment was keener, remained motionless, with their eyes fixed on Nero, who, as he still reclined in seeming unconsciousness, said that this was a common occurrence, from a periodical epilepsy, with which Britannicus had been afflicted from his earliest infancy, and that his sight and senses would gradually return. As for Agrippina, her terror and confusion, though her countenance struggled to hide it, so visibly appeared, that she was clearly just as ignorant as was Octavia, Britannicus's own sister. She saw, in fact, that she was robbed of her only remaining refuge, and that here was a precedent for parricide. Even Octavia, notwithstanding her youthful inexperience, had learnt to hide her grief, her affection, and indeed every emotion.

17

AND so after a brief pause the company resumed its mirth. One and the same night witnessed Britannicus's death and funeral, preparations having been already made for his obsequies, which were on a humble scale. He was however buried in the Campus Martius, amid storms so violent, that in the popular belief they portended the wrath of heaven against a crime which many were even inclined to forgive when they remembered the immemorial feuds of brothers and the impossibility of a divided throne. It is related by several writers of the period that many days before the murder, Nero had offered the worst insult to the boyhood of Britannicus; so that his death could no longer seem a premature or dreadful event, though it happened at the sacred board, without even a moment for the embraces of his sisters, hurried on too, as it was, under the eyes of an enemy, on the sole surviving offspring of the Claudii, the victim first of dishonour, then of poison. The emperor apologized for the hasty funeral by reminding people that it was the practice of our ancestors to withdraw from view any grievously untimely death, and not to dwell on it with panegyrics or display. For himself, he said, that as he had now lost a brother's help, his remaining hopes centred in the State, and all the more tenderness ought to be shown by the Senate and people towards a prince who was the only survivor of a family born to the highest greatness.

18

HE then enriched his most powerful friends with liberal presents. Some there were who reproached men of austere professions with having on such an occasion divided houses and estates among themselves, like so much spoil. It was the belief of others that a pressure had been put on them by the emperor, who, conscious as he was of guilt, hoped for merciful consideration if he could secure the most important men by wholesale bribery. But his mother's rage no lavish bounty could allay. She would clasp Octavia to her arms, and have many a secret interview with her friends; with more than her natural rapacity, she clutched at money everywhere, seemingly for a reserve, and courteously received tribunes and centurions. She honoured the names and virtues of the nobles who still were left, seeking apparently a party and a leader. Of this Nero became aware, and he ordered the departure of the military guard now kept for the emperor's mother, as it had formerly been for the imperial consort, along with some German troops, added as a further honour. He also gave her a separate establishment, that throngs of visitors might no longer wait on her, and removed her to what had been Antonia's house; and whenever he went there himself, he was surrounded by a crowd of centurions, and used to leave her after a hurried kiss.

19

OF all things human, the most precarious and transitory is a reputation for power which has no strong support of its own. In a moment Agrippina's doors were deserted; there was no one to comfort or to go near her, except a few ladies, whether out of love or malice was doubtful. One of these was Junia Silana, whom Messalina had driven from her husband, Caius Silius, as I have already related. Conspicuous for her birth, her beauty, and her wantonness, she had long been a special favourite of Agrippina, till after a while there were secret mutual dislikes, because Sextius Africanus, a noble youth, had been deterred from marrying Silana by Agrippina, who repeatedly spoke of her as an immodest woman in the decline of life, not to secure Africanus for herself, but to keep the childless and wealthy widow out of a husband's control. Silana having now a prospect of vengeance, suborned as accusers two of her creatures, Iturius and Calvisius, not with the old and often-repeated charges about Agrippina's mourning the death of Britannicus or publishing the wrongs of Octavia, but with a hint that it was her purpose to encourage in revolutionary designs Rubellius Plautus, who his mother's side was as nearly connected as Nero with the Divine Augustus; and then, by marrying him and making him emperor, again seize the control of the State. All this Iturius and Calvisius divulged to Atimetus, a freedman of Domitia, Nero's aunt. Exulting in the opportunity, for Agrippina and Domitia were in bitter rivalry, Atimetus urged Paris, who was himself also a freedman of Domitia, to go at once and put the charge in the most dreadful form.

20

NIGHT was far advanced and Nero was still sitting over his cups, when Paris entered, who was generally wont at such times to heighten the emperor's enjoyments, but who now wore a gloomy expression. He went through the whole evidence in order, and so frightened his hearer as to make him resolve not only on the destruction of his mother and of Plautus, but also on the removal of Burrus from the command of the guards, as a man who had been promoted by Agrippina's interest, and was now showing his gratitude. We have it on the authority of Fabius Rusticus that a note was written to Caecina Tuscus, entrusting to him the charge of the praetorian cohorts, but that through Seneca's influence that distinguished post was retained for Burrus. According to Plinius and Cluvius, no doubt was felt about the commander's loyalty. Fabius certainly inclines to the praise of Seneca, through whose friendship he rose to honour. Proposing as I do to follow the consentient testimony of historians, I shall give the differences in their narratives under the writers' names. Nero, in his bewilderment and impatience to destroy his mother, could not be put off till Burrus answered for her death, should she be convicted of the crime, but "any one," he said, "much more a parent, must be allowed a defense. Accusers there were none forthcoming; they had before them only the word of a single person from an enemy's house, and this the night with its darkness and prolonged festivity and everything savouring of recklessness and folly, was enough to refute."

21

HAVING thus allayed the prince's fears, they went at daybreak to Agrippina, that she might know the charges against her, and either rebut them or suffer the penalty. Burrus fulfilled his instructions in Seneca's presence, and some of the freedmen were present to witness the interview. Then Burrus, when he had fully explained the charges with the authors' names, assumed an air of menace. Instantly Agrippina, calling up all her high spirit, exclaimed, "I wonder not that Silana, who has never borne offspring, knows nothing of a mother's feelings. Parents do not change their children as lightly as a shameless woman does her paramours. And if Iturius and Calvisius, after having wasted their whole fortunes, are now, as their last resource, repaying an old hag for their hire by undertaking to be informers, it does not follow that I am to incur the infamy of plotting a son's murder, or that a Caesar is to have the consciousness of like guilt. As for Domitia's enmity, I should be thankful for it, were she to vie with me in goodwill towards my Nero. Now through her paramour, Atimetus, and the actor, Paris, she is, so to say, concocting a drama for the stage. She at her Baiae was increasing the magnificence of her fishponds, when I was planning in my counsels his adoption with a proconsul's powers and a consul-elect's rank and every other step to empire. Only let the man come forward who can charge me with having tampered with the praetorian cohorts in the capital, with having sapped the loyalty of the provinces, or, in a word, with having bribed slaves and freedmen into any wickedness. Could I have lived with Britannicus in the possession of power? And if Plautus or any other were to become master of the State so as to sit in judgment on me, accusers forsooth would not be forthcoming, to charge me not merely with a few incautious expressions prompted by the eagerness of affection, but with guilt from which a son alone could absolve me." There was profound excitement among those present, and they even tried to soothe her agitation, but she insisted on an interview with her son. Then, instead of pleading her innocence, as though she lacked confidence, or her claims on him by way of reproach, she obtained vengeance on her accusers and rewards for her friends.

22

THE superintendence of the corn supply was given to Faenius Rufus, the direction of the games which the emperor was preparing, to Arruntius Stella, and the province of Egypt to Caius Balbillus. Syria was to be assigned to Publius Anteius, but he was soon put off by various artifices and finally detained at Rome. Silana was banished; Calvisius and Iturius exiled for a time; Atimetus was capitally punished, while Paris was too serviceable to the emperor's profligacy to allow of his suffering any penalty. Plautus for the present was silently passed over.

23

NEXT Pallas and Burrus were accused of having conspired to raise Cornelius Sulla to the throne, because of his noble birth and connection with Claudius, whose son-in-law he was by his marriage with Antonia. The promoter of the prosecution was one Paetus, who had become notorious by frequent purchases of property confiscated to the exchequer and was now convicted clearly of imposture.

But the proved innocence of Pallas did Pallas did not please men so much, as his arrogance offended them. When his freedmen, his alleged accomplices, were called, he replied that at home he signified his wishes only by a nod or a gesture, or, if further explanation was required, he used writing, so as not to degrade his voice in such company. Burrus, though accused, gave his verdict as one of the judges. The prosecutor was sentenced to exile, and the account books in which he was reviving forgotten claims of the exchequer, were burnt.

24

AT the end of the year the cohort usually on guard during the games was withdrawn, that there might be a greater show of freedom, that the soldiery too might be less demoralized when no longer in contact with the license of the theatre, and that it might be proved whether the populace, in the absence of a guard, would maintain their self-control. The emperor, on the advice of the augurs, purified Rome by a lustration, as the temples of Jupiter and Minerva had been struck by lightning.

25

IN the consulship of Quintus Volusius and Publius Scipio, there was peace abroad, but a disgusting licentiousness at home on the part of Nero, who in a slave's disguise, so as to be unrecognised, would wander through the streets of Rome, to brothels and taverns, with comrades, who seized on goods exposed for sale and inflicted wounds on any whom they encountered, some of these last knowing him so little that he even received blows himself, and showed the marks of them in his face. When it was notorious that the emperor was the assailant, and the insults on men and women of distinction were multiplied, other persons too on the strength of a license once granted under Nero's name, ventured with impunity on the same practices, and had gangs of their own, till night presented the scenes of a captured city. Julius Montanus, a senator, but one who had not yet held any office, happened to encounter the prince in the darkness, and because he fiercely repulsed his attack and then on recognizing him begged for mercy, as though this was a reproach, forced to destroy himself. Nero was for the future more timid, and surrounded himself with soldiers and a number of gladiators, who, when a fray began on a small scale and seemed a private affair, were to let it alone, but, if the injured persons resisted stoutly, they rushed in with their swords. He also turned the license of the games and the enthusiasm for the actors into something like a battle by the impunity he allowed, and the rewards he offered, and especially by looking on himself, sometimes concealed, but often in public view, till, with the people at strife and the fear of a worse commotion, the only remedy which could be devised was the expulsion of the offending actors from Italy, and the presence once more of the soldiery in the theatre.

Book XIV

1

IN the consulship of Quintus Volusius and Publius Scipio, there was peace abroad, but a disgusting licentiousness at home on the part of Nero, who in a slave's disguise, so as to be unrecognised, would wander through the streets of Rome, to brothels and taverns, with comrades, who seized on goods exposed for sale and inflicted wounds on any whom they encountered, some of these last knowing him so little that he even received blows himself, and showed the marks of them in his face. When it was notorious that the emperor was the assailant, and the insults on men and women of distinction were multiplied, other persons too on the strength of a license once granted under Nero's name, ventured with impunity on the same practices, and had gangs of their own, till night presented the scenes of a captured city. Julius Montanus, a senator, but one who had not yet held any office, happened to encounter the prince in the darkness, and because he fiercely repulsed his attack and then on recognizing him begged for mercy, as though this was a reproach, forced to destroy himself. Nero was for the future more timid, and surrounded himself with soldiers and a number of gladiators, who, when a fray began on a small scale and seemed a private affair, were to let it alone, but, if the injured persons resisted stoutly, they rushed in with their swords. He also turned the license of the games and the enthusiasm for the actors into something like a battle by the impunity he allowed, and the rewards he offered, and especially by looking on himself, sometimes concealed, but often in public view, till, with the people at strife and the fear of a worse commotion, the only remedy which could be devised was the expulsion of the offending actors from Italy, and the presence once more of the soldiery in the theatre.

2

CLUVIUS relates that Agrippina in her eagerness to retain her influence went so far that more than once at midday, when Nero, even at that hour, was flushed with wine and feasting, she presented herself attractively attired to her half intoxicated son and offered him her person, and that when kinsfolk observed wanton kisses and caresses, portending infamy, it was Seneca who sought a female's aid against a woman's fascinations, and hurried in Acte, the freed-girl, who alarmed at her own peril and at Nero's disgrace, told him that the incest was notorious, as his mother boasted of it, and that the soldiers would never endure the rule of an impious sovereign. Fabius Rusticus tells us that it was not Agrippina, but Nero, who lusted for the crime, and that it was frustrated by the adroitness of that same freed-girl. Cluvius's account, however, is also that of all other authors, and popular belief inclines to it, whether it was that Agrippina really conceived such a monstrous wickedness in her heart, or perhaps because the thought of a strange passion seemed comparatively credible in a woman, who in her girlish years had allowed herself to be seduced by Lepidus in the hope of winning power, had stooped with a like ambition to the lust of Pallas, and had trained herself for every infamy by her marriage with her uncle.

3

NERO accordingly avoided secret interviews with her, and when she withdrew to her gardens or to her estates at Tusculum and

Antium, he praised her for courting repose. At last, convinced that she would be too formidable, wherever she might dwell, he resolved to destroy her, merely deliberating whether it was to be accomplished by poison, or by the sword, or by any other violent means. Poison at first seemed best, but, were it to be administered at the imperial table, the result could not be referred to chance after the recent circumstances of the death of Britannicus. Again, to tamper with the servants of a woman who, from her familiarity with crime, was on her guard against treachery, appeared to be extremely difficult, and then, too, she had fortified her constitution by the use of antidotes. How again the dagger and its work were to be kept secret, no one could suggest, and it was feared too that whoever might be chosen to execute such a crime would spurn the order. An ingenious suggestion was offered by Anicetus, a freedman, commander of the fleet at Misenum, who had been tutor to Nero in boyhood and had a hatred of Agrippina which she reciprocated. He explained that a vessel could be constructed, from which a part might by a contrivance be detached, when out at sea, so as to plunge her unawares into the water. "Nothing," he said, "allowed of accidents so much as the sea, and should she be overtaken by shipwreck, who would be so unfair as to impute to crime an offence committed by the winds and waves? The emperor would add the honour of a temple and of shrines to the deceased lady, with every other display of filial affection."

4

NERO liked the device, favoured as it also was by the particular time, for he was celebrating Minerva's five days' festival at Baiae. Thither he enticed his mother by repeated assurances that children ought to bear with the irritability of parents and to soothe their tempers, wishing thus to spread a rumour of reconciliation and to secure Agrippina's acceptance through the feminine credulity, which easily believes what joy. As she approached, he went to the shore to meet her (she was coming from Antium), welcomed her with outstretched hand and embrace, and conducted her to Bauli. This was the name of a country house, washed by a bay of the sea, between the promontory of Misenum and the lake of Baiae. Here was a vessel distinguished from others by its equipment, seemingly meant, among other things, to do honour to his mother; for she had been accustomed to sail in a trireme, with a crew of marines. And now she was invited to a banquet, that night might serve to conceal the crime. It was well known that somebody had been found to betray it, that Agrippina had heard of the plot, and in doubt whether she was to believe it, was conveyed to Baiae in her litter. There some soothing words allayed her fear; she was graciously received, and seated at table above the emperor. Nero prolonged the banquet with various conversation, passing from a youth's playful familiarity to an air of constraint, which seemed to indicate serious thought, and then, after protracted festivity, escorted her on her departure, clinging with kisses to her eyes and bosom, either to crown his hypocrisy or because the last sight of a mother on the even of destruction caused a lingering even in that brutal heart.

5

A NIGHT of brilliant starlight with the calm of a tranquil sea was granted by heaven, seemingly, to convict the crime. The vessel had not gone far, Agrippina having with her two of her intimate attendants, one of whom, Crepereius Gallus, stood near the helm, while Acerronia, reclining at Agrippina's feet as she reposed herself, spoke joyfully of her son's repentance and of the recovery of the mother's influence, when at a given signal the ceiling of the place, which was loaded with a quantity of lead, fell in, and Crepereius was crushed and instantly killed. Agrippina and Acerronia were protected by the projecting sides of the couch, which happened to be too strong to yield under the weight. But this was not followed by the breaking up of the vessel; for all were bewildered, and those too, who were in the plot, were hindered by the unconscious majority. The crew then thought it best to throw the vessel on one side and so sink it, but they could not themselves promptly unite to face the emergency, and others, by counteracting the attempt, gave an opportunity of a gentler fall into the sea. Acerronia, however, thoughtlessly exclaiming that she was Agrippina, and imploring help for the emperor's mother, was despatched with poles and oars, and such naval implements as chance offered. Agrippina was silent and was thus the less recognised; still, she received a wound in her shoulder. She swam, then met with some small boats which conveyed her to the Lucrine lake, and so entered her house.

6

THERE she reflected how for this very purpose she had been invited by a lying letter and treated with conspicuous honour, how also it was near the shore, not from being driven by winds or dashed on rocks, that the vessel had in its upper part collapsed, like a mechanism anything but nautical. She pondered too the death of Acerronia; she looked at her own wound, and saw that her only safeguard against treachery was to ignore it. Then she sent her freedman Agerinus to tell her son how by heaven's favour and his good fortune she had escaped a terrible disaster; that she begged him, alarmed, as he might be, by his mother's peril, to put off the duty of a visit, as for the present she needed repose. Meanwhile, pretending that she felt secure, she applied remedies to her wound, and fomentations to her person. She then ordered search to be made for the will of Acerronia, and her property to be sealed, in this alone throwing off disguise.

7

NERO, meantime, as he waited for tidings of the consummation of the deed, received information that she had escaped with the injury of a slight wound, after having so far encountered the peril that there could be no question as to its author. Then, paralysed with terror and protesting that she would show herself the next moment eager for vengeance, either arming the slaves or stirring up the soldiery, or hastening to the Senate and the people, to charge him with the wreck, with her wound, and with the destruction of her friends, he asked what resource he had against all this, unless something could be at once devised by Burrus and Seneca. He had instantly summoned both of them, and possibly they were already in the secret. There was a long silence on their part; they feared they might remonstrate in vain, or believed the crisis to be such that Nero must perish, unless Agrippina were at once crushed. Thereupon Seneca was so far the more prompt as to glance back on Burrus, as if to ask him whether the bloody deed must be required of the soldiers. Burrus replied "that the praetorians were attached to the whole family of the Caesars, and remembering Germanicus would not dare a savage deed on his offspring. It was for Anicetus to accomplish his promise." Anicetus, without a pause, claimed for himself the consummation of the crime. At those words, Nero declared that that day gave him empire, and that a freedman was the author of this mighty boon. "Go," he said, "with all speed and take with you the men readiest to execute your orders." He himself, when he had heard of the arrival of Agrippina's messenger, Agerinus, contrived a theatrical mode of accusation, and, while the man was repeating his message, threw down a sword at his feet, then ordered him to be put in irons, as a detected criminal, so that he might invent a story how his mother had plotted the emperor's destruction and in the shame of discovered guilt had by her own choice sought death.

8

MEANTIME, Agrippina's peril being universally known and taken to be an accidental occurrence, everybody, the moment he heard of it, hurried down to the beach. Some climbed projecting piers; some the nearest vessels; others, as far as their stature allowed, went into the sea; some, again, stood with outstretched arms, while the whole shore rung with wailings, with prayers and cries, as different questions were asked and uncertain answers given. A vast multitude streamed to the spot with torches, and as soon as all knew that she was safe, they at once prepared to wish her joy, till the sight of an armed and threatening force scared them away. Anicetus then surrounded the house with a guard, and having burst open the gates, dragged off the slaves who met him, till he came to the door of her chamber, where a few still stood, after the rest had fled in terror at the attack. A small lamp was in the room, and one slave-girl with Agrippina, who grew more and more anxious, as no messenger came from her son, not even Agerinus, while the appearance of the shore was changed, a solitude one moment, then sudden bustle and tokens of the worst catastrophe. As the girl rose to depart, she exclaimed,

"Do you too forsake me?" and looking round saw Anicetus, who had with him the captain of the trireme, Herculeius, and Obaritus, a centurion of marines. "If," said she, "you have come to see me, take back word that I have recovered, but if you are here to do a crime, I believe nothing about my son; he has not ordered his mother's murder." The assassins closed in round her couch, and the captain of the trireme first struck her head violently with a club. Then, as the centurion bared his sword for the fatal deed, presenting her person, she exclaimed, "Smite my womb," and with many wounds she was slain.

9

SO far our accounts agree. That Nero gazed on his mother after her death and praised her beauty, some have related, while others deny it. Her body was burnt that same night on a dining couch, with a mean funeral; nor, as long as Nero was in power, was the earth raised into a mound, or even decently closed. Subsequently, she received from the solicitude of her domestics, a humble sepulchre on the road to Misenum, near the country house of Caesar the Dictator, which from a great height commands a view of the bay beneath. As soon as the funeral pile was lighted, one of her freedmen, surnamed Mnester, ran himself through with a sword, either from love of his mistress or from the fear of destruction. Many years before Agrippina had anticipated this end for herself and had spurned the thought. For when she consulted the astrologers about Nero, they replied that he would be emperor and kill his mother. "Let him kill her," she said, "provided he is emperor."

10

BUT the emperor, when the crime was at last accomplished, realized its portentous guilt. The rest of the night, now silent and stupefied, now and still oftener starting up in terror, bereft of reason, he awaited the dawn as if it would bring with it his doom. He was first encouraged to hope by the flattery addressed to him, at the prompting of Burrus, by the centurions and tribunes, who again and again pressed his hand and congratulated him on his having escaped an unforeseen danger and his mother's daring crime. Then his friends went to the temples, and, an example having once been set, the neighbouring towns of Campania testified their joy with sacrifices and deputations. He himself, with an opposite phase of hypocrisy, seemed sad, and almost angry at his own deliverance, and shed tears over his mother's death. But as the aspects of places change not, as do the looks of men, and as he had ever before his eyes the dreadful sight of that sea with its shores (some too believed that the notes of a funereal trumpet were heard from the surrounding heights, and wailings from the mother's grave), he retired to Neapolis and sent a letter to the Senate, the drift of which was that Agerinus, one of Agrippina's confidential freedmen, had been detected with the dagger of an assassin, and that in the consciousness of having planned the crime she had paid its penalty.

11

HE even revived the charges of a period long past, how she had aimed at a share of empire, and at inducing the praetorian cohorts to swear obedience to a woman, to the disgrace of the Senate and people; how, when she was disappointed, in her fury with the soldiers, the Senate, and the populace, she opposed the usual donative and largess, and organized perilous prosecutions against distinguished citizens. What efforts had it cost him to hinder her from bursting into the Senate-house and giving answers to foreign nations! He glanced too with indirect censure at the days of Claudius, and ascribed all the abominations of that reign to his mother, thus seeking to show that it was the State's good fortune which had destroyed her. For he actually told the story of the shipwreck; but who could be so stupid as to believe that it was accidental, or that a shipwrecked woman had sent one man with a weapon to break through an emperor's guards and fleets? So now it was not Nero, whose brutality was far beyond any remonstrance, but Seneca who was in ill repute, for having written a confession in such a style.

12

STILL there was a marvelous rivalry among the nobles in decreeing thanksgivings at all the shrines, and the celebration with annual games of Minerva's festival, as the day on which the plot had been discovered; also, that a golden image of Minerva with a statue of the emperor by its side should be set up in the Senate-house, and that Agrippina's birthday should be classed among the inauspicious days. Thrasea Paetus, who had been used to pass over previous flatteries in silence or with brief assent, then walked out of the Senate, thereby imperiling himself, without communicating to the other senators any impulse towards freedom. There occurred too a thick succession of portents, which meant nothing. A woman gave birth to a snake, and another was killed by a thunderbolt in her husband's embrace. Then the sun was suddenly darkened and the fourteen districts of the city were struck by lightning. All this happened quite without any providential design; so much so, that for many subsequent years Nero prolonged his reign and his crimes. Still, to deepen the popular hatred towards his mother, and prove that since her removal, his clemency had increased, he restored to their ancestral homes two distinguished ladies, Junia and Calpurnia, with two ex-praetors, Valerius Capito and Licinius Gabolus, whom Agrippina had formerly banished. He also allowed the ashes of Lollia Paulina to be brought back and a tomb to be built over them. Iturius and Calvisius, whom he had himself temporarily exiled, he now released from their penalty. Silana indeed had died a natural death at Tarentum, whither she had returned from her distant exile, when the power of Agrippina, to whose enmity she owed her fall, began to totter, or her wrath was at last appeased.

13

WHILE Nero was lingering in the towns of Campania, doubting how he should enter Rome, whether he would find the Senate submissive and the populace enthusiastic, all the vilest courtiers, and of these never had a court a more abundant crop, argued against his hesitation by assuring him that Agrippina's name was hated and that her death had heightened his popularity. "He might go without a fear," they said, "and experience in his person men's veneration for him." They insisted at the same time on preceding him. They found greater enthusiasm than they had promised, the tribes coming forth to meet him, the Senate in holiday attire, troops of their children and wives arranged according to sex and age, tiers of seats raised for the spectacle, where he was to pass, as a triumph is witnessed. Thus elated and exulting over his people's slavery, he proceeded to the Capitol, performed the thanksgiving, and then plunged into all the excesses, which, though ill-restrained, some sort of respect for his mother had for a while delayed.

14

HE had long had a fancy for driving a four-horse chariot, and a no less degrading taste for singing to the harp, in a theatrical fashion, when he was at dinner. This he would remind people was a royal custom, and had been the practice of ancient chiefs; it was celebrated too in the praises of poets and was meant to show honour to the gods. Songs indeed, he said, were sacred to Apollo, and it was in the dress of a singer that that great and prophetic deity was seen in Roman temples as well as in Greek cities. He could no longer be restrained, when Seneca and Burrus thought it best to concede one point that he might not persist in both. A space was enclosed in the Vatican valley where he might manage his horses, without the spectacle being public. Soon he actually invited all the people of Rome, who extolled him in their praises, like a mob which craves for amusements and rejoices when a prince draws them the same way. However, the public exposure of his shame acted on him as an incentive instead of sickening him, as men expected. Imagining that he mitigated the scandal by disgracing many others, he brought on the stage descendants of noble families, who sold themselves because they were paupers. As they have ended their days, I think it due to their ancestors not to hand down their names. And indeed the infamy is his who gave them wealth to reward their degradation rather than to deter them from degrading themselves. He prevailed too on some well-known Roman knights, by immense presents, to offer their services in the amphitheatre; only pay from one who is able to command, carries with it the force of compulsion.

15

STILL, not yet wishing to disgrace himself on a public stage, he instituted some games under the title of "juvenile sports," for which people of every class gave in their names. Neither rank nor age nor previous high promotion hindered any one from practicing the art of a Greek or Latin actor and even stooping to gestures and songs unfit for a man. Noble ladies too actually played disgusting parts, and in the grove, with which Augustus had surrounded the lake for the naval fight, there were erected places for meeting and refreshment, and every incentive to excess was offered for sale. Money too was distributed, which the respectable had to spend under sheer compulsion and which the profligate gloried in squandering. Hence a rank growth of abominations and of all infamy. Never did a more filthy rabble add a worse licentiousness to our long corrupted morals. Even, with virtuous training, purity is not easily upheld; far less amid rivalries in vice could modesty or propriety or any trace of good manners be preserved. Last of all, the emperor himself came on the stage, tuning his lute with elaborate care and trying his voice with his attendants. There were also present, to complete the show, a guard of soldiers with centurions and tribunes, and Burrus, who grieved and yet applauded. Then it was that Roman knights were first enrolled under the title of Augustani, men in their prime and remarkable for their strength, some, from a natural frivolity, others from the hope of promotion. Day and night they kept up a thunder of applause, and applied to the emperor's person and voice the epithets of deities. Thus they lived in fame and honour, as if on the strength of their merits.

16

NERO however, that he might not be known only for his accomplishments as an actor, also affected a taste for poetry, and drew round him persons who had some skill in such compositions, but not yet generally recognised. They used to sit with him, stringing together verses prepared at home, or extemporised on the spot, and fill up his own expressions, such as they were, just as he threw them off. This is plainly shown by the very character of the poems, which have no vigour or inspiration, or unity in their flow. He would also bestow some leisure after his banquets on the teachers of philosophy, for he enjoyed the wrangles of opposing dogmatists. And some there were who liked to exhibit their gloomy faces and looks, as one of the amusements of the court.

17

ABOUT the same time a trifling beginning led to frightful bloodshed between the inhabitants of Nuceria and Pompeii, at a gladiatorial show exhibited by Livineius Regulus, who had been, as I have related, expelled from the Senate. With the unruly spirit of townsfolk, they began with abusive language of each other; then they took up stones and at last weapons, the advantage resting with the populace of Pompeii, where the show was being exhibited. And so there were brought to Rome a number of the people of Nuceria, with their bodies mutilated by wounds, and many lamented the deaths of children or of parents. The emperor entrusted the trial of the case to the Senate, and the Senate to the consuls, and then again the matter being referred back to the Senators, the inhabitants of Pompeii were forbidden to have any such public gathering for ten years, and all associations they had formed in defiance of the laws were dissolved. Livineius and the others who had excited the disturbance, were punished with exile.

18

PEDIUS Blaesus was also expelled from the Senate on the accusation of the people of Cyrene, that he had violated the treasury of Aesculapius and had tampered with a military levy by bribery and corruption. This same people prosecuted Acilius Strabo who had held the office of praetor, and had been sent by Claudius to adjudicate on some lands which were bequeathed by king Apion, their former possessor, together with his kingdom to the Roman people, and which had since been seized by the neighbouring proprietors, who trusted to a long continued license in wrong, as if it constituted right and justice. Consequently, when the adjudication was against them, there arose a bitter feeling towards the judge, but the Senate replied that they knew nothing of the instructions given by Claudius, and that the emperor must be consulted. Nero, though he approved Strabo's decision, wrote word that nevertheless he was for relieving the allies, and that he waived all claim to what had been taken into possession.

19

THEN followed the deaths of two illustrious men, Domitius Afer and Marcus Servilius, who had flourished through a career of the highest honours and great eloquence. The first was a pleader; Servilius, after long practice in the courts, distinguished himself by his history of Rome and by the refinement of his life, which the contrast of his character to that of Afer, whom he equaled in genius, rendered the more conspicuous.

20

IN Nero's fourth consulship with Cornelius Cossus for his colleague, a theatrical entertainment to be repeated every five years was established at Rome in imitation of the Greek festival. Like all novelties, it was variously canvassed. There were some who declared that even Cnius Pompeius was censured by the older men of the day for having set up a fixed and permanent theatre. "Formerly," they said, "the games were usually exhibited with hastily erected tiers of benches and a temporary stage, and the people stood to witness them, that they might not, by having the chance of sitting down, spend a succession of entire days in idleness. Let the ancient character of these shows be retained, whenever the praetors exhibited them, and let no citizen be under the necessity of competing. As it was, the morality of their fathers, which had by degrees been forgotten, was utterly subverted by the introduction of a lax tone, so that all which could suffer or produce corruption was to be seen at Rome, and a degeneracy bred by foreign tastes was infecting the youth who devoted themselves to athletic sports, to idle loungings and low intrigues, with the encouragement of the emperor and Senate, who not only granted license to vice, but even applied a compulsion to drive Roman nobles into disgracing themselves on the stage, under the pretense of being orators and poets. What remained for them but to strip themselves naked, put on the boxing-glove, and practice such battles instead of the arms of legitimate warfare? Would justice be promoted, or would they serve on the knights' commissions for the honourable office of a judge, because they had listened with critical sagacity to effeminate strains of music and sweet voices? Night too was given up to infamy, so that virtue had not a moment left to her, but all the vilest of that promiscuous throng dared to do in the darkness anything they had lusted for in the day."

21

MANY people liked this very license, but they screened it under respectable names. "Our ancestors," they said, "were not averse to the attractions of shows on a scale suited to the wealth of their day, and so they introduced actors from the Etruscans and horse-races from Thurii. When we had possessed ourselves of Achaia and Asia, games were exhibited with greater elaboration, and yet no one at Rome of good family had stooped to the theatrical profession during the 200 years following the triumph of Lucius Mummius, who first displayed this kind of show in the capital. Besides, even economy had been consulted, when a permanent edifice was erected for a theatre, in preference to a structure raised and fitted up yearly at vast expense. Nor would the magistrates, as hitherto, exhaust their substance, or would the populace have the same motive for demanding of them the Greek contests, when once the State undertakes the expenditure. The victories won by orators and poets would furnish a stimulus to genius, and it could not be a burden for any judge to bestow his attention on graceful pursuits or on legitimate recreations. It was to mirth rather than to profligacy that a few nights every five years were devoted, and in these amid such a blaze of illumination no lawless conduct could be concealed." This entertainment, it is true, passed off without any notorious scandal. The enthusiasm too of the populace was not even slightly kindled, for the pantomimic actors, though permitted to return to the stage, were excluded from the sacred contests. No one gained the first prize for eloquence, but it was publicly announced that the emperor was victorious. Greek dresses, in which most people showed themselves during this festival, had then gone out of fashion.

22

A COMET meantime blazed in the sky, which in popular opinion always portends revolution to kingdoms. So people began to ask, as if Nero was already dethroned, who was to be elected. In every one's mouth was the name of Rubellius Blandus, who inherited through his mother the high nobility of the Julian family. He was himself attached to the ideas of our ancestors; his manners were austere, his home was one of purity and seclusion, and the more he lived in retirement from fear, the more fame did he acquire. Popular talk was confirmed by an interpretation put with similar credulity on a flash of lightning. While Nero was reclining at dinner in his house named Sublaqueum on the Simbruine lake, the table with the banquet was struck and shattered, and as this happened close to Tibur, from which town Plautus derived his origin on his father's side, people believed him to be the man marked out by divine providence; and he was encouraged by that numerous class, whose eager and often mistaken ambition it is to attach themselves prematurely to some new and hazardous cause. This alarmed Nero, and he wrote a letter to Plautus, bidding "him consider the tranquility of Rome and withdraw himself from mischievous gossip. He had ancestral possessions in Asia, where he might enjoy his youth safely and quietly." And so thither Plautus retired with his wife Antistia and a few intimate friends. About the same time an excessive love of luxurious gratification involved Nero in disgrace and danger. He had plunged for a swim into the source of the stream which Quintus Marcius conveyed to Rome, and it was thought that, by thus immersing his person in it, he had polluted the sacred waters and the sanctity of the spot. A fit of illness which followed, convinced people of the divine displeasure.

51

BUT while the miseries of the State were daily growing worse, its supports were becoming weaker. Burrus died, whether from illness or from poison was a question. It was supposed to be illness from the fact that from the gradual swelling of his throat inwardly and the closing up of the passage he ceased to breathe. Many positively asserted that by Nero's order his throat was smeared with some poisonous drug under the pretense of the application of a remedy, and that Burrus, who saw through the crime, when the emperor paid him a visit, recoiled with horror from his gaze, and merely replied to his question, "I indeed am well." Rome felt for him a deep and lasting regret, because of the remembrance of his worth, because too of the merely passive virtue of one of his successors and the very flagrant iniquities of the other. For the emperor had appointed two men to the command of the praetorian cohorts, Faenius Rufus, for a vulgar popularity, which he owed to his administration of the corn-supplies without profit to himself; and Sofonius Tigellinus, whose inveterate shamelessness and infamy were an attraction to him. As might have been expected from their known characters, Tigellinus had the greater influence with the prince, and was the associate of his most secret profligacy, while Rufus enjoyed the favour of the people and of the soldiers, and this, he found, prejudiced him with Nero.

52

THE death of Burrus was a blow to Seneca's power, for virtue had not the same strength when one of its companions, so to say, was removed, and Nero too began to lean on worse advisers. They assailed Seneca with various charges, representing that he continued to increase a wealth which was already so vast as to be beyond the scale of a subject, and was drawing to himself the attachment of the citizens, while in the picturesqueness of his gardens and the magnificence of his country houses he almost surpassed the emperor. They further alleged against him that he claimed for himself alone the honours of eloquence, and composed poetry more assiduously, as soon as a passion for it had seized on Nero. "Openly inimical to the prince's amusements, he disparaged his ability in driving horses, and ridiculed his voice whenever he sang. When was there to be an end of nothing being publicly admired but what Seneca was thought to have originated? Surely Nero's boyhood was over, and he was all but in the prime of youthful manhood. He ought to shake off a tutor, furnished as he was with sufficiently noble instructors in his own ancestors."

53

SENECA, meanwhile, aware of these slanders, which were revealed to him by those who had some respect for merit, coupled with the fact that the emperor more and more shunned his intimacy, besought the opportunity of an interview. This was granted, and he spoke as follows: "It is fourteen years ago, Caesar, that I was first associated with your prospects, and eight years since you have been emperor. In the interval, you have heaped on me such honours and riches that nothing is wanting to my happiness but a right use of it. I will refer to great examples taken not from my own but from your position. Your great-grandfather Augustus granted to Marcus Agrippa the calm repose of Mitylene, to Caius Maecenas what was nearly equivalent to a foreign retreat in the capital itself. One of these men shared his wars; the other struggled with many laborious duties at Rome; both received awards which were indeed splendid, but only proportioned to their great merits. For myself, what other recompense had I for your munificence, than a culture nursed, so to speak, in the shade of retirement, and to which a glory attaches itself, because I thus seem to have helped on the early training of your youth, an ample reward for the service. "You on the other hand have surrounded me with vast influence and boundless wealth, so that I often think within myself, Am I, who am but of an equestrian and provincial family, numbered among the chief men of Rome? Among nobles who can show a long succession of glories, has my new name become famous? Where is the mind once content with a humble lot? Is this the man who is building up his garden terraces, who paces grandly through these suburban parks, and revels in the affluence of such broad lands and such widely-spread investments? Only one apology occurs to me, that it would not have been right in me to have thwarted your bounty.

54

"AND yet we have both filled up our respective measures, you in giving as much as a prince can bestow on a friend, and I in receiving as much as a friend can receive from a prince. All else only fosters envy, which, like all things human, sinks powerless beneath your greatness, though on me it weighs heavily. To me relief is a necessity. Just as I should implore support if exhausted by warfare or travel, so in this journey of life, old as I am and unequal even to the lightest cares, since I cannot any longer bear the burden of my wealth, I crave assistance. Order my property to be managed by your agents and to be included in your estate. Still I shall not sink myself into poverty, but having surrendered the splendours which dazzle me, I will henceforth again devote to my mind all the leisure and attention now reserved for my gardens and country houses. You have yet before you a vigorous prime, and that on which for so many years your eyes were fixed, supreme power. We, your older friends, can answer for our quiet behaviour. It will likewise redound to your honour that you have raised to the highest places men who could also bear moderate fortune."

55

NERO'S reply was substantially this: "My being able to meet your elaborate speech with an instant rejoinder is, I consider, primarily your gift, for you taught me how to express myself not only after reflection but at a moment's notice. My great-grandfather Augustus allowed Agrippa and Maecenas to enjoy rest after their labours, but he did it at an age carrying with it an authority sufficient to justify any boon, of any sort, he might have bestowed. But neither of them did he strip of the rewards he had given. It was by war and its perils they had earned them; for in these the youth of Augustus was spent. And if I had passed my years in arms, your sword and right hand would not have failed me. But, as my actual condition required, you watched over my boyhood, then over my youth, with wisdom, counsel, and advice. And indeed your gifts to me will, as long as life holds out, be lasting possessions; those which you owe to me, your parks, investments, your country houses, are liable to accidents. Though they seem much, many far inferior to you in merit have obtained more. I am ashamed to quote the names of freedmen who parade a greater wealth. Hence I actually blush to think that, standing as you do first in my affections, you do not as yet surpass all in fortune.

56

"YOURS too is a still vigorous manhood, quite equal to the labours of business and to the fruit of those labours; and, as for myself, I am but treading the threshold of empire. But perhaps you count yourself inferior to Vitellius, thrice a consul, and me to Claudius. Such wealth as long thrift has procured for Volusius, my bounty, you think, cannot fully make up to you. Why not rather, if the frailty of my youth goes in any respect astray, call me back and guide yet more zealously with your help the manhood which you have instructed? It will not be your moderation, if you restore me your wealth, not your love of quiet, if you forsake your emperor, but my avarice, the fear of my cruelty, which will be in all men's mouths. Even if your self-control were praised to the utmost, still it would not be seemly in a wise man to get glory for himself in the very act of bringing disgrace on his friend." To these words the emperor added embraces and kisses; for he was formed by nature and trained by habit to veil his hatred under delusive flattery. Seneca thanked him, the usual end of an interview with a despot. But he entirely altered the practices of his former greatness; he kept the crowds of his visitors at a distance, avoided trains of followers, seldom appeared in Rome, as though weak health or philosophical studies detained him at home.

57

WHEN Seneca had fallen, it was easy to shake the position of Faenius Rufus by making Agrippina's friendship a charge against him. Tigellinus, who was daily becoming more powerful and who thought that the wicked schemings which alone gave him strength, would be better liked if he could secure the emperor's complicity in guilt, dived into Nero's most secret apprehensions, and, as soon as he had ascertained that Plautus and Sulla were the men he most dreaded, Plautus having been lately sent away to Asia, Sulla to Gallia Narbonensis, he spoke much of their noble rank and of their respective proximity to the armies of the East and of Germany. "I have no eye," he said, "like Burrus, to two conflicting aims, but only to Nero's safety, which is at least secured against treachery in Rome by my presence. As for distant commotions, how can they be checked? Gaul is roused at the name of the great dictator, and I distrust no less the nations of Asia, because of the renown of such a grandfather as Drusus. Sulla is poor, and hence comes his surpassing audacity; he shams apathy, while he is seeking an opening for his reckless ambition. Plautus again, with his great wealth, does not so much as affect a love of repose, but he flaunts before us his imitations of the old Romans, and assumes the self-consciousness of the Stoics along with a philosophy, which makes men restless, and eager for a busy life." There was not a moment's delay. Sulla, six days afterwards, was murdered by assassins brought over to Massilia, while he was reclining at the dinner-table, before he feared or heard of his danger. The head was taken to Rome, and Nero scoffed at its premature grey hairs as if they were a disfigurement.

58

IT was less of a secret that there was a design to murder Plautus, as his life was dear to many. The distance too by land and sea, and the interval of time, had given rise to rumours, and the popular story was that he had tampered with Corbulo, who was then at the head of great armies, and would be a special mark for danger, if illustrious and innocent men were to be destroyed. Again Asia, it was said, from its partiality for the young man, had taken up arms, and the soldiers sent to do the crime, not being sufficient in number or decided in purpose, and, finding themselves unable to execute their orders, had gone over to the new cause. These absurdities, like all popular gossip, gathered strength from the idle leisure of a credulous society. As it was, one of Plautus's freedmen, thanks to swift winds, arrived before the centurion and brought him a message from his father-in-law, Lucius Antistius. "He was to avoid the obvious refuge of a coward's death, and in the pity felt for a noble name he would soon find good men to help him, and daring spirits would rally round him. Meantime no resource was to be rejected. If he did but repel sixty soldiers (this was the number on the way), while tidings were being carried back to Nero, while another force was on its march, many events would follow which would ripen into war. Finally, by this plan he either secured safety, or he would suffer nothing worse by daring than by cowardice."

59

BUT all this had no effect on Plautus. Either he saw no resource before him, an unarmed exile as he was, or he was weary of an uncertain hope, or was swayed by his love of his wife and of his children, to whom he thought the emperor, if harassed by no anxiety, would be more merciful. Some say that another message came to him from his father-in-law, representing that no dreadful peril hung over him, and that two teachers of philosophy, Coeranus from Greece and Musonius from Etruria, advised him to await death with firmness rather than lead a precarious and anxious life. At all events, he was surprised at midday, when stripped for exercise. In that state the centurion slew him in the presence of Pelago, an eunuch, whom Nero had set over the centurion and his company, like a despot's minister over his satellites. The head of the murdered man was brought to Rome. At its sight the emperor exclaimed (I give his very words), "Why would you have been a Nero?" Then casting off all fear he prepared to hurry on his marriage with Poppaea, hitherto deferred because of such alarms as I have described, and to divorce his wife Octavia, notwithstanding her virtuous life, because her father's name and the people's affection for her made her an offence to him. He wrote, however, a letter to the Senate, confessing nothing about the murders of Sulla and Plautus, but merely hinting that both had a restless temper, and that he gave the most anxious thought to the safety of the State. On this pretext a thanksgiving was decreed, and also the expulsion from the Senate of Sulla and Plautus, more grievous, however, as a farce than as an actual calamity.

60

NERO, on receiving this decree of the Senate and seeing that every piece of his wickedness was regarded as a conspicuous merit, drove Octavia from him, alleging that she was barren, and then married Poppaea. The woman who had long been Nero's mistress and ruled him first as a paramour, then as her husband, instigated one of Octavia's servants to accuse her an intrigue with a slave. The man fixed on as the guilty lover was one by name Eucaerus, an Alexandrine by birth, skilled in singing to the flute. As a consequence, her slave-girls were examined under torture, and though some were forced by the intensity of agony into admitting falsehoods, most of them persisted in upholding the virtue of their mistress. One of them said, in answer to the furious menaces of Tigellinus, that Octavia's person was purer than his mouth. Octavia, however, was dismissed under the form of an ordinary divorce, and received possession of the house of Burrus and of the estates of Plautus, an ill-starred gift. She was soon afterwards banished to Campania under military surveillance. This led to incessant and outspoken remonstrances among the common people, who have less discretion and are exposed to fewer dangers than others from the insignificance of their position. Upon this Nero, though he did not repent of his outrage, restored to Octavia her position as wife.

61

THEN people in their joy went up to the Capitol and, at last, gave thanks to the gods. They threw down the statues of Poppaea; they bore on their shoulders the images of Octavia, covering them with flowers, and setting them up in the forum and in the temples. There was even a burst of applause for the emperor, men hailing the recalled Octavia. And now they were pouring into the Palace in crowds, with loud shoutings, when some companies of soldiers rushed out and dispersed the tumultuous throng with blows, and at the point of the sword. Whatever changes had been made in the riot, were reversed, and Poppaea's honours restored. Ever relentless in her hatred, she was now enraged by the fear that either the violence of the mob would burst on her with yet fiercer fury, or that Nero would be swayed by the popular bias, and so, flinging herself at his knees, she exclaimed that she was not in the position of a rival fighting for marriage, though that was dearer to her than life, but that her very life was brought into jeopardy by the dependents and slaves of Octavia, who had assumed the name of the people, and dared in peace what could hardly happen in war. "Those arms," she said, "have been taken up against the emperor; a leader only is wanting, and he will easily be found in a commotion. Only let her whose mere beck, though she is far away, stirs up tumult, quit Campania, and make her way in person to Rome. And, again, what is my sin? What offense have I caused any one? Is it that I am about to give to the house of the Caesars a lawful heir? Do the people of Rome prefer that the offspring of an Egyptian flute player should be raised to the imperial throne? In a word, if it be expedient, Nero should of his own choice rather than on compulsion send for her who ruled him, or else secure his safety by a righteous vengeance. The beginning of a commotion has often been quieted by slight precautions; but if people once despair of Octavia being Nero's wife, they will soon find her a husband."

62

HER various arguments, tending both to frighten and to enrage, at once alarmed and incensed her listener. But the suspicion about the slave was of little weight, and the torture of the slave-girls exposed its absurdity. Consequently it was decided to procure a confession from some one on whom could also be fastened a charge of revolutionary designs. Fittest for this seemed the perpetrator of the mother's murder, Anicetus, commander, as I have already mentioned, of the fleet at Misenum, who got but scant gratitude after that atrocious deed, and subsequently all the more vehement hatred, inasmuch as men look on their instruments in crime as a sort of standing reproach to them. The emperor accordingly sent for Anicetus, and reminded him of his former service. "He alone," he said, "had come to the rescue of the prince's life against a plotting mother. Close at hand was a chance of winning no less gratitude by ridding him of a malignant wife. No violence or weapons were needed; only let him confess to an intrigue with Octavia." Nero then promised him a secret but ample immediate recompense, and some delightful retreat, while he threatened him with death in case of refusal. Anicetus, with the moral insensibility of his nature and a promptness inspired by previous atrocities, invented even more than was required of him, and confessed before friends whom the prince had called in, as a sort of judicial council. He was then banished to Sardinia, where he endured exile without poverty, and died a natural death.

63

NERO meanwhile declared by edict that the prefect had been corrupted into a design of gaining over the fleet, and added, in forgetfulness of his late charge of barrenness against Octavia, that, conscious of her profligacies, she had procured abortion, a fact he had himself ascertained. Then he confined her in the island of Pandataria. No exile ever filled the eyes of beholders with tears of greater compassion. Some still remembered Agrippina, banished by Tiberius, and the yet fresher memory of Julia, whom Claudius exiled, was present to men's thoughts. But they had life's prime for their stay; they had seen some happiness, and the horror of the moment was alleviated by recollections of a better lot in the past. For Octavia, from the first, her marriage-day was a kind of funeral, brought, as she was, into a house where she had nothing but scenes of mourning, her father and, an instant afterwards, her brother, having been snatched from her by poison; then, a slave-girl raised above the mistress; Poppaea married only to insure a wife's ruin, and, to end all, an accusation more horrible than any death.

64

AND now the girl, in her twentieth year, with centurions and soldiers around her, already removed from among the living by the forecast of doom, still could not reconcile herself to death. After an interval of a few days, she received an order that she was to die, although she protested that she was now a widow and only a sister, and appealed to their common ancestors, the Germanici, and finally to the name of Agrippina, during whose life she had endured a marriage, which was miserable enough indeed, but not fatal. She was then tightly bound with cords, and the veins of every limb were opened; but as her blood was congealed by terror and flowed too slowly, she was killed outright by the steam of an intensely hot bath. To this was added the yet more appalling horror of Poppaea beholding the severed head which was conveyed to Rome. And for all this offerings were voted to the temples. I record the fact with a special object. Whoever would study the calamities of that period in my pages or those of other authors, is to take it for granted that as often as the emperor directed banishments or executions, so often was there a thanksgiving to the gods, and what formerly commemorated some prosperous event, was then a token of public disaster. Still, if any decree of the Senate was marked by some new flattery, or by the lowest servility, I shall not pass it over in silence.

65

THAT same year Nero was believed to have destroyed by poison two of his most powerful freedmen, Doryphorus, on the pretext of his having opposed the marriage with Poppaea, Pallas for still keeping his boundless wealth by a prolonged old age. Romanus had accused Seneca in stealthy calumnies, of having been an accomplice of Caius Piso, but he was himself crushed more effectually by Seneca on the same charge. This alarmed Piso, and gave rise to a huge fabric of unsuccessful conspiracies against Nero.

Book XV

30

TO military glory Corbulo added courtesy and hospitality. When the king continually asked the reason of whatever he noticed which was new to him, the announcements, for example, by a centurion of the beginnings of each watch, the dismissal of the guests by the sound of a trumpet, and the lighting by a torch from beneath of an altar in front of the headquarters, Corbulo, by exaggerating everything, filled him with admiration of our ancient system. Next day Tiridates begged for time which, as he was about to enter on so long a journey, might suffice for a previous visit to his brothers and his mother. Meanwhile he gave up his daughter as a hostage, and prepared a suppliant letter to Nero.

31

HE then departed, and found Pacorus in Media, and Vologeses at Ecbatana, who was by no means unconcerned for his brother. In fact, Vologeses had entreated Corbulo by special messengers, that Tiridates might not have to endure any badge of slavery, or have to deliver up his sword, or be debarred the honour of embracing the governors of the provinces, or have to present himself at their doors, and that he might be treated at Rome with as much respect as the consuls. Accustomed, forsooth, to foreign arrogance, he had no knowledge of us, who value the reality of empire and disregard its empty show.

32

THAT same year the emperor put into possession of the Latin franchise the tribes of the maritime Alps. To the Roman knights he assigned places in the circus in front of the seats of the people, for up to that time they used to enter in a promiscuous throng, as the Roscian law extended only to fourteen rows in the theatre. The same year witnessed shows of gladiators as magnificent as those of the past. Many ladies of distinction, however, and senators, disgraced themselves by appearing in the amphitheatre.

33

IN the year of the consulship of Caius Laecanius and Marcus Licinius a yet keener impulse urged Nero to show himself frequently on the public stage. Hitherto he had sung in private houses or gardens, during the juvenile games, but these he now despised, as being but little frequented, and on too small a scale for so fine a voice. As, however, he did not venture to make a beginning at Rome, he chose Neapolis, because it was a Greek city. From this as his starting point he might cross into Achaia, and there, winning the well-known and sacred garlands of antiquity, evoke, with increased fame, the enthusiasm of the citizens. Accordingly, a rabble of the townsfolk was brought together, with those whom the excitement of such an event had attracted from the neighbouring towns and colonies, and such as followed in the emperor's train to pay him honour or for various objects. All these, with some companies of soldiers, filled the theatre at Neapolis.

34

THERE an incident occurred, which many thought unlucky, though to the emperor it seemed due to the providence of auspicious deities. The people who had been present, had quitted the theatre, and the empty building then fell in without harm to anyone. Thereupon Nero in an elaborate ode thanked the gods, celebrating the good luck which attended the late downfall, and as he was on his way to cross the sea of Hadria, he rested awhile at Beneventum, where a crowded gladiatorial show was being exhibited by Vatinius. The man was one of the most conspicuously infamous sights in the imperial court, bred, as he had been, in a shoemaker's shop, of a deformed person and vulgar wit, originally introduced as a butt. After a time he grew so powerful by accusing all the best men, that in influence, wealth, and ability to injure, he was preeminent even in that bad company.

35

WHILE Nero was frequently visiting the show, even amid his pleasures there was no cessation to his crimes. For during the very same period Torquatus Silanus was forced to die, because over and above his illustrious rank as one of the Junian family he claimed to be the great-grandson of Augustus. Accusers were ordered to charge him with prodigality in lavishing gifts, and with having no hope but in revolution. They said further that he had nobles about him for his letters, books, and accounts, titles all and rehearsals of supreme power. Then the most intimate of his freedmen were put in chains and torn from him, till, knowing the doom which impended, Torquatus divided the arteries in his arms. A speech from Nero followed, as usual, which stated that though he was guilty and with good reason distrusted his defense, he would yet have lived, had he awaited the clemency of the judge.

36

SOON afterwards, giving up Achaia for the present (his reasons were not certainly known), he returned to Rome, there dwelling in his secret imaginations on the provinces of the east, especially Egypt. Then having declared in a public proclamation that his absence would not be long and that all things in the State would remain unchanged and prosperous, he visited the temple of the Capitol for advice about his departure. There he adored the gods; then he entered also the temple of Vesta, and there feeling a sudden trembling throughout his limbs, either from terror inspired by the deity or because, from the remembrance of his crimes, he was never free from fear, he relinquished his purpose, repeatedly saying that all his plans were of less account than his love of his country. "He had seen the sad countenances of the citizens, he heard their secret complainings at the prospect of his entering on so long a journey, when they could not bear so much as his brief excursions, accustomed as they were to cheer themselves under mischances by the sight of the emperor. Hence, as in private relationships the closest ties were the strongest, so the people of Rome had the most powerful claims and must be obeyed in their wish to retain him." These and the like sentiments suited the people, who craved amusement, and feared, always their chief anxiety, scarcity of corn, should he be absent. The Senate and leading citizens were in doubt whether to regard him as more terrible at a distance or among them. After a while, as is the way with great terrors, they thought what happened the worst alternative.

37

NERO, to win credit for himself of enjoying nothing so much as the capital, prepared banquets in the public places, and used the whole city, so to say, as his private house. Of these entertainments the most famous for their notorious profligacy were those furnished by Tigellinus, which I will describe as an illustration, that I may not have again and again to narrate similar extravagance. He had a raft constructed on Agrippa's lake, put the guests on board and set it in motion by other vessels towing it. These vessels glittered with gold and ivory; the crews were arranged according to age and experience in vice. Birds and beasts had been procured from remote countries, and sea monsters from the ocean. On the margin of the lake were set up brothels crowded with noble ladies, and on the opposite bank were seen naked prostitutes with obscene gestures and movements. As darkness approached, all the adjacent grove and surrounding buildings resounded with song, and shone brilliantly with lights. Nero, who polluted himself by every lawful or lawless indulgence, had not omitted a single abomination which could heighten his depravity, till a few days afterwards he stooped to marry himself to one of that filthy herd, by name Pythagoras, with all the forms of regular wedlock. The bridal veil was put over the emperor; people saw the witnesses of the ceremony, the wedding dower, the couch and the nuptial torches; everything in a word was plainly visible, which, even when a woman weds, darkness hides.

38

A DISASTER followed, whether accidental or treacherously contrived by the emperor, is uncertain, as authors have given both accounts, worse, however, and more dreadful than any which have ever happened to this city by the violence of fire. It had its beginning in that part of the circus which adjoins the Palatine and Caelian hills, where, amid the shops containing inflammable wares, the conflagration both broke out and instantly became so fierce and so rapid from the wind that it seized in its grasp the entire length of the circus. For here there were no houses fenced in by solid masonry, or temples surrounded by walls, or any other obstacle to interpose delay. The blaze in its fury ran first through the level portions of the city, then rising to the hills, while it again devastated every place below them, it outstripped all preventive measures; so rapid was the mischief and so completely at its mercy the city, with those narrow winding passages and irregular streets, which characterized old Rome. Added to this were the wailings of terror-stricken women, the feebleness of age, the helpless inexperience of childhood, the crowds who sought to save themselves or others, dragging out the infirm or waiting for them, and by their hurry in the one case, by their delay in the other, aggravating the confusion. Often, while they looked behind them, they were intercepted by flames on their side or in their face. Or if they reached a refuge close at hand, when this too was seized by the fire, they found that, even places, which they had imagined to be remote, were involved in the same calamity. At last, doubting what they should avoid or whither betake themselves, they crowded the streets or flung themselves down in the fields, while some who had lost their all, even their very daily bread, and others out of love for their kinsfolk, whom they had been unable to rescue, perished, though escape was open to them. And no one dared to stop the mischief, because of incessant menaces from a number of persons who forbade the extinguishing of the flames, because again others openly hurled brands, and kept shouting that there was one who gave them authority, either seeking to plunder more freely, or obeying orders.

39

NERO at this time was at Antium, and did not return to Rome until the fire approached his house, which he had built to connect the palace with the gardens of Maecenas. It could not, however, be stopped from devouring the palace, the house, and everything around it. However, to relieve the people, driven out homeless as they were, he threw open to them the Campus Martius and the public buildings of Agrippa, and even his own gardens, and raised temporary structures to receive the destitute multitude. Supplies of food were brought up from Ostia and the neighbouring towns, and the price of corn was reduced to three sesterces a peck. These acts, though popular, produced no effect, since a rumour had gone forth everywhere that, at the very time when the city was in flames, the emperor appeared on a private stage and sang of the destruction of Troy, comparing present misfortunes with the calamities of antiquity.

40

AT last, after five days, an end was put to the conflagration at the foot of the Esquiline hill, by the destruction of all buildings on a vast space, so that the violence of the fire was met by clear ground and an open sky. But before people had laid aside their fears, the flames returned, with no less fury this second time, and especially in the spacious districts of the city. Consequently, though there was less loss of life, the temples of the gods, and the porticoes which were devoted to enjoyment, fell in a yet more widespread ruin. And to this conflagration there attached the greater infamy because it broke out on the Aemilian property of Tigellinus, and it seemed that Nero was aiming at the glory of founding a new city and calling it by his name. Rome, indeed, is divided into fourteen districts, four of which remained uninjured, three were leveled to the ground, while in the other seven were left only a few shattered, half-burnt relics of houses.

41

IT would not be easy to enter into a computation of the private mansions, the blocks of tenements, and of the temples, which were lost. Those with the oldest ceremonial, as that dedicated by Servius Tullius to Luna, the great altar and shrine raised by the Arcadian Evander to the visibly appearing Hercules, the temple of Jupiter the Stayer, which was vowed by Romulus, Numa's royal palace, and the sanctuary of Vesta, with the tutelary deities of the Roman people, were burnt. So too were the riches acquired by our many victories, various beauties of Greek art, then again the ancient and genuine historical monuments of men of genius, and, notwithstanding the striking splendour of the restored city, old men will remember many things which could not be replaced. Some persons observed that the beginning of this conflagration was on the 19th of July, the day on which the Senones captured and fired Rome. Others have pushed a curious inquiry so far as to reduce the interval between these two conflagrations into equal numbers of years, months, and days.

42

NERO meanwhile availed himself of his country's desolation, and erected a mansion in which the jewels and gold, long familiar objects, quite vulgarised by our extravagance, were not so marvelous as the fields and lakes, with woods on one side to resemble a wilderness, and, on the other, open spaces and extensive views. The directors and contrivers of the work were Severus and Celer, who had the genius and the audacity to attempt by art even what nature had refused, and to fool away an emperor's resources. They had actually undertaken to sink a navigable canal from the lake Avernus to the mouths of the Tiber along a barren shore or through the face of hills, where one meets with no moisture which could supply water, except the Pomptine marshes. The rest of the country is broken rock and perfectly dry. Even if it could be cut through, the labour would be intolerable, and there would be no adequate result. Nero, however, with his love of the impossible, endeavoured to dig through the nearest hills to Avernus, and there still remain the traces of his disappointed hope.

43

OF Rome meanwhile, so much as was left unoccupied by his mansion, was not built up, as it had been after its burning by the Gauls, without any regularity or in any fashion, but with rows of streets according to measurement, with broad thoroughfares, with a restriction on the height of houses, with open spaces, and the further addition of colonnades, as a protection to the frontage of the blocks of tenements. These colonnades Nero promised to erect at his own expense, and to hand over the open spaces, when cleared of the debris, to the ground landlords. He also offered rewards proportioned to each person's position and property, and prescribed a period within which they were to obtain them on the completion of so many houses or blocks of building. He fixed on the marshes of Ostia for the reception of the rubbish, and arranged that the ships which had brought up corn by the Tiber, should sail down the river with cargoes of this rubbish. The buildings themselves, to a certain height, were to be solidly constructed, without wooden beams, of stone from Gabii or Alba, that material being impervious to fire. And to provide that the water which individual license had illegally appropriated, might flow in greater abundance in several places for the public use, officers were appointed, and everyone was to have in the open court the means of stopping a fire. Every building, too, was to be enclosed by its own proper wall, not by one common to others. These changes which were liked for their utility, also added beauty to the new city. Some, however, thought that its old arrangement had been more conducive to health, inasmuch as the narrow streets with the elevation of the roofs were not equally penetrated by the sun's heat, while now the open space, unsheltered by any shade, was scorched by a fiercer glow.

44

SUCH indeed were the precautions of human wisdom. The next thing was to seek means of propitiating the gods, and recourse was had to the Sibylline books, by the direction of which prayers were offered to Vulcanus, Ceres, and Proserpina. Juno, too, was entreated by the matrons, first, in the Capitol, then on the nearest part of the coast, whence water was procured to sprinkle the fane and image of the goddess. And there were sacred banquets and nightly vigils celebrated by married women. But all human efforts, all the lavish gifts of the emperor, and the propitiations of the gods, did not banish the sinister belief that the conflagration was the result of an order. Consequently, to get rid of the report, Nero fastened the guilt and inflicted the most exquisite tortures on a class hated for their abominations, called Christians by the populace. Christus, from whom the name had its origin, suffered the extreme penalty during the reign of Tiberius at the hands of one of our procurators, Pontius Pilatus, and a most mischievous superstition, thus checked for the moment, again broke out not only in Judaea, the first source of the evil, but even in Rome, where all things hideous and shameful from every part of the world find their centre and become popular. Accordingly, an arrest was first made of all who pleaded guilty; then, upon their information, an immense multitude was convicted, not so much of the crime of firing the city, as of hatred against mankind. Mockery of every sort was added to their deaths. Covered with the skins of beasts, they were torn by dogs and perished, or were nailed to crosses, or were doomed to the flames and burnt, to serve as a nightly illumination, when daylight had expired. Nero offered his gardens for the spectacle, and was exhibiting a show in the circus, while he mingled with the people in the dress of a charioteer or stood aloft on a car. Hence, even for criminals who deserved extreme and exemplary punishment, there arose a feeling of compassion; for it was not, as it seemed, for the public good, but to glut one man's cruelty, that they were being destroyed.

45

MEANWHILE Italy was thoroughly exhausted by contributions of money, the provinces were ruined, as also the allied nations and the free states, as they were called. Even the gods fell victims to the plunder; for the temples in Rome were despoiled and the gold carried off, which, for a triumph or a vow, the Roman people in every age had consecrated in their prosperity or their alarm. Throughout Asia and Achaia not only votive gifts, but the images of deities were seized, Acratus and Secundus Carinas having been sent into those provinces. The first was a freedman ready for any wickedness; the latter, as far as speech went, was thoroughly trained in Greek learning, but he had not imbued his heart with sound principles. Seneca, it was said, to avert from himself the obloquy of sacrilege, begged for the seclusion of a remote rural retreat, and, when it was refused, feigning ill health, as though he had a nervous ailment, would not quit his chamber. According to some writers, poison was prepared for him at Nero's command by his own freedman, whose name was Cleonicus. This Seneca avoided through the freedman's disclosure, or his own apprehension, while he used to support life on the very simple diet of wild fruits, with water from a running stream when thirst prompted.

46

DURING the same time some gladiators in the town of Praeneste, who attempted to break loose, were put down by a military guard stationed on the spot to watch them, and the people, ever desirous and yet fearful of change, began at once to talk of Spartacus, and of bygone calamities. Soon afterwards, tidings of a naval disaster was received, but not from war, for never had there been so profound a peace. Nero, however, had ordered the fleet to return to Campania on a fixed day, without making any allowance for the dangers of the sea. Consequently the pilots, in spite of the fury of the waves, started from Formiae, and while they were struggling to double the promontory of Misenum, they were dashed by a violent south-west wind on the shores of Cumae, and lost, in all directions, a number of their triremes with some smaller vessels.

47

AT the close of the year people talked much about prodigies, presaging impending evils. Never were lightning flashes more frequent, and a comet too appeared, for which Nero always made propitiation with noble blood. Human and other births with two heads were exposed to public view, or were discovered in those sacrifices in which it is usual to immolate victims in a pregnant condition. And in the district of Placentia, close to the road, a calf was born with its head attached to its leg. Then followed an explanation of the diviners, that another head was preparing for the world, which however would be neither mighty nor hidden, as its growth had been checked in the womb, and it had been born by the wayside.

48

SILIUS Nerva and Atticus Vestinus then entered on the consulship, and now a conspiracy was planned, and at once became formidable, for which senators, knights, soldiers, even women, had given their names with eager rivalry, out of hatred of Nero as well as a liking for Caius Piso. A descendant of the Calpurnian house, and embracing in his connections through his father's noble rank many illustrious families, Piso had a splendid reputation with the people from his virtue or semblance of virtue. His eloquence he exercised in the defense of fellow-citizens, his generosity towards friends, while even for strangers he had a courteous address and demeanour. He had, too, the fortuitous advantages of tall stature and a handsome face. But solidity of character and moderation in pleasure were wholly alien to him. He indulged in laxity, in display, and occasionally in excess. This suited the taste of that numerous class who, when the attractions of vice are so powerful, do not wish for strictness or special severity on the throne.

49

THE origin of the conspiracy was not in Piso's personal ambition. But I could not easily narrate who first planned it, or whose prompting inspired a scheme into which so many entered. That the leading spirits were Subrius Flavus, tribune of a praetorian cohort, and Sulpicius Asper, a centurion, was proved by the fearlessness of their death. Lucanus Annaeus, too, and Plautius Lateranus, imported into it an intensely keen resentment. Lucanus had the stimulus of personal motives, for Nero tried to disparage the fame of his poems and, with the foolish vanity of a rival, had forbidden him to publish them. As for Lateranus, a consul-elect, it was no wrong, but love of the State which linked him with the others. Flavius Scaevinus and Afranius Quintianus, on the other hand, both of senatorian rank, contrary to what was expected of them, undertook the beginning of this daring crime. Scaevinus, indeed, had enfeebled his mind by excess, and his life, accordingly, was one of sleepy languor. Quintianus, infamous for his effeminate vice, had been satirized by Nero in a lampoon, and was bent on avenging the insult.

50

SO, while they dropped hints among themselves or among their friends about the emperor's crimes, the approaching end of empire, and the importance of choosing some one to rescue the State in its distress, they associated with them Tullius Senecio, Cervarius Proculus, Vulcatius Araricus, Julius Augurinus, Munatius Gratus, Antonius Natalis, and Marcius Festus, all Roman knights. Of these Senecio, one of those who was specially intimate with Nero, still kept up a show of friendship, and had consequently to struggle with all the more dangers. Natalis shared with Piso all his secret plans. The rest built their hopes on revolution. Besides Subrius and Sulpicius, whom I have already mentioned, they invited the aid of military strength, of Gavius Silvanus and Statius Proximus, tribunes of praetorian cohorts, and of two centurions, Maximus Scaurus and Venetus Paulus. But their mainstay, it was thought, was Faenius Rufus, the commander of the guard, a man of esteemed life and character, to whom Tigellinus with his brutality and shamelessness was superior in the emperor's regard. He harassed him with calumnies, and had often put him in terror by hinting that he had been Agrippina's paramour, and from sorrow at her loss was intent on vengeance. And so, when the conspirators were assured by his own repeated language that the commander of the praetorian guard had come over to their side, they once more eagerly discussed the time and place of the fatal deed. It was said that Subrius Flavus had formed a sudden resolution to attack Nero when singing on the stage, or when his house was in flames and he was running hither and thither, unattended, in the darkness. In the one case was the opportunity of solitude; in the other, the very crowd which would witness so glorious a deed, had roused a singularly noble soul; it was only the desire of escape, that foe to all great enterprises, which held him back.

51

MEANWHILE, as they hesitated in prolonged suspense between hope and fear, a certain Epicharis (how she informed herself is uncertain, as she had never before had a thought of anything noble) began to stir and upbraid the conspirators. Wearied at last of their long delay, she endeavoured, when staying in Campania, to shake the loyalty of the officers of the fleet at Misenum, and to entangle them in a guilty complicity. She began thus. There was a captain in the fleet, Volusius Proculus, who had been one of Nero's instruments in his mother's murder, and had not, as he thought, been promoted in proportion to the greatness of his crime. Either, as an old acquaintance of the woman, or on the strength of a recent intimacy, he divulged to her his services to Nero and their barren result to himself, adding complaints, and his determination to have vengeance, should the chance arise. He thus inspired the hope that he could be persuaded, and could secure many others. No small help was to be found in the fleet, and there would be numerous opportunities, as Nero delighted in frequent enjoyment of the sea off Puteoli and Misenum. Epicharis accordingly said more, and began the history of all the emperor's crimes. "The Senate," she affirmed, "had no power left it; yet means had been provided whereby he might pay the penalty of having destroyed the State. Only let Proculus gird himself to do his part and bring over to their side his bravest soldiers, and then look for an adequate recompense." The conspirators' names, however, she withheld. Consequently the information of Proculus was useless, even though he reported what he had heard to Nero. For Epicharis being summoned and confronted with the informer easily silenced him, unsupported as he was by a single witness. But she was herself detained in custody, for Nero suspected that even what was not proved to be true, was not wholly false.

52

THE conspirators, however, alarmed by the fear of disclosure, resolved to hurry on the assassination at Baiae, in Piso's villa, whither the emperor, charmed by its loveliness, often went, and where, unguarded and without the cumbrous grandeur of his rank, he would enjoy the bath and the banquet. But Piso refused, alleging the odium of an act which would stain with an emperor's blood, however bad he might be, the sanctity of the hospitable board and the deities who preside over it. "Better," he said, "in the capital, in that hateful mansion which was piled up with the plunder of the citizens, or in public, to accomplish what on the State's behalf they had undertaken." So he said openly, with however a secret apprehension that Lucius Silanus might, on the strength of his distinguished rank and the teachings of Caius Cassius, under whom he had been trained, aspire to any greatness and seize an empire, which would be promptly offered him by all who had no part in the conspiracy, and who would pity Nero as the victim of a crime. Many thought that Piso shunned also the enterprising spirit of Vestinus, the consul, who might, he feared, rise up in the cause of freedom, or, by choosing another emperor, make the State his own gift. Vestinus, indeed, had no share in the conspiracy, though Nero on that charge gratified an old resentment against an innocent man.

53

AT last they decided to carry out their design on that day of the circus games, which is celebrated in honour of Ceres, as the emperor, who seldom went out, and shut himself up in his house or gardens, used to go to the entertainments of the circus, and access to him was the easier from his keen enjoyment of the spectacle. They had so arranged the order of the plot, that Lateranus was to throw himself at the prince's knees in earnest entreaty, apparently craving relief for his private necessities, and, being a man of strong nerve and huge frame, hurl him to the ground and hold him down. When he was prostrate and powerless, the tribunes and centurions and all the others who had sufficient daring were to rush up and do the murder, the first blow being claimed by Scaevinus, who had taken a dagger from the Temple of Safety, or, according to another account, from that of Fortune, in the town of Ferentum, and used to wear the weapon as though dedicated to some noble deed. Piso, meanwhile, was wait in the sanctuary of Ceres, whence he was to be summoned by Faenius, the commander of the guard, and by the others, and then conveyed into the camp, accompanied by Antonia, the daughter of Claudius Caesar, with a view to evoke the people's enthusiasm. So it is related by Caius Pliny. Handed down from whatever source, I had no intention of suppressing it, however absurd it may seem, either that Antonia should have lent her name at her life's peril to a hopeless project, or that Piso, with his well-known affection for his wife, should have pledged himself to another marriage, but for the fact that the lust of dominion inflames the heart more than any other passion.

54

IT was however wonderful how among people of different class, rank, age, sex, among rich and poor, everything was kept in secrecy till betrayal began from the house of Scaevinus. The day before the treacherous attempt, after a long conversation with Antonius Natalis, Scaevinus returned home, sealed his will, and, drawing from its sheath the dagger of which I have already spoken, and complaining that it was blunted from long disuse, he ordered it to be sharpened on a stone to a keen and bright point. This task he assigned to his freedman Milichus. At the same time sat down to a more than usually sumptuous banquet, and gave his favourite slaves their freedom, and money to others. He was himself depressed, and evidently in profound thought, though he affected gaiety in desultory conversation. Last of all, he directed ligatures for wounds and the means of stanching blood to be prepared by the same Milichus, who either knew of the conspiracy and was faithful up to this point, or was in complete ignorance and then first caught suspicions, as most authors have inferred from what followed. For when his servile imagination dwelt on the rewards of perfidy, and he saw before him at the same moment boundless wealth and power, conscience and care for his patron's life, together with the remembrance of the freedom he had received, fled from him. From his wife, too, he had adopted a womanly and yet baser suggestion; for she even held over him a dreadful thought, that many had been present, both freedmen and slaves, who had seen what he had; that one man's silence would be useless, whereas the rewards would be for him alone who was first with the information.

55

ACCORDINGLY at daybreak Milichus went to the Servilian gardens, and, finding the doors shut against him, said again and again that he was the bearer of important and alarming news. Upon this he was conducted by the gatekeepers to one of Nero's freedmen, Epaphroditus, and by him to Nero, whom he informed of the urgent danger, of the formidable conspiracy, and of all else which he had heard or inferred. He showed him too the weapon prepared for his destruction, and bade him summon the accused. Scaevinus on being arrested by the soldiers began his defense with the reply that the dagger about which he was accused, had of old been regarded with a religious sentiment by his ancestors, that it had been kept in his chamber, and been stolen by a trick of his freedman. He had often, he said, signed his will without heeding the observance of particular days, and had previously given presents of money as well as freedom to some of his slaves, only on this occasion he gave more freely, because, as his means were now impoverished and his creditors were pressing him, he distrusted the validity of his will. Certainly his table had always been profusely furnished, and his life luxurious, such as rigid censors would hardly approve. As to the bandages for wounds, none had been prepared at his order, but as all the man's other charges were absurd, he added an accusation in which he might make himself alike informer and witness.

56

HE backed up his words by an air of resolution. Turning on his accuser, he denounced him as an infamous and depraved wretch, with so fearless a voice and look that the information was beginning to collapse, when Milichus was reminded by his wife that Antonious Natalis had had a long secret conversation with Scaevinus, and that both were Piso's intimate friends. Natalis was therefore summoned, and they were separately asked what the conversation was, and what was its subject. Then a suspicion arose because their answers did not agree, and they were both put in irons. They could not endure the sight and the threat of torture. Natalis however, taking the initiative, knowing as he did more of the whole conspiracy, and being also more practiced in accusing, first confessed about Piso, next added the name of Annaeus Seneca, either as having been a messenger between him and Piso, or to win the favour of Nero, who hated Seneca and sought every means for his ruin. Then Scaevinus too, when he knew the disclosure of Natalis, with like pusillanimity, or under the impression that everything now divulged, and that there could be no advantage in silence, revealed the other conspirators. Of these, Lucanus, Quintianus, and Senecio long persisted in denial; after a time, when bribed by the promise of impunity, anxious to excuse their reluctance, Lucanus named his mother Atilla, Quintianus and Senecio, their chief friends, respectively, Glitius Gallus and Annius Pollio.

57

NERO, meanwhile, remembering that Epicharis was in custody on the information of Volusius Proculus, and assuming that a woman's frame must be unequal to the agony, ordered her to be torn on the rack. But neither the scourge nor fire, nor the fury of the men as they increased the torture that they might not be a woman's scorn, overcame her positive denial of the charge. Thus the first day's inquiry was futile. On the morrow, as she was being dragged back on a chair to the same torments (for with her limbs all dislocated she could not stand), she tied a band, which she had stripped off her bosom, in a sort of noose to the arched back of the chair, put her neck in it, and then straining with the whole weight of her body, wrung out of her frame its little remaining breath. All the nobler was the example set by a freedwoman at such a crisis in screening strangers and those whom she hardly knew, when freeborn men, Roman knights, and senators, yet unscathed by torture, betrayed, every one, his dearest kinsfolk. For even Lucanus and Senecio and Quintianus failed not to reveal their accomplices indiscriminately, and Nero was more and more alarmed, though he had fenced his person with a largely augmented guard.

58

EVEN Rome itself he put, so to say, under custody, garrisoning its walls with companies of soldiers and occupying with troops the coast and the river-banks. Incessantly were there flying through the public places, through private houses, country fields, and the neighbouring villages, horse and foot soldiers, mixed with Germans, whom the emperor trusted as being foreigners. In long succession, troops of prisoners in chains were dragged along and stood at the gates of his gardens. When they entered to plead their cause, a smile of joy on any of the conspirators, a casual conversation, a sudden meeting, or the fact of having entered a banquet or a public show in company, was construed into a crime, while to the savage questionings of Nero and Tigellinus were added the violent menaces of Faenius Rufus, who had not yet been named by the informers, but who, to get the credit of complete ignorance, frowned fiercely on his accomplices. When Subius Flavus at his side asked him by a sign whether he should draw his sword in the middle of the trial and perpetrate the fatal deed, Rufus refused, and checked the man's impulse as he was putting his hand to his sword-hilt.

59

SOME there were who, as soon as the conspiracy was betrayed, urged Piso, while Milichus' story was being heard, and Scaevinus was hesitating, to go to the camp or mount the Rostra and test the feelings of the soldiers and of the people. "If," said they, "your accomplices join your enterprise, those also who are yet undecided, will follow, and great will be the fame of the movement once started, and this in any new scheme is all-powerful. Against it Nero has taken no precaution. Even brave men are dismayed by sudden perils; far less will that stage-player, with Tigellinus forsooth and his concubines in his train, raise arms against you. Many things are accomplished on trial which cowards think arduous. It is vain to expect secrecy and fidelity from the varying tempers and bodily constitutions of such a host of accomplices. Torture or reward can overcome everything. Men will soon come to put you also in chains and inflict on you an ignominious death. How much more gloriously will you die while you cling to the State and invoke aid for liberty. Rather let the soldiers fail, the people be traitors, provided that you, if prematurely robbed of life, justify your death to your ancestors and descendants." Unmoved by these considerations, Piso showed himself a few moments in public, then sought the retirement of his house, and there fortified his spirit against the worst, till a troop of soldiers arrived, raw recruits, or men recently enlisted, whom Nero had selected, because he was afraid of the veterans, imbued, though they were, with a liking for him. Piso expired by having the veins in his arms severed. His will, full of loathsome flatteries of Nero, was a concession to his love of his wife, a base woman, with only a beautiful person to recommend her, whom he had taken away from her husband, one of his friends. Her name was Atria Galla; that of her former husband, Domitius Silus. The tame spirit of the man, the profligacy of the woman, blazoned Piso's infamy.

60

IN quick succession Nero added the murder of Plautius Lateranus, consul-elect, so promptly that he did not allow him to embrace his children or to have the brief choice of his own death. He was dragged off to a place set apart for the execution of slaves, and butchered by the hand of the tribune Statius, maintaining a resolute silence, and not reproaching the tribune with complicity in the plot. Then followed the destruction of Annaeus Seneca, a special joy to the emperor, not because he had convicted him of the conspiracy, but anxious to accomplish with the sword what poison had failed to do. It was, in fact, Natalis alone who divulged Seneca's name, to this extent, that he had been sent to Seneca when ailing, to see him and remonstrate with him for excluding Piso from his presence, when it would have been better to have kept up their friendship by familiar intercourse; that Seneca's reply was that mutual conversations and frequent interviews were to the advantage of neither, but still that his own life depended on Piso's safety. Gavius Silvanus, tribune of a praetorian cohort, was ordered to report this to Seneca and to ask him whether he acknowledged what Natalis said and his own answer. Either by chance or purposely Seneca had returned on that day from Campania, and had stopped at a country house four miles from Rome. Thither the tribune came next evening, surrounded the house with troops of soldiers, and then made known the emperor's message to Seneca as he was at dinner with his wife, Pompeia Paulina, and two friends.

61

SENECA replied that Natalis had been sent to him and had complained to him in Piso's name because of his refusal to see Piso, upon which he excused himself on the ground of failing health and the desire of rest. "He had no reason," he said, for "preferring the interest of any private citizen to his own safety, and he had no natural aptitude for flattery. No one knew this better than Nero, who had oftener experienced Seneca's outspokenness than his servility." When the tribune reported this answer in the presence of Poppaea and Tigellinus, the emperor's most confidential advisers in his moments of rage, he asked whether Seneca was meditating suicide. Upon this the tribune asserted that he saw no signs of fear, and perceived no sadness in his words or in his looks. He was accordingly ordered to go back and to announce sentence of death. Fabius Rusticus tells us that he did not return the way he came, but went out of his course to Faenius, the commander of the guard, and having explained to him the emperor's orders, and asked whether he was to obey them, was by him admonished to carry them out, for a fatal spell of cowardice was on them all. For this very Silvanus was one of the conspirators, and he was now abetting the crimes which he had united with them to avenge. But he spared himself the anguish of a word or of a look, and merely sent in to Seneca one of his centurions, who was to announce to him his last doom.

62

SENECA, quite unmoved, asked for tablets on which to inscribe his will, and, on the centurion's refusal, turned to his friends, protesting that as he was forbidden to requite them, he bequeathed to them the only, but still the noblest possession yet remaining to him, the pattern of his life, which, if they remembered, they would win a name for moral worth and steadfast friendship. At the same time he called them back from their tears to manly resolution, now with friendly talk, and now with the sterner language of rebuke. "Where," he asked again and again, "are your maxims of philosophy, or the preparation of so many years' study against evils to come? Who knew not Nero's cruelty? After a mother's and a brother's murder, nothing remains but to add the destruction of a guardian and a tutor."

63

HAVING spoken these and like words, meant, so to say, for all, he embraced his wife; then softening awhile from the stern resolution of the hour, he begged and implored her to spare herself the burden of perpetual sorrow, and, in the contemplation of a life virtuously spent, to endure a husband's loss with honourable consolations. She declared, in answer, that she too had decided to die, and claimed for herself the blow of the executioner. There upon Seneca, not to thwart her noble ambition, from an affection too which would not leave behind him for insult one whom he dearly loved, replied: "I have shown you ways of smoothing life; you prefer the glory of dying. I will not grudge you such a noble example. Let the fortitude of so courageous an end be alike in both of us, but let there be more in your decease to win fame." Then by one and the same stroke they sundered with a dagger the arteries of their arms. Seneca, as his aged frame, attenuated by frugal diet, allowed the blood to escape but slowly, severed also the veins of his legs and knees. Worn out by cruel anguish, afraid too that his sufferings might break his wife's spirit, and that, as he looked on her tortures, he might himself sink into irresolution, he persuaded her to retire into another chamber. Even at the last moment his eloquence failed him not; he summoned his secretaries, and dictated much to them which, as it has been published for all readers in his own words, I forbear to paraphrase.

64

NERO meanwhile, having no personal hatred against Paulina and not wishing to heighten the odium of his cruelty, forbade her death. At the soldiers' prompting, her slaves and freedmen bound up her arms, and stanched the bleeding, whether with her knowledge is doubtful. For as the vulgar are ever ready to think the worst, there were persons who believed that, as long as she dreaded Nero's relentlessness, she sought the glory of sharing her husband's death, but that after a time, when a more soothing prospect presented itself, she yielded to the charms of life. To this she added a few subsequent years, with a most praise worthy remembrance of her husband, and with a countenance and frame white to a degree of pallor which denoted a loss of much vital energy. Seneca meantime, as the tedious process of death still lingered on, begged Statius Annaeus, whom he had long esteemed for his faithful friendship and medical skill, to produce a poison with which he had some time before provided himself, same drug which extinguished the life of those who were condemned by a public sentence of the people of Athens. It was brought to him and he drank it in vain, chilled as he was throughout his limbs, and his frame closed against the efficacy of the poison. At last he entered a pool of heated water, from which he sprinkled the nearest of his slaves, adding the exclamation, "I offer this liquid as a libation to Jupiter the Deliverer." He was then carried into a bath, with the steam of which he was suffocated, and he was burnt without any of the usual funeral rites. So he had directed in a codicil of his will, when even in the height of his wealth and power he was thinking of his life's close.

65

THERE was a rumour that Sabrius Flavus had held a secret consultation with the centurions, and had planned, not without Seneca's knowledge, that when Nero had been slain by Piso's instrumentality, Piso also was to be murdered, and the empire handed over to Seneca, as a man singled out for his splendid virtues by all persons of integrity. Even a saying of Flavus was popularly current, "that it mattered not as to the disgrace if a harp-player were removed and a tragic actor succeeded him." For as Nero used to sing to the harp, so did Piso in the dress of a tragedian.

66

THE soldiers' part too in the conspiracy no longer escaped discovery, some in their rage becoming informers to betray Faenius Rufus, whom they could not endure to be both an accomplice and a judge. Accordingly Scaevinus, in answer to his browbeating and menaces, said with a smile that no one knew more than he did, and actually urged him to show gratitude to so good a prince. Faenius could not meet this with either speech or silence. Halting in his words and visibly terror-stricken, while the rest, especially Cervarius Proculus, a Roman knight, did their utmost to convict him, he was, at the emperor's bidding, seized and bound by Cassius, a soldier, who because of his well-known strength of limb was in attendance.

67

SHORTLY afterwards, the information of the same men proved fatal to Subrius Flavus. At first he grounded his defense on his moral contrast to the others, implying that an armed soldier, like himself, would never have shared such an attempt with unarmed and effeminate associates. Then, when he was pressed, he embraced the glory of a full confession. Questioned by Nero as to the motives which had led him on to forget his oath of allegiance, "I hated you," he replied; "yet not a soldier was more loyal to you while you deserved to be loved. I began to hate you when you became the murderer of your mother and your wife, a charioteer, an actor, and an incendiary." I have given the man's very words, because they were not, like those of Seneca, generally published, though the rough and vigorous sentiments of a soldier ought to be no less known. Throughout the conspiracy nothing, it was certain, fell with more terror on the ears of Nero, who was as unused to be told of the crimes he perpetrated as he was eager in their perpetration. The punishment of Flavus was entrusted to Veianius Niger, a tribune. At his direction, a pit was dug in a neighbouring field. Flavus, on seeing it, censured it as too shallow and confined, saying to the soldiers around him, "Even this is not according to military rule." When bidden to offer his neck resolutely, "I wish," said he, "that your stroke may be as resolute." The tribune trembled greatly, and having only just severed his head at two blows, vaunted his brutality to Nero, saying that he had slain him with a blow and a half.

68

SULPICIUS Asper, a centurion, exhibited the next example of

fortitude. To Nero's question why he had conspired to murder him, he briefly replied that he could not have rendered a better service to his infamous career. He then underwent the prescribed penalty. Nor did the remaining centurions forget their courage in suffering their punishment. But Faenius Rufus had not equal spirit; he even put his laments into his will. Nero waited in the hope that Vestinus also, the consul, whom he thought an impetuous and deeply disaffected man, would be involved in the charge. None however of the conspirators had shared their counsels with him, some from old feuds against him, most because they considered him a reckless and dangerous associate. Nero's hatred of him had had its origin in intimate companionship, Vestinus seeing through and despising the emperor's cowardice, while Nero feared the high spirit of his friend, who often bantered him with that rough humour which, when it draws largely on facts, leaves a bitter memory behind it. There was too a recent aggravation in the circumstance of Vestinus having married Statilia Messalina, without being ignorant that the emperor was one of her paramours.

69

AS neither crime nor accuser appeared, Nero, being thus unable to assume the semblance of a judge, had recourse to the sheer might of despotism, and despatched Gerellanus, a tribune, with a cohort of soldiers, and with orders to forestall the designs of the consul, to seize what he might call his fortress, and crush his train of chosen youths. For Vestinus had a house towering over the Forum, and a host of handsome slaves of the same age. On that day he had performed all his duties as consul, and was entertaining some guests, fearless of danger, or perhaps by way of hiding his fears, when the soldiers entered and announced to him the tribune's summons. He rose without a moment's delay, and every preparation was at once made. He shut himself into his chamber; a physician was at his side; his veins were opened; with life still strong in him, he was carried into a bath, and plunged into warm water, without uttering a word of pity for himself. Meanwhile the guards surrounded those who had sat at his table, and it was only at a late hour of the night that they were dismissed, when Nero, having pictured to himself and laughed over their terror at the expectation of a fatal end to their banquet, said that they had suffered enough punishment for the consul's entertainment.

70

NEXT he ordered the destruction of Marcus Annaeus Lucanus. As the blood flowed freely from him, and he felt a chill creeping through his feet and hands, and the life gradually ebbing from his extremities, though the heart was still warm and he retained his mental power, Lucanus recalled some poetry he had composed in which he had told the story of a wounded soldier dying a similar kind of death, and he recited the very lines. These were his last words. After him, Senecio, Quintianus, and Scaevinus perished, not in the manner expected from the past effeminacy of their life, and then the remaining conspirators, without deed or word deserving record.

71

ROME all this time was thronged with funerals, the Capitol with sacrificial victims. One after another, on the destruction of a brother, a kinsman, or a friend, would return thanks to the gods, deck his house with laurels, prostrate himself at the knees of the emperor, and weary his hand with kisses. He, in the belief that this was rejoicing, rewarded with impunity the prompt informations of Antonius Natalis and Cervarius Proculus. Milichus was enriched with gifts and assumed in its Greek equivalent the name of Saviour. Of the tribunes, Gavius Silvanus, though acquitted, perished by his own hand; Statius Proximus threw away the benefit of the pardon he had accepted from the emperor by the folly of his end. Cornelius Martialis, Flavius Nepos, Statius Domitius were then deprived of the tribuneship, on the ground, not of actually hating the emperor, but of having the credit of it. Novius Priscus, as Seneca's friend, Glitius Gallus, and Annius Pollio, as men disgraced rather than convicted, escaped with sentences of banishment. Priscus and Gallus were accompanied respectively by their wives, Artoria Flaccilla and Egnatia Maximilla. The latter possessed at first a great fortune, still unimpaired, and was subsequently deprived of it, both which circumstances enhanced her fame. Rufius Crispinus too was banished, on the opportune pretext of the conspiracy, but he was in fact hated by Nero, because he had once been Poppaea's husband. It was the splendour of their name which drove Verginius Flavus and Musonius Rufus into exile. Verginius encouraged the studies of our youth by his eloquence; Rufus by the teachings of philosophy. Cluvidienus Quietus, Julius Agrippa, Blitius Catulinus, Petronius Priscus, Julius Altinus, mere rank and file, so to say, had islands in the Aegean Sea assigned to them. Caedicia, the wife of Scaevinus, and Caesonius Maximus were forbidden to live in Italy, their penalty being the only proof they had of having been accused. Atilla, the mother of Annaeus Lucanus, without either acquittal or punishment, was simply ignored.

72

ALL this having been completed, Nero assembled the troops and distributed two thousand sesterces to every common soldier, with an addition of as much corn without payment, as they had previously the use of at the market price. Then, as if he was going to describe successes in war, he summoned the Senate, and awarded triumphal honours to Petronius Turpilianus, an ex-consul, to Cocceius Nerva, praetor-elect, and to Tigellinus, commander of the praetorians. Tigellinus and Nerva he so distinguished as to place busts of them in the palace in addition to triumphal statues in the Forum. He granted a consul's decorations to Nymphidius, on whose origin, as he now appears for the first time, I will briefly touch. For he too will be a part of Rome's calamities. The son of a freed-woman, who had prostituted a handsome person among the slaves and freedmen of the emperors, he gave out that he was the offspring of Caius Caesar, for he happened to be of tall stature and to have a fierce look, or possibly Caius Caesar, who liked even harlots, had also amused himself with the man's mother.

73

NERO meanwhile summoned the Senate, addressed them in a speech, and further added a proclamation to the people, with the evidence which had been entered on records, and the confessions of the condemned. He was indeed perpetually under the lash of popular talk, which said that he had destroyed men perfectly innocent out of jealousy or fear. However, that a conspiracy was begun, matured, and conclusively proved was not doubted at the time by those who took pains to ascertain the truth, and is admitted by those who after Nero's death returned to the capital. When every one in the Senate, those especially who had most cause to mourn, abased himself in flattery, Salienus Clemens denounced Junius Gallio, who was terror-stricken at his brother Seneca's death was pleading for his life. He called him an enemy and traitor to the State, till the unanimous voice of the senators deterred him from perverting public miseries into an occasion for a personal resentment, and thus importing fresh bitterness into what by the prince's clemency had been hushed up or forgotten.

74

THEN offerings and thanksgivings to the gods were decreed, with special honours to the Sun, who has an ancient temple in the circus where the crime was planned, as having revealed by his power the secrets of the conspiracy. The games too of Ceres in the circus were to be celebrated with more horse-races, and the month of April was to be called after the name of Nero. A temple also was to be erected to Safety, on the spot whence Scaevinus had taken his dagger. The emperor himself dedicated the weapon in the temple of the capital, and inscribed on it, "To Jupiter the Avenger." This passed without notice at the moment, but after the war of Julius Vindex it was construed as an omen and presage of impending vengeance. I find in the registers of the Senate that Cerialis Anicius, consul-elect, proposed a motion that a temple should as soon as possible be built at the public expense to the Divine Nero. He implied indeed by this proposal that the prince had transcended all mortal grandeur and deserved the adoration of mankind. Some however interpreted it as an omen of his death, seeing that divine honours are not paid to an emperor till he has ceased to live among men.

Lives

Plutarch

Translated by John Dryden

Life of Demosthenes

WHOEVER it was, Sosius, that wrote the poem in honor of Alcibiades, upon his winning the chariot race at the Olympian Games, whether it were Euripides, as is most commonly thought, or some other person, he tells us, that to a man's being happy it is in the first place requisite he should be born in "some famous city." But for him that would attain to true happiness, which for the most part is placed in the qualities and disposition of the mind, it is, in my opinion, of no other disadvantage to be of a mean, obscure country, than to be born of a small or plain-looking woman. For it were ridiculous to think that Iulis, a little part of Ceos, which itself is no great island, and Aegina, which an Athenian once said ought to be removed, like a small eye-sore, from the port of Piraeus, should breed good actors and poets, and yet should never be able to produce a just, temperate, wise, and high-minded man. Other arts, whose end it is to acquire riches or honor, are likely enough to wither and decay in poor and undistinguished towns; but virtue, like a strong and durable plant, may take root and thrive in any place where it can lay hold of an ingenuous nature, and a mind that is industrious. I, for my part, shall desire that for any deficiency of mine in right judgment or action, I myself may be, as in fairness, held accountable, and shall not attribute it to the obscurity of my birthplace.

But if any man undertake to write a history, that has to be collected from materials gathered by observation and the reading of works not easy to be got in all places, nor written always in his own language, but many of them foreign and dispersed in other hands, for him, undoubtedly, it is in the first place and above all things most necessary, to reside in some city of good note, addicted to liberal arts, and populous; where he may have plenty of all sorts of books, and upon inquiry may hear and inform himself of such particulars as, having escaped the pens of writers, are more faithfully preserved in the memories of men, lest his work be deficient in many things, even those which it can least dispense with.

But for me, I live in a little town, where I am willing to continue, lest it should grow less; and having had no leisure, while I was in Rome and other parts of Italy, to exercise myself in the Roman language, on account of public business and of those who came to be instructed by me in philosophy, it was very late, and in the decline of my age, before I applied myself to the reading of Latin authors. Upon which that which happened to me, may seem strange, though it be true; for it was not so much by the knowledge of words, that I came to the understanding of things, as by my experience of things I was enabled to follow the meaning of words. But to appreciate the graceful and ready pronunciation of the Roman tongue, to understand the various figures and connection of words, and such other ornaments, in which the beauty of speaking consists, is, I doubt not, an admirable and delightful accomplishment; but it requires a degree of practice and study, which is not easy, and will better suit those who have more leisure, and time enough yet before them for the occupation.

And so in this fifth book of my Parallel Lives, in giving an account of Demosthenes and Cicero, my comparison of their natural dispositions and their characters will be formed upon their actions and their lives as statesmen, and I shall not pretend to criticize their orations one against the other, to show which of the two was the more charming or the more powerful speaker. For there, as Ion says, "We are but like a fish upon dry land"—a proverb which Caecilius perhaps forgot, when he employed his always adventurous talents in so ambitious an attempt as a comparison of Demosthenes and Cicero: and, possibly, if it were a thing obvious and easy for every man to know himself, the precept had not passed for an oracle.

The divine power seems originally to have designed Demosthenes and Cicero upon the same plan, giving them many similarities in their natural characters, as their passion for distinction and their love of liberty in civil life, and their want of courage in dangers and war, and at the same time also to have added many accidental resemblances. I think there can hardly be found two other orators, who, from small and obscure beginnings, became so great and mighty; who both contested with kings and tyrants; both lost their daughters, were driven out of their country, and returned with honor; who, flying from thence again, were both seized upon by their enemies, and at last ended their lives with the liberty of their countrymen. So that if we were to suppose there had been a trial of skill between nature and fortune, as there is sometimes between artists, it would be hard to judge, whether that succeeded best in making them alike in their dispositions and manners, or this, in the coincidences of their lives. We will speak of the eldest first.

Demosthenes, the father of Demosthenes, was a citizen of good rank and quality, as Theopompus informs us, surnamed the Swordmaker, because he had a large workhouse, and kept servants skillful in that art at work. But of that which Aeschines, the orator, said of his mother, that she was descended of one Gylon, who fled his country upon an accusation of treason, and of a barbarian woman, I can affirm nothing, whether he spoke true, or slandered and maligned her. This is certain, that Demosthenes, being as yet but seven years old, was left by his father in affluent circumstances, the whole value of his estate being little short of fifteen talents, and that he was wronged by his guardians, part of his fortune being embezzled by them, and the rest neglected; insomuch that even his teachers were defrauded of their salaries. This was the reason that he did not obtain the liberal education that he should have had; besides that on account of weakness and delicate health, his mother would not let him exert himself, and his teachers forbore to urge him. He was meager and sickly from the first, and hence had his nickname of Batalus, given him, it is said, by the boys, in derision of his appearance; Batalus being, as some tell us, a certain enervated flute-player, in ridicule of whom Antiphanes wrote a play. Others speak of Batalus as a writer of wanton verses and drinking songs. And it would seem that some part of the body, not decent to be named, was at that time called "batalus" by the Athenians. But the name of Argas, which also they say was a nickname of Demosthenes, was given him for his behavior, as being savage and spiteful, "argas" being one of the poetical words for a snake; or for his disagreeable way of speaking, Argas being the name of a poet, who composed very harshly and disagreeably. So much, as Plato says, for such matters.

The first occasion of his eager inclination to oratory they say, was this. Callistratus, the orator, being to plead in open court for Oropus, the expectation of the issue of that cause was very great, as well for the ability of the orator, who was then at the height of his reputation, as also for the fame of the action itself. Therefore, Demosthenes, having heard the tutors and schoolmasters agreeing among themselves to be present at this trial, with much importunity persuades his tutor to take him along with him to the hearing; who, having some acquaintance with the doorkeepers, procured a place where the boy might sit unseen, and hear what was said. Callistratus having got the day, and being much admired, the boy began to look upon his glory with a kind of emulation, observing how he was courted on all hands, and attended on his way by the multitude; but his wonder was more than all excited by the power of his eloquence, which seemed able to subdue and win over anything. From this time, therefore, bidding farewell to other sorts of learning and study, he now began to exercise himself, and to take pains in declaiming, as one that meant to be himself also an orator. He made use of Isaeus as his guide to the art of speaking, though Isocrates at that time was giving lessons;

whether, as some say, because he was an orphan, and was not able to pay Isocrates his appointed fee of ten minae, or because he preferred Isaeus's speaking, as being more business-like and effective in actual use. Hermippus says, that he met with certain memoirs without any author's name, in which it was written that Demosthenes was a scholar to Plato, and learnt much of his eloquence from him; and he also mentions Ctesibius, as reporting from Callias of Syracuse and some others, that Demosthenes secretly obtained a knowledge of the systems of Isocrates and Alcidamas, and mastered them thoroughly.

As soon, therefore, as he was grown up to man's estate, he began to go to law with his guardians, and to write orations against them; who, in the meantime, had recourse to various subterfuges and pleas for new trials, and Demosthenes, though he was thus, as Thucydides says, taught his business in dangers, and by his own exertions was successful in his suit, was yet unable for all this to recover so much as a small fraction of his patrimony. He only attained some degree of confidence in speaking, and some competent experience in it. And having got a taste of the honor and power which are acquired by pleadings, he now ventured to come forth, and to undertake public business. And, as it is said of Laomedon, the Orchomenian, that by advice of his physician, he used to run long distances to keep off some disease of his spleen, and by that means having, through labor and exercise, framed the habit of his body, he betook himself to the great garland games, and became one of the best runners at the long race; so it happened to Demosthenes, who, first venturing upon oratory for the recovery of his own private property, by this acquired ability in speaking, and at length, in public business, as it were in the great games, came to have the preeminence of all competitors in the assembly. But when he first addressed himself to the people, he met with great discouragements, and was derided for his strange and uncouth style, which was cumbered with long sentences and tortured with formal arguments to a most harsh and disagreeable excess. Besides, he had, it seems, a weakness in his voice, a perplexed and indistinct utterance and a shortness of breath, which, by breaking and disjointing his sentences much obscured the sense and meaning of what he spoke. So that in the end, being quite disheartened, he forsook the assembly; and as he was walking carelessly and sauntering about the Piraeus, Eunomus, the Thriasian, then a very old man, seeing him, upbraided him, saying that his diction was very much like that of Pericles, and that he was wanting to himself through cowardice and meanness of spirit, neither bearing up with courage against popular outcry, nor fitting his body for action, but suffering it to languish through mere sloth and negligence.

Another time, when the assembly had refused to hear him, and he was going home with his head muffled up, taking it very heavily, they relate that Satyrus, the actor, followed him, and being his familiar acquaintance, entered into conversation with him. To whom, when Demosthenes bemoaned himself, that having been the most industrious of all the pleaders, and having almost spent the whole strength and vigor of his body in that employment, he could not yet find any acceptance with the people, that drunken sots, mariners, and illiterate fellows were heard, and had the hustings for their own, while he himself was despised, "You say true, Demosthenes," replied Satyrus, "but I will quickly remedy the cause of all this, if you will repeat to me some passage out of Euripides or Sophocles." Which when Demosthenes had pronounced, Satyrus presently taking it up after him gave the same passage, in his rendering of it, such a new form, by accompanying it with the proper mien and gesture, that to Demosthenes it seemed quite another thing. By this being convinced how much grace and ornament language acquires from action, he began to esteem it a small matter, and as good as nothing for a man to exercise himself in declaiming, if he neglected enunciation and delivery. Hereupon he built himself a place to study in underground, (which was still remaining in our time,) and hither he would come constantly every day to form his action, and to exercise his voice; and here he would continue, oftentimes without intermission, two or three months together, shaving one half of his head, that so for shame he might not go abroad, though he desired it ever so much.

Nor was this all, but he also made his conversation with people abroad, his common speech, and his business, subservient to his studies, taking from hence occasions and arguments as matter to work upon. For as soon as he was parted from his company, down he would go at once into his study, and run over everything in order that had passed, and the reasons that might be alleged for and against it. Any speeches, also, that he was present at, he would go over again with himself, and reduce into periods; and whatever others spoke to him, or he to them, he would correct, transform, and vary several ways. Hence it was, that he was looked upon as a person of no great natural genius, but one who owed all the power and ability he had in speaking to labor and industry. Of the truth of which it was thought to be no small sign, that he was very rarely heard to speak upon the occasion, but though he were by name frequently called upon by the people, as he sat in the assembly, yet he would not rise unless he had previously considered the subject, and came prepared for it. So that many of the popular pleaders used to make it a jest against him; and Pytheas once, scoffing at him, said that his arguments smelt of the lamp. To which Demosthenes gave the sharp answer, "It is true, indeed, Pytheas, that your lamp and mine are not conscious of the same things." To others, however, he would not much deny it, but would admit frankly enough, that he neither entirely wrote his speeches beforehand, nor yet spoke wholly extempore. And he would affirm, that it was the more truly popular act to use premeditation, such preparation being a kind of respect to the people; whereas, to slight and take no care how what is said is likely to be received by the audience, shows something of an oligarchical temper, and is the course of one that intends force rather than persuasion. Of his want of courage and assurance to speak off-hand, they make it also another argument, that when he was at a loss, and discomposed, Demades would often rise up on the sudden to support him, but he was never observed to do the same for Demades.

Whence then, may some say, was it, that Aeschines speaks of him as a person so much to be wondered at for his boldness in speaking? Or, how could it be, when Python, the Byzantine, "with so much confidence and such a torrent of words inveighed against" the Athenians, that Demosthenes alone stood up to oppose him? Or, when Lamachus, the Myrinaean, had written a panegyric upon king Philip and Alexander, in which he uttered many things in reproach of the Thebans and Olynthians, and at the Olympic Games recited it publicly, how was it, that he, rising up, and recounting historically and demonstratively what benefits and advantages all Greece had received from the Thebans and Chalcidians, and on the contrary, what mischiefs the flatterers of the Macedonians had brought upon it, so turned the minds of all that were present that the sophist, in alarm at the outcry against him, secretly made his way out of the assembly? But Demosthenes, it should seem, regarded other points in the character of Pericles to be unsuited to him; but his reserve and his sustained manner, and his forbearing to speak on the sudden, or upon every occasion, as being the things to which principally he owed his greatness, these he followed, and endeavored to imitate, neither wholly neglecting the glory which present occasion offered, nor yet willing too often to expose his faculty to the mercy of chance. For, in fact, the orations which were spoken by him had much more of boldness and confidence in them than those that he wrote, if we may believe Eratosthenes, Demetrius the Phalerian, and the Comedians. Eratosthenes says that often in his speaking he would be transported into a kind of ecstasy, and Demetrius, that he uttered the famous metrical adjuration to the people,

> By the earth, the springs, the rivers, and the streams,

as a man inspired, and beside himself. One of the comedians calls him a rhopoperperethras, and another scoffs at him for his use of antithesis:

> And what he took, took back; a phrase to please
> The very fancy of Demosthenes.

Unless, indeed, this also is meant by Antiphanes for a jest upon the speech on Halonesus, which Demosthenes advised the Athenians not to take at Philip's hands, but to take back.

All, however, used to consider Demades, in the mere use of his natural gifts, an orator impossible to surpass, and that in what he spoke on the sudden, he excelled all the study and preparation of Demosthenes. And Ariston the Chian, has recorded a judgment which Theophrastus passed upon the orators; for being asked what kind of orator he accounted Demosthenes, he answered, "Worthy of the city of Athens;" and then, what he thought of Demades, he answered, "Above it." And the same philosopher reports, that Polyeuctus, the Sphettian, one of the Athenian politicians about that time, was wont to say that Demosthenes was the greatest orator, but Phocion the ablest, as he expressed the most sense in the fewest words. And, indeed, it is related, that Demosthenes himself, as often as Phocion stood up to plead against him, would say to his acquaintance, "Here comes the knife to my speech." Yet it does not appear whether he had this feeling for his powers of speaking, or for his life and character, and meant to say that one word or nod from a man who was really trusted, would go further than a thousand lengthy periods from others.

Demetrius, the Phalerian, tells us, that he was informed by Demosthenes himself, now grown old, that the ways he made use of to remedy his natural bodily infirmities and defects were such as these; his inarticulate and stammering pronunciation he overcame and rendered more distinct by speaking with pebbles in his mouth; his voice he disciplined by declaiming and reciting speeches or verses when he was out of breath, while running or going up steep places; and that in his house he had a large looking-glass, before which he would stand and go through his exercises. It is told that someone once came to request his assistance as a pleader, and related how he had been assaulted and beaten. "Certainly," said Demosthenes, "nothing of the kind can have happened to you." Upon which the other, raising his voice, exclaimed loudly, "What, Demosthenes, nothing has been done to me?" "Ah," replied Demosthenes, "now I hear the voice of one that has been injured and beaten." Of so great consequence towards the gaining of belief did he esteem the tone and action of the speaker. The action which he used himself was wonderfully pleasing to the common people; but by well-educated people, as, for example, by Demetrius, the Phalerian, it was looked upon as mean, humiliating, and unmanly. And Hermippus says of Aesion, that, being asked his opinion concerning the ancient orators and those of his own time, he answered that it was admirable to see with what composure and in what high style they addressed themselves to the people; but that the orations of Demosthenes, when they are read, certainly appear to be superior in point of construction, and more effective. His written speeches, beyond all question, are characterized by austere tone and by their severity. In his extempore retorts and rejoinders, he allowed himself the use of jest and mockery. When Demades said, "Demosthenes teach me! So might the sow teach Minerva!" he replied, "Was it this Minerva, that was lately found playing the harlot in Collytus?" When a thief, who had the nickname of the Brazen, was attempting to upbraid him for sitting up late, and writing by candlelight, "I know very well," said he, "that you had rather have all lights out; and wonder not, O ye men of Athens, at the many robberies which are committed, since we have thieves of brass and walls of clay." But on these points, though we have much more to mention, we will add nothing at present. We will proceed to take an estimate of his character from his actions and his life as a statesman.

His first entering into public business was much about the time of the Phocian war, as himself affirms, and may be collected from his Philippic orations. For of these, some were made after that action was over, and the earliest of them refer to its concluding events. It is certain that he engaged in the accusation of Midias when he was but two and thirty years old, having as yet no interest or reputation as a politician. And this it was, I consider, that induced him to withdraw the action, and accept a sum of money as a compromise. For of himself

> He was no easy or good-natured man,

but of a determined disposition, and resolute to see himself righted; however, finding it a hard matter and above his strength to deal with Midias, a man so well secured on all sides with money, eloquence, and friends, he yielded to the entreaties of those who interceded for him. But had he seen any hopes or possibility of prevailing, I cannot believe that three thousand drachmas could have taken off the edge of his revenge. The object which he chose for himself in the commonwealth was noble and just, the defense of the Grecians against Philip; and in this he behaved himself so worthily that he soon grew famous, and excited attention everywhere for his eloquence and courage in speaking. He was admired through all Greece, the king of Persia courted him, and by Philip himself he was more esteemed than all the other orators. His very enemies were forced to confess that they had to do with a man of mark; for such a character even Aeschines and Hyperides give him, where they accuse and speak against him.

So that I cannot imagine what ground Theopompus had to say, that Demosthenes was of a fickle, unsettled disposition, and could not long continue firm either to the same men or the same affairs; whereas the contrary is most apparent, for the same party and post in politics which he held from the beginning, to these he kept constant to the end; and was so far from leaving them while he lived, that he chose rather to forsake his life than his purpose. He was never heard to apologize for shifting sides like Demades, who would say, he often spoke against himself, but never against the city; nor as Melanopus, who, being generally against Callistratus, but being often bribed off with money, was wont to tell the people, "The man indeed is my enemy, but we must submit for the good of our country;" nor again as Nicodemus, the Messenian, who having first appeared on Cassander's side, and afterwards taken part with Demetrius, said the two things were not in themselves contrary, it being always most advisable to obey the conqueror. We have nothing of this kind to say against Demosthenes, as one who would turn aside or prevaricate, either in word or deed. There could not have been less variation in his public acts if they had all been played, so to say, from first to last, from the same score. Panaetius, the philosopher, said, that most of his orations are so written, as if they were to prove this one conclusion, that what is honest and virtuous is for itself only to be chosen; as that of the Crown, that against Aristocrates, that for the Immunities, and the Philippics; in all which he persuades his fellow citizens to pursue not that which seems most pleasant, easy, or profitable; but declares over and over again, that they ought in the first place to prefer that which is just and honorable, before their own safety and preservation. So that if he had kept his hands clean, if his courage for the wars had been answerable to the generosity of his principles, and the dignity of his orations, he might deservedly have his name placed, not in the number of such orators as Moerocles, Polyeuctus, and Hyperides, but in the highest rank with Cimon, Thucydides, and Pericles.

Certainly amongst those who were contemporary with him, Phocion, though he appeared on the less commendable side in the commonwealth, and was counted as one of the Macedonian party, nevertheless, by his courage and his honesty, procured himself a name not inferior to those of Ephialtes, Aristides, and Cimon. But Demosthenes, being neither fit to be relied on for courage in arms, as Demetrius says, nor on all sides inaccessible to bribery (for how invincible soever he was against the gifts of Philip and the Macedonians, yet elsewhere he lay open to assault, and was overpowered by the gold which came down from Susa and Ecbatana), was therefore esteemed better able to recommend than to imitate the virtues of past times. And yet (excepting only Phocion), even in his life and manners, he far surpassed the other orators of his time. None of them addressed the people so boldly; he attacked the faults, and opposed himself to the unreasonable desires of the multitude, as may be seen in his orations. Theopompus writes, that the Athenians having by name selected Demosthenes, and called upon him to accuse a certain person, he refused to do it; upon which the assembly being all in an uproar, he rose up and said, "Your counselor, whether you will or no, O ye men of Athens, you shall always have me; but a sycophant or false accuser, though you would have me, I shall never be." And his conduct in the case of Antiphon was perfectly aristocratical; whom, after he had been acquitted in the assembly, he took and brought before the court of Areopagus, and, setting at naught the displeasure of the people, convicted him there of having promised Philip to burn the arsenal; whereupon the man was condemned by that court, and suffered for it. He accused, also, Theoris, the priestess, amongst other misdemeanors, of having instructed and taught the slaves to deceive and cheat their masters, for which the sentence of death passed upon her, and she was executed.

The oration which Apollodorus made use of, and by it carried the cause against Timotheus, the general, in an action of debt, it is said was written for him by Demosthenes; as also those against Phormion and Stephanus, in which latter case he was thought to have acted dishonorably, for the speech which Phormion used against Apollodorus was also of his making; he, as it were, having simply furnished two adversaries out of the same shop with weapons to wound one another. Of his orations addressed to the public assemblies, that against Androtion, and those against Timocrates and Aristocrates, were written for others, before he had come forward himself as a politician. They were composed, it seems, when he was but seven or eight and twenty years old. That against Aristogiton, and that for the Immunities, he spoke himself, at the request, as he says, of Ctesippus, the son of Chabrias, but, as some say, out of courtship to the young man's mother. Though, in fact, he did not marry her, for his wife was a woman of Samos, as Demetrius, the Magnesian, writes, in his book on Persons of the same Name. It is not certain whether his oration against Aeschines, for Misconduct as Ambassador, was ever spoken; although Idomeneus says that Aeschines wanted only thirty voices to condemn him. But this seems not to be correct, at least so far as may be conjectured from both their orations concerning the Crown; for in these, neither of them speaks clearly or directly of it, as a cause that ever came to trial. But let others decide this controversy.

It was evident, even in time of peace, what course Demosthenes would steer in the commonwealth; for whatever was done by the Macedonian, he criticized and found fault with, and upon all occasions was stirring up the people of Athens, and inflaming them against him. Therefore, in the court of Philip, no man was so much talked of, or of so great account as he; and when he came thither, one of the ten ambassadors who were sent into Macedonia, though all had audience given them, yet his speech was answered with most care and exactness. But in other respects, Philip entertained him not so honorably as the rest, neither did he show him the same kindness and civility with which he applied himself to the party of Aeschines and Philocrates. So that, when the others commended Philip for his able speaking, his beautiful person, nay, and also for his good companionship in drinking, Demosthenes could not refrain from caviling at these praises; the first, he said, was a quality which might well enough become a rhetorician, the second a woman, and the last was only the property of a sponge; no one of them was the proper commendation of a prince.

But when things came at last to war, Philip on the one side being not able to live in peace, and the Athenians, on the other side, being stirred up by Demosthenes, the first action he put them upon was the reducing of Euboea, which, by the treachery of the tyrants, was brought under subjection to Philip. And on his proposition, the decree was voted, and they crossed over thither and chased the Macedonians out of the island. The next, was the relief of the Byzantines and Perinthians, whom the Macedonians at that time were attacking. He persuaded the people to lay aside their enmity against these cities, to forget the offenses committed by them in the Confederate War, and to send them such succors as eventually saved and secured them. Not long after, he undertook an embassy through the States of Greece, which he solicited and so far incensed against Philip, that, a few only excepted, he brought them all into a general league. So that, besides the forces composed of the citizens themselves, there was an army consisting of fifteen thousand foot and two thousand horse, and the money to pay these strangers was levied and brought in with great cheerfulness. On which occasion it was, says Theophrastus, on the allies requesting that their contributions for the war might be ascertained and stated, Crobylus, the orator, made use of the saying, "War can't be fed at so much a day." Now was all Greece up in arms, and in great expectation what would be the event. The Euboeans, the Achaeans, the Corinthians, the Megarians, the Leucadians, and Corcyraeans, their people and their cities, were all joined together in a league. But the hardest task was yet behind, left for Demosthenes, to draw the Thebans into this confederacy with the rest. Their country bordered next upon Attica, they had great forces for the war, and at that time they were accounted the best soldiers of all Greece, but it was no easy matter to make them break with Philip, who, by many good offices, had so lately obliged them in the Phocian war; especially considering how the subjects of dispute and variance between the two cities were continually renewed and exasperated by petty quarrels, arising out of the proximity of their frontiers.

But after Philip, being now grown high and puffed up with his good success at Amphissa, on a sudden surprised Elatea and possessed himself of Phocis, and the Athenians were in a great consternation, none durst venture to rise up to speak, no one knew what to say, all were at a loss, and the whole assembly in silence and perplexity, in this extremity of affairs, Demosthenes was the only man who appeared, his counsel to them being alliance with the Thebans. And having in other ways encouraged the people, and, as his manner was, raised their spirits up with hopes, he, with some others, was sent ambassador to Thebes. To oppose him, as Marsyas says, Philip also sent thither his envoys, Amyntas and Clearellus, two Macedonians, besides Daochus, a Thessalian, and Thrasydaeus. Now the Thebans, in their consultations, were well enough aware what suited best with their own interest, but everyone had before his eyes the terrors of war, and their losses in the Phocian troubles were still recent: but such was the force and power of the orator, fanning up, as Theopompus says, their courage, and firing their emulation, that casting away every thought of prudence, fear, or obligation, in a sort of divine possession, they chose the path of honor, to which his words invited them. And this success, thus accomplished by an orator, was thought to be so glorious and of such consequence, that Philip immediately sent heralds to treat and petition for a peace: all Greece was aroused, and up in arms to help. And the commanders-in-chief, not only of Attica, but of Boeotia, applied themselves to Demosthenes, and observed his directions. He managed all the assemblies of the Thebans, no less than those of the Athenians; he was beloved both by the one and by the other, and exercised the same supreme authority with both; and that not by unfair means, or without just cause, as Theopompus professes, but indeed it was no more than was due to his merit.

But there was, it should seem, some divinely-ordered fortune, commissioned, in the revolution of things, to put a period at this time to the liberty of Greece, which opposed and thwarted all their actions, and by many signs foretold what should happen. Such were the sad predictions uttered by the Pythian priestess, and this old oracle cited out of the Sibyl's verses:

> The battle on Thermodon that shall be
> Safe at a distance I desire to see,
> Far, like an eagle, watching in the air.
> Conquered shall weep, and conqueror perish there.

This Thermodon, they say, is a little rivulet here in our country in Chaeronea, running into the Cephisus. But we know of none that is so called at the present time; and can only conjecture that the streamlet which is now called Haemon, and runs by the Temple of Hercules, where the Grecians were encamped, might perhaps in those days be called Thermodon, and after the fight, being filled with blood and dead bodies, upon this occasion, as we guess, might change its old name for that which it now bears. Yet Duris says that this Thermodon was no river, but that some of the soldiers, as they were pitching their tents and digging trenches about them, found a small stone statue, which, by the inscription, appeared to be the figure of Thermodon, carrying a wounded Amazon in his arms; and that there was another oracle current about it, as follows:

> The battle on Thermodon that shall be,
> Fail not, black raven, to attend and see;
> The flesh of men shall there abound for thee.

In fine, it is not easy to determine what is the truth. But of Demosthenes it is said, that he had such great confidence in the Grecian forces, and was so excited by the sight of the courage and resolution of so many brave men ready to engage the enemy, that he would by no means endure they should give any heed to oracles, or hearken to prophecies, but gave out that he suspected even the prophetess herself, as if she had been tampered with to speak in favor of Philip. The Thebans he put in mind of Epaminondas, the Athenians, of Pericles, who always took their own measures and governed their actions by reason, looking upon things of this kind as mere pretexts for cowardice. Thus far, therefore, Demosthenes acquitted himself like a brave man. But in the fight he did nothing honorable, nor was his performance answerable to his speeches. For he fled, deserting his place disgracefully, and throwing away his arms, not ashamed, as Pytheas observed, to belie the inscription written on his shield, in letters of gold, "With good fortune."

In the meantime Philip, in the first moment of victory, was so transported with joy, that he grew extravagant, and going out, after he had drunk largely, to visit the dead bodies, he chanted the first words of the decree that had been passed on the motion of Demosthenes,

> The motion of Demosthenes, Demosthenes's son,
> Dividing it metrically into feet, and marking the beats.

But when he came to himself, and had well considered the danger he was lately under, he could not forbear from shuddering at the wonderful ability and power of an orator who had made him hazard his life and empire on the issue of a few brief hours. The fame of it also reached even to the court of Persia, and the king sent letters to his lieutenants, commanding them to supply Demosthenes with money, and to pay every attention to him, as the only man of all the Grecians who was able to give Philip occupation and find employment for his forces near home, in the troubles of Greece. This afterwards came to the knowledge of Alexander, by certain letters of Demosthenes which he found at Sardis, and by other papers of the Persian officers, stating the large sums which had been given him.

At this time, however, upon the ill success which now happened to the Grecians, those of the contrary faction in the commonwealth fell foul upon Demosthenes, and took the opportunity to frame several informations and indictments against him. But the people not only acquitted him of these accusations, but continued towards him their former respect, and still invited him, as a man that meant well, to take a part in public affairs. Insomuch that when the bones of those who had been slain at Chaeronea were brought home to be solemnly interred, Demosthenes was the man they chose to make the funeral oration. They did not show, under the misfortunes which befell them, a base or ignoble mind, as Theopompus writes in his exaggerated style, but, on the contrary, by the honor and respect paid to their counselor, they made it appear that they were noway dissatisfied with the counsels he had given them. The speech, therefore, was spoken by Demosthenes. But the subsequent decrees he would not allow to be passed in his own name, but made use of those of his friends, one after another, looking upon his own as unfortunate and inauspicious; till at length he took courage again after the death of Philip, who did not long outlive his victory at Chaeronea. And this, it seems, was that which was foretold in the last verse of the oracle,

> Conquered shall weep, and conqueror perish there.

Demosthenes had secret intelligence of the death of Philip, and laying hold of this opportunity to prepossess the people with courage and better hopes for the future, he came into the assembly with a cheerful countenance, pretending to have had a dream that presaged some great good fortune for Athens; and, not long after, arrived the messengers who brought the news of Philip's death. No sooner had the people received it but immediately they offered sacrifice to the gods, and decreed that Pausanias should be presented with a crown. Demosthenes appeared publicly in a rich dress, with a chaplet on his head, though it were but the seventh day since the death of his daughter, as is said by Aeschines, who upbraids him upon this account, and rails at him as one void of natural affection towards his children. Whereas, indeed, he rather betrays himself to be of a poor, low spirit, and effeminate mind, if he really means to make wailings and lamentation the only signs of a gentle and affectionate nature, and to condemn those who bear such accidents with more temper and less passion. For my own part, I cannot say that the behavior of the Athenians on this occasion was wise or honorable, to crown themselves with garlands and to sacrifice to the Gods for the death of a Prince who, in the midst of his success and victories, when they were a conquered people, had used them with so much clemency and humanity. For besides provoking fortune, it was a base thing, and unworthy in itself, to make him a citizen of Athens, and pay him honors while he lived, and yet as soon as he fell by another's hand, to set no bounds to their jollity, to insult over him dead, and to sing triumphant songs of victory, as if by their own valor they had vanquished him. I must at the same time commend the behavior of Demosthenes, who, leaving tears and lamentations and domestic sorrows to the women, made it his business to attend to the interests of the commonwealth. And I think it the duty of him who would be accounted to have a soul truly valiant, and fit for government, that, standing always firm to the common good, and letting private griefs and troubles find their compensation in public blessings, he should maintain the dignity of his character and station, much more than actors who represent the persons of kings and tyrants, who, we see, when they either laugh or weep on the stage, follow, not their own private inclinations, but the course consistent with the subject and with their position. And if, moreover, when our neighbor is in misfortune, it is not our duty to forbear offering any consolation, but rather to say whatever may tend to cheer him, and to invite his attention to any agreeable objects, just as we tell people who are troubled with sore eyes, to withdraw their sight from bright and offensive colors to green, and those of a softer mixture, from whence can a man seek, in his own case, better arguments of consolation for afflictions in his family, than from the prosperity of his country, by making public and domestic chances count, so to say, together, and the better fortune of the state obscure and conceal the less happy circumstances of the individual. I have been induced to say so much, because I have known many readers melted by Aeschines's language into a soft and unmanly tenderness.

But now to return to my narrative. The cities of Greece were inspirited once more by the efforts of Demosthenes to form a league together. The Thebans, whom he had provided with arms, set upon their garrison, and slew many of them; the Athenians made preparations to join their forces with them; Demosthenes ruled supreme in the popular assembly, and wrote letters to the Persian officers who commanded under the king in Asia, inciting them to make war upon the Macedonian, calling him child and simpleton. But as soon as Alexander had settled matters in his own country, and came in person with his army into Boeotia, down fell the courage of the Athenians, and Demosthenes was hushed; the Thebans, deserted by them, fought by themselves, and lost their city. After which, the people of Athens, all in distress and great perplexity, resolved to send ambassadors to Alexander, and amongst others, made choice of Demosthenes for one; but his heart failing him for fear of the king's anger, he returned back from Cithaeron, and left the embassy. In the meantime, Alexander sent to Athens, requiring ten of their orators to be delivered up to him, as Idomeneus and Duris have reported, but as the most and best historians say, he demanded these eight only: Demosthenes, Polyeuctus, Ephialtes, Lycurgus, Moerocles, Demon, Callisthenes, and Charidemus. It was upon this occasion that Demosthenes related to them the fable in which the sheep are said to deliver up their dogs to the wolves; himself and those who with him contended for the people's safety, being, in his comparison, the dogs that defended the flock, and Alexander "the Macedonian arch wolf." He further told them, "As we see corn-masters sell their whole stock by a few grains of wheat which they carry about with them in a dish, as a sample of the rest, so you, by delivering up us, who are but a few, do at the same time unawares surrender up yourselves all together with us;" so we find it related in the history of Aristobulus, the Cassandrian. The Athenians were deliberating, and at a loss what to do, when Demades, having agreed with the persons whom Alexander had demanded, for five talents, undertook to go ambassador, and to intercede with the king for them; and, whether it was that he relied on his friendship and kindness, or that he hoped to find him satiated, as a lion glutted with slaughter, he certainly went, and prevailed with him both to pardon the men, and to be reconciled to the city.

So he and his friends, when Alexander went away, were great men, and Demosthenes was quite put aside. Yet when Agis, the Spartan, made his insurrection, he also for a short time attempted a movement in his favor; but he soon shrunk back again, as the Athenians would not take any part in it, and, Agis being slain, the Lacedaemonians were vanquished. During this time it was that the indictment against Ctesiphon, concerning the Crown, was brought to trial. The action was commenced a little before the battle in Chaeronea, when Chaerondas was archon, but it was not proceeded with till about ten years after, Aristophon being then archon. Never was any public cause more celebrated than this, alike for the fame of the orators, and for the generous courage of the judges, who, though at that time the accusers of Demosthenes were in the height of power, and supported by all the favor of the Macedonians, yet would not give judgment against him, but acquitted him so honorably, that Aeschines did not obtain the fifth part of their suffrages on his side, so that, immediately after, he left the city, and spent the rest of his life in teaching rhetoric about the island of Rhodes, and upon the continent in Ionia.

It was not long after that Harpalus fled from Alexander, and came to Athens out of Asia; knowing himself guilty of many misdeeds into which his love of luxury had led him, and fearing the king, who was now grown terrible even to his best friends. Yet this man had no sooner addressed himself to the people, and delivered up his goods, his ships, and himself to their disposal, but the other orators of the town had their eyes quickly fixed upon his money, and came in to his assistance, persuading the Athenians to receive and protect their suppliant. Demosthenes at first gave advice to chase him out of the country, and to beware lest they involved their city in a war upon an unnecessary and unjust occasion. But some few days after, as they were taking an account of the treasure, Harpalus, perceiving how much he was pleased with a cup of Persian manufacture, and how curiously he surveyed the sculpture and fashion of it, desired him to poise it in his hand, and consider the weight of the gold. Demosthenes, being amazed to feel how heavy it was, asked him what weight it came to. "To you," said Harpalus, smiling, "it shall come with twenty talents." And presently after, when night drew on, he sent him the cup with so many talents. Harpalus, it seems, was a person of singular skill to discern a man's covetousness by the air of his countenance, and the look and movements of his eyes. For Demosthenes could not resist the temptation, but admitting the present, like an armed garrison, into the citadel of his house, he surrendered himself up to the interest of Harpalus. The next day, he came into the assembly with his neck swathed about with wool and rollers, and when they called on him to rise up and speak, he made signs as if he had lost his voice. But the wits, turning the matter to ridicule, said that certainly the orator had been seized that night with no other than a silver quinsy. And soon after, the people, becoming aware of the bribery, grew angry, and would not suffer him to speak, or make any apology for himself, but ran him down with noise; and one man stood up, and cried out, "What, ye men of Athens, will you not hear the cup-bearer?" So at length they banished Harpalus out of the city; and fearing lest they should be called to account for the treasure which the orators had purloined, they made a strict inquiry, going from house to house; only Callicles, the son of Arrhenidas, who was newly married, they would not suffer to be searched, out of respect, as Theopompus writes, to the bride, who was within.

Demosthenes resisted the inquisition, and proposed a decree to refer the business to the court of Areopagus, and to punish those whom that court should find guilty. But being himself one of the first whom the court condemned, when he came to the bar, he was fined fifty talents, and committed to prison; where, out of shame of the crime for which he was condemned, and through the weakness of his body, growing incapable of supporting the confinement, he made his escape, by the carelessness of some and by the connivance of others of the citizens. We are told, at least, that he had not fled far from the city, when, finding that he was pursued by some of those who had been his adversaries, he endeavored to hide himself. But when they called him by his name, and coming up nearer to him, desired he would accept from them some money which they had brought from home as a provision for his journey, and to that purpose only had followed him, when they entreated him to take courage, and to bear up against his misfortune, he burst out into much greater lamentation, saying, "But how is it possible to support myself under so heavy an affliction, since I leave a city in which I have such enemies, as in any other it is not easy to find friends." He did not show much fortitude in his banishment, spending his time for the most part in Aegina and Troezen, and, with tears in his eyes, looking towards the country of Attica. And there remain upon record some sayings of his, little resembling those sentiments of generosity and bravery which he used to express when he had the management of the commonwealth. For, as he was departing out of the city, it is reported, he lifted up his hands towards the Acropolis, and said, "O Lady Minerva, how is it that thou takest delight in three such fierce untractable beast, the owl, the snake, and the people?" The young men that came to visit and converse with him, he deterred from meddling with state affairs, telling them, that if at first two ways had been proposed to him, the one leading to the speaker's stand and the assembly, the other going direct to destruction, and he could have foreseen the many evils which attend those who deal in public business, such as fears, envies, calumnies, and contentions, he would certainly have taken that which led straight on to his death.

But now happened the death of Alexander, while Demosthenes was in this banishment which we have been speaking of. And the Grecians were once again up in arms, encouraged by the brave attempts of Leosthenes, who was then drawing a circumvallation about Antipater, whom he held close besieged in Lamia. Pytheas, therefore, the orator, and Callimedon, called the Crab, fled from Athens, and taking sides with Antipater, went about with his friends and ambassadors to keep the Grecians from revolting and taking part with the Athenians. But, on the other side, Demosthenes, associating himself with the ambassadors that came from Athens, used his utmost endeavors and gave them his best assistance in persuading the cities to fall unanimously upon the Macedonians, and to drive them out of Greece. Phylarchus says that in Arcadia there happened an encounter between Pytheas and Demosthenes, which came at last to downright railing, while the one pleaded for the Macedonians, and the other for the Grecians. Pytheas said, that as we always suppose there is some disease in the family to which they bring asses' milk, so wherever there comes an embassy from Athens, that city must needs be indisposed. And Demosthenes answered him, retorting the comparison: "Asses' milk is brought to restore health, and the Athenians come for the safety and recovery of the sick." With this conduct the people of Athens were so well pleased, that they decreed the recall of Demosthenes from banishment. The decree was brought in by Demon the Paeanian, cousin to Demosthenes. So they sent him a ship to Aegina, and he landed at the port of Piraeus, where he was met and joyfully received by all the citizens, not so much as an Archon or a priest staying behind. And Demetrius, the Magnesian, says, that he lifted up his hands towards heaven, and blessed this day of his happy return, as far more honorable than that of Alcibiades; since he was recalled by his countrymen, not through any force or constraint put upon them, but by their own good-will and free inclinations. There remained only his pecuniary fine, which, according to law, could not be remitted by the people. But they found out a way to elude the law. It was a custom with them to allow a certain quantity of silver to those who were to furnish and adorn the altar for the sacrifice of Jupiter Soter. This office, for that turn, they bestowed on Demosthenes, and for the performance of it ordered him fifty talents, the very sum in which he was condemned.

Yet it was no long time that he enjoyed his country after his return, the attempts of the Greeks being soon all utterly defeated. For the battle at Cranon happened in Metagitnion, in Boedromion the garrison entered into Munychia, and in the Pyanepsion following died Demosthenes after this manner.

Upon the report that Antipater and Craterus were coming to Athens, Demosthenes with his party took their opportunity to escape privily out of the city; but sentence of death was, upon the motion of Demades, passed upon them by the people. They dispersed themselves, flying some to one place, some to another; and Antipater sent about his soldiers into all quarters to apprehend them. Archias was their captain, and was thence called the exile-hunter. He was a Thurian born, and is reported to have been an actor of tragedies, and they say that Polus, of Aegina, the best actor of his time, was his scholar; but Hermippus reckons Archias among the disciples of Lacritus, the orator, and Demetrius says, he spent some time with Anaximenes. This Archias finding Hyperides the orator, Aristonicus of Marathon, and Himeraeus, the brother of Demetrius the Phalerian, in Aegina, took them by force out of the temple of Aeacus, whither they were fled for safety, and sent them to Antipater, then at Cleonae, where they were all put to death; and Hyperides, they say, had his tongue cut out.

Demosthenes, he heard, had taken sanctuary at the temple of Neptune in Calauria, and, crossing over thither in some light vessels, as soon as he had landed himself, and the Thracian spear-men that came with him, he endeavored to persuade Demosthenes to accompany him to Antipater, as if he should meet with no hard usage from him. But Demosthenes, in his sleep the night before, had a strange dream. It seemed to him that he was acting a tragedy, and contended with Archias for the victory; and though he acquitted himself well, and gave good satisfaction to the spectators, yet for want of better furniture and provision for the stage, he lost the day. And so, while Archias was discoursing to him with many expressions of kindness, he sat still in the same posture, and looking up steadfastly upon him, "O Archias," said he, "I am as little affected by your promises now as I used formerly to be by your acting." Archias at this beginning to grow angry and to threaten him, "Now," said Demosthenes, "you speak like the genuine Macedonian oracle; before you were but acting a part. Therefore forbear only a little, while I write a word or two home to my family." Having thus spoken, he withdrew into the temple, and taking a scroll, as if he meant to write, he put the reed into his mouth, and biting it, as he was wont to do when he was thoughtful or writing, he held it there for some time. Then he bowed down his head and covered it. The soldiers that stood at the door, supposing all this to proceed from want of courage and fear of death, in derision called him effeminate, and faint-hearted, and coward. And Archias, drawing near, desired him to rise up, and repeating the same kind things he had spoken before, he once more promised him to make his peace with Antipater. But Demosthenes, perceiving that now the poison had pierced and seized his vitals, uncovered his head, and fixing his eyes upon Archias, "Now," said he, "as soon as you please you may commence the part of Creon in the tragedy, and cast out this body of mine unburied. But, O gracious Neptune, I, for my part, while I am yet alive, arise up and depart out of this sacred place; though Antipater and the Macedonians have not left so much as thy temple unpolluted." After he had thus spoken and desired to be held up, because already he began to tremble and stagger, as he was going forward, and passing by the altar, he fell down, and with a groan gave up the ghost.

Ariston says that he took the poison out of a reed, as we have shown before. But Pappus, a certain historian whose history was recovered by Hermippus, says, that as he fell near the altar, there was found in his scroll this beginning only of a letter, and nothing more, "Demosthenes to Antipater." And that when his sudden death was much wondered at, the Thracians who guarded the doors reported that he took the poison into his hand out of a rag, and put it in his mouth, and that they imagined it had been gold which he swallowed; but the maid that served him, being examined by the followers of Archias, affirmed that he had worn it in a bracelet for a long time, as an amulet. And Eratosthenes also says that he kept the poison in a hollow ring, and that that ring was the bracelet which he wore about his arm. There are various other statements made by the many authors who have related the story, but there is no need to enter into their discrepancies; yet I must not omit what is said by Demochares, the relation of Demosthenes, who is of opinion, it was not by the help of poison that he met with so sudden and so easy a death, but that by the singular favor and providence of the gods he was thus rescued from the cruelty of the Macedonians. He died on the sixteenth of Pyanepsion, the most sad and solemn day of the Thesmophoria, which the women observe by fasting in the temple of the goddess.

Soon after his death, the people of Athens bestowed on him such honors as he had deserved. They erected his statue of brass; they decreed that the eldest of his family should be maintained in the Prytaneum; and on the base of his statue was engraven the famous inscription:

> Had you for Greece been strong, as wise you were,
> The Macedonian had not conquered her.

For it is simply ridiculous to say, as some have related, that Demosthenes made these verses himself in Calauria, as he was about to take the poison.

A little before we went to Athens, the following incident was said to have happened. A soldier, being summoned to appear before his superior officer, and answer to an accusation brought against him, put that little gold which he had into the hands of Demosthenes's statue. The fingers of this statue were folded one within another, and near it grew a small plane-tree, from which many leaves, either accidentally blown thither by the wind, or placed so on purpose by the man himself falling together, and lying round about the gold, concealed it for a long time. In the end, the soldier returned, and found his treasure entire, and the fame of this incident was spread abroad. And many ingenious persons of the city competed with each other, on this occasion, to vindicate the integrity of Demosthenes, in several epigrams which they made on the subject.

As for Demades, he did not long enjoy the new honors he now came in for, divine vengeance for the death of Demosthenes pursuing him into Macedonia, where he was justly put to death by those whom he had basely flattered. They were weary of him before, but at this time the guilt he lay under was manifest and undeniable. For some of his letters were intercepted, in which he had encouraged Perdiccas to fall upon Macedonia, and to save the Grecians, who, he said, hung only by an old rotten thread, meaning Antipater. Of this he was accused by Dinarchus, the Corinthian, and Cassander was so enraged, that he first slew his son in his bosom, and then gave orders to execute him; who might-now at last, by his own extreme misfortunes, learn the lesson, that traitors, who make sale of their country, sell themselves first; a truth which Demosthenes had often foretold him, and he would never believe. Thus, Sosius, you have the life of Demosthenes, from such accounts as we have either read or heard concerning him.

Life of Cicero

IT is generally said, that Helvia, the mother of Cicero, was both well born and lived a fair life; but of his father nothing is reported but in extremes. For whilst some would have him the son of a fuller, and educated in that trade, others carry back the origin of his family to Tullus Attius, an illustrious king of the Volscians, who waged war not without honor against the Romans. However, he who first of that house was surnamed Cicero seems to have been a person worthy to be remembered; since those who succeeded him not only did not reject, but were fond of that name, though vulgarly made a matter of reproach. For the Latins call a vetch Cicer, and a nick or dent at the tip of his nose, which resembled the opening in a vetch, gave him the surname of Cicero.

Cicero, whose story I am writing, is said to have replied with spirit to some of his friends, who recommended him to lay aside or change the name when he first stood for office and engaged in politics, that he would make it his endeavor to render the name of Cicero more glorious than that of the Scauri and Catuli. And when he was quaestor in Sicily, and was making an offering of silver plate to the gods, and had inscribed his two names, Marcus and Tullius, instead of the third he jestingly told the artificer to engrave the figure of a vetch by them. Thus much is told us about his name.

Of his birth it is reported, that his mother was delivered without pain or labor, on the third of the new Calends, the same day on which now the magistrates of Rome pray and sacrifice for the emperor. It is said, also, that a vision appeared to his nurse, and foretold the child she then suckled should afterwards become a great benefit to the Roman States. To such presages, which might in general be thought mere fancies and idle talk, he himself erelong gave the credit of true prophecies. For as soon as he was of an age to begin to have lessons, he became so distinguished for his talent, and got such a name and reputation amongst the boys, that their fathers would often visit the school, that they might see young Cicero, and might be able to say that they themselves had witnessed the quickness and readiness in learning for which he was renowned. And the more rude among them used to be angry with their children, to see them, as they walked together, receiving Cicero with respect into the middle place. And being, as Plato would have, the scholar-like and philosophical temper, eager for every kind of learning, and indisposed to no description of knowledge or instruction, he showed, however, a more peculiar propensity to poetry; and there is a poem now extant, made by him when a boy, in tetrameter verse, called Pontius Glaucus. And afterwards, when he applied himself more curiously to these accomplishments, he had the name of being not only the best orator, but also the best poet of Rome. And the glory of his rhetoric still remains, notwithstanding the many new modes in speaking since his time; but his verses are forgotten and out of all repute, so many ingenious poets having followed him.

Leaving his juvenile studies, he became an auditor of Philo the Academic, whom the Romans, above all the other scholars of Clitomachus, admired for his eloquence and loved for his character. He also sought the company of the Mucii, who were eminent statesmen and leaders in the senate, and acquired from them a knowledge of the laws. For some short time he served in arms under Sylla, in the Marsian war. But perceiving the commonwealth running into factions, and from faction all things tending to an absolute monarchy, he betook himself to a retired and contemplative life, and conversing with the learned Greeks, devoted himself to study, till Sylla had obtained the government, and the commonwealth was in some kind of settlement.

At this time, Chrysogonus, Sylla's emancipated slave, having laid an information about an estate belonging to one who was said to have been put to death by proscription, had bought it himself for two thousand drachmas. And when Roscius, the son and heir of the dead, complained, and demonstrated the estate to be worth two hundred and fifty talents, Sylla took it angrily to have his actions questioned, and preferred a process against Roscius for the murder of his father, Chrysogonus managing the evidence. None of the advocates durst assist him, but fearing the cruelty of Sylla, avoided the cause. The young man, being thus deserted, came for refuge to Cicero. Cicero's friends encouraged him, saying he was not likely ever to have a fairer and more honorable introduction to public life; he therefore undertook the defense, carried the cause, and got much renown for it.

But fearing Sylla, he traveled into Greece, and gave it out that he did so for the benefit of his health. And indeed he was lean and meager, and had such a weakness in his stomach, that he could take nothing but a spare and thin diet, and that not till late in the evening. His voice was loud and good, but so harsh and unmanaged that in vehemence and heat of speaking he always raised it to so high a tone, that there seemed to be reason to fear about his health.

When he came to Athens, he was a hearer of Antiochus of Ascalon, with whose fluency and elegance of diction he was much taken, although he did not approve of his innovations in doctrine. For Antiochus had now fallen off from the New Academy, as they call it, and forsaken the sect of Carneades, whether that he was moved by the argument of manifestness and the senses, or, as some say, had been led by feelings of rivalry and opposition to the followers of Clitomachus and Philo to change his opinions, and in most things to embrace the doctrine of the Stoics. But Cicero rather affected and adhered to the doctrines of the New Academy; and purposed with himself, if he should be disappointed of any employment in the commonwealth, to retire hither from pleading and political affairs, and to pass his life with quiet in the study of philosophy.

But after he had received the news of Sylla's death, and his body, strengthened again by exercise, was come to a vigorous habit, his voice managed and rendered sweet and full to the ear and pretty well brought into keeping with his general constitution, his friends at Rome earnestly soliciting him by letters, and Antiochus also urging him to return to public affairs, he again prepared for use his orator's instrument of rhetoric, and summoned into action his political faculties, diligently exercising himself in declamations, and attending the most celebrated rhetoricians of the time. He sailed from Athens for Asia and Rhodes. Amongst the Asian masters, he conversed with Xenocles of Adramyttium, Dionysius of Magnesia, and Menippus of Caria; at Rhodes, he studied oratory with Apollonius, the son of Molon, and philosophy with Posidonius. Apollonius, we are told, not understanding Latin, requested Cicero to declaim in Greek. He complied willingly, thinking that his faults would thus be better pointed out to him. And after he finished, all his other hearers were astonished, and contended who should praise him most, but Apollonius, who had shown no signs of excitement whilst he was hearing him, so also now, when it was over, sat musing for some considerable time, without any remark. And when Cicero was discomposed at this, he said, "You have my praise and admiration, Cicero, and Greece my pity and commiseration, since those arts and that eloquence which are the only glories that remain to her, will now be transferred by you to Rome."

And now when Cicero, full of expectation, was again bent upon political affairs, a certain oracle blunted the edge of his inclination; for consulting the god of Delphi how he should attain most glory, the Pythoness answered, by making his own genius and not the opinion of the people the guide of his life; and therefore at first he passed his time in Rome cautiously, and was very backward in pretending to public offices, so that he was at that time in little esteem, and had got the names, so readily given by low and ignorant people in Rome, of Greek and Scholar. But when his own desire of fame and the eagerness of his father and relations had made him take in earnest to pleading, he made no slow or gentle advance to the first place, but shone out in full luster at once, and far surpassed all the advocates of the bar. At first, it is said, he, as well as Demosthenes, was defective in his delivery, and on that account paid much attention to the instructions, sometimes of Roscius the comedian, and sometimes of Aesop the tragedian. They tell of this Aesop, that whilst he was representing on the theater Atreus deliberating the revenge of Thyestes, he was so transported beyond himself in the heat of action, that he struck with his scepter one of the servants, who was running across the stage, so violently, that he laid him dead upon the place. And such afterwards was Cicero's delivery, that it did not a little contribute to render his eloquence persuasive. He used to ridicule loud speakers, saying that they shouted because they could not speak, like lame men who get on horseback because they cannot walk. And his readiness and address in sarcasm, and generally in witty sayings, was thought to suit a pleader very well, and to be highly attractive, but his using it to excess offended many, and gave him the repute of ill nature.

He was appointed quaestor in a great scarcity of corn, and had Sicily for his province, where, though at first he displeased many, by compelling them to send in their provisions to Rome, yet after they had had experience of his care, justice, and clemency, they honored him more than ever they did any of their governors before. It happened, also, that some young Romans of good and noble families, charged with neglect of discipline and misconduct in military service, were brought before the praetor in Sicily. Cicero undertook their defense, which he conducted admirably, and got them acquitted. So returning to Rome with a great opinion of himself for these things, a ludicrous incident befell him, as he tells us himself. Meeting an eminent citizen in Campania, whom he accounted his friend, he asked him what the Romans said and thought of his actions, as if the whole city had been filled with the glory of what he had done. His friend asked him in reply, "Where is it you have been, Cicero?" This for the time utterly mortified and cast him down, to perceive that the report of his actions had sunk into the city of Rome as into an immense ocean, without any visible effect or result in reputation. And afterwards considering with himself that the glory he contended for was an infinite thing, and that there was no fixed end nor measure in its pursuit, he abated much of his ambitious thoughts. Nevertheless, he was always excessively pleased with his own praise, and continued to the very last to be passionately fond of glory; which often interfered with the prosecution of his wisest resolutions.

On beginning to apply himself more resolutely to public business, he remarked it as an unreasonable and absurd thing that artificers, using vessels and instruments inanimate, should know the name, place, and use of every one of them, and yet the statesman, whose instruments for carrying out public measures are men, should be negligent and careless in the knowledge of persons. And so he not only acquainted himself with the names, but also knew the particular place where every one of the more eminent citizens dwelt, what lands he possessed, the friends he made use of, and those that were of his neighborhood, and when he traveled on any road in Italy, he could readily name and show the estates and seats of his friends and acquaintance. Having so small an estate, though a sufficient competency for his own expenses, it was much wondered at that he took neither fees nor gifts from his clients, and more especially, that he did not do so when he undertook the prosecution of Verres. This Verres, who had been praetor of Sicily, and stood charged by the Sicilians of many evil practices during his government there, Cicero succeeded in getting condemned, not by speaking, but in a manner by holding his tongue. For the praetors, favoring Verres, had deferred the trial by several adjournments to the last day, in which it was evident there could not be sufficient time for the advocates to be heard, and the cause brought to an issue. Cicero, therefore, came forward, and said there was no need of speeches; and after producing and examining witnesses, he required the judges to proceed to sentence. However, many witty sayings are on record, as having been used by Cicero on the occasion. When a man named Caecilius, one of the freed slaves, who was said to be given to Jewish practices, would have put by the Sicilians, and undertaken the prosecution of Verres himself, Cicero asked, "What has a Jew to do with swine?" ("verres" being the Roman word for a boar). And when Verres began to reproach Cicero with effeminate living, "You ought," replied he, "to use this language at home, to your sons;" Verres having a son who had fallen into disgraceful courses. Hortensius the orator, not daring directly to undertake the defense of Verres, was yet persuaded to appear for him at the laying on of the fine, and received an ivory sphinx for his reward; and when Cicero, in some passage of his speech, obliquely reflected on him, and Hortensius told him he was not skillful in solving riddles, "No," said Cicero, "and yet you have the Sphinx in your house!"

Verres was thus convicted; though Cicero, who set the fine at seventy-five myriads, lay under the suspicion of being corrupted by bribery to lessen the sum. But the Sicilians, in testimony of their gratitude, came and brought him all sorts of presents from the island, when he was aedile; of which he made no private profit himself, but used their generosity only to reduce the public price of provisions.

He had a very pleasant seat at Arpi, he had also a farm near Naples, and another about Pompeii, but neither of any great value. The portion of his wife, Terentia, amounted to ten myriads, and he had a bequest valued at nine myriads of denarii; upon these he lived in a liberal but temperate style, with the learned Greeks and Romans that were his familiars. He rarely, if at any time, sat down to meat till sunset, and that not so much on account of business, as for his health and the weakness of his stomach. He was otherwise in the care of his body nice and delicate, appointing himself, for example, a set number of walks and rubbings. And after this manner managing the habit of his body, he brought it in time to be healthful, and capable of supporting many great fatigues and trials. His father's house he made over to his brother, living himself near the Palatine hill, that he might not give the trouble of long journeys to those that made suit to him. And, indeed, there were not fewer daily appearing at his door, to do their court to him, than there were that came to Crassus for his riches, or to Pompey for his power amongst the soldiers, these being at that time the two men of the greatest repute and influence in Rome. Nay, even Pompey himself used to pay court to Cicero, and Cicero's public actions did much to establish Pompey's authority and reputation in the state.

Numerous distinguished competitors stood with him for the praetor's office; but he was chosen before them all, and managed the decision of causes with justice and integrity. It is related that Licinius Macer, a man himself of great power in the city, and supported also by the assistance of Crassus, was accused before him of extortion, and that, in confidence on his own interest and the diligence of his friends, whilst the judges were debating about the sentence, he went to his house, where hastily trimming his hair and putting on a clean gown, as already acquitted, he was setting off again to go to the Forum; but at his hall door meeting Crassus, who told him that he was condemned by all the votes, he went in again, threw himself upon his bed, and died immediately. This verdict was considered very creditable to Cicero, as showing his careful management of the courts of justice. On another occasion, Vatinius, a man of rude manners and often insolent in court to the magistrates, who had large swellings on his neck, came before his tribunal and made some request, and on Cicero's desiring further time to consider it, told him that he himself would have made no question about it, had he been praetor. Cicero, turning quickly upon him, answered, "But I, you see, have not the neck that you have."

When there were but two or three days remaining in his office, Manilius was brought before him, and charged with peculation. Manilius had the good opinion and favor of the common people, and was thought to be prosecuted only for Pompey's sake, whose particular friend he was. And therefore, when he asked a space of time before his trial, and Cicero allowed him but one day, and that the next only, the common people grew highly offended, because it had been the custom of the praetors to allow ten days at least to the accused: and the tribunes of the people having called him before the people, and accused him, he, desiring to be heard, said, that as he had always treated the accused with equity and humanity, as far as the law allowed, so he thought it hard to deny the same to Manilius, and that he had studiously appointed that day of which alone, as praetor, he was master, and that it was not the part of those that were desirous to help him, to cast the judgment of his cause upon another praetor. These things being said made a wonderful change in the people, and, commending him much for it, they desired that he himself would undertake the defense of Manilius; which he willingly consented to, and that principally for the sake of Pompey, who was absent. And, accordingly, taking his place before the people again, he delivered a bold invective upon the oligarchical party and on those who were jealous of Pompey.

Yet he was preferred to the consulship no less by the nobles than the common people, for the good of the city; and both parties jointly assisted his promotion, upon the following reasons. The change of government made by Sylla, which at first seemed a senseless one, by time and usage had now come to be considered by the people no unsatisfactory settlement. But there were some that endeavored to alter and subvert the whole present state of affairs not from any good motives, but for their own private gain; and Pompey being at this time employed in the wars with the kings of Pontus and Armenia, there was no sufficient force at Rome to suppress any attempts at a revolution. These people had for their head a man of bold, daring, and restless character, Lucius Catiline, who was accused, besides other great offenses, of deflowering his virgin daughter, and killing his own brother; for which latter crime, fearing to be prosecuted at law, he persuaded Sylla to set him down, as though he were yet alive, amongst those that were to be put to death by proscription. This man the profligate citizens choosing for their captain, gave faith to one another, amongst other pledges, by sacrificing a man and eating of his flesh; and a great part of the young men of the city were corrupted by him, he providing for everyone pleasures, drink, and women, and profusely supplying the expense of these debauches. Etruria, moreover, had all been excited to revolt, as well as a great part of Gaul within the Alps. But Rome itself was in the most dangerous inclination to change, on account of the unequal distribution of wealth and property, those of highest rank and greatest spirit having impoverished themselves by shows, entertainments, ambition of offices, and sumptuous buildings, and the riches of the city having thus fallen into the hands of mean and low-born persons. So that there wanted but a slight impetus to set all in motion, it being in the power of every daring man to overturn a sickly commonwealth.

Catiline, however, being desirous of procuring a strong position to carry out his designs, stood for the consulship, and had great hopes of success, thinking he should be appointed, with Caius Antonius as his colleague, who was a man fit to lead neither in a good cause nor in a bad one, but might be a valuable accession to another's power. These things the greatest part of the good and honest citizens apprehending, put Cicero upon standing for the consulship; whom the people readily receiving, Catiline was put by, so that he and Caius Antonius were chosen, although amongst the competitors he was the only man descended from a father of the equestrian, and not of the senatorial order.

Though the designs of Catiline were not yet publicly known, yet considerable preliminary troubles immediately followed upon Cicero's entrance upon the consulship. For, on the one side, those who were disqualified by the laws of Sylla from holding any public offices, being neither inconsiderable in power nor in number, came forward as candidates and caressed the people for them; speaking many things truly and justly against the tyranny of Sylla, only that they disturbed the government at an improper and unseasonable time; on the other hand, the tribunes of the people proposed laws to the same purpose, constituting a commission of ten persons, with unlimited powers, in whom as supreme governors should be vested the right of selling the public lands of all Italy and Syria and Pompey's new conquests, of judging and banishing whom they pleased, of planting colonies, of taking moneys out of the treasury, and of levying and paying what soldiers should be thought needful. And several of the nobility favored this law, but especially Caius Antonius, Cicero's colleague, in hopes of being one of the ten. But what gave the greatest fear to the nobles was, that he was thought privy to the conspiracy of Catiline, and not to dislike it, because of his great debts.

Cicero, endeavoring in the first place to provide a remedy against this danger, procured a decree assigning to him the province of Macedonia, he himself declining that of Gaul, which was offered to him. And this piece of favor so completely won over Antonius, that he was ready to second and respond to, like a hired player, whatever Cicero said for the good of the country. And now, having made his colleague thus tame and tractable, he could with greater courage attack the conspirators. And, therefore, in the senate, making an oration against the law of the ten commissioners, he so confounded those who proposed it, that they had nothing to reply. And when they again endeavored, and, having prepared things beforehand, had called the consuls before the assembly of the people, Cicero, fearing nothing, went first out, and commanded the senate to follow him, and not only succeeded in throwing out the law, but so entirely overpowered the tribunes by his oratory, that they abandoned all thought of their other projects.

For Cicero, it may be said, was the one man, above all others, who made the Romans feel how great a charm eloquence lends to what is good, and how invincible justice is, if it be well spoken; and that it is necessary for him who would dexterously govern a commonwealth, in action, always to prefer that which is honest before that which is popular, and in speaking, to free the right and useful measure from everything that may occasion offense. An incident occurred in the theater, during his consulship, which showed what his speaking could do. For whereas formerly the knights of Rome were mingled in the theater with the common people, and took their places amongst them as it happened, Marcus Otho, when he was praetor, was the first who distinguished them from the other citizens, and appointed them a proper seat, which they still enjoy as their special place in the theater. This the common people took as an indignity done to them, and, therefore, when Otho appeared in the theater, they hissed him; the knights, on the contrary, received him with loud clapping. The people repeated and increased their hissing; the knights continued their clapping. Upon this, turning upon one another, they broke out into insulting words, so that the theater was in great disorder. Cicero, being informed of it, came himself to the theater, and summoning the people into the temple of Bellona, he so effectually chid and chastised them for it, that, again returning into the theater, they received Otho with loud applause, contending with the knights who should give him the greatest demonstrations of honor and respect.

The conspirators with Catiline, at first cowed and disheartened, began presently to take courage again. And assembling themselves together, they exhorted one another boldly to undertake the design before Pompey's return, who, as it was said, was now on his march with his forces for Rome. But the old soldiers of Sylla were Catiline's chief stimulus to action. They had been disbanded all about Italy, but the greatest number and the fiercest of them lay scattered among the cities of Etruria, entertaining themselves with dreams of new plunder and rapine amongst the hoarded riches of Italy. These, having for their leader Manlius, who had served with distinction in the wars under Sylla, joined themselves to Catiline, and came to Rome to assist him with their suffrages at the election. For he again pretended to the consulship, having resolved to kill Cicero in a tumult at the elections. Also, the divine powers seemed to give intimation of the coming troubles, by earthquakes, thunderbolts, and strange appearances. Nor was human evidence wanting, certain enough in itself, though not sufficient for the conviction of the noble and powerful Catiline. Therefore Cicero, deferring the day of election, summoned Catiline into the senate, and questioned him as to the charges made against him. Catiline, believing there were many in the senate desirous of change, and to give a specimen of himself to the conspirators present, returned an audacious answer, "What harm," said he, "when I see two bodies, the one lean and consumptive with a head, the other great and strong without one, if I put a head to that body which wants one?" This covert representation of the senate and the people excited yet greater apprehensions in Cicero. He put on armor, and was attended from his house by the noble citizens in a body; and a number of the young men went with him into the Plain. Here, designedly letting his tunic slip partly off from his shoulders, he showed his armor underneath, and discovered his danger to the spectators; who, being much moved at it, gathered round about him for his defense. At length, Catiline was by a general suffrage again put by, and Silanus and Murena chosen consuls.

Not long after this, Catiline's soldiers got together in a body in Etruria, and began to form themselves into companies, the day appointed for the design being near at hand. About midnight, some of the principal and most powerful citizens of Rome, Marcus Crassus, Marcus Marcellus, and Scipio Metellus went to Cicero's house, where, knocking at the gate, and calling up the porter, they commended him to awake Cicero, and tell him they were there. The business was this: Crassus's porter after supper had delivered to him letters brought by an unknown person. Some of them were directed to others, but one to Crassus, without a name; this only Crassus read, which informed him that there was a great slaughter intended by Catiline, and advised him to leave the city. The others he did not open, but went with them immediately to Cicero, being affrighted at the danger, and to free himself of the suspicion he lay under for his familiarity with Catiline. Cicero, considering the matter, summoned the senate at break of day. The letters he brought with him, and delivered them to those to whom they were directed, commanding them to read them publicly; they all alike contained an account of the conspiracy. And when Quintus Arrius, a man of praetorian dignity, recounted to them, how soldiers were collecting in companies in Etruria, and Manlius stated to be in motion with a large force, hovering about those cities, in expectation of intelligence from Rome, the senate made a decree, to place all in the hands of the consuls, who should undertake the conduct of everything, and do their best to save the state. This was not a common thing, but only done by the senate in case of imminent danger.

After Cicero had received this power, he committed all affairs outside to Quintus Metellus, but the management of the city he kept in his own hands. Such a numerous attendance guarded him every day when he went abroad, that the greatest part of the market-place was filled with his train when he entered it. Catiline, impatient of further delay, resolved himself to break forth and go to Manlius, but he commanded Marcius and Cethegus to take their swords, and go early in the morning to Cicero's gates, as if only intending to salute him, and then to fall upon him and slay him. This a noble lady, Fulvia, coming by night, discovered to Cicero, bidding him beware of Cethegus and Marcius. They came by break of day, and being denied entrance, made an outcry and disturbance at the gates, which excited all the more suspicion. But Cicero, going forth, summoned the senate into the temple of Jupiter Stator, which stands at the end of the Sacred Street, going up to the Palatine. And when Catiline with others of his party also came, as intending to make his defense, none of the senators would sit by him, but all of them left the bench where he had placed himself. And when he began to speak, they interrupted him with outcries. At length Cicero, standing up, commanded him to leave the city, for since one governed the commonwealth with words, the other with arms, it was necessary there should be a wall betwixt them. Catiline, therefore, immediately left the town, with three hundred armed men; and assuming, as if he had been a magistrate, the rods, axes, and military ensigns, he went to Manlius, and having got together a body of near twenty thousand men, with these he marched to the several cities, endeavoring to persuade or force them to revolt. So it being now come to open war, Antonius was sent forth to fight him.

The remainder of those in the city whom he had corrupted, Cornelius Lentulus kept together and encouraged. He had the surname Sura, and was a man of a noble family, but a dissolute liver, who for his debauchery was formerly turned out of the senate, and was now holding the office of praetor for the second time, as the custom is with those who desire to regain the dignity of senator. It is said that he got the surname Sura upon this occasion; being quaestor in the time of Sylla, he had lavished away and consumed a great quantity of the public moneys, at which Sylla being provoked, called him to give an account in the senate; he appeared with great coolness and contempt, and said he had no account to give, but they might take this, holding up the calf of his leg, as boys do at ball, when they have missed. Upon which he was surnamed Sura, sura being the Roman word for the calf of the leg. Being at another time prosecuted at law, and having bribed some of the judges, he escaped only by two votes, and complained of the needless expense he had gone to in paying for a second, as one would have sufficed to acquit him. This man, such in his own nature, and now inflamed by Catiline, false prophets and fortune-tellers had also corrupted with vain hopes, quoting to him fictitious verses and oracles, and proving from the Sibylline prophecies that there were three of the name Cornelius designed by fate to be monarchs of Rome; two of whom, Cinna and Sylla, had already fulfilled the decree, and that divine fortune was now advancing with the gift of monarchy for the remaining third Cornelius; and that therefore he ought by all means to accept it, and not lose opportunity by delay, as Catiline had done.

Lentulus, therefore, designed no mean or trivial matter, for he had resolved to kill the whole senate, and as many other citizens as he could, to fire the city, and spare nobody, except only Pompey's children, intending to seize and keep them as pledges of his reconciliation with Pompey. For there was then a common and strong report that Pompey was on his way homeward from his great expedition. The night appointed for the design was one of the Saturnalia; swords, flax, and sulfur they carried and hid in the house of Cethegus; and providing one hundred men, and dividing the city into as many parts, they had allotted to every one singly his proper place, so that in a moment many kindling the fire, the city might be in a flame all together. Others were appointed to stop up the aqueducts, and to kill those who should endeavor to carry water to put it out. Whilst these plans were preparing, it happened there were two ambassadors from the Allobroges staying in Rome; a nation at that time in a distressed condition, and very uneasy under the Roman government. These Lentulus and his party judging useful instruments to move and seduce Gaul to revolt, admitted into the conspiracy, and they gave them letters to their own magistrates, and letters to Catiline; in those they promised liberty, in these they exhorted Catiline to set all slaves free, and to bring them along with him to Rome. They sent also to accompany them to Catiline, one Titus, a native of Croton, who was to carry those letters to him.

These counsels of inconsidering men, who conversed together over wine and with women, Cicero watched with sober industry and forethought, and with most admirable sagacity, having several emissaries abroad, who observed and traced with him all that was done, and keeping also a secret correspondence with many who pretended to join in the conspiracy. He thus knew all the discourse which passed betwixt them and the strangers; and lying in wait for them by night, he took the Crotonian with his letters, the ambassadors of the Allobroges acting secretly in concert with him.

By break of day, he summoned the senate into the temple of Concord, where he read the letters and examined the informers. Junius Silanus further stated, that several persons had heard Cethegus say, that three consuls and four praetors were to be slain; Piso, also, a person of consular dignity, testified other matters of the like nature; and Caius Sulpicius, one of the praetors, being sent to Cethegus's house, found there a quantity of darts and of armor, and a still greater number of swords and daggers, all recently whetted. At length, the senate decreeing indemnity to the Crotonian upon his confession of the whole matter, Lentulus was convicted, abjured his office (for he was then praetor), and put off his robe edged with purple in the senate, changing it for another garment more agreeable to his present circumstances. He, thereupon, with the rest of his confederates present, was committed to the charge of the praetors in free custody.

It being evening, and the common people in crowds expecting without, Cicero went forth to them, and told them what was done, and then, attended by them, went to the house of a friend and near neighbor; for his own was taken up by the women, who were celebrating with secret rites the feast of the goddess whom the Romans call the Good, and the Greeks, the Women's goddess. For a sacrifice is annually performed to her in the consul's house, either by his wife or mother, in the presence of the vestal virgins. And having got into his friend's house privately, a few only being present, he began to deliberate how he should treat these men. The severest, and the only punishment fit for such heinous crimes, he was somewhat shy and fearful of inflicting, as well from the clemency of his nature, as also lest he should be thought to exercise his authority too insolently, and to treat too harshly men of the noblest birth and most powerful friendships in the city; and yet, if he should use them more mildly, he had a dreadful prospect of danger from them. For there was no likelihood, if they suffered less than death, they would be reconciled, but rather, adding new rage to their former wickedness, they would rush into every kind of audacity, while he himself, whose character for courage already did not stand very high with the multitude, would be thought guilty of the greatest cowardice and want of manliness.

Whilst Cicero was doubting what course to take, a portent happened to the women in their sacrificing. For on the altar, where the fire seemed wholly extinguished, a great and bright flame issued forth from the ashes of the burnt wood; at which others were affrighted, but the holy virgins called to Terentia, Cicero's wife, and bade her haste to her husband, and command him to execute what he had resolved for the good of his country, for the goddess had sent a great light to the increase of his safety and glory. Terentia, therefore, as she was otherwise in her own nature neither tender-hearted nor timorous, but a woman eager for distinction (who, as Cicero himself says, would rather thrust herself into his public affairs, than communicate her domestic matters to him), told him these things, and excited him against the conspirators. So also did Quintus his brother, and Publius Nigidius, one of his philosophical friends, whom he often made use of in his greatest and most weighty affairs of state.

The next day, a debate arising in the senate about the punishment of the men, Silanus, being the first who was asked his opinion, said, it was fit they should be all sent to the prison, and there suffer the utmost penalty. To him all consented in order till it came to Caius Caesar, who was afterwards dictator. He was then but a young man, and only at the outset of his career, but had already directed his hopes and policy to that course by which he afterwards changed the Roman state into a monarchy. Of this others foresaw nothing; but Cicero had seen reason for strong suspicion, though without obtaining any sufficient means of proof. And there were some indeed that said that he was very near being discovered, and only just escaped him; others are of opinion that Cicero voluntarily overlooked and neglected the evidence against him, for fear of his friends and power; for it was very evident to everybody, that if Caesar was to be accused with the conspirators, they were more likely to be saved with him, than he to be punished with them.

When, therefore, it came to Caesar's turn to give his opinion, he stood up and proposed that the conspirators should not be put to death, but their estates confiscated, and their persons confined in such cities in Italy as Cicero should approve, there to be kept in custody till Catiline was conquered. To this sentence, as it was the most moderate, and he that delivered it a most powerful speaker, Cicero himself gave no small weight, for he stood up and, turning the scale on either side, spoke in favor partly of the former, partly of Caesar's sentence. And all Cicero's friends, judging Caesar's sentence most expedient for Cicero, because he would incur the less blame if the conspirators were not put to death, chose rather the latter; so that Silanus, also, changing his mind, retracted his opinion, and said he had not declared for capital, but only the utmost punishment, which to a Roman senator is imprisonment. The first man who spoke against Caesar's motion was Catulus Lutatius. Cato followed, and so vehemently urged in his speech the strong suspicion about Caesar himself, and so filled the senate with anger and resolution, that a decree was passed for the execution of the conspirators. But Caesar opposed the confiscation of their goods, not thinking it fair that those who had rejected the mildest part of his sentence should avail themselves of the severest. And when many insisted upon it, he appealed to the tribunes, but they would do nothing; till Cicero himself yielding, remitted that part of the sentence.

After this, Cicero went out with the senate to the conspirators; they were not all together in one place, but the several praetors had them, some one, some another, in custody. And first he took Lentulus from the Palatine, and brought him by the Sacred Street, through the middle of the marketplace, a circle of the most eminent citizens encompassing and protecting him. The people, affrighted at what was doing, passed along in silence, especially the young men; as if, with fear and trembling; they were undergoing a rite of initiation into some ancient, sacred mysteries of aristocratic power. Thus passing from the market-place, and coming to the gaol, he delivered Lentulus to the officer, and commanded him to execute him; and after him Cethegus, and so all the rest in order, he brought and delivered up to execution. And when he saw many of the conspirators in the market-place, still standing together in companies, ignorant of what was done, and waiting for the night, supposing the men were still alive and in a possibility of being rescued, he called out in a loud voice, and said, "They did live;" for so the Romans, to avoid inauspicious language, name those that are dead.

It was now evening, when he returned from the market-place to his own house, the citizens no longer attending him with silence, nor in order, but receiving him, as he passed, with acclamations and applauses, and saluting him as the savior and founder of his country. A bright light shone through the streets from the lamps and torches set up at the doors, and the women showed lights from the tops of the houses, to honor Cicero, and to behold him returning home with a splendid train of the most principal citizens; amongst whom were many who had conducted great wars, celebrated triumphs, and added to the possessions of the Roman empire, both by sea and land. These, as they passed along with him, acknowledged to one another, that though the Roman people were indebted to several officers and commanders of that age for riches, spoils, and power, yet to Cicero alone they owed the safety and security of all these, for delivering them from so great and imminent a danger. For though it might seem no wonderful thing to prevent the design, and punish the conspirators, yet to defeat the greatest of all conspiracies with so little disturbance, trouble, and commotion, was very extraordinary. For the greater part of those who had flocked in to Catiline, as soon as they heard the fate of Lentulus and Cethegus, left and forsook him, and he himself, with his remaining forces, joining battle with Antonius, was destroyed with his army.

And yet there were some who were very ready both to speak ill of Cicero, and to do him hurt for these actions; and they had for their leaders some of the magistrates of the ensuing year, as Caesar, who was one of the praetors, and Metellus and Bestia, the tribunes. These, entering upon their office some few days before Cicero's consulate expired, would not permit him to make any address to the people, but, throwing the benches before the Rostra, hindered his speaking, telling him he might, if he pleased, make the oath of withdrawal from office, and then come down again. Cicero, accordingly, accepting the conditions, came forward to make his withdrawal; and silence being made, he recited his oath, not in the usual, but in a new and peculiar form, namely, that he had saved his country, and preserved the empire; the truth of which oath all the people confirmed with theirs. Caesar and the tribunes, all the more exasperated by this, endeavored to create him further trouble, and for this purpose proposed a law for calling Pompey home with his army, to put an end to Cicero's usurpation. But it was a very great advantage for Cicero and the whole commonwealth that Cato was at that time one of the tribunes. For he, being of equal power with the rest, and of greater reputation, could oppose their designs. He easily defeated their other projects, and, in an oration to the people, so highly extolled Cicero's consulate, that the greatest honors were decreed him, and he was publicly declared the Father of his Country, which title he seems to have obtained, the first man who did so, when Cato gave it him in this address to the people.

At this time, therefore, his authority was very great in the city; but he created himself much envy, and offended very many, not by any evil action, but because he was always lauding and magnifying himself. For neither senate, nor assembly of the people, nor court of judicature could meet, in which he was not heard to talk of Catiline and Lentulus. Indeed, he also filled his books and writings with his own praises, to such an excess as to render a style, in itself most pleasant and delightful, nauseous and irksome to his hearers; this ungrateful humor, like a disease, always cleaving to him. Nevertheless, though he was intemperately fond of his own glory, he was very free from envying others, and was, on the contrary, most liberally profuse in commending both the ancients and his contemporaries, as anyone may see in his writings. And many such sayings of his are also remembered; as that he called Aristotle a river of flowing gold, and said of Plato's Dialogues, that if Jupiter were to speak, it would be in language like theirs. He used to call Theophrastus his special luxury. And being asked which of Demosthenes's orations he liked best, he answered, the longest. And yet some affected imitators of Demosthenes have complained of some words that occur in one of his letters, to the effect that Demosthenes sometimes falls asleep in his speeches; forgetting the many high encomiums he continually passes upon him, and the compliment he paid him when he named the most elaborate of all his orations, those he wrote against Antony, Philippics. And as for the eminent men of his own time, either in eloquence or philosophy, there was not one of them whom he did not, by writing or speaking favorably of him, render more illustrious. He obtained of Caesar, when in power, the Roman citizenship for Cratippus, the Peripatetic, and got the court of Areopagus, by public decree, to request his stay at Athens, for the instruction of their youth, and the honor of their city. There are letters extant from Cicero to Herodes, and others to his son, in which he recommends the study of philosophy under Cratippus. There is one in which he blames Gorgias, the rhetorician, for enticing his son into luxury and drinking, and, therefore, forbids him his company. And this, and one other to Pelops, the Byzantine, are the only two of his Greek epistles which seem to be written in anger. In the first, he justly reflects on Gorgias, if he were what he was thought to be, a dissolute and profligate character; but in the other, he rather meanly expostulates and complains with Pelops, for neglecting to procure him a decree of certain honors from the Byzantines.

Another illustration of his love of praise is the way in which sometimes, to make his orations more striking, he neglected decorum and dignity. When Munatius, who had escaped conviction by his advocacy, immediately prosecuted his friend Sabinus, he said in the warmth of his resentment, "Do you suppose you were acquitted for your own meets, Munatius, and was it not that I so darkened the case, that the court could not see your guilt?" When from the Rostra he had made an eulogy on Marcus Crassus, with much applause, and within a few days after again as publicly reproached him, Crassus called to him, and said, "Did not you yourself two days ago, in this same place, commend me?" "Yes," said Cicero, "I exercised my eloquence in declaiming upon a bad subject." At another time, Crassus had said that no one of his family had ever lived beyond sixty years of age, and afterwards denied it, and asked, "What should put it into my head to say so?" "It was to gain the people's favor," answered Cicero; "you knew how glad they would be to hear it." When Crassus expressed admiration of the Stoic doctrine, that the good man is always rich, "Do you not mean," said Cicero, "their doctrine that all things belong to the wise?" Crassus being generally accused of covetousness. One of Crassus's sons, who was thought so exceedingly like a man of the name of Axius as to throw some suspicion on his mother's honor, made a successful speech in the senate. Cicero on being asked how he liked it, replied with the Greek words, Axios Crassou.

When Crassus was about to go into Syria, he desired to leave Cicero rather his friend than his enemy, and, therefore, one day saluting him, told him he would come and sup with him, which the other as courteously received. Within a few days after, on some of Cicero's acquaintances interceding for Vatinius, as desirous of reconciliation and friendship, for he was then his enemy, "What," he replied, "does Vatinius also wish to come and sup with me?" Such was his way with Crassus. When Vatinius, who had swellings in his neck, was pleading a cause, he called him the tumid orator; and having been told by someone that Vatinius was dead, on hearing presently after that he was alive, "May the rascal perish," said he, "for his news not being true."

Upon Caesar's bringing forward a law for the division of the lands in Campania amongst the soldiers, many in the senate opposed it; amongst the rest, Lucius Gellius, one of the oldest men in the house, said it should never pass whilst he lived. "Let us postpone it," said Cicero, "Gellius does not ask us to wait long." There was a man of the name of Octavius, suspected to be of African descent. He once said, when Cicero was pleading, that he could not hear him; "Yet there are holes," said Cicero, "in your ears." When Metellus Nepos told him, that he had ruined more as a witness, than he had saved as an advocate, "I admit," said Cicero, "that I have more truth than eloquence." To a young man who was suspected of having given a poisoned cake to his father, and who talked largely of the invectives he meant to deliver against Cicero, "Better these," replied he, "than your cakes." Publius Sextius, having amongst others retained Cicero as his advocate in a certain cause, was yet desirous to say all for himself, and would not allow anybody to speak for him; when he was about to receive his acquittal from the judges, and the ballots were passing, Cicero called to him, "Make haste, Sextius, and use your time; tomorrow you will be nobody." He cited Publius Cotta to bear testimony in a certain cause, one who affected to be thought a lawyer, though ignorant and unlearned; to whom, when he had said, "I know nothing of the matter," he answered, "You think, perhaps, we ask you about a point of law." To Metellus Nepos, who, in a dispute between them, repeated several times, "Who was your father, Cicero?" he replied, "Your mother has made the answer to such a question in your case more difficult;" Nepos's mother having been of ill repute. The son, also, was of a giddy, uncertain temper. At one time, he suddenly threw up his office of tribune, and sailed off into

Syria to Pompey; and immediately after, with as little reason, came back again. He gave his tutor, Philagrus, a funeral with more than necessary attention, and then set up the stone figure of a crow over his tomb. "This," said Cicero, "is really appropriate; as he did not teach you to speak, but to fly about." When Marcus Appius, in the opening of some speech in a court of justice, said that his friend had desired him to employ industry, eloquence, and fidelity in that cause, Cicero answered, "And how have you had the heart not to accede to any one of his requests?"

To use this sharp raillery against opponents and antagonists in judicial pleading seems allowable rhetoric. But he excited much ill feeling by his readiness to attack anyone for the sake of a jest. A few anecdotes of this kind may be added. Marcus Aquinius, who had two sons-in-law in exile, received from him the name of king Adrastus. Lucius Cotta, an intemperate lover of wine, was censor when Cicero stood for the consulship. Cicero, being thirsty at the election, his friends stood round about him while he was drinking. "You have reason to be afraid," he said, "lest the censor should be angry with me for drinking water." Meeting one day Voconius with his three very ugly daughters, he quoted the verse,

> He reared a race without Apollo's leave.

When Marcus Gellius, who was reputed the son of a slave, had read several letters in the senate with a very shrill, and loud voice, "Wonder not," said Cicero, "he comes of the criers." When Faustus Sylla, the son of Sylla the dictator, who had, during his dictatorship, by public bills proscribed and condemned so many citizens, had so far wasted his estate, and got into debt, that he was forced to publish his bills of sale, Cicero told him that he liked these bills much better than those of his father. By this habit he made himself odious with many people.

But Clodius's faction conspired against him upon the following occasion. Clodius was a member of a noble family, in the flower of his youth, and of a bold and resolute temper. He, being in love with Pompeia, Caesar's wife, got privately into his house in the dress and attire of a music-girl; the women being at that time offering there the sacrifice which must not be seen by men, and there was no man present. Clodius, being a youth and beardless, hoped to get to Pompeia among the women without being taken notice of. But coming into a great house by night, he missed his way in the passages, and a servant belonging to Aurelia, Caesar's mother, spying him wandering up and down, inquired his name. Thus being necessitated to speak, he told her he was seeking for one of Pompeia's maids, Abra by name; and she, perceiving it not to be a woman's voice, shrieked out, and called in the women; who, shutting the gates, and searching every place, at length found Clodius hidden in the chamber of the maid with whom he had come in. This matter being much talked about, Caesar put away his wife, Pompeia, and Clodius was prosecuted for profaning the holy rites.

Cicero was at this time his friend, for he had been useful to him in the conspiracy of Catiline, as one of his forwardest assistants and protectors. But when Clodius rested his defense upon this point, that he was not then at Rome, but at a distance in the country, Cicero testified that he had come to his house that day, and conversed with him on several matters; which thing was indeed true, although Cicero was thought to testify it not so much for the truth's sake as to preserve his quiet with Terentia his wife. For she bore a grudge against Clodius on account of his sister Clodia's wishing, as it was alleged, to marry Cicero, and having employed for this purpose the intervention of Tullus, a very intimate friend of Cicero's; and his frequent visits to Clodia, who lived in their neighborhood, and the attentions he paid to her had excited Terentia's suspicions, and, being a woman of a violent temper, and having the ascendant over Cicero, she urged him on to taking a part against Clodius, and delivering his testimony. Many other good and honest citizens also gave evidence against him, for perjuries, disorders, bribing the people, and debauching women. Lucullus proved, by his women-servants, that he had debauched his youngest sister when she was Lucullus's wife; and there was a general belief that he had done the same with his two other sisters, Tertia, whom Marcius Rex, and Clodia, whom

Metellus Celer had married; the latter of whom was called Quadrantia, because one of her lovers had deceived her with a purse of small copper money instead of silver, the smallest copper coin being called a quadrant. Upon this sister's account, in particular, Clodius's character was attacked. Notwithstanding all this, when the common people united against the accusers and witnesses and the whole party, the judges were affrighted, and a guard was placed about them for their defense; and most of them wrote their sentences on the tablets in such a way, that they could not well be read. It was decided, however, that there was a majority for his acquittal, and bribery was reported to have been employed; in reference to which Catulus remarked, when he next met the judges, "You were very right to ask for a guard, to prevent your money being taken from you." And when Clodius upbraided Cicero that the judges had not believed his testimony, "Yes," said he, "five and twenty of them trusted me, and condemned you, and the other thirty did not trust you, for they did not acquit you till they had got your money."

Caesar, though cited, did not give his testimony against Clodius, and declared himself not convinced of his wife's adultery, but that he had put her away because it was fit that Caesar's house should not be only free of the evil fact, but of the fame too.

Clodius, having escaped this danger, and having got himself chosen one of the tribunes, immediately attacked Cicero, heaping up all matters and inciting all persons against him. The common people he gained over with popular laws; to each of the consuls he decreed large provinces, to Piso, Macedonia, and to Gabinius, Syria; he made a strong party among the indigent citizens, to support him in his proceedings, and had always a body of armed slaves about him. Of the three men then in greatest power, Crassus was Cicero's open enemy, Pompey indifferently made advances to both, and Caesar was going with an army into Gaul. To him, though not his friend (what had occurred in the time of the conspiracy having created suspicions between them), Cicero applied, requesting an appointment as one of his lieutenants in the province. Caesar accepted him, and Clodius, perceiving that Cicero would thus escape his tribunician authority, professed to be inclinable to a reconciliation, laid the greatest fault upon Terentia, made always a favorable mention of him, and addressed him with kind expressions, as one who felt no hatred or ill-will, but who merely wished to urge his complaints in a moderate and friendly way. By these artifices, he so freed Cicero of all his fears, that he resigned his appointment to Caesar, and betook himself again to political affairs. At which Caesar being exasperated, joined the party of Clodius against him, and wholly alienated Pompey from him; he also himself declared in a public assembly of the people, that he did not think Lentulus and Cethegus, with their accomplices, were fairly and legally put to death without being brought to trial. And this, indeed, was the crime charged upon Cicero, and this impeachment he was summoned to answer. And so, as an accused man, and in danger for the result, he changes his dress, and went round with his hair untrimmed, in the attire of a suppliant, to beg the people's grace. But Clodius met him in every corner, having a band of abusive and daring fellows about him, who derided Cicero for his change of dress and his humiliation, and often, by throwing dirt and stones at him, interrupted his supplication to the people.

However, first of all, almost the whole equestrian order changed their dress with him, and no less than twenty thousand young gentlemen followed him with their hair untrimmed, and supplicating with him to the people. And then the senate met, to pass a decree that the people should change their dress as in time of public sorrow. But the consuls opposing it, and Clodius with armed men besetting the senate-house, many of the senators ran out, crying out and tearing their clothes. But this sight moved neither shame nor pity; Cicero must either fly or determine it by the sword with Clodius. He entreated Pompey to aid him, who was on purpose gone out of the way, and was staying at his country-house in the Alban hills; and first he sent his son-in-law Piso to intercede with him, and afterwards set out to go himself. Of which Pompey being informed, would not stay to see him, being ashamed at the remembrance of the many conflicts in the commonwealth which Cicero had undergone in his behalf, and how much of his policy he had directed for his advantage. But being now Caesar's son-in-law, at his instance he had set aside all former kindness, and, slipping out at another door, avoided the interview. Thus being forsaken by Pompey, and left alone to himself, he fled to the consuls. Gabinius was rough with him, as usual, but Piso spoke more courteously, desiring him to yield and give place for a while to the fury of Clodius, and to await a change of times, and to be now, as before, his country's savior from the peril of these troubles and commotions which Clodius was exciting.

Cicero, receiving this answer, consulted with his friends. Lucullus advised him to stay, as being sure to prevail at last; others to fly, because the people would soon desire him again, when they should have enough of the rage and madness of Clodius. This last Cicero approved. But first he took a statue of Minerva, which had been long set up and greatly honored in his house, and carrying it to the capitol, there dedicated it, with the inscription, "To Minerva, Patroness of Rome." And receiving an escort from his friends, about the middle of the night he left the city, and went by land through Lucania, intending to reach Sicily.

But as soon as it was publicly known that he was fled, Clodius proposed to the people a decree of exile, and by his own order interdicted him fire and water, prohibiting any within five hundred miles in Italy to receive him into their houses. Most people, out of respect for Cicero, paid no regard to this edict, offering him every attention and escorting him on his way. But at Hipponium, a city of Lucania, now called Vibo, one Vibius, a Sicilian by birth, who, amongst many other instances of Cicero's friendship, had been made head of the state engineers when he was consul, would not receive him into his house, sending him word he would appoint a place in the country for his reception. Caius Vergilius, the praetor of Sicily, who had been on the most intimate terms with him, wrote to him to forbear coming into Sicily. At these things Cicero being disheartened, went to Brundusium, whence putting forth with a prosperous wind, a contrary gale blowing from the sea carried him back to Italy the next day. He put again to sea, and having reached Dyrrachium, on his coming to shore there, it is reported that an earthquake and a convulsion in the sea happened at the same time, signs which the diviners said intimated that his exile would not be long, for these were prognostics of change. Although many visited him with respect, and the cities of Greece contended which should honor him most, he yet continued disheartened and disconsolate, like an unfortunate lover, often casting his looks back upon Italy; and, indeed, he was become so poor-spirited, so humiliated and dejected by his misfortunes, as none could have expected in a man who had devoted so much of his life to study and learning. And yet he often desired his friends not to call him orator, but philosopher, because he had made philosophy his business, and had only used rhetoric as an instrument for attaining his objects in public life. But the desire of glory has great power in washing the tinctures of philosophy out of the souls of men, and in imprinting the passions of the common people, by custom and conversation, in the minds of those that take a part in governing them, unless the politician be very careful so to engage in public affairs as to interest himself only in the affairs themselves, but not participate in the passions that are consequent to them.

Clodius, having thus driven away Cicero, fell to burning his farms and villas, and afterwards his city house, and built on the site of it a temple to Liberty. The rest of his property he exposed to sale by daily proclamation, but nobody came to buy. By these courses he became formidable to the noble citizens, and, being followed by the commonalty, whom he had filled with insolence and licentiousness, he began at last to try his strength against Pompey, some of whose arrangements in the countries he conquered, he attacked. The disgrace of this made Pompey begin to reproach himself for his cowardice in deserting Cicero, and, changing his mind, he now wholly set himself with his friends to contrive his return. And when Clodius opposed it, the senate made a vote that no public measure should be ratified or passed by them till Cicero was recalled. But when Lentulus was consul, the commotions grew so high upon this matter, that the tribunes were wounded in the Forum, and Quintus, Cicero's brother, was left as dead, lying unobserved amongst the slain. The people began to change in their feelings; and Annius Milo, one of their tribunes, was the first who took confidence to summon Clodius to trial for acts of violence. Many of the common people and out of the neighboring cities formed a party with Pompey, and he went with them, and drove Clodius out of the Forum, and summoned the people to pass their vote. And, it is said, the people never passed any suffrage more unanimously than this. The senate, also, striving to outdo the people, sent letters of thanks to those cities which had received Cicero with respect in his exile, and decreed that his house and his country-places, which Clodius had destroyed, should be rebuilt at the public charge.

Thus Cicero returned sixteen months after his exile, and the cities were so glad, and people so zealous to meet him, that what he boasted of afterwards, that Italy had brought him on her shoulders home to Rome, was rather less than the truth. And Crassus himself, who had been his enemy before his exile, went then voluntarily to meet him, and was reconciled, to please his son Publius, as he said, who was Cicero's affectionate admirer.

Cicero had not been long at Rome, when, taking the opportunity of Clodius's absence, he went, with a great company, to the capitol, and there tore and defaced the tribunician tables, in which were recorded the acts done in the time of Clodius. And on Clodius calling him in question for this, he answered, that he, being of the patrician order, had obtained the office of tribune against law, and, therefore, nothing done by him was valid. Cato was displeased at this, and opposed Cicero, not that he commended Clodius, but rather disapproved of his whole administration; yet, he contended, it was an irregular and violent course for the senate to vote the illegality of so many decrees and acts, including those of Cato's own government in Cyprus and at Byzantium. This occasioned a breach between Cato and Cicero, which, though it came not to open enmity, yet made a more reserved friendship between them.

After this, Milo killed Clodius, and, being arraigned for the murder, he procured Cicero as his advocate. The senate, fearing lest the questioning of so eminent and high-spirited a citizen as Milo might disturb the peace of the city, committed the superintendence of this and of the other trials to Pompey, who should undertake to maintain the security alike of the city and of the courts of justice. Pompey, therefore, went in the night, and occupying the high grounds about it, surrounded the Forum with soldiers. Milo, fearing lest Cicero, being disturbed by such an unusual sight, should conduct his cause the less successfully, persuaded him to come in a litter into the Forum, and there repose himself till the judges were set, and the court filled. For Cicero, it seems, not only wanted courage in arms, but, in his speaking also, began with timidity, and in many cases scarcely left off trembling and shaking when he had got thoroughly into the current and the substance of his speech. Being to defend Licinius Murena against the prosecution of Cato, and being eager to outdo Hortensius, who had made his plea with great applause, he took so little rest that night, and was so disordered with thought and over-watching, that he spoke much worse than usual. And so now, on quitting his litter to commence the cause of Milo, at the sight of Pompey, posted, as it were, and encamped with his troops above, and seeing arms shining round about the Forum, he was so confounded, that he could hardly begin his speech, for the trembling of his body, and hesitance of his tongue; whereas Milo, meantime, was bold and intrepid in his demeanor, disdaining either to let his hair grow, or to put on the mourning habit. And this, indeed, seems to have been one principal cause of his condemnation. Cicero, however, was thought not so much to have shown timidity for himself, as anxiety about his friend.

He was made one of the priests, whom the Romans call Augurs, in the room of Crassus the younger, dead in Parthia. Then he was appointed, by lot, to the province of Cilicia, and set sail thither with twelve thousand foot and two thousand six hundred horse. He had orders to bring back Cappadocia to its allegiance to Ariobarzanes, its king; which settlement he effected very completely without recourse to arms. And perceiving the Cilicians, by the great loss the Romans had suffered in Parthia, and the commotions in Syria, to have become disposed to attempt a revolt, by a gentle course of government he soothed them back into fidelity. He would accept none of the presents that were offered him by the kings; he remitted the charge of public entertainments, but daily, at his own house, received the ingenious and accomplished persons of the province, not sumptuously, but liberally. His house had no porter, nor was he ever found in bed by any man, but early in the morning, standing or walking before his door, he received those who came to offer their salutations. He is said never once to have ordered any of those under his command to be beaten with rods, or to have their garments rent. He never gave contumelious language in his anger, nor inflicted punishment with reproach. He detected an embezzlement, to a large amount, in the public money, and thus relieved the cities from their burdens, at the same time that he allowed those who made restitution, to retain without further punishment their rights as citizens. He engaged too, in war, so far as to give a defeat to the banditti who infested Mount Amanus, for which he was saluted by his army Imperator. To Caecilius, the orator, who asked him to send him some panthers from Cilicia, to be exhibited on the theater at Rome, he wrote, in commendation of his own actions, that there were no panthers in Cilicia, for they were all fled to Caria, in anger that in so general a peace they had become the sole objects of attack. On leaving his province, he touched at Rhodes, and tarried for some length of time at Athens, longing much to renew his old studies. He visited the eminent men of learning, and saw his former friends and companions; and after receiving in Greece the honors that were due to him, returned to the city, where everything was now just as it were in a flame, breaking out into a civil war.

When the senate would have decreed him a triumph, he told them he had rather, so differences were accommodated, follow the triumphal chariot of Caesar. In private, he gave advice to both, writing many letters to Caesar, and personally entreating Pompey; doing his best to soothe and bring to reason both the one and the other. But when matters became incurable, and Caesar was approaching Rome, and Pompey durst not abide it, but, with many honest citizens, left the city, Cicero, as yet, did not join in the flight, and was reputed to adhere to Caesar. And it is very evident he was in his thoughts much divided, and wavered painfully between both, for he writes in his epistles, "To which side should I turn? Pompey has the fair and honorable plea for war; and Caesar, on the other hand, has managed his affairs better, and is more able to secure himself and his friends. So that I know whom I should fly, not whom I should fly to." But when Trebatius, one of Caesar's friends, by letter signified to him that Caesar thought it was his most desirable course to join his party, and partake his hopes, but if he considered himself too old a man for this, then he should retire into Greece, and stay quietly there, out of the way of either party, Cicero, wondering that Caesar had not written himself, gave an angry reply, that he should not do anything unbecoming his past life. Such is the account to be collected from his letters.

But as soon as Caesar was marched into Spain, he immediately sailed away to join Pompey. And he was welcomed by all but Cato; who, taking him privately, chid him for coming to Pompey. As for himself, he said, it had been indecent to forsake that part in the commonwealth which he had chosen from the beginning; but Cicero might have been more useful to his country and friends, if, remaining neuter, he had attended and used his influence to moderate the result, instead of coming hither to make himself, without reason or necessity, an enemy to Caesar, and a partner in such great dangers. By this language, partly, Cicero's feelings were altered, and partly, also, because Pompey made no great use of him. Although, indeed, he was himself the cause of it, by his not denying that he was sorry he had come, by his depreciating Pompey's resources, finding fault underhand with his counsels, and continually indulging in jests and sarcastic remarks on his fellow-soldiers. Though he went about in the camp with a gloomy and melancholy face himself, he was always trying to raise a laugh in others, whether they wished it or not. It may not be amiss to mention a few instances. To Domitius, on his preferring to a command one who was no soldier, and saying, in his defense, that he was a modest and prudent person, he replied, "Why did not you keep him for a tutor for your children?" On hearing Theophanes, the Lesbian, who was master of the engineers in the army, praised for the admirable way in which he had consoled the Rhodians for the loss of their fleet, "What a thing it is," he said, "to have a Greek in command!" When Caesar had been acting successfully, and in a manner blockading Pompey, Lentulus was saying it was reported that Caesar's friends were out of heart; "Because," said Cicero, "they do not wish Caesar well." To one Marcius, who had just come from Italy, and told them that there was a strong report at Rome that Pompey was blocked up, he said, "And you sailed hither to see it with your own eyes." To Nonius, encouraging them after a defeat to be of good hope, because there were seven eagles still left in Pompey's camp, "Good reason for encouragement," said Cicero, "if we were going to fight with jackdaws." Labienus insisted on some prophecies to the effect that Pompey would gain the victory; "Yes," said Cicero, "and the first step in the campaign has been losing our camp."

After the battle of Pharsalia was over, at which he was not present for want of health, and Pompey was fled, Cato, having considerable forces and a great fleet at Dyrrachium, would have had Cicero commander-in-chief, according to law, and the precedence of his consular dignity. And on his refusing the command, and wholly declining to take part in their plans for continuing the war, he was in the greatest danger of being killed, young Pompey and his friends calling him traitor, and drawing their swords upon him; only that Cato interposed, and hardly rescued and brought him out of the camp.

Afterwards, arriving at Brundusium, he tarried there sometime in expectation of Caesar, who was delayed by his affairs in Asia and Egypt. And when it was told him that he was arrived at Tarentum, and was coming thence by land to Brundusium, he hastened towards him, not altogether without hope, and yet in some fear of making experiment of the temper of an enemy and conqueror in the presence of many witnesses. But there was no necessity for him either to speak or do anything unworthy of himself; for Caesar, as soon as he saw him coming a good way before the rest of the company, came down to meet him, saluted him, and, leading the way, conversed with him alone for some furlongs. And from that time forward he continued to treat him with honor and respect; so that, when Cicero wrote an oration in praise of Cato, Caesar, in writing an answer to it, took occasion to commend Cicero's own life and eloquence, comparing him to Pericles and Theramenes. Cicero's oration was called Cato; Caesar's, anti-Cato.

So also, it is related that when Quintus Ligarius was prosecuted for having been in arms against Caesar, and Cicero had undertaken his defense, Caesar said to his friends, "Why might we not as well once more hear a speech from Cicero? Ligarius, there is no question, is a wicked man and an enemy." But when Cicero began to speak, he wonderfully moved him, and proceeded in his speech with such varied pathos, and such a charm of language, that the color of Caesar's countenance often changed, and it was evident that all the passions of his soul were in commotion. At length, the orator touching upon the Pharsalian battle, he was so affected that his body trembled, and some of the papers he held dropped out of his hands. And thus he was overpowered, and acquitted Ligarius.

Henceforth, the commonwealth being changed into a monarchy, Cicero withdrew himself from public affairs, and employed his leisure in instructing those young men that would, in philosophy; and by the near intercourse he thus had with some of the noblest and highest in rank, he again began to possess great influence in the city. The work and object which he set himself was to compose and translate philosophical dialogues and to render logical and physical terms into the Roman idiom. For he it was, as it is said, who first or principally gave Latin names to phantasia, syncatathesis, epokhe, catalepsis, atomon, ameres, kenon, and other such technical terms, which, either by metaphors or other means of accommodation, he succeeded in making intelligible and expressible to the Romans. For his recreation, he exercised his dexterity in poetry, and when he was set to it, would make five hundred verses in a night. He spent the greatest part of his time at his country-house near Tusculum. He wrote to his friends that he led the life of Laertes, either jestingly, as his custom was, or rather from a feeling of ambition for public employment, which made him impatient under the present state of affairs. He rarely went to the city, unless to pay his court to Caesar. He was commonly the first amongst those who voted him honors, and sought out new terms of praise for himself and for his actions. As, for example, what he said of the statues of Pompey, which had been thrown down, and were afterwards by Caesar's orders set up again: that Caesar, by this act of humanity, had indeed set up Pompey's statues, but he had fixed and established his own.

He had a design, it is said, of writing the history of his country, combining with it much of that of Greece, and incorporating in it all the stories and legends of the past that he had collected. But his purposes were interfered with by various public and various private unhappy occurrences and misfortunes; for most of which he was himself in fault. For first of all, he put away his wife Terentia, by whom he had been neglected in the time of the war, and sent away destitute of necessaries for his journey; neither did he find her kind when he returned into Italy, for she did not join him at Brundusium, where he stayed a long time, nor would allow her young daughter, who undertook so long a journey, decent attendance, or the requisite expenses; besides, she left him a naked and empty house, and yet had involved him in many and great debts. These were alleged as the fairest reasons for the divorce. But Terentia, who denied them all, had the most unmistakable defense furnished her by her husband himself, who not long after married a young maiden for the love of her beauty, as Terentia upbraided him; or as Tiro, his emancipated slave, has written, for her riches, to discharge his debts. For the young woman was very rich, and Cicero had the custody of her estate, being left guardian in trust; and being indebted many myriads of money, he was persuaded by his friends and relations to marry her, notwithstanding his disparity of age, and to use her money to satisfy his creditors. Antony, who mentions this marriage in his answer to the Philippics, reproaches him for putting away a wife with whom he had lived to old age; adding some happy strokes of sarcasm on Cicero's domestic, inactive, unsoldier-like habits. Not long after this marriage, his daughter died in child-bed at Lentulus's house, to whom she had been married after the death of Piso, her former husband. The philosophers from all parts came to comfort Cicero; for his grief was so excessive, that he put away his new-married wife, because she seemed to be pleased at the death of Tullia. And thus stood Cicero's domestic affairs at this time.

He had no concern in the design that was now forming against Caesar, although, in general, he was Brutus's most principal confidant, and one who was as aggrieved at the present, and as desirous of the former state of public affairs, as any other whatsoever. But they feared his temper, as wanting courage, and his old age, in which the most daring dispositions are apt to be timorous.

As soon, therefore, as the act was committed by Brutus and Cassius, and the friends of Caesar were got together, so that there was fear the city would again be involved in a civil war, Antony, being consul, convened the senate, and made a short address recommending concord. And Cicero, following with various remarks such as the occasion called for, persuaded the senate to imitate the Athenians, and decree an amnesty for what had been done in Caesar's case, and to bestow provinces on Brutus and Cassius. But neither of these things took effect. For as soon as the common people, of themselves inclined to pity, saw the dead body of Caesar borne through the marketplace, and Antony showing his clothes filled with blood, and pierced through in every part with swords, enraged to a degree of frenzy, they made a search for the murderers, and with firebrands in their hands ran to their houses to burn them. They, however, being forewarned, avoided this danger; and expecting many more and greater to come, they left the city.

Antony on this was at once in exultation, and everyone was in alarm with the prospect that he would make himself sole ruler, and Cicero in more alarm than anyone. For Antony, seeing his influence reviving in the commonwealth, and knowing how closely he was connected with Brutus, was ill-pleased to have him in the city. Besides, there had been some former jealousy between them, occasioned by the difference of their manners. Cicero, fearing the event, was inclined to go as lieutenant with Dolabella into Syria. But Hirtius and Pansa, consuls elect as successors of Antony, good men and lovers of Cicero, entreated him not to leave them, undertaking to put down Antony if he would stay in Rome. And he, neither distrusting wholly, nor trusting them, let Dolabella go without him, promising Hirtius that he would go and spend his summer at Athens, and return again when he entered upon his office. So he set out on his journey; but some delay occurring in his passage, new intelligence, as often happens, came suddenly from Rome, that Antony had made an astonishing change, and was doing all things and managing all public affairs at the will of the senate, and that there wanted nothing but his presence to bring things to a happy settlement. And therefore, blaming himself for his cowardice, he returned again to Rome, and was not deceived in his hopes at the beginning. For such multitudes flocked out to meet him, that the compliments and civilities which were paid him at the gates, and at his entrance into the city, took up almost one whole day's time.

On the morrow, Antony convened the senate, and summoned Cicero thither. He came not, but kept is bed, pretending to be ill with his journey; but the true reason seemed the fear of some design against him, upon a suspicion and intimation given him on his way to Rome. Antony, however, showed great offense at the affront, and sent soldiers, commanding them to bring him or burn his house; but many interceding and supplicating for him, he was contented to accept sureties. Ever after, when they met, they passed one another with silence, and continued on their guard, till Caesar, the younger, coming from Apollonia, entered on the first Caesar's inheritance, and was engaged in a dispute with Antony about two thousand five hundred myriads of money, which Antony detained from the estate.

Upon this, Philippus, who married the mother, and Marcellus, who married the sister of young Caesar, came with the young man to Cicero, and agreed with him that Cicero should give them the aid of his eloquence and political influence with the senate and people, and Caesar give Cicero the defense of his riches and arms. For the young man had already a great party of the soldiers of Caesar about him. And Cicero's readiness to join him was founded, it is said, on some yet stronger motives; for it seems, while Pompey and Caesar were yet alive, Cicero, in his sleep, had fancied himself engaged in calling some of the sons of the senators into the capitol, Jupiter being about, according to the dream, to declare one of them the chief ruler of Rome. The citizens, running up with curiosity, stood about the temple, and the youths, sitting in their purple-bordered robes, kept silence. On a sudden the doors opened, and the youths, arising one by one in order, passed round the god, who reviewed them all, and, to their sorrow, dismissed them; but when this one was passing by, the god stretched forth his right hand and said, "O ye Romans, this young man, when he shall be lord of Rome, shall put an end to all your civil wars." It is said that Cicero formed from his dream a distinct image of the youth, and retained it afterwards perfectly, but did not know who it was. The next day, going down into the Campus Martius, he met the boys resuming from their gymnastic exercises, and the first was he, just as he had appeared to him in his dream. Being astonished at it, he asked him who were his parents. And it proved to be this young Caesar, whose father was a man of no great eminence, Octavius, and his mother, Attia, Caesar's sister's daughter; for which reason, Caesar, who had no children, made him by will the heir of his house and property. From that time, it is said that Cicero studiously noticed the youth whenever he met him, and he as kindly received the civility; and by fortune he happened to be born when Cicero was consul.

These were the reasons spoken of; but it was principally Cicero's hatred of Antony, and a temper unable to resist honor, which fastened him to Caesar, with the purpose of getting the support of Caesar's power for his own public designs. For the young man went so far in his court to him, that he called him Father; at which Brutus was so highly displeased, that, in his epistles to Atticus he reflected on Cicero saying, it was manifest, by his courting Caesar for fear of Antony, he did not intend liberty to his country, but an indulgent master to himself. Notwithstanding, Brutus took Cicero's son, then studying philosophy at Athens, gave him a command, and employed him in various ways, with a good result. Cicero's own power at this time was at the greatest height in the city, and he did whatsoever he pleased; he completely overpowered and drove out Antony, and sent the two consuls, Hirtius and Pansa, with an army, to reduce him; and, on the other hand, persuaded the senate to allow Caesar the lictors and ensigns of a praetor, as though he were his country's defender. But after Antony was defeated in battle, and the two consuls slain, the armies united, and ranged themselves with Caesar. And the senate, fearing the young man, and his extraordinary fortune, endeavored, by honors and gifts, to call off the soldiers from him, and to lessen his power; professing there was no further need of arms, now Antony was put to flight.

This giving Caesar an affright, he privately sends some friends to entreat and persuade Cicero to procure the consular dignity for them both together; saying he should manage the affairs as he pleased, should have the supreme power, and govern the young man who was only desirous of name and glory. And Caesar himself confessed, that in fear of ruin, and in danger of being deserted, he had seasonably made use of Cicero's ambition, persuading him to stand with him, and to accept the offer of his aid and interest for the consulship.

And now, more than at any other time, Cicero let himself be carried away and deceived, though an old man, by the persuasions of a boy. He joined him in soliciting votes, and procured the good-will of the senate, not without blame at the time on the part of his friends; and he, too, soon enough after, saw that he had ruined himself, and betrayed the liberty of his country. For the young man, once established, and possessed of the office of consul, bade Cicero farewell; and, reconciling himself to Antony and Lepidus, joined his power with theirs, and divided the government, like a piece of property, with them. Thus united, they made a schedule of above two hundred persons who were to be put to death. But the greatest contention in all their debates was on the question of Cicero's case. Antony would come to no conditions, unless he should be the first man to be killed. Lepidus held with Antony, and Caesar opposed them both. They met secretly and by themselves, for three days together, near the town of Bononia. The spot was not far from the camp, with a river surrounding it. Caesar, it is said, contended earnestly for Cicero the first two days; but on the third day he yielded, and gave him up.

The terms of their mutual concessions were these; that Caesar should desert Cicero, Lepidus his brother Paulus, and Antony, Lucius Caesar, his uncle by his mother's side. Thus they let their anger and fury take from them the sense of humanity, and demonstrated that no beast is more savage than man, when possessed with power answerable to his rage.

Whilst these things were contriving, Cicero was with his brother at his country-house near Tusculum; whence, hearing of the proscriptions, they determined to pass to Astura, a villa of Cicero's near the sea, and to take shipping from thence for Macedonia to Brutus, of whose strength in that province news had already been heard. They traveled together in their separate litters, overwhelmed with sorrow; and often stopping on the way till their litters came together, condoled with one another. But Quintus was the more disheartened, when he reflected on his want of means for his journey; for, as he said, he had brought nothing with him from home. And even Cicero himself had but a slender provision. It was judged, therefore, most expedient that Cicero should make what haste he could to fly, and Quintus return home to provide necessaries, and thus resolved, they mutually embraced, and parted with many tears.

Quintus, within a few days after, betrayed by his servants to those who came to search for him, was slain, together with his young son. But Cicero was carried to Astura, where, finding a vessel, he immediately went on board her, and sailed as far as Circaeum with a prosperous gale; but when the pilots resolved immediately to set sail from thence, whether fearing the sea, or not wholly distrusting the faith of Caesar, he went on shore, and passed by land a hundred furlongs, as if he was going for Rome. But losing resolution and changing his mind, he again returned to the sea, and there spent the night in fearful and perplexed thoughts. Sometimes he resolved to go into Caesar's house privately, and there kill himself upon the altar of his household gods, to bring divine vengeance upon him; but the fear of torture put him off this course. And after passing through a variety of confused and uncertain counsels, at last he let his servants carry him by sea to Capitae, where he had a house, an agreeable place to retire to in the heat of summer, when the Etesian winds are so pleasant.

There was at that place a chapel of Apollo, not far from the seaside, from which a flight of crows rose with a great noise, and made towards Cicero's vessel as it rowed to land, and lighting on both sides of the yard, some croaked, others pecked the ends of the ropes. This was looked upon by all as an ill omen; and, therefore, Cicero went again ashore, and entering his house, lay down upon his bed to compose himself to rest. Many of the crows settled about the window, making a dismal cawing; but one of them alighted upon the bed where Cicero lay covered up, and with its bill by little and little pecked off the clothes from his face. His servants, seeing this, blamed themselves that they should stay to be spectators of their master's murder, and do nothing in his defense, whilst the brute creatures came to assist and take care of him in his undeserved affliction; and, therefore, partly by entreaty, partly by force, they took him up, and carried him in his litter towards the sea-side.

But in the meantime the assassins were come with a band of soldiers, Herennius, a centurion, and Popillius, a tribune, whom Cicero had formerly defended when prosecuted for the murder of his father. Finding the doors shut, they broke them open, and Cicero not appearing and those within saying they knew not where he was, it is stated that a youth, who had been educated by Cicero in the liberal arts and sciences, an emancipated slave of his brother Quintus, Philologus by name, informed the tribune that the litter was on its way to the sea through the close and shady walks. The tribune, taking a few with him, ran to the place where he was to come out. And Cicero, perceiving Herennius running in the walks, commanded his servants to set down the litter; and stroking his chin, as he used to do, with his left hand, he looked steadfastly upon his murderers, his person covered with dust, his beard and hair untrimmed, and his face worn with his troubles. So that the greatest part of those that stood by covered their faces whilst Herennius slew him. And thus was he murdered, stretching forth his neck out of the litter, being now in his sixty-fourth year. Herennius cut off his head, and, by Antony's command, his hands also, by which his Philippics were written; for so Cicero styled those orations he wrote against Antony, and so they are called to this day.

When these members of Cicero were brought to Rome, Antony was holding an assembly for the choice of public officers; and when he heard it, and saw them, he cried out, "Now let there be an end of our proscriptions." He commanded his head and hands to be fastened up over the Rostra, where the orators spoke; a sight which the Roman people shuddered to behold, and they believed they saw there not the face of Cicero, but the image of Antony's own soul. And yet amidst these actions he did justice in one thing, by delivering up Philologus to Pomponia, the wife of Quintus; who, having got his body into her power, besides other grievous punishments, made him cut off his own flesh by pieces, and roast and eat it; for so some writers have related. But Tiro, Cicero's emancipated slave, has not so much as mentioned the treachery of Philologus.

Some long time after, Caesar, I have been told, visiting one of his daughter's sons, found him with a book of Cicero's in his hand. The boy for fear endeavored to hide it under his gown; which Caesar perceiving, took it from him, and turning over a great part of the book standing, gave it him again, and said, "My child, this was a learned man, and a lover of his country." And immediately after he had vanquished Antony, being then consul, he made Cicero's son his colleague in the office; and under that consulship, the senate took down all the statues of Antony, and abolished all the other honors that had been given him, and decreed that none of that family should thereafter bear the name of Marcus; and thus the final acts of the punishment of Antony were, by the divine powers, devolved upon the family of Cicero.

Comparison of Demosthenes and Cicero

THESE are the most memorable circumstances recorded in history of Demosthenes and Cicero which have come to our knowledge. But omitting an exact comparison of their respective faculties in speaking, yet thus much seems fit to be said; that Demosthenes, to make himself a master in rhetoric, applied all the faculties he had, natural or acquired, wholly that way; that he far surpassed in force and strength of eloquence all his contemporaries in political and judicial speaking, in grandeur and majesty all the panegyrical orators, and in accuracy and science all the logicians and rhetoricians of his day; that Cicero was highly educated, and by his diligent study became a most accomplished general scholar in all these branches, having left behind him numerous philosophical treatises of his own on Academic principles; as, indeed, even in his written speeches, both political and judicial, we see him continually trying to show his learning by the way. And one may discover the different temper of each of them in their speeches. For Demosthenes's oratory was without all embellishment and jesting, wholly composed for real effect and seriousness; not smelling of the lamp, as Pytheas scoffingly said, but of the temperance, thoughtfulness, austerity, and grave earnestness of his temper. Whereas Cicero's love of mockery often ran him into scurrility; and in his love of laughing away serious arguments in judicial cases by jests and facetious remarks, with a view to the advantage of his clients, he paid too little regard to what was decent: saying, for example, in his defense of Caelius, that he had done no absurd thing in such plenty and affluence to indulge himself in pleasures, it being a kind of madness not to enjoy the things we possess, especially since the most eminent philosophers have asserted pleasure to be the chiefest good. So also we are told, that when Cicero, being consul, undertook the defense of Murena against Cato's prosecution, by way of bantering Cato, he made a long series of jokes upon the absurd paradoxes, as they are called, of the Stoic sect; so that a loud laughter passing from the crowd to the judges, Cato, with a quiet smile, said to those that sat next him, "My friends, what an amusing consul we have."

And, indeed, Cicero was by natural temper very much disposed to mirth and pleasantry, and always appeared with a smiling and serene countenance. But Demosthenes had constant care and thoughtfulness in his look, and a serious anxiety, which he seldom, if ever, laid aside; and, therefore, was accounted by his enemies, as he himself confessed, morose and ill-mannered.

Also, it is very evident, out of their several writings, that Demosthenes never touched upon his own praises but decently and without offense when there was need of it, and for some weightier end; but, upon other occasions modestly and sparingly. But Cicero's immeasurable boasting of himself in his orations argues him guilty of an uncontrollable appetite for distinction, his cry being evermore that arms should give place to the gown, and the soldier's laurel to the tongue. And at last we find him extolling not only his deeds and actions, but his orations also, as well those that were only spoken, as those that were published; as if he were engaged in a boyish trial of skill, who should speak best, with the rhetoricians, Isocrates and Anaximenes, not as one who could claim the task to guide and instruct the Roman nation, the

> Soldier full-armed, terrific to the foe.

It is necessary, indeed, for a political leader to be an able speaker; but it is an ignoble thing for any man to admire and relish the glory of his own eloquence. And, in this matter, Demosthenes had a more than ordinary gravity and magnificence of mind, accounting his talent in speaking nothing more than a mere accomplishment and matter of practice, the success of which must depend greatly on the good-will and candor of his hearers, and regarding those who pride themselves on such accounts to be men of a low and petty disposition.

The power of persuading and governing the people did, indeed, equally belong to both, so that those who had armies and camps at command stood in need of their assistance; as Chares, Diopithes, and Leosthenes of Demosthenes's, Pompey and young Caesar of Cicero's, as the latter himself admits in his Memoirs addressed to Agrippa and Maecenas. But what are thought and commonly said most to demonstrate and try the tempers of men, namely, authority and place, by moving every passion, and discovering every frailty, these are things which Demosthenes never received; nor was he ever in a position to give such proof of himself, having never obtained any eminent office, nor led any of those armies into the field against Philip which he raised by his eloquence. Cicero, on the other hand, was sent quaestor into Sicily, and proconsul into Cilicia and Cappadocia, at a time when avarice was at the height, and the commanders and governors who were employed abroad, as though they thought it a mean thing to steal, set themselves to seize by open force; so that it seemed no heinous matter to take bribes, but he that did it most moderately was in good esteem. And yet he, at this time, gave the most abundant proofs alike of his contempt of riches and of his humanity and good-nature. And at Rome, when he was created consul in name, but indeed received sovereign and dictatorial authority against Catiline and his conspirators, he attested the truth of Plato's prediction, that then the miseries of states would be at an end, when by a happy fortune supreme power, wisdom, and justice should be united in one.

It is said, to the reproach of Demosthenes, that his eloquence was mercenary; that he privately made orations for Phormion and Apollodorus, though adversaries in the same cause; that he was charged with moneys received from the king of Persia, and condemned for bribes from Harpalus. And should we grant that all those (and they are not few) who have made these statements against him have spoken what is untrue, yet that Demosthenes was not the character to look without desire on the presents offered him out of respect and gratitude by royal persons, and that one who lent money on maritime usury was likely to be thus indifferent, is what we cannot assert. But that Cicero refused, from the Sicilians when he was quaestor, from the king of Cappadocia when he was proconsul, and from his friends at Rome when he was in exile, many presents, though urged to receive them, has been said already.

Moreover, Demosthenes's banishment was infamous, upon conviction for bribery; Cicero's very honorable, for ridding his country of a set of villains. Therefore, when Demosthenes fled his country, no man regarded it; for Cicero's sake the senate changed their habit, and put on mourning, and would not be persuaded to make any act before Cicero's return was decreed. Cicero, however, passed his exile idly in Macedonia. But the very exile of Demosthenes made up a great part of the services he did for his country; for he went through the cities of Greece, and everywhere, as we have said, joined in the conflict on behalf of the Grecians, driving out the Macedonian ambassadors, and approving himself a much better citizen than Themistocles and Alcibiades did in the like fortune. And, after his return, he again devoted himself to the same public service, and continued firm to his opposition to Antipater and the Macedonians. Whereas Laelius reproached Cicero in the senate for sitting silent when Caesar, a beardless youth, asked leave to come forward, contrary to the law, as a candidate for the consulship; and Brutus, in his epistles, charges him with nursing and rearing a greater and more heavy tyranny than that they had removed.

Finally, Cicero's death excites our pity; for an old man to be miserably carried up and down by his servants, flying and hiding himself from that death which was, in the course of nature, so near at hand; and yet at last to be murdered. Demosthenes, though he seemed at first a little to supplicate, yet, by his preparing and keeping the poison by him, demands our admiration; and still more admirable was his using it. When the temple of the god no longer afforded him a sanctuary, he took refuge, as it were, at a mightier altar, freeing himself from arms and soldiers, and laughing to scorn the cruelty of Antipater.

Life of Alexander the Great

1

IT is the life of Alexander the king, and of Caesar, who overthrew Pompey, that I am writing in this book, and the multitude of the deeds to be treated is so great that I shall make no other preface than to entreat my readers, in case I do not tell of all the famous actions of these men, nor even speak exhaustively at all in each particular case, but in epitome for the most part, not to complain. For it is not Histories that I am writing, but Lives; and in the most illustrious deeds there is not always a manifestation of virtue or vice, nay, a slight thing like a phrase or a jest often makes a greater revelation of character than battles when thousands fall, or the greatest armaments, or sieges of cities. Accordingly, just as painters get the likenesses in their portraits from the face and the expression of the eyes, wherein the character shows itself, but make very little account of the other parts of the body, so I must be permitted to devote myself rather to the signs of the soul in men, and by means of these to portray the life of each, leaving to others the description of their great contests.

2

AS for the lineage of Alexander, on his father's side he was a descendant of Heracles through Caranus, and on his mother's side a descendant of Aeacus through Neoptolemus; this is accepted without any question. And we are told that Philip, after being initiated into the mysteries of Samothrace at the same time with Olympias, he himself being still a youth and she an orphan child, fell in love with her and betrothed himself to her at once with the consent of her brother, Arymbas. Well, then, the night before that on which the marriage was consummated, the bride dreamed that there was a peal of thunder and that a thunder-bolt fell upon her womb, and that thereby much fire was kindled, which broke into flames that traveled all about, and then was extinguished. At a later time, too, after the marriage, Philip dreamed that he was putting a seal upon his wife's womb; and the device of the seal, as he thought, was the figure of a lion. The other seers, now, were led by the vision to suspect that Philip needed to put a closer watch upon his marriage relations; but Aristander of Telmessus said that the woman was pregnant, since no seal was put upon what was empty, and pregnant of a son whose nature would be bold and lion-like. Moreover, a serpent was once seen lying stretched out by the side of Olympias as she slept, and we are told that this, more than anything else, dulled the ardour of Philip's attentions to his wife, so that he no longer came often to sleep by her side, either because he feared that some spells and enchantments might be practiced upon him by her, or because he shrank for her embraces in the conviction that she was the partner of a superior being.

But concerning these matters there is another story to this effect: all the women of these parts were addicted to the Orphic rites and the orgies of Dionysus from very ancient times (being called Klodones and Mimallones) and imitated in many ways the practices of the Edonian women and the Thracian women about Mount Haemus, from whom, as it would seem, the word "threskeuein" came to be applied to the celebration of extravagant and superstitious ceremonies. Now Olympias, who affected these divine possessions more zealously than other women, and carried out these divine inspirations in wilder fashion, used to provide the reveling companies with great tame serpents, which would often lift their heads from out the ivy and the mystic winnowing-baskets, or coil themselves about the wands and garlands of the women, thus terrifying the men.

3

HOWEVER, after his vision, as we are told, Philip sent Chaeron of Megalopolis to Delphi, by whom an oracle was brought to him from Apollo, who bade him sacrifice to Ammon and hold that god in greatest reverence, but told him he was to lose that one of his eyes which he had applied to the chink in the door when he espied the god, in the form of a serpent, sharing the couch of his wife. Moreover, Olympias, as Eratosthenes says, when she sent Alexander forth upon his great expedition, told him, and him alone, the secret of his begetting, and bade him have purposes worthy of his birth. Others, on the contrary, say that she repudiated the idea, and said: "Alexander must cease slandering me to Hera."

Be that as it may, Alexander was born early in the month Hecatombaeon, the Macedonian name for which is Loüs, on the sixth day of the month, and on this day the temple of Ephesian Artemis was burnt. It was apropos of this that Hegesias the Magnesian made an utterance frigid enough to have extinguished that great conflagration. He said, namely, it was no wonder that the temple of Artemis was burned down, since the goddess was busy bringing Alexander into the world. But all the Magi who were then at Ephesus, looking upon the temple's disaster as a sign of further disaster, ran about beating their faces and crying aloud that woe and great calamity for Asia had that day been born. To Philip, however, who had just taken Potidaea, there came three messages at the same time: the first that Parmenio had conquered the Illyrians in a great battle, the second that his race-horse had won a victory at the Olympic games, while a third announced the birth of Alexander. These things delighted him, of course, and the seers raised his hopes still higher by declaring that the son whose birth coincided with three victories would be always victorious.

4

THE outward appearance of Alexander is best represented by the statues of him which Lysippus made, and it was by this artist alone that Alexander himself thought it fit that he should be modeled. For those peculiarities which many of his successors and friends afterwards tried to imitate, namely, the poise of the neck, which was bent slightly to the left, and the melting glance of his eyes, this artist has accurately observed. Apelles, however, in painting him as wielder of the thunder-bolt, did not reproduce his complexion, but made it too dark and swarthy. Whereas he was of a fair colour, as they say, and his fairness passed into ruddiness on his breast particularly, and in his face. Moreover, that a very pleasant odour exhaled from his skin and that there was a fragrance about his mouth and all his flesh, so that his garments were filled with it, this we have read in the Memoirs of Aristoxenus.

Now, the cause of this, perhaps, was the temperament of his body, which was a very warm and fiery one; for fragrance is generated, as Theophrastus thinks, where moist humours are acted upon by heat. Wherefore the dry and parched regions of the world produce the most and best spices; for the sun draws away the moisture which, like material of corruption, abounds in vegetable bodies. And in Alexander's case, it was the heat of his body, as it would seem, which made him prone to drink, and choleric.

But while he was still a boy his self-restraint showed itself in the fact that, although he was impetuous and violent in other matters, the pleasures of the body had little hold upon him, and he indulged in them with great moderation, while his ambition kept his spirit serious and lofty in advance of his years. For it was neither every kind of fame nor fame from every source that he courted, as Philip did, who plumed himself like a sophist on the power of his oratory, and took care to have the victories of his chariots at Olympia engraved upon his coins; nay, when those about him inquired whether he would be willing to contend in the foot-race at the Olympic games, since he was swift of foot, "Yes," said he, "if I could have kings as my contestants." And in general, too, Alexander appears to have been averse to the whole race of athletes; at any rate, though he instituted very many contests, not only for tragic poets and players on the flute and players on the lyre, but also for rhapsodists, as well as for hunting of every sort and for fighting with staves, he took no interest in offering prizes either for boxing or for the pancratium.

5

HE once entertained the envoys from the Persian king who came during Philip's absence, and associated with them freely. He won upon them by his friendliness, and by asking no childish or trivial questions, but by inquiring about the length of the roads and the character of the journey into the interior, about the king himself, what sort of a warrior he was, and what the prowess and might of the Persians. The envoys were therefore astonished and regarded the much-talked-of ability of Philip as nothing compared with his son's eager disposition to do great things. At all events, as often as tidings were brought that Philip had either taken a famous city or been victorious in some celebrated battle, Alexander was not very glad to hear them, but would say to his comrades: "Boys, my father will anticipate everything; and for me he will leave no great or brilliant achievement to be displayed to the world with your aid." For since he did not covet pleasure, nor even wealth, but excellence and fame, he considered that the more he should receive from his father the fewer would be the successes won by himself. Therefore, considering that increase in prosperity meant the squandering upon his father of opportunities for achievement, he preferred to receive from him a realm which afforded, not wealth nor luxury and enjoyment, but struggles and wars and ambitions.

In the work of caring for him, then, many persons, as was natural, were appointed to be his nurturers, tutors, and teachers, but over them all stood Leonidas, a man of stern temperament and a kinsman of Olympias. Although he did not himself shun the title of tutor, since the office afforded an honourable and brilliant occupation, yet by other people, owing to his dignity and his relationship, he was called Alexander's foster-father and preceptor. The man, however, who assumed the character and the title of tutor was Lysimachus, a native of Acarnania, who had no general refinement, but because he called himself Phoenix, Alexander Achilles, and Philip Peleus, was highly regarded and held a second place.

6

ONCE upon a time Philoneicus the Thessalian brought Bucephalas, offering to sell him to Philip for thirteen talents, and they went down into the plain to try the horse, who appeared to be savage and altogether intractable, neither allowing any one to mount him, nor heeding the voice of any of Philip's attendants, but rearing up against all of them. Then Philip was vexed and ordered the horse to be led away, believing him to be altogether wild and unbroken; but Alexander, who was near by, said: "What a horse they are losing, because, for lack of skill and courage, they cannot manage him!" At first, then, Philip held his peace; but as Alexander many times let fall such words and showed great distress, he said: "Dost thou find fault with thine elders in the belief that thou knowest more than they do or art better able to manage a horse?" "This horse, at any rate," said Alexander, "I could manage better than others have." "And if thou shouldst not, what penalty wilt thou undergo for thy rashness?" "Indeed," said Alexander, "I will forfeit the price of the horse." There was laughter at this, and then an agreement between father and son as to the forfeiture, and at once Alexander ran to the horse, took hold of his bridle-rein, and turned him towards the sun; for he had noticed, as it would seem, that the horse was greatly disturbed by the sight of his own shadow falling in front of him and dancing about. And after he had calmed the horse a little in this way, and had stroked him with his hand, when he saw that he was full of spirit and courage, he quietly cast aside his mantle and with a light spring safely bestrode him. Then, with a little pressure of the reins on the bit, and without striking him or tearing his mouth, he held him in hand; but when he saw that the horse was rid of the fear that had beset him, and was impatient for the course, he gave him his head, and at last urged him on with sterner tone and thrust of foot. Philip and his company were speechless with anxiety at first; but when Alexander made the turn in proper fashion and came back to them proud and exultant, all the rest broke into loud cries, but his father, as we are told, actually shed tears of joy, and when Alexander had dismounted, kissed him, saying: "My son, seek thee out a kingdom equal to thyself; Macedonia has not room for thee."

7

AND since Philip saw that his son's nature was unyielding and that he resisted compulsion, but was easily led by reasoning into the path of duty, he himself tried to persuade rather than to command him; and because he would not wholly entrust the direction and training of the boy to the ordinary teachers of poetry and the formal studies, feeling that it was a matter of too great importance, and, in the words of Sophocles,

> "A task for many bits and rudder-sweeps as well,"

he sent for the most famous and learned of philosophers, Aristotle, and paid him a noble and appropriate tuition-fee. The city of Stageira, that is, of which Aristotle was a native, and which he had himself destroyed, he peopled again, and restored to it those of its citizens who were in exile or slavery.

Well, then, as a place where master and pupil could labour and study, he assigned them the precinct of the nymphs near Mieza, where to this day the visitor is shown the stone seats and shady walks of Aristotle. It would appear, moreover, that Alexander not only received from his master his ethical and political doctrines, but also participated in those secret and more profound teachings which philosophers designate by the special terms "acroamatic" and "epoptic," and do not impart to many. For after he had already crossed into Asia, and when he learned that certain treatises on these recondite matters had been published in books by Aristotle, he wrote him a letter on behalf of philosophy, and put it in plain language. And this is a copy of the letter. "Alexander, to Aristotle, greeting. Thou hast not done well to publish thy acroamatic doctrines; for in what shall I surpass other men if those doctrines wherein I have been trained are to be all men's common property? But I had rather excel in my acquaintance with the best things than in my power. Farewell." Accordingly, in defending himself, Aristotle encourages this ambition of Alexander by saying that the doctrines of which he spoke were both published and not published; for in truth his treatise on metaphysics is of no use for those who would either teach or learn the science, but is written as a memorandum for those already trained therein.

8

MOREOVER, in my opinion Alexander's love of the art of healing was inculcated in him by Aristotle preeminently. For he was not only fond of the theory of medicine, but actually came to the aid of his friends when they were sick, and prescribed for them certain treatments and regimens, as one can gather from his letters. He was also by nature a lover of learning and a lover of reading. And since he thought and called the Iliad a viaticum of the military art, he took with him Aristotle's recension of the poem, called the Iliad of the Casket, and always kept it lying with his dagger under his pillow, as Onesicritus informs us; and when he could find no other books in the interior of Asia, he ordered Harpalus to send him some. So Harpalus sent him the books of Philistus, a great many of the tragedies of Euripides, Sophocles, and Aeschylus, and the dithyrambic poems of Telestes and Philoxenus. Aristotle he admired at the first, and loved him, as he himself used to say, more than he did his father, for that the one had given him life, but the other had taught him a noble life; later, however, he held him in more or less of suspicion, not to the extent of doing him any harm, but his kindly attentions lacked their former ardour and affection towards him, and this was proof of estrangement. However, that eager yearning for philosophy which was embedded in his nature and which ever grew with his growth, did not subside from his soul, as is testified by the honour in which he held Anaxarchus, by his gift of fifty talents to Xenocrates, and by the attentions which he so lavishly bestowed upon Dandamis and Calanus.

9

WHILE Philip was making an expedition against Byzantium, Alexander, though only sixteen years of age, was left behind as regent in Macedonia and keeper of the royal seal, and during this time he subdued the rebellious Maedi, and after taking their city, drove out the Barbarians, settled there a mixed population, and named the city Alexandropolis. He was also present at Chaeroneia and took part in the battle against the Greeks, and he is said to have been the first to break the ranks of the Sacred Band of the Thebans. And even down to our own day there was shown an ancient oak by the Cephisus, called Alexander's oak, near which at that time he pitched his tent; and the general sepulchre of the Macedonians is not far away.

In consequence of these exploits, then, as was natural, Philip was excessively fond of his son, so that he even rejoiced to hear the Macedonians call Alexander their king, but Philip their general. However, the disorders in his household, due to the fact that his marriages and amours carried into the kingdom the infection, as it were, which reigned in the women's apartments, produced many grounds of offence and great quarrels between father and son, and these the bad temper of Olympias, who was a jealous and sullen woman, made still greater, since she spurred Alexander on. The most open quarrel was brought on by Attalus at the marriage of Cleopatra, a maiden whom Philip was taking to wife, having fallen in love with the girl when he was past the age for it. Attalus, now, was the girl's uncle, and being in his cups, he called upon the Macedonians to ask of the gods that from Philip and Cleopatra there might be born a legitimate successor to the kingdom. At this Alexander was exasperated, and with the words, "But what of me, base wretch? Dost thou take me for a bastard?" threw a cup at him. Then Philip rose up against him with drawn sword, but, fortunately for both, his anger and his wine made him trip and fall. Then Alexander, mocking over him, said: "Look now, men! here is one who was preparing to cross from Europe into Asia; and he is upset in trying to cross from couch to couch." After this drunken broil Alexander took Olympias and established her in Epirus, while he himself tarried in Illyria.

Meanwhile Demaratus the Corinthian, who was a guest-friend of the house and a man of frank speech, came to see Philip. After the first greetings and welcomes were over, Philip asked him how the Greeks were agreeing with one another, and Demaratus replied: "It is surely very fitting, Philip, that thou shouldst be concerned about Greece, when thou hast filled thine own house with such great dissension and calamities." Thus brought to his senses, Philip sent and fetched Alexander home, having persuaded him to come through the agency of Demaratus.

10

BUT when Pixodarus, the satrap of Caria, trying by means of a tie of relationship to steal into a military alliance with Philip, wished to give his eldest daughter in marriage to Arrhidaeus the son of Philip, and sent Aristocritus to Macedonia on this errand, once more slanderous stories kept coming to Alexander from his friends and his mother, who said that Philip, by means of a brilliant marriage and a great connexion, was trying to settle the kingdom upon Arrhidaeus. Greatly disturbed by these stories, Alexander sent Thessalus, the tragic actor, to Caria, to argue with Pixodarus that he ought to ignore the bastard brother, who was also a fool, and make Alexander his connection by marriage. And this plan was vastly more pleasing to Pixodarus than the former. But Philip, becoming aware of this, went to Alexander's chamber, taking with him one of Alexander's friends and companions, Philotas the son of Parmenio, and upbraided his son severely, and bitterly reviled him as ignoble and unworthy of his high estate, in that he desired to become the son-in-law of a man who was a Carian and a slave to a barbarian king. And as for Thessalus, Philip wrote to the Corinthians that they should send him back to Macedonia in chains. Moreover, of the other companions of Alexander, he banished from Macedonia Harpalus and Nearchus, as well as Erigyius and Ptolemy, men whom Alexander afterwards recalled and had in the highest honours.

And so when Pausanias, who had been outrageously dealt with at the instance of Attalus and Cleopatra and could get no justice at Philip's hands, slew Philip, most of the blame devolved upon Olympias, on the ground that she had added her exhortations to the young man's anger and incited him to the deed; but a certain amount of accusation attached itself to Alexander also. For it is said that when Pausanias, after the outrage that he had suffered, met Alexander, and bewailed his fate, Alexander recited to him the iambic verse of the "Medeia":

> "The giver of the bride, the bridegroom, and the bride."

However, he did seek out the participants in the plot and punished them, and was angry with Olympias for her savage treatment of Cleopatra during his absence.

11

THUS it was that at the age of twenty years Alexander received the kingdom, which was exposed to great jealousies, dire hatreds, and dangers on every hand. For the neighbouring tribes of Barbarians would not tolerate their servitude, and longed for their hereditary kingdoms; and as for Greece, although Philip had conquered her in the field, he had not had time enough to make her tame under his yoke, but had merely disturbed and changed the condition of affairs there, and then left them in a great surge and commotion, owing to the strangeness of the situation. The Macedonian counselors of Alexander had fears of the crisis, and thought he should give up the Greek states altogether and use no more compulsion there, and that he should call the revolting Barbarians back to their allegiance by mild measures and try to arrest the first symptoms of their revolutions; but he himself set out from opposite principles to win security and safety for his realm by boldness and a lofty spirit, assured that, were he seen to abate his dignity even but a little, all his enemies would set upon him. Accordingly, he put a speedy stop to the disturbances and wars among the Barbarians by overrunning their territories with an army as far as to the river Danube, where he fought a great battle with Syrmus, the king of the Triballi, and defeated him; and on learning that the Thebans had revolted and that the Athenians were in sympathy with them, he immediately led his forces through the pass of Thermopylae, declaring that since Demosthenes had called him a boy while he was among the Illyrians and Triballians, and a stripling when he had reached Thessaly, he wished to show him that before the walls of Athens he was a man.

Arrived before Thebes, and wishing to give her still a chance to repent of what she had done, he merely demanded the surrender of Phoenix and Prothytes, and proclaimed an amnesty for those who came over to his side. But the Thebans made a counter-demand that he should surrender to them Philotas and Antipater, and made a counter-proclamation that all who wished to help in setting Greece free should range themselves with them; and so Alexander set his Macedonians to the work of war. On the part of the Thebans, then, the struggle was carried on with a spirit and valour beyond their powers, since they were arrayed against an enemy who was many times more numerous than they; but when the Macedonian garrison also, leaving the citadel of the Cadmeia, fell upon them in the rear, most of them were surrounded, and fell in the battle itself, and their city was taken, plundered, and razed to the ground. This was done, in the main, because Alexander expected that the Greeks would be terrified by so great a disaster and cower down in quiet, but apart from this, he also plumed himself on gratifying the complaints of his allies; for the Phocians and Plataeans had denounced the Thebans. So after separating out the priests, all who were guest-friends of the Macedonians, the descendants of Pindar, and those who had voted against the revolt, he sold the rest into slavery, and they proved to be more than thirty thousand; those who had been slain were more than six thousand.

12

AMONG the many and grievous calamities which thus possessed the city, some Thracians broke into the house of Timocleia, a woman of high repute and chastity, and while the rest were plundering her property, their leader shamefully violated her, and then asked her if she had gold or silver concealed anywhere. She admitted that she had, and after leading him by himself into the garden and showing him a well, told him that when the city was taken she had with her own hands cast in there her most valuable possessions. Then, as the Thracian was bending over and inspecting the place, she came behind him and pushed him in, cast many stones upon him, and killed him. And when the Thracians led her, with hands bound, to Alexander, she showed by her mien and gait that she was a person of great dignity and lofty spirit, so calmly and fearlessly did she follow her conductors; and when the king asked her who she was, she replied that she was a sister of Theagenes, who drew up the forces which fought Philip in behalf of the liberty of the Greeks, and fell in command at Chaeroneia. Amazed, therefore, at her reply and at what she had done, Alexander bade her depart in freedom with her children.

13

FURTHERMORE, he was reconciled with the Athenians, although they showed exceeding sorrow at the misfortunes of Thebes; for although they had begun the festival of the mysteries, they gave it up in consequence of their grief, and upon the Thebans who sought refuge in their city they bestowed every kindness. But notwithstanding this, whether his rage was now sated, as a lion's might be, or whether he wished to offset a deed of the most sullen savagery with one that was merciful, he not only remitted all his charges against the city, but even bade it give good heed to its affairs, since, if anything should happen to him, it would have the rule over Greece. In later times, moreover, as we are told, the calamity of the Thebans often gave him remorse, and made him milder towards many people. And certainly the murder of Cleitus, which he committed in his cups, and the cowardly refusal of his Macedonians to follow him against the Indians, whereby they as it were robbed his expedition and his glory of their consummation, he was wont to attribute to the vengeful wrath of Dionysus. And there was not a Theban of those that survived who afterwards came to him with any request and did not get what he wanted from him. Thus much concerning Thebes.

14

AND now a general assembly of the Greeks was held at the Isthmus, where a vote was passed to make an expedition against Persia with Alexander, and he was proclaimed their leader. Thereupon many statesmen and philosophers came to him with their congratulations, and he expected that Diogenes of Sinope also, who was tarrying in Corinth, would do likewise. But since that philosopher took not the slightest notice of Alexander, and continued to enjoy his leisure in the suburb Craneion, Alexander went in person to see him; and he found him lying in the sun. Diogenes raised himself up a little when he saw so many persons coming towards him, and fixed his eyes upon Alexander. And when that monarch addressed him with greetings, and asked if he wanted anything, "Yes," said Diogenes, "stand a little out of my sun." It is said that Alexander was so struck by this, and admired so much the haughtiness and grandeur of the man who had nothing but scorn for him, that he said to his followers, who were laughing and jesting about the philosopher as they went away, "But verily, if I were not Alexander, I would be Diogenes."

And now, wishing to consult the god concerning the expedition against Asia, he went to Delphi; and since he chanced to come on one of the inauspicious days, when it is not lawful to deliver oracles, in the first place he sent a summons to the prophetess. And when she refused to perform her office and cited the law in her excuse, he went up himself and tried to drag her to the temple, whereupon, as if overcome by his ardour, she said: "Thou art invincible, my son!" On hearing this, Alexander said he desired no further prophecy, but had from her the oracle which he wanted.

Moreover, when he set out upon his expedition, it appears that there were many signs from heaven, and, among them, the image of Orpheus at Leibethra (it was made of cypress-wood) sweated profusely at about that time. Most people feared the sign, but Aristander bade Alexander be of good cheer, assured that he was to perform deeds worthy of song and story, which would cost poets and musicians much toil and sweat to celebrate.

15

AS to the number of his forces, those who put it at the smallest figure mention thirty thousand foot and four thousand horse; those who put it at the highest, forty-three thousand foot and five thousand horse. To provision these forces, Aristobulus says he had not more than seventy talents; Duris speaks of maintenance for only thirty days; and Onesicritus says he owed two hundred talents besides. But although he set out with such meagre and narrow resources, he would not set foot upon his ship until he had enquired into the circumstances of his companions and allotted to one a farm, to another a village, and to another the revenue from some hamlet or harbour. And when at last nearly all of the crown property had been expended or allotted, Perdiccas said to him: "But for thyself, O king, what art thou leaving?" And when the king answered, "My hopes," "In these, then," said Perdiccas, "we also will share who make the expedition with thee." Then he declined the possessions which had been allotted to him, and some of the other friends of Alexander did likewise. But upon those who wanted and would accept his favours Alexander bestowed them readily, and most of what he possessed in Macedonia was used up in these distributions. Such was the ardour and such the equipment with which he crossed the Hellespont.

Then, going up to Ilium, he sacrificed to Athena and poured libations to the heroes. Furthermore, the gravestone of Achilles he anointed with oil, ran a race by it with his companions, naked, as is the custom, and then crowned it with garlands, pronouncing the hero happy in having, while he lived, a faithful friend, and after death, a great herald of his fame. As he was going about and viewing the sights of the city, someone asked him if he wished to see the lyre of Paris. "For that lyre," said Alexander, "I care very little; but I would gladly see that of Achilles, to which he used to sing the glorious deeds of brave men."

16

MEANWHILE the generals of Dareius had assembled a large

force and set it in array at the crossing of the river Granicus, so that it was practically necessary to fight, as it were at the gates of Asia, for entrance and dominion there. But most of the Macedonian officers were afraid of the depth of the river, and of the roughness and unevenness of the farther banks, up which they would have to climb while fighting. Some, too, thought they ought to observe carefully the customary practice in regard to the month (in the month of Daesius the kings of Macedonia were not wont to take the field with an army). This objection Alexander removed by bidding them call the month a second Artemisius; and when Parmenio, on the ground that it was too late in the day, objected to their risking the passage, he declared that the Hellespont would blush for shame, if, after having crossed that strait, he should be afraid of the Granicus, and plunged into the stream with thirteen troops of horsemen. And since he was charging against hostile missiles and precipitous positions covered with infantry and cavalry, and through a stream that swept men off their feet and surged about them, he seemed to be acting like a frenzied and foolish commander rather than a wise one. However, he persisted in his attempt to cross, gained the opposite banks with difficulty and much ado, though they were moist and slippery with mud, and was at once compelled to fight pell-mell and engage his assailants man by man, before his troops who were crossing could form into any order. For the enemy pressed upon them with loud shouts, and matching horse with horse, plied their lances, and their swords when their lances were shattered. Many rushed upon Alexander, for he was conspicuous by his buckler and by his helmet's crest, on either side of which was fixed a plume of wonderful size and whiteness. But although a javelin pierced the joint of his breastplate, he was not wounded; and when Rhoesaces and Spithridates, two Persian commanders, made at him together, he avoided the one, and smote Rhoesaces, who wore a breastplate, with his spear; and when this weapon snapped in two with the blow, he took to his sword. Then, while he was thus engaged with Rhoesaces, Spithridates rode up from one side, raised himself up on his horse, and with all his might came down with a barbarian battle-axe upon Alexander's head. Alexander's crest was broken off, together with one of its plumes, and his helmet could barely and with difficulty resist the blow, so that the edge of the battle-axe touched the topmost hair of his head. But while Spithridates was raising his arm again for another stroke, Cleitus, "Black Cleitus," got the start of him and ran him through the body with his spear. At the same time Rhoesaces also fell, smitten by Alexander's sword.

While Alexander's cavalry were making such a dangerous and furious fight, the Macedonian phalanx crossed the river and the infantry forces on both sides engaged. The enemy, however, did not resist vigorously, nor for a long time, but fled in a rout, all except the Greek mercenaries. These made a stand at a certain eminence, and asked that Alexander should promise them quarter. But he, influenced by anger more than by reason, charged foremost upon them and lost his horse, which was smitten through the ribs with a sword (it was not Bucephalas, but another); and most of the Macedonians who were slain or wounded fought or fell there, since they came to close quarters with men who knew how to fight and were desperate.

Of the Barbarians, we are told, twenty thousand footmen fell, and twenty-five hundred horsemen. But on Alexander's side, Aristobulus says there were thirty-four dead in all, of whom nine were footmen. Of these, then, Alexander ordered statues to be set up in bronze, and Lysippus wrought them. Moreover, desiring to make the Greeks partners in his victory, he sent to the Athenians in particular three hundred of the captured shields, and upon the rest of the spoils in general he ordered a most ambitious inscription to be wrought: "Alexander the son of Philip and all the Greeks except the Lacedaemonians from the Barbarians who dwell in Asia." But the drinking vessels and the purple robes and whatever things of this nature he took from the Persians, all these, except a few, he sent to his mother.

17

THIS contest at once made a great change in the situation to Alexander's advantage, so that he received the submission even of Sardis, the bulwark of the barbarian dominion on the sea-coast, and added the rest of the country to his conquests. Halicarnassus alone withstood him, and Miletus, which cities he took by storm and subdued all the territories about them. Then he was in doubt as to his future course. Many times he was eager to encounter Dareius and put the whole issue to hazard, and many times he would make up his mind to practice himself first, as it were, and strengthen himself by acquiring the regions along the sea with their resources, and then to go up against that monarch. Now, there is in Lycia, near the city of Xanthus, a spring, which at this time, as we are told, was of its own motion upheaved from its depths, and overflowed, and cast forth a bronze tablet bearing the prints of ancient letters, in which it was made known that the empire of the Persians would one day be destroyed by the Greeks and come to an end. Encouraged by this prophecy, Alexander hastened to clear up the sea-coast as far as Cilicia and Phoenicia. His rapid passage along the coasts of Pamphylia has afforded many historians material for bombastic and terrifying description. They imply that by some great and heaven-sent good fortune the sea retired to make way for Alexander, although at other times it always came rolling in with violence from the main, and scarcely ever revealed to sight the small rocks which lie close up under the precipitous and riven sides of the mountain. And Menander, in one of his comedies, evidently refers jestingly to this marvel:

> "How Alexander-like, indeed, this is; and if I seek some one,
> Spontaneous he'll present himself; and if I clearly must
> Pass through some place by sea, this will lie open to my steps."

Alexander himself, however, made no such prodigy out of it in his letters, but says that he marched by way of the so-called Ladder, and passed through it, setting out from Phaselis. This was the reason for his spending several days in that city, during which he noticed that a statue of Theodectas, a deceased citizen of Phaselis, had been erected in the market-place. Once, therefore, after supper and in his cups, he led a band of revelers to the statue and crowned it with many of their garlands, thus in pleasantry returning no ungraceful honour for the past association with the man which he owed to Aristotle and philosophy.

18

AFTER this, he overpowered such of the Pisidians as had offered him resistance, and subdued Phrygia; and after he had taken the city of Gordium, reputed to have been the home of the ancient Midas, he saw the much-talked-of wagon bound fast to its yoke with the bark of the cornel-tree, and heard a story confidently told about it by the Barbarians, to the effect that whosoever loosed the fastening was destined to become king of the whole world. Well, then, most writers say that since the fastenings had their ends concealed, and were intertwined many times in crooked coils, Alexander was at a loss how to proceed, and finally loosened the knot by cutting it through with his sword, and that when it was thus smitten many ends were to be seen. But Aristobulus says that he undid it very easily, by simply taking out the so-called "hestor," or pin, of the wagon-pole, by which the yoke-fastening was held together, and then drawing away the yoke.

Setting out from there, he subdued Paphlagonia and Cappadocia, and on hearing of the death of Memnon, one of the commanders of Dareius on the sea-board, who was thought likely to give Alexander abundant trouble and infinite annoyance, he was all the more encouraged for his expedition into the interior. Moreover, Dareius was already coming down to the coast from Susa, exalted in spirit by the magnitude of his forces (for he was leading an army of six hundred thousand men), and also encouraged by a certain dream, which the Magi interpreted in a way to please him rather than as the probabilities demanded. For he dreamed that the Macedonian phalanx was all on fire, and that Alexander, attired in a robe which he himself formerly used to wear when he was a royal courier, was waiting upon him, after which service he passed into the temple of Belus and disappeared. By this means, as it would seem, it was suggested to Dareius from Heaven that the exploits of the Macedonians would be conspicuous and brilliant, that Alexander would be master of Asia, just as Dareius became its master when he was made king instead of royal courier, and would speedily end his life with glory.

19

DAREIUS was still more encouraged by Alexander's long delay in Cilicia, which he attributed to cowardice. The delay was due, however, to a sickness, which assailed him in consequence of fatigues, according to some, but according to others, because he took a bath in the river Cydnus, whose waters were icy cold. Be that as it may, none of the other physicians had the courage to administer remedies, but thinking that the danger was too great to be overcome by any remedy whatever, they were afraid of the charges which would be made against them by the Macedonians in consequence of their failure; but Philip the Acarnanian, who saw that the king was in an evil plight, put confidence in his friendship, and thinking it a shameful thing not to share his peril by exhausting the resources of art in trying to help him even at great risk, prepared a medicine and persuaded him to drink it boldly, if he was anxious to regain his strength for the war. Meanwhile, however, Parmenio sent a letter to Alexander from the camp, urging him to be on his guard against Philip, for the reason that he had been persuaded by Dareius, with the promise of large gifts and a marriage with his daughter, to kill Alexander. Alexander read the letter and placed it under his pillow, without showing it to any one of his friends. When the time appointed was at hand, and Philip came in with the king's companions, carrying the medicine in a cup, Alexander handed him the letter, while he himself took the medicine from him with readiness and no sign of suspicion. It was an amazing sight, then, and one worthy of the stage—the one reading the letter, the other drinking the medicine, and then both together turning their eyes upon one another, but not with the same expression; for Alexander, by his glad and open countenance, showed his good will towards Philip and his trust in him, while Philip was beside himself at the calumny, now lifting up his hands towards heaven and calling upon the gods to witness his innocence, and now falling upon the couch on which Alexander lay and beseeching him to be of good courage and obey his physician. For at first the medicine mastered the patient, and as it were drove back and buried deep his bodily powers, so that his voice failed, he fell into a swoon, and became almost wholly unconscious.

However, he was speedily restored to his senses by Philip, and when he had recovered strength he showed himself to the Macedonians, who refused to be comforted until they had seen Alexander.

20

NOW, there was in the army of Dareius a certain Macedonian who had fled from his country, Amyntas by name, and he was well acquainted with the nature of Alexander. This man, when he saw that Dareius was eager to attack Alexander within the narrow passes of the mountains, begged him to remain where he was, that he might fight a decisive battle with his vast forces against inferior numbers in plains that were broad and spacious. And when Dareius replied that he was afraid the enemy would run away before he could get at them, and Alexander thus escape him, "Indeed," said Amyntas, "on this point, O king, thou mayest be without fear; for he will march against thee, nay, at this very moment, probably, he is on the march." Dareius would not listen to these words of Amyntas, but broke camp and marched into Cilicia, and at the same time Alexander marched into Syria against him. But having missed one another in the night, they both turned back again, Alexander rejoicing in his good fortune, and eager to meet his enemy in the passes, while Dareius was as eager to extricate his forces from the passes and regain his former camping ground. For he already saw that he had done wrong to throw himself into places which were rendered unfit for cavalry by sea and mountains and a river running through the middle (the Pinarus), which were broken up in many parts, and favoured the small numbers of his enemy. And not only was the place for the battle a gift of Fortune to Alexander, but his generalship was better than the provisions of Fortune for his victory. For since he was so vastly inferior in numbers to the Barbarians, he gave them no opportunity to encircle him, but leading his right wing in person, extended it past the enemy's left, got on their flank, and routed the Barbarians who were opposed to him fighting among the foremost, so that he got a sword-wound in the thigh. Chares says this wound was given him by Dareius, with whom he had a hand-to-hand combat, but Alexander, in a letter to Antipater about the battle, did not say who it was that gave him the wound;

he wrote that he had been wounded in the thigh with a dagger, but that no serious harm resulted from the wound.

Although he won a brilliant victory and destroyed more than a hundred and ten thousand of his enemies, he did not capture Dareius, who got a start of four or five furlongs in his flight; but he did take the king's chariot, and his bow, before he came back from the pursuit. He found his Macedonians carrying off the wealth from the camp of the Barbarians, and the wealth was of surpassing abundance, although its owners had come to the battle in light marching order and had left most of their baggage in Damascus; he found, too, that his men had picked out for him the tent of Dareius, which was full to overflowing with gorgeous servitors and furniture, and many treasures. Straightway, then, Alexander put off his armour and went to the bath, saying: "Let us go and wash off the sweat of the battle in the bath of Dareius." "No, indeed," said one of his companions, "but rather in that of Alexander; for the property of the conquered must belong to the conqueror, and be called his." And when he saw the basins and pitchers and tubs and caskets, all of gold, and curiously wrought, while the apartment was marvelously fragrant with spices and unguents, and when he passed from this into a tent which was worthy of admiration for its size and height, and for the adornment of the couch and tables and banquet prepared for him, he turned his eyes upon his companions and said: "This, as it would seem, is to be a king."

21

AS he was betaking himself to supper, someone told him that among the prisoners were the mother, wife, and two unmarried daughters of Dareius, and that at sight of his chariot and bow they beat their breasts and lamented, believing that he was dead. Accordingly, after a considerable pause, more affected by their affliction than by his own success, he sent Leonnatus, with orders to tell them that Dareius was not dead, and that they need have no fear of Alexander; for it was Dareius upon whom he was waging war for supremacy, but they should have everything which they used to think their due when Dareius was undisputed king. If this message was thought by the women to be mild and kindly, still more did the actions of Alexander prove to be humane. For he gave them permission to bury whom they pleased of the Persians, and to use for this purpose raiment and adornment from the spoils, and he abated not one jot of their honourable maintenance, nay, they enjoyed even larger allowances than before. But the most honourable and most princely favour which these noble and chaste women received from him in their captivity was that they neither heard, nor suspected, nor awaited anything that could disgrace them, but lived, as though guarded in sacred and inviolable virgins' chambers instead of in an enemy's camp, apart from the speech and sight of men. And yet it is said that the wife of Dareius was far the most comely of all royal women, just as Dareius himself also was handsomest and tallest of men, and the daughters resembled their parents.

But Alexander, as it would seem, considering the mastery of himself a more kingly thing than the conquest of his enemies, neither laid hands upon these women, nor did he know any other before marriage, except Barsiné. This woman, Memnon's widow, was taken prisoner at Damascus. And since she had received a Greek education, and was of an agreeable disposition, and since her father, Artabazus, was son of a king's daughter, Alexander determined (at Parmenio's instigation, as Aristobulus says) to attach himself to a woman of such high birth and beauty. But as for the other captive women, seeing that they were surpassingly stately and beautiful, he merely said jestingly that Persian women were torments to the eyes. And displaying in rivalry with their fair looks the beauty of his own sobriety and self-control, he passed them by as though they were lifeless images for display.

22

MOREOVER, when Philoxenus, the commander of his forces on the sea-board, wrote that there was with him a certain Theodorus, of Tarentum, who had two boys of surpassing beauty to sell, and inquired whether Alexander would buy them, Alexander was incensed, and cried out many times to his friends, asking them what shameful thing Philoxenus had ever seen in him that he should spend his time in making such disgraceful proposals. And on Philoxenus himself he heaped so much reproach in a letter, bidding him send Theodorus to perdition, merchandize and all. He severely rebuked Hagnon also for writing to him that he wanted to buy Crobylus, whose beauty was famous in Corinth, as a present for him. Furthermore, on learning that Damon and Timotheus, two Macedonian soldiers under Parmenio's command, had ruined the wives of certain mercenaries, he wrote to Parmenio ordering him, in case the men were convicted, to punish them and put them to death as wild beasts born for the destruction of mankind. In this letter he also wrote expressly concerning himself: "As for me, indeed, it will be found not only that I have not seen the wife of Dareius or desired to see her, but that I have not even allowed people to speak to me of her beauty." And he used to say that sleep and sexual intercourse, more than any thing else, made him conscious that he was mortal, implying that both weariness and pleasure arise from one and the same natural weakness.

He had also the most complete mastery over his appetite, and showed this both in many other ways, and especially by what he said to Ada, whom he honoured with the title of Mother and made queen of Caria. When, namely, in the kindness of her heart, she used to send him day by day many viands and sweetmeats, and finally offered him bakers and cooks reputed to be very skillful, he said he wanted none of them, for he had better cooks which had been given him by his tutor, Leonidas; for his breakfast, namely, a night march, and for his supper, a light breakfast. "And this same Leonidas," he said, "used to come and open my chests of bedding and clothing, to see that my mother did not hide there for me some luxury or superfluity."

23

TO the use of wine also he was less addicted than was generally believed. The belief arose from the time which he would spend over each cup, talking than in drinking, always holding some long discourse, and this too when he had abundant leisure. For in the stress of affairs he was not to be detained, as other commanders were, either by wine, or sleep, or any sport, or amour, or spectacle. This is proved by his life, which, though altogether brief, he filled to overflowing with the greatest exploits. In his times of leisure, however, after rising and sacrificing to the gods, he immediately took breakfast sitting; then, he would spend the day in hunting, or administering justice, or arranging his military affairs, or reading. If he were making a march which was not very urgent, he would practice, as he went along, either archery or mounting and dismounting from a chariot that was under way. Often, too, for diversion, he would hunt foxes or birds, as may be gathered from his journals. After he had taken quarters for the night, and while he was enjoying bath or anointing, he would inquire of his chief cooks and bakers whether the arrangements for his supper were duly made. When it was late and already dark, he would begin his supper, reclining on a couch, and marvelous was his care and circumspection at table, in order that everything might be served impartially and without stint; but over the wine, as I have said, he would sit long, for conversation's sake. And although in other ways he was of all princes most agreeable in his intercourse, and endowed with every grace, at this time his boastfulness would make him unpleasant and very like a common soldier. Not only was he himself carried away into blustering, but he suffered himself to be ridden by his flatterers. There were a great annoyance to the finer spirits in the company, who desired neither to vie with the flatterers, nor yet to fall behind them in praising Alexander. The one course they thought disgraceful, the other had its perils. After the drinking was over, he would take a bath and sleep, frequently until midday; and sometimes he would actually spend the entire day in sleep.

In the matter of delicacies, too, he himself, at all events, was master of his appetite, so that often, when the rarest fruits or fish were brought to him from the sea-coast, he would distribute them to each of his companions until he was the only one for whom nothing remained. His suppers, however, were always magnificent, and the outlay upon them increased with his successes until it reached the sum of ten thousand drachmas. There it stood, and that was the prescribed limit of expenditure for those who entertained Alexander.

24

AFTER the battle at Issus, he sent to Damascus and seized the money and baggage of the Persians together with their wives and children. And most of all did the Thessalian horsemen enrich themselves, for they had shown themselves surpassingly brave in the battle, and Alexander sent them on this expedition purposely, wishing to have them enrich themselves. But the rest of the army also was filled with wealth. Then for the first time the Macedonians got a taste of gold and silver and women and barbaric luxury of life, and now that they had struck the trail, they were like dogs in their eagerness to pursue and track down the wealth of the Persians.

However, Alexander determined first to make himself master of the sea-coasts. As for Cyprus, then, its kings came at once and put the island in his hands, together with Phoenicia, with the exception of Tyre. But Tyre he besieged for seven months, with moles, and engines-of-war, and two hundred triremes by sea. During this siege he had a dream in which he saw Heracles stretching out his hand to him from the wall and calling him. And many of the Tyrians dreamed that Apollo told them he was going away to Alexander, since he was displeased at what was going on in the city. Whereupon, as if the god had been a common deserter caught in the act of going over to the enemy, they encircled his colossal figure with cords and nailed it down to its pedestal, calling him an Alexandrist. In another dream, too, Alexander thought he saw a satyr who mocked him at a distance, and eluded his grasp when he tried to catch him, but finally, after much coaxing and chasing, surrendered. The seers, dividing the word "satyros" into two parts, said to him, plausibly enough, "Tyre is to be thine." And a spring is pointed out, near which Alexander dreamed he saw the satyr.

While the siege of the city was in progress, he made an expedition against the Arabians who dwelt in the neighbourhood of Mount Antilibanus. On this expedition he risked his life to save his tutor, Lysimachus, who insisted on following him, declaring himself to be neither older nor weaker than Phoenix. But when the force drew near the mountains, they abandoned their horses and proceeded on foot, and most of them got far on in advance. Alexander himself, however, would not consent to abandon the worn and weary Lysimachus, since evening was already coming on and the enemy were near, but sought to encourage him and carry him along. Before he was aware of it, therefore, he was separated from the army with a few followers, and had to spend a night of darkness and intense cold in a region that was rough and difficult. In this plight, he saw far off a number of scattered fires which the enemy were burning. So, since he was confident in his own agility, and was ever wont to cheer the Macedonians in their perplexities by sharing their toils, he ran to the nearest camp-fire. Two Barbarians who were sitting at the fire he despatched with his dagger, and snatching up a fire-brand, brought it to his own party. These kindled a great fire and at once frightened some of the enemy into flight, routed others who came up against them, and spent the night without further peril. Such, then, is the account we have from Chares.

25

THE siege of the city had the following issue. While Alexander was giving the greater part of his forces a rest from the many struggles which they had undergone, and was leading up only a few men to attack the walls, in order that the enemy might have no respite, Aristander the seer made a sacrifice, and after taking the omens, declared very confidently to the bystanders that the city would certainly be captured during that month. His words produced laughter and jesting, since it was then the last day of the month, and the king, seeing that he was perplexed, and being always eager to support his prophecies, gave orders to reckon that day, not as the thirtieth of the month, but as the twenty-eighth; and then, after the trumpet had sounded the signal, he attacked the walls with greater vigour than he had at first intended. The assault became fierce, and even those troops which had been left in camp could not restrain themselves, but ran in throngs to help the assailants, and the Tyrians gave up the fight. So Alexander took the city on that day.

After this, as he was giving siege to Gaza, the principal city of Syria, a clod of earth, which had been dropped from on high by a bird, struck him on the shoulder. The bird alighted on one of the battering-engines, and was at once caught in the network of sinews which were used to give a twist to the ropes. And the omen was fulfilled as Aristander predicted; for though Alexander was wounded in the shoulder, he took the city. Moreover, as he was dispatching great quantities of the spoils home to Olympias and Cleopatra and his friends, he sent also to Leonidas his tutor five hundred talents' weight of frankincense and a hundred of myrrh, in remembrance of the hope which that teacher had inspired his boyhood. It would seem, namely, that Leonidas, as Alexander was one day sacrificing and taking incense with both hands to throw upon the altar-fire, said to him: "Alexander, when thou hast conquered the spice-bearing regions thou canst be thus lavish with thine incense; now, however, use sparingly what thou hast." Accordingly, Alexander now wrote him: "I have sent thee myrrh and frankincense in abundance, that thou mayest stop dealing parsimoniously with the gods."

26

WHEN a small coffer was brought to him, which those in charge of the baggage and wealth of Dareius thought the most precious thing there, he asked his friends what valuable object they thought would most fittingly be deposited in it. And when many answered and there were many opinions, Alexander himself said he was going to deposit the Iliad there for safe keeping. This is attested by many trustworthy authorities. And if what the Alexandrians tell us on the authority of Heracleides is true, then it would seem that Homer was no idle or unprofitable companion for him in his expedition. They say, namely, that after his conquest of Egypt he wished to found a large and populous Greek city which should bear his name, and by the advice of his architects was on the point of measuring off and enclosing a certain site for it. Then, in the night, as he lay asleep, he saw a wonderful vision. A man with very hoary locks and of a venerable aspect appeared to stand by his side and recite these verses:

"Now, there is an island in the much-dashing sea,
In front of Egypt; Pharos is what men call it."

Accordingly, he rose up at once and went to Pharos, which at that time was still an island, a little above the Canobic mouth of the Nile, but now it has been joined to the mainland by a causeway. And when he saw a site of surpassing natural advantages (for it is a strip of land like enough to a broad isthmus, extending between a great lagoon and a stretch of sea which terminates in a large harbour), he said he saw now that Homer was not only admirable in other ways, but also a very wise architect, and ordered the plan of the city to be drawn in conformity with this site. There was no chalk at hand, so they took barley-meal and marked out with it on the dark soil a rounded area, to whose inner arc straight lines extended so as to produce the figure of a chlamys, or military cloak, the lines beginning from the skirts (as one may say), and narrowing the breadth of the area uniformly. The king was delighted with the design; but suddenly birds from the river and the lagoon, infinite in number and of every sort and size, settled down upon the place like clouds and devoured every particle of the barley-meal, so that even Alexander was greatly disturbed at the omen.

However, the seers exhorted him to be of good cheer, since the city here founded by him would have most abundant and helpful resources and be a nursing mother for men of every nation, and so he ordered those in charge of the work to proceed with it, while he himself set out for the temple of Ammon. The journey thither was long, full of toils and hardships, and had two perils. One is the dearth of water, which leaves the traveler destitute of it for many days; the other arises when a fierce south wind smites men traveling in sand of boundless depth, as is said to have been the case with the army of Cambyses, long ago; the wind raised great billows of sand all over the plain and buried up fifty thousand men, to their utter destruction. Almost all of Alexander's followers took all these things into consideration, but it was difficult to turn him aside from any course so ever when he had once set out upon it. For Fortune, by yielding to his onsets, was making his purpose obstinate, and the high spirit which he carried into his undertakings rendered his ambition finally invincible, so that it subdued not only enemies, but even times and places.

50

NOT long afterwards came the affair of Cleitus, which those who simply learn the immediate circumstances will think more savage than that of Philotas; if we take into consideration, however, alike the cause and the time, we find that it did not happen of set purpose, but through some misfortune of the king, whose anger and intoxication furnished occasion for the evil genius of Cleitus. It happened on this wise. Some people came bringing Greek fruit to the king from the sea-board. He admired its perfection and beauty and called Cleitus, wishing to show it to him and share it with him. It chanced that Cleitus was sacrificing, but he gave up the sacrifice and came; and three of the sheep on which libations had already been poured came following after him. When the king learned of this circumstance, he imparted it to his soothsayers, Aristander and Cleomantis the Lacedaemonian. Then, on their telling him that the omen was bad, he ordered them to sacrifice in all haste for the safety of Cleitus. For he himself, two days before this, had seen a strange vision in his sleep; he thought he saw Cleitus sitting with the sons of Parmenio in black robes, and all were dead. However, Cleitus did not finish his sacrifice, but came at once to the supper of the king, who had sacrificed to the Dioscuri. After boisterous drinking was under way, verses were sung which had been composed by a certain Pranichus, or, as some say, Pierio, to shame and ridicule the generals who had lately been defeated by the Barbarians. The older guests were annoyed at this and railed at both the poet and the singer, but Alexander and those about him listened with delight and bade the singer go on. Then Cleitus, who was already drunk and naturally of a harsh temper and willful, was more than ever vexed, and insisted that it was not well done, when among Barbarians and enemies, to insult Macedonians who were far better men than those who laughed at them, even though they had met with misfortune. And when Alexander declared that Cleitus was pleading his own cause when he gave cowardice the name of misfortune, Cleitus sprang to his feet and said: "It was this cowardice of mine, however, that saved thy life, god-born as thou art, when thou wast already turning thy back upon the spear of Spithridates; and it is by the blood of Macedonians, and by these wounds, that thou art become so great as to disown Philip and make thyself son to Ammon."

51

THOROUGHLY incensed, then, Alexander said: "Base fellow, dost thou think to speak thus of me at all times, and to raise faction among Macedonians, with impunity?" "Nay," said Cleitus, "not even now do we enjoy impunity, since such are the rewards we get for our toils; and we pronounce those happy who are already dead, and did not live to see us Macedonians thrashed with Median rods, or begging Persians in order to get audience with our king." So spake Cleitus in all boldness, and those about Alexander sprang up to confront him and reviled him, while the elder men tried to quell the tumult. Then Alexander, turning to Xenodochus of Cardia and Artemus of Colophon, said: "Do not the Greeks appear to you to walk about among Macedonians like demi-gods among wild beasts?" Cleitus, however, would not yield, but called on Alexander to speak out freely what he wished to say, or else not to invite to supper men who were free and spoke their minds, but to live with Barbarians and slaves, who would do obeisance to his white tunic and Persian girdle. Then Alexander, no longer able to restrain his anger, threw one of the apples that lay on the table at Cleitus and hit him, and began looking about for his sword. But one of his body-guards, Aristophanes, conveyed it away before he could lay his hands on it, and the rest surrounded him and begged him to desist, whereupon he sprang to his feet and called out in Macedonian speech a summons to his corps of guards (and this was a sign of great disturbance), and ordered the trumpeter to sound, and smote him with his fist because he hesitated and was unwilling to do so. This man, then, was afterwards held in high esteem on the ground that it was due to him more than to any one else that the camp was not thrown into commotion. But Cleitus would not give in, and with much ado his friends pushed him out of the banquet-hall.

He tried to come in again, however, by another door, very boldly and contemptuously reciting these iambics from the "Andromache" of Euripides:

> "Alas! in Hellas what an evil government!"

And so, at last, Alexander seized a spear from one of his guards, met Cleitus as he was drawing aside the curtain before the door, and ran him through. No sooner had Cleitus fallen with a roar and a groan than the king's anger departed from him. And when he was come to himself and beheld his friends standing speechless, he drew the spear from the dead body and would have dashed it into his own throat, had not his body-guards prevented this by seizing his hands and carrying him by force to his chamber.

52

HERE he spent the night and the following day in bitter lamentations, and at last lay speechless, worn out with his cries and wailing, heaving deep groans. Then his friends, alarmed at his silence, forced their way in. To what the others said he would pay no attention, but when Aristander the seer reminded him of the vision he had seen concerning Cleitus, and of the omen, assuring him that all this had long ago been decreed by fate, he seemed to be less obdurate. Therefore they brought in to him Callisthenes the philosopher, who was a relative of Aristotle, and Anaxarchus of Abdera. Of these, Callisthenes tried by considerate and gentle methods to alleviate the king's suffering, employing insinuation and circumlocution so as to avoid giving pain; but Anaxarchus, who had always taken a path of his own in philosophy, and had acquired a reputation for despising and slighting his associates, shouted out as soon as he came in: "Here is Alexander, to whom the whole world is now looking; but he lies on the floor weeping like a slave, in fear of the law and the censure of men, unto whom he himself should be a law and a measure of justice, since he has conquered the right to rule and mastery, instead of submitting like a slave to the mastery of a vain opinion. Knowest thou not," said he, "that Zeus had Justice and Law seated beside him, in order that everything that is done by the master of the world may be lawful and just?" By using some such arguments as these Anaxarchus succeeded in lightening the suffering of the king, it is true, but rendered his disposition in many ways more vainglorious and lawless; he also made himself wonderfully liked by the king, and brought the intercourse of Callisthenes with him, which had always been unpleasant because of the man's austerity, into additional disfavour.

It is said that once at supper the conversation turned upon seasons and weather, and that Callisthenes, who held with those who maintain that it is more cold and wintry there than in Greece, was stoutly opposed by Anaxarchus, whereupon he said: "You surely must admit that it is colder here than there; for there you used to go about in winter in a cloak merely, but here you recline at table with three rugs thrown over you." Of course this also added to the irritation of Anaxarchus.

57

ALEXANDER was now about to cross the mountains into India, and since he saw that his army was by this time cumbered with much booty and hard to move, at break of day, after the baggage-wagons had been loaded, he burned first those which belonged to himself and his companions, and then gave orders to set fire to those of the Macedonians. And the planning of the thing turned out to be a larger and more formidable matter than its execution. For it gave annoyance to a few only of the soldiers, while the most of them, with rapturous shouts and war-cries, shared their necessaries with those who were in need of them, and what was superfluous they burned and destroyed with their own hands, thus filling Alexander with zeal and eagerness. Besides, he was already greatly feared, and inexorable in the chastisement of a transgressor. For instance, when a certain Menander, one of his companions, who had been put in command of a garrison, refused to remain there, he put him to death; and Orsodates, a Barbarian who had revolted from him, he shot down with his own hand.

When a sheep yeaned a lamb which had upon its head what looked like a tiara in form and colour, with testicles on either side of it, Alexander was filled with loathing at the portent, and had himself purified by the Babylonians, whom he was accustomed to take along with him for such purposes; and in conversation with his friends he said that he was not disturbed for his own sake, but for theirs, fearing lest after his death Heaven might devolve his power upon an ignoble and impotent man. However, a better portent occurred and put an end to his dejection. The Macedonian, namely, who was set over those in charge of the royal equipage, Proxenus by name, as he was digging a place for the king's tent along the river Oxus, uncovered a spring of liquid which was oily and fatty; but when the top of it was drawn off, there flowed at once a pure and clear oil, which appeared to differ from olive oil neither in odour nor in flavour, and in smoothness and lustre was altogether the same, and that too though the country produced no olive trees. It is said, indeed, that Oxus itself also has a very soft water, which gives sleekness to the skin of those who bathe in it. However, that Alexander was marvelously pleased is clear from what he writes to Antipater, where he speaks of this as one of the greatest omens vouchsafed to him from Heaven. The seers, however, held that the omen foreshadowed an expedition which would be glorious, but difficult and toilsome; for oil, they said, was given to men by Heaven as an aid to toil.

58

AND so it proved; for he encountered many perils in the battles which he fought, and received very severe wounds; but the greatest losses which his army suffered were caused by lack of necessary provisions and severity of weather. Still, he was eager to overcome fortune by boldness and force by valour, and thought nothing invincible for the courageous, and nothing secure for the cowardly. It is said that when he was besieging the citadel of Sisimithres, which was steep and inaccessible, so that his soldiers were disheartened, he asked Oxyartes what sort of a man Sisimithres himself was in point of spirit. And when Oxyartes replied that he was most cowardly of men, "Thy words mean," said Alexander, "that we can take the citadel, since he who commands it is a weak thing." And indeed he did take the citadel by frightening Sisimithres. Again, after attacking another citadel equally precipitous, he was urging on the younger Macedonians, and addressing one who bore the name of Alexander, said: "It behooves thee, at least, to be a brave man, even for thy name's sake." And when the young man, fighting gloriously, fell, the king was pained beyond measure. And at another time, when his Macedonians hesitated to advance upon the citadel called Nysa because there was a deep river in front of it, Alexander, halting on the bank, cried: "Most miserable man that I am, why, pray, have I not learned to swim?" and at once, carrying his shield, he would have tried to cross. And when, after he had put a stop to the fighting, ambassadors came from the beleaguered cities to beg for terms, they were amazed, to begin with, to see him in full armour and without an attendant; and besides, when a cushion was brought to him for his use, he ordered the eldest of the ambassadors, Acuphis by name, to take it for his seat. Acuphis, accordingly, astonished at his magnanimity and courtesy, asked what he wished them to do in order to be his friends. "Thy countrymen," said Alexander, "must make thee their ruler, and send me a hundred of their best men." At this Acuphis laughed, and said: "Nay, O King, I shall rule better if I send to thee the worst men rather than the best."

59

TAXILES, we are told, had a realm in India as large as Egypt, with good pasturage, too, and in the highest degree productive of beautiful fruits. He was also a wise man in his way, and after he had greeted Alexander, said: "Why must we war and fight with one another, Alexander, if thou art not come to rob us of water or of necessary sustenance, the only things for which men of sense are obliged to fight obstinately? As for other wealth and possessions, so-called, if I am thy superior therein, I am ready to confer favours; but if thine inferior, I will not object to thanking you for favours conferred." At this Alexander was delighted, and clasping the king's hand, said: "Canst thou think, pray, that after such words of kindness our interview is to end without a battle? Nay, thou shalt not get the better of me; for I will contend against thee and fight to the last with my favours, that thou mayest not surpass me in generosity." So, after receiving many gifts and giving many more, at last he lavished upon him a thousand talents in coined money. This conduct greatly vexed Alexander's friends, but it made many of the Barbarians look upon him more kindly.

The best fighters among the Indians, however, were mercenaries, and they used to go about to the different cities and defend them sturdily, and wrought much harm to Alexander's cause. Therefore, after he had made a truce with them in a certain city and allowed them to depart, he fell upon them as they marched and slew them all. And this act adheres like a stain to his military career; in all other instances he waged war according to usage and like a king. The philosophers, too, no less than the mercenaries, gave him trouble, by abusing those of the native princes who attached themselves to his cause, and by inciting the free peoples to revolt. He therefore took many of these also and hanged them.

60

OF his campaign against Porus he himself has given an account in his letters. He says, namely, that the river Hydaspes flowed between the two camps, and that Porus stationed his elephants on the opposite bank and kept continual watch of the crossing. He himself, accordingly, day by day caused a great din and tumult to be made in his camp, and thereby accustomed the Barbarians not to be alarmed. Then, on a dark and stormy night, he took a part of his infantry and the best of his horsemen, and after proceeding along the river to a distance from where the enemy lay, crossed over to a small island. Here rain fell in torrents, and many tornadoes and thunder-bolts dashed down upon his men; but nevertheless, although he saw that many of them were being burned to death by the thunder-bolts, he set out from the islet and made for the opposite banks. But the Hydaspes, made violent by the storm and dashing high against its bank, made a great breach in it, and a large part of the stream was setting in that direction; and the shore between the two currents gave his men no sure footing, since it was broken and slippery. And here it was that he is said to have cried: "O Athenians, can ye possibly believe what perils I am undergoing to win glory in your eyes?" This, however, is the story of Onesicritus; Alexander himself says that they left their rafts and crossed the breach with their armour on, wading breast-high in water, and that after he had crossed he led his horsemen twenty furlongs in advance of his infantry, calculating that, in case the enemy attacked with their cavalry, he would be far superior to them, and in case they moved up their men-at-arms, his infantry would join him in good season. And one of these suppositions came to pass. For after routing a thousand of the enemy's horsemen and sixty of their chariots which engaged him, he captured all the chariots, and slew four hundred of the horsemen. And now Porus, thus led to believe that Alexander himself had crossed the river, advanced upon him with all his forces, except the part he left behind to impede the crossing of the remaining Macedonians. But Alexander, fearing the elephants and the great numbers of the enemy, himself assaulted their left wing, and ordered Coenus to attack their right. Both wings having been routed, the vanquished troops retired in every case upon the elephants in the centre, and were there crowded together with them, and from this point on the battle was waged at close quarters, and it was not until the eighth hour that the enemy gave up. Such then, is the account of the battle which the victor himself has given in his letters.

Most historians agree that Porus was four cubits and a span high, and that the size and majesty of his body made his elephant seem as fitting a mount for him as a horse for the horseman. And yet his elephant was of the largest size; and it showed remarkable intelligence and solicitude for the king, bravely defending him and beating back his assailants while he was still in full vigour, and when it perceived that its master was worn out with a multitude of missiles and wounds, fearing he should fall off, it knelt softly on the ground, and with its proboscis gently took each spear and drew it out of his body. Porus was taken prisoner, and when Alexander asked him how he would be treated, said: "Like a king"; and to another question from Alexander whether he had anything else to say, replied: "All things are included in my 'like a king.'" Accordingly, Alexander not only permitted him to govern his former kingdom, giving him the title of satrap, but also added to it the territory of the independent peoples whom he subdued, in which there are said to have been fifteen nations, five thousand cities of considerable size, and a great multitude of villages. He subdued other territory also thrice as large as this and appointed Philip, one of his companions, satrap over it.

61

AFTER the battle with Porus, too, Bucephalas died,—not at once, but some time afterwards,—as most writers say, from wounds for which he was under treatment, but according to Onesicritus, from old age, having become quite worn out; for he was thirty years old when he died. His death grieved Alexander mightily, who felt that he had lost nothing less than a comrade and a friend; he also built a city in his memory on the banks of the Hydaspes and called it Bucephalia. It is said, too, that when he lost a dog also, named Peritas, which had been reared by him and was loved by him, he founded a city and gave it the dog's name. Sotion says he heard this from Potamon the Lesbian.

62

AS for the Macedonians, however, their struggle with Porus blunted their courage and stayed their further advance into India. For having had all they could do to repulse an enemy who mustered only twenty thousand infantry and two thousand horse, they violently opposed Alexander when he insisted on crossing the river Ganges also, the width of which, as they learned, was thirty-two furlongs, its depth a hundred fathoms, while its banks on the further side were covered with multitudes of men-at-arms and horsemen and elephants. For they were told that the kings of the Ganderites and Praesii were awaiting them with eighty thousand horsemen, two hundred thousand footmen, eight thousand chariots, and six thousand fighting elephants. And there was no boasting in these reports. For Androcottus, who reigned there not long afterwards, made a present to Seleucus of five hundred elephants, and with an army of six hundred thousand men overran and subdued all India.

At first, then, Alexander shut himself up in his tent from displeasure and wrath and lay there, feeling no gratitude for what he had already achieved unless he should cross the Ganges, nay, counting retreat a confession of defeat. But his friends gave him fitting consolation, and his soldiers crowded about his door and besought him with loud cries and wailing, until at last he relented and began to break camp, resorting to many deceitful and fallacious devices for the enhancement of his fame. For instance, he had armour prepared that was larger than usual, and mangers for horses that were higher, and bits that were heavier than those in common use, and left them scattered up and down. Moreover, he erected altars for the gods, which down to the present time are revered by the kings of the Praesii when they cross the river, and on them they offer sacrifices in the Hellenic manner. Androcottus, when he was a stripling, saw Alexander himself, and we are told that he often said in later times that Alexander narrowly missed making himself master of the country, since its king was hated and despised on account of his baseness and low birth.

63

FROM thence, being eager to behold the ocean, and having built many passage-boats equipped with oars, and many rafts, he was conveyed down the rivers in a leisurely course. And yet his voyage was not made without effort nor even without war, but he would land and assault the cities on his route and subdue everything. However, in attacking the people called Malli, who are said to have been the most warlike of the Indians, he came within a little of being cut down. For after dispersing the inhabitants from the walls with missiles, he was the first to mount upon the wall by a scaling ladder, and since the ladder was broken to pieces and he was exposed to the missiles of the Barbarians who stood along the wall below, almost alone as he was, he crouched and threw himself into the midst of the enemy, and by good fortune alighted on his feet. Then, as he brandished his arms, the Barbarians thought that a shape of gleaming fire played in front of his person. Therefore at first they scattered and fled; but when they saw that he was accompanied by only two of his guards, they ran upon him, and some tried to wound him by thrusting their swords and spears through his armour as he defended himself, while one, standing a little further off, shot an arrow at him with such accuracy and force that it cut its way through his breastplate and fastened itself in his ribs at the breast. Such was the force of the blow that Alexander recoiled and sank to his knees, whereupon his assailant ran at him with drawn scimitar, while Peucestas and Limnaeus defended him. Both of them were wounded, and Limnaeus was killed; but Peucestas held out, and at last Alexander killed the Barbarian. But he himself received many wounds, and at last was smitten on the neck with a cudgel, and leaned against the wall, his eyes still fixed upon his foes. At this instant the Macedonians flocked about him, caught him up, already unconscious of what was going on about him, and carried him to his tent. And straightway a report that he was dead prevailed in the camp; but when with much difficulty and pains they had sawn off the shaft of the arrow, which was of wood, and had thus succeeded at last in removing the king's breastplate, they came to the excision of the arrow-head, which was buried in one of the ribs. We are told, moreover, that it was three fingers broad and four long. Its removal, therefore, threw the king into swoons and brought him to death's door, but nevertheless he recovered. And after he was out of danger, though he was still weak and kept himself for a long time under regimen and treatment, perceiving from their tumult at his door that his Macedonians were yearning to see him, he took his cloak and went out to them. And after sacrificing to the gods he went on board ship again and dropped down the river, subduing much territory and great cities as he went.

64

HE captured ten of the Gymnosophists who had done most to get Sabbas to revolt, and had made the most trouble for the Macedonians. These philosophers were reputed to be clever and concise in answering questions, and Alexander therefore put difficult questions to them, declaring that he would put to death him who first made an incorrect answer, and then the rest, in an order determined in like manner; and he commanded one of them, the oldest, to be the judge in the contest. The first one, accordingly, being asked which, in his opinion, were more numerous, the living or the dead, said that the living were, since the dead no longer existed. The second, being asked whether the earth or the sea produced larger animals, said the earth did, since the sea was but a part of the earth. The third, being asked what animal was the most cunning, said: "That which up to this time man has not discovered." The fourth, when asked why he had induced Sabbas to revolt, replied: "Because I wished him either to live nobly or to die nobly." The fifth, being asked which, in his opinion, was older, day or night, replied: "Day, by one day"; and he added, upon the king expressing amazement, that hard questions must have hard answers. Passing on, then, to the sixth, Alexander asked how a man could be most loved; "If," said the philosopher, "he is most powerful, and yet does not inspire fear." Of the three remaining, he who was asked how one might become a god instead of man, replied: "By doing something which a man cannot do"; the one who was asked which was the stronger, life or death, answered: "Life, since it supports so many ills." And the last, asked how long it were well for a man to live, answered: "Until he does not regard death as better than life." So, then, turning to the judge, Alexander bade him give his opinion. The judge declared that they had answered one worse than another. "Well, then," said Alexander, "thou shalt die first for giving such a verdict." "That cannot be, O King," said the judge, "unless thou falsely saidst that thou wouldst put to death first him who answered worst."

65

THESE philosophers, then, he dismissed with gifts; but to those who were in the highest repute and lived quietly by themselves he sent Onesicritus, asking them to pay him a visit. Now, Onesicritus was a philosopher of the school of Diogenes the Cynic. And he tells us that Calanus very harshly and insolently bade him strip off his tunic and listen naked to what he had to say, otherwise he would not converse with him, not even if he came from Zeus; but he says that Dandamis was gentler, and that after hearing fully about Socrates, Pythagoras, and Diogenes, he remarked that the men appeared to him to have been of good natural parts but to have passed their lives in too much awe of the laws. Others, however, say that the only words uttered by Dandamis were these "Why did Alexander make such a long journey hither?" Calanus, nevertheless, was persuaded by Taxiles to pay a visit to Alexander. His real name was Sphines, but because he greeted those whom he met with "Cale," the Indian word of salutation, the Greeks called him Calanus. It was Calanus, as we are told, who laid before Alexander the famous illustration of government. It was this. He threw down upon the ground a dry and shriveled hide, and set his foot upon the outer edge of it; the hide was pressed down in one place, but rose up in others. He went all round the hide and showed that this was the result wherever he pressed the edge down, and then at last he stood in the middle of it, and lo! it was all held down firm and still. The similitude was designed to show that Alexander ought to put most constraint upon the middle of his empire and not wander far away from it.

66

HIS descent of the rivers to the sea consumed seven months' time. And after emerging with his fleet into the ocean, he sailed out to an island to which he himself gave the name of Scillustis, others that of Psiltucis. Here he landed and sacrificed to the gods, and studied the nature of the sea and of all the sea-coast that was accessible. Then, after praying that no man after him might pass beyond the bounds of his expedition, he turned to go back. His fleet he ordered to go round by sea, keeping India on the right; Nearchus was appointed admiral of the fleet, Onesicritus its chief-pilot. But he himself proceeded by land through the country of the Oreites, where he was reduced to the direst straits and lost a multitude of men, so that not even the fourth part of his fighting force was brought back from India. And yet his infantry had once numbered a hundred and twenty thousand, and his cavalry fifteen thousand. But grievous diseases, wretched food, parching heats, and, worst of all, famine destroyed them, since they traversed an untilled country of men who dragged out a miserable existence, who possessed but few sheep and those of a miserable sort, since the sea-fish which they ate made their flesh unsavoury and rank. It was with difficulty, then, that Alexander passed through this country in sixty days; but as soon as he reached Gedrosia he had all things in abundance, for the nearest satraps and princes had provided them.

67

ACCORDINGLY, after refreshing his forces here, he set out and marched for seven days through Carmania in a reveling rout. He himself was conveyed slowly along by eight horses, while he feasted day and night continuously with his companions on a dais built upon a lofty and conspicuous scaffolding of oblong shape; and wagons without number followed, some with purple and embroidered canopies, others protected from the sun by boughs of trees which were kept fresh and green, conveying the rest of his friends and commanders, who were all garlanded and drinking. Not a shield was to be seen, not a helmet, not a spear, but along the whole march with cups and drinking-horns and flagons the soldiers kept dipping wine from huge casks and mixing-bowls and pledging one another, some as they marched along, others lying down; while pipes and flutes, stringed instruments and song, with reveling cries of women, filled every place with abundant music. Then, upon this disordered and straggling procession there followed also the sports of bacchanalian license, as though Bacchus himself were present and conducting the revel. Moreover, when he came to the royal palace of Gedrosia, he once more gave his army time for rest and held high festival. We are told, too, that he was once viewing some contests in singing and dancing, being well heated with wine, and that his favourite, Bagoas, won the prize for song and dance, and then, all in his festal array, passed through the theatre and took his seat by Alexander's side; at sight of which the Macedonians clapped their hands and loudly bade the king kiss the victor, until at last he threw his arms about him and kissed him tenderly.

68

HERE Nearchus came up to meet him, and Alexander was so delighted to hear of his voyage that he eagerly desired to sail down the Euphrates himself with a large fleet, and then, after circumnavigating Arabia and Africa, to enter the Mediterranean by way of the pillars of Heracles. And vessels of every sort were built for him at Thapsacus, and sailors and pilots were assembled from all parts. But the increasing difficulties of his march back, his wound among the Malli, and the losses in his army, which were reported to be heavy, led men to doubt his safe return, inclined subject peoples to revolt, and bred great injustice, rapacity, and insolence in the generals and satraps whom he had appointed. In a word, restlessness and a desire for change spread everywhere. For even against Antipater, Olympias and Cleopatra had raised a faction, Olympias taking Epirus, and Cleopatra Macedonia. When he heard of this, Alexander said that his mother had made the better choice; for the Macedonians would not submit to be reigned over by a woman.

For these reasons he sent Nearchus back to the sea, determined to fill all the regions along the sea with wars, while he himself, marching down from Upper Asia, chastised those of his commanders who had done wrong. One of the sons of Abuletes, Oxyartes, he slew with his own hand, running him through with a spear; and when Abuletes failed to furnish him with the necessary provisions, but brought him instead three thousand talents in coin, Alexander ordered the money to be thrown to his horses. And when they would not touch it, "Of what use to us, then," he cried, "is the provision you have made?" and threw Abuletes into prison.

69

IN Persia, to begin with, he distributed the money among the women, just as their kings were accustomed, as often as they came into Persia, to give each one a gold piece. And this reason, it is said, some of their kings did not come often into Persia, and Ochus not even once, being so penurious as to expatriate himself. In the second place, having discovered that the tomb of Cyrus had been rifled, he put to death the perpetrator of the deed, although the culprit was a prominent Macedonian native of Pella, by name Polymachus. After reading the inscription upon this tomb, he ordered it to be repeated below in Greek letters. It ran thus: "O man, whosoever thou art and whencesoever thou comest, for I know that thou wilt come, I am Cyrus, and I won for the Persians their empire. Do not, therefore, begrudge me this little earth which covers my body." These words, then, deeply affected Alexander, who was reminded of the uncertainty and mutability of life.

In Persia, too, Calanus, who had suffered for a little while from intestinal disorder, asked that a funeral pyre might be prepared for him. To this he came on horseback, and after offering prayers, sprinkling himself, and casting some of his hair upon the pyre, he ascended it, greeting the Macedonians who were present, and exhorting them to make that day one of pleasure and revelry with the king, whom, he declared, he should soon see in Babylon. After thus speaking, he lay down and covered his head, nor did he move as the fire approached him, but continued to lie in the same posture as at first, and so sacrificed himself acceptably, as the wise men of his country had done from of old. The same thing was done many years afterwards by another Indian who was in the following of Caesar, at Athens; and the "Indian's Tomb" is shown there to this day.

Life of Caesar

1

THE wife of Caesar was Cornelia, the daughter of the Cinna who had once held the sole power at Rome, and when Sulla became master of affairs, he could not, either by promises or threats, induce Caesar to put her away, and therefore confiscated her dowry. Now, the reason for Caesar's hatred of Sulla was Caesar's relationship to Marius. For Julia, a sister of Caesar's father, was the wife of Marius the Elder, and the mother of Marius the Younger, who was therefore Caesar's cousin. Moreover, Caesar was not satisfied to be overlooked at first by Sulla, who was busy with a multitude of proscriptions, but he came before the people as candidate for the priesthood, although he was not yet much more than a stripling. To this candidacy Sulla secretly opposed himself, and took measures to make Caesar fail in it, and when he was deliberating about putting him to death and some said there was no reason for killing a mere boy like him, he declared that they had no sense if they did not see in this boy many Mariuses. When this speech was reported to Caesar, he hid himself for some time, wandering about in the country of the Sabines. Then, as he was changing his abode by night on account of sickness, he fell in with soldiers of Sulla who were searching those regions and arresting the men in hiding there. Caesar gave their leader, Cornelius, two talents to set him free, and at once went down to the sea and sailed to King Nicomedes in Bithynia. With him he tarried a short time, and then, on his voyage back, was captured, near the island Pharmacusa, by pirates, who already at that time controlled the sea with large armaments and countless small vessels.

2

TO begin with, then, when the pirates demanded twenty talents for his ransom, he laughed at them for not knowing who their captive was, and of his own accord agreed to give them fifty. In the next place, after he had sent various followers to various cities to procure the money and was left with one friend and two attendants among Cilicians, most murderous of men, he held them in such disdain that whenever he lay down to sleep he would send and order them to stop talking. For eight and thirty days, as if the men were not his watchers, but his royal body-guard, he shared in their sports and exercises with great unconcern. He also wrote poems and sundry speeches which he read aloud to them, and those who did not admire these he would call to their faces illiterate Barbarians, and often laughingly threatened to hang them all. The pirates were delighted at this, and attributed his boldness of speech to a certain simplicity and boyish mirth. But after his ransom had come from Miletus and he had paid it and was set free, he immediately manned vessels and put to sea from the harbour of Miletus against the robbers. He caught them, too, still lying at anchor off the island, and got most of them into his power. Their money he made his booty, but the men themselves he lodged in the prison at Pergamum, and then went in person to Junius, the governor of Asia, on the ground that it belonged to him, as praetor of the province, to punish the captives. But since the praetor cast longing eyes on their money, which was no small sum, and kept saying that he would consider the case of the captives at his leisure, Caesar left him to his own devices, went to Pergamum, took the robbers out of prison, and crucified them all, just as he had often warned them on the island that he would do, when they thought he was joking.

3

AFTER this, Sulla's power being now on the wane, and Caesar's friends at home inviting him to return, Caesar sailed to Rhodes to study under Apollonius the son of Molon, an illustrious rhetorician with the reputation of a worthy character, of whom Cicero also was a pupil. It is said, too, that Caesar had the greatest natural talent for political oratory, and cultivated his talent most ambitiously, so that he had an undisputed second rank; the first rank, however, he renounced, because he devoted his efforts to being first as a statesman and commander rather, and did not achieve that effectiveness in oratory to which his natural talent directed him, in consequence of his campaigns and of his political activities, by means of which he acquired the supremacy. And so it was that, at a later time, in his reply to Cicero's "Cato," he himself deprecated comparison between the diction of a soldier and the eloquence of an orator who was gifted by nature and had plenty of leisure to pursue his studies.

4

AFTER his return to Rome he impeached Dolabella for maladministration of his province, and many of the cities of Greece supplied him with testimony. Dolabella, it is true, was acquitted, but Caesar, in return for the zealous efforts of the Greeks in his behalf, served as their advocate when they prosecuted Publius Antonius for corruption before Marcus Lucullus, the praetor of Macedonia. And he was so effective that Antonius appealed to the tribunes at Rome, alleging that he could not have a fair trial in Greece against Greeks. At Rome, moreover, Caesar won a great and brilliant popularity by his eloquence as an advocate, and much good will from the common people for the friendliness of his manners in intercourse with them, since he was ingratiating beyond his years. He had also a large and gradually increasing political influence in consequence of his lavish hospitality and the general splendour of his mode of life. At first his enemies thought this influence would quickly vanish when his expenditures ceased, and therefore suffered it to thrive among the common people; but later on when it had become great and hard to subvert, and aimed directly at a complete revolution in the state, they perceived that no beginnings should be considered too small to be quickly made great by continuance, after contempt of them has left them unobstructed. At all events, the man who is thought to have been the first to see beneath the surface of Caesar's public policy and to fear it, as one might fear the smiling surface of the sea, and who comprehended the powerful character hidden beneath his kindly and cheerful exterior, namely Cicero, said that in most of Caesar's political plans and projects he saw a tyrannical purpose; "On the other hand," said he, "when I look at his hair, which is arranged with so much nicety, and see him scratching his head with one finger, I cannot think that this man would ever conceive of so great a crime as the overthrow of the Roman constitution." This, it is true, belongs to a later period.

5

THE first proof of the people's good will towards him he received when he competed against Caius Popilius for a military tribuneship and was elected over him; a second and more conspicuous proof he received when, as nephew of Julia the deceased wife of Marius, he pronounced a splendid encomium upon her in the forum, and in her funeral procession ventured to display images of Marius, which were then seen for the first time since the administration of

Sulla, because Marius and his friends had been pronounced public enemies. When, namely, some cried out against Caesar for this procedure, the people answered them with loud shouts, received Caesar with applause, and admired him for bringing back after so long a time, as it were from Hades, the honours of Marius into the city. Now, in the case of elderly women, it was ancient Roman usage to pronounce funeral orations over them; but it was not customary in the case of young women, and Caesar was the first to do so when his own wife died. This also brought him much favour, and worked upon the sympathies of the multitude, so that they were fond of him, as a man who was gentle and full of feeling.

After the funeral of his wife, he went out to Spain as quaestor under Vetus, one of the praetors, whom he never ceased to hold in high esteem, and whose son, in turn, when he himself was praetor, he made his quaestor. After he had served in this office, he married for his third wife Pompeia, having already by Cornelia a daughter who was afterwards married to Pompey the Great. He was unsparing in his outlays of money, and was thought to be purchasing a transient and short-lived fame at a great price, though in reality he was buying things of the highest value at a small price. We are told, accordingly, that before he entered upon any public office he was thirteen hundred talents in debt. Again, being appointed curator of the Appian Way, he expended upon it vast sums of his own money; and again, during his aedileship, he furnished three hundred and twenty pairs of gladiators, and by lavish provision besides for theatrical performances, processions, and public banquets, he washed away all memory of the ambitious efforts of his predecessors in the office. By these means he put the people in such a humour that every man of them was seeking out new offices and new honours with which to requite him.

15

SUCH, then, is said to have been the course of Caesar's life before his Gallic campaigns. But the period of the wars which he afterwards fought, and of the campaigns by which he subjugated Gaul, as if he had made another beginning and entered upon a different path of life and one of new achievements, proved him to be inferior as soldier and commander to no one soever of those who have won most admiration for leadership and shown themselves greatest therein. Nay, if one compare him with such men as Fabius and Scipio and Metellus, and with the men of his own time or a little before him, like Sulla, Marius, the two Luculli, or even Pompey himself, whose fame for every sort of military excellence was at this time flowering out and reaching to the skies, Caesar will be found to surpass them all in his achievements. One he surpassed in the difficulty of the regions where he waged his wars; another in the great extent of country which he acquired; another in the multitude and might of the enemies over whom he was victorious; another in the savage manners and perfidious dispositions of the people whom he conciliated; another in his reasonableness and mildness towards his captives; another still in the gifts and favours which he bestowed upon his soldiers; and all in the fact that he fought the most battles and killed the most enemies. For although it was not full ten years that he waged war in Gaul, he took by storm more than eight hundred cities, subdued three hundred nations, and fought pitched battles at different times with three million men, of whom he slew one million in hand to hand fighting and took as many more prisoners.

16

HIS soldiers showed such good will and zeal in his service that those who in their previous campaigns had been in no way superior to others were invincible and irresistible in confronting every danger to enhance Caesar's fame. Such a man, for instance, was Acilius, who, in the sea-fight at Massalia, boarded a hostile ship and had his right hand cut off with a sword, but clung with the other hand to his shield, and dashing it into the faces of his foes, routed them all and got possession of the vessel. Such a man, again, was Cassius Scaeva, who, in the battle at Dyrrhachium, had his eye struck out with an arrow, his shoulder transfixed with one javelin and his thigh with another, and received on his shield the blows of one hundred and thirty missiles. In this plight, he called the enemy to him as though he would surrender. Two of them, accordingly, coming up, he lopped off the shoulder of one with his sword, smote the other in the face and put him to flight, and came off safely himself with the aid of his comrades. Again, in Britain, when the enemy had fallen upon the foremost centurions, who had plunged into a watery marsh, a soldier, while Caesar in person was watching the battle, dashed into the midst of the fight, displayed many conspicuous deeds of daring, and rescued the centurions, after the Barbarians had been routed. Then he himself, making his way with difficulty after all the rest, plunged into the muddy current, and at last, without his shield, partly swimming and partly wading, got across. Caesar and his company were amazed and came to meet the soldier with cries of joy; but he, in great dejection, and with a burst of tears, cast himself at Caesar's feet, begging pardon for the loss of his shield. Again, in Africa, Scipio captured a ship of Caesar's in which Granius Petro, who had been appointed quaestor, was sailing. Of the rest of the passengers Scipio made booty, but told the quaestor that he offered him his life. Granius, however, remarking that it was the custom with Caesar's soldiers not to receive but to offer mercy, killed himself with a blow of his sword.

17

SUCH spirit and ambition Caesar himself created and cultivated in his men, in the first place, because he showed, by his unsparing bestowal of rewards and honours, that he was not amassing wealth from his wars for his own luxury or for any life of ease, but that he treasured it up carefully as a common prize for deeds of valour, and had no greater share in the wealth than he offered to the deserving among his soldiers; and in the second place, by willingly undergoing every danger and refusing no toil. Now, at his love of danger his men were not astonished, knowing his ambition; but that he should undergo toils beyond his body's apparent powers of endurance amazed them, because he was of a spare habit, had a soft and white skin, suffered from distemper in the head, and was subject to epileptic fits, a trouble which first attacked him, we are told, in Corduba. Nevertheless, he did not make his feeble health an excuse for soft living, but rather his military service a cure for his feeble health, since by wearisome journeys, simple diet, continuously sleeping in the open air, and enduring hardships, he fought off his trouble and kept his body strong against its attacks. Most of his sleep, at least, he got in cars or litters, making his rest conduce to action, and in the day-time he would have himself conveyed to garrisons, cities, or camps, one slave who was accustomed to write from dictation as he traveled sitting by his side, and one soldier standing behind him with a sword. And he drove so rapidly that, on his first journey from Rome to Gaul, he reached the Rhone in seven days.

Horsemanship, moreover, had been easy for him from boyhood; for he was wont to put his hands behind his back and, holding them closely there, to ride his horse at full speed. And in the Gallic campaigns he practiced dictating letters on horseback and keeping two scribes at once busy, or, as Oppius says, even more. We are told, moreover, that Caesar was the first to devise intercourse with his friends by letter, since he could not wait for personal interviews on urgent matters owing to the multitude of his occupations and the great size of the city. Of his indifference in regard to his diet the following circumstance also is brought in proof. When the host who was entertaining him in Mediolanum, Valerius Leo, served up asparagus dressed with myrrh instead of olive oil, Caesar ate of it without ado, and rebuked his friends when they showed displeasure. "Surely," said he, "it were enough not to eat what you don't like; but he who finds fault with ill-breeding like this is ill-bred himself." Once, too, upon a journey, he and his followers were driven by a storm into a poor man's hut, and when he found that it consisted of one room only, and that one barely able to accommodate a single person, he said to his friends that honours must be yielded to the strongest, but necessities to the weakest, and bade Oppius lie down there, while he himself with the rest of his company slept in the porch.

28

NOW, Caesar had long ago decided to put down Pompey, just as, of course, Pompey also had decided to put Caesar down. For now that Crassus, who was only waiting for the issue of their struggle to engage the victor, had perished among the Parthians, it remained for him who would be greatest to put down him who was, and for him who was greatest, if he would not be put down, to take off in time the man he feared. This fear had only recently come upon Pompey, who till then despised Caesar, feeling that it was no hard task to put down again the man whom he himself had raised on high. But Caesar had from the outset formed this design, and like an athlete had removed himself to a great distance from his antagonists, and by exercising himself in the Gallic wars had practiced his troops and increased his fame, lifting himself by his achievements to a height where he could vie with the successes of Pompey. He laid hold of pretexts which were furnished partly by Pompey himself, and partly by the times and the evil state of government at Rome, by reason of which candidates for office set up counting-tables in public and shamelessly bribed the multitudes, while the people went down into the forum under pay, contending in behalf of their paymaster, not with votes, but with bows and arrows, swords, and slings. Often, too, they would defile the rostra with blood and corpses before they separated, leaving the city to anarchy like a ship drifting about without a steersman, so that men of understanding were content if matters issued in nothing worse for them than monarchy, after such madness and so great a tempest. And there were many who actually dared to say in public that nothing but monarchy could now cure the diseases of the state, and that this remedy ought to be adopted when offered by the gentlest of physicians, hinting at Pompey. And when even Pompey, although in words he affected to decline the honour, in fact did more than any one else to effect his appointment as dictator, Cato saw through his design and persuaded the senate to appoint him sole consul, solacing him with a more legal monarchy that he might not force his way to the dictatorship. They also voted him additional time in which to hold his provinces; and he had two, Spain, and all Africa, which he managed by sending legates thither and maintaining armies there, for which he received from the public treasury a thousand talents annually.

29

CONSEQUENTLY, Caesar canvassed by proxy for a consulship, and likewise for an extension of time in which to hold his own provinces. At first, then, Pompey held his peace, while Marcellus and Lentulus opposed these plans; they hated Caesar on other grounds, and went beyond all bounds in their efforts to bring dishonour and abuse upon him. For instance, the inhabitants of Novum Comum, a colony recently established by Caesar in Gaul, were deprived of citizenship by them; and Marcellus, while he was consul, beat with rods a senator of Novum Comum who had come to Rome, telling him besides that he put these marks upon him to prove that he was not a Roman, and bade him go back and show them to Caesar. But after the consulship of Marcellus, Caesar having now sent his Gallic wealth for all those in public life to draw from in copious streams, and having freed Curio the tribune from many debts, and having given Paulus the consul fifteen hundred talents, out of which he adorned the forum with the Basilica, a famous monument, erected in place of the Fulvia,—under these circumstances Pompey took fright at the coalition, and openly now, by his own efforts and those of his friends, tried to have a successor appointed to Caesar in his government, and sent a demand to him for the return of the soldiers whom he had lent him for his Gallic contests. Caesar sent the soldiers back, after making a present to each man of two hundred and fifty drachmas. But the officers who brought these men to Pompey spread abroad among the multitude stories regarding Caesar which were neither reasonable nor true, and ruined Pompey himself with vain hopes. They told him that Caesar's army yearned for him, and that while he was with difficulty controlling affairs in the city owing to the disease of envy which festered in the body politic, the forces in Gaul were ready to serve him, and had but to cross into Italy when they would at once be on his side; so obnoxious to them had Caesar become by reason of the multitude of his campaigns, and so suspicious of him were they made by their fear of a monarchy. All this fed Pompey's vanity, and he neglected to provide himself with soldiers, as though he had no fears; while with speeches and resolutions of the senate he was carrying the day against Caesar, as he supposed, although he was merely getting measures rejected about which Caesar cared naught. Nay, we are told that one of the centurions sent to Rome by Caesar, as he stood in front of the senate house and learned that the senate would not give Caesar an extension of his term of command, slapped the handle of his sword and said: "But this will give it."

30

HOWEVER, the demands which came from Caesar certainly had a striking resemblance of fairness. He demanded, namely, that if he himself laid down his arms, Pompey should do the same, and that both, thus become private men, should find what favour they could with their fellow citizens; arguing that if they took away his forces from him, but confirmed Pompey in the possession of his, they would be accusing one of seeking a tyranny and making the other a tyrant. When Curio laid these proposals before the people in behalf of Caesar, he was loudly applauded, and some actually cast garlands of flowers upon him as if he were a victorious athlete. Antony, too, who was a tribune, brought before the people a letter of Caesar's on these matters which he had received, and read it aloud, in defiance of the consuls. But in the senate, Scipio, the father-in-law of Pompey, introduced a motion that if by a fixed day Caesar did not lay down his arms he should be declared a public enemy. And when the consuls put the question whether Pompey should dismiss his soldiers, and again whether Caesar should, very few senators voted for the first, and all but a few for the second; but when Antony again demanded that both should give up their commands, all with one accord assented. Scipio, however, made violent opposition, and Lentulus the consul cried out that against a robber there was need of arms, not votes; whereupon the senate broke up, and the senators put on the garb of mourning in view of the dissension.

31

BUT presently letters came from Caesar in which he appeared to take a more moderate position, for he agreed to surrender everything else, but demanded that Cisalpine Gaul and Illyricum together with two legions should be given him until he stood for his second consulship. Cicero the orator, too, who had just returned from Cilicia and was busy with a reconciliation, tried to mollify Pompey, who yielded everything else, but insisted on taking away Caesar's soldiers. Cicero also tried to persuade the friends of Caesar to compromise and come to a settlement on the basis of the provinces mentioned and only six thousand soldiers, and Pompey was ready to yield and grant so many. Lentulus the consul, however, would not let him, but actually heaped insults upon Antony and Curio and drove them disgracefully from the senate, thus himself contriving for Caesar the most specious of his pretexts, and the one by means of which he most of all incited his soldiers, showing them men of repute and high office who had fled the city on hired carts and in the garb of slaves. For thus they had arrayed themselves in their fear and stolen out of Rome.

32

NOW, Caesar had with him not more than three hundred horsemen and five thousand legionaries; for the rest of his army had been left beyond the Alps, and was to be brought up by those whom he had sent for the purpose. He saw, however, that the beginning of his enterprise and its initial step did not require a large force at present, but must take advantage of the golden moment by showing amazing boldness and speed, since he could strike terror into his enemies by an unexpected blow more easily than he could overwhelm them by an attack in full force. He therefore ordered his centurions and other officers, taking their swords only, and without the rest of their arms, to occupy Ariminum, a large city of Gaul, avoiding commotion and bloodshed as far as possible; and he entrusted this force to Hortensius.

He himself spent the day in public, attending and watching the exercises of gladiators; but a little before evening he bathed and dressed and went into the banqueting hall. Here he held brief converse with those who had been invited to supper, and just as it was getting dark and went away, after addressing courteously most of his guests and bidding them await his return. To a few of his friends, however, he had previously given directions to follow him, not all by the same route, but some by one way and some by another. He himself mounted one of his hired carts and drove at first along another road, then turned towards Ariminum. When he came to the river which separates Cisalpine Gaul from the rest of Italy (it is called the Rubicon), and began to reflect, now that he drew nearer to the fearful step and was agitated by the magnitude of his ventures, he checked his speed. Then, halting in his course, he communed with himself a long time in silence as his resolution wavered back and forth, and his purpose then suffered change after change. For a long time, too, he discussed his perplexities with his friends who were present, among whom was Asinius Pollio, estimating the great evils for all mankind which would follow their passage of the river, and the wide fame of it which they would leave to posterity. But finally, with a sort of passion, as if abandoning calculation and casting himself upon the future, and uttering the phrase with which men usually prelude their plunge into desperate and daring fortunes, "Let the die be cast," he hastened to cross the river; and going at full speed now for the rest of the time, before daybreak he dashed into Ariminum and took possession of it. It is said, moreover, that on the night before he crossed the river he had an unnatural dream; he thought, namely, that he was having incestuous intercourse with his own mother.

33

AFTER the seizure of Ariminum, as if the war had opened with broad gates to cover the whole earth and sea alike, and the laws of the state were confounded along with the boundaries of the province, one would not have thought that men and women, as at other times, were hurrying through Italy in consternation, but that the very cities had risen up in flight and were rushing one through another; while Rome herself, deluged as it were by the inhabitants of the surrounding towns who were fleeing from their homes, neither readily obeying a magistrate nor listening to the voice of reason, in the surges of a mighty sea narrowly escaped being overturned by her own internal agitations. For conflicting emotions and violent disturbances prevailed everywhere. Those who rejoiced did not keep quiet, but in many places, as was natural in a great city, encountered those who were in fear and distress, and being filled with confidence as to the future came into strife with them; while Pompey himself, who was terror-stricken, was assailed on every side, being taken to task by some for having strengthened Caesar against himself and the supreme power of the state, and denounced by others for having permitted Lentulus to insult Caesar when he was ready to yield and was offering reasonable terms of settlement. Favonius bade him stamp on the ground; for once, in a boastful speech to the senate, he told them to take no trouble or anxious thought about preparations for the war, since when it came he had but to stamp upon the earth to fill Italy with armies.

However, even then Pompey's forces were more numerous than Caesar's; but no one would suffer him to exercise his own judgment; and so, under the influence of many false and terrifying reports, believing that the war was already close at hand and prevailed everywhere, he gave way, was swept along with the universal tide, issued an edict declaring a state of anarchy, and forsook the city, commanding the senate to follow, and forbidding any one to remain who preferred country and freedom to tyranny.

34

ACCORDINGLY, the consuls fled, without even making the sacrifices usual before departure; most of the senators also fled, after seizing, in a sort of robbery, whatever came to hand of their own possessions, as though it were the property of others. Some, too, who before this had vehemently espoused the cause of Caesar, were now frightened out of their wits, and were carried along, when there was no need of it, by the sweep of the great tide. But most pitiful was the sight of the city, now that so great a tempest was bearing down upon her, carried along like a ship abandoned of her helmsmen to dash against whatever lay in her path. Still, although their removal was so pitiful a thing, for the sake of Pompey men considered exile to be their country, and abandoned Rome with the feeling that it was Caesar's camp. For even Labienus, one of Caesar's greatest friends, who had been his legate and had fought most zealously with him in all his Gallic wars, now ran away from him and came to Pompey.

But Caesar sent to Labienus his money and his baggage; against Domitius, however, who was holding Corfinium with thirty cohorts under his command, he marched, and pitched his camp near by. Domitius, despairing of his enterprise, asked his physician, who was a slave, for a poison; and taking what was given him, drank it, intending to die. But after a little, hearing that Caesar showed most wonderful clemency towards his prisoners, he bewailed his fate, and blamed the rashness of his purpose. Then his physician bade him be of good cheer, since what he had drunk was a sleeping-potion and not deadly; whereupon Domitius rose up overjoyed and went to Caesar, the pledge of whose right hand he received, only to desert him and go back to Pompey. When tidings of these things came to Rome, men were made more cheerful, and some of the fugitives turned back.

35

CAESAR took over the troops of Domitius, as well as all the other levies of Pompey which he surprised in the various cities. Then, since his forces were already numerous and formidable, he marched against Pompey himself. Pompey, however, did not await his approach, but fled to Brundisium, sent the consuls before him with an army to Dyrrhachium, and shortly afterwards, as Caesar drew near, sailed off himself, as shall be set forth circumstantially in his Life. Caesar wished to pursue him at once, but was destitute of ships; so he turned back to Rome, having in sixty days and without bloodshed become master of all Italy.

He found the city more tranquil than he was expecting, and many senators in it. With these, therefore, he conferred in a gentle and affable manner, inviting them even to send a deputation to Pompey suitable terms of agreement. But no one would listen to him, either because they feared Pompey, whom they had abandoned, or because they thought that Caesar did not mean what he said, but was indulging in specious talk. When the tribune Metellus tried to prevent Caesar's taking money from the reserve funds of the state, and cited certain laws, Caesar said that arms and laws had not the same season. "But if thou art displeased at what is going on, for the present get out of the way, since war has no use for free speech; when, however, I have come to terms and laid down my arms, then thou shalt come before the people with thy harangues. And in saying this I waive my own just rights; for thou art mine, thou and all of the faction hostile to me whom I have caught." After this speech to Metellus, Caesar walked towards the door of the treasury, and when the keys were not to be found, he sent for smiths and ordered them to break in the door. Metellus once more opposed him, and was commended by some for so doing; but Caesar, raising his voice, threatened to kill him if he did not cease his troublesome interference. "And thou surely knowest, young man," said he, "that it is more unpleasant for me to say this than to do it." Then Metellus, in consequence of this speech, went off in a fright, and henceforth everything was speedily and easily furnished to Caesar for the war.

36

SO he made an expedition into Spain, having resolved first to drive out from there Afranius and Varro, Pompey's legates, and bring their forces there and the provinces into his power, and then to march against Pompey, leaving not an enemy in his rear. And though his life was often in peril from ambuscades, and his army most of all from hunger, he did not cease from pursuing, challenging, and besieging the men until he had made himself by main force master of their camps and their forces. The leaders, however, made their escape to Pompey.

37

WHEN Caesar came back to Rome, Piso, his father-in-law, urged him to send a deputation to Pompey with proposals for a settlement; but Isauricus, to please Caesar, opposed the project. So, having been made dictator by the senate, he brought home exiles, restored to civic rights the children of those who had suffered in the time of Sulla, relieved the burdens of the debtor-class by a certain adjustment of interest, took in hand a few other public measures of like character, and within eleven days abdicated the sole power, had himself declared consul with Servilius Isauricus, and entered upon his campaign.

The rest of his forces he passed by in a forced march, and with six hundred picked horsemen and five legions, at the time of the winter solstice, in the early part of January (this month answers nearly to the Athenian Poseideon), put to sea, and after crossing the Ionian gulf took Oricum and Apollonia, and sent his transports back again to Brundisium for the soldiers who had been belated on their march. These, as long as they were on the road, since they were now past their physical prime and worn out with their multitudinous wars, murmured against Caesar. "Whither, pray, and to what end will this man bring us, hurrying us about and treating us like tireless and lifeless things? Even a sword gets tired out with smiting, and shield and breastplate are spared a little after so long a time of service. Will not even our wounds, then, convince Caesar that he commands mortal men, and that we are mortal in the endurance of pain and suffering? Surely the wintry season and the occasion of a storm at sea not even a god can constrain; yet this man takes risks as though he were not pursuing, but flying from, enemies." With such words as these they marched in a leisurely way to Brundisium. But when they got there and found that Caesar had put to sea, they quickly changed their tone and reviled themselves as traitors to the Imperator; they reviled their officers, too, for not having quickened their march. Then, sitting on the cliffs, they looked off towards the open sea and Epirus, watching for the ships which were to carry them across to their commander.

38

AT Apollonia, since the force which he had with him was not a match for the enemy and the delay of his troops on the other side caused him perplexity and distress, Caesar conceived the dangerous plan of embarking in a twelve-oared boat, without any one's knowledge, and going over to Brundisium, though the sea was encompassed by such large armaments of the enemy. At night, accordingly, after disguising himself in the dress of a slave, he went on board, threw himself down as one of no account, and kept quiet. While the river Aoüs was carrying the boat down towards the sea, the early morning breeze, which at that time usually made the mouth of the river calm by driving back the waves, was quelled by a strong wind which blew from the sea during the night; the river therefore chafed against the inflow of the sea and the opposition of its billows, and was rough, being beaten back with a great din and violent eddies, so that it was impossible for the master of the boat to force his way along. He therefore ordered the sailors to come about in order to retrace his course. But Caesar, perceiving this, disclosed himself, took the master of the boat by the hand, who was terrified at sight of him, and said: "Come, good man, be bold and fear naught; thou carryest Caesar and Caesar's fortune in thy boat." The sailors forgot the storm, and laying to their oars, tried with all alacrity to force their way down the river. But since it was impossible, after taking much water and running great hazard at the mouth of the river, Caesar very reluctantly suffered the captain to put about. When he came back, his soldiers met him in throngs, finding much fault and sore displeased with him because he did not believe that even with them alone he was able to conquer, but was troubled, and risked his life for the sake of the absent as though distrusting those who were present.

39

AFTER this, Antony put in from Brundisium with his forces, and Caesar was emboldened to challenge Pompey to battle. Pompey was well posted and drew ample supplies both from land and sea; while Caesar had no great abundance at first, and afterwards was actually hard pressed for want of provisions. But his soldiers dug up a certain root, mixed it with milk, and ate it. Once, too, they made loaves of it, and running up to the enemy's outposts, threw the loaves inside or tossed them to one another, adding by way of comment that as long as the earth produced such roots, they would not stop besieging Pompey. Pompey, however, would not allow either the loaves or these words to reach the main body of his army. For his soldiers were dejected, fearing the ferocity and hardiness of their enemies, who were like wild beasts in their eyes.

There were constant skirmishings about the fortifications of Pompey, and in all of them Caesar got the better except one, where there was a great rout of his men and he was in design of losing his camp. For when Pompey attacked not one of Caesar's men stood his ground, but the moats were filled with the slain, and others were falling at their own ramparts and walls, whither they had been driven in headlong flight. And though Caesar met the fugitives and tried to turn them back, he availed nothing, nay, when he tried to lay hold of the standards the bearers threw them away, so that the enemy captured thirty-two of them. Caesar himself, too, narrowly escaped being killed. For as a tall and sturdy man was running away past him, he laid his hand upon him and bade him stay and face about upon the enemy; and the fellow, full of panic at the threatening danger, raised his sword to smite Caesar, but before he could do so Caesar's shield-bearer lopped off his arm at the shoulder. So completely had Caesar given up his cause for lost that, when Pompey, either from excessive caution or by some chance, did not follow up his great success, but withdrew after he had shut up the fugitives within their entrenchments, Caesar said to his friends as he left them: "To-day victory had been with the enemy, if they had had a victor in command." Then going by himself to his tent and lying down, he spent that most distressful of all nights in vain reflections, convinced that he had shown bad generalship. For while a fertile country lay waiting for him, and the prosperous cities of Macedonia and Thessaly, he had neglected to carry the war thither, and had posted himself here by the sea, which his enemies controlled with their fleets, being thus held in siege by lack of provisions rather than besieging with his arms. Thus his despondent thoughts of the difficulty and perplexity of his situation kept him tossing upon his couch, and in the morning he broke camp, resolved to lead his army into Macedonia against Scipio; for he would either draw Pompey after him to a place where he would give battle without drawing his supplies as he now did from the sea, or Scipio would be left alone and he would overwhelm him.

40

THIS emboldened the soldiers of Pompey and the leaders by whom he was surrounded to keep close to Caesar, whom they thought defeated and in flight. For Pompey himself was cautious about hazarding a battle for so great a stake, and since he was most excellently provided with everything necessary for a long war, he thought it best to wear out and quench the vigour of the enemy, which must be short-lived. For the best fighting men in Caesar's army had experience, it is true, and a daring which was irresistible in combat; but what with their long marches and frequent encampments and siege-warfare and night-watches, they were beginning to give out by reason of age, and were too unwieldy for labour, having lost their ardour from weakness. At that time, too, a kind of pestilential disease, occasioned by the strangeness of their diet, was said to be prevalent in Caesar's army. And what was most important of all, since Caesar was neither strong in funds or well supplied with provisions, it was thought that within a short time his army would break up of itself.

41

FOR these reasons Pompey did not wish to fight, but Cato was the only one to commend his course, and this from a desire to spare the lives of his fellow citizens; for when he saw even those of the enemy who had fallen in battle, to the number of a thousand, he burst into tears, muffled up his head, and went away. All the rest, however, reviled Pompey for trying to avoid a battle, and sought to goad him on by calling him Agamemnon and King of Kings, implying that he did not wish to lay aside his sole authority, but plumed himself on having so many commanders dependent on him and coming constantly to his tent. And Favonius, affecting Cato's boldness of speech, complained like a mad man because that year also they would be unable to enjoy the figs of Tusculum because of Pompey's love of command. Afranius, too, who had lately come from Spain, where he had shown bad generalship, when accused of betraying his army for a bribe, asked why they did not fight with the merchant who had bought the provinces for him. Driven on by all these importunities, Pompey reluctantly sought a battle and pursued Caesar.

Caesar accomplished most of his march with difficulty, since no one would sell him provisions, and everybody despised him on account of his recent defeat; but after he had taken Gomphi, a city of Thessaly, he not only provided food for his soldiers, but also relieved them of their disease unexpectedly. For they fell in with plenty of wine, and after drinking freely of it, and then reveling and rioting on their march, by means of their drunkenness they drove away and got rid of their trouble, since they brought their bodies into a different habit.

57

HOWEVER, the Romans gave way before the good fortune of the man and accepted the bit, and regarding the monarchy as a respite from the evils of the civil wars, they appointed him dictator for life. This was confessedly a tyranny, since the monarchy, besides the element of irresponsibility, now took on that of permanence. It was Cicero who proposed the first honours for him in the senate, and their magnitude was, after all, not too great for a man; but others added excessive honours and vied with one another in proposing them, thus rendering Caesar odious and obnoxious even to the mildest citizens because of the pretension and extravagance of what was decreed for him. It is thought, too, that the enemies of Caesar no less than his flatterers helped to force these measures through, in order that they might have as many pretexts as possible against him and might be thought to have the best reasons for attempting his life. For in all other ways, at least, after the civil wars were over, he showed himself blameless; and certainly it is thought not inappropriate that the temple of Clemency was decreed as a thank-offering in view of his mildness. For he pardoned many of those who had fought against him, and to some he even gave honours and offices besides, as to Brutus and Cassius, both of whom were now praetors. The statues of Pompey, which had been thrown down, he would not suffer to remain so, but set them up again, at which Cicero said that in setting up Pompey's statues Caesar firmly fixed his own. When his friends thought it best that he should have a body-guard, and many of them volunteered for this service, he would not consent, saying that it was better to die once for all than to be always expecting death. And in the effort to surround himself with men's good will as the fairest and at the same time the securest protection, he again courted the people with banquets and distributions of grain, and his soldiers with newly planted colonies, the most conspicuous of which were Carthage and Corinth. The earlier capture of both these cities, as well as their present restoration, chanced to fall at one and the same time.

58

AS for the nobles, to some of them he promised consulships and praetorships in the future, others he appeased with sundry other powers and honours, and in all he implanted hopes, since he ardently desired to rule over willing subjects. Therefore, when Maximus the consul died, he appointed Caninius Revilius consul for the one day still remaining of the term of office. To him, as we are told, many were going with congratulations and offers of escort, whereupon Cicero said: "Let us make haste, or else the man's consulship will have expired."

Caesar's many successes, however, did not divert his natural spirit of enterprise and ambition to the enjoyment of what he had laboriously achieved, but served as fuel and incentive for future achievements, and begat in him plans for greater deeds and a passion for fresh glory, as though he had used up what he already had. What he felt was therefore nothing else than emulation of himself, as if he had been another man, and a sort of rivalry between what he had done and what he purposed to do. For he planned and prepared to make an expedition against the Parthians; and after subduing these and marching around the Euxine by way of Hyrcania, the Caspian Sea, and the Caucasus, to invade Scythia; and after overrunning the countries bordering on Germany and Germany itself, to come back by way of Gaul to Italy, and so to complete this circuit of his empire, which would then be bounded on all sides by the ocean. During this expedition, moreover, he intended to dig through the isthmus of Corinth, and had already put Anienus in charge of this work; he intended also to divert the Tiber just below the city into a deep channel, give it a bend towards Circeium, and make it empty into the sea at Terracina, thus contriving for merchantmen a safe as well as an easy passage to Rome; and besides this, to convert marshes about Pomentinum and Setia into a plain which many thousands of men could cultivate; and further, to build moles which should barricade the sea where it was nearest to Rome, to clear away the hidden dangers on the shore of Ostia, and then construct harbours and roadsteads sufficient for the great fleets that would visit them. And all these things were in preparation.

59

THE adjustment of the calendar, however, and the correction of the irregularity in the computation of time, were not only studied scientifically by him, but also brought to completion, and proved to be of the highest utility. For not only in very ancient times was the relation of the lunar to the solar year in great confusion among the Romans, so that the sacrificial feasts and festivals, diverging gradually, at last fell in opposite seasons of the year, but also at this time people generally had no way of computing the actual solar year; the priests alone knew the proper time, and would suddenly and to everybody's surprise insert the intercalary month called Mercedonius. Numa the king is said to have been the first to intercalate this month, thus devising a slight and short-lived remedy for the error in regard to the sidereal and solar cycles, as I have told in his Life. But Caesar laid the problem before the best philosophers and mathematicians, and out of the methods of correction which were already at hand compounded one of his own which was more accurate than any. This the Romans use down to the present time, and are thought to be less in error than other peoples as regards the inequality between the lunar and solar years. However, even this furnished occasion for blame to those who envied Caesar and disliked his power. At any rate, Cicero the orator, we are told, when some one remarked that Lyra would rise on the morrow, said: "Yes, by decree," implying that men were compelled to accept even this dispensation.

60

BUT the most open and deadly hatred towards him was produced by his passion for the royal power. For the multitude this was a first cause of hatred, and for those who had long smothered their hate, a most specious pretext for it. And yet those who were advocating this honour for Caesar actually spread abroad among the people a report that from the Sibylline books it appeared that Parthia could be taken if the Romans went up against it with a king, but otherwise could not be assailed; and as Caesar was coming down from Alba into the city they ventured to hail him as king. But at this the people were confounded, and Caesar, disturbed in mind, said that his name was not King, but Caesar, and seeing that his words produced an universal silence, he passed on with no very cheerful or contented looks. Moreover, after sundry extravagant honours had been voted him in the senate, it chanced that he was sitting above the rostra, and as the praetors and consuls drew near, with the whole senate following them, he did not rise to receive them, but as if he were dealing with mere private persons, replied that his honours needed curtailment rather than enlargement. This vexed not only the senate, but also the people, who felt that in the persons of the senators the state was insulted, and in a terrible dejection they went away at once, all who were not obliged to remain, so that Caesar too, when he was aware of his mistake, immediately turned to go home, and drawing back his toga from his neck, cried in loud tones to his friends that he was ready to offer his throat to any one who wished to kill him. But afterwards he made his disease an excuse for his behaviour, saying that the senses of those who are thus afflicted do not usually remain steady when they address a multitude standing, but are speedily shaken and whirled about, bringing on giddiness and insensibility. However, what he said was not true; on the contrary, he was very desirous of rising to receive the senate; but one of his friends, as they say, or rather one of his flatterers, Cornelius

Balbus, restrained him, saying: "Remember that thou art Caesar, and permit thyself to be courted as a superior."

61

THERE was added to these causes of offence his insult to the tribunes. It was, namely, the festival of the Lupercalia, of which many write that it was anciently celebrated by shepherds, and has also some connection with the Arcadian Lycaea. At this time many of the noble youths and of the magistrates run up and down through the city naked, for sport and laughter striking those they meet with shaggy thongs. And many women of rank also purposely get in their way, and like children at school present their hands to be struck, believing that the pregnant will thus be helped to an easy delivery, and the barren to pregnancy. These ceremonies Caesar was witnessing, seated upon the rostra on a golden throne, arrayed in triumphal attire. And Antony was one of the runners in the sacred race; for he was consul. Accordingly, after he had dashed into the forum and the crowd had made way for him, he carried a diadem, round which a wreath of laurel was tied, and held it out to Caesar. Then there was applause, not loud, but slight and preconcerted. But when Caesar pushed away the diadem, all the people applauded; and when Antony offered it again, few, and when Caesar declined it again, all, applauded. The experiment having thus failed, Caesar rose from his seat, after ordering the wreath to be carried up to the Capitol; but then his statues were seen to have been decked with royal diadems. So two of the tribunes, Flavius and Maryllus, went up to them and pulled off the diadems, and after discovering those who had first hailed Caesar as king, led them off to prison. Moreover, the people followed the tribunes with applause and called them Brutuses, because Brutus was the man who put an end to the royal succession and brought the power into the hands of the senate and people instead of a sole ruler. At this, Caesar was greatly vexed, and deprived Maryllus and Flavius of their office, while in his denunciation of them, although he at the same time insulted the people, he called them repeatedly Brutes and Cymaeans.

62

UNDER these circumstances the multitude turned their thoughts towards Marcus Brutus, who was thought to be a descendant of the elder Brutus on his father's side, on his mother's side belonged to the Servilii, another illustrious house, and was a son-in-law and nephew of Cato. The desires which Brutus felt to attempt of his own accord the abolition of the monarchy were blunted by the favours and honours that he had received from Caesar. For not only had his life been spared at Pharsalus after Pompey's flight, and the lives of many of his friends at his entreaty, but also he had great credit with Caesar. He had received the most honourable of the praetorships for the current year, and was to be consul three years later, having been preferred to Cassius, who was a rival candidate. For Caesar, as we are told, said that Cassius urged the juster claims to the office, but that for his own part he could not pass Brutus by. Once, too, when certain persons were actually accusing Brutus to him, the conspiracy being already on foot, Caesar would not heed them, but laying his hand upon his body said to the accusers: "Brutus will wait for this shriveled skin," implying that Brutus was worthy to rule because of his virtue, but that for the sake of ruling he would not become a thankless villain. Those, however, who were eager for the change, and fixed their eyes on Brutus alone, or on him first, did not venture to talk with him directly, but by night they covered his praetorial tribune and chair with writings, most of which were of this sort: "Thou art asleep, Brutus," or, "Thou art not Brutus." When Cassius perceived that the ambition of Brutus was somewhat stirred by these things, he was more urgent with him than before, and pricked him on, having himself also some private grounds for hating Caesar; these I have mentioned in the Life of Brutus. Moreover, Caesar actually suspected him, so that he once said to his friends: "What, think ye, doth Cassius want? I like him not over much, for he is much too pale." And again, we are told that when Antony and Dolabella were accused to him of plotting revolution, Caesar said: "I am not much in fear of these fat, long-haired fellows, but rather of those pale, thin ones," meaning Brutus and Cassius.

63

BUT destiny, it would seem, is not so much unexpected as it is unavoidable, since they say that amazing signs and apparitions were seen. Now, as for lights in the heavens, crashing sounds borne all about by night, and birds of omen coming down into the forum, it is perhaps not worth while to mention these precursors of so great an event; but Strabo the philosopher says that multitudes of men all on fire were seen rushing up, and a soldier's slave threw from his hand a copious flame and seemed to the spectators to be burning, but when the flame ceased the man was uninjured; he says, moreover, that when Caesar himself was sacrificing, the heart of the victim was not to be found, and the prodigy caused fear, since in the course of nature, certainly, an animal without a heart could not exist. The following story, too, is told by many. A certain seer warned Caesar to be on his guard against a great peril on the day of the month of March which the Romans call the Ides; and when the day had come and Caesar was on his way to the senate-house, he greeted the seer with a jest and said: "Well, the Ides of March are come," and the seer said to him softly: "Ay, they are come, but they are not gone." Moreover, on the day before, when Marcus Lepidus was entertaining him at supper, Caesar chanced to be signing letters, as his custom was, while reclining at table, and the discourse turned suddenly upon the question what sort of death was the best; before any one could answer Caesar cried out: "That which is unexpected." After this, while he was sleeping as usual by the side of his wife, all the windows and doors of the chamber flew open at once, and Caesar, confounded by the noise and the light of the moon shining down upon him, noticed that Calpurnia was in a deep slumber, but was uttering indistinct words and inarticulate groans in her sleep; for she dreamed, as it proved, that she was holding her murdered husband in her arms and bewailing him.

Some, however, say that this was not the vision which the woman had; but that there was attached to Caesar's house to give it adornment and distinction, by vote of the senate, a gable-ornament, as Livy says, and it was this which Calpurnia in her dreams saw torn down, and therefore, as she thought, wailed and wept. At all events, when day came, she begged Caesar, if it was possible, not to go out, but to postpone the meeting of the senate; if, however, he had no concern at all for her dreams, she besought him to inquire by other modes of divination and by sacrifices concerning the future. And Caesar also, as it would appear, was in some suspicion and fear. For never before had he perceived in Calpurnia any womanish superstition, but now he saw that she was in great distress. And when the seers also, after many sacrifices, told him that the omens were unfavourable, he resolved to send Antony and dismiss the senate.

64

BUT at this juncture Decimus Brutus, surnamed Albinus, who was so trusted by Caesar that he was entered in his will as his second heir, but was partner in the conspiracy of the other Brutus and Cassius, fearing that if Caesar should elude that day, their undertaking would become known, ridiculed the seers and chided Caesar for laying himself open to malicious charges on the part of the senators, who would think themselves mocked at; for they had met at his bidding, and were ready and willing to vote as one man that he should be declared king of the provinces outside of Italy, and might wear a diadem when he went anywhere else by land or sea; but if some one should tell them at their session to be gone now, but to come back again when Calpurnia should have better dreams, what speeches would be made by his enemies, or who would listen to his friends when they tried to show that this was not slavery and tyranny? But if he was fully resolved (Albinus said) to regard the day as inauspicious, it was better that he should go in person and address the senate, and then postpone its business. While saying these things Brutus took Caesar by the hand and began to lead him along. And he had gone but a little way from his door when a slave belonging to some one else, eager to get at Caesar, but unable to do so for the press of numbers about him, forced his way into the house, gave himself into the hands of Calpurnia, and bade her keep him secure until Caesar came back, since he had important matters to report to him.

65

FURTHERMORE, Artemidorus, a Cnidian by birth, a teacher of Greek philosophy, and on this account brought into intimacy with some of the followers of Brutus, so that he also knew most of what they were doing, came bringing to Caesar in a small roll the disclosures which he was going to make; but seeing that Caesar took all such rolls and handed them to his attendants, he came quite near, and said: "Read this, Caesar, by thyself, and speedily; for it contains matters of importance and of concern to thee." Accordingly, Caesar took the roll and would have read it, but was prevented by the multitude of people who engaged his attention, although he set out to do so many times, and holding in his hand and retaining that roll alone, he passed on into the senate. Some, however, say that another person gave him this roll, and that Artemidorus did not get to him at all, but was crowded away all along the route.

66

SO far, perhaps, these things may have happened of their own accord; the place, however, which was the scene of that struggle and murder, and in which the senate was then assembled, since it contained a statue of Pompey and had been dedicated by Pompey as an additional ornament to his theatre, made it wholly clear that it was the work of some heavenly power which was calling and guiding the action thither. Indeed, it is also said that Cassius, turning his eyes toward the statue of Pompey before the attack began, invoked it silently, although he was much addicted to the doctrines of Epicurus; but the crisis, as it would seem, when the dreadful attempt was now close at hand, replaced his former cool calculations with divinely inspired emotion.

Well, then, Antony, who was a friend of Caesar's and a robust man, was detained outside by Brutus Albinus, who purposely engaged him in a lengthy conversation; but Caesar went in, and the senate rose in his honour. Some of the partisans of Brutus took their places round the back of Caesar's chair, while others went to meet him, as though they would support the petition which Tullius Cimber presented to Caesar in behalf of his exiled brother, and they joined their entreaties to his and accompanied Caesar up to his chair. But when, after taking his seat, Caesar continued to repulse their petitions, and, as they pressed upon him with greater importunity, began to show anger towards one and another of them, Tullius seized his toga with both hands and pulled it down from his neck. This was the signal for the assault. It was Casca who gave him the first blow with his dagger, in the neck, not a mortal wound, nor even a deep one, for which he was too much confused, as was natural at the beginning of a deed of great daring; so that Caesar turned about, grasped the knife, and held it fast. At almost the same instant both cried out, the smitten man in Latin: "Accursed Casca, what does thou?" and the smiter, in Greek, to his brother: "Brother, help!"

So the affair began, and those who were not privy to the plot were filled with consternation and horror at what was going on; they dared not fly, nor go to Caesar's help, nay, nor even utter a word. But those who had prepared themselves for the murder bared each of them his dagger, and Caesar, hemmed in on all sides, whichever way he turned confronting blows of weapons aimed at his face and eyes, driven hither and thither like a wild beast, was entangled in the hands of all; for all had to take part in the sacrifice and taste of the slaughter. Therefore Brutus also gave him one blow in the groin. And it is said by some writers that although Caesar defended himself against the rest and darted this way and that and cried aloud, when he saw that Brutus had drawn his dagger, he pulled his toga down over his head and sank, either by chance or because pushed there by his murderers, against the pedestal on which the statue of Pompey stood. And the pedestal was drenched with his blood, so that one might have thought that Pompey himself was presiding over this vengeance upon his enemy, who now lay prostrate at his feet, quivering from a multitude of wounds. For it is said that he received twenty-three; and many of the conspirators were wounded by one another, as they struggled to plant all those blows in one body.

67

CAESAR thus done to death, the senators, although Brutus came forward as if to say something about what had been done, would not wait to hear him, but burst out of doors and fled, thus filling the people with confusion and helpless fear, so that some of them closed their houses, while others left their counters and places of business and ran, first to the place to see what had happened, then away from the place when they had seen. Antony and Lepidus, the chief friends of Caesar, stole away and took refuge in the houses of others. But Brutus and his partisans, just as they were, still warm from the slaughter, displaying their daggers bare, went all in a body out of the senate-house and marched to the Capitol, not like fugitives, but with glad faces and full of confidence, summoning the multitude to freedom, and welcoming into their ranks the most distinguished of those who met them. Some also joined their number and went up with them as though they had shared in the deed, and laid claim to the glory of it, of whom were Caius Octavius and Lentulus Spinther. These men, then, paid the penalty for their imposture later, when they were put to death by Antony and the young Caesar, without even enjoying the fame for the sake of which they died, owing to the disbelief of their fellow men. For even those who punished them did not exact a penalty for what they did, but for what they wished they had done.

On the next day Brutus came down and held a discourse, and the people listened to what was said without either expressing resentment at what had been done or appearing to approve of it; they showed, however, by their deep silence, that while they pitied Caesar, they respected Brutus. The senate, too, trying to make a general amnesty and reconciliation, voted to give Caesar divine honours and not to disturb even the most insignificant measure which he had adopted when in power; while to Brutus and his partisans it distributed provinces and gave suitable honours, so that everybody thought that matters were decided and settled in the best possible manner.

68

BUT when the will of Caesar was opened and it was found that he had given every Roman citizen a considerable gift, and when the multitude saw his body carried through the forum all disfigured with its wounds, they no longer kept themselves within the restraints of order and discipline, but after heaping round the body benches, railings, and tables from the forum they set fire to them and burned it there; then, lifting blazing brands on high, they ran to the houses of the murderers with intent to burn them down, while others went every whither through the city seeking to seize the men themselves and tear them to pieces. Not one of these came in their way, but all were well barricaded. There was a certain Cinna, however, one of the friends of Caesar, who chanced, as they say, to have seen during the previous night a strange vision. He dreamed, that is, that he was invited to supper by Caesar, and that when he excused himself, Caesar led him along by the hand, although he did not wish to go, but resisted. Now, when he heard that they were burning the body of Caesar in the forum, he rose up and went thither out of respect, although he had misgivings arising from his vision, and was at the same time in a fever. At sight of him, one of the multitude told his name to another who asked him what it was, and he to another, and at once word ran through the whole throng that this man was one of the murderers of Caesar. For there was among the conspirators a man who bore this same name of Cinna, and assuming this man was he, the crowd rushed upon him and tore him in pieces among them. This more than anything else made Brutus and Cassius afraid, and not many days afterwards they withdrew from the city. What they did and suffered before they died, has been told in the Life of Brutus.

69

AT the time of his death Caesar was fully fifty-six years old, but he had survived Pompey not much more than four years, while of the power and dominion which he had sought all his life at so great risks, and barely achieved at last, of this he had reaped no fruit but the name of it only, and a glory which had awakened envy on the part of his fellow citizens. However, the great guardian-genius of the man, whose help he had enjoyed through life, followed upon him even after death as an avenger of his murder, driving and tracking down his slayers over every land and sea until not one of them was left, but even those who in any way soever either put hand to the deed or took part in the plot were punished.

Among events of man's ordering, the most amazing was that which befell Cassius; for after his defeat at Philippi he slew himself with that very dagger which he had used against Caesar; and among events of divine ordering, there was the great comet, which showed itself in great splendour for seven nights after Caesar's murder, and then disappeared; also, the obscuration of the sun's rays. For during all that year its orb rose pale and without radiance, while the heat that came down from it was slight and ineffectual, so that the air in its circulation was dark and heavy owing to the feebleness of the warmth that penetrated it, and the fruits, imperfect and half ripe, withered away and shriveled up on account of the coldness of the atmosphere. But more than anything else the phantom that appeared to Brutus showed that the murder of Caesar was not pleasing to the gods; and it was on this wise. As he was about to take his army across from Abydos to the other continent, he was lying down at night, as his custom was, in his tent, not sleeping, but thinking of the future; for it is said that of all generals Brutus was least given to sleep, and that he naturally remained awake a longer time than anybody else. And now he thought he heard a noise at the door, and looking towards the light of the lamp, which was slowly going out, he saw a fearful vision of a man of unnatural size and harsh aspect. At first he was terrified, but when he saw that the visitor neither did nor said anything, but stood in silence by his couch, he asked him who he was. Then the phantom answered him: "I am thy evil genius, Brutus, and thou shalt see me at Philippi." At the time, then, Brutus said courageously: "I shall see thee;" and the heavenly visitor at once went away. Subsequently, however, when arrayed against Antony and Caesar at Philippi, in the first battle he conquered the enemy in his front, routed and scattered them, and sacked the camp of Caesar;

but as he was about to fight the second battle, the same phantom visited him again at night, and though it said nothing to him, Brutus understood his fate, and plunged headlong into danger. He did not fall in battle, however, but after the rout retired to a crest of ground, put his naked sword to his breast (while a certain friend, as they say, helped to drive the blow home), and so died.

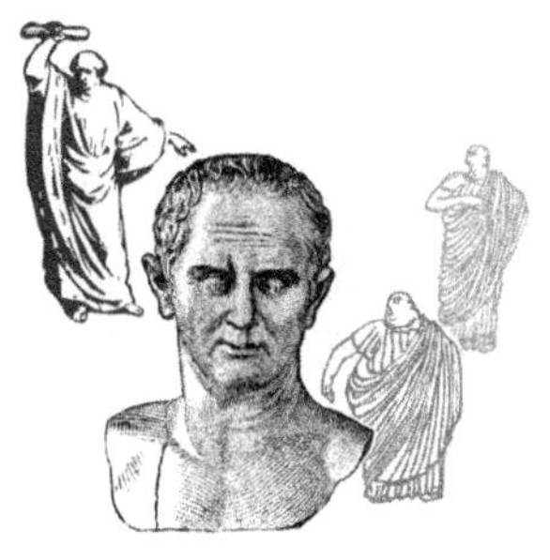

CICERO

AGAINST VERRES

CICERO

1

THAT which was above all things to be desired, O judges, and which above all things was calculated to have the greatest influence toward allaying the unpopularity of your order, and putting an end to the discredit into which your judicial decisions have fallen, appears to have been thrown in your way, and given to you not by any human contrivance, but almost by the interposition of the gods, at a most important crisis of the republic. For an opinion has now become established, pernicious to us, and pernicious to the republic, which has been the common talk of every one, not only at Rome, but among foreign nations also,—that in the courts of law as they exist at present, no wealthy man, however guilty he may be, can possibly be convicted.

2

NOW at this time of peril to your order and to your tribunal, when men are ready to attempt by harangues, and by the proposal of new laws, to increase the existing unpopularity of the senate, Caius Verres is brought to trial as a criminal—a man condemned in the opinion of every one by his life and actions, but acquitted by the enormousness of his wealth according to his own hope and boast. I, O judges, have undertaken this cause as prosecutor with the greatest good wishes and expectation on the part of the Roman people, not in order to increase the unpopularity of the senate, but to relieve it from the discredit which I share with it. For I have brought before you a man, by acting justly in whose case you have an opportunity of retrieving the lost credit of your judicial proceedings, of regaining your credit with the Roman people, and of giving satisfaction to foreign nations; a man, the embezzler of the public funds, the petty tyrant of Asia and Pamphylia, the robber who deprived the city of its rights, the disgrace and ruin of the province of Sicily. And if you come to a decision about this man with severity and a due regard to your oaths, that authority which ought to remain in you will cling to you still; but if that man's vast riches shall break down the sanctity and honesty of the courts of justice, at least I shall achieve this, that it shall be plain that it was rather honest judgment that was wanting to the republic, than a criminal to the judges or an accuser to the criminal.

3

I, INDEED, that I may confess to you the truth about myself, O judges, tho many snares were laid for me by Caius Verres, both by land and sea, which I partly avoided by my own vigilance, and partly warded off by the zeal and kindness of my friends, yet I never seemed to be incurring so much danger, and I never was in such a state of great apprehension, as I am now in this very court of law. Nor does the expectation which people have formed of my conduct of this prosecution, nor this concourse of so vast a multitude as is here assembled, influence me (tho indeed I am greatly agitated by these circumstances) so much as his nefarious plots which he is endeavoring to lay at one and the same time against me, against you, against Marcus Glabrio, the pretor, and against the allies, against foreign nations, against the senate, and even against the very name of senator; whose favorite saying it is that they have got to fear who have stolen only as much as is enough for themselves, but that he has stolen so much that it may easily be plenty for many; that nothing is so holy that it can not be corrupted, or so strongly fortified that it can not be stormed by money. But if he were as secret in acting as he is audacious in attempting, perhaps in some particular he might some time or other have escaped our notice.

4

BUT it happens very fortunately that to his incredible audacity there is joined a most unexampled folly. For as he was unconcealed in committing his robberies of money, so in his hope of corrupting the judges he has made his intentions and endeavors visible to every one. He says that only once in his life has he felt fear, at the time when he was first impeached as a criminal by me; because he was only lately arrived from his province, and was branded with unpopularity and infamy, not modern but ancient and of long standing; and, besides that, the time was unlucky, being very ill-suited for corrupting the judges. Therefore, when I had demanded a very short time to prosecute my inquiries in Sicily, he found a man to ask for two days less to make investigations in Achaia; not with any real intention of doing the same with his diligence and industry, that I have accomplished by my labor, and daily and nightly investigations. For the Achæan inquisitor never even arrived at Brundusium. I in fifty days so traveled over the whole of Sicily that I examined into the records and injuries of all the tribes and of all private individuals, so that it was easily visible to every one, that he had been seeking out a man not really for the purpose of bringing the defendant whom he accused to trial, but merely to occupy the time which ought to belong to me.

5

NOW that most audacious and most senseless man thinks this. He is aware that I am come into court so thoroughly prepared and armed, that I shall fix all his thefts and crimes not only in your ears, but in the very eyes of all men. He sees that many senators are witnesses of his audacity; he sees that many Roman knights are so, too, and many citizens, and many of the allies besides to whom he has done unmistakable injuries. He sees also that very numerous and very important deputations have come here at the same time from most friendly cities, armed with the public authority and evidence collected by their states.

6

IN truth, what genius is there so powerful, what faculty of speaking, what eloquence so mighty, as to be in any particular able to defend the life of that man convicted as it is of so many vices and crimes, and long since condemned by the inclinations and private sentiments of every one. And, to say nothing of the stains and disgraces of his youth, what other remarkable event is there in his questorship, that first step to honor, except that Cnæus Carbo was robbed by his questor of the public money? that the consul was plundered and betrayed? his army deserted? his province abandoned? the holy nature and obligations imposed on him by lot violated?—whose lieutenancy was the ruin of all Asia and Pamphylia, in which provinces he plundered many houses, very many cities, all the shrines and temples; when he renewed and repeated against Cnæus Dolabella his ancient wicked tricks when he had been questor, and did not only in his danger desert, but even attack and betray the man to whom he had been lieutenant, and proquestor, and whom he had brought into odium by his crimes; whose city pretorship was the destruction of the sacred temples and the public works, and, as to his legal decisions, was the adjudging and awarding of property contrary to all established rules and precedents. But now he has established great and numerous monuments and proofs of all his vices in the province of Sicily, which he for three years so harassed and ruined that it can by no possibility be restored to its former condition, and appears scarcely able to be at all recovered after a long series of years, and a long succession of virtuous pretors. While this man was pretor the Sicilians enjoyed neither their own laws, nor the decrees of our senate, nor the common rights of every nation. Every one in Sicily has only so much left as either escaped the notice or was disregarded by the satiety of that most avaricious and licentious man

7

NO legal decision for three years was given on any other ground but his will; no property was so secure to any man, even if it had descended to him from his father and grandfather, but he was deprived of it at his command; enormous sums of money were exacted from the property of the cultivators of the soil by a new and nefarious system. The most faithful of the allies were classed in the number of enemies. Roman citizens were tortured and put to death like slaves; the greatest criminals were acquitted in the courts of justice through bribery; the most upright and honorable men, being prosecuted while absent, were condemned and banished without being heard in their own defense; the most fortified harbors, the greatest and strongest cities, were laid open to pirates and robbers; the sailors and soldiers of the Sicilians, our own allies and friends, died of hunger; the best built fleets on the most important stations were lost and destroyed, to the great disgrace of the Roman people. This same man while pretor plundered and stripped those most ancient monuments, some erected by wealthy monarchs and intended by them as ornaments for their cities; some, too, the work of our own generals, which they either gave or restored as conquerors to the different states in Sicily. And he did this not only in the case of public statues and ornaments, but he also plundered all the temples consecrated in the deepest religious feelings of the people. He did not leave, in short, one god to the Sicilians which appeared to him to be made in a tolerable workmanlike manner, and with any of the skill of the ancients.

8

I AM prevented by actual shame from speaking of his nefarious licentiousness as shown in rapes and other such enormities; and I am unwilling also to increase the distress of those men who have been unable to preserve their children and their wives unpolluted by his wanton lust. But, you will say, these things were done by him in such a manner as not to be notorious to all men. I think there is no man who has heard his name who cannot also relate wicked actions of his; so that I ought rather to be afraid of being thought to omit many of his crimes, than to invent any charges against him. And indeed I do not think that this multitude which has collected to listen to me wishes so much to learn of me what the facts of the case are, as to go over it with me, refreshing its recollection of what it knows already.

9

AND as this is the case, that senseless and profligate man attempts to combat me in another manner. He does not seek to oppose the eloquence of any one else to me; he does not rely on the popularity, or influence, or authority of any one. He pretends that he trusts to these things; but I see what he is really aiming at (and indeed he is not acting with any concealment). He sets before me empty titles of nobility—that is to say, the names of arrogant men, who do not hinder me so much by being noble, as assist me by being notorious; he pretends to rely on their protection, when he has in reality been contriving something else this long time. What hope he now has, and what he is endeavoring to do, I will now briefly explain to you, O judges.

19

AND I beg you, in the name of the immortal gods, O judges, think of and guard against this; I warn you, I give notice to you, of what I am well assured, that this most seasonable opportunity has been given to you by the favor of the gods, for the purpose of delivering your whole order from hatred, from unpopularity, from infamy, and from disgrace. There is no severity believed to exist in the tribunals, nor any scruples with regard to religion; in short, there are not believed to be any tribunals at all. Therefore we are despised and scorned by the Roman people; we are branded with a heavy and now long standing infamy. Nor, in fact, is there any other reason for which the Roman people has with so much earnestness sought the restoration of the tribunician power: but when it was demanding that in words, it seemed to be asking for that, but in reality it was asking for tribunals which it could trust.

20

BUT now men are on the watch-towers; they observe how every one of you behaves himself in respecting religion and observing the laws. They see that, ever since the passing of the law for restoring the power of the tribunes, only one senator, and he, too, a very insignificant one, has been condemned. And tho they do not blame this, yet they have nothing which they can very much commend. For there is no credit in being upright in a case where there is no one who is either able or who endeavors to corrupt one. This is a trial in which you will be deciding about the defendant, the Roman people about you;—by the example of what happens to this man it will be determined whether, when senators are the judges, a very guilty and a very rich man can be condemned.

21

ON which account, in the first place, I beg this of the immortal gods, which I seem to myself to have hopes of, too—that in this trial no one may be found to be wicked except he who has long since been found to be such; secondly, if there are many wicked men, I promise this to you, O judges, I promise this to the Roman people, that my life shall fail rather than my vigor and perseverance in prosecuting their iniquity. But that iniquity, which, if it should be committed, I promise to prosecute severely, with however much trouble and danger to myself, and whatever enmities I may bring on myself by so doing, you, O Marcus Glabrio, can guard against ever taking place by your wisdom, and authority, and diligence. Do you undertake the cause of the tribunals. Do you undertake the cause of impartiality, of integrity, of good faith and religion. Do you undertake the cause of the senate, that, being proved worthy by its conduct in this trial, it may come into favor and popularity with the Roman people. Think who you are and in what a situation you are placed; what you ought to give to the Roman people and what you ought to repay to your ancestors. Let the recollection of the Acilian Law passed by your father occur to your mind, owing to which law the Roman people has had this advantage of most admirable decisions and very strict judges in cases of extortion.

22

I AM resolved not to permit the pretor or the judges to be changed in this cause. I will not permit the matter to be delayed till the lictors of the consuls can go and summon the Sicilians, whom the servants of the consuls-elect did not influence before, when by an unprecedented course of proceeding they sent for them all; I will not permit those miserable men, formerly the allies and friends of the Roman people, now their slaves and supplicant, to lose not only their rights and fortunes by their tyranny, but to be deprived of even the power of bewailing their condition; I will not, I say, when the cause has been summed up by me, permit them after a delay of forty days has intervened, then at last to reply to me when my accusation has already fallen into oblivion through lapse of time; I will not permit the decision to be given when this crowd collected from all Italy has departed from Rome, which has assembled from all quarters at the same time on account of the *comitia*, of the games, and of the census.

23

THE reward of the credit gained by your decision, or the danger arising from the unpopularity which will accrue to you if you decide unjustly, I think ought to belong to you; the labor and anxiety to me; the knowledge of what is done and the recollection of what has been said by every one, to all. I will adopt this course, not an unprecedented one, but one that has been adopted before, by those who are now the chief men of our state,—the course, I mean, of at once producing the witnesses.

24

WHAT you will find novel, O judges, is this, that I will so marshal my witnesses as to unfold the whole of my accusation; that when I have established it by examining my witnesses, by arguments, and by my speech, then I shall show the agreement of the evidence with my accusation: so that there shall be no difference between the established mode of prosecuting, and this new one, except that, according to the established mode, when everything has been said which is to be said, then the witnesses are produced; here they shall be produced as each count is brought forward, so that the other side shall have the same opportunity of examining them, of arguing and making speeches on their evidence. If there be any one who prefers an uninterrupted speech and the old mode of conducting a prosecution without any break, he shall have it in some other trial. But for this time let him understand that what we do is done by us on compulsion (for we only do it with the design of opposing the artifice of the opposite party by our prudence). This will be the first part of the prosecution. We say that Caius Verres has not only done many licentious acts, many cruel ones, toward Roman citizens, and toward some of the allies, many wicked acts against both gods and men; but especially that he has taken away four hundred thousand sesterces out of Sicily contrary to the laws. We will make this so plain to you by witnesses, by private documents, and by public records, that you shall decide that, even if we had abundant space and leisure days for making a long speech without any inconvenience, still there was no need at all of a long speech in this matter.

CICERO

SECOND PHILIPPIC AGAINST ANTONY

CICERO

1

TO what destiny of mine, O conscript fathers, shall I say that it is owing, that none for the last twenty years has been an enemy to the republic without at the same time declaring war against me? Nor is there any necessity for naming any particular person; you yourselves recollect instances in proof of my statement. They have all hitherto suffered severer punishments than I could have wished for them; but I marvel that you, O Antonius, do not fear the end of those men whose conduct you are imitating. And in others I was less surprised at this. None of those men of former times was a voluntary enemy to me; all of them were attacked by me for the sake of the republic. But you, who have never been injured by me, not even by a word, in order to appear more audacious than Catiline, more frantic than Clodius, have of your own accord attacked me with abuse, and have considered that your alienation from me would be a recommendation of you to impious citizens.

2

WHAT am I to think?—that I have been despised? I see nothing either in my life, or in my influence in the city, or in my exploits, or even in the moderate abilities with which I am endowed, which Antonius can despise. Did he think that it was easiest to disparage me in the senate?—a body which has borne its testimony in favor of many most illustrious citizens that they governed the republic well, but in favor of me alone, of all men, that I preserved it. Or did he wish to contend with me in a rivalry of eloquence? This, indeed, is an act of generosity; for what could be a more fertile or richer subject for me, than to have to speak in defense of myself, and against Antonius? This, in fact, is the truth. He thought it impossible to prove to the satisfaction of those men who resembled himself, that he was an enemy to his country, if he was not also an enemy to me. And before I make him any reply on the other topics of his speech, I will say a few words respecting the friendship formerly subsisting between us, which he has accused me of violating—for that I consider a most serious charge.

3

HE has complained that I pleaded once against his interest. Was I not to plead against one with whom I was quite unconnected, in behalf of an intimate acquaintance, of a dear friend? Was I not to plead against interest acquired not by hopes of virtue, but by the disgrace of youth? Was I not to plead against an injustice which that man procured to be done by the obsequiousness of a most iniquitous interposer of his veto, not by any law regulating the privileges of the pretor? But I imagine that this was mentioned by you, in order that you might recommend yourself to the citizens, if they all recollected that you were the son-in-law of a freedman, and that your children were the grandsons of Quintus Fabius, a freedman.

4

BUT you had entirely devoted yourself to my principles (for this is what you said); you had been in the habit of coming to my house. In truth, if you had done so, you would more have consulted your own character and your reputation for chastity. But you did not do so, nor, if you had wished it, would Caius Curio have ever suffered you to do so.

5

BUT I availed myself of your friendly assistance. Of what assistance? Altho the instance which you cite I have myself at all times openly admitted. I preferred confessing that I was under obligations to you, to letting myself appear to any foolish person not sufficiently grateful. However, what was the kindness that you did me? not killing me at Brundusium? Would you then have slain the man whom the conqueror himself, who conferred on you, as you used to boast, the chief rank among all his robbers, had desired to be safe, and had enjoined to go to Italy? Grant that you could have slain him, is not this, O conscript fathers, such a kindness as is done by banditti, who are contented with being able to boast that they have granted their lives to all those men whose lives they have not taken? and if that were really a kindness, then those who slew that man by whom they themselves had been saved, and whom you yourself are in the habit of styling most illustrious men, would never have acquired such immortal glory. But what sort of kindness is it, to have abstained from committing nefarious wickedness? It is a case in which it ought not to appear so delightful to me not to have been killed by you, as miserable, that it should have been in your power to do such a thing with impunity. However, grant that it was a kindness, since no greater kindness could be received from a robber; still in what point can you call me ungrateful? Ought I not to complain of the ruin of the republic, lest I should appear ungrateful toward you?

6

BUT he also read letters which he said that I had sent to him, like a man devoid of humanity and ignorant of the common usages of life. For who ever, who was even but slightly acquainted with the habits of polite men, produced in an assembly and openly read letters which had been sent to him by a friend, just because some quarrel had arisen between them? Is not this destroying all companionship in life, destroying the means by which absent friends converse together? How many jests are frequently put in letters, which, if they were produced in public, would appear stupid! How many serious opinions, which, for all that, ought not to be published! Let this be a proof of your utter ignorance of courtesy. Now mark, also, his incredible folly. What have you to oppose to me, O you eloquent man, as you seem at least to Mustela Tamisus, and to Tiro Numisius? And while these men are standing at this very time in the sight of the senate with drawn swords, I, too, will think you an eloquent man if you will show how you would defend them if they were charged with being assassins. However, what answer would you make if I were to deny that I ever sent those letters to you? By what evidence could you convict me? By my handwriting? Of handwriting indeed you have a lucrative knowledge. How can you prove it in that manner? for the letters are written by an amanuensis. By this time I envy your teacher, who for all that payment which I shall mention presently, has taught you to know nothing.

7

YOU have said that Publius Clodius was slain by my contrivance. What would men have thought if he had been slain at the time when you pursued him in the forum with a drawn sword, in the sight of all the Roman people; and when you would have settled his business if he had not thrown himself up the stairs of a bookseller's shop, and shutting them against you, checked your attack by that means? And I confess that at that time I favored you, but even you yourself do not say that I had advised your attempt. But as for Milo, it was not possible even for me to favor his action; for he had finished the business before any one could suspect that he was going to do it. Oh, but I advised it! I suppose Milo was a man of such a disposition that he was not able to do a service to the republic if he had not some one to advise him to do it. But I rejoiced at it! Well, suppose I did; was I to be the only sorrowful person in the city, when every one else was in such delight? Although that inquiry into the death of Publius Clodius was not instituted with any great wisdom. For what was the reason for having a new law to inquire into the conduct of the man who had slain him, when there was a form of inquiry already established by the laws? However, an inquiry was instituted. And have you now been found, so many years afterward, to say a thing which, at the time that the affair was under discussion, no one ventured to say against me? But as to the assertion that you have dared to make, and that at great length, too, that it was by my means that Pompeius was alienated from his friendship with Cæsar, and that on that account it was my fault that the civil war was originated; in that you have not erred so much in the main facts, as (and that is of the greatest importance) in the times.

8

WHEN Marcus Bibulus, a most illustrious citizen, was consul, I omitted nothing which I could possibly do or attempt to draw off Pompeius from his union with Cæsar. In which, however, Cæsar was more fortunate than I, for he himself drew off Pompeius from his intimacy with me. But afterward, when Pompeius joined Cæsar with all his heart, what could have been my object in attempting to separate them then? It would have been the part of a fool to hope to do so, and of an impudent man to advise it. However, two occasions did arise, on which I gave Pompeius advice against Cæsar. You are at liberty to find fault with my conduct on those occasions if you can. One was when I advised him not to continue Cæsar's government for five years more. The other, when I advised him not to permit him to be considered as a candidate for the consulship when he was absent. And if I had been able to prevail on him in either of these particulars, we should never have fallen into our present miseries.

9

MOREOVER, I also, when Pompeius had now devoted to the service of Cæsar all his own power, and all the power of the Roman people, and had begun when it was too late to perceive all those things which I had foreseen long before, and when I saw that a nefarious war was about to be waged against our country, I never ceased to be the adviser of peace, and concord, and some arrangement. And that language of mine was well known to many people: "I wish, O Cnæus Pompeius, that you had either never joined in a confederacy with Caius Cæsar, or else that you had never broken it off. The one conduct would have become your dignity, and the other would have been suited to your prudence." This, O Marcus Antonius, was at all times my advice both respecting Pompeius and concerning the republic. And if it had prevailed, the republic would still be standing, and you would have perished through your own crimes, and indigence, and infamy.

10

BUT these are all old stories now. This charge, however, is quite a modern one: that Cæsar was slain by my contrivance. I am afraid, O conscript fathers, lest I should appear to you to have brought up a sham accuser against myself (which is a most disgraceful thing to do); a man not only to distinguish me by the praises which are my due, but to load me also with those which do not belong to me. For who ever heard my name mentioned as an accomplice in that most glorious action? and whose name has been concealed who was in the number of that gallant band? Concealed, do I say? Whose name was there which was not at once made public? I should sooner say that some men had boasted in order to appear to have been concerned in that conspiracy, tho they had in reality known nothing of it, than that any one who had been an accomplice in it could have wished to be concealed.

11

MOREOVER, how likely it is, that among such a number of men, some obscure, some young men who had not the wit to conceal any one, my name could possibly have escaped notice? Indeed, if leaders were wanted for the purpose of delivering the country, what need was there of my instigating the Bruti, one of whom saw every day in his house the image of Lucius Brutus, and the other saw also the image of Ahala? Were these the men to seek counsel from the ancestors of others rather than from their own? and out of doors rather than at home? What! Caius Cassius, a man of that family which could not endure, I will not say the domination, but even the power of any individual,—he, I suppose, was in need of me to instigate him? a man who, even without the assistance of these other most illustrious men, would have accomplished this same deed in Cilicia, at the mouth of the river Cydnus, if Cæsar had brought his ships to that bank of the river which he had intended, and not to the opposite one. Was Cnæus Domitius spurred on to seek to recover his dignity, not by the death of his father, a most illustrious man, nor by the death of his uncle, nor by the deprivation of his own dignity, but by my advice and authority? Did I persuade Caius Trebonius, a man whom I should not have ventured even to advise? On which account the republic owes him even a larger debt of gratitude, because he preferred the liberty of the Roman people to the friendship of one man, and because he preferred overthrowing arbitrary power to sharing it. Was I the instigator whom Lucius Tillius Cimber followed? a man whom I admired for having performed that action, rather than ever expected that he would perform it; and I admired him on this account, that he was unmindful of the personal kindnesses which he had received, but mindful of his country. What shall I say of the two Servilii? Shall I call them Cascas, or Ahalas? And do you think that those men were instigated by my authority rather than by their affection for the republic? It would take a long time to go through all the rest; and it is a glorious thing for the republic that they were so numerous, and a most honorable thing also for themselves.

12

BUT recollect, I pray you, how that clever man convicted me of being an accomplice in the business. When Cæsar was slain, says he, Marcus Brutus immediately lifted up on high his bloody dagger, and called on Cicero by name, and congratulated him on liberty being recovered. Why on me above all men? Because I knew of it beforehand? Consider rather whether this was not his reason for calling on me, that, when he had performed an action very like those which I myself had done, he called me above all men to witness that he had been an imitator of my exploits. But you, O stupidest of all men, do not you perceive, that if it is a crime to have wished that Cæsar should be slain—which you accuse me of having wished—it is a crime also to have rejoiced at his death? For what is the difference between a man who has advised an action, and one who has approved of it? or what does it signify whether I wished it to be done, or rejoice that it has been done? Is there any one then, except you yourself and those men who wished him to become a king, who was unwilling that that deed should be done, or who disapproved of it after it was done? All men, therefore, are guilty as far as this goes. In truth, all good men, as far as it depended on them, bore a part in the slaying of Cæsar. Some did not know how to contrive it, some had not courage for it, some had no opportunity,—every one had the inclination.

13

SHALL we then examine your conduct from the time when you were a boy? I think so. Let us begin at the beginning. Do you recollect that, while you were still clad in the pretexta, you became a bankrupt? That was the fault of your father, you will say. I admit that. In truth, such a defense is full of filial affection. But it is peculiarly suited to your own audacity, that you sat among the fourteen rows of the knights, tho by the Roscian law there was a place appointed for bankrupts, even if any one had become such by the fault of fortune and not by his own. You assumed the manly gown, which you soon made a womanly one; at first a public prostitute, with a regular price for your wickedness, and that not a low one. But very soon Curio stepped in, who carried you off from your public trade, and, as if he had bestowed a matron's robe upon you, settled you in a steady and durable wedlock. No boy bought for the gratification of passion was ever so wholly in the power of his master as you were in Curio's. How often has his father turned you out of his house? How often has he placed guards to prevent you from entering? while you, with night for your accomplice, lust for your encourager, and wages for your compeller, were let down through the roof. That house could no longer endure your wickedness.

14

DO you not know I am speaking of matters with which I am thoroughly acquainted? Remember that time when Curio, the father, lay weeping in his bed; his son throwing himself at my feet with tears recommended to me you; he entreated me to defend you against his own father, if he demanded six millions of sesterces of you; for that he had been bail for you to that amount. And he himself, burning with love, declared positively that because he was unable to bear the misery of being separated from you, he should go into banishment. And at that time what misery of that most flourishing family did I allay, or rather did I remove! persuaded the father to pay the son's debts; to release the young man, endowed as he was with great promise of courage and ability, by the sacrifice of part of his family estate; and to use his privileges and authority as a father to prohibit him not only from all intimacy with, but from every opportunity of meeting you. When you recollected that all this was done by me, would you have dared to provoke me by abuse if you had not been trusting to those swords which we behold.

15

BUT let us say no more of your profligacy and debauchery. There are things which it is not possible for me to mention with honor; but you are all the more free for that, inasmuch as you have not scrupled to be an actor in scenes which a modest enemy can not bring himself to mention.

16

MARK now, O conscript fathers, the rest of his life, which I will touch upon rapidly. For my inclination hastens to arrive at those things which he did in the time of the civil war, amid the greatest miseries of the republic, and at those things which he does every day. And I beg of you, tho they are far better known to you than they are to me, still to listen attentively, as you are doing, to my relation of them. For in such cases as this, it is not the mere knowledge of such actions that ought to excite the mind, but the recollection of them also. And we must at once go into the middle of them, lest otherwise we should be too long in coming to the end.

17

HE was very intimate with Clodius at the time of his tribuneship—he, who now enumerates the kindnesses which he did me. He was the firebrand to handle all conflagrations; and even in his house he attempted something. He himself well knows what I allude to. From thence he made a journey to Alexandria, in defiance of the authority of the senate, and against the interests of the republic, and in spite of religious obstacles; but he had Gabinius for his leader, with whom whatever he did was sure to be right. What were the circumstances of his return from thence? What sort of return was it? He went from Egypt to the farthest extremity of Gaul before he returned home. And what was his home? For at that time every man had possession of his own house; and you had no house anywhere, O Antonius. House, do you say? What place was there in the whole world where you could set your foot on anything that belonged to you, except Mienum, which you farmed with your partners, as if it had been Sisapo?

18

YOU came from Gaul to stand for the questorship. Dare to say that you went to your own father before you came to me. I had already received Cæsar's letters, begging me to allow myself to accept of your excuses; and, therefore, I did not allow you even to mention thanks. After that, I was treated with respect by you, and you received attentions from me in your canvass for the questorship. And it was at that time, indeed, that you endeavored to slay Publius Clodius in the forum, with the approbation of the Roman people; and tho you made the attempt of your own accord, and not at my instigation, still you clearly alleged that you did not think, unless you slew him, that you could possibly make amends to me for all the injuries which you had done me. And this makes me wonder why you should say that

Milo did that deed at my instigation; when I never once exhorted you to do it, who of your own accord attempted to do me the same service. Although, if you had persisted in it, I should have preferred allowing the action to be set down entirely to your own love of glory rather than to my influence.

19

IT was you, you, I say, O Marcus Antonius, who gave Caius Cæsar, desirous as he already was to throw everything into confusion, the principal pretext for waging war against his country. For what other pretense did he allege? What cause did he give for his own most frantic resolution and action, except that the power of interposition by the veto had been disregarded, the privileges of the tribunes taken away, and Antonius's rights abridged by the senate? I say nothing of how false, how trivial these pretenses were; especially when there could not possibly be any reasonable cause whatever to justify any one in taking up arms against his country. But I have nothing to do with Cæsar. You must unquestionably allow, that the cause of that ruinous war existed in your person.

31

WHEN you behold those beaks of ships in the vestibule, and those warlike trophies, do you fancy that you are entering into a house which belongs to you? It is impossible. Although you are devoid of all sense and all feeling—as in truth you are—still you are acquainted with yourself, and with your trophies, and with your friends. Nor do I believe that you, either waking or sleeping, can ever act with quiet sense. It is impossible but that, were you ever so drunk and frantic—as in truth you are—when the recollection of the appearance of that illustrious man comes across you, you should be roused from sleep by your fears, and often stirred up to madness if awake. I pity even the walls and the roof. For what had that house ever beheld except what was modest, except what proceeded from the purest principles and from the most virtuous practice. For that man was, O conscript fathers, as you yourselves know, not only illustrious abroad, but also admirable at home; and not more praiseworthy for his exploits in foreign countries, than for his domestic arrangements. Now in his house every bedchamber is a brothel, and every dining-room a cookshop. Although he denies this—do not, do not make inquiries: he is become economical. He desired that mistress of his to take possession of whatever belonged to her, according to the laws of the Twelve Tables. He has taken his keys from her, and turned her out of doors. What a well-tried citizen! of what proved virtue is he! the most honorable passage in whose life is the one when he divorced himself from this actress.

32

THOUGH you yourself took no personal share in it, partly through timidity, partly through profligacy, you had tasted, or rather had sucked in, the blood of fellow citizens: you had been in the battle of Pharsalia as a leader; you had slain Lucius Domitius, a most illustrious and highborn man; you had pursued and put to death in the most barbarous manner many men who had escaped from the battle, and whom Cæsar would perhaps have saved, as he did some other.

33

AND, after having performed these exploits, what was the reason why you did not follow Cæsar into Africa—especially when so large a portion of the war was still remaining? And accordingly, what place did you obtain about Cæsar's person after his return from Africa? What was your rank? He whose questor you had been when general, whose master of the horse when he was dictator, to whom you had been the chief cause of war, the chief instigator of cruelty, the sharer of his plunder, his son, as you yourself said, by inheritance, proceeded against you for the money which you owed for the house and gardens, and for the other property which you had bought at that sale. At first you answered fiercely enough; and that I may not appear prejudiced against you in every particular, you used a tolerably just and reasonable argument. "What, does Caius Cæsar demand money of me? Why should he do so, any more than

I should claim it of him? Was he victorious without my assistance? No; and he never could have been. It was I who supplied him with a pretext for civil war; it was I who proposed mischievous laws; it was I who took up arms against the consuls and generals of the Roman people, against the senate and people of Rome, against the gods of the country, against its altars and hearths, against the country itself. Has he conquered for himself alone? Why should not those men whose common work the achievement is, have the booty also in common?" You were only claiming your right, but what had that to do with it? He was the more powerful of the two.

34

OH, how splendid was that eloquence of yours, when you harangued the people stark naked! What could be more foul than this? more shameful than this? more deserving of every sort of punishment? Are you waiting for me to prick you more? This that I am saying must tear you and bring blood enough if you have any feeling at all. I am afraid that I may be detracting from the glory of some most eminent men. Still my indignation shall find a voice. What can be more scandalous than for that man to live who placed a diadem on a man's head when every one confesses that that man was deservedly slain who rejected it? And, moreover, he caused it to be recorded in the annals, under the head of Lupercalia, "That Marcus Antonius, the consul, by command of the people, had offered the kingdom to Caius Cæsar, perpetual dictator; and that Cæsar had refused to accept it." I now am not much surprised at your seeking to disturb the general tranquility; at your hating not only the city but the light of day; and at your living with a pack of abandoned robbers, disregarding the day, and yet regarding nothing beyond the day. For where can you be safe in peace? What place can there be for you where laws and courts of justice have sway, both of which you, as far as in you lay, destroyed by the substitution of kingly power? Was it for this that Lucius Tarquinius was driven out; that Spurius Cassius, and Spurius Mælius, and Marcus Manlius were slain; that many years afterward a king might be established at Rome by Marcus Antonius, tho the bare idea was impiety? However, let us return to the auspices.

35

OH, what a splendid progress of yours was that in the months of April and May, when you attempted even to lead a colony to Capua! How you made your escape from thence, or rather how you barely made your escape, we all know. And now you are still threatening that city. I wish you would try, and we should not then be forced to say "barely." However, what a splendid progress of yours that was! Why need I mention your preparations for banquets, why your frantic hard drinking? Those things are only an injury, to yourself; these are injuries to us. We thought that a great blow was inflicted on the republic when the Campanian district was released from the payment of taxes, in order to be given to the soldiery, but you have divided it among your partners in drunkenness and gambling. I tell you, O conscript fathers, that a lot of buffoons and actresses have been settled in the district of Campania. Why should I now complain of what has been done in the district of Leontini? Altho formerly these lands of Campania and Leontini were considered part of the patrimony of the Roman people, and were productive of great revenue, and very fertile. You gave your physician three thousand acres; what would you have done if he had cured you? and two thousand to your master of oratory; what would you have done if he had been able to make you eloquent?

36

IN public transactions nothing is more authoritative than law; in private affairs the most valid of all deeds is a will. Of the laws, some he abolished without giving the least notice; others he gave notice of bills to abolish. Wills he annulled; tho they have been at all times held sacred even in the case of the very meanest of the citizens. As for the statues and pictures which Cæsar bequeathed to the people, together with his gardens, those he carried away, some to the house which belonged to Pompeius, and some to Scipio's villa.

37

AND are you then diligent in doing honor to Cæsar's memory? Do you love him even now that he is dead? What greater honor had he obtained than that of having a holy cushion, an image, a temple, and a priest? As then Jupiter, and Mars, and Quirinus have priests, so Marcus Antonius is the priest of the god Julius. Why then do you delay? why are you not inaugurated? Choose a day. select some one to inaugurate you; we are colleagues; no one will refuse, O you detestable man, whether you are the priest of a tyrant, or of a dead man! I ask you, then, whether you are ignorant what day this is? Are you ignorant that yesterday was the fourth day of the Roman games in the Circus? and that you yourself submitted a motion to the people, that a fifth day should be added besides, in honor of Cæsar? Why are we not all clad in the pretexta? Why are we permitting the honor which by your law was appointed for Cæsar to be deserted? Had you no objection to so holy a day being polluted by the addition of supplications, while you did not choose it to be so by the addition of ceremonies connected with a sacred cushion? Either take away religion in every case, or preserve it in every case.

38

RECOLLECT then, O Marcus Antonius, that day on which you abolished the dictatorship. Set before you the joy of the senate and people of Rome; compare it with this infamous market held by you and by your friends, and then you will understand how great is the difference between praise and profit. But in truth, just as some people, through some disease which has blunted the senses, have no conception of the niceness of food, so men who are lustful, avaricious, and criminal, have no taste for true glory. But if praise can not allure you to act rightly, still can not even fear turn you away from the most shameful actions? You are not afraid of the courts of justice. If it is because you are innocent, I praise you; if because you trust in your power of overbearing them by violence, are you ignorant of what that man has to fear, who on such an account as that does not fear the courts of justice?

39

BUT if you are not afraid of brave men and illustrious citizens, because they are prevented from attacking you by your armed retinue, still believe me, your own fellows will not long endure you. And what a life is it, day and night to be fearing danger from one's own people! Unless, indeed, you have men who are bound to you by greater kindnesses than some of those men by whom he was slain were bound to Cæsar; or unless there are points in which you can be compared with him.

40

IN that man were combined genius, method, memory, literature, prudence, deliberation, and industry. He had performed exploits in war which, tho calamitous for the republic, were nevertheless mighty deeds. Having for many years aimed at being a king, he had with great labor, and much personal danger, accomplished what he intended. He had conciliated the ignorant multitude by presents, by monuments, by largesses of food, and by banquets; he had bound his own party to him by rewards, his adversaries by the appearance of clemency. Why need I say much on such a subject? He had already brought a free city, partly by fear, partly by patience, into a habit of slavery.

41

WITH him I can, indeed, compare you as to your desire to reign; but in all other respects you are in no degree to be compared to him. But from the many evils which by him have been burnt into the republic, there is still this good: that the Roman people has now learnt how much to believe every one, to whom to trust itself, and against whom to guard. Do you never think on these things? And do you not understand that it is enough for brave men to have learnt how noble a thing it is as to the act, how grateful it is as to the benefit done, how glorious as to the fame acquired, to slay a tyrant? When men could not bear him, do you think they will bear you? Believe me, the time will come when men will race with one another to do this deed, and when no one will wait for the tardy arrival of an opportunity.

42

CONSIDER, I beg you, Marcus Antonius, do some time or other consider the republic: think of the family of which you are born, not of the men with whom you are living. Be reconciled to the republic. However, do you decide on your conduct. As to mine, I myself will declare what that shall be. I defended the republic as a young man; I will not abandon it now that I am old. I scorned the sword of Catiline; I will not quail before yours. No; I will rather cheerfully expose my own person, if the liberty of the city can be restored by my death.

CICERO

On Duties

Cicero

Translated by Walter Miller

Book III

5

WELL then, for a man to take something from his neighbour and to profit by his neighbour's loss is more contrary to Nature than is death or poverty or pain or anything else that can affect either our person or our property. For, in the first place, injustice is fatal to social life and fellowship between man and man. For, if we are so disposed that each, to gain some personal profit, will defraud or injure his neighbour, then those bonds of human society, which are most in accord with Nature's laws, must of necessity be broken. Suppose, by way of comparison, that each one of our bodily members should conceive this idea and imagine that it could be strong and well if it should draw off to itself the health and strength of its neighbouring member, the whole body would necessarily be enfeebled and die; so, if each one of us should seize upon the property of his neighbours and take from each whatever he could appropriate to his own use, the bonds of human society must inevitably be annihilated. For, without any conflict with Nature's laws, it is granted that everybody may prefer to secure for himself rather than for his neighbour what is essential for the conduct of life; but Nature's laws do forbid us to increase our means, wealth, and resources by despoiling others.

But this principle is established not by Nature's laws alone (that is, by the common rules of equity), but also by the statutes of particular communities, in accordance with which in individual states the public interests are maintained. In all these it is with one accord ordained that no man shall be allowed for the sake of his own advantage to injure his neighbour. For it is to this that the laws have regard; this is their intent, that the bonds of union between citizens should not be impaired; and any attempt to destroy these bonds is repressed by the penalty of death, exile, imprisonment, or fine.

Again, this principle follows much more effectually directly from the Reason which is in Nature, which is the law of gods and men. If anyone will hearken to that voice (and all will hearken to it who wish to live in accord with Nature's laws), he will never be guilty of coveting anything that is his neighbour's or of appropriating to himself what he has taken from his neighbour. Then, too, loftiness and greatness of spirit, and courtesy, justice, and generosity are much more in harmony with Nature than are selfish pleasure, riches, and life itself; but it requires a great and lofty spirit to despise these latter and count them as naught, when one weighs them over against the common weal. [But for anyone to rob his neighbour for his own profit is more contrary to Nature than death, pain, and the like.]

In like manner it is more in accord with Nature to emulate the great Hercules and undergo the greatest toil and trouble for the sake of aiding or saving the world, if possible, than to live in seclusion, not only free from all care, but reveling in pleasures and abounding in wealth, while excelling others also in beauty and strength. Thus Hercules denied himself and underwent toil and tribulation for the world, and, out of gratitude for his services, popular belief has given him a place in the council of the gods.

The better and more noble, therefore, the character with which a man is endowed, the more does he prefer the life of service to the life of pleasure. Whence it follows that man, if he is obedient to Nature, cannot do harm to his fellow-man.

Finally, if a man wrongs his neighbour to gain some advantage for himself, he must either imagine that he is not acting in defiance of Nature or he must believe that death, poverty, pain, or even the loss of children, kinsmen, or friends, is more to be shunned than an act of injustice against another. If he thinks he is not violating the laws of Nature, when he wrongs his fellow-men, how is one to argue with the individual who takes away from man all that makes him man? But if he believes that, while such a course should be avoided, the other alternatives are much worse—namely, death, poverty, pain—he is mistaken in thinking that any ills affecting either his person or his property are more serious than those affecting his soul.

6

THIS, then, ought to be the chief end of all men, to make the interest of each individual and of the whole body politic identical. For, if the individual appropriates to selfish ends what should be devoted to the common good, all human fellowship will be destroyed.

And further, if Nature ordains that one man shall desire to promote the interests of a fellow-man, whoever he may be, just because he is a fellow-man, then it follows, in accordance with that same Nature, that there are interests that all men have in common. And, if this is true, we are all subject to one and the same law of Nature; and, if this also is true, we are certainly forbidden by Nature's law to wrong our neighbour. Now the first assumption is true; therefore the conclusion is likewise true. For that is an absurd position which is taken by some people, who say that they will not rob a parent or a brother for their own gain, but that their relation to the rest of their fellow-citizens is quite another thing. Such people contend in essence that they are bound to their fellow-citizens by no mutual obligations, social ties, or common interests. This attitude demolishes the whole structure of civil society.

Others again who say that regard should be had for the rights of fellow citizens, but not of foreigners, would destroy the universal brotherhood of mankind; and, when this is annihilated, kindness, generosity, goodness, and justice must utterly perish; and those who work all this destruction must be considered as wickedly rebelling against the immortal gods. For they uproot the fellowship which the gods have established between human beings, and the closest bond of this fellowship is the conviction that it is more repugnant to Nature for man to rob a fellow-man for his own gain than to endure all possible loss, whether to his property or to his person... or even to his very soul—so far as these losses are not concerned with justice; for this virtue is the sovereign mistress and queen of all the virtues.

But, perhaps, someone may say: "Well, then, suppose a wise man were starving to death, might he not take the bread of some perfectly useless member of society?" [Not at all; for my life is not more precious to me than that temper of soul which would keep me from doing wrong to anybody for my own advantage.] "Or again; supposing a righteous man were in a position to rob the cruel and inhuman tyrant Phalaris of clothing, might he not do it to keep himself from freezing to death?"

These cases are very easy to decide. For, if merely for one's own benefit one were to take something away from a man, though he were a perfectly worthless fellow, it would be an act of meanness and contrary to Nature's law. But suppose one would be able, by remaining alive, to render signal service to the state and to human society—if from that motive one should take something from another, it would not be a matter for censure. But, if such is not the case, each one must bear his own burden of distress rather than rob a neighbour of his rights. We are not to say, therefore, that sickness or want or any evil of that sort is more repugnant to Nature than to covet and to appropriate what is one's neighbour's; but we do maintain that disregard of the common interests is repugnant to Nature; for it is unjust. And therefore Nature's law itself, which protects and conserves human interests, will surely determine that a man who is wise, good, and brave, should in emergency have the necessaries of life transferred to him from a person who is idle and worthless; for the good man's death would be a heavy loss to the common weal; only let him beware that self-esteem and self-love do not find in such a transfer of possessions a pretext for wrong-doing. But, thus guided in his decision, the good man will always perform his duty, promoting the general interests of human society on which I am so fond of dwelling.

As for the case of Phalaris, a decision is quite simple: we have no ties of fellowship with a tyrant, but rather the bitterest feud; and it is not opposed to Nature to rob, if one can, a man whom it is morally right to kill;—nay, all that pestilent and abominable race should be exterminated from human society. And this may be done by proper measures; for, as certain members are amputated, if they show signs themselves of being bloodless and virtually lifeless and thus jeopardize the health of the other parts of the body, so those fierce and savage monsters in human form should be cut off from what may be called the common body of humanity.

Of this sort are all those problems in which we have to determine what moral duty is, as it varies with varying circumstances.

7

IT is subjects of this sort that I believe Panaetius would have followed up, had not some accident or business interfered with his design. For the elucidation of these very questions there are in his former books rules in plenty, from which one can learn what should be avoided because of its immorality and what does not have to be avoided for the reason that it is not immoral at all.

We are now putting the capstone, as it were, upon our structure, which is unfinished, to be sure, but still almost completed; and, as mathematicians make a practice of not demonstrating every proposition, but require that certain axioms be assumed as true, in order more easily to explain their meaning, so, my dear Cicero, I ask you to assume with me, if you can, that nothing is worth the seeking for its own sake except what is morally right. But if Cratippus does not permit this assumption, you will still grant this at least—that what is morally right is the object most worth the seeking for its own sake. Either alternative is sufficient for my purposes; first the one and then the other seems to me the more probable; and, besides these, there no other alternative that seems probable at all.

In the first place, I must undertake the defense of Panaetius on this point; for he has said, not that the truly expedient could under certain circumstances clash with the morally right (for he could not have said that conscientiously), but only that what seemed expedient could do so. For he often bears witness to the fact that nothing is really expedient that is not at the same time morally right, and nothing morally right that is not at the same time expedient; and he says that no greater curse has ever assailed human life than the doctrine of those who have separated these two conceptions. And so he introduced an apparent, not a real, conflict between them, not to the end that we should under certain circumstances give the expedient preference over the moral, but that, in case they ever should get in each other's way, we might decide between them without uncertainty. This part, therefore, which was passed over by Panaetius, I will carry to completion without any auxiliaries, but fighting my own battle, as the saying is. For, of all that has been worked out on this line since the time of Panaetius, nothing that has come into my hands is at all satisfactory to me.

8

NOW when we meet with expediency in some specious form or other, we cannot help being influenced by it. But if upon closer inspection one sees that there is some immorality connected with what presents the appearance of expediency, then one is not necessarily to sacrifice expediency but to recognize that there can be no expediency where there is immorality. But if there is nothing so repugnant to Nature as immorality (for Nature demands right and harmony and consistency and abhors their opposites), and if nothing is so thoroughly in accord with Nature as expediency, then surely expediency and immorality cannot coexist in one and the same object.

Again: if we are born for moral rectitude and if that is either the only thing worth seeking, as Zeno thought, or at least to be esteemed as infinitely outweighing everything else, as Aristotle holds, then it necessarily follows that the morally right is either the sole good or the supreme good. Now, that which is good is certainly expedient; consequently, that which is morally right is also expedient.

Thus it is the error of men who are not strictly upright to seize upon something that seems to be expedient and straightway to dissociate that from the question of moral right. To this error the assassin's dagger, the poisoned cup, the forged wills owe their origin; this gives rise to theft, embezzlement of public funds, exploitation and plundering of provincials and citizens; this engenders also the lust for excessive wealth, for despotic power, and finally for making oneself king even in the midst of a free people; and anything more atrocious or repulsive than such a passion cannot be conceived. For with a false perspective they see the material rewards but not the punishment—I do not mean the penalty of the law, which they often escape, but the heaviest penalty of all, their own demoralization.

Away, then, with questioners of this sort (for their whole tribe is wicked and ungodly), who stop to consider whether to pursue the course which they see is morally right or to stain their hands with what they know is crime. For there is guilt in their very deliberation, even though they never reach the performance of the deed itself. Those actions, therefore, should not be considered at all, the mere consideration of which is itself morally wrong.

Furthermore, in any such consideration we must banish any vain hope and thought that our action may be covered up and kept secret. For if we have only made some real progress in the study of philosophy, we ought to be quite convinced that, even though we may escape the eyes of gods and men, we must still do nothing that savours of greed or of injustice, of lust or of intemperance.

9

BY way of illustrating this truth Plato introduces the familiar story of Gyges: Once upon a time the earth opened in consequence of heavy rains; Gyges went down into the chasm and saw, so the story goes, a horse of bronze; in its side was a door. On opening this door he saw the body of a dead man of enormous size with a gold ring upon his finger. He removed this and put it on his own hand and then repaired to an assembly of the shepherds, for he was a shepherd of the king. As often as he turned the bezel of the ring inwards toward the palm of his hand, he became invisible to everyone, while lie himself saw everything; but as often as he turned it back to its proper position, he became visible again. And so, with the advantage which the ring gave him, he debauched the queen, and with her assistance he murdered his royal master and removed all those who he thought stood in his way, without anyone's being able to detect him in his crimes. Thus, by virtue of the ring, he shortly rose to be king of Lydia.

Now, suppose a wise man had just such a ring, he would not imagine that he was free to do wrong any more than if he did not have it; for good men aim to secure not secrecy but the right.

And yet on this point certain philosophers, who are not at all vicious but who are not very discerning, declare that the story related by Plato is fictitious and imaginary. As if he affirmed that it was actually true or even possible! But the force of the illustration of the ring is this: if nobody were to know or even to suspect the truth, when you do anything to gain riches or power or sovereignty or sensual gratification—if your act should be hidden for ever from the knowledge of gods and men, would you do it? The condition, they say, is impossible. Of course it is. But my question is, if that were possible which they declare to be impossible, what, pray, would one do? They press their point with right boorish obstinacy: they assert that it is impossible and insist upon it; they refuse to see the meaning of my words, "if possible." For when we ask what they would do, if they could escape detection, we are not asking whether they can escape detection; but we put them as it were upon the rack:

should they answer that, if impunity were assured, they would do what was most to their selfish interest, that would be a confession that they are criminally minded; should they say that they would not do so, they would be granting that all things in and of themselves immoral should be avoided.

But let us now return to our theme.

10

MANY cases oftentimes arise to perplex our minds with a specious appearance of expediency: the question raised in these cases is not whether moral rectitude is to be sacrificed to some considerable advantage (for that would of course be wrong), but whether the apparent advantage can be secured without moral wrong. When Brutus deposed his colleague Collatinus from the consular office, his treatment of him might have been thought unjust; for Collatinus had been his associate, and had helped him with word and deed in driving out the royal family. But when the leading men of the state had determined that all the kindred of Superbus and the very name of the Tarquins and every reminder of the monarchy should be obliterated, then the course that was expedient—namely, to serve the country's interests—was so pre-eminently right, that it was even Collatinus's own duty to acquiesce in its justice. And so expediency gained the day because of its moral rightness; for without moral rectitude there could have been no possible expediency.

Not so in the case of the king who founded the city: it was the specious appearance of expediency that actuated him; and when he decided that it was more expedient for him to reign alone than to share the throne with another, he slew his brother. He threw to the winds his brotherly affection and his human feelings, to secure what seemed to him—but was not—expedient; and yet in defense of his deed he offered the excuse about his wall—a specious show of moral rectitude, neither reasonable nor adequate at all. He committed a crime, therefore, with due respect to him let me say so, be he Quirinus or Romulus.

And yet we are not required to sacrifice our own interests and surrender to others what we need for ourselves, but each one should consider his own interests, as far as he may without injury to his neighbour's. "When a man enters the foot-race," says Chrysippus with his usual aptness, "it is his duty to put forth all his strength and strive with all his might to win; but he ought never with his foot to trip, or with his hand to foul a competitor. Thus in the stadium of life, it is not unfair for anyone to seek to obtain what is needful for his own advantage, but he has no right to wrest it from his neighbour."

It is in the case of friendships, however, that men's conceptions of duty are most confused; for it is a breach of duty either to fail to do for a friend what one rightly can do, or to do for him what is not right. But for our guidance in all such cases we have a rule that is short and easy to master: apparent advantages—political preferment, riches, sensual pleasures, and the like—should never be preferred to the obligations of friendship. But an upright man will never for a friend's sake do anything in violation of his country's interests or his oath or his sacred honour, not even if he sits as judge in a friend's case; for he lays aside the role of friend when he assumes that of judge. Only so far will he make concessions to friendship, that he will prefer his friend's side to be the juster one and that he will set the time for presenting his case, as far as the laws will allow, to suit his friend's convenience. But when he comes to pronounce the verdict under oath, he should remember that he has God as his witness—that is, as I understand it, his own conscience, than which God himself has bestowed upon man nothing more divine. From this point of view it is a fine custom that we have inherited from our forefathers (if we were only true to it now), to appeal to the juror with this formula—"to do what he can consistently with his sacred honour." This form of appeal is in keeping with what I said a moment ago would be morally right for a judge to concede to a friend. For supposing that we were bound to do everything that our friends desired, such relations would have to be accounted not friendships but conspiracies. But I am speaking here of ordinary friendships; for among men who are ideally wise and perfect such situations cannot arise.

They say that Damon and Phintias, of the Pythagorean school, enjoyed such ideally perfect friendship, that when the tyrant Dionysius had appointed a day for the execution of one of them, and the one who had been condemned to death requested a few days' respite for the purpose of putting his loved ones in the care of friends, the other became surety for his appearance, with the understanding that if his friend did not return, he himself should be put to death. And when the friend returned on the day appointed, the tyrant in admiration for their faithfulness begged that they would enroll him as a third partner in their friendship.

Well then, when we are weighing what seems to be expedient in friendship against what is morally right, let apparent expediency be disregarded and moral rectitude prevail; and when in friendship requests are submitted that are not morally right, let conscience and scrupulous regard for the right take precedence of the obligations of friendship. In this way we shall arrive at a proper choice between conflicting duties—the subject of this part of our investigation.

11

THROUGH a specious appearance of expediency wrong is very often committed in transactions between state and state, as by our own country in the destruction of Corinth. A more cruel wrong was perpetrated by the Athenians in decreeing that the Aeginetans, whose strength lay in their navy, should have their thumbs cut off. This seemed to be expedient; for Aegina was too grave a menace, as it was close to the Piraeus. But no cruelty can be expedient; for cruelty is most abhorrent to human nature, whose lead we ought to follow. They, too, do wrong who would debar foreigners from enjoying the advantages of their city and would exclude them from its borders, as was done by Pennus in the time of our fathers, and in recent times by Papius. It may not be right, of course, for one who is not a citizen to exercise the rights and privileges of citizenship; and the law on this point was secured by two of our wisest consuls, Crassus and Scaevola. Still, to debar foreigners from enjoying the advantages of the city is altogether contrary to the laws of humanity.

There are splendid examples in history where the apparent expediency of the state has been set at naught out of regard for moral rectitude. Our own country has many instances to offer throughout her history, and especially in the Second Punic War, when news came of the disaster at Cannae, Rome displayed a loftier courage than ever she did in success; never a trace of faintheartedness, never a mention of making terms. The influence of moral right is so potent, that it eclipses the specious appearance of expediency.

When the Athenians could in no way stem the tide of the Persian invasion and determined to abandon their city, bestow their wives and children in safety at Troezen, embark upon their ships, and fight on the sea for the freedom of Greece, a man named Cyrsilus proposed that they should stay at home and open the gates of their city to Xerxes. They stoned him to death for it. And yet he was working for what he thought was expediency; but it was not—not at all, for it clashed with moral rectitude.

After the victorious close of that war with Persia, Themistocles announced in the Assembly that he had a plan for the welfare of the state, but that it was not politic to let it be generally known. He requested the people to appoint someone with whom he might discuss it. They appointed Aristides. Themistocles confided to him that the Spartan fleet, which had been hauled up on shore at Gytheum, could be secretly set on fire; this done, the Spartan power would inevitably be crushed. When Aristides heard the plan, he came into the Assembly amid the eager expectation of all and reported that the plan proposed by Themistocles was in the highest degree expedient, but anything but morally right. The result was that the Athenians concluded that what was not morally right was likewise not expedient, and at the instance of Aristides they rejected the whole proposition without even listening to it. Their attitude was better than ours; for we let pirates go scot-free, while we make our allies pay tribute.

12

LET it be set down as an established principle, then, that what is morally wrong can never be expedient—not even when one secures by means of it that which one thinks expedient; for the mere act of thinking a course expedient, when it is morally wrong, is demoralizing. But, as I said above, cases often arise in which expediency may seem to clash with moral rectitude; and so we should examine in carefully and see whether their conflict is inevitable or whether they may be reconciled. The following are problems of this sort: suppose, for example, a time of dearth and famine at Rhodes, with provisions at fabulous prices; and suppose that an honest man has imported a large cargo of grain from Alexandria and that to his certain knowledge also several other importers have set sail from Alexandria, and that on the voyage he has sighted their vessels laden with grain and bound for Rhodes; is he to report the fact to the Rhodians or is he to keep his own counsel and sell his own stock at the highest market price? I am assuming the case of a virtuous, upright man, and I am raising the question how a man would think and reason who would not conceal the facts from the Rhodians if he thought that it was immoral to do so, but who might be in doubt whether such silence would really be immoral.

In deciding cases of this kind Diogenes of Babylonia, a great and highly esteemed Stoic, consistently holds one view; his pupil Antipater, a most profound scholar, holds another. According to Antipater all the facts should be disclosed, that the buyer may not be uninformed of any detail that the seller knows; according to Diogenes the seller should declare any defects in his wares, in so far as such a course is prescribed by the common law of the land; but for the rest, since he has goods to sell, he may try to sell them to the best possible advantage, provided he is guilty of no misrepresentation.

"I have imported my stock," Diogenes's merchant will say; "I have offered it for sale; I sell at a price no higher than my competitors—perhaps even lower, when the market is overstocked. Who is wronged?" "What say you?" comes Antipater's argument on the other side; "it is your duty to consider the interests of your fellow-men and to serve society; you were brought into the world under these conditions and have these inborn principles which you are in duty bound to obey and follow, that your interest shall be the interest of the community and conversely that the interest of the community shall be your interest as well; will you, in view of all these facts, conceal from your fellow-men what relief in plenteous supplies is close at hand for them?"

"It is one thing to conceal," Diogenes will perhaps reply; "not to reveal is quite a different thing. At this present moment I am not concealing from you, even if I am not revealing to you, the nature of the gods or the highest good; and to know these secrets would be of more advantage to you than to know that the price of wheat was down. But I am under no obligation to tell you everything that it may be to your interest to be told."

"Yea," Antipater will say, "but you are, as you must admit, if you will only bethink you of the bonds of fellowship forged by Nature and existing between man and man.""I do not forget them," the other will reply; "but do you mean to say that those bonds of fellowship are such that there is no such thing as private property? If that is the case, we should not sell anything at all, but freely give everything away."

13

IN this whole discussion, you see, no one says, "However wrong morally this or that may be, still, since it is expedient, I will do it"; but the one side asserts that a given act is expedient, without being morally wrong, while the other insists that the act should not be done, because it is morally wrong.

Suppose again that an honest man is offering a house for sale on account of certain undesirable features of which he himself is aware but which nobody else knows; suppose it is unsanitary, but has the reputation of being healthful; suppose it is not generally known that vermin are to be found in all the bedrooms; suppose, finally, that it is built of unsound timber and likely to collapse, but that no one knows about it except the owner; if the vendor does not tell the purchaser these facts but sells him the house for far more than he could reasonably have expected to get for it, I ask whether his transaction is unjust or dishonourable.

"Yes," says Antipater, "it is; for to allow a purchaser to be hasty in closing a deal and through mistaken judgment to incur a very serious loss, if this is not refusing ' to set a man right when he has lost his way' (a crime which at Athens is prohibited on pain of public execration), what is? It is even worse than refusing to set a man on his way: it is deliberately leading a man astray."

"Can you say," answers Diogenes, "that he compelled you to purchase, when he did not even advise it? He advertised for sale what he did not like; you bought what you did like. If people are not considered guilty of swindling when they place upon their placards FOR SALE: A FINE VILLA, WELL BUILT, even when it is neither good nor properly built, still less guilty are they who say nothing in praise of their house. For where the purchaser may exercise his own judgment, what fraud can there be on the part of the vendor? But if, again, not all that is expressly stated has to be made good, do you think a man is bound to make good what has not been said? What, pray, would be more stupid than for a vendor to recount all the faults in the article he is offering for sale? And what would be so absurd as for an auctioneer to cry, at the owner's bidding, 'Here is an unsanitary house for sale'?"

In this way, then, in certain doubtful cases moral rectitude is defended on the one side, while on the other side the case of expediency is so presented as to make it appear not only morally right to do what seems expedient, but even morally wrong not to do it. This is the contradiction that seems often to arise between the expedient and the morally right. But I must give my decision in these two cases; for I did not propound them merely to raise the questions, but to offer a solution. I think, then, that it was the duty of that grain-dealer not to keep back the facts from the Rhodians, and of this vendor of the house to deal in the same way with his purchaser, the fact is that merely holding one's peace about a thing does not constitute concealment, but concealment consists in trying for your own profit to keep others from finding out something that you know, when it is for their interest to know it. And who fails to discern what manner of concealment that is and what sort of person would be guilty of it? At all events he would be no candid or sincere or straightforward or upright or honest man, but rather one who is shifty, sly, artful, shrewd, underhand, cunning, one grown old in fraud and subtlety. Is it not inexpedient to subject oneself to all these terms of reproach and many more besides?

14

IF, then, they are to be blamed who suppress the truth, what are we to think of those who actually state what is false? Gaius Canius, a Roman a man of considerable wit and literary culture, once went to Syracuse for a vacation, as he himself used to say, and not for business. He gave out that he had a mind to purchase a little country seat, where he could invite his friends and enjoy himself, uninterrupted by troublesome visitors. When this fact was spread abroad, one Pythius, a banker of Syracuse, informed him that he had such an estate; that it was not for sale, however, but Canius might make himself at home there, if he pleased; and at the same time he invited him to the estate to dinner next day. Canius accepted. Then Pythius, who, as might be expected of a moneylender, could command favours of all classes, called the fishermen together and asked them to do their fishing the next day out in front of his villa, and told them what he wished them to do. Canius came to dinner at the appointed hour; Pythius had a sumptuous banquet prepared; there was a whole fleet of boats before their eyes; each fisherman brought in in turn the catch that he had made; and the fishes were deposited at the feet of Pythius.

"Pray, Pythius," said Canius thereupon, "what does this mean?—all these fish?—all these boats?"

"No wonder," answered Pythius; "this is where all the fish in Syracuse are; here is where the fresh water comes from; the fishermen cannot get along without this estate."

Inflamed with desire for it, Canius insisted upon Pythius's selling it to him. At first he demurred. To make a long story short, Canius gained his point. The man was rich, and, in his desire to own the country seat, he paid for it all that Pythius asked; and he bought the entire equipment, too. Pythius entered the amount upon his ledger and completed the transfer. The next day Canius invited his friends; he came early himself. Not so much as a thole-pin was in sight. He asked his next-door neighbour whether it was a fishermen's holiday, for not a sign of them did he see.

"Not so far as I know," said he; "but none are in the habit of fishing here. And so I could not make out what was the matter yesterday."

Canius was furious; but what could he do? For not yet had my colleague and friend, Gaius Aquilius, introduced the established forms to apply to criminal fraud. When asked what he meant by "criminal fraud," as specified in these forms, he would reply:

"Pretending one thing and practicing another"—a very felicitous definition, as one might expect from an expert in making them. Pythius, therefore, and all others who do one thing while they pretend another are faithless, dishonest, and unprincipled scoundrels. No act of theirs can be expedient, when what they do is tainted with so many vices.

15

BUT if Aquilius's definition is correct, pretence and concealment should be done away with in all departments of our daily life. Then an honest man will not be guilty of either pretence or concealment in order to buy or to sell to better advantage. Besides, your "criminal fraud" had previously been prohibited by the statutes: the penalty in the matter of trusteeships, for example, is fixed by the Twelve Tables; for the defrauding of minors, by the Plaetorian law. The same prohibition is effective, without statutory enactment, in equity cases, in which it is added that the decision shall be "as good faith requires." In all other cases in equity, moreover, the following phrases are most noteworthy: in a case calling for arbitration in the matter of a wife's dowry: what is "the fairer is the better"; in a suit for the restoration of a trust: "honest dealing, as between honest parties." Pray, then, can there be any element of fraud in what is adjusted for the "better and fairer"? Or can anything fraudulent or unprincipled be done, when "honest dealing between honest parties" is stipulated? But "criminal fraud," as Aquilius says, consists in false pretence. We must, therefore, keep misrepresentation entirely out of business transactions: the seller will not engage a bogus bidder to run prices up nor the buyer one to bid low against himself to keep them down; and each, if they come to naming a price, will state once for all what he will give or take. Why, when Quintus Scaevola, the son of Publius Scaevola, asked that the price of a farm that he desired to purchase be definitely named and the vendor named it, he replied that he considered it worth more, and paid him 100,000 sesterces over and above what he asked. No one could say that this was not the act of an honest man; but people do say that it was not the act of a worldly-wise man, any more than if he had sold for a smaller amount than he could have commanded. Here, then, is that mischievous idea—the world accounting some men upright, others wise; and it is this fact that gives Ennius occasion to say:

> "In vain is the wise man wise, who cannot benefit himself."

And Ennius is quite right, if only he and I were agreed upon the meaning of "benefit."

Now I observe that Hecaton of Rhodes, a pupil of Panaetius, says in his books on "Moral Duty" dedicated to Quintus Tubero that "it is a wise man's duty to take care of his private interests, at the same time doing nothing contrary to the civil customs, laws, and institutions. But that depends on our purpose in seeking prosperity; for we do not aim to be rich for ourselves alone but for our children, relatives, friends, and, above all, for our country. For the private fortunes of individuals are the wealth of the state." Hecaton could not for a moment approve of Scaevola's act, which I cited a moment ago; for he openly avows that he will abstain from doing for his own profit only what the law expressly forbids. Such a man deserves no great praise nor gratitude.

Be that as it may, if both pretense and concealment constitute "criminal fraud," there are very few transactions into which "criminal fraud" does not enter; or, if he only is a good man who help all he can, and harms no one, it will certainly be no easy matter for us to find the good man as thus defined.

To conclude, then, it is never expedient to do wrong, because wrong is always immoral; and it is always expedient to be good, because goodness is always moral.

16

IN the laws pertaining to the sale of real property it is stipulated in our civil code that when a transfer of any real estate is made, all its defects shall be declared as far as they are known to the vendor. According to the laws of the Twelve Tables it used to be sufficient that such faults as had been expressly declared should be made good and that for any flaws which the vendor expressly denied, when questioned, he should be assessed double damages. A like penalty for failure to make such declaration also has now been secured by our jurisconsults: they have decided that any defect in a piece of real estate, if known to the vendor but not expressly stated, must be made good by him. For example, the augurs were proposing to take observations from the citadel and they ordered Tiberius Claudius Centumalus, who owned a house upon the Caelian Hill, to pull down such parts of the building as obstructed the augurs' view by reason of their height. Claudius at once advertised his block for sale, and Publius Calpurnius Lanarius bought it. The same notice was served also upon him. And so, when Calpurnius had pulled down those parts of the building and discovered that Claudius had advertised it for sale only after the augurs had ordered them to be pulled down, he summoned the former owner before a court of equity to decide "what indemnity the owner was under obligation 'in good faith' to pay and deliver to him." The verdict was pronounced by Marcus Cato, the father of our Cato (for as other men receive a distinguishing name from their fathers, so he who bestowed upon the world so bright a luminary must have his distinguishing name from his son); he, as I was saying, was presiding judge and pronounced the verdict that "since the augurs' mandate was known to the vendor at the time of making the transfer and since he had not made it known, he was bound to make good the purchaser's loss."

With this verdict he established the principle that it was essential to good faith that any defect known to the vendor must be made known to the purchaser. If his decision was right, our grain-dealer and the vendor of the unsanitary house did not do right to suppress the facts in those cases. But the civil code cannot be made to include all cases where facts are thus suppressed; but those cases which it does include are summarily dealt with. Marcus Marius Gratidianus, a kinsman of ours, sold back to Gaius Sergius Orata the house which he himself had bought a few years before from that same Orata. It was subject to an encumbrance, but Marius had said nothing about this fact in stating the terms of sale. The case was carried to the courts. Crassus was counsel for Orata; Antonius was retained by Gratidianus. Crassus pleaded the letter of the law that "the vendor was bound to make good the defect, for he had not declared it, although he was aware of it"; Antonius laid stress upon the equity of the case, pleading that, "inasmuch as the defect in question had not been unknown to Sergius (for it was the same house that he had sold to Marius), no declaration of it was needed, and in purchasing it back he had not been imposed upon, for he knew to what legal liability his purchase was subject."

What is the purpose of these illustrations? To let you see that our forefathers did not countenance sharp practice.

17

NOW the law disposes of sharp practices in one way, philosophers in another: the law deals with them as far as it can lay its strong arm upon them; philosophers, as far as they can be apprehended by reason and conscience. Now reason demands that nothing be done with unfairness, with false pretense, or with misrepresentation. Is it not deception, then, to set snares, even if one does not mean to start the game or to drive it into them? Why, wild creatures often fall into snares undriven and unpursued. Could one in the same way advertise a house for sale, post up a notice "To be sold," like a snare, and have somebody run into it unsuspecting?

Owing to the low ebb of public sentiment, such a method of procedure, I find, is neither by custom accounted morally wrong nor forbidden either by statute or by civil law; nevertheless it is forbidden by the moral law. For there is a bond of fellowship—although I have often made this statement, I must still repeat it again and again—which has the very widest application, uniting all men together and each to each. This bond of union is closer between those who belong to the same nation, and more intimate still between those who are citizens of the same city-state. It is for this reason that our forefathers chose to understand one thing by the universal law and another by the civil law. The civil law is not necessarily also the universal law; but the universal law ought to be also the civil law. But we possess no substantial, life-like image of true Law and genuine Justice; a mere outline sketch is all that we enjoy. I only wish that we were true even to this; for, even as it is, it is drawn from the excellent models which Nature and Truth afford. For how weighty are the words: "That I be not deceived and defrauded through you and my confidence in you"! How precious are these: "As between honest people there ought to be honest dealing, and no deception"! But who are "honest people," and what is "honest dealing"—these are serious questions.

It was Quintus Scaevola, the pontifex maximus, who used to attach the greatest importance to all questions of arbitration to which the formula was appended "as good faith requires"; and he held that the expression "good faith" had a very extensive application, for it was employed in trusteeships and partnerships, in trusts and commissions, in buying and selling, in hiring and letting—in a word, in all the transactions on which the social relations of daily life depend; in these, he said, it required a judge of great ability to decide the extent of each individual's obligation to the other, especially when counter-claims were admissible in most cases.

Away, then, with sharp practice and trickery, which desires, of course, to pass for wisdom, but is far from it and totally unlike it. For the function of wisdom is to discriminate between good and evil; whereas, inasmuch as all things morally wrong are evil, trickery prefers the evil to the good.

It is not only in the case of real estate transfers that the civil law,based upon a natural feeling for the right, punishes trickery and deception, but also in the sale of slaves every form of deception on the vendor's part is disallowed. For by the aediles' ruling the vendor is answerable for any deficiency in the slave he sells, for he is supposed to know if his slave is sound, or if he is a runaway, or a thief. The case of those who have just come into the possession of slaves by inheritance is different.

From this we come to realize that since Nature is the source of right, it is not in accord with Nature that anyone should take advantage of his neighbour's ignorance. And no greater curse in life can be found than knavery that wears the mask of wisdom. Thence come those countless cases in which the expedient seems to conflict with the right. For how few will be found who can refrain from wrong-doing, if assured of the power to keep it an absolute secret and to run no risk of punishment!

18

LET us put our principle to the test, if you please, and see if it holds good in those instances in which, perhaps, the world in general finds no wrong; for in this connection we do not need to discuss cutthroats, poisoners, forgers of wills, thieves, and embezzlers of public moneys, who should be repressed not by lectures and discussions of philosophers, but by chains and prison walls; but let us study here the conduct of those who have the reputation of being honest men.

Certain individuals brought from Greece to Rome a forged will, purporting to be that of the wealthy Lucius Minucius Basilus. The more easily to procure validity for it, they made joint-heirs with themselves two of the most influential men of the day, Marcus Crassus and Quintus Hortensius. Although these men suspected that the will was a forgery, still, as they were conscious of no personal guilt in the matter, they did not spurn the miserable boon procured through the crime of others. What shall we say, then? Is this excuse competent to acquit them of guilt? I cannot think so, although I loved the one while he lived, and do not hate the other now that he is dead. Be that as it may, Basilus had in fact desired that his nephew Marcus Satrius should bear his name and inherit his property. (I refer to the Satrius who is the present patron of Picenum and the Sabine country—and oh, what a shameful stigma it is upon the times!) And therefore it was not right that two of the leading citizens of Rome should take the estate and Satrius succeed to nothing except his uncle's name. For if he does wrong who does not ward off and repel injury when he can—as I explained in the course of the First Book—what is to be thought of the man who not only does not try to prevent wrong, but actually aids and abets it? For my part, I do not believe that even genuine legacies are moral, if they are sought after by designing flatteries and by attentions hypocritical rather than sincere.

And yet in such cases there are times when one course is likely to appear expedient and another morally right. The appearance is deceptive; for our standard is the same for expediency and for moral rectitude. And the man who does not accept the truth of this will be capable of any sort of dishonesty, any sort of crime. For if he reasons, "That is, to be sure, the right course, but this course brings advantage," he will not hesitate in his mistaken judgment to divorce two conceptions that Nature has made one; and that spirit opens the door to all sorts of dishonesty, wrong-doing, and crime.

19

SUPPOSE, then, that a good man had such power that at a snap of his fingers his name could steal into rich men's wills, he would not avail himself of that power—no, not even though he could be perfectly sure that no one would ever suspect it. Suppose, on the other hand, that one were to offer a Marcus Crassus the power, by the mere snapping of his fingers, to get himself named as heir, when he was not really an heir, he would, I warrant you, dance in the forum. But the righteous man, the one whom we feel to be a good man, would never rob anyone of anything to enrich himself. If anybody is astonished at this doctrine, let him confess that he does not know what a good man is. If, on the other hand, anyone should desire to unfold the idea of a good man which lies wrapped up in his own mind, he would then at once make it clear to himself that a good man is one who helps all whom he can and harms nobody, unless provoked by wrong. What shall we say, then? Would he not be doing harm who by a kind of magic spell should succeed in displacing the real heirs to an estate and pushing himself into their place? "Well," someone may say, "is he not to do what is expedient, what is advantageous to himself?" Nay, verily; he should rather be brought to realize that nothing that is unjust is either advantageous or expedient; if he does not learn this lesson, it will never be possible for him to be a "good man."

When I was a boy, I used to hear my father tell that Gaius Fimbria, an ex-consul, was judge in a case of Marcus Lutatius Pinthia, a Roman knight of irreproachable character. On that occasion Pinthia had laid a wager to be forfeited "if he did not prove in court that he was a good man." Fimbria declared that he would never render a decision in such a case, for fear that he might either rob a reputable man of his good name, if he decided against him, or be thought to have pronounced someone a good man, when such a character is, as he said, established by the performance of countless duties and the possession of praiseworthy qualities without number.

To this type of good man, then, known not only to a Socrates but even to a Fimbria, nothing can possibly seem expedient that is not morally right. Such a man, therefore, will never venture to think—to say nothing of doing—anything that he would not dare openly to proclaim. Is it not a shame that philosophers should be in doubt about moral questions on which even peasants have no doubts at all? For it is with peasants that the proverb, already trite with age, originated: when they praise a man's honour and honesty, they say, "He is a man with whom you can safely play at odd and even in the dark." What is the point of the proverb but this—that what is not proper brings no advantage, even if you can gain your end without anyone's being able to convict you of wrong?

Do you not see that in the light of this proverb no excuse is available either for the Gyges of the story or for the man who I assumed a moment ago could with a snap of his fingers sweep together everybody's inheritance at once? For as the morally wrong cannot by any possibility be made morally right, however successfully it may be covered up, so what is not morally right cannot be made expedient, for Nature refuses and resists.

20

"BUT stay," someone will object, "when the prize is very great, there is excuse for doing wrong." Gaius Marius had been left in obscurity for more than six whole years after his praetorship and had scarcely the remotest hope of gaining the consulship. It looked as if he would never even be a candidate for that office. He was now a lieutenant under Quintus Metellus, who sent him on a furlough to Rome. There before the Roman People he accused his own general, an eminent man and one of our first citizens, of purposely protracting the war and declared that if they would make him consul, he would within a short time deliver Jugurtha alive or dead into the hands of the Roman People. And so he was elected consul, it is true, but he was a traitor to his own good faith and to justice; for by a false charge he subjected to popular disfavour an exemplary and highly respected citizen, and that too, although he was his lieutenant and under leave of absence from him.

Even our kinsman Gratidianus failed on one occasion to perform what would be a good man's duty: in his praetorship the tribunes of the people summoned the college of praetors to council, in order to adopt by joint resolution a standard of value for our currency; for at that time the value of money was so fluctuating that no one could tell how much he was worth. In joint session they drafted an ordinance, defining the penalty and the methods of procedure in cases of violation of the ordinance, and agreed that they should all appear together upon the rostra in the afternoon to publish it. And while all the rest withdrew, some in one direction, some in another, Marius (Gratidianus) went straight from the council-chamber to the rostra and published individually what had been drawn up by all together. And that coup, if you care to know, brought him vast honour; in every street statues of him were erected; before these incense and candles burned. In a word, no one ever enjoyed greater popularity with the masses.

It is such cases as these that sometimes perplex us in our consideration, when the point in which justice is violated does not seem so very significant, but the consequences of such slight transgression seem exceedingly important. For example, it was not so very wrong morally, in the eyes of Marius, to overreach his colleagues and the tribunes in turning to himself alone all the credit with the people; but to secure by that means his election to the consulship, which was then the goal of his ambition, seemed very greatly to his interest. But for all cases we have one rule, with which I desire you to be perfectly familiar: that which seems expedient must not be morally wrong; or, if it is morally wrong, it must not seem expedient. What follows? Can we account either the great Marius or our Marius Gratidianus a good man? Work out your own ideas and sift your thoughts so as to see what conception and idea of a good man they contain. Pray, tell me, does it coincide with the character of your good man to lie for his own profit, to slander, to overreach, to deceive? Nay, verily; anything but that!

Is there, then, any object of such value or any advantage so worth the winning that, to gain it, one should sacrifice the name of a "good man" and the lustre of his reputation? What is there that your so called expediency can bring to you that will compensate for what it can take away, if it steals from you the name of a "good man" and causes you to lose your sense of honour and justice? For what difference does it make whether a man is actually transformed into a beast or whether, keeping the outward appearance of a man, he has the savage nature of a beast within?

21

AGAIN, when people disregard everything that is morally right and true, if only they may secure power thereby, are they not pursuing the same course as he who wished to have as a father-in-law the man by whose effrontery he might gain power for himself? He thought it advantageous to secure supreme power while the odium of it fell upon another; and he failed to see how unjust to his country this was, and how wrong morally. But the father-in-law himself used to have continually upon his lips the Greek verses from the Phoenissae, which I will reproduce as well as I can—awkwardly, it may be, but still so that the meaning can be understood:

> If wrong may e'er be right, for a throne's sake
> Were wrong most right:—be God in all else feared![1]

Our tyrant deserved his death for having made an exception of the one thing that was the blackest crime of all. Why do we gather instances of petty crime—legacies criminally obtained and fraudulent buying and selling? Behold, here you have a man who was ambitious to be king of the Roman People and master of the whole world; and he achieved it! The man who maintains that such an ambition is morally right is a madman; for he justifies the destruction of law and liberty and thinks their hideous and detestable suppression glorious. But if anyone agrees that it is not morally right to be kind in a state that once was free and that ought to be free now, and yet imagines that it is advantageous for him who can reach that position, with what remonstrance or rather with what appeal should I try to tear him away from so strange a delusion? For, oh ye immortal gods! can the most horrible and hideous of all murders—that of fatherland—bring advantage to anybody, even though he who has committed

1 From A.S. Way's translation.

such a crime receives from his enslaved fellow-citizens the title of "Father of his Country"? Expediency, therefore, must be measured by the standard of moral rectitude, and in such a way, too, that these two words shall seem in sound only to be different but in real meaning to be one and the same.

What greater advantage one could have, according to the standard of popular opinion, than to be a king, I do not know; when, however, I begin to bring the question back to the standard of truth, then I find nothing more disadvantageous for one who has risen to that height by injustice. For can occasions for worry, anxiety, fear by day and by night, and a life all beset with plots and perils be of advantage to anybody?

> "Thrones have many foes and friends untrue,
> but few devoted friends"

says Accius. But of what sort of throne was he speaking? Why, one that was held by right, handed down from Tantalus and Pelops. Aye, but how many more foes, think you, had that king who with the Roman People's army brought the Roman People themselves into subjection and compelled a state that not only had been free but had been mistress of the world to be his slave? What stains do you think he had upon his conscience, what scars upon his heart? But whose life can be advantageous to himself, if that life is his on the condition that the man who takes it shall be held in undying gratitude and glory? But if these things which seem so very advantageous are not advantageous because they are full of shame and moral wrong, we ought to be quite convinced that nothing can be expedient that is not morally right.

22

AND yet this very question has been decided on many occasions before and since; but in the war with Pyrrhus the decision rendered by Gaius Fabricius, in his second consulship, and by our senate was particularly striking. Without provocation King Pyrrhus had declared war upon the Roman People; the struggle was against a generous and powerful prince, and the supremacy of power was the prize; a deserter came over from him to the camp of Fabricius and promised, if Fabricius would assure him of a reward, to return to the camp of Pyrrhus as secretly as he had come, administer poison to the king, and bring about his death. Fabricius saw to it that this fellow was taken back to Pyrrhus; and his action was commended by the senate. And yet, if the mere show of expediency and the popular conception of it are all we want, this one deserter would have put an end to that wasting war and to a formidable foe of our supremacy; but it would have been a lasting shame and disgrace to us to have overcome not by valour but by crime the man with whom we had a contest for glory.

Which course, then, was more expedient for Fabricius, who was to our city what Aristides was to Athens, or for our senate, who never divorced expediency from honour—to contend against the enemy with the sword or with poison? If supremacy is to be sought for the sake of glory, crime should be excluded, for there can be no glory in crime; but if it is power for its own sake that is sought, whatever the price, it cannot be expedient if it is linked with shame.

That well-known measure, therefore, introduced by Philippus, the son of Quintus, was not expedient. With the authority of the senate, Lucius Sulla had exempted from taxation certain states upon receipt of a lump sum of money from them. Philippus proposed that they should again be reduced to the condition of tributary states, without repayment on our part of the money that they had paid for their exemption. And the senate accepted his proposal. Shame upon our government! The pirates' sense of honour is higher than the senate's. "But," someone will say, "the revenues were increased, and therefore it was expedient." How long will people venture to say that a thing that is not morally right can be expedient? Furthermore, can hatred and shame be expedient for any government? For government ought to be founded upon fair fame and the loyalty of allies.

On this point I often disagreed even with my friend Cato; it seemed to me that he was too rigorous in his watchful care over the claims of the treasury and the revenues; he refused everything that the farmers of the revenue asked for and much that the allies desired; whereas, as I insisted, it was our duty to be generous to the allies and to treat the publicans as we were accustomed individually to treat our tenants—and all the more, because harmony between the orders was essential to the welfare of the republic. Curio, too, was wrong, when he pleaded that the demands of the people beyond the Po were just, but never failed to add, "Let expediency prevail." He ought rather to have proved that the claims were not just, because they were not expedient for the republic, than to have admitted that they were just, when, as he maintained, they were not expedient.

23

THE sixth book of Hecaton's "Moral Duties" is full of questions like the following: "Is it consistent with a good man's duty to let his slaves go hungry when provisions are at famine prices?"

Hecaton gives the argument on both sides of the question; but still in the end it is by the standard of expediency, as he conceives it, rather than by one of human feeling, that he decides the question of duty.

Then he raises this question: supposing a man had to throw part of his cargo overboard in a storm, should he prefer to sacrifice a high-priced horse or a cheap and worthless slave? In this case regard for his property interest inclines him one way, human feeling the other.

"Suppose that a foolish man has seized hold of a plank from a sinking ship, shall a wise man wrest it away from him if he can?"

"No," says Hecaton; "for that would be unjust."

"But how about the owner of the ship? Shall he take the plank away because it belongs to him?"

"Not at all; no more than he would be willing when far out at sea to throw a passenger overboard on the ground that the ship was his. For until they reach the place for which the ship is chartered, she belongs to the passengers, not to the owner."

"Again; suppose there were two to be saved from the sinking ship—both of them wise men—and only one small plank, should both seize it to save themselves? Or should one give place to the other?"

"Why of course, one should give place to the other, but that other must be the one whose life is more valuable either for his own sake or for that of his country."

"But what if these considerations are of equal weight in both?"

"Then there will be no contest, but one will give place to the other, as if the point were decided by lot or at a game of odd and even."

"Again, suppose a father were robbing temples or making underground passages to the treasury, should a son inform the officers of it?"

"Nay; that were a crime; rather should he defend his father, in case he were indicted."

"Well, then, are not the claims of country paramount to all other duties?"

"Aye, verily; but it is to our country's interest to have citizens who are loyal to their parents."

"But once more—if the father attempts to make himself king, or to betray his country, shall the son hold his peace?"

"Nay, verily; he will plead with his father not to do so. If that accomplishes nothing, he will take him to task; he will even threaten;

and in the end, if things point to the destruction of the state, he will sacrifice his father to the safety of his country."

Again, he raises the question: "If a wise man should inadvertently accept counterfeit money for good, will he offer it as genuine in payment of a debt after he discovers his mistake?" Diogenes says, "Yes"; Antipater, "No," and I agree with him.

If a man knowingly offers for sale wine that is spoiling, ought he to tell his customers? Diogenes thinks that it is not required; Antipater holds that an honest man would do so. These are like so many points of the law disputed among the Stoics. "In selling a slave, should his faults be declared—not those only which the seller is bound by the civil law to declare or have the slave returned to him, but also the fact that he is untruthful, or disposed to gamble, or steal, or get drunk?" The one thinks such facts should be declared, the other does not.

"If a man thinks that he is selling brass, when he is actually selling gold, should an upright man inform him that his stuff is gold, or go on buying for one shilling what is worth a thousand?"

It is clear enough by this time what my views are on these questions, and what are the grounds of dispute between the above-named philosophers.

24

THE question arises also whether agreements and promises must always be kept, "when," in the language of the praetors' edicts, "they have not been secured through force or criminal fraud."

If one man gives another a remedy for the dropsy, with the stipulation that, if he is cured by it, he shall never make use of it again; suppose the patient's health is restored by the use of it, but some years later he contracts the same disease once more; and suppose he cannot secure from the man with whom he made the agreement permission to use the remedy again, what should he do? That is the question. Since the man is unfeeling in refusing the request, and since no harm could be done to him by his friend's using the remedy, the sick man is justified in doing what he can for his own life and health.

Again: suppose that a millionaire is making some wise man his heir and leaving him in his will a hundred million sesterces; and suppose that he has asked the wise man, before he enters upon his inheritance, to dance publicly in broad daylight in the forum; and suppose that the wise man has given his promise to do so, because the rich man would not leave him his fortune on any other condition; should he keep his promise or not? I wish he had made no such promise; that, I think, would have been in keeping with his dignity. But, seeing that he has made it, it will be morally better for him, if he believes it morally wrong to dance in the forum, to break his promise and refuse to accept his inheritance rather than to keep his promise and accept it—unless, perhaps, he contributes the money to the state to meet some grave crisis. In that case, to promote thereby the interests of one's country, it would not be morally wrong even to dance, if you please, in the forum.

25

NO more binding are those promises which are inexpedient for the persons themselves to whom they have been given. To go back to the realm of story, the sun god promised his son Phaethon to do for him whatever he should wish. His wish was to be allowed to ride in his father's chariot. It was granted. And before he came back to the ground he was consumed by a stroke of lightning. How much better had it been, if in his case the father's promise had not been kept. And what of that promise, the fulfillment of which Theseus required from Neptune? When Neptune offered him three wishes, he wished for the death of his son Hippolytus, because the father was suspicious of the son's relations with his step-mother. And when this wish was granted, Theseus was overwhelmed with grief. And once more; when Agamemnon had vowed to Diana the most beautiful creature born that year within his realm, he was brought to sacrifice Iphigenia; for in that year nothing was born more beautiful than she. He ought to have broken his vow rather than commit so horrible a crime.

Promises are, therefore, sometimes not to be kept; and trusts are not always to be restored. Suppose that a person leaves his sword with you when he is in his right mind, and demands it back in a fit of insanity; it would be criminal to restore it to him; it would be your duty not to do so. Again, suppose that a man who has entrusted money to you proposes to make war upon your common country, should you restore the trust? I believe you should not; for you would be acting against the state, which ought to be the dearest thing in the world to you. Thus there are many things which in and of themselves seem morally right, but which under certain circumstances prove to be not morally right: to keep a promise, to abide by an agreement, to restore a trust may, with a change of expediency, cease to be morally right.

With this I think I have said enough about those actions which masquerade as expedient under the guise of prudence, while they are really contrary to justice.

Since, however, in Book One we derived moral duties from the four sources of moral rectitude, let us continue the same fourfold division here in pointing out how hostile to virtue are those courses of conduct which seem to be, but really are not, expedient. We have discussed wisdom, which cunning seeks to counterfeit, and likewise justice, which is always expedient. There remain for our discussion two divisions of moral rectitude, the one of which is discernible in the greatness and preeminence of a superior soul, the other, in the shaping and regulation of it by temperance and self-control.

SUETONIUS

THE LIVES OF THE TWELVE CAESARS

SUETONIUS

The Life of Augustus

5

AUGUSTUS was born just before sunrise on the ninth day before the Kalends of October in the consulship of Marcus Tullius Cicero and Gaius Antonius, at the Ox-Heads in the Palatine quarter, where he now has a shrine, built shortly after his death. For it is recorded in the proceedings of the senate, that when Gaius Laetorius, a young man of patrician family, was pleading for a milder punishment for adultery because of his youth and position, he further urged upon the senators that he was the possessor and as it were the warden of the sport which the deified Augustus first touched at his birth, begged that he be pardoned for the sake of what might be called his own special god. Whereupon it was decreed that that part of his house should be consecrated.

6

A SMALL room like a pantry is shown to this day as the emperor's nursery in his grandfather's country-house near Velitrae, and the opinion prevails in the neighbourhood that he was actually born there. No one ventures to enter this room except of necessity and after purification, since there is a conviction of long-standing that those approach it without ceremony are seized with shuddering who and terror; and what is more, this has recently been shown to be true. For when a new owner, either by chance or to test the matter, went to bed in that room, it came to pass that, after a very few hours of the night, he was thrown out by a sudden mysterious force and was found bedclothes and all half-dead before the door.

7

IN his infancy he was given the surname Thurinus in memory of the home of his ancestors, or else because it was near Thurii that his father Octavius, shortly after the birth of his son, had gained his victory over the runaway slaves. That he was surnamed Thurinus I may assert on very trustworthy evidence, since I once obtained a bronze statuette, representing him as a boy and inscribed with that name in letters of iron almost illegible from age. This I presented to the emperor, who cherishes it among the Lares of his bed-chamber. Furthermore, he is often called Thurinus in Mark Antony's letters by way of insult; to which Augustus merely replied that he was surprised that his former name was thrown in his face as a reproach. Later he took the name of Gaius Caesar and then the surname Augustus, the former by the will of his great-uncle, the latter on the motion of Munatius Plancus. For when some expressed the opinion that he ought to be called Romulus as a second founder of the city, Plancus carried the proposal that this was not merely a new title but a more honorable one, inasmuch as sacred places too, and those in which anything is consecrated by augural rites are called "august" (*augusta*), from the increase (*auctus*) in dignity, or front movements or feeding of the birds (*avium*, *gestus*, *gustuve*), as Ennius also shows when he writes: "After by augury august illustrious Rome had been founded."

13

THEN, forming a league with Antony and Lepidus, he finished the war of Philippi also in two battles, although weakened by illness, being driven from his camp in the first battle and barely making his escape by fleeing to Antony's division. He did not use his victory with moderation, but after sending Brutus's head to Rome, to be cast at the feet of Caesar's statue, he vented his spleen upon the most distinguished of his captives, not even sparing them insulting language. For instance, to one man who begged humbly for burial, he is said to have replied: "The birds will soon settle that question." When two others, father and son, begged for their lives, he is said to have bidden them cast lots or play mora, to decide which should be spared and then to have looked on while both died, since the father was executed because he offered to die for his son, and the latter thereupon took his own life. Because of this the rest, including Marucs Favonius, the well-known imitator of Cicero, saluted Antony respectfully as Imperator, when they were led out in chains, but lashed Augustus to his face with the foulest abuse. When the duties of administration were divided after the victory, Antony undertaking to restore order in the East, and Augustus to lead the veterans back to Italy and assign them lands in the municipalities, he could neither satisfy the veterans nor the landowners, since the latter complained that they were driven from their homes, and the former that they were not being treated as their services had led them to hope.

14

WHEN Lucius Antonius at this juncture attempted a revolution, relying on his position as consul and his brother's power, he forced him to take refuge in Perusia, and starved him into surrender, not, however, without great personal danger both before and during the war. For at an exhibition of games, when he had given orders that a common soldier who was sitting in the fourteen rows be put out by an attendant, the report was spread by his detractors that he had had the man killed later and tortured as well; whereupon he all but lost his life in a furious mob of soldiers, owing his escape to the sudden appearance of the missing man safe and sound. Again, when he was sacrificing near the walls of Perusia, he was well nigh cut by a band of gladiators, who had made a sally from the town.

15

AFTER the capture of Perusia he took vengeance on many, meeting all attempts to beg for pardon or to make excuses with the one reply, "You must die." Some write that three hundred men of both orders were selected from the prisoners of war and sacrificed on the Ides of March like so many victims at the altar raised to the Deified Julius. Some have written that he took up arms of a set purpose, to unmask his secret opponents and those whom fear rather than good-will kept faithful to him, by giving them the chance to follow the lead of Lucius Antonius; and then by vanquishing them and confiscating their estates to pay the rewards promised to his veterans.

16

THE Sicilian war was among the first that he began, but it was long drawn out by many interruptions, now for the purpose of rebuilding his fleets, which he twice lost by shipwreck due to storms, and that, too, in the summer; and again by making peace at the demand of the people, when supplies were cut off and there was a severe famine. Finally, after new ships had been built and twenty thousand slaves set free and trained as oarsmen, he made the Julian harbour at Baiae by letting the sea into the Lucrine lake and lake Avernus. After drilling his forces there all winter, he defeated Pompey between Mylae and Naulochus, though just before the battle he was suddenly held fast by so deep a sleep that his friends had to awaken him to give the signal. And it was this, I think, that gave Antony opportunity for the taunt: "He could not even look with steady eyes at the fleet when it was ready for battle, but lay in a stupor on his back, looking up at the sky, and did not rise or appear before the soldiers until the enemy's ships had been put to flight by Marcus Agrippa." Some censured an act and saying of his, declaring that when his fleets were lost in the storm, he cried out, "I will have the victory spite of Neptune," and that on the day when games in the Circus next occurred, he removed the statue of the god from the sacred procession. And it is safe to say that in none of his wars did he encounter more dangers or greater ones. For when he had transported an army to Sicily and was on his way back to the rest of his forces on the mainland, he was surprised by Pompey's admirals Demochares and Apollophanes and barely escaped with but a single ship. Again, as he was going on foot to Regium by way of Locri, he saw some of Pompey's biremes coasting along the shore, and taking them for his own ships and going down the beach, narrowly escaped capture. At that same time, too, as he was making his escape by narrow bypaths, a slave of his companion Aemilius Paulus, nursing a grudge because Augustus had proscribed his master's father some time before, and thinking that he had an opportunity for revenge, attempted to slay him. After Pompey's flight, Augustus' other colleague, Marcus Lepidus, whom he had summoned from Africa to help him, was puffed up by confidence in his twenty legions and claimed the first place with terrible threats; but Augustus stripped him of his army; and though he granted him his life when he sued for it, he banished him for all time to Circei.

18

ABOUT this time he had the sarcophagus and body of Alexander the Great brought forth from its shrine, and after gazing on it, showed his respect by placing upon it a golden crown and strewing it with flowers; and being then asked whether he wished to see the tomb of the Ptolemies as well, he replied, "My wish was to see a king, not corpses." He reduced Egypt to the form of a province, and then to make it more fruitful and better adapted to supply the city with grain, he set his soldiers at work cleaning out all the canals into which the Nile overflows, which in the course of many years had become choked with mud. To extend the fame of his victory at Actium and perpetuate his memory, he founded a city called Nicopolis near Actium, and provided for the celebration of games there every five years; enlarged the ancient temple of Apollo; and after adorning the site of the camp which he had occupied with naval trophies, consecrated it to Neptune and Mars.

19

AFTER this he nipped in the bud at various times several outbreaks, attempts at revolution, and conspiracies, which were betrayed before they became formidable. The ringleaders were, first the young Lepidus, then Varro Murena and Fannius Caepio, later Marcus Egnatius, next Plautius Rufus and Lucius Paulus, husband of the emperor's granddaughter, and besides these Lucius Audasius, who had been charged with forgery, and was most old and feeble; also Asinius Epicadus, a half-breed of Parthian descent, and finally Telephus, slave and page of a woman; for even men of the lowest condition conspired against him and imperiled his safety. Audasius and Epicadus had planned to take his daughter Julia and his grandson Agrippa by force to the armies from the islands where they were confined, Telephus to set upon both Augustus and the senate, under the delusion that he himself was destined for empire. Even a soldier's servant from the army in Illyricum, who had escaped the vigilance of the door-keepers, was caught at night near the emperor's bed-room, armed with a hunting knife; but whether the fellow was crazy or feigned madness is a question, since nothing could be wrung from him by torture.

20

HE carried on but two foreign wars in person: in Dalmatia, when he was but a youth, and with the Cantabarians after the overthrow of Antony. He was wounded, too, in the former campaign, being struck on the right knee with a stone in one battle, and in another having a leg and both arms severely injured by the collapse of a bridge. His other wars he carried on through his generals, although he was either present at some of those in Pannonia and Germany, or was not far from the front, since he went from the city as far as Ravenna, Mediolanum, or Aquileia.

21

IN part as leader, and in part with armies serving under his auspices, he subdued Cantabria, Aquitania, Pannonia, Dalmatia, and all Illyricum, as well as Raetia and the Vindelici and Salassi, which are Alpine tribes. He also put a stop to the inroads of the Dacians, slaying great numbers of them, together with three of their leaders, and force the Germans back to the farther side of the river Albis, with the exception of the Suebi and the Sigambri, who submitted to him and were taken into Gaul and settled in lands near the Rhine. He reduced to submission other peoples, too, that were in a state of unrest. But he never made war on any nation without just and due cause, and he was so far from desiring to increase his dominion or his military glory at any cost, that he forced the chiefs of certain barbarians to take oath in the temple of Mars the Avenger that they would faithfully keep the peace for which they asked; in some case, indeed, he tried exacting a new kind of hostages, namely women, realizing that the barbarians disregarded pledges secured by males; but all were given the privilege of reclaiming their hostages whenever they wished. On those who rebelled often or under circumstances of especial treachery he never inflicted any severer punishment than that of selling the prisoners, with the condition that they should not pass their term of slavery in a country near their own, nor be set free within thirty years. The reputation for prowess and moderation which he thus gained led even the Indians and the Scythians, nations known to us only by hearsay, to send envoys of their own free will and sue for his friendship and that of the Roman people. The Parthians, too, readily yielded to him, when he laid claim to Armenia, and at his demand surrendered the standards which they had taken from Marcus Crassus and Marcus Antonius; they offered him hostages besides, and once when there were several claimants of the throne, they would accept only the one whom he selected.

22

THE temple of Janus Quirinus, which had been closed but twice before his time since the founding of the city, he closed three times in a far shorter period, having won peace on land and sea. He twice entered the city in an ovation, after the war of Philippi, again after that in Sicily, and he celebrated three regular triumphs for his victories in Dalmatia, at Actium, and at Alexandria, all on three successive days.

23

HE suffered but two severe and ignominious defeats, those of Lollius and Varus, both of which were in Germany. Of these the former was more humiliating than serious, but the latter was almost fatal, since three legions were cut to pieces with their general, his lieutenants, and all the auxiliaries. When the news of this came, he ordered that watch be kept by night throughout the city, to prevent outbreak, and prolonged the terms of the governors of the provinces, that the allies might be held to their allegiance by experienced men with whom they were acquainted. He also vowed great games to Jupiter Optimus Maximus, in case the condition of the commonwealth should improve, a thing which had been done in the Cimbric and Marsic wars. In fact, they saw that he was so greatly affected that for several month in succession he cut neither his beard nor his hair, and sometimes he would dash his head against a door, crying: "Quintilius Varus, give me back my legions!" And he observed the day of the disaster each year as one of sorrow and mourning.

24

HE made many changes and innovations in the army, besides reviving some usages of former times. He exacted the strictest discipline. It was with great reluctance that he allowed even his generals to visit their wives, and then only in the winter season. He sold a Roman knight and his property at public auction, because he had cut off the thumbs of two young sons, to make them unfit for military service; but when he saw that some tax-gatherers were intent upon buying him, he knocked him down to a freedman of his own, with the understanding that he should be banished to the country districts, but allowed to live in freedom. He dismissed the entire tenth legion in disgrace, because they were insubordinate, and others, too, that demanded their discharge in an insolent fashion, he disbanded without the rewards which would have been due for faithful service. If any cohorts gave way in battle, he decimated them, and fed the rest on barley. When centurions left their posts, he punished them with death, just as he did the rank and file; for faults of other kinds he imposed various ignominious penalties, such as ordering to stand all day long before the general's tent, sometimes in their tunics without their sword-belts, or again holding ten-foot poles or even a clod of earth.

25

AFTER the civil war he never called any of the troops "comrades," either in the assembly or in an edict, but always "soldiers"; and he would not allow them to be addressed otherwise, even by those of his sons or stepsons who held military commands, thinking the former term too flattering for the requirements of discipline, the peaceful state of the times, and his own dignity and that of his household. Except as a fire-brigade in Rome, and when there was fear of riots in time of scarcity, he employed freedmen as soldiers only twice: once as a guard for the colonies in the vicinity of Illyricum, and again to defend the bank of the river Rhine; even these he levied, when they were slaves, from men and women of means, and at once gave them freedom; and he kept them under their original standard, not mingling them with the soldiers of free birth or arming them in the same fashion. As military prizes he was somewhat more ready to give trappings or collars, valuable for their gold and silver, than crowns for scaling ramparts or walls, which conferred high honour; the latter he gave as sparingly as possible and without favouritism, often even to the common soldiers. He presented Marcus Agrippa with a blue banner in Sicily after his naval victory. Those who had celebrated triumphs where the only one whom he thought ineligible for prizes, even though they had been the companions of his campaigns and shared in his victories, on the ground that they themselves had the privilege of bestowing such honours whenever they wished. He thought nothing less becoming in a well-trained leader than haste and rashness and, accordingly, favourite saying of his were: "More haste, less speed"; "Better a safe commander than a bold"; and "That is done quickly enough which is done well enough." He used to say that a war or a battle should not be begun under any circumstances, unless the hope of gain was clearly greater than the fear of loss; for he likened such as grasped at slight gains with no slight risk to those who finished with a golden hook, the loss of which, if it were carried off, could not be make good by any catch.

28

HE twice thought of restoring the republic; first immediately after the overthrow of Antony, remembering that his rival had often made the charge that it was his fault that it was not restored; and again in the weariness of a lingering illness, when he went so far as to summon the magistrates and the senate to his house, and submit an account of the general condition of the empire. Reflecting, however, that as he himself would not be free from danger if he should retire, so too it would be hazardous to trust the State to the control of more than one, he continued to keep it in his hands; and it is not easy to say whether his intentions or their results were better. His good intentions he not only expressed from time to time, but put them on record as well as in an edict in the following words: "May it be my privilege to establish the State in a firm and secure position, and reap from that act the fruit that I desire; but only if I may be called the author of the best possible government, and bear with me the hope when I die that the foundations which I have laid for the State will remain unshaken." And he realized his hope by making every effort to prevent any dissatisfaction with the new regime. Since the city was not adorned as the dignity of the empire demanded, and was exposed to flood and fire, he so beautified it that he could justly boast that he had found it built of brick and left it in marble. He made it safe too for the future, so far as human foresight could provide for this.

43

HE surpassed all his predecessors in the frequency, variety, and magnificence of his public shows. He says that he gave games four times in his own name and twenty-three times for other magistrates, who were either away from Rome or lacked means. He gave them sometimes in all the wards and on many stages with actors in all languages, and combats of gladiators not only in the Forum or the amphitheatre, but in the Circus and in the Saepta; sometimes, however, he gave nothing except a fight with wild beasts. He gave athletic contests too in the Campus Martius, erecting wooden seats; also a sea-fight, constructing an artificial lake near the Tiber, where the grove of the Caesars now stands. On such occasions he stationed guards in various parts of the city, to prevent it from falling a prey to footpads because of the few people who remained at home. In the Circus he exhibited charioteers, runners, and slayers of wild animals, who were sometimes young men of the highest rank. Besides he gave frequent performances of the game of Troy by older and younger boys, thinking it a time-honoured and worthy custom for the flower of the nobility to become known in this way. When Nonius Asprenas was lamed by a fall while taking part in this game, he presented him with a golden necklace and allowed him and his descendants to bear the surname Torquatus. But soon after he gave up that form of entertainment, because Asinius Pollio the orator complained bitterly and angrily in the senate of an accident to his grandson Aeserninus, who also had broken his leg. He sometimes employed even Roman knights in scenic and gladiatorial performances, but only before it was forbidden by decree of the senate. After that he exhibited no one of respectable parentage, with the exception of a young man named Lycius, whom he showed merely as a curiosity; for he was less than two feet tall, weighed but seventeen pounds, yet had a stentorian voice. He did however on the day of one of the shows make a display of the first Parthian hostages that had ever been sent to Rome, by leading them through the middle of the arena and placing them in the second row above his own seat. Furthermore, if anything rare and worth seeing was ever brought to the city, it was his habit to make a special exhibit of it in any convenient place on days when no shows were appointed. For example a rhinoceros in the Saepta, a tiger on the stage and a snake of fifty cubits in front of the Comitium. It chanced that at the time of the games which he had vowed to give in the circus, he was taken ill and headed the sacred procession lying in a litter; again, at the opening of the games with which he dedicated the theater of Marcellus, it happened that the joints of his curule chair gave way and he fell on his back. At the games for his grandsons, when the people were in a panic that the theater should fall, and he could not calm them or encourage them in any way, he left his own place and took his seat in the part which appeared most dangerous.

44

HE put a stop by special regulations to the disorderly and indiscriminate fashion of viewing the games, through exasperation at the insult to a senator, to whom no one offered a seat in a crowded house at some largely attended games in Puteoli. In consequence of this the senate decreed that, whenever any public show was given anywhere, the first row of seats should be reserved for senators; and at Rome he would not allow the envoys of the free and allied nations to sit in the orchestra, since he was informed that even freedmen were sometimes appointed. He separated the soldiery from the people. He assigned special seats to the married men of the commons, to boys under age their own section and the adjoining one to their preceptors; and he decreed that no one wearing a dark cloak should sit in the middle of the house. He would not allow women to view even the gladiators except from the upper seats, though it had been the custom for men and women to sit together at such shows. Only the Vestal virgins were assigned a place to themselves, opposite the praetor's tribunal. As for the contests of the athletes, he excluded women from them so strictly, that when a contest between a pair of boxers had been called for at the games in honour of his appointment as *pontifex maximus*, he postponed it until early the following day, making proclamation that it was his desire that women should not come to the theatre before the fifth hour.

45

HE himself usually watched the games in the Circus from the upper rooms of his friends and freedmen, but sometimes from the imperial box, and even in company with his wife and children. He was sometimes absent for several hours, and now and then for whole days, making his excuses and appointing presiding officers to take his place. But whenever he was present, he gave his entire attention to the performance, either to avoid the censure to which he realized that his father Caesar had been generally exposed, because he spent his time in reading or answering letters and petitions; or from his interest and pleasure in the spectacle, which he never denied but often frankly confessed. Because of this he used to offer special prizes and numerous valuable gifts from his own purse at games given by others, and he appeared at no contest in the Grecian fashion without making a present to each of the participants according to his deserts. He was especially given to watching boxers, particularly those of Latin birth, not merely such as were recognised and classed as professionals, whom he was wont to match even with Greeks, but the common untrained townspeople that fought rough and tumble and without skill in the narrow streets. In fine, he followed with his interest all classes of performers who took part in the public shows; maintained the privileges of the athletes and even increased them; forbade the matching of gladiators without the right of appeal for quarter; and deprived the magistrates of the power allowed them by an ancient law of punishing actors anywhere and everywhere, restricting it to the time of games and to the theatre. Nevertheless he exacted the severest discipline in the contests in the wrestling halls and the combats of the gladiators. In particular he was so strict in curbing the lawlessness of the actors, that when he learned that Stephanio, an actor of Roman plays, was waited on by a matron with hair cut short to look like a boy, he had him whipped with rods through the three theatres and then banished him. Hylas, a pantomimic actor, was publicly scourged in the atrium of his own house, on complaint of a praetor, and Pylades was expelled from the city and from Italy as well, because by pointing at him with his finger he turned all eyes upon a spectator who was hissing him.

46

AFTER having thus set the city and its affairs in order, he added to the population of Italy by personally establishing twenty-eight colonies; furnished many parts of it with public buildings and revenues; and even gave it, at least to some degree, equal rights and dignity with the city of Rome, by devising a kind of votes which the members of the local senate were to cast in each colony for candidates for the city offices and send under seal to Rome against the day of the elections. To keep up the supply of men of rank and induce the commons to increase and multiply, he admitted to the equestrian military career those who were recommended by any town, while to those commons who could lay claim to legitimate son or daughters when he made his rounds of the districts he distributed a thousand sesterces for each child.

47

THE stronger provinces, which could neither easily nor safely be guarded by annual meetings, he took to himself; the others he assigned to proconsular governors selected by lot. But he changed some of them at times from one class to the other, and often visited many of both sorts. Certain of the cities which had treaties with Rome, but were on the road to ruin through their lawlessness, he deprived of their independence; he relieved others that were overwhelmed with debt, rebuilt some which had been destroyed by earthquakes, and gave Latin rights or full citizenship to such as could point to services rendered the Roman people. I believe there is no province, excepting only Africa and Sardinia, which he did not visit; and he was planning to cross to these from Sicily after his defeat of Sextus Pompeius, but was prevented by a series of violent storms, and later had neither the opportunity nor occasion to make the voyage.

48

EXCEPT in a few instances he restored the kingdoms of which he gained possession by the right of conquest to those from whom he had taken them or joined them with other foreign nations. He also united the kings with whom he was in alliance by mutual ties, and was very ready to propose or favour intermarriages or friendships among them. He never failed to treat them all with consideration as integral parts of the empire, regularly appointing a guardian for such as were too young to rule or whose minds were affected, until they grew up or recovered; and he brought up the children of many of them and educated them with his own.

49

OF his military forces he assigned legions and auxiliaries to the various provinces, stationed a fleet at Misenum and another at Ravenna, to defend the Upper and Lower seas, and employed the remainder partly in the defense of the city and partly in that of his own person, disbanding a troop of Calagurritani which had formed a part of his body-guard until the overthrow of Antony, and also one of the Germans, which he had retained until the defeat of Varus. However, he never allowed more than three cohorts to remain in the city and even those were without a permanent camp; the rest he regularly sent to winter or summer quarters in the towns near Rome. Furthermore, he restricted all the soldiery everywhere to a fixed scale of pay and allowances, designating the duration of their service and the rewards on its completion according to each man's rank, in order to keep them from being tempted to revolution after their discharge either by age or poverty. To have funds ready at all times without difficulty for maintaining the soldiers and paying the rewards due to them, he established a military treasury, supported by new taxes. To enable what was going on in each of the provinces to be reported and known more speedily and promptly, he at first stationed young men at short intervals along the military roads, and afterwards post chaises. The latter has seemed the more convenient arrangement, since the same men who bring the dispatches from any place can, if occasion demands, be questioned as well.

50

IN passports, dispatches, and private letters he used as his seal at first a sphinx, later an image of Alexander the Great, and finally his own, carved by the hand of Dioscurides; and this his successors continued to use as their seal. He always attached to all letters the exact hour, not only of the day, but even of the night, to indicate precisely when they were written.

51

THE evidences of his clemency and moderation are numerous and strong. Not to give the full list of the men of the opposite faction whom he not only pardoned and spared, but allowed to hold high positions in the state, I may say that he thought it enough to punish two plebeians, Junius Novatus and Cassius Patavinus, with a fine and with a mild form of banishment respectively, although the former had circulated a most scathing letter about him under the name of the young Agrippa, while the latter had openly declared at a large dinner party that he lacked neither the earnest desire nor the courage to kill him. Again, when he was hearing a case against Aemilius Aelianus of Corduba and it was made the chief offence, amongst other charges, that he was in the habit of expressing a bad opinion of Caesar, Augustus turned to the accused with assumed anger and said: "I wish you could prove the truth of that. I'll let Aelianus know that I have a tongue as well as he, for I'll say even more about him"; and he made no further inquiry either at that time or afterwards. When Tiberius complained to him of the same thing in a letter, but in more forcible language, he replied as follows: "My dear Tiberius, do not be carried away by the ardour of youth in this matter, or take it too much to heart that anyone speak evil of me; we must be content if we can stop anyone from doing evil to us."

52

ALTHOUGH well aware that it was usual to vote temples even to proconsuls, he would not accept one even in a province save jointly in his own name and that of Rome. In the city itself he refused this honour most emphatically, even melting down the silver statues which had been set up in his honour in former times and with the money coined from them dedicating golden tripods to Apollo of the Palatine. When the people did their best to force the dictatorship upon him, he knelt down, threw off his toga from his shoulders and with bare breast begged them not to insist.

53

HE always shrank from the title of Lord as reproachful and insulting. When the word "O just and gracious Lord!" were uttered in a farce at which he was a spectator and all the people sprang to their feet and applauded as if they were said of him, he at once checked their unseemly flattery by look and gesture, and on the following day sharply reproved them in an edict. After that he would not suffer himself to be called Sire even by his children or his grandchildren either in jest or in earnest, and he forbade them to use such flattering terms even among themselves. He did not if he could help it leave or enter any city or town except in the evening or at night, to avoid disturbing anyone by the obligations of ceremony. In his consulship he commonly went through the streets on foot, and when he was not consul, generally in a closed litter. His morning receptions were open to all, including even the commons, and he met the requests of those who approached him with great affability, jocosely reproving one man because he had presented a petition to him with as much hesitation "as he would a penny to an elephant." On the day of a meeting of the senate he always greeted the members in the House and in their seats, calling each man by name without a prompter; and when he left the House, he used to take leave of them in the same manner, while they remained seated. He exchanged social calls with many, and did not cease to attend all their anniversaries, until he was well on in years and was once incommoded by the crowd on the day of a betrothal. When Gallus Cerrinius, a senator with whom he was not at all intimate, had suddenly become blind and therefore resolved to end his life by starvation, Augustus called on him and by his consoling words induced him to live.

54

AS he was speaking in the senate someone said to him: "I did not understand," and another: "I would contradict you if I had an opportunity." Several times when he was rushing from the House in anger at the excessive bickering of the disputants, some shouted after him: "Senators ought to have the right of speaking their mind on public affairs." At the selection of senators when each member chose another, Antistius Labeo named Marcus Lepidus, an old enemy of the emperor's who was at the time in banishment; and when Augustus asked him whether there were not other more deserving of the honour, Labeo replied that every man had his own opinion. Yet for all that no one suffered for his freedom of speech or insolence.

55

HE did not even dread the lampoons against him which were scattered in the senate house, but took great pains to refute them; and without trying to discover the authors, he merely proposed that thereafter such as published notes or verses defamatory of anyone under a false name should be called to account.

56

WHEN he was assailed with scurrilous or spiteful jests by certain men, he made reply in a public proclamation; yet he vetoed a law to check freedom of speech in wills. Whenever he took part in the election of magistrates, he went the round of the tribes with his candidates and appealed for them in the traditional manner. He also cast his own vote in his tribe, as one of the people. When he gave testimony in court, he was most patient in submitting to questions and even to contradiction. He made his forum narrower than he had planned, because he did not venture to eject the owners of the neighbouring houses. He never recommended his sons for office without adding "If they be worthy of it." When they were still under age and the audience at the theatre rose as one man in their honour, and stood up and applauded them, he expressed strong disapproval. He wished his friends to be prominent and influential in the state, but to be bound by the same laws as the rest and equally liable to prosecution. When Nonius Asprenas, a close friend of his, was meeting a charge of poisoning made by Cassius Severus, Augustus asked the senate what they thought he ought to do; for he hesitated, he said, for fear that if he should support him, it might be thought that he was shielding a guilty man, but if he failed to do so, that he was proving false to a friend and prejudicing his case. Then, since all approved of his appearing in the case, he sat on the benches for several hours, but in silence and without even speaking in praise of the defendant. He did however defend some of his clients, for instance a certain Scutarius, one of his former officers, who was accused of slander. But he secured the acquittal of no more than one single man, and then only by entreaty, making a successful appeal to the accuser in the presence of the jurors; this was Castricius, through whom he had learned of Murena's conspiracy.

57

IT may readily be imagined how much he was beloved because of this admirable conduct. I say nothing of decrees of the senate, which might seem to have been dictated by necessity or by awe. The Roman knights celebrated his birthday of their own accord by common consent, and always for two successive days. All sorts and conditions of men, in fulfillment of a vow for his welfare, each year threw a small coin into the Lacus Curtius, and also brought a New Year's gift to the Capitol on the Kalends of January, even when he was away from Rome. With this sum he bought and dedicated in each of the city wards costly statues of the gods, such as Apollo Sandalarius, Jupiter Tragoedus, and others. To rebuild his house on the Palatine, which had been destroyed by fire, the veterans, the guilds, the tribes, and even individuals of other conditions gladly contributed money, each according to his means; but he merely took a little from each pile as a matter of form, not more than a denarius from any of them. On his return from a province they received him not only with prayers and good wishes, but with songs. It was the rule, too, that whenever he entered the city, no one should suffer punishment.

72

IN the other detail of his life it is generally agreed that he was most temperate and without even the suspicion of any fault. He lived at first near the Forum Romanum, above the Stairs of the Ringmakers, in a house which had belonged to the orator Calvus;

afterwards, on the Palatine, but in the no less modest dwelling of Hortensius, which was remarkable neither for size nor elegance, having but short colonnades with columns of Alban stone, and rooms without any marble decorations or handsome pavements. For more than forty years too he used the same bedroom in winter and summer; although he found the city unfavourable to his health in the winter, yet continued to winter there. If ever he planned to do anything in private or without interruption, he had a retired place at the top of the house, which he called "Syracuse" and "technyphion." In this he used to take refuge, or else in the villa of one of his freedmen in the suburbs; but whenever he was not well, he slept at Maecenas's house. For retirement he went most frequently to places by the sea and the islands of Campania, or to the towns near Rome, such as Lanuvium, Praeneste or Tibur, where he very often held court in the colonnades of the Temple of Hercules. He disliked large and sumptuous country palaces, actually razing to the ground one which his granddaughter Julia built on a lavish scale. His own villas, which were modest enough, he decorated not so much with handsome statues and pictures as with terraces, groves, and objects noteworthy for their antiquity and rarity; for example, at Capreae the monstrous bones of huge sea monsters and wild beasts, called the "bones of the giants," and the weapons of the heroes.

73

THE simplicity of his furniture and household goods may be seen from couches and tables still in existence, many of which are scarcely fine enough for a private citizen. They say that he always slept on a low and plainly furnished bed. Except on special occasions he wore common clothes for the house, made by his sister, wife, daughter or granddaughters; his togas were neither close nor full, his purple stripe neither narrow nor broad, and his shoes somewhat high-soled, to make him look taller than he really was. But he always kept shoes and clothing to wear in public ready in his room for sudden and unexpected occasions.

74

HE gave dinner parties constantly and always formally, with great regard to the rank and personality of his guests. Valerius Messala writes that he never invited a freedman to dinner with the exception of Menas, and then only when he had been enrolled among the freeborn after betraying the fleet of Sextus Pompey. Augustus himself writes that he once entertained a man at whose villa he used to stop, who had been one of his body-guard. He would sometimes come to table late on these occasions and leave early, allowing his guests to begin to dine before he took his place and keep their places after he went out. He served a dinner of three courses or of six when he was most lavish, without needless extravagance but with the greatest good fellowship. For he drew into the general conversation those who were silent or chatted under their breath, and introduced music and actors, or even strolling players from the circus, and especially story-tellers.

75

FESTIVALS and holidays he celebrated lavishly as a rule, but sometimes only in a spirit of fun. On the Saturnalia, and at any other time when he took it into his head, he would now give gifts of clothing or gold and silver; again coins of every device, including old pieces of the kings and foreign money; another time nothing but hair cloth, sponges, pokers and tongs, and other such things under misleading names of double meaning. He used also at a dinner party to put up for auction lottery-tickets for articles of most unequal value, and paintings of which only the back was shown, thus by the caprice of fortune disappointing or filling to the full the expectations of the purchasers, requiring however that all the guests should take part in the bidding and share the loss or gain.

76

HE was a light eater (for I would not omit even this detail) and as a rule ate of plain food. He particularly liked coarse bread, small fishes, hand-made moist cheese, and green figs of the second crop; and he would eat even before dinner, wherever and whenever he felt hungry. I quote word for word from some of his letters: "I ate a little bread and some dates in my carriage." And again: "As I was on my homeward way from the Regia in my litter, I devoured an ounce of bread and a few berries from a cluster of hard-fleshed grapes." Once more: "Not even a Jew, my dear Tiberius, fasts so scrupulously on his Sabbaths as I have to-day; for it was not until after the first hour of the night that I ate two mouthfuls of bread in the bath before I began to be anointed." Because of this irregularity he sometimes ate alone either before a dinner party began or after it was over, touching nothing while it was in progress.

77

HE was by nature most sparing also in his use of wine. Cornelius Nepos writes that in camp before Mutina it was his habit to drink not more than three times at dinner. Afterwards, when he indulged most freely he never exceeded a pint; or if he died, he used to throw it up. He like Raetian wine best, but rarely drank before dinner. Instead he would take a bit of bread soaked in cold water, a slice of cucumber, a spring of young lettuce, or an apple with a tart flavour, either fresh or dried.

78

AFTER his midday meal he used to rest for a while just as he was, without taking off his clothes or his shoes, with his feet uncovered and his hand to his eyes. After dinner he went to a couch in his study, where he remained to late at night, until he had attended to what was left of the day's business, either wholly or in great part. Then he went to bed and slept not more than seven hours at most, and not even that length of time without a break, but waking three or four times. If he could not resume his sleep when it was interrupted, as would happen, he sent for readers or story-tellers, and when sleep came to him he often prolonged it until after daylight. He would never lie awake in the dark without having someone sit by his side. He detested early rising and when he had to get up earlier than usual because of some official or religious duty, to avoid inconveniencing himself he spent the night in the room of one of his friends near the appointed place. Even so, he often suffered from want of sleep, and he would drop off while he was being carried through the streets and when his litter was set down because of some delay.

79

HE was unusually handsome and exceedingly graceful at all periods of his life, though he cared nothing for personal adornment. He was so far from being particular about the dressing of his hair, that he would have several barbers working in a hurry at the same time, and as for his beard he now had it clipped and now shaved, while at the very same time he would either be reading or writing something. His expression, whether in conversation or when he was silent, was so calm and mild, that one of the leading men of the Gallic provinces admitted to his countrymen that it softened his heart, and kept him from carrying out his design of pushing the emperor over a cliff, when he had been allowed to approach him under the pretense of a conference, as he was crossing the Alps. He had clear, bright eyes, in which he liked to have it thought that there was a kind of divine power, and it greatly pleased him, whenever he would look keenly at anyone, if he let his face fall as if before the radiance of the sun; but in his old age he could not see very well with his left eye. His teeth were wide apart, small, and ill-kept; his hair was slightly curly and inclining to golden; his eyebrows met. His ears were of moderate size, and his nose projected a little at the top and then bent slightly inward. His complexion was between dark and fair. He was short of stature (although Julius Marathus, his freedman and keeper of his records, says that he was five feet and nine inches in height), but this was concealed by the fine proportion and symmetry of his figure, and was noticeable only by comparison with some taller person standing beside him.

80

IT is said that his body was covered with spots and that he had birthmarks scattered over his breast and belly, corresponding in form, order and number with the stars of the Bear in the heavens; also numerous callous places resembling ringworm, caused by a constant itching of his body and a vigorous use of the strigil. He was not very strong in his left hip, and leg, and even limped slightly at times; but he strengthened them by treatment with sand and reeds. He sometimes found the forefinger of his right hand so weak, when it was numb and shrunken with the cold, that he could hardly use it for writing even with the aid of a finger-stall of horn. He complained of his bladder too, and was relieved of the pain only after passing stones in his urine.

81

IN the course of his life he suffered from several severe and dangerous illnesses, especially after the subjugation of Cantabria, when he was in such a desperate plight from abscesses of the liver, that he was forced to submit to an unprecedented and hazardous course of treatment. Since hot fomentations gave him no relief, he was led by the advice of his physician Antonius Musa to try cold ones.

He experienced also some disorders which recurred every year at definite times; for he was commonly ailing just before his birthday; and at the beginning of spring he was troubled with an enlargement of the diaphragm, and when the wind was in the south, with catarrh. Hence his constitution was so weakened that he could not readily endure either cold or heat.

82

IN winter he protected himself with four tunics and a heavy toga, besides an undershirt, a woolen chest-protector and wraps for his thighs and shins, while in summer he slept with the doors of his bedroom open, oftentimes in the open court near a fountain, besides having someone to fan him. Yet he could not endure the sun even in winter, and never walked in the open air without wearing a broad-brimmed hat, even at home. He traveled in a litter, usually at night, and by such slow and easy stages that he took two days to go to Praeneste or Tibur; and if he could reach his destination by sea, he preferred to sail. Yet in spite of all he made good his weakness by great care, especially by moderation in bathing; for as a rule he was anointed or took sweat by a fire, after which he was doused with water either lukewarm or tepid from long exposure to the sun. When however he had to use hot salt water and sulphur baths for rheumatism, he contented himself with sitting on a wooden bath seat, which he called by the Spanish name *dureta*, and plunging his hands and feet in the water one after the other.

83

IMMEDIATELY after the civil war he gave up exercise with horses and arms in the Campus Martius, at first turning to pass-ball and balloon-ball, but soon confining himself to riding or taking a walk, ending the latter by running and leaping, wrapped in a mantle or a blanket. To divert his mind he sometimes angled with little boys, searching everywhere for such as were attractive for their pretty faces or their prattle, especially Syrians and Moors; for he abhorred dwarfs, cripples, and everything of that sort, as freaks of nature and of ill omen.

84

FROM early youth he devoted himself eagerly and with utmost diligence to oratory and liberal studies. During the war at Mutina, amid such a press of affairs, he is said to have read, written and declaimed every day. In fact he never afterwards spoke in the senate, or to the people or the soldiers, except in a studied and written address, although he did not lack the gift for speaking offhand without preparation. Moreover, to avoid the danger of forgetting what he was to say, or wasting time in committing it to memory, he adopted the practice of reading everything from a manuscript. Even his conversations with individuals and the more important of those with his own wife Livia, he always wrote out and read from a notebook, for fear of saying too much or too little if he spoke offhand. He had an agreeable and rather characteristic enunciation, and he practiced constantly with a teacher of elocution; but sometimes because of weakness of the throat he addressed the people through a herald.

85

HE wrote numerous works of various kinds in prose, some of which he read to a group of his intimate friends, as others did in a lecture room; for example, his "Reply to Brutus on Cato." At the reading of these volumes he had all but come to the end, when he grew tired and handed them to Tiberius to finish, for he was well on in years. He also wrote "Exhortations to Philosophy" and some volumes of an Autobiography, giving an account of his life in thirteen books up to the time of the Cantabrian war, but no farther. His essays in poetry were but slight. One book has come down to us written in hexameter verse, of which the subject and the title is "Sicily." There is another, equally brief, of "Epigrams," which he composed for the most part at the time of the bath. Though he began a tragedy with much enthusiasm, he destroyed it because his style did not satisfy him, and when some of his friends asked him what in the world had become of Ajax, he answered that "his Ajax had fallen on his sponge."

90

THIS is what we are told of his attitude towards matters of religion. He was somewhat weak in his fear of thunder and lightning, for he always carried a seal-skin about with him everywhere as a protection, and at any sign of a violent storm took refuge in an underground vaulted room; for as I have said, he was once badly frightened by a narrow escape from lightning during a journey by night.

91

HE was not indifferent to his own dreams or to those which others dreamed about him. At the battle of Philippi, though he had made up his mind not to leave his tent because of illness, he did so after all when warned by a friend's dream; fortunately, as it turned out, for his camp was taken and when the enemy rushed in, his litter was stabbed through and through and torn to pieces, in the belief that he was still lying there ill. All through the spring his own dreams were very numerous and fearful, but idle and unfulfilled; during the rest of the year they were less frequent and more reliable. Being in the habit of making constant visits to the temple of Jupiter the Thunderer, which he had founded on the Capitol, he dreamed that Jupiter Capitolinus complained that his worshipers were being taken from him, and that he answered that he had placed the Thunderer hard by to be his doorkeeper; and accordingly he presently festooned the gable of the temple with bells, because these commonly hung at house-doors. It was likewise because of a dream that every year on an appointed day he begged alms of the people, holding out his open hand to have pennies dropped in it.

92

CERTAIN auspices and omens he regarded as infallible. If his shoes were put on in the wrong way in the morning, the left instead of the right, he considered it a bad sign. If there chanced to be a drizzle of rain when he was starting on a long journey by land or sea, he thought it a good omen, betokening a speedy and prosperous return. But he was especially affected by prodigies. When a palm tree sprang up between the crevices of the pavement before his house, he transplanted it to the inner court beside his household gods and took great pains to make it grow. He was so pleased that the branches of an old oak, which had already drooped to the ground and were withering, became vigorous again on his arrival in the island of Capreae, that he arranged with the city of Naples to give him the island in exchange for Aenaria. He also had regard to certain days, refusing ever to begin a journey on the day after a market day, or to take up any important business on the Nones; though in the latter case, as he writes Tiberius, he merely dreaded the unlucky sound of the name.

93

HE treated with great respect such foreign rites as were ancient and well established, but held the rest in contempt. For example, having been initiated in Athens and afterwards sitting in judgment of a case at Rome involving the privileges of the priests of Attic Ceres, in which certain matters of secrecy of bystanders and heard the disputants in private. But on the other hand he not only omitted to make a slight detour to visit Apis, when he was traveling through Egypt, but highly commended his grandson Gaius for not offering prayers at Jerusalem as he passed by Judaea.

94

HAVING reached this point, it will not be out of place to add an account of the omens which occurred before he was born, on the very day of his birth, and afterwards, from which it was possible to anticipate and perceive his future greatness and uninterrupted good fortune.

In ancient days, when a part of the wall of Velitrae had been struck by lightning, the prediction was made that a citizen of that town would one day rule the world. Through their confidence in this the people of Velitrae had at once made war on the Roman people and fought with them many times after that almost to their utter destruction; but at last long afterward the event proved that the omen had foretold the rule of Augustus.

According to Julius Marathus, a few months before Augustus was born a portent was generally observed at Rome, which gave warning that nature was pregnant with a king for the Roman people; thereupon the senate in consternation decreed that no male child born that year should be reared; but those whose wives with child saw to it that the decree was not filed in the treasury, since each one appropriated the prediction to his own family.

I have read the following story in the books of Asclepias of Mendes entitled Theologumena. When Atia had come in the middle of the night to the solemn service of Apollo, she had her litter set down in the temple and fell asleep, while the rest of the matrons also slept. On a sudden a serpent glided up to her and shortly went away. When she awoke, she purified herself, as if after the embraces of her husband, and at once there appeared on her body a mark in colours like a serpent, and she could never get rid of it; so that presently she ceased ever to go to the public baths. In the tenth month after that Augustus was born and was therefore regarded as the son of Apollo. Atia too, before she gave him birth, dreamed that her vitals were borne up to the stars and spread over the whole extent of the land and sea, while Octavius dreamed that the sun rose from Atia's womb.

The day he was born the conspiracy of Catiline was before the House, and Octavius came late because of his wife's confinement; then Publius Nigidius, as everyone knows, learning the reason for his tardiness and being informed also of the hour of the birth, declared that the ruler of the world had been born. Later, when Octavius was leading an army through remote parts of Thrace, and in the grove of Father Liber consulted the priests about his son with barbarian rites, they made the same prediction; since such a pillar of flame sprang forth from the wine that was poured over the altar, that it rose above the temple roof and mounted to the very sky, and such an omen had befallen no one save Alexander the Great, when he offered sacrifice at the same altar. Moreover, the very next night he dreamt that his son appeared to him in a guise more majestic than that of a mortal man, with the thunderbolt, sceptre, and insignia of Jupiter Optimus Maximus, wearing a crown begirt with rays and mounted upon a laurel-wreathed chariot drawn by twelve horses of surpassing whiteness. When Augustus was still an infant, as is recorded by the hand of Gaius Drusus, he was placed by his nurse at evening in his cradle on the ground floor and the next morning had disappeared; but after a long search he was at last found on a lofty tower with his face towards the rising sun.

As soon as he began to talk, it chanced that the frogs were making a great noise at his grandfather's country place; he bade them be silent, and they say that since then no frog has ever croaked there. As he was lunching in a grove at the fourth milestone on the Campanian road, an eagle surprised him by snatching his bread from his hand, after flying to a great height, equally to his surprise dropped gently down again and gave it back to him.

After Quintus Catulus had dedicated the Capitol, he had dreams on two nights in succession: first, that Jupiter Optimus Maximus called aside a number of boys of good family, who were playing around his altar, and put in the fold of his toga an image of Roma, which he was carrying in his hand; the next night he dreamt that he saw this same boy in the lap of Jupiter of the Capitol, and that when he had ordered that he be removed, the god warned him to desist, declaring that the boy was being reared to be the saviour of his country. When Catulus next day met Augustus, whom he had never seen before, he looked at him in great surprise and said that he was very like the boy of whom he had dreamed.

Some give a different account of Catulus's first dream: when a large group of well-born children asked Jupiter for a guardian, he pointed out one of their number, to whom they were to refer all their wishes, and then, after lightly touching the boy's mouth with his fingers, laid them on his own lips.

As Marcus Cicero was attending Gaius Caesar to the Capitol, he happened to tell his friends a dream of the night before; that a boy of noble countenance was let down from heaven on a golden chain and, standing by the door of the temple, was given a whip by Jupiter. Just then suddenly catching sight of Augustus, who was still unknown to the greater number of those present and had been brought to the ceremony by his uncle Caesar, he declared that he was the very one whose form had appeared to him in his dream.

When Augustus was assuming the gown of manhood, his senatorial tunic was ripped apart on both sides and fell at his feet, which some interpreted as a sure sign that the order of which the tunic was the badge would one day be brought to his feet.

As the Deified Julius was cutting down a wood at Munda and preparing a place for his camp, coming across a palm tree, he cause it to be spared as an omen of victory. From this a shoot at once sprang forth and in a few days grew so great that it not only equaled the parent tree, but even overshadowed it; moreover many doves built their nests there, although that kind of bird especially avoids hard and rough foliage. Indeed, it was that omen in particular, they say, that led Caesar to wish that none other than his sister's grandson should be his successor.

While in retirement at Apollonia, Augustus mounted with Agrippa to the studio of the astrologer Theogenes. Agrippa was the first to try his fortune, and when a great and almost incredible career was predicted for him, Augustus persisted in concealing the time of his birth and in refusing to disclose it, through diffidence and fear that he might be found to be less eminent. When he at last gave it unwillingly and hesitatingly, and only after many requests, Theogenes sprang up and threw himself at his feet. From that time on Augustus had such faith in his destiny, that he made his horoscope public and issued a silver coin stamped with the sign of the constellation Capricornus, under which he was born.

95

AS he was entering the city on his return from Apollonia after Caesar's death, though the heaven was clear and cloudless, a circle like a rainbow suddenly formed around the sun's disc, and straightaway the tomb of Caesar's daughter Julia was struck by lightning. Again, as he was taking the auspices in his first consulship, twelve vultures appeared to him, as to Romulus, and when he slew the victims, the livers within all of them were found to be doubled inward at the lower end, which all those who were skilled in such matter unanimously declared to be an omen of a great and happy future.

96

HE even divined beforehand the outcome of all his wars. When the forces of the triumvirs were assembled at Bononia, an eagle that had perched upon his tent made a dash at two ravens, which attacked it on either side, and struck them to the ground. From this the whole army inferred that there would one day be discord among the colleagues, as actually came to pass, and divined its result. As he was on his way to Philippi, a Thessalian gave him notice of his coming victory on the authority of the deified Caesar, whose shade had met him on a lonely road. When he was sacrificing at Perusia without getting a favourable omen, and so had ordered more victims to be brought, the enemy made a sudden sally and carried off all the equipment of the sacrifice; whereupon the soothsayers agreed that all the dangers and disasters with which the sacrificer had been threatened would recoil on the heads of those who were in possession of the entrails; and so it turned out. As he was walking on the shore the day before the sea-fight off Sicily, a fish sprang from the sea and fell at his feet. At Actium, as he was going down to begin the battle, he met an ass with his driver, the man having the name Eutychus and the beast that of Nicon; and after the victory he set up bronze images of the two in the sacred enclosure into which he converted the site of his camp.

97

HIS death, too, of which I shall speak next, and his deification after death, were known in advance by unmistakable signs. As he was bringing the lustrum to an end in the Campus Martius before a great throng of people, an eagle flew several times about him and then going across to the temple hard by, perched above the first letter of Agrippa's name. On noticing this, Augustus bade his colleague recite the vows which it is usual to offer for the next five years for although he had them prepared and written out on a tablet, he declared that he would not be responsible for vows which he should never pay. At about the same time the first letter of his name was melted from the inscription on one of his statues by a flash of lightning; this was interpreted to mean that he would live only a hundred days from that time, the number indicated by the letter C, and that he would be numbered with the gods, since *aesar* (that is, the part of the name Caesar which was left) is the word for god in the Etruscan tongue.

Then, too, when he was on the point of sending Tiberius to Illyricum and was proposing to escort him as far as Beneventum, and litigants detained him on the judgment seat by bringing forward case after case, he cried out that he would stay no longer in Rome, even if everything conspired to delay him--and this too was afterwards looked upon as one of the omens of his death. When he had begun the journey, he went on as far as Astura and from then, contrary to his custom, took ship by night since it chanced that there was a favourable breeze, and thus contracted an illness beginning with diarrhoea.

98

THEN after skirting the coast of Campania and the neighbouring islands, he spent four more days at his villa in Capreae, where he gave himself up wholly to rest and social diversions. As he sailed by the gulf of Puteoli, it happened that an Alexandrian ship which had just arrived there, the passengers and crew, clad in white, crowned with garlands, and burning incense, lavished upon him good wishes and the highest praise, saying that it was through him that they lived, through him that they sailed the seas, and through him that they enjoyed their liberty and their fortunes. Exceedingly pleased at this, he gave forty gold pieces to each of his companions, exacting from every one of them a pledge under oath not to spend the sum that had been given them in any other way than in buying wares from Alexandria. More than that, for the several remaining days of his stay, among little presents of various kinds, he distributed togas and cloaks as well, stipulating that Romans should use the Greek dress and language and the Greeks the Roman. He continually watched the exercises of the ephebi, of whom there was still a goodly number at Capreae according to the ancient usage. He also gave these youths a banquet at which he himself was present, and not only allowed, but even required perfect freedom in jesting and in scrambling for tickets for fruit, dainties and all kinds of things, which he threw to them. In short, there was no form of gaiety in which he did not indulge.

He called the neighbouring part of the island of Capreae Apragopolis from the laziness of some of his company who sojourned there. Beside he used to call one his favourites, Masgaba by name, Ktistes, as if he were the founder of the island. Noticing from his dining-room that the tomb of this Masgaba, who had died the year before, was visited by a large crowd with many torches, he uttered aloud this verse, composed offhand: "I see the founder's tomb alight with fire"; and turning to Thrasyllus, one of the suite of Tiberius who was reclining opposite him and knew nothing about the matter, he asked of what poet he thought it was the work. When Thrasyllus hesitated, he added another verse: "See you with lights Masgaba honoured now?" and asked his opinion of this one also. When Thrasyllus could say nothing except that they were very good, whoever made them, he burst into a laugh and fell a joking above it.

Presently he crossed over to Naples, although his bowels were still weak from intermittent attacks. In spite of this he witnessed a quinquennial gymnastic contest which had been established in his honour, and then started with Tiberius for his destination. But as he was returning his illness increased and he at last took to his bed at Nola, calling back Tiberius, who was on his way to Illyricum, and keeping him for a long time in private conversation, after which he gave attention to no business of importance.

99

ON the last day of his life he asked every now and then whether there was any disturbance without on his account; then calling for a mirror, he had his hair combed and his falling jaws set straight. After that, calling in his friends and asking whether it seemed to them that he had played the comedy of life fitly, he added the tag: "Since well I've played my part, all clap your hands/ And from the stage dismiss me with applause." Then he sent them all off, and while he was asking some newcomers from the city about the daughter of Drusus, who was ill, he suddenly passed away as he was kissing Livia, uttering these last words: "Live mindful of our wedlock, Livia, and farewell," thus blessed with an easy death and such a one as he had always longed for. For almost always on hearing that anyone had died swiftly and painlessly, he prayed that he and his might have a like euthanasia, for that was the term he was wont to use. He gave but one single sign of wandering before he breathed his last, calling out in sudden terror that forty men were carrying him off. And even this was rather a premonition than a delusion, since it was that very number of soldiers of the pretorian guard that carried him forth to lie in state.

100

HE died in the same room as his father Octavius, in the consulship of two Sextuses, Pompeius and Appuleius, on the fourteenth day before the Kalends of September at the ninth hour, just thirty-five days before his seventy-sixth birthday.

His body was carried by the senators of the municipalities and colonies from Nola all the way to Bovillae, in the night time because of the season of the year, being placed by day in the basilica of the town at which they arrived or in its principal temple. At Bovillae the members of the equestrian order met it and bore it to the city, where they placed it in the vestibule of his house.

In their desire to give him a splendid funeral and honour his memory the senators so vied with one another that among many other suggestions some proposed that his cortege pass through the triumphal gate, preceded by a statue of Victory which stands in the House, while a dirge was sung by childred of both sexes belonging to the leading families; others, that one the day of the obsequies golden rings be laid aside and iron ones worn; and some, that his ashes be collected by the priests of the highest colleges. One man proposed that the name of the month of August be transferred to September, because Augustus was born in the latter, but died in the former; another, that all the period from the day of his birth until his demise be called the Augustan Age, and so entered in the Calendar. But though a limit was set to the honours paid him, his eulogy was twice delivered: before the temple of the Deified Julius by Tiberius, and from the old rostra by Drusus, son of Tiberius; and he was carried on the shoulders of senators to the Campus Martius and there cremated. There was even an ex-praetor who took oath that he had seen the form of the Emperor, after he had been reduced to ashes, on its way to heaven. His remains were gathered up by the leading men of the equestrian order, bare-footed and in ungirt tunics, and placed in the Mausoleum. This structure he had built in his sixth consulship between the Via Flaminia and the bank of the Tiber, and at the same time opened to the public the groves and walks by which it was surrounded.

101

HE had made a will in the consulship of Lucius Plancus and Gaius Silius on the third day before the Nones of April, a year and four months before he died, in two note-books, written in part in his own hand and in part that of his freedmen Polybius and Hilarion. These the Vestal virgins, with whom they had been deposited, now produced, together with three rolls, which were sealed in the same way. All these were opened and read in the senate. He appointed as his chief heirs Tiberius, to receive two-thirds of the estate, and Livia, one-third; these he also bade assume his name. His heirs in the second degree were Drusus, son of Tiberius, for one-third, and for the rest Germanicus and his three male children. In the third grade he mentioned many of his relatives and friends. He left to the Roman people forty million sesterces; to the tribes three million five hundred thousand; to the soldiers of the pretorian guard a thousand each; to the city cohorts five hundred; and to the legionaries three hundred. This sum he ordered to be paid at once, for he had always kept the amount at hand and ready for the purpose. He gave other legacies to various individuals, some amounting to as much as twenty thousand sesterces, and provided for the payment of these a year later, giving as his excuse for the delay the small amount of his property, and declaring that not more than a hundred and fifty millions would come to his heirs; for though he had received fourteen hundred millions during the last twenty years from the wills of his friends, he said that he had spent nearly all of it, as well as the estates left him by his natural and his adoptive father, for the benefit of the State. He gave orders that his daughter and his granddaughter Julia should not be put in his Mausoleum, if anything befell them. In one of the three rolls he included directions for his funeral; in the second, an account of what he had accomplished, which he desired to have cut upon bronze tablets and set up at the entrance to the Mausoleum; in the third, a summary of the condition of the whole empire; how many soldiers there were in active service in all parts of it, how much money there was in the public treasury and in the privy-purse, and what revenues were in arrears. He added, besides, the names of the freedmen and slaves from whom the details could be demanded.

Correspondence of Pliny and Trajan

Pliny the Younger to the Emperor Trajan

IT is my practice, my lord, to refer to you all matters concerning which I am in doubt. For who can better give guidance to my hesitation or inform my ignorance? I have never participated in trials of Christians. I therefore do not know what offenses it is the practice to punish or investigate, and to what extent. And I have been not a little hesitant as to whether there should be any distinction on account of age or no difference between the very young and the more mature; whether pardon is to be granted for repentance, or, if a man has once been a Christian, it does him no good to have ceased to be one; whether the name itself, even without offenses, or only the offenses associated with the name are to be punished.

Meanwhile, in the case of those who were denounced to me as Christians, I have observed the following procedure: I interrogated these as to whether they were Christians; those who confessed I interrogated a second and a third time, threatening them with punishment; those who persisted I ordered executed. For I had no doubt that, whatever the nature of their creed, stubbornness and inflexible obstinacy surely deserve to be punished. There were others possessed of the same folly; but because they were Roman citizens, I signed an order for them to be transferred to Rome.

Soon accusations spread, as usually happens, because of the

proceedings going on, and several incidents occurred. An anonymous document was published containing the names of many persons. Those who denied that they were or had been Christians, when they invoked the gods in words dictated by me, offered prayer with incense and wine to your image, which I had ordered to be brought for this purpose together with statues of the gods, and moreover cursed Christ—none of which those who are really Christians, it is said, can be forced to do—these I thought should be discharged. Others named by the informer declared that they were Christians, but then denied it, asserting that they had been but had ceased to be, some three years before, others many years, some as much as twenty-five years. They all worshiped your image and the statues of the gods, and cursed Christ.

They asserted, however, that the sum and substance of their fault or error had been that they were accustomed to meet on a fixed day before dawn and sing responsively a hymn to Christ as to a god, and to bind themselves by oath, not to some crime, but not to commit fraud, theft, or adultery, not falsify their trust, nor to refuse to return a trust when called upon to do so. When this was over, it was their custom to depart and to assemble again to partake of food—but ordinary and innocent food. Even this, they affirmed, they had ceased to do after my edict by which, in accordance with your instructions, I had forbidden political associations. Accordingly, I judged it all the more necessary to find out what the truth was by torturing two female slaves who were called deaconesses. But I discovered nothing else but depraved, excessive superstition.

I therefore postponed the investigation and hastened to consult you. For the matter seemed to me to warrant consulting you, especially because of the number involved. For many persons of every age, every rank, and also of both sexes are and will be endangered. For the contagion of this superstition has spread not only to the cities but also to the villages and farms. But it seems possible to check and cure it. It is certainly quite clear that the temples, which had been almost deserted, have begun to be frequented, that the established religious rites, long neglected, are being resumed, and that from everywhere sacrificial animals are coming, for which until now very few purchasers could be found. Hence it is easy to imagine what a multitude of people can be reformed if an opportunity for repentance is afforded.

Trajan to Pliny the Younger

YOU observed proper procedure, my dear Pliny, in sifting the cases of those who had been denounced to you as Christians. For it is not possible to lay down any general rule to serve as a kind of fixed standard. They are not to be sought out; if they are denounced and proved guilty, they are to be punished, with this reservation, that whoever denies that he is a Christian and really proves it—that is, by worshiping our gods—even though he was under suspicion in the past, shall obtain pardon through repentance. But anonymously posted accusations ought to have no place in any prosecution. For this is both a dangerous kind of precedent and out of keeping with the spirit of our age.

QUINTILIAN

Institutes of Oratory

Quintilian

Book I: Chapter I

1

LET a father, then, as soon as his son is born, conceive first of all the best possible hopes of him, for he will thus grow the more solicitous about his improvement from the very beginning. It is a complaint without foundation that "to very few people is granted the faculty of comprehending what is imparted to them, and that most, through dullness of understanding, lose their labor and their time." On the contrary, you will find the greater number of men both ready in conceiving and quick in learning, since such quickness is natural to man. As birds are born to fly, horses to run, and wild beasts to show fierceness, so to us peculiarly belong activity and sagacity of understanding; hence the origin of the mind is thought to be from heaven.

2

BUT dull and unteachable persons are no more produced in the course of nature than are persons marked by monstrosity and deformities, such are certainly but few. It will be a proof of this assertion that among boys, good promise is shown in the far greater number; and if it passes off in the progress of time, it is manifest that it was not natural ability, but care, that was wanting.

3

BUT one surpasses another, you will say, in ability. I grant that this is true, but only so far as to accomplish more or less; there is no one who has not gained something by study. Let him who is convinced of this truth, bestow, as soon as he becomes a parent, the most vigilant possible care on cherishing the hopes of a future orator.

4

BEFORE all things, let the talk of the child's nurses not be ungrammatical. Chrysippus wished them, if possible, to be women of some knowledge; at any rate he would have the best chosen, as far as circumstances would allow. To their morals, doubtless, attention is first to be paid, but let them also speak with propriety.

5

IT is they that the child will hear first; it is their words that he will try to form by imitation. We are by nature most tenacious of what we have imbibed in our infant years, as the flavor with which you scent vessels when new remains in them, nor can the colors of wool, for which its plain whiteness has been exchanged, be effaced. Those very habits, which are of a more objectionable nature, adhere with the greater tenacity, for good ones are easily changed for the worse, but when will you change bad ones into good? Let the child not be accustomed, therefore, even while he is yet an infant, to phraseology which must be unlearned.

6

IN parents I should wish that there should be as much learning as possible. Nor do I speak, indeed, merely of fathers, for we have heard that Cornelia, the mother of the Gracchi (whose very learned writing in her letters has come down to posterity), contributed greatly to their eloquence; the daughter of Laelius is said to have exhibited her father's elegance in her conversation; and the oration of the daughter of Quintus Hortensius, delivered before the Triumviri, is read not merely as an honor to her sex.

7

NOR let those parents, who have not had the fortune to get learning themselves, bestow the less care on the instruction of their children, but let them, on this very account, be more solicitous as to other particulars.

Of the boys, among whom he who is destined to this prospect is to be educated, the same may be said as concerning nurses.

8

OF *paedagogi* this further may be said, that they should either be men of acknowledged learning, which I should wish to be the first object, or that they should be conscious of their want of learning; for none are more pernicious than those who, having gone some little beyond the first elements, clothe themselves in a mistaken persuasion of their own knowledge. Since they disdain to yield to those who are skilled in teaching and, growing imperious, and sometimes fierce, in a certain right, as it were, of exercising their authority (with which that sort of men are generally puffed up), they teach only their own folly.

9

NOR is their misconduct less prejudicial to the manners of their pupils; for Leonides, the tutor of Alexander, as is related by Diogenes of Babylon, tinctured him with certain bad habits, which adhered to him, from his childish education, even when he was grown up and become the greatest of kings.

10

IF I seem to my reader to require a great deal, let him consider that it is an orator that is to be educated, an arduous task even when nothing is deficient for the formation of his character; and that more and more difficult labours yet remain. There is need of constant study, the most excellent teachers, and a variety of mental exercises.

11

THE best of rules, therefore, are to be laid down, and if any one shall refuse to observe them, the fault will lie not in the method, but in the man.

If, however, it should not be the good fortune of children to have such nurses as I should wish, let them at least have one attentive *paedagogus*, not unskilled in language, who, if anything is spoken incorrectly by the nurse in the presence of his pupil, may at once correct it and not let it settle in his mind. But let it be understood that what I prescribed at first is the right course, and this only a remedy.

12

I PREFER that a boy should begin with the Greek language, because he will acquire the Latin in general use, even though we tried to prevent him, and because, at the same time, he ought first to be instructed in Greek learning, from which ours is derived.

13

YET I should not wish this rule to be so superstitiously observed that he should for a long time speak or learn only Greek, as is the custom with most people; for hence arise many faults of pronunciation, which is viciously adapted to foreign sounds, and also of language, in which when Greek idioms have become inherent by constant usage, they keep their place most pertinaciously even when we speak a different tongue.

14

THE study of Latin ought, therefore, to follow at no long interval, and soon after to keep pace with the Greek; thus it will happen that when we have begun to attend to both tongues with equal care, neither will impede the other.

15

SOME have thought that boys, as long as they are under seven years of age, should not be set to learn, because that is the earliest age that can understand what is taught, and endure the labor of learning. Of which opinion a great many writers say that Hesiod was, at least such writers as lived before Aristophanes the grammarian, for he was the first to deny that the *Hypothecae*, in which this opinion is found, was the work of that poet.

16

BUT other writers likewise, among whom is Erastothenes, have given the same advice. Those, however, advise better, who, like Chrysippus, think that no part of a child's life should be exempt from tuition; for Chrysippus, though he has allowed three years to the nurses, is of opinion that the minds of children may be imbued with excellent instruction even by them.

17

AND why should not that age, which is now confessedly subject to moral influence, be under the influence of learning? I am not indeed ignorant that during the whole time of which I am speaking, scarcely as much can be done as one year may afterwards accomplish. Yet those who are of the opinion which I have mentioned appear, with regard to this part of life, to have spared not so much the learners as the teachers.

18

WHAT else, after they are able to speak, will children do better, for they must do something? Or why should we despise the gain, how little so ever it be, previous to the age of seven years? For certainly, small as may be the proficiency which an earlier age exhibits, the child will yet learn something greater during the very year in which he would have been learning something less.

19

THIS advancement, extended through each year, is a profit on the whole, and whatever is gained in infancy is an acquisition to youth. The same rule should be prescribed as to the following years, so that what every boy has to learn, he may not be too late in beginning to learn. Let us not then lose even the earliest period of life, and so much the less, as the elements of learning depend on the memory alone, which not only exists in children, but is at that time of life even most tenacious.

20

YET I am not so unacquainted with differences of age as to think that we should urge those of tender years severely or exact a full complement of work from them. For it will be necessary, above all things, to take care lest the child should conceive a dislike to the application which he cannot yet love, and continue to dread the bitterness which he has once tasted, even beyond the years of infancy. Let his instruction be an amusement to him; let him be questioned and praised; let him never feel pleased that he does not know a thing; and sometimes, if he is unwilling to learn, let another be taught before him, of whom he may be envious. Let him strive for victory now and then, and generally suppose that he gains it; and let his powers be called forth by rewards such as that age prizes.

21

WE are giving small instructions, while professing to educate an orator. But even studies have their infancy, and as the rearing of the very strongest bodies commenced with milk and the cradle, so he, who was to be the most eloquent of men, once uttered cries, tried to speak at first with a stuttering voice, and hesitated at the shapes of the letters. Nor, if it is impossible to learn a thing completely, is it therefore unnecessary to learn it at all.

22

IF no one blames a father who thinks that these matters are not to be neglected in regard to his son, why should he be blamed who communicates to the public what he would practice to advantage in his own house? And this is so much more the case, as younger minds more easily take in small things. And as bodies cannot be formed to certain flexures of the limbs unless while they are tender, so even strength itself makes our minds likewise more unyielding to most things.

23

WOULD Philip, king of Macedonia, have wished the first principles of learning to be communicated to his son Alexander by Aristotle, the greatest philosopher of that age, or would Aristotle have undertaken that office if they had not both thought that the first rudiments of instruction are best treated by the most accomplished teacher and have an influence on the whole course?

24

LET us suppose, then, that Alexander were committed to me, and laid in my lap, an infant worthy of so much solicitude (though every man thinks his own son worthy of similar solicitude), should I be ashamed, even in teaching him his very letters, to point out some compendious methods of instruction?

For that which I see practiced in regard to most children by no means pleases me, namely, that they learn the names and order of the letters before they learn their shapes.

25

THIS method hinders their recognition of them, as, while they follow their memory that takes the lead, they do not fix their attention on the forms of the letters. This is the reason why teachers, even when they appear to have fixed them sufficiently in the minds of children, in the straight order in which they are usually first written, make them go over them again the contrary way, and confuse them by variously changing the arrangement, until their pupils know them by their shape, not by their place. It will be best for children therefore, to be taught the appearances and names of the letters at once, as they are taught those of men.

26

BUT that which is hurtful with regard to letters, will be no impediment with regard to syllables. I do not disapprove, however, the practice, which is well known, of giving children, for the sake of stimulating them to learn, ivory figures of letters to play with, or whatever else can be invented, in which that infantile age may take delight, and which may be pleasing to handle, look at, or name.

27

BUT as soon as the child shall have begun to trace the forms of the letters, it will not be improper that they should be cut for him, as exactly as possible, on a board, that his stylus may be guided along them as along grooves, for he will then make no mistakes, as on wax (since he will be kept in by the edge on each side, and will be unable to stray beyond the boundary). By following these sure traces rapidly and frequently, he will form his hand and not require the assistance of a person to guide his hand with his own hand placed over it.

28

THE accomplishment of writing well and expeditiously, which is commonly disregarded by people of quality, is by no means an indifferent matter. Writing itself is the principal thing in our studies, and by it alone sure proficiency, resting on the deepest roots, is secured. A too slow way of writing retards thought, and a rude and confused hand cannot be read; and hence follows another task, that of reading off what is to be copied from the writing.

29

AT all times, therefore, and in all places, and especially in writing private and familiar letters, it will be a source of pleasure to us not to have neglected even this acquirement.

30

FOR learning syllables there is no short way. They must all be learned throughout, nor are the most difficult of them, as is the general practice, to be postponed, that children may be at a loss, forsooth, in writing words.

31

MOREOVER, we must not even trust to the first learning by heart; it will be better to have syllables repeated and to impress them long upon the memory; and in reading too, not to hurry on, in order to make it continuous or quick, until the clear and certain connection of the letters become familiar, without at least any necessity to stop for recollection. Let the pupil then begin to form words from syllables and to join phrases together from words.

32

IT is incredible how much retardation is caused to reading by haste; for hence arise hesitation, interruption, and repetition, as children attempt more than they can manage; and then, after making mistakes, they become distrustful even of what they know.

33

LET reading, therefore, be at first sure, then continuous, and for a long time slow, until, by exercise, a correct quickness is gained.

34

FOR to look to the right, as everybody teaches, and to look forward, depends not merely on rule, but on habit, since, while the child is looking to what follows, he has to pronounce what goes before, and, what is very difficult, the direction of his thoughts must be divided, so that one duty may be discharged with his voice, and another with his eyes.

When the child shall have begun, as is the practice, to write words, it will cause no regret if we take care that he may not waste his efforts on common words, and such was perpetually occur.

35

FOR he may readily learn the explanations of obscure terms, which the Greeks call γλώσσαι (*glosses*), while some other occupation is before him, and acquire, amidst his first rudiments, a knowledge of that which would afterwards demand a special time for it. Since, too, we are still attending to small matters, I would express a wish that even the lines that are set him for his imitation in writing should not contain useless sentences, but such as convey some moral instruction.

36

THE remembrance of such admonitions will attend him to old age and will be of use even for the formation of his character. It is possible for him, also, to learn the sayings of eminent men, and select passages, chiefly from the poets (for the reading of poets is more pleasing to the young), in his play-time. Memory (as I shall show in its proper place) is most necessary to an orator and is eminently strengthened and nourished by exercise; and, at the age of which we are now speaking, and which cannot, as yet, produce anything of itself, it is almost the only faculty that can be improved by the aid of teachers.

37

IT will not be improper, however, to require of boys of this age (in order that their pronunciation may be fuller and their speech more distinct) to roll forth, as rapidly as possible, certain words and lines of studied difficulty, composed of several syllables, and those roughly clashing together, and, as it were, rugged-sounding; the Greeks call them χαλινοί (*chalinoi*). This may seem a trifling matter to mention, but when it is neglected, many faults of pronunciation, unless they are removed in the years of youth, are fixed by incorrigible ill habit for the rest of life.

Chapter II

1

BUT let us suppose that the child now gradually increases in size, leaves the lap, and applies himself to learning in earnest. In this place, accordingly, must be considered the question whether it is more advantageous to confine the learner at home and within the walls of a private house, or to commit him to the large numbers of a school and, as it were, to public teachers.

2

THE latter mode, I observe, has had the sanction of those by whom the polity of the most eminent states was settled, as well as that of the most illustrious authors.

Yet it is not to be concealed that there are some, who from certain notions of their own, disapprove of this almost public mode of instruction. These persons appear to be swayed chiefly by two reasons: one, that they take better precautions for the morals of the young by avoiding a concourse of human beings of that age which is most prone to vice (from which cause I wish it were falsely asserted that provocations to immoral conduct arise); the other, that whoever may be the teacher, he is likely to bestow his time more liberally on one pupil than if he has to divide it among several.

3

THE first reason indeed deserves great consideration, for if it were certain that schools, though advantageous to studies, are pernicious to morals, a virtuous course of life would seem to me preferable to one even of the most distinguished eloquence. But in my opinion, the two are combined and inseparable; I am convinced that no one can be an orator who is not a good man, and even if anyone could, I should be unwilling that he should be. On this point, therefore, I shall speak first.

4

PEOPLE think that morals are corrupted in schools; indeed they are at times corrupted, but such may be the case even at home. Many proofs of this fact may be adduced; proofs of character having been vitiated, as well as preserved, with the utmost purity under both modes of education. It is the disposition of the individual pupil, and the care taken of him, that make the whole difference. Suppose that his mind be prone to vice, suppose that there be neglect in forming and guarding his morals in early youth. Seclusion would afford no less opportunity for immorality than publicity, for the private tutor may be himself of bad character, nor is intercourse with vicious slaves at all safer than that with immodest free-born youths.

5

BUT if his disposition is good, and if there is not a blind and indolent negligence on the part of his parents, it will be possible for them to select a tutor of irreproachable character (a matter to which the utmost attention is paid by sensible parents) and to fix on a course of instruction of the very strictest kind. They may at the same time place at the elbow of their son some influential friend or faithful freedman whose constant attendance may improve even those of whom apprehensions may be entertained.

6

THE remedy for this object of fear is easy. Would that we ourselves did not corrupt the morals of our children! We enervate their very infancy with luxuries. That delicacy of education which we call fondness weakens all the powers, both of body and mind. What luxury will he not covet in his manhood who crawls about on purple! He can not yet articulate his first words, but he already distinguishes scarlet and wants his purple.

7

WE form the palate of children before we form their pronunciation. They grow up in sedan chairs; if they touch the ground, they hang by the hands of attendants supporting them on each side. We are delighted if they utter anything immodest. We hear from them with a smile and a kiss expressions which would not be tolerated even from the effeminate youths of Alexandria. Nor is this wonderful. We have taught them; they have heard such language from ourselves.

8

THEY see our mistresses, our male objects of affection; every dining room rings with impure songs; things shameful to be told are objects of sight. From such practices springs habit, and afterwards nature. The unfortunate children learn these vices before they know that they are vices. Hence, rendered effeminate and luxurious, they do not imbibe immorality from schools, but carry it themselves into schools.

9

BUT, it is said, one tutor will have more time for one pupil. First of all, however, nothing prevents that one pupil, whoever he may be, from being the same with him who is taught in the school. But if the two objects cannot be united, I should still prefer the daylight of an honorable seminary to darkness and solitude, for every eminent teacher delights in a large concourse of pupils and thinks himself worthy of a still more numerous auditory.

10

BUT inferior teachers, from a consciousness of their inability, do not disdain to fasten on single pupils and to discharge the duty, as it were, of *paedagogi*.

11

BUT supposing that either interest, or friendship, or money, should secure to any parent a domestic tutor of the highest learning, and in every respect unrivaled, will he, however, spend the whole day on one pupil? Or can the application of any pupil be so constant as not to be sometimes wearied, like the sight of the eyes, by continued direction to one object, especially as study requires the far greater portion of time to be solitary.

12

FOR the tutor does not stand by the pupil while he is writing, or learning by heart, or thinking; and when he is engaged in any of those exercises, the company of any person whatsoever is a hindrance to him. Nor does every kind of reading require at all times a praelector or interpreter, for if such were the case, when would the knowledge of so many authors be gained? Therefore, the time during which the work, as it were, may be laid out for the whole day is but short.

13

THUS the instructions which are to be given to each may reach to many. Most of them, indeed, are of such a nature that they may be communicated to all at once with the same exertion of the voice. I say nothing of the topics and declamations of rhetoricians, at which, certainly, whatever be the number of the audience, each will still carry off the whole.

14

FOR the voice of the teacher is not like a meal, which will not suffice for more than a certain number, but like the sun, which diffuses the same portion of light and heat to all. If a grammarian, too, discourses on the art of speaking, solves questions, explains matters of history, or illustrates poems, as many as shall hear him will profit by his instructions.

15

BUT, it may be said, number is an obstacle to correction and explanation. Suppose that this is a disadvantage in a number (for what in general satisfies us in every respect?); we will soon compare that disadvantage with other advantages.

Yet I would not wish a boy to be sent to a place where he will be neglected. Nor should a good master encumber himself with a greater number of scholars than he can manage. It is to be a chief object with us, also, that the master may be in every way our kind friend and may have regard in his teaching, not so much to duty, as to affection. Thus we shall never be confounded with the multitude.

16

NOR will any master, who is in the slightest degree tinctured with literature, fail particularly to cherish that pupil in whom he shall observe application and genius, even for his own honor. But even if great schools ought to be avoided (a position to which I cannot assent, if numbers flock to a master on account of his merit), the rule is not to be carried so far that schools should be avoided altogether. It is one thing to shun schools, and another to choose from them.

17

IF I have now refuted the objections which are made to schools, let me next state what opinions I myself entertain.

18

FIRST of all, let him who is to be an orator and who must live amidst the greatest publicity and in the full daylight of public affairs, accustom himself, from his boyhood, not to be abashed at the sight of men, nor pine in a solitary and, as it were, recluse way of life. The mind requires to be constantly excited and roused, while in such retirement it either languishes and contracts rust, as it were, in the shade, or, on the other hand, becomes swollen with empty conceit, since he who compares himself to no one else will necessarily attribute too much to his own powers.

19

BESIDES, when his acquirements are to be displayed in public, he is blinded at the light of the sun and stumbles at every new object, as having learned in solitude that which is to be done in public.

20

I SAY nothing of friendships formed at school, which remain in full force even to old age, as if cemented with a certain religious obligation, for to have been initiated in the same studies is a not less sacred bond than to have been initiated in the same sacred rites. That sense, too, which is called common sense, where shall a young man learn when he has separated himself from society, which is natural not to men only, but even to dumb animals?

21

ADD to this, that at home, he can learn only what is taught himself; at school, even what is taught others.

22

HE will daily hear many things commended, many things corrected. The idleness of a fellow student, when reproved, will be a warning to him; the industry of anyone, when commended, will be a stimulus. Emulation will be excited by praise, and he will think it a disgrace to yield to his equals in age and an honor to surpass his seniors. All these matters excite the mind, and though ambition itself is a vice, it is often the parent of virtues.

23

I REMEMBER a practice that was observed by my masters, not without advantage. Having divided the boys into classes, they assigned them their order in speaking in conformity to the abilities of each, and thus each stood in the higher place to declaim according as he appeared to excel in proficiency.

24

JUDGMENTS were pronounced on the performances, and great was the strife among us for distinction, but to take the lead of the class was by far the greatest honor. Nor was sentence given on our merits only once; the 30th day brought the vanquished an opportunity of contending again. Thus, he who was most successful did not relax his efforts, while uneasiness incited the unsuccessful to retrieve his honor.

25

I SHOULD be inclined to maintain, as far as I can form a judgment from what I conceive in my own mind, that this method furnished stronger incitements to the study of eloquence than the exhortations of preceptors, the watchfulness of *paedagogi*, or the wishes of parents.

26

BUT as emulation is of use to those who have made some advancement in learning, so, to those who are but beginning and are still of tender age, to imitate their schoolfellows is more pleasant than to imitate their master, for the very reason that it is easier. They who are learning the first rudiments will scarcely dare to exalt themselves to the hope of attaining that eloquence which they regard as the highest; they will rather fix on what is nearest to them, as vines attached to trees gain the top by taking hold of the lower branches first.

27

THIS is an observation of such truth that it is the care even of the master himself, when he has to instruct minds that are still unformed, not (if he prefer at least the useful to the showy) to overburden the weakness of his scholars, but to moderate his strength and to let himself down to the capacity of the learner.

28

FOR as narrow-necked vessels reject a great quantity of the liquid that is poured upon them, but are filled by that which flows or is poured into them by degrees, so it is for us to ascertain how much the minds of boys can receive, since what is too much for their grasp of intellect will not enter their minds, as not being sufficiently expanded to admit it.

29

IT is of advantage, therefore, for a boy to have schoolfellows whom he may first imitate and afterwards try to surpass. Thus will he gradually conceive hope of higher excellence.

To these observations I shall add that masters themselves, when they have but one pupil at a time with them, cannot feel the same degree of energy and spirit in addressing him as when they are excited by a large number of hearers.

30

ELOQUENCE depends in a great degree on the state of the mind, which must conceive images of objects and transform itself, so to speak, to the nature of the things of which we discourse. Besides, the more noble and lofty a mind is, by the more powerful springs, as it were, is it moved. Accordingly, it is both strengthened by praise and enlarged by effort, and filled with joy at achieving something great.

31

BUT a certain secret disdain is felt at lowering the power of eloquence, acquired by so much labor, to one auditor, and the teacher is ashamed to raise his style above the level of ordinary conversation. Let anyone imagine, indeed, the air of a man haranguing, or the voice of one entreating, the gesture, the pronunciation, the agitation of mind and body, the exertion, and, to mention nothing else, the fatigue, while he has but one auditor. Would not he seem to be affected with something like madness? There would be no eloquence in the world if we were to speak only with one person at a time.

Chapter III

1

LET him that is skilled in teaching ascertain first of all, when a boy is entrusted to him, his ability and disposition. The chief symptom of ability in children is memory, the excellence of which is twofold: to receive with ease and retain with fidelity. The next symptom is imitation, for that is an indication of a teachable disposition, but with this provision: that it express merely what it is taught, and not a person's manner or walk, for instance, or whatever may be remarkable for deformity.

2

THE boy who shall make it his aim to raise a laugh by his love of mimicry, will afford me no hope of good capacity. For he who is possessed of great talent will be well disposed, else I should think it not at all worse to be of a dull, than of a bad, disposition. But he who is honorably inclined will be very different from the stupid or idle.

3

SUCH a pupil as I would have will easily learn what is taught him and will ask questions about some things, but will still rather follow than run on before. That precocious sort of talent scarcely ever comes to good fruit.

4

SUCH are those who do little things easily and, impelled by impudence, show at once all that they can accomplish in such matters. But they succeed only in what is ready to their hand; they string words together, uttering them with an intrepid countenance, not in the least discouraged by bashfulness, and do little, but do it readily.

5

THERE is no real power behind, or any that rests on deeply fixed roots, but they are like seeds which have been scattered on the surface of the ground and shoot up prematurely, like grass that resembles corn and grows yellow, with empty ears, before the time of harvest. Their efforts give pleasure, as compared with their years, but their progress comes to a stand, and our wonder diminishes.

6

WHEN a tutor has observed these indications, let him next consider how the mind of his pupil is to be managed. Some boys are indolent unless you stimulate them; some are indignant at being commanded; fear restrains some and unnerves others; continued labor forms some; with others, hasty efforts succeed better.

7

LET the boy be given to me whom praise stimulates, whom honor delights, who weeps when he is unsuccessful. His powers must be cultivated under the influence of ambition; reproach will sting him to the quick; honor will incite him; and in such a boy I shall never be apprehensive of indifference.

8

YET some relaxation is to be allowed to all; not only because there is nothing that can bear perpetual labor (and even those things that are without sense and life are unbent by alternate rest, as it were, in order that they may preserve their vigor), but because application to learning depends on the will, which cannot be forced.

9

BOYS, accordingly, when reinvigorated and refreshed, bring more sprightliness to their learning and a more determined spirit, which for the most part spurns compulsion.

10

NOR will play in boys displease me; it is also a sign of vivacity, and I cannot expect that he who is always dull and spiritless will be of an eager disposition in his studies, when he is indifferent even to that excitement which is natural to his age.

11

THERE must, however, be bounds set to relaxation, lest the refusal of it beget an aversion to study, or too much indulgence in it a habit of idleness. There are some kinds of amusement, too, not unserviceable for sharpening the wits of boys, as when they contend with each other by proposing all sorts of questions in turn.

12

IN their plays, also, their moral dispositions show themselves more plainly, supposing that there is no age so tender that it may not readily learn what is right and wrong. The tender age may best be formed at a time when it is ignorant of dissimulation and most willingly submits to instructors, for you may break, sooner than mend, that which has hardened into deformity.

13

THEREFORE, a child is to be admonished, as early as possible, that he must do nothing too eagerly, nothing dishonestly, nothing without self-control, and we must always keep in mind the maxim of Virgil, *Adeo in teneris consuescere multum est*, "of so much importance is the acquirement of habit in the young."

14

BUT that boys should suffer corporal punishment, though it be a received custom, and Chrysippus makes no objection to it, I by no means approve; first, because it is a disgrace and a punishment for slaves, and in reality (as will be evident if you imagine the age changed) an affront; secondly, because, if a boy's disposition be so abject as not to be amended by reproof, he will be hardened, like the worst of slaves, even to stripes; and lastly, because, if one who regularly exacts his tasks be with him, there will not be the least need of any such chastisement.

15

AT present, the negligence of *paedagogi* seems to be made amends for in such a way that boys are not obliged to do what is right, but are punished whenever they have not done it. Besides, after you have coerced a boy with stripes, how will you treat him when he becomes a young man, to whom such terror cannot be held out, and by whom more difficult studies must be pursued?

16

ADD to these considerations that many things unpleasant to be mentioned, and likely afterwards to cause shame, often happen to boys while being whipped, under the influence of pain or fear. Such shame enervates and depresses the mind, and makes them shun people's sight and feel a constant uneasiness.

17

IF, moreover, there has been too little care in choosing governors and tutors of reputable character, I am ashamed to say how scandalously unworthy men may abuse their privilege of punishing, and what opportunity also the terror of the unhappy children may sometimes accord to others. I will not dwell upon this point; what is already understood is more than enough. It will be sufficient, therefore, to intimate that no man should be allowed too much authority over an age so weak and so unable to resist ill treatment.

18

I WILL now proceed to show in what studies he who is to be so trained that he may become an orator must be instructed, and which of them must be commenced at each particular period of youth.

Chapter V

1

SINCE all language has three kinds of excellence, to be correct, perspicuous, and elegant (for to speak with propriety, which is its highest quality, most writers include under elegance), and the same number of faults, which are the opposites of the excellences just mentioned, let the grammarian consider well the rules for correctness which constitute the first part of grammar.

2

THESE rules are required to be observed, *verbis aut singulis aut pluribus*, in regard to one or more words. The word *verbum* I wish to be here understood in a general sense, for it has two significations: the one, which includes all words of which language is composed, as in the verse of Horace,

Verbaque provisam rem non invita sequentur,

"And words, not unwilling, will follow provided matter"; the other, under which is comprehended only one part of speech, as *lego, scribo*. To avoid this ambiguity, some have preferred the terms *voces, dictiones, locutiones*.

3

WORDS, considered singly, are either our own, or foreign, simple or compound, proper or metaphorical, in common use or newly invented.

A word taken singly is more often objectionable than faultless, for however we may express anything with propriety, elegance, and sublimity, none of these qualities arise from anything but the connection and order of the discourse, since we commend single words merely as being well suited to the matter.

4

THE only good quality which can be remarked in them is their *vocalitas*, so to speak, called εὐφωνία (*euphony*). This depends upon selection, when, of two words which have the same signification and are of equal force, we make choice of the one that has the better sound.

5

FIRST of all, let the offensiveness of barbarisms and solecisms be put away. But as these faults are sometimes excused, either from custom, or authority, or perhaps from their nearness to beauties (for it is often difficult to distinguish faults from figures of speech), let the grammarian, that so uncertain a subject of observation may deceive no one, give his earnest attention to that nice discrimination of which we shall speak more fully in the part where we shall have to treat of figures of speech.

6

MEANWHILE, let an offense committed in regard to a single word be called a barbarism.

But some one may stop me with the remark, what is there here worthy of the promise of so great a work? Or who does not know that barbarisms are committed, some in writing, others in speaking? (Because what is written incorrectly must also be spoken incorrectly, though he who speaks incorrectly may not necessarily make mistakes in writing). The first sort is caused by addition, curtailment, substitution, or transposition; the second by separation or confusion of syllables, aspiration, or other faults of sound.

7

BUT though these may be small matters, boys are still to be taught, and we put grammarians in mind of their duty. If any one of them, however, shall not be sufficiently accomplished, but shall have just entered the vestibule of the art, he will have to confine himself within those rules which are published in the little manuals of professors. The more learned will add many other instructions, the very first of which will be this, that we understand barbarisms as being of several kinds.

8

ONE, with reference to country, such as is committed when a person inserts an African or Spanish term in Latin composition, as when the iron ring with which wheels are bound is called *canthus*, though Persius uses this as a received word; as when Catullus got the word *ploxenum*, "a box," on the banks of the Po; and in the speech of Labienus (if it be not rather the speech of Cornelius Gallus), the word *casnar*, "a parasite," is brought from Gaul against Pollio; as to *mastruca*, "a shaggy garment," which is a Sardinian word, Cicero has used it purposely in jest.

9

ANOTHER kind of barbarism is that which we regard as proceeding from the natural disposition, when he, by whom anything has been uttered insolently or threateningly or cruelly, is said to have spoken like a barbarian.

10

THE third kind of barbarism is that of which examples are everywhere abundant and which every one can form for himself, by adding a letter or syllable to any word he pleases, or taking one away, or substituting one for another, or putting one in a place where it is not right for it to be.

11

BUT some grammarians, to make a show of learning, are accustomed, for the most part, to take examples of these from the poets and find fault with the authors whom they interpret. A boy ought to know, however, that such forms of speech, in writers of poetry, are considered as deserving of excuse or even of praise, and learners must be taught less common instances.

12

THUS Tinca of Placentia (if we believe Hortensius, who finds fault with him) was guilty of two barbarisms in one word, saying *precula* instead of *pergula*; first, by the change of a letter, putting *c* for *g*, and secondly, by transposition, placing *r* before the preceding *e*. But Ennius, when committing a like double fault, by saying *Metoeo Fufetioeo*, is defended on the ground of poetic license.

13

IN prose, too, there are certain received changes, for Cicero speaks of an army of Canopitae, though the people of the city call it Canobus; and many writers have authorized Trasumennus for Tarsumennus, although there is a transposition in it. Other words suffer similar treatment; for if *assentior*, "I assent," be thought the proper way of spelling that word, Sisenna has said *assentio*, and many have followed him on analogy; or, if *assentio* be deemed the right method, the other form, *assentior*, is supported by common practice.

14

YET the prim and dull teacher will suppose that there is either curtailment in the one case or addition in the other. I need hardly add that some forms, which taken singly, are doubtless faulty, are used in composition without blame.

15

FOR *dua*, *tre*, and *pondo*, are barbarisms of discordant gender; yet the compounds *duapondo*, "two pounds," and *trepondo*, "three pounds," have been used by everybody down to our own times, and Messala maintains that they are used with propriety.

16

IT may perhaps seem absurd to say that a barbarism, which is incorrectness in a single word, may be committed in number and gender, like a solecism; yet *scala*, "stairs," and *scopa*, "a broom," in the singular, and *hordea*, "barley," and *mulsa*, "mead," in the plural, as they are attended with no change, withdrawal, or addition of letters, are objectionable only because plurals are expressed in the singular, and singulars in the plural; and those who have used *gladia*, "swords," have committed a fault in gender.

17

BUT this point, too, I am satisfied with merely noticing, that I myself may not appear to have added another question to a branch of study already perplexed through the fault of certain obstinate grammarians.

Faults which are committed in speaking require more sagacity in criticizing them, because examples of them cannot be given from writing except when they have occurred in verses, as the division of the diphthong in Europaï, and the irregularity of the opposite kind, which the Greeks call συναίρεσιν (*synaeresis*) and ἐπισυναλοιφήν (*episynaloiphê*), and we *conflexio*, "combination," as in the verse in Publius Varro, *Quum te flagranti dejectum fulmine Phaeton.*

18

FOR if it were prose, it would be possible to enunciate those letters by their proper syllables. Those peculiarities, also, which occur in quantity, whether when a short syllable is made long, as in *Ītaliam fato profugus*, or when a long one is made short, as in *Unĭus ob noxam et furias*, you would not remark except in verse; and even in verse they are not to be regarded as faults.

19

THOSE which are committed in sound are judged only by the ear; as to the aspirate, whether it be added or retrenched in variation from common practice, it may be a question with us whether it be a fault in writing, if *h* indeed be a letter and not merely a mark, as to which point opinion has often changed with time.

20

THE ancients used it very sparingly even before vowels, as they said *aedos* and *ircos,* and it was long afterwards withheld from conjunction with consonants, as in *Graccas* and *triumpus.* But suddenly an excessive use of it became prevalent, so that *choronae*, *chenturiones*, *praechones*, are still to be seen in certain inscriptions, on which practice there is a well-known epigram of Catullus.

21

HENCE there remain, even to our times, *vehementer*, *conprehendere*, and *mihi.* Among the ancient writers, also, especially those of tragedy, we find in old copies *mehe* for me.

22

STILL more difficult is the marking of faults in respect to the *tenores*, "tones" (which I find called by the old writers *tonores*, as if, forsooth, the word were derived from the Greeks who call them τόνους (*tonos*)), or accents, which the Greeks call προσῳδίας (*prosodiai*) when the acute is put for the grave, or the grave for the acute; as if, in the word *Camillus*, the first syllable should receive the acute accent;

23

OR if the grave is put for the circumflex, as when the first syllable of *Cethegus* has the acute, for thus the quantity of the middle syllable is altered; or if the circumflex is put for the grave, as when the second syllable is circumflexed in *Appi*, by contracting which from two syllables into one, and then circumflexing it, people commit two errors.

24

BUT this happens far more frequently in Greek words, as *Atreus*, which, when I was young, the most learned old men used to pronounce with an acute on the first syllable, so that the second was necessarily grave, as was also that of *Tereus* and *Nereus*. Such have been the rules respecting accents.

25

BUT I am quite aware that certain learned men, and some grammarians also, teach and speak in such a manner as to terminate a word at times with an acute sound, for the sake of preserving certain distinctions in words, as in *circum* in these lines,

> *Quae circum litora, circum*
> *Piscosos scopulos,*

lest, if they make the second syllable in *circum* grave, a *circus* might seem to be meant, not a *circuit*.

26

QUANTUM and *quale*, also, when asking a question, they conclude with a grave accent; when making a comparison, with an acute; this is a practice, however, which they observe almost only in adverbs and pronouns, in other words they follow the old custom.

27

TO me it appears to make a difference that in these phrases we join the words, for when I say *circum litora*, I enunciate the words as one, without making any distinction between them; thus one syllable only, as in a single word, is acute. The same is the case in this hemistich,

Trojae qui primus ab oris.

28

IT sometimes happens, too, that the law of the meter alters the accent: as,

Pecudes, pictaeque volucres;

For I shall pronounce *volucres* with an acute on the middle syllable, because, though it be short by nature, it is long by position, that it may not form an iambus, which a heroic verse does not admit.

29

BUT these words, taken separately, will not vary from the rule, or if custom shall triumph, the old law of the language will be abolished. The observation of which law is more difficult among the Greeks (because they have several modes of speaking, which they call dialects, and because what is wrong in one is sometimes right in another). But among us, the principle of accentuation is very simple.

30

FOR in every word the acuted syllable is confined within the number of three syllables, whether those three be the only syllables in the word or the three last; and of these, the acuted syllable is either the next, or next but one, to the last. Of the three syllables of which I am speaking, moreover, the middle one will be long, acute, or circumflex; a short syllable in that position will, of course, have a grave sound and will accordingly acute the one that stands before it, that is, the third from the end.

31

BUT in every word there is an acute syllable, though never more than one; nor is that one ever the last, and consequently in dissyllables it is the first. Besides, there is never in the same word one syllable circumflexed and another acuted, for the same syllable that is circumflexed is also acuted; neither of the two, therefore, will terminate a Latin word. Those words, however, which consist but of one syllable will be either acuted or circumflexed that there may be no word without an acute.

32

IN sounds also occur those faults of utterance and pronunciation, of which specimens cannot be given in writing; the Greeks, who are more happy in inventing names, call them *iotacisms*, l*ambdacisms*, ἰσχνότητες (*ischnotētes*), and πλατείασμοι (*plateiasmoi*); as also κοιλοστομία (*koilostomia*), when the voice is heard, as it were, in the depths of the throat.

33

THERE are also certain peculiar and inexpressible sounds, for which we sometimes find fault with whole nations. All the incorrectnesses, then, which we have mentioned above, being removed, there will result that which is called ὀρθοέπαι (*orthoepia*), that is, a correct and clear utterance of words with an agreeableness of sound; for so may a right pronunciation be termed.

34

ALL other faults arise out of more words than one; among

these faults is the solecism, though about this also there has been controversy. For even those who admit that it lies in the composition of words, yet contend that, because it may be corrected by the amendment of a single word, it is the incorrectness of a word and not a fault in composition;

35

SINCE, whether *amarae corticis* or *medio cortice* constitutes a fault in gender (to neither of which do I object, Virgil being the author of both; but let us suppose that one of the two is incorrect), the alteration of one word, in which the fault lay, produces correctness of phraseology, so that we have *amari corticis* or *mediâ cortice*. This is a manifest misrepresentation, for neither of the words is wrong, taken separately, but the fault lies in them when put together, and it is a fault therefore of phrase.

36

IT is, however, a question of greater sagacity whether a solecism can be committed in a single word, as if a man, calling one person to him, should say *venite*, or, sending several away from him, should say *abi*, or *discede*; or, moreover, when an answer does not agree with the question, as if to a person saying *quem vides*? you should reply *ego*. Some also think that the same fault is committed in gesture when one thing is signified by the voice and another by a nod or by the hand.

37

WITH this opinion I do not altogether agree, nor do I altogether dissent from it, for I allow that a solecism may occur in one word, but not unless there be something having the force of another word to which the incorrect word may be referred. A solecism arises from the union of things by which something is signified or some intention manifested, and, that I may avoid all caviling, it sometimes occurs in one word, but never in a word by itself.

38

BUT under how many, and what forms, the solecism occurs, is not sufficiently agreed. Those who speak of it most fully make the nature of it fourfold, like that of the barbarism, so that it may be committed by addition (as *nam enim, de susum, in Alexandriam*); by retrenchment (as *Ambulo viam, Aegypto venio, ne hoc fecit*);

39

BY transposition, by which the order of words is confused (as, *Quoque ego, Enim hoc voluit, Autem non habuit*). Whether *igitur*, placed at the beginning of a phrase, ought to be included may be a matter of dispute, because I see that eminent authors have been of opposite opinions as to the practice, it being common among some, while it is never found in others.

40

THESE three sorts of irregularity some distinguish from the solecism, and call a fault of addition "a pleonasm," of retrenchment "an ellipsis," of inversion "an anastrophe," and allege that if these fall under the head of solecism, the hyperbaton may be included under the same title.

41

SUBSTITUTION is without dispute when one thing is put for another; it is an irregularity which we find affecting all the parts of speech, but most frequently the verb, because it has most modifications. Accordingly, under the head of substitution, occur solecisms in gender, tense, persons, moods, (or states or qualities, if any one wish that they should be so called), being six, or, as some will have it, eight in number (since into however many forms you distinguish each of the parts of speech of which mention has just been made, there will be so many sorts of errors liable to be committed), as well as in numbers, of which we have the singular and plural, the Greeks also the dual.

42

THERE have, indeed, been some who assigned us also a dual, *scripsere*, *legere*, a termination which was merely a softening for the sake of avoiding roughness of sound, as, among the old writers, *male merere* for *male mereris*. What they call the dual consists in that one sort of termination only, whereas among the Greeks it is found not only through almost the whole system of the verb, but also in nouns, though even so the use of it is very rare.

43

BUT in no one of our authors is this distinction of ending to be discovered; on the contrary, the phrases, *Devenere locos* and *Conticuere omnes* and *Consedere duces* show us plainly that no one of them refers to two persons only; *dixere*, too, though Antonius Rufus gives it as an example of the contrary, the crier pronounces concerning more advocates than two.

44

DOES not Livy, also, near the beginning of his first book, say, *Tenuere arcem Sabini*, and a little afterwards, *In adversum Romani subiere*? But whom shall I follow in preference to Cicero, who, in his Orator, says, "I do not object to *scripsere*, though I consider *scripserunt* to be preferable"?

45

IN appellative and other nouns, likewise, the solecism shows itself in regard to gender and to number, but especially to case. Whichsoever of those three shall be put in the place of another, the error may be placed under this head, as also incorrectnesses in the use of comparatives and superlatives, as well as cases in which the patronymic is put for the possessive or the contrary.

46

AS to a fault committed in regard to quantity, such as *magnum peculiolum*, there will be some who will think it a solecism, because a diminution is used instead of the integral word, but for my own part, I doubt whether I should not rather call it a misapplication of a word, for it is a departure from the signification. The impropriety of a solecism is not an error as to the sense of a word, but in the junction of words.

47

IN respect to the participle, errors are committed in gender and case, as in the noun; in tense, as in the verb; and in number, as in both. The pronoun, also, has gender, number, and case, all of which admit mistakes of this kind.

48

SOLECISMS are committed, too, and in great numbers, as to parts of speech, but it is not enough merely to remark this generally, lest the pupil should think a solecism committed only where one part of speech is put for another, as a verb where there ought to have been a noun, or an adverb where there ought to have been a pronoun, and the like.

49

FOR there are some nouns cognate, as they say, that is, of the same kind, in regard to which he who shall use another species than that which he ought to use, will be guilty of no less an error than if he were to use a word of another genus.

50

THUS *an* and *aut* are both conjunctions, yet you would be incorrect in asking, *hic, aut ille, sit? Ne* and *non* are both adverbs, yet he who should say *non feceris* for *ne feceris* would fall into a similar error, since the one is an adverb of denying, the other of forbidding. I will add another example: *intro* and *intus* are both adverbs of place, yet *eo intus* and *intro sum* are solecisms.

51

THE same faults may be committed in regard to the different sorts of pronouns, interjections, and prepositions. The discordant collocation of preceding and following words, also, in a sentence of one clause, is a solecism.

52

THERE are expressions, however, which have the appearance of solecisms and yet cannot be called faulty, as *tragoedia Thyestes*, *ludi Floralia*, and *Megalesia*, for though these modes of expression have fallen into disuse in later times, there was never any variation from them among the ancients. They shall therefore be called figures, which are more common among the poets, but allowable also to writers and speakers in prose.

53

BUT a figure will generally have something right for its basis, as I shall show in that part of my work which I just before promised. Yet what is now called a figure will not be free from the fault of solecism, if it be used by any one unknowingly.

54

OF the same sort, though, as I have already said, they have

nothing of figure, are names with a feminine termination which males have, and those with a masculine termination which females have. But of the solecism I shall say no more, for I have not undertaken to write a treatise on grammar, though, as grammar met me in my road, I was unwilling to pass it without paying my respects to it.

55

IN continuation, that I may follow the course which I prescribed to myself, let me repeat that words are either Latin or foreign. Foreign words, like men, and like many of our institutions, have come to us, I might almost say, from all nations.

56

I SAY nothing of the Tuscans, Sabines, and Praenestines, for though Lucilius attacks Vectius for using their dialect, as Pollio discovers Patavinity in Livy, I would consider every part of Italy as Roman.

57

MANY Gallic words have prevailed among us, as *rheda*, "a chariot," and *petorritum*, "a four-wheeled carriage," of which, however, Cicero uses one, and Horace the other. *Mappa*, "a napkin," too, a term much used in the circus, the Carthaginians claim as theirs; *andgurdus*, a word which the common people use for foolish, had, I have heard, its origin in Spain.

58

BUT this division of mine is intended to refer chiefly to the Greek language, for it is from thence that the Roman language is, in a very great degree, derived, and we use even pure Greek words where our own fail, as they also sometimes borrow from us. Hence arises the question, whether it is proper that foreign words should be declined with cases in the same way as our own.

59

IF you meet with a grammarian who is a lover of the ancients, he will say that there should be no departure from the Latin method, because, as there is in our language an ablative case, which the Greeks have not, it is by no means becoming for us to use one case of our own and five Greek cases.

60

AND he would also praise the merit of those who studied to increase the resources of the Latin language, and asserted that they need not introduce foreign practices; under the influence of which notion they said *Castorem*, with the middle syllable long, because such was the case with all our nouns whose nominative case ends in the same letters as *Castor*; and they retained the practice, moreover, of saying *Palaemo*, *Telamo*, and *Plato* (for so Cicero also called him), because they found no Latin word that terminated with the letters *-o* and *-n*.

61

NOR did they willingly allow masculine Greek nouns to end in as in the nominative case, and accordingly, we read in Caelius, *Pelia Cincinnatus*; in Messala, *Bene fecit Euthia*; in Cicero, H*ermagora*; so that we need not wonder that the forms *Aenea* and *Anchisa* were used by most of the old writers: for, said they, if those words were written as *Maecenas*, *Suffenas*, *Asprenas*, they would end in the genitive case, not with the letter *-e*, but with the syllable *-tis*.

62

HENCE, to *Olympus* and *tyrannus* they gave an acuted middle syllable because our language does not permit the first syllable of a word, if short, to have an acute accent when two long syllables follow.

63

THUS the genitive had the forms *Achilli* and *Ulixi*, and many others similar. The modern grammarians have now made it a practice rather to give Greek declensions to Greek nouns, a practice which cannot, however, always be observed. For myself, I prefer following the Latin method, as far as propriety allows, for I would not now say *Calypsonem*, like *Junonem*, though Caius Caesar, following the older writers, uses this mode of declining.

64

BUT custom has prevailed over authority. In other words, which may be declined without impropriety in either way, he who shall prefer to use the Greek form will speak, not indeed like a Roman, but without incurring blame.

65

SIMPLE words are what they are in their first position, that is, in their own nature. Compound words are either formed by subjoining words to prepositions, as *innocens* (care being taken that there be not two prepositions inconsistent with each other, as *imperterritus*, otherwise two may be at times joined together, as *incompositus*, *reconditus*, and, a word which Cicero uses, *subabsurdum*); or they coalesce, as it were, from two bodies into one, as *maleficus*.

66

FOR to form words out of three constituent parts, I should certainly not grant to our language; though Cicero says that *capsis* is compounded of *cape si vis*, and some are found to maintain that *Lupercalia* also consists of three parts of speech, *luere per caprum*.

67

AS to *solitaurilia*, it is now believed that it is for *suovetaurilia*, and such indeed is the sacrifice, as it is described also in Homer. But these words are constructed, not so much of three words, as of parts of three words. *Pacuvius*, however, appears to have formed compounds, most inelegantly of a preposition and two other words:

Nerei
Repandirostrum, incurvicervicum pecus,

"The broad-nosed, crook-necked flock of Nereus."

68

COMPOUNDS, however, are formed either of two entire Latin words, as *superfui*, *subterfugi* (though it is a question whether these are indeed formed of entire words), of an entire and incomplete word, as *malevolus*; of an incomplete and entire word, *asnoctivagus*; of two incomplete words, as *pedissequus*; of a Latin and a foreign word, as *biclinium*; of a foreign and a Latin word, as *epitogium* and *Anticato*; or of two foreign words, as *epirhedium*, for though the preposition *epi-* is Greek, and *rheda* Gallic, and though neither the Greek nor the Gaul uses the compound, yet the Romans have formed their word of the two foreign words.

69

FREQUENTLY, too, the union causes a change in the prepositions, as *abstulit*, *aufugit*, *amisit*, though the preposition is merely *ab-*, and *coit*, the preposition being *con-*; and so *ignavi*, *erepti*, and similar compounds.

70

BUT the composition of words in general is better suited to

the Greeks; with us it is less successful, though I do not think that this results from the nature of the language; but we look with more favor on foreign compounds, and, accordingly, while we admire the Greek κυρταύχενα (*kurtauchena*), we hardly defend *incurvicervicum* from derision.

71

WORDS are proper when they signify that to which they were first applied; metaphorical, when they have one signification by nature, and another in the place in which they are used. Common words we use with greater safety; new ones we do not form without some danger; for if they are well received, they add but little merit to our style, and, if rejected, they turn to jokes against us.

72

YET we must make attempts; for, as Cicero says, even words which have seemed harsh at first, become softened by use.

As to the onomatopoeia, it is by no means granted to our language; for, if we should venture to produce anything like those justly admired Greek expressions λίγξε βιός (*linxe bios*), "the bow twanged," and σίζε ὀψθαλμός (*siz ophthalmos*), "the eye hissed," who would endure it? We should not even dare to *saybalare*, "to bleat" or *hinnire*, "to neigh," unless those words were supported by the sanction of antiquity.

Chapter VI

1

BY speakers, as well as writers, there are certain rules to be observed. Language is based on reason, antiquity, authority, custom.

It is analogy, and sometimes etymology, that affords the chief support to reason. A certain majesty, and, if I may so express myself, religion, graces the antique.

2

AUTHORITY is commonly sought in orators or historians. As to the poets, the obligation of the meter excuses their phraseology, unless, when the measure of the feet offers no impediment to the choice of either of two expressions, they fancifully prefer one to the other, as in the following phrases: *Imo de stirpe recisum*, *Aeriae quo congessere palumbes*, *Silice in nuda*, and the like. Since the judgment of men eminent in eloquence is in place of reason, then even error is without dishonor in following illustrious guides.

3

CUSTOM, however, is the surest preceptor in speaking, and we must use phraseology, like money, which has the public stamp.

But all these particulars require great judgment, especially analogy, which, translating it closely from Greek into Latin, people have called proportion.

4

WHAT it requires is that a writer or speaker should compare whatever is at all doubtful with something similar concerning which there is no doubt, so as to prove the uncertain by the certain. This is done in two ways: by a comparison of similar words, in respect chiefly to their last syllables (for which reason the words that have but one syllable are said not to be accountable to analogy), and by looking to diminutives.

5

COMPARISON in nouns shows either their gender or their declension; their gender, as when it is inquired whether *funis* be masculine or feminine, *panis* may be an object of comparison with it; their declension as, if it should be a subject of doubt whether we should say *hac domu* or *hac domo*, and *domuum* or *domorum*, *domus*, *anus*, *manus* may be compared with each other.

6

THE formation of diminutives shows only the gender of words, as (that I may take the same word for an example) *funiculus* proves that *funis* is masculine.

7

THERE is also similar reason for comparison in verbs; as if any one, following the old writers, should pronounce *fervere* with the middle syllable short, he would be convicted of speaking incorrectly, since all verbs which end with the letters *-eo* in the indicative mood, when they have assumed the letter *-e* in the middle syllables in the infinitive, have it necessarily long, as *prandeo*, *pendeo*, *spondeo*, *prandēre*, *pendēre*, *spondēre*.

8

BUT those which have *-o* only in the indicative, when they end with the same letter *-e* in the infinitive, shorten it, as *lego*, *dico*, *curro*, *legĕre*, *dicĕre*, *currĕre*; although there occurs in Lucilius,

Fervit aqua et fervet; fervit nunc, fervet ad annum.

The water boils and will boil; it boils now, and will boil for a year.

9

BUT with all respect to a man of such eminent learning, if he thinks *fervit* similar to *currit* and *legit*, *fervo* will be a word like *curro* and *lego*, a word which has never been heard by me. But this is not a just comparison, for *servit* is like *fervit*, and he that follows this analogy must say *fervire* as well as *servire*.

10

THE present indicative also is sometimes discovered from the other moods and tenses. For I remember that some people who had blamed me for using the word *pepigi* were convinced by me of their error; they had allowed, indeed, that the best authors had used *pepigi*, but denied that analogy permitted its use, since the present indicative *paciscor*, as it had the form of a passive verb, made in the perfect tense *pactus sum*.

11

BUT I, besides adducing the authority of orators and historians, maintained that *pepigi* was also supported by analogy; for, as we read in the Twelve Fables, *ni ita pagunt*, I found *cadunt* similar to *pagunt*, whence the present indicative, though it had fallen into disuse through time, was evidently *pago*, like *cado*, and it was therefore certain that we say *pepigi* like *cecidi*.

12

BUT we must remember that the course of analogy cannot be traced through all the parts of speech, as it is in many cases at variance with itself. Learned men, indeed, endeavor to justify some departures from it, as when it is remarked how much *lepus* and *lupus*, though of similar terminations in the nominative, differ in their cases and numbers, they reply that they are not of the same sort, since *lepus* is epicene, and *lupus* masculine; yet Varro, in the book in which he relates the origin of the city of Rome, uses *lupus* as feminine, following Ennius and Fabius Pictor.

13

BUT those same grammarians, when they are asked why *aper* makes *apri*, and *pater patris*, assert that the first is declined absolutely, and the second with reference to something; and, besides, as both are derived from the Greek, they recur to the rule thatπατρός (*patros*) gives *patris*, and κάπρου (*kaprou*) *apri*.

14

BUT how will they escape from the fact that nouns, which end with the letters *-u* and *-s* in the nominative singular, never, even though feminine, end with the syllable *-ris* in the genitive, yet that *Venus* makes *Veneris*; and that, though nouns ending in *-es* have various endings in the genitive, yet their genitive never ends in that same syllable *-ris*, when, nevertheless, *Ceres* obliges us to say *Cereris*?

15

AND what shall I say of those parts of speech, which, though all of similar commencement, proceed with different inflections, as *Alba* makes *Albani* and *Albenses*, and *Volo* has *volui* and *volavi*? For analogy itself admits that verbs which end with the letter *-oin* the first person singular are variously formed in the perfect, as *cado* makes *cecidi*; *spondeo* makes *spopondi*; *pingo* makes *pinxi*; *lego*, *legi*; *pono*, *posui*; *frango*, *fregi*; and *laudo*, *laudavi*.

16

SINCE analogy was not sent down from heaven, when men were first made, to give them rules for speaking, but was discovered after men had begun to speak and after it was observed how each word in speaking terminated, it is not therefore founded on reason, but on example. Nor is it a law for speaking, but the mere result of observation, so that nothing but custom has been the origin of analogy.

17

YET some people adhere to it with a most unpleasantly perverse attachment to exactness, so that they will say *audaciter* in preference to *audacter*, though all orators adopt the latter, and *emicavit* instead of *emicuit*, and *conire* instead of *coire*. Such persons we may allow to say *audivisse*, and *scivisse*, *tribunale*, and *faciliter*; let them also have their *frugalis*, instead of *frugi*, for how else can *frugalitas* be formed?

18

LET them also prove that *centum millia nummum* and *fidem Deum* are two solecisms, since they err in both case and number; for we were ignorant of this and were not merely complying with custom and convenience, as in most cases, of which Cicero treats nobly, as of everything else, in his *De Oratore*.

19

AUGUSTUS, too, in his letters written to Caius Caesar, corrects him for preferring to say *calidum* rather than *caldum*, not because *calidum* is not Latin, but because it is unpleasing, and, as he has himself expressed it by a Greek word, περίεργον (*periergon*).

20

ALL this indeed they consider as mere ὀρθοέπειαν (*orthopeia*), which I by no means set aside, for what is so necessary as correctness of speech? I think that we ought to adhere to it as far as possible and to make persevering resistance against innovators; but to retain words that are obsolete and disused is a species of impertinence and puerile ostentation in little things.

21

LET the extremely learned man, who has saluted you without an aspirate and with the second syllable lengthened (for the verb, he will say, is *avēte*) say also *calefacere* and *conservavisse* rather than what we say, and with these let him join *face*, *dice*, and the like.

22

HIS way is the right way; who will deny it? But a smoother and more beaten road is close by the side of it. There is nothing, however, with which I am more offended than that these men, led away by oblique cases, permit themselves, I do not say not to find, but even to alter nominative cases, as when *ebur androbur*, so spoken and written by the greatest authors, are made to change the vowel of the second syllable into *-o*, because their genitives are *roboris* and *eboris*, and because *sulfur* and *guttur* preserve the vowel *-u* in the genitive. For which reason also *jecur* and *femur* have raised disputes.

23

THIS change of theirs is no less audacious than if they were to substitute the letter *-o* for *-u* in the genitive case of *sulfur* and *guttur*, because *eboris* and *roboris* are formed with *-o*. Consider the example of Antonius Gnipho, who acknowledges that *robur* and *ebur* are proper words, and even *marmur*, but would have the plurals of them to be *robura*, *ebura*, *marmura*.

24

BUT if they had paid attention to the affinity of letters, they would have understood that *roboris* is as fairly formed from *robur* as *militis*, *limitis*, *frommiles*, *limes*, or *judicis*, *vindicis*, from *judex*, *vindex*, and would have observed some other forms to which I have adverted above.

25

DO not similar nominative cases, as I remarked, diverge into very dissimilar forms in the oblique cases, as *Virgo*, *Juno*; *fusus*, *lusus*; *cuspis*, *puppis*; and a thousand others? It happens, too, that some nouns are not used in the plural, others not in the singular; some are indeclinable; some depart altogether from the form of their nominatives, as *Jupiter*.

26

THE same peculiarity happens in verbs, as *fero*, *tuli*, of which the preterperfect is found and nothing more. Nor is it of much importance whether those unused parts are actually not in existence or whether they are too harsh to be used, for what, for example, will *progenies* make in the genitive singular, or what will *spes* make in the genitive plural? Or how will *quire* and *ruere* form themselves in the perfect passive or in the passive participles?

27

IT is needless to advert to other words, when it is even uncertain whether *senatus* makes *senatus senatui*, or *senati senato*. It appears to me, therefore, to have been not unhappily remarked that it is one thing to speak Latin and another to speak grammar. Of analogy I have now said enough, and more than enough.

28

ETYMOLOGY, which inquires into the origin of words, is called by Cicero *notatio*, because its designation in Aristotle is σύμβολον (*symbolon*), that is, *nota*; for to a literal rendering of etymology, which would be *veriloquium* ("word for word"), Cicero himself, who formed that word, is averse. There are some, who looking rather to the meaning of the word, call it "origination."

29

THIS part of grammar is sometimes of the utmost use; as often, indeed, as the matter, concerning which there is any dispute, stands in need of interpretation; as when Marcus Caelius would prove that he was a homo *frugi*, "a frugal man," not because he was temperate (for on that point he could not speak falsely), but because he was profitable to many, that is *fructuosus*, from whence, he said, was derived *frugality*. A place is accordingly assigned to etymology in definitions.

30

SOMETIMES, also, it endeavors to distinguish barbarous from polite words, as when a question arises whether Sicily should be called *Triquetra* or *Triquedra*, and whether we should say *meridies* or *medidies*, and similar questions concerning other words which yield to custom.

31

BUT it carries with it much learning, whether we employ it in treating of words sprung from the Greek, which are very numerous, especially those inflected according to the Aeolic dialect to which our language has most similitude, or in inquiring, from our knowledge of ancient history, into the names of men, places, nations, and cities. Whence come the names of the *Bruti*, *Publicolae*, *Pici*; why we say *Latium*, *Italia*, *Beneventum*; and what is our reason for using the terms *Capitol*, *Quirinal* hill, and *Argiletum*.

32

I WOULD now allude also to those minuter points on which the greatest lovers of etymology weary themselves: men who bring back to their true derivation, by various and manifold arts, words that have become a little distorted, shortening or lengthening, adding, taking away, or interchanging letters or syllables. In this pursuit, through weakness or judgment, they run into the most contemptible absurdities. Let *consul* be (I make no objection) from "consulting" or from "judging," for the ancients called *consulere* "judicare," whence still remains the phrase *rogat boni consulas*, that is, *bonum judices*.

33

LET it be old age that has given a name to the senate, for the senators are fathers; let *rex*, *rector*, and abundance of other words be indisputably from *rego*; nor would I dispute the ordinary derivation of *tegula*, *regula*, and other words similar to them; let *classis*, also, be from *calare*, "to call together," and let *lepus* be for *levipes*, and *vulpes* for *volipes*.

34

BUT shall we also allow words to be derived from contraries, as *lucus*, "a grove," from *luceo,* "to shine," because, being thick with shade, *parum lucet*, it does not shine? As *ludus*, "a school," from *ludo*, "to play," because it is as far as possible from play? As *Ditis*, "Pluto," from *dives*, "rich," because he is by no means rich? Or shall we allow *homo*, "man," to be from *humus*, "the ground," because he was sprung from the ground, as if all animals had not the same origin, or as if the first men had given a name to the ground before they gave one to themselves? Shall we allow *verba*, "words," to be from *aer verberatus*, "beaten air?"

35

LET us go on and we shall get so far that *stella*, "a star," will be believed to be *luminis stilla*, "a drop of light," the author of which derivation, an eminent man in literature, it would be ungenerous for me to name in regard to a point on which he is censured by me.

36

BUT those who have recorded such etymologies in books have

themselves set their names to them; and Caius Granius thought himself extremely clever for saying that *caelibes*, "bachelors," was the same as *caelites*, "inhabitants of heaven," because they are alike free from a most heavy burden, resting his derivation, too, on an argument from the Greek, for he affirmed that ἠιθέους (*ēitheoi*) was used in the same sense. Nor does Modestus yield to him in imagination, for he says that because Saturn cut off the genitalia of Caelus, men who have no wives are therefore called *caelibes.*

37

LUCIUS Aelius declares that *pituita*, "phlegm," is so called *quia petat vitam*, because "it aims at life." But who may not be pardoned after Varro, who wished to persuade Cicero (for it was to him that he wrote this), that *ager*, "a field," is so called because in *eo agatur aliquid*, "something is done in it," and that *graculos*, "jackdaws," are so named because they fly *gregatim*, "in flocks," though it is evident that the one is derived from the Greek and the other from the cries of the birds themselves?

38

BUT of such importance was it to Varro to derive that *merula*, "a blackbird," he declared, was so named because it flies alone, as if *mera volans*. Some have not hesitated to apply to etymology for the origin of every name or word; deducing *Longus* and *Rufus*, as I remarked, from personal peculiarities; *strepere* and *murmurare* from particular sounds; with which they join, also, certain derivatives, as *velox*, "swift," deduced from *velocitas*, "swiftness," and the greater number of compounds (as being similar to them), which, doubtless, have their origin from something, but demand no exercise of ingenuity for which, indeed, except on doubtful points, there is no opportunity in these investigations.

39

WORDS derived from antiquity have not only illustrious patrons, but also confer on style a certain majesty not unattended with pleasure, for they have the authority of age and, as they have been disused for a time, bring with them a charm similar to that of novelty.

40

BUT there is need of moderation in the use of them, in order that they may not occur too frequently nor show themselves too manifestly since nothing is more detestable than affectation; nor should they be taken from a remote and already forgotten age, as are *topper*, "quickly," *antigerio*, "very much," *exanclare*, "to draw out," *prosapia*, "a race," and the verses of the Salii, which are scarcely understood by the priests themselves.

41

THOSE verses, however, religion forbids to be changed, and we must use what has been consecrated; but how faulty is speech, of which the greatest virtue is perspicuity, if it needs an interpreter! Consequently, as the oldest of new words will be the best, so the newest of old words will be the best.

42

THE case is similar with regard to authority, for though he may seem to commit no fault who uses those words which the greatest writers have handed down to him, yet it is of much importance for him to consider, not only what words they used, but how far they gave a sanction to them. No one would now tolerate from us *tuburchinabundus*, "devouring," or *lurchinabundus*, "voracious," though Cato was the father of them; nor would people endure *lodices*, "blankets," in the masculine gender, though that gender pleases Pollio; nor *gladiola* for "little swords," though Messala has used it; nor *parricidatus*, "parricide," which was thought scarcely endurable in Caelius; nor would Calvus induce me to use *collos*, "necks"; all which words, indeed, those authors themselves would not now use.

43

THERE remains, therefore, custom, for it would be almost ridiculous to prefer the language which men have spoken rather than that which they now speak. What else, indeed, is old language, but the old manner of speaking? But even for following custom judgment is necessary, and we must settle, in the first place, what that is which we call custom.

44

IF custom be merely termed that which the greater number do, it will furnish a most dangerous rule, not only for language, but, what is of greater importance, for life. For where is there so much virtue that what is right can please the majority? As, therefore, to pluck out hairs, to cut the hair of the head in a succession of rings, and to drink to excess in the bath, whatever country those practices may have invaded, will not become the custom, because no one of them is undeserving of censure. Though we bathe and clip our hair, and take our meals together according to custom, so, in speaking, it is not whatever has become a vicious practice with many that is to be received as a rule of language.

45

FOR, not to mention how the ignorant commonly speak, we know that whole theaters and all the crowd of the circus have frequently uttered barbarous exclamations. Custom in speaking, therefore, I shall call the agreement of the educated, as I call custom in living the agreement of the good.

Chapter VII

1

SINCE we have mentioned what rules are to be followed in speaking, we must now specify what are to be observed by writers. What the Greeks call ὀρθογραφία (*orthographia*), we may call the art of writing correctly, an art which does not consist in knowing of what letters every syllable is composed (for this study is beneath the profession even of the grammarian), but exercises its whole subtlety, in my opinion, on dubious points.

2

AS it is the greatest of folly to place a mark on all long syllables, since most of them are apparent from the very nature of the word that is written, yet it is at times necessary to mark them, as when the same letter gives sometimes one sense and sometimes another, according as it is short or long; thus *malus* is distinguished by a mark to show whether it means "a tree" or "a bad man;"

3

PALUS, too, signifies one thing when its first syllable is long, and another when its second is so; and when the same letter is short in the nominative and long in the ablative, we have generally to be informed by this mark which quantity we are to adopt.

4

GRAMMARIANS have in like manner thought that the following distinction should be observed: namely, that we should write the preposition ex, if the word *specto* was compounded with it, with the addition of *-s* in the second syllable, *exspecto*; if *pecto*, without the *-s*.

5

IT has been a distinction, also, observed by many, that *ad*, when it was a preposition, should take the letter *-d*, but when a conjunction, the letter *-t*; and that *cum*, if it signified time, should be written with a *-q* and two *-u*'s following, but if it meant accompaniment, with a *-c*.

6

SOME other things were even more trifling than these, as that *quicquid* should have a *-c* for the fourth letter, lest we should seem to ask a double question, and that we should write *quotidie*, not *cotidie*, to show that it was for *quot diebus*. But these notions have already passed away among other puerilities.

7

IT is, however, a question in writing prepositions whether it is proper to observe the sound which they make when joined to another word, or that which they make when separate, as for instance when I pronounce the word *obtinuit*, for our method of writing requires that the second letter should be *-b*, while the ear catches rather the sound of *-p*;

8

OR when I say *immunis*, for the letter *-n*, which the composition of the word requires, is influenced by the sound of the following syllable and changed into another *-m*.

9

IT is also to be observed, in dividing compound words, whether you ought to attach the middle consonant to the first or to the second syllable; for *aruspex*, as its latter part is from *spectare*, will assign the letter *-s* to the third syllable; *abstemius*, as it is formed of *abstinentia temeti*, "abstinence from wine," will leave the *-s* to the first syllable.

10

AS to *-k*, I think it should not be used in any words, except those which it denotes of itself, so that it may be put alone. This remark I have not omitted to make because there are some who think *-k* necessary when *-a* follows; though there is the letter *-c*, which suits itself to all vowels.

11

BUT orthography submits to custom and has therefore frequently been altered. I say nothing of those ancient times when there were fewer letters and when their shapes were different from these of ours, and their natures also different, as that of *-o* among the Greeks, which was sometimes long and sometimes short, and *-as* among us was sometimes put for the syllable which it expresses by its mere name.

12

I SAY nothing also of *-d*, among the ancient Latins, being added as the last letter to a great number of words, as is apparent from the rostral pillar erected to Calus Duellius in the forum; nor do I speak of *-g* being used in the same manner, as on the pulvinar of the Sun, which is worshiped near the temple of Romulus, is read *vesperug*, which we take for *vesperugo*.

13

NOR is it necessary to say anything here of the interchange of letters, of which I have spoken above, for perhaps as they wrote they also spoke.

14

IT was for a long time a very common custom not to double the semivowels, while, on the other hand, even down to the time of Accius and later, they wrote, as I have remarked, long syllables with two vowels.

15

STILL longer continued the practice of using *-e* and *-i* together, joining them in the same manner as the Greeks in the diphthong *-ei.* This practice was adopted for a distinction in cases and numbers, as Lucilius admonishes us:

> *Jam pueri venere: E postremum facito, atque I,*
> *Ut puerei plures fiant*;

and afterwards,

> *Mendaci furique addes E, quum dare furei*
> *Jusseris.*

16

HOWEVER this addition of *-e* is both superfluous, since *-i* has the nature of a long as well as of a short letter, and also sometimes inconvenient; for in those words which have *-e* immediately before the last syllable, and end with *-i* long, we should use, if we adopted that method, a double *-e*, as *aureei*, *argenteei*, and the like; and this would be extremely embarrassing to those who are being taught to read.

17

THIS happens also among the Greeks by the addition of the letter *-i*, which they not only write at the end of dative cases, but sometimes even in the middle of a word, as ΛΗΙΣΤΗΙ (*LĒISTĒI*), because etymology, in making a division of the word into three syllables, requires that letter.

18

THE diphthong *-ae,* for the second letter of which we now substitute *-e*, our ancestors expressed with a varied pronunciation, by *-a* and *-i*, some using it in all cases like the Greeks, others only in the singular when they had to form a genitive or dative case. Whence Virgil, a great lover of antiquity, has inserted in his verses *pictai vestis* and *aquai*, but in the plural number of such nouns they use *-e*, as *Syllae*, *Galbae*.

19

THERE is on this point also a precept of Lucilius, which, as it is expressed in a great number of verses, whoever is incredulous about it may seek in his ninth book.

20

I MAY mention, too, that in the time of Cicero and some what later, the letter *-s*, as often as it occurred between two long vowels or followed a long vowel, was doubled, as *caussae*, *cassus*, *divissiones*, for that both he and Virgil wrote in this way, their own hands show.

21

BUT those of a somewhat earlier period wrote the word *jussi*, which we express with two *-s*'s, with only one. That *optimus*, *maximus*, should take *-i* as their middle letter which among the ancients was *-u*, is said to have been brought about by an inscription to Caius Caesar.

22

THE word here we now end with the letter *-e*; but I still find in the books of the old comic writers *Heri ad me venit*, which same mode of spelling is found in the letters of Augustus, which he wrote or corrected with his own hand.

23

DID not Cato the Censor, also, for *dicam* and *faciam*, write *dicem* and *faciem*? And did he not observe the same method in other verbs which terminate in a similar way? This is indeed manifest from his old writings and is remarked by Messala in his book on the letter *-s*.

24

SIBE and *quase* occur in the writings of many authors, but whether the authors themselves intended them to be written thus, I do not know. That Livy spelled them in that way, I learn from Pedianus, who himself imitated Livy; we end those words with the letter *-i*.

25

WHY need I allude to *vortices* and *vorsus* and other similar words, in which Scipio Africanus is said to have first changed the second letter into *-e*?

26

OUR tutors wrote *cervum* and *servum* with the letters *-u* and *-o*, *ceruom*, *seruom*, in order that the same two vowels, following each other, might not coalesce and be confounded in the same sound; they are now written with two *-u*'s on the principle which I have stated, though in neither way is the word which we conceive exactly expressed. Nor was it without advantage that Claudius introduced the Aeolic letter for such cases.

27

IT is an improvement of the present day that we spell *cui* with the three letters which I have just written; for in this word, when we were boys, they used, making a very offensive sound, *qu* and *oi*, only that it might be distinguished from *qui*.

28

WHAT shall I say, too, of words that are written otherwise than they are pronounced? *Gaius* is spelled with the letter *-c*, which, inverted, means a woman; for that women were called *Caiae*, as well as men *Caii*, appears even from our nuptial ceremonies.

29

NOR does *Gneius* assume that letter, in designating a *praenomen*, with which it is sounded. We read, too, *columna* and *consules* with the letter *-n* omitted, and *Sabura*, when it is designated by three letters, takes *-c* as the third. There are many other peculiarities of this kind, but I fear that those which I have noticed have exceeded the limits of so unimportant a subject.

30

ON all such points let the grammarian use his own judgment, for in this department it ought to be of the greatest authority. For myself, I think that all words (unless custom has ordered otherwise) should be written in conformity with their sound.

31

FOR this is the use of letters, to preserve words, and to restore them, like a deposit, to readers; and they ought, therefore, to express exactly what we are to say.

32

THESE are the most important points as to speaking and writing correctly. The other two departments, those of speaking with significance and elegance, I do not indeed take away from the grammarians, but as the duties of the rhetorician remain for me to explain, I reserve them for a more important part of my work.

33

YET the reflection recurs to me that some will regard those matters of which I have just treated as extremely trifling and even as impediments to the accomplishment of anything greater. Nor do I myself think that we ought to descend to extreme solicitude and puerile disputations about them; I even consider that the mind may be weakened and contracted by being fixed upon them.

34

BUT no part of grammar will be hurtful, except what is superfluous. Was Cicero the less of an orator because he was most attentive to the study of grammar and because, as appears from his letters, he was a rigid exactor, on all occasions, of correct language from his son? Did the writings of Julius Caesar *On Analogy* diminish the vigor of his intellect? Or was Messala less elegant as a writer because he devoted whole books, not merely to single words, but even to single letters? These studies are injurious not to those who pass through them, but to those who dwell immoderately upon them.

Chapter VIII

1

READING remains to be considered. Only practice can teach a boy to know when to take breath, where to divide a verse, where the sense is concluded, where it begins, when the voice is to be raised or lowered, what is to be uttered with any particular inflection of sound, or what is to be pronounced with greater slowness or rapidity, with greater animation or gentleness than other passages.

2

THERE is but one direction, therefore, which I have to give in this part of my work, namely, that he may be able to do all this successfully, let him understand what he reads.

Let his mode of reading, however, be, above all, manly, uniting gravity with a certain degree of sweetness. Let not his reading of the poets be like that of prose, for it is verse, and the poets say that they sing. Yet let it not degenerate into sing-song or be rendered effeminate with unnatural softness, as is now the practice among most readers; on which sort of reading we hear that Caius Caesar, while he was still under age, observed happily to some one that was practicing it, "If you are singing, you sing badly; if you pretend to read, you nevertheless sing."

3

NOR would I have *prosopopeiae* pronounced, as some would wish them, after the manner of actors, though I think there should be a certain alteration of the voice by which they may be distinguished from those passages in which the poet speaks in his own person.

4

OTHER points demand much admonition to be given on them, and care is to be taken, above all things, that tender minds, which will imbibe deeply whatever has entered them while rude and ignorant of everything, may learn not only what is eloquent, but, still more, what is morally good.

5

IT has accordingly been an excellent custom that reading should commence with Homer and Virgil, although to understand their merits, there is need of maturer judgment. But for the acquisition of judgment there is abundance of time, for they will not be read once only. In the meantime, let the mind of the pupil be exalted with the sublimity of the heroic verse, conceive ardor from the magnitude of the subjects, and be imbued with the noblest sentiments.

6

THE reading of tragedies is beneficial; the lyric poets nourish the mind, provided that you select from them not merely authors, but portions of their works; for the Greeks are licentious in many of their writings, and I should be loath to interpret Horace in certain passages. As to elegy, at least that which treats of love, and hendecasyllables, and poems in which there are portions of Sotadic verses (for concerning Sotadic verses themselves no precept need even be mentioned) let them be altogether kept away, if it be possible; if not, let them at least be reserved for the greater strength of mature age.

7

OF comedy, which may contribute very much to eloquence, as it extends to all sorts of characters and passions, I will state a little further on, in the proper place, the good which I think it may do to boys; when their morals are out of danger, it will be among the subjects to be chiefly read. It is of Menander that I speak, though I would not set aside other comic writers, for the Latin authors, too, will confer some benefit.

8

BUT those writings should be the subjects of lectures for boys, which may best nourish the mind and enlarge the thinking powers; for reading other books, which relate merely to erudition, advanced life will afford sufficient time. The old Latin authors, however, will be of great use, though most of them, indeed, were stronger in genius than in art. Above all they will supply a *copia verborum*, while in their tragedies may be found a weightiness of thought, and in their comedies elegance, and something as it were of Atticism.

9

THERE will be seen in them, too, a more careful regard to regularity of structure than in most of the moderns, who have considered that the merit of every kind of composition lies solely in the thoughts. Purity, certainly, and that I may so express myself, manliness, is to be gained from them, since we ourselves have fallen into all the vices of refinement, even in our manner of speaking.

10

LET us, moreover, trust to the practice of the greatest orators, who have recourse to the poems of the ancients, as well for the support of their arguments, as for the adornment of their eloquence.

11

FOR in Cicero, most of all, and frequently, also, in Asinius and others nearest to his times, we see verses of Ennius, Accius, Pacuvius, Lucilius, Terence, Caecilius, and other poets, introduced with the best effect, not only for showing the learning of the speakers, but for giving pleasure to the hearers, whose ears find in the charms of poetry a relief from the want of elegance in forensic pleading.

12

TO this is to be added no mean advantage, as the speakers confirm what they have stated by the sentiments of the poets, as by so many testimonies. But those first observations of mine have reference rather to boys, the latter to more advanced students, for the love of letters and the benefit of reading are bounded not by the time spent at school, but by the extent of life.

13

IN lecturing on the poets, the grammarian must attend also to minor points, so that after taking a verse to pieces, he may require the parts of speech to be specified, and the peculiarities of the feet, which are necessary to be known, not merely for writing poetry, but even for prose composition. He may also distinguish what words are barbarous, or misapplied, or used contrary to the rules of the language.

14

NOT that the poets may thus be disparaged (to whom, as they are commonly forced to obey the meter, so much indulgence is granted, that even solecisms are designated by other names in poetry, for we call them, as I have remarked, metaplasms, schematisms, and schemata, and give to necessity the praise of merit), but that the tutor may instruct the pupil in figurative terms and exercise his memory.

15

IT is likewise useful, among the first rudiments of instruction, to show in how many senses each word may be understood. About glossemata, too, that is, words not in general use, no small attention is requisite in the grammatical profession.

16

WITH still greater care, however, let him teach all kinds of tropes from which not only poetry, but even prose, receives the greatest ornament, as well as the two sorts of schemata or figures, called figures of speech and figures of thought. My observations on these figures, as well as those on tropes, I put off to that portion of my work in which I shall have to speak of the embellishments of composition.

17

BUT let the tutor, above all things, impress upon the minds of his pupils what merit there is in a just disposition of parts, and a becoming treatment of subjects; what is well suited to each character; what is to be commended in the thoughts, and what in the words; where diffuseness is appropriate, and where contraction.

18

TO these duties will be added explanations of historical points, which must be sufficiently minute, but not carried into superfluous disquisitions; for it will suffice to lecture on facts which are generally admitted, or which are at least related by eminent authors. To examine, indeed, what all writers, even the most contemptible, have ever related is a proof either of extravagant laboriousness or of useless ostentation, and chains and overloads the mind, which might give its attention to other things with more advantage.

19

FOR he who makes researches into all sorts of writings, even such as are unworthy to be read, is capable of giving his time even to old women's tales. Yet the writings of grammarians are full of noxious matters of this kind, scarcely known even to the very men who wrote them.

20

SINCE it is known to have happened to Didymus, than whom no man wrote more books, that, when he denied a certain story as unworthy of belief, his own book containing it was laid before him.

21

THIS occurs chiefly in fabulous stories, descending even to what is ridiculous, and sometimes licentious; whence every unprincipled grammarian has the liberty of inventing many of his comments, so that he may lie with safety concerning whole books and authors, as it may occur to him, for writers that never existed cannot be produced against him. In the better known class of authors they are often exposed by the curious. Hence it shall be accounted by me among the merits of a grammarian to be ignorant of some things.

FIN

www.ingramcontent.com/pod-product-compliance
Lightning Source LLC
Chambersburg PA
CBHW070331170726
48291CB00001B/10

* 9 7 8 1 9 4 4 4 8 2 0 5 3 *